THE WRITER'S WORKPLACE
with Readings

THE WRITER'S WORKPLACE

with Readings

Building College Writing Skills

Sixth Edition

SANDRA SCARRY

Formerly with the Office of Academic Affairs
City University of New York

JOHN SCARRY

Hostos Community College
City University of New York

WADSWORTH
CENGAGE Learning™

Australia • Brazil • Japan • Korea • Mexico • Singapore • Spain • United Kingdom • United States

WADSWORTH
CENGAGE Learning

**The Writer's Workplace with Readings:
Building College Writing Skills, Sixth Edition**
Sandra Scarry/John Scarry

Publisher: Lyn Uhl

Acquisitions Editor: Annie Todd

Development Editor: Laurie Runion

Editorial Assistant: Dan DeBonis

Marketing Manager: Kate Edwards

Marketing Communications Manager:
Darlene Amidon-Brent

Associate Content Project Manager: Sarah Sherman

Senior Art Director: Cate Rickard Barr

Print/Media Buyer: Mary Beth Hennebury

Permissions Editor: Ronald Montgomery
and Timothy Sisler

Permissions Researcher: Writer's Research Group LLC

Production Service: Newgen

Text Designer: Joyce Weston Design

Sr. Permissions Account Manager, Images:
Sheri Blaney

Photo Researcher: Cheri Throop

Cover Designer: Anne Carter

Printer: C&C Offset Printing, Co., Ltd.

Cover Illustration: © Steven Chorney 2008

For product information and technology assistance, contact us at
Cengage Learning Customer & Sales Support, 1-800-354-9706
For permission to use material from this text or product,
submit all requests online at **www.cengage.com/permissions**
Further permissions questions can be emailed to
permissionrequest@cengage.com

Library of Congress Control Number: 2006932521

Student Edition ISBN-10: 1-4130-3068-8

Student Edition ISBN-13: 978-1-4130-3068-6

Wadsworth
25 Thomson Place
Boston, MA 02210-1202
USA

Cengage Learning is a leading provider of customized learning solutions with office locations around the globe, including Singapore, the United Kingdom, Australia, Mexico, Brazil, and Japan. Locate your local office at:
international.cengage.com/region

Cengage Learning products are represented in Canada by Nelson Education, Ltd.

For your course and learning solutions, visit **academic.cengage.com**

Purchase any of our products at your local college store or at our preferred online store **www.ichapters.com**

Credits appear on pages C1–C2, which constitute a continuation of the copyright page.

Printed in China.
4 5 6 7 11 10 09 08

For Our Students

What shall I do this year? What shall I become? What shall I learn—truly learn and know that I have learned by the time I look at these pages next year?

Lorraine Hansberry
Journal entry of August 23, 1962

Contents

PART 2   CREATING EFFECTIVE SENTENCES   33

CHAPTER 3   Finding Subjects and Verbs in Simple Sentences   34

CHAPTER 4   Making Subjects and Verbs Agree   57

CHAPTER 24 Developing Paragraphs:
Definition and Classification   **443**

PART 5   STRUCTURING THE COLLEGE ESSAY   **455**

CHAPTER 25   Moving from the Paragraph to the Essay   **456**

CHAPTER 26   Following the Progress of a Student Essay   **474**

CHAPTER 27 ## Writing an Essay Using Examples, Illustrations, or Anecdotes   489

CHAPTER 28 ## Writing an Essay Using Narration   499

CHAPTER 29 ## Writing an Essay Using Process Analysis   509

CHAPTER 30 Writing an Essay Using Comparison/Contrast   520

CHAPTER 31 Writing an Essay Using Persuasion   533

CHAPTER 32 Other College Writing: The Research Paper and the Essay Exam   547

PART 6   FURTHER READINGS FOR THE COLLEGE WRITER   567

Preface

The *Writer's Workplace* and *The Writer's Workplace with Readings* are the result of many years of classroom teaching, and for the past twenty years have served the needs of **more than half a million** students in two-year and four-year colleges throughout the country. Our textbook in both its forms has established itself as a time-tested leader in the field of grammar and composition, supporting the classroom work of teachers and providing inspiration and guidance for students. The students who have used the book have been helped in many of their college courses, as they have pursued their majors and headed directly into their careers.

Each chapter of *The Writer's Workplace with Readings* marks an important step in mastering the grammar and writing skills needed in college and in the world of work. Many of our developmental students find themselves already working while they go to school, and others are returning to school after some years away from the classroom. No matter what their school or work situations, these students need a textbook that is flexible enough to meet a variety of needs. Whether the student using this book works only in the classroom and at home, or gets support in a writing center or a lab, or even participates in the increasingly popular online courses, the structure of *The Writer's Workplace with Readings*, along with the wealth of ancillary materials available for use, make for a total support system that benefits every user of the book in virtually every learning situation.

We were gratified by the enthusiastic response to the features added in the Fifth Edition of *The Writer's Workplace with Readings*. This new Sixth Edition retains all of these features (including the answer key for selected exercises, the ESOL section, editing exercises, and a lively four-color design) while updating content and adding many refinements. The opening chapter has been streamlined; the chapter introducing the essay has been completely redesigned to involve more student hands-on activities; many new exercises have been added; lesson presentations have been refined; and eight new selections have been chosen for the Further Readings section. We are confident that both teacher and student will continue to find this latest edition engaging, flexible, and comprehensive, a supportive resource for developing writers everywhere.

New! Customize *The Writer's Workplace* to Fit Your Course

This edition also introduces *The Writer's Workplace: Custom Edition*. Instructors often find that they cannot cover the entire text in a semester-long course. We are offering the opportunity to pick and choose exactly which chapters you use in a semester, and create a customized text for your course. This allows you the ability to provide your students with the resources that they need—without paying for parts of the book they won't use.

Organization

PART 1   AN INVITATION TO WRITING

The two chapters in the opening section set the invitational tone of this textbook. Students are immediately introduced to the idea that writing is a process. From the very start, they are engaged in short skill-building activities that give them actual practice using the techniques and concepts taught in these chapters. Whether the skill is brainstorming, freewriting, or revising to avoid the use of the second person *you*, students will experience first hand important stages of the writing process.

PART 2   CREATING EFFECTIVE SENTENCES

Part 2 examines a variety of sentence-level topics, all of which lead to student awareness of sentence structure. A careful sequencing of topics builds from less complex to more complex concepts, from phrases to clauses, and from the fragments to the sentences composed of multiple clauses. Most of the exercises in this section are written in continuous discourse; that is, all of the sentences in an exercise relate to a single subject. As a result, students enjoy engaging content while they learn the fundamental skills needed for writing clear and complete sentences. Multiple exercises on each topic give students more than one opportunity to grasp a concept, and by using the answer key to selected exercises, students will be able to judge their need for further work. Instructors who have concentrated on this sentence-building section of the book report that our text provides the most comprehensive and easy-to-follow presentation for building a foundation that prepares students to edit and revise their own work.

PART 3   UNDERSTANDING THE POWER OF WORDS

All writing is strengthened by a more careful attention to word choice. This can range from choosing between commonly confused words such as *its* and *it's*, to understanding why the word *kid* is inappropriate in formal writing. The chapters in this section contain challenging and enjoyable lessons that demonstrate the need for such precise and appropriate language.

PART 4   CREATING EFFECTIVE PARAGRAPHS

Strong paragraphs are the solid blocks of any good piece of writing, and students need to build on such a foundation to produce successful college essays. Many instructors who have used earlier editions of the text have judged this section the heart of the book. Each chapter explains the basic elements needed to develop a paragraph using a particular rhetorical pattern. After practicing with these elements, students are guided in a step-by-step construction of their own paragraphs. Finally, students are given model paragraphs for analysis. These models are outstanding professional examples that serve to inspire more creative approaches to student writing and are accompanied by a list of carefully selected and clearly related writing topics.

PART 5 STRUCTURING THE COLLEGE ESSAY

The goal of *The Writer's Workplace with Readings* is to give students the skills needed for constructing effective college essays. The work of this section relies on a student's grasp of sentence mechanics and paragraph development (skills taught in the preceding sections) and adds the more demanding requirements needed for a longer piece of writing: logical organization of the material, a strong thesis statement and introduction, use of transitions wherever needed, effective paragraph development, appropriate use of outside sources, and a satisfying conclusion. This section includes a chapter that deals with one of a writer's most difficult challenges: developing the essay of argument or persuasion, an effort that always demands careful logic and critical thinking. Part 5 ends with two final concerns: the research paper and the essay exam.

PART 6 FURTHER READINGS FOR THE COLLEGE WRITER

In addition to the carefully chosen professional models used throughout the first five parts of *The Writer's Workplace with Readings*, twenty high-interest essays support the work of the book, with each reading giving the student further opportunity for study and enjoyment. Each reading illustrates a rhetorical mode, thus reinforcing the work of an earlier chapter. Brief introductory notes help students understand and appreciate the background and context of each reading. Finally, two sets of questions guide the instructor through classroom work. The first set, "Questions for Critical Thinking," concentrates on the structure of each piece, while the second set, "Writing in Response," stimulates critical reaction to the themes and leads to a number of challenging writing opportunities.

Features

A PROCESS WRITING APPROACH

Whether the student is working on a single paragraph of comparison and contrast or is developing a complete essay using the student model in Chapter 26, the book encourages a step-by-step approach to the writing process. Whenever possible, students are also encouraged to collaborate. Most developing writers need input from their peers and instructors. In the prewriting stages, in-class brainstorming and discussion of ideas for specific writing topics are especially productive to help students get started. Collaborative work is again useful during the stages of editing and revision.

THE COMPREHENSIVENESS OF A GRAMMAR HANDBOOK

Students come to college writing classes from a wide range of educational backgrounds. Many of these students expect that the gaps in their knowledge of grammar will be addressed. This textbook satisfies those expectations. Almost alone among the many writing textbooks in the field, *The Writer's Workplace with Readings* contains an unusually comprehensive language development section. Carefully crafted definitions, charts, and rules provide visual aids for students as they learn the underlying elements of sentence structure and punctuation. After students have absorbed this material, they will be better able to discuss, analyze, and edit their own writing, as well as better understand the comments made by instructors on returned papers.

CAREFULLY CHOSEN PRACTICES, ACTIVITIES, EXERCISES, AND MASTERY TESTS TO ADDRESS DIFFERENT RATES OF LEARNING

Because every student learns at a different rate, some students need more practice opportunities than others in order to fully absorb a particular concept. Whether the concept is subordination or parallel structure, our textbook offers three exercises to practice each particular rule or concept. The quality and quantity of these exercises are seldom encountered in a textbook of this kind. Students are grateful for the additional practice opportunities, which save them from having to search for resources elsewhere.

EDITING TESTS

"Editing Student Writing" is a feature that appears in Chapters 4 through 13. In each of these exercises, students are asked to analyze student writing by using editing symbols to locate errors and correct them. While students enjoy the search for a number of specified errors, the activity serves as an excellent review of the material learned up to that point in the book. Students also become familiar with the use of editing symbols, a critical tool for interpreting the comments instructors or peers make when evaluating student work. Finally, we have included these editing exercises because many students have grown accustomed to handing in papers without taking the necessary step of editing for errors. These exercises encourage students to focus on the types of errors they must learn to spot in their own writing.

CONTINUOUS DISCOURSE

To create maximum interest in the material, many exercises have been written using continuous discourse. This ensures that the exercises not only teach the skill being presented, but also hold other benefits for the student, including touches of irony or humor, or the telling of a story that is filled with human interest.

PATTERNS OF RHETORICAL DEVELOPMENT

The chapters of Parts 4 and 5 are organized around the classical rhetorical modes, the most commonly accepted method of introducing developmental students to the discipline of college writing. Students first study the specific features of each mode. Then, students are guided using a step-by-step method to construct basic paragraphs or essays. Finally, with the confidence they have gained, they will be challenged by the study of professional models. Given a list of suggested topics on themes suggested by each professional model, students will have a wealth of possible writing assignments from which to choose.

PROFESSIONAL WRITING MODELS WITH CHALLENGING CONTENT

Each of the book's engaging and provocative professional models has the immediate goal of demonstrating some aspect of writing. Each example has also been chosen to enrich our students' lives and increase their love of reading. Our students are mature individuals who need and deserve the challenge of stimulating and sometimes controversial content.

STUDENT MODELS

Students learn from professional writing, and they also learn from other students' writing. Examples of student writing occur throughout the text. The first chapter, for instance, gives an excerpt from a journal written by a young girl struggling with adolescent issues; the chapter also includes a student essay developed from a brainstorming list. Beyond student writing within the text, we encourage instructors to use the writing that comes out of their own classrooms, as opportunities for discussion, analysis, and editing.

THE UNIQUE *WORKING TOGETHER* FEATURE

At the end of every chapter, the Working Together activity provides the instructor with an additional or alternative lesson plan that encourages critical thinking and collaborative learning. These activities tend to stress job-related issues such as sexual harassment (Chapter 29) or integrity in the workplace (Chapter 12). The skill might focus on brainstorming, peer editing, or class discussion to help students gather information for writing. Each of these Working Together projects is designed to provide an engaging full instructional class period that will stimulates class discussion and individual thinking.

MANY PORTFOLIO SUGGESTIONS

The portfolio feature at the conclusion of each chapter encourages students to gather and save all their writing efforts, not only for evaluation purposes, but also for ongoing and future writing projects. Students are encouraged to save journal entries, brainstorming lists, paragraphs, and drafts for essays. All these materials have real potential for development later in the term or in other courses throughout the student's college career.

SIX APPENDICES

The six appendices at the end of the book offer a wealth of pertinent and useful reference material. This section is an especially valuable resource for speakers of English as a Second Language. The first appendix deals with specific issues for ESOL, while the other appendices include material on parts of speech, irregular verbs, spelling, and transitions. All of these sections together serve as a resource for students who find themselves in a variety of other courses that require coherent writing.

ACTIVE READING APPROACH

While *The Writer's Workplace with Readings* is a book that depends heavily on student participation in the process of writing, no successful writing is produced without significant attention being paid to reading and study skills. Beginning Part 6, a section entitled "Strategies for the Active Reader" emphasizes the importance of those skills for the developmental writing student. One of the essays new to this edition, "How to Mark a Book" by Mortimer Adler, also makes the case for active reading. Students are encouraged to become more engaged in the texts they are reading and to place more emphasis on their critical thinking skills. These are skills that will take students far beyond the experience of a particular writing class, and will enrich many other parts of their lives.

EXPLORING ONLINE

Students can now access the website for *The Writer's Workplace with Readings* to find additional help with the topics covered in each chapter. At the website, students will find a chapter-by-chapter glossary, along with quizzes, and other suggested activities.

AN ANSWER KEY TO PRACTICES AND SELECTED EXERCISES

The answer key provides answers to all the practices and approximately one-third of the exercises in the book. For instance, where three exercises are given on a topic, the answers to the first exercise will always be given. This answer key allows students to work more independently. Of course, answers to the Mastery Tests are given only in the Annotated Instructor's Edition.

INSIDE FRONT AND BACK COVER CHARTS

The inside front and back cover charts provide material on two important subjects for easy reference: options for coordination and subordination and common editing symbols.

New to This Edition

10 NEW WORKING TOGETHER COLLABORATIVE ACTIVITIES

These fresh activities are intended to evoke lively classroom discussion while they focus on skills that are conducive to collaborative work, such as brainstorming or editing. Many topics are purposely job related and provide students with helpful information about careers and the world of work.

A MORE CONCISE CHAPTER 1

The first chapter of any textbook should not be overwhelming. Although note taking, with its emphasis on summarizing and paraphrasing, is important for many prewriting efforts, we have moved this material to Chapter 32, where these skills are already part of the work of that chapter. The Instructor's Resource Manual also provides texts for teachers to utilize if their course design calls for more practice in the skill of summarizing.

A WIDE RANGE OF NEW EXERCISES AND PRACTICES

Many new practices and exercises bring fresh content to this edition. Chapter 3, for example, has ten new practices and exercises, which maintain continuous discourse wherever possible and use current topics (video gaming, best sellers, human interest stories) that reflect the interests of our students and pay attention to controversial national trends. Throughout our chapters, we continue to offer freshly chosen paragraphs filled with humor and irony.

TEXT REFINEMENTS THROUGHOUT THE BOOK

Many changes occur throughout the text: tightened definitions, more clearly designed presentations of concepts, expanded explanations and examples where needed, rewritten questions, and numerous other small and some not-so-small improvements. For many of these refinements, we must thank our users and reviewers for their thoughtful suggestions.

EXPANDED USE OF PHOTOGRAPHS

Our students' world is increasingly visual. The book's four-color design now has a greater number of color photographs that will add to students' enjoyment as they work with the text.

AN ENTIRELY NEW CHAPTER 26 THAT ENSURES STUDENT PARTICIPATION

In this newly written chapter, each student will develop an essay following the same process used by our model student writer. Everyone is assigned the same topic (the description of a school once attended). Students begin with prewriting activities and finish with their final drafts. At each step, students will observe how the student writer handled the corresponding step in the writing assignment. Working through this chapter impresses on students not only the degree of thought required to construct an adequate thesis statement, but also the amount of effort needed to arrive at the topic sentences that will correctly state the main ideas of paragraphs. By the conclusion of this process-centered chapter, students will have experienced the many changes that inevitably take place between the first freewriting effort and the final draft.

EIGHT NEW READINGS

The Further Reading section has been expanded from sixteen readings to twenty. Of these twenty readings, eight are new to this edition. Each of these readings has been chosen for its high-interest level, for its value as an example of a particular rhetorical mode, and for its theme, which reinforces another lesson in the text. For instance, Mortimer Adler's Essay "How to Mark a Book" will reinforce the section that shows students how to become active readers, while Elizabeth Berg's essay on "Heroes" will enrich the discussion in the Working Together activity that addresses how to define the term *hero*.

Ancillaries

The Writer's Workplace with Readings is supported by a wide range of instructional materials, each one designed to aid the teacher's classroom work. These materials include:

Annotated Instructor's Edition

This book provides answers to the practices and exercises in the versions of the text used by students.

Instructor's Resource Manual

This Instructor's Resource Manual supports instructors teaching with *The Writer's Workplace*, Eighth Edition, and *The Writer's Workplace with Readings*, Sixth Edition. Teachers using this manual will find a variety of materials geared toward enhancing, reinforcing, and complementing students' experience with the primary text.

This manual has been revised and expanded in order to support the new editions of *The Writer's Workplace*, with a view toward integrating ancillary material more closely with the objectives, chapter content, and readings in the textbook. Instructors will find comprehensive support for planning and organizing their courses in Part 1, including specific sample syllabi that leverage the exciting new material from the text. This section also includes in-depth discussion on incorporating collaborative learning and the use of journals into the classroom, as well as a section on grading and responding to student writing. Teachers looking for additional assignments to give their students will benefit from the revised chapter guides in Part 2, which offer in-class activities, journal assignments, and responding to reading assignments designed with the goals of each chapter in mind. New instructional essays, drawn from respected colleagues in the field of composition studies, have been added to Part 3 and cover such topics as integrating the teaching of grammar into the composition classroom and using a hybrid model of online and in-classroom learning for composition students. Part 4 now includes a full and revised set of handouts and transparency masters that complement the entire text. Part 5 provides a variety of evaluation handouts that may prove useful for both teachers and students. Two appendices complete the manual, offering sample student writings and a compendium of the more than one hundred assignments presented in the manual.

Exercise and Test Book

This book contains numerous multiple-choice grammar and sentence structure exercises, giving instructors the option of providing additional practices to students as the need arises. The topics for these exercises are carefully keyed to the chapters of *The Writer's Workplace* and *The Writer's Workplace with Readings*.

WebTutor™ ToolBox for Blackboard and WebCT

Preloaded with content and available free via pincode when packaged with this text, WebTutor ToolBox pairs all the content of this text's rich Book Companion Web Site with all the sophisticated course management functionality of a Blackboard or WebCT product. Instructors can assign materials (including online quizzes) and have the results flow automatically to their gradebook. Students have access only to student resources on the Web site; instructors enter a pincode for access to password-protected instructor resources.

Book Companion Web Site
academic.cengage.com/devenglish/scarry

The Book Companion Web Site features a wealth of text-specific resources for students. For each chapter of the text, students have access to chapter objectives, an "Exploring Online" section that provides links to additional online resources, a glossary of important terms, online activities that build on chapter material by leveraging the depth and breadth of content available on the Web, and interactive online grammar quizzes.

CengageNOW for Writing

Another way to incorporate new media into the composition classroom is by using *CengageNOW for Writing*, available from Cengage Learning. This online multimedia program covers all aspects of the writing process, from pointers on prewriting techniques to grammar exercises to help with the college essay. Incorporating this media ancillary as part of the curriculum may prove useful in adding dimensionality and currency to composition courses.

The Writer's Resources CD-ROM, Version 2.0

The first interactive CD-ROM that teaches the grammar and mechanics of writing, *Writer's Resources* provides writing instruction, extensive examples (with animation and audio clips), and over 4,500 interactive exercises with immediate feedback and additional explanation.

"Salvation" by Langston Hughes DVD

A free DVD of the famous Langston Hughes story "Salvation" is available with the purchase of *The Writer's Workplace with Readings*, Sixth Edition. (A copy of the DVD may also be ordered separately for a modest charge.) This professionally produced version of the Hughes story provides further insight into the selection and into the author's life and work. Integrating this outstanding production into a semester's coursework quickly leads to lively class discussion, stimulating writing prompts, or even more extensive essay or report assignments.

Acknowledgments

With our new edition, we find ourselves again indebted to a host of people, those who have inspired us and those who have worked behind the scenes to make certain that our initial vision of the book would be realized. First of all, we thank some wonderful colleagues (Professors Vermell Blanding and Cynthia Jones chief among them) and all the amazing students we have taught at Hostos Community College. Their inspiration has been a constant source of energy and creativity. One of them in particular, Raluca Tanasescu, especially is to be thanked for her contribution to the new Chapter 26 of this edition. It is first and foremost the hard work and courage of our students, and indeed all the students who have used our textbook, that motivate us to constantly refine our work. We have come to realize that the skills taught in this book have the ability to empower people and change their lives. Our gratitude to our team at Wadsworth is not easy to measure. Through the previous editions and including the present work, we have had the good fortune to benefit from the energy and talent of professionals who have patiently and attentively addressed the needs of the book. Our publisher, Michael Rosenberg, has been with us from the start, and we recall with pleasure all of our working collaborations. We also owe a genuine debt of gratitude to Steve Dalphin, Acquisitions Editor, whose faith in our work and guiding insights over the years have made our rethinking and revision much less stressful than otherwise might have been; his presence and personality have been much appreciated. Our book has benefited tremendously because of the professionalism and expertise of these two men. We are enjoying our association with Annie Todd, new acquisitions editor, and look forward to working with her on this and future editions. Another piece of our good fortune deserves special mention. We have had the benefit of the day-to-day problem solving accomplished by our Developmental Editor, Laurie Runion. We could not have hoped for anyone with more careful attention to every detail. We will always be grateful for her total support and encouragement every step of the way. Every author should be as fortunate!

Other members of the Wadsworth family have been supportive in so many other ways. We thank Sarah Sherman, our Content Project Manager, for her page-by-page expert attention. To Kate Edwards, our Marketing Manager, our gratitude to her responsiveness to our needs as they have arisen. Karen Judd has been our Managing Development Editor once again and with the results we as always deeply appreciate. We also have been fortunate to have had help in the selection of photographs and the securing of literary texts by Cheri Throop. We understand all too well the detailed work required for these tasks and how important such good work has been for the finished product. Stephanie Gregoire Technology Project Manager, has directed the work of the vast technological support system which accompanies our book; we have only profound admiration for all this work.

Two other people have played major roles in the creation of materials that accompany our text, and to both of them we must express how much their work has meant to us and to instructors everywhere. Preparing materials to help teachers is very important to us. Valerie Russell, of Valencia Community College, has again undertaken the daunting task of the careful work needed to prepare the Exercise and Test Book. Siobhán Scarry, now at the University of Buffalo, has again updated the Instructor's Resource Manual, which we believe is filled with a wealth of helpful material for our instructors. We have never seen a better Instructor's Resource Manual. For this and for so much more, we thank her.

We would not be achieving the degree of success with each new edition without the invaluable insights of our professional reviewers. The fruits of their many years of collective experience, and their individual perceptions for the needs of this latest revised manuscript, have made our efforts for this new edition possible. To each of them, our sincerest gratitude. They include:

Becky Ament, *Muskingum Area Technical College*

Karen Antill, *Heald CollegeHonolulu*

Karin L. Blaske, *Arapahoe Community College*

Helen Chester, *Milwaukee Area Technical College*

Shelly Dorsey, *Pima Community College*

Raymond W. Foster, *Scottsdale Community College*

Irene Gilliam, *Tallahassee Community College*

Aaron Goldweber, *Heald College*

Carmen Hall, *St. Petersburg College*

Joel Henderson, *Chattanooga State Technical Community College*

Bonnie Hilton, *Broward Community College*

Teri Maddox, *Jackson State Community College*

Valerie Russell, *Valencia Community College*

Verne Underwood, *Rogue Community College*

Stephanie L. R. Van Lear, *Heald CollegeHonolulu*

Rick Williams, *Rogue Community College*

THE WRITER'S WORKPLACE
with Readings

PART

1

An Invitation to Writing

Part 1 invites you to explore the beginning stages of the writing process and examine the essential elements of any effective piece of writing. Begin your work in this writing course with the kind of spirit that spells success.

- **Begin with a positive attitude.** You know more than you think. You have unique life experiences, and your ideas are worth writing about. Fortunately, writing is a skill that can be developed. No matter what your present skills are, practice can greatly help you improve those skills.

- **Be receptive to new techniques and approaches.** As a student beginning this course, you undoubtedly have not yet explored all the various techniques writers use to generate ideas on paper, and you may still have to learn how to incorporate other people's ideas in your writing. Be willing to experiment with the techniques given in this section of the book. Once you practice these proven techniques, you will feel a new confidence as you tackle your own writing assignments.

- **Actively reach out and welcome help from others.** When we learn new skills, we are not expected to figure out everything by ourselves. Most students need help getting started, and because learning styles are different, students need to explore whatever methods work best for them. At every stage of the process, writers need each other to brainstorm, to read and comment on drafts, and to help revise, edit, and proofread each other's work. Part 1 of this book will help you extend your own thinking as you work beyond your first thoughts on a topic.

- **Respect the ideas of others.** Communication goes two ways. In the process of exploring and expressing your ideas, you must be open to other points of view, whether they come from your instructors, your classmates, or your own reading. You can debate opposing ideas without criticizing the people who hold those ideas.

- **Finally, practice, practice, practice.** This means being willing to put in the necessary time and effort to achieve the needed results.

Gathering Ideas for Writing

In this first chapter, you will practice several **prewriting techniques** used by professional writers as well as student writers as they gather material and generate ideas for writing:

CHAPTER OBJECTIVES

- journal writing
- focused freewriting
- brainstorming, clustering, and outlining
- conducting interviews and surveys

Overview of the Writing Process

The following chart shows the stages a writer goes through to produce a finished piece of writing. Writers may differ slightly in how they approach a task, but for most of us the following steps are necessary.

The Writing Process

Prewriting Stages

1. Choose the topic and consider what aspect of that topic interests you.
2. Gather ideas, using prewriting techniques.

Writing and Revising

3. Compose a first draft and then set it aside for a time.
4. Reread your first draft and, if possible, ask the instructor or classmates for input.
5. Revise the first draft by adding, cutting, and moving material. Continue to revise, correcting grammar errors and producing new drafts, until you are satisfied.

Proofreading

6. Proofread the final copy, looking especially for typographical errors (typos), misspellings, and omitted words.

BEGINNING TO WRITE: CARING ABOUT YOUR TOPIC

Whether you are writing a college paper or a report on the job, your belief in the importance of your topic and confidence in your own ideas will be major factors in your success as a writer. Sometimes a college writing assignment can seem to have little or no relevance beyond a requirement for a passing grade. In this course, however, you should consider each assignment as an opportunity to do the following:

- discover that you have ideas worth expressing
- explore topics that you care about
- incorporate the ideas of others into your own work

PREWRITING TECHNIQUES: THE FIRST STEP IN THE WRITING PROCESS

> **Prewriting,** the earliest stage of the writing process, uses techniques such as brainstorming, clustering, and outlining to transform thoughts into words.

Very few writers ever sit down and start writing immediately. To produce effective work, most writers begin by using a variety of strategies called *prewriting techniques.* These techniques help writers generate ideas and gather material about topics that are of interest to them or that they are required to write about for their work. Prewriting techniques are a way to explore and give some order to what might otherwise be a confusing hodgepodge of different thoughts on a topic. These techniques reassure every writer who feels the stress of looking at a blank page or an empty computer screen, knowing it has to be filled. Not only will the writer have needed material but he or she can also plan how to develop that material: what the major ideas will be, what the order of those ideas will be, and what specific details will be used. The rest of this chapter will describe these prewriting techniques and provide opportunities to practice them.

Journal Writing

> **Journal writing** is the written record of a person's observations, thoughts, reactions, or opinions. Kept daily, or nearly so, the journal usually draws on everyday experiences.

A great many people keep a diary or journal at some point in their lives. Keeping a journal shows that a person feels the need to make a record of day-to-day events or wishes to put down on paper some important thoughts, reactions, or opinions about what is happening in life. If the journal is a personal one, the writer does not have to worry about making a mistake or being misunderstood. The journal writer does not have to worry about handwriting or how thoughts are organized, because the writer is the only person who will be reading the pages of that journal. A personal journal allows a person to be totally honest and write about anything he or she wishes.

For some people, a journal is a kind of scrapbook of meaningful written expressions they find around them. These journals could include drawings, quotations from books and articles, snippets of overheard conversations, or information heard on the radio or television. Over time, journals help students grow as writers and add to their overall success in college.

If you keep a journal, you might want to record events that happen around you, focus on problems you are trying to solve, or note your personal reactions to the people you know. Until you actually put your thoughts into words, you may not be fully aware of all your feelings and opinions. Most writers are surprised and pleased with the results of their personal explorations in writing.

Another type of journal is the one that will definitely have an audience, even if it is only the instructor. In many writing classes, instructors require students to keep a more public journal as part of a semester's work. In this more public journal, handwriting will be important and some topics might be considered inappropriate. Sometimes this journal contributes to the final grade for a course. Instructors who make a journal part of their semester's assignments understand how such writing, done frequently, gives students valuable practice in setting thoughts down on paper.

ENTRY FROM *THE DIARY OF LATOYA HUNTER*

Keeping a journal is especially popular during adolescence, partly because these years are usually a time of uncertainty when young people try to discover themselves as individuals. The following selection is from the published diary of a junior high school student, Latoya Hunter, who kept a journal when she was only twelve years old. The diary reports on her growing need for independence and her changing perceptions of the world around her.

Today my friend Isabelle had a fit in her house. It was because of her mother. She's never home and she expects Isabelle to stay by herself. Today she was extra late because she was out with her boyfriend. Isabelle was really mad. She called her father and told him she wanted to live with him because her mother only cared about one person—her boyfriend. She was so upset. She was throwing things all over the place and crying. I never saw her like that before. It was really sad to see. I felt bad when I had to leave her all by herself. I hope she and her mother work it out but all mothers are the same. They think that you're young and shouldn't have an opinion. It's really hard to communicate with my parents. They'll listen to me but that's about it. They hardly take me seriously and it's because of my age. It's like discrimination! If you do speak your mind, you end up getting beaten. The real pain doesn't come from the belt though, it comes from inside. That's the worst pain you could ever feel.

ACTIVITY 1

Writing a Journal Entry of Your Own

In the selection you have just read, Latoya Hunter sadly observes a friend going through an emotional crisis. Latoya uses her journal to explore her own feelings about parent-child relationships and to express what she thinks are some of the common failings of parents.

Write a journal entry of your own. Report an incident in which you were successful or unsuccessful in communicating with someone you know. The person could be a family member or someone from outside your family. Looking back on the incident, think about what contributed to the success or failure of that communication. What part did each person play that led to the final outcome?

_____

_____

_____

_____

_____

_____

_____

_____

_____

_____

_____

_____

_____

_____

_____

_____

_____

_____

_____

Focused Freewriting

Focused freewriting offers another way to explore writing topics. With this technique, the writer keeps on writing for a predetermined amount of time and does not stop, no matter what. The goal of this technique is to put words on paper, and even if nothing new comes to mind, the writer keeps going by repeating a particular idea. This approach is one way to free a writer from what is often called "writer's block," that moment in the writing process when a person runs out of words and becomes paralyzed by the blank page or computer screen.

> **Focused freewriting** is a prewriting technique in which the writer explores a topic by writing for a predetermined amount of time without stopping, even if it means repeating the same ideas.

Here, for example, is what one young man wrote when he was asked to write for five minutes on the topic of *keeping a journal:*

> I'm supposed to write about journal writing. I've never kept a journal so how can I say anything about it? But I broke into my younger sister's diary once and found out about a boy she had kissed. It was one of those diaries with those little keys and I ruined the lock. She didn't speak to me for over a month and my parents were mad at me. I thought it was funny at the time. After that she didn't keep a diary anymore. So now what should I say? Now what should I say? I don't really know. I guess I might keep a journal to keep track of important things that happen to me, like the day my dad came home with a used car for me—now that was really cool. Of course, it had a lot of problems that we had to fix over the next year little by little, but that was really an awesome day.

ACTIVITY 2

Focused Freewriting

For this exercise, consider the topic *My attitude toward writing* as an opportunity to practice focused freewriting. Write for at least five minutes without stopping, making sure that you keep going even if you have to repeat some thoughts.

_____

_____

_____

_____

_____

_____

_____

_____

_____

_____

_____

_____

_____

_____

_____

_____

_____

Brainstorming, Clustering, and Outlining

BRAINSTORMING

Of all the prewriting techniques, brainstorming is perhaps the most widely used. Brainstorming is an exercise in free association. You allow a thought or phrase to lead you from one idea to the next until you feel you have fully explored your topic. Many writers find brainstorming liberating because item order is unimportant and no special connection is needed between items. The main goal is to jot down everything while your mind explores different paths. Later, you can sort the items, grouping some and eliminating others. Unless you are doing outside research, brainstorming is probably the best way to discover ideas for writing.

> **Brainstorming** is a prewriting technique in which the writer uses free association to create a list of whatever words, phrases, or ideas come to mind on a given topic. It can be done alone or in a group.

The following list shows a college student's initial brainstorming on the topic of *parent-teen communication*.

> Problems talking with my father
>   Called me immature sometimes
>   Occasionally shouted
>   Too tense
>   Seemed overly critical
> Stacy's father
>   Seemed to have a sense of humor about everything, not so serious,
>   easygoing

Guidance counselor
    Always calm, no hurry, always listened
What prevents a good talk with a parent?
    person's voice—loud, soft, angry, calm
    namecalling, putdowns
    words that hurt
    bad language
    body language—no eye contact, frowning, glaring
    authoritarian or controlling
    monopolizing the conversation
    tense
    withdrawal or the silent treatment
    teens can act worse than parents—disrespectful and rude
    rushed, not listening
    rigid, won't consider any other viewpoint
    sarcastic

Below is a revised brainstorming list showing how the student has reorganized the initial list.

Advice to Parents: How to Communicate with Your Teen

Choose your words carefully
    do not call people names
    do not belittle them—use example of my father
    do not use bad language
    do not be disrespectful
    do not be mean or sarcastic
    do not use the silent treatment or monopolize the talk
Listen to the way you sound, your tone, your attitude
    watch the volume of your voice—use example of Stacy's father
    wait until you have calmed down so you do not sound angry and
        tense
    don't sound rushed and hurried, as if you have no time to listen
    don't sound too controlling
Take a look at your body language
    work at being calm and relaxed
    do not withdraw; if possible give the person a hug or a pat on the
        shoulder
    no physical abuse—pushing, shoving, slapping
    what is your facial expression (frowning, glaring, smirking, no eye
        contact)?

CLUSTERING

Clustering is another method of gathering ideas during the prewriting stage. Clustering is very similar to brainstorming, except that when you cluster, you produce a visual map of your ideas rather than a list. You begin by placing a key idea (usually a single word or phrase) in the center of the page. Then you jot down other words and phrases that come to mind as you think about this key idea. As you work, you draw lines, or branches, to connect the items.

Here is how the writer might have explored the topic using a clustering technique:

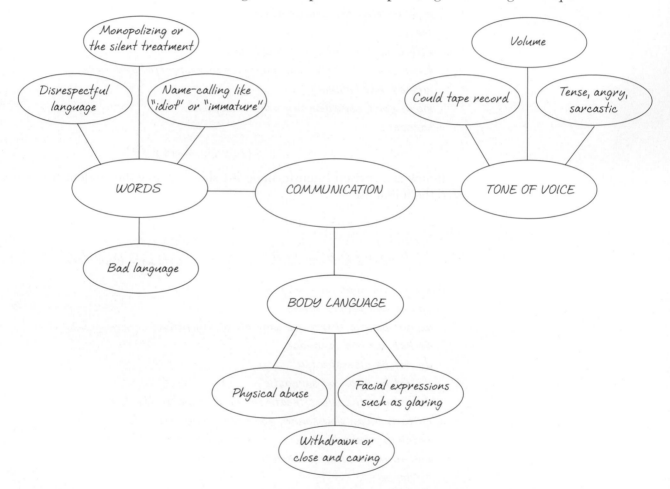

Clustering is a prewriting technique that emphasizes the connections among items on a brainstorming list. The topic is written in the middle of the page and has a circle drawn around it. As details or ideas are generated, they are circled and then lines are drawn to connect them to related details or ideas. This process continues until the topic has been fully explored. Variations of clustering are *mapping, webbing,* and *branching.*

ACTIVITY 3   **Using Brainstorming or Clustering to Develop a Topic of Your Own**

Use either brainstorming or clustering to develop your ideas on one of the following topics:

● communicating with teachers and classmates
● communicating on a cell phone
● communicating on the Internet (e-mail and chat rooms)

Create your brainstorming list or cluster on a separate sheet of paper.

OUTLINING

Outlining is the most formal method of organizing prewriting ideas. It is more difficult than the other prewriting techniques and usually comes after a good bit of brainstorming and rearranging of ideas. In a formal outline you must distinguish between major points and supporting details and put them in the order of your presentation of ideas. Because organization and order are important in outlining, there are rules for the outline so that you can tell by looking at it which ideas are major and which are supporting details. In the sample outline that follows, notice the use of capital roman numerals (I, II, III) for major points, indented capital letters (A, B, C) for details, and arabic numbers (1, 2, 3) where further details fall under the secondary points.

> **Outlining,** the most formal method of organizing prewriting ideas, uses numerals and letters to distinguish between major points and supporting details of a planned piece of writing.

Here is how the student's outline of his material might have developed:

```
              Advice to Parents:
   How to Communicate with Your Teens

   I.  Introduction
       Topic Sentence: Parents need to consider their
       words, tone, and body language when they talk to
       their teens.
   II. Choose your words carefully.
       A. Do not call people names.
          1. My father called me immature.
          2. Parents sometimes use words like "idiot."
       B. Do not use bad language.
       C. Do not be disrespectful.
       D. Do not monopolize the conversation.
       E. Do not use the silent treatment.
```

```
III. Listen to your tone.
     A. Wait until you have calmed down so you do not
        sound angry and tense.
     B. Watch the volume of your voice.
        1. Stacy's father speaks softly.
        2. Stacy's father speaks reassuringly.
     C. Taping a conversation would reveal tone.
IV. Observe your body language.
     A. Notice your facial expression.
        1. Are you glaring?
        2. Are you full of rage?
     B. Make eye contact.
     C. Do not withdraw; if possible, give the person
        a hug or hold that person's hand.
     D. Physical abuse is never appropriate.
 V. Conclusion
    Parents who think about these three factors of
    communication will be able to avoid a lot of pain
    and heartache.
```

ACTIVITY **Making an Outline**

Using the title "Communication in the Twenty-First Century," make an outline for an essay that would describe modern forms of communication. You may want to consider the following items: Internet, e-mail, instant messaging, online courses, blogs, fax machines, printers, digital cameras, cell phones, and iPods.

_____

_____

_____

_____

_____

_____

_____

_____

_____

_____

STUDENT ESSAY

Now we are ready to look at the student essay that evolved from the initial brainstorming list. Notice that the writer is not bound to follow the brainstorming list or the outline word for word. As the student wrote, a certain creative flow occurred.

Advice to Parents:
How to Communicate with Your Teens

When parents and teens cannot sit down and talk together, parents should take a long hard look at themselves to see if part of the blame might lie with them. Parents need to consider three factors: the words they choose, the tone of voice they use, and the message their body language gives.

One usually thinks of words as being at the center of communication, and of course, words are important. The wrong words can unintentionally put people in a bad mood. Parents very often belittle their children or call them names. My father, for example, sometimes used the word "immature" to describe me when I made a mistake. I felt put down. It would probably have been better if he would have talked with me about the situation and explained why he thought I had made a bad choice. I've heard parents call their children "idiots" and even worse. Name-calling only makes teens angry and defensive. It's hard after being attacked to feel open to any discussion at all. I've heard teens and parents use bad language and speak disrespectfully to each other. Speaking in the heat of the moment, people often say things they really don't mean, but when they calm down, it is too late to take the words back. The harm is done. Then there is the parent who monopolizes the discussion, giving the teen no opportunity to explain his or her position. Finally, there is the complete opposite of the wrong words, and that is no words at all. Have you ever experienced the silent treatment? With this approach, everyone feels terrible and there is no chance to work out a problem.

A parent's tone of voice is a second factor in communicating with a teenager. Something said in a tense, harsh, or angry voice creates unnecessary bad feelings. The same words said with a firm but soft and reassuring voice can make for a completely different conversation. Even the volume of a person's voice can make a tremendous difference when people talk. My friend Stacy, for example, has a lot of disagreements with her father, but I have never heard their disagreements turn into angry arguments. Her father is from another country where people speak very softly. His voice is so calm and soft that I suppose this is one reason why Stacy never seems to get angry with him. He also uses a lot of humor, and they can laugh about her occasional outrageous behavior. I think it would be a good idea for some parents to tape themselves when they are talking with their teenagers. They might be very surprised to hear their tone. They might then have a better understanding of why their teenagers suddenly become upset or withdrawn.

I also wish some parents could see themselves when they are talking to their teens. Their body language really communicates "I am angry at you!" Facial expressions can be glaring or even full of rage. To communicate with your teen, you need to make eye contact and if possible even give an affectionate hug or hold the teen's hand; in other words, let your body language say that you care about him or her even though you have a serious concern about your teen's behavior. Obviously, any kind of physical abuse is never appropriate. Slapping, hitting, or punching is absolutely unacceptable. If you cannot control your teen without physical restraint, you need to seek outside help.

If only parents would understand the importance of words, tone, and body language the next time they faced a conflict with their teens, much needless pain and heartache could be avoided.

Conducting Interviews and Surveys

Journal writing, focused freewriting, brainstorming, and outlining are all techniques that you can use to explore your thoughts and ideas. Often, however, a writer needs to go further and obtain information from outside sources. An excellent way to obtain such information is to conduct an interview or prepare and distribute a survey or questionnaire. News reporters, marketing people, social workers, and government workers are only a few of the people who use these techniques in their everyday work.

INTERVIEWS

Interviews are useful in many situations. Speaking to a single individual can provide information that you might not be able to get any other way. For example, you might want to interview an older family member to preserve stories of your family's past. You might want to talk to someone in a career that interests you. If you were considering a career in law, for example, speaking to a lawyer in your community might be more revealing than reading a book about the legal profession. An interview is also an excellent way to find information on very current topics, material you might have trouble finding in the library or even on the Internet.

The secret of a good interview lies in what happens before the interview. You must prepare properly. First of all, make an appointment with the person you want to interview. Let that person know how long the interview will take. If you intend to bring a tape recorder, be sure to ask for permission in advance. It is important for the person being interviewed to know what to expect so he or she can be relaxed and in a receptive frame of mind. Most importantly, the interviewer should always have a number of questions prepared beforehand. Few interviews go well without some structure and a sense of direction. This is not to say that every question must be asked in the way and order in which it was prepared; an interviewer is not restricted to a fixed set of questions. An interview can often take an interesting and unexpected turn with a single good question that leads to a surprising exploration of a subject.

When you prepare your questions, compose them in such a way that the answers require some thought. You do not want to ask questions that can be answered with a simple yes or no; such replies are not useful because they do not encourage any in-depth discussion of the answer.

ACTIVITY **Preparing Questions for an Interview**

The following five pairs of sentences could have been used in an interview in which a person was trying to learn about a lawyer's work. In each case, check which question would more likely lead to a thoughtful interview response.

_____   1.   What is a typical day at work like?
_____   How many hours a day do you work?

_____   2.   How much do you earn in a year?
_____   What is the range of salaries that a person could expect to earn as a lawyer?

_____   3.   What kind of law do you practice?
_____   What are the different areas of law practice, and how did you choose which one you wanted to pursue?

_____   4.   What is the most interesting case you have ever had?
_____   Have you ever had an interesting case?

_____   5.   Do you ever have a bad day?
_____   What are some of your greatest challenges and how do you handle them?

SURVEYS

Taking a survey is an especially helpful prewriting technique when you want to write about a certain group's attitudes, practices, or experiences. For instance, you could do a survey on your classmates' attitudes toward binge drinking, your family's attitudes about how to share the household chores, or your community's attitudes about the need for a teen center. A survey is somewhat like an interview in that the person conducting it prepares a set of questions. However, an interview is conducted one-on-one, and the conversation has great flexibility. A survey, on the other hand, is usually written in advance. A number of participants agree to answer a set of questions. If they write their answers, the survey takes the form of a questionnaire. They may or may not complete the survey in your presence. What you will get will be the briefest answers to your questions—no more, no less. Obviously, you will run into difficulty if you realize later on that you should have asked different questions. Therefore, in a survey, most of the work lies in the preparation of the questions and in experimenting with different ways of presenting questions so as to get the best answers. Unlike the interview, the survey may include questions that can be answered with a yes or a no. You may also want to ask questions that call for precise facts and figures. Here are a few other considerations:

1. Will people give their names, or will they be anonymous?
2. How will the surveys be returned? Will you give people a deadline and collect the surveys yourself, or will you give them a self-addressed stamped envelope so that they can mail the survey to you?
3. Be prepared for some people who may not answer the survey's questions at all. If it is too long or too complicated, people may decide they don't have time to do it. After all, most people volunteer to answer a survey, and they will be doing it as a favor to you.
4. The more responses there are to a survey, the more valid the results of that survey will be. For example, if you want to know the attitudes of your classmates toward journal writing, the closer you come to having 100 percent response, the more valid the survey will be.
5. How will you tally the answers? Will the results be presented as a chart, or will you write a report in which you explain the results?

ACTIVITY **Composing Questions for a Survey**

Several serious problems on college campuses today relate to the use of alcohol. Underage drinking, binge drinking, drunken fights, and vandalism of school property are some of the problems college administrations face. Compose five questions that could be included in a survey of your classmates to determine their drinking habits. Construct each question so that it asks for personal experience, not a person's opinion about what other students are doing. Here is an example:

Which of the following best describes how often you have an alcoholic drink?

a. never
b. only on holidays and other special occasions
c. two or three times a month
d. once or twice a week
e. three or more times a week
f. every day

1. _____
_____
_____
_____
_____
_____
_____
_____

2. _____
_____
_____
_____

3. _____

_____

_____

_____

_____

_____

_____

_____

_____

_____

4. _____

_____

_____

_____

_____

_____

_____

_____

_____

_____

_____

5. _____

_____

_____

_____

_____

_____

_____

_____

Exploring Online

Go to academic.cengage.com/devenglish/scarry to find the **Writer's
Online Workplace,** a website designed for students using this book.
You will find links to handouts, interactive quizzes, and other online
resources as you explore the following topics:

- the writing process
- prewriting techniques
- journaling

Taking a Survey:
Student Attitudes about Writing

Writers gather material for their work in a number of ways. One way is to conduct a survey, drawing on the experiences of people who have something in common. For this prewriting exercise, you will participate in a survey with all the students in your class. The survey asks students about their experiences with writing and their attitudes toward writing. As a class, you may add to or change the questions suggested here, but everyone should answer exactly the same questions.

Use the following procedure:

1. Remove the survey on page 19 from your textbook.

2. Put your name or an assigned number in the top right corner of the survey for purposes of identification.

3. Answer the survey questions as completely and honestly as possible.

4. Select two people who will collect all the surveys and lead the class in tallying the information. One person can read off the responses; the other person can put the information on a blackboard where everyone can view the information and take notes on it.

Portfolio Suggestion

A **portfolio** is a collection of materials representing a person's best work and intended to help in the evaluation of that work, often for a grade in a course. A writer may also include materials to use in future work.

To start building your portfolio, take back your own page of responses to the survey and add it to any notes you took about the results of the class survey. Jot down any other ideas that might have come to you as you thought about the topic. Place all these in your portfolio and keep them for possible use in future writing assignments.

Consider using the interview and the survey as techniques for gathering material that can be transformed quite easily into an essay. Remember that people who write for a living—newspaper and magazine writers, for example—depend heavily on these techniques for their material.

1. How would you describe the ideal place for a writer to work?

   _____

   _____

   _____

   _____

2. Where do you do your best writing—in the library, at home, or someplace else?

   _____

   _____

3. Is a certain time of day better for you than other times? When do you concentrate best?

   _____

4. How long can you write with concentration before you need a break?

   _____

5. What concerns do you have when you write?

   _____

6. Have you ever kept a journal?

   _____

7. Do you prefer composing on a computer or writing by hand?

   _____

8. In high school, how many of your classes included writing opportunities? How often were you required to write?

   _____

9. Keeping in mind that most people today use a telephone or e-mail to keep in touch, how often do you find yourself writing a letter?

   a. never   b. almost never   c. sometimes   d. often

10. At this point in your school career, which of the following best describes your attitude about writing?

    _____ I enjoy writing most of the time.

    _____ I occasionally like to write.

    _____ I usually do not like to write.

    _____ I don't have any opinion about writing at all.

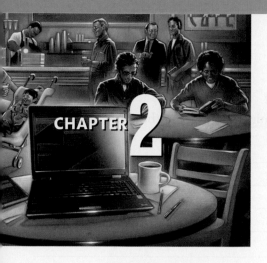

CHAPTER 2

Recognizing the Elements of Good Writing

In this chapter, you will learn how each of the following elements helps to create an effective piece of writing:

CHAPTER OBJECTIVES

- a carefully chosen **subject;** or what the writing is about
- a clear **purpose;** or the writer's intention
- a targeted **audience;** or the writer's intended readers
- a consistent and appropriate **voice;** or how the writer's attitude is revealed
- an overall **unity;** or all parts relating to the central theme
- a basic **coherence;** or clear and logical progression of thought

The Subject: What the Writing Is About

The subject of a piece of writing is also called the *topic* or the *central theme.* The subject can be chosen by the writer or assigned by someone else. We've all heard the student who complains, "I don't have anything to say." Not true! It may be that the student hasn't yet developed the skill to put ideas into writing, but we all know more than we think we do. We all know about our families, our homes, our friends, our opinions, our experiences. We have childhood memories, interests, activities we participate in, and dreams. When we write, we need to tap into these life experiences and life lessons to find topics that interest us. We also need to remember that we can gather more information by consulting others.

Even with an assigned topic, a writer can often find an aspect of the subject that is of interest. For example, on the subject of *binge drinking in college,* a writer might choose to narrow the subject to one of the following aspects:

Tell a personal story:	The story of my friend Tom who flunked out of college last semester
Provide statistical information:	The facts about drinking on college campuses
Discuss the effects:	The effects of binge drinking on college campuses
Explain how to do something:	How to avoid substance abuse in college
Take a stand on an issue:	The need for colleges to enforce the laws on underage drinking

ACTIVITY **Choosing an Aspect of a Subject**

Give five possible approaches a writer might take, given the topic of *working while going to school.*

1. _____

2. _____

3. _____

4. _____

5. _____

Purpose: The Writer's Intention

In school, when a student hands in a writing assignment, that student's primary purpose may be to get a good grade. At work, an employee may produce a written document with the purpose of getting ahead in a job. These examples are not what we mean by *purpose.* In writing, *purpose* is what the piece of writing itself is intended to accomplish, apart from any other personal aims of the writer. The main purposes for writing are entertainment, information, and persuasion.

ENTERTAINMENT

A writer may want to entertain an audience. One way to do this is by telling a good story. We all remember, as children, how much fun it was when someone read us

a story. We were being entertained. Most of the stories we see on television are shown for the purpose of entertainment. The novels we buy in bookstores were written to entertain us. What we call *narrative writing* (the telling of stories) is mostly in this category.

INFORMATION—PRESENTATION OF FACTS

Most of the writing you will do in school and in your future career will be informational in nature. In school, you will take written tests and write papers to explain what you know about a subject; at work, you might find yourself explaining why your company's profits have diminished or increased. In formal writing, these explanations can be developed in more than one way, depending on the type of information required. The methods of development that you will learn in this book include the following:

- illustration (giving examples)
- process (explaining how to do something)
- comparison and contrast
- cause and effect
- definition and analysis
- classification (putting material into mutually exclusive groups)

PERSUASION OR ARGUMENTATION

Persuasive writing, or argumentation, tries to convince the reader to agree with the writer's point of view on a topic. In our daily lives, the newspaper editorial is the most common example of persuasive writing. Such writing gives facts and examples and uses logical reasoning to support the writer's claim. An argument seeks to change the reader's mind or confirm beliefs already there. Often, the conclusion pleads for a plan of action to be taken.

ACTIVITY **Understanding Purpose in Writing**

If your instructor told you that your assignment was to write an essay on some aspect of technology, each person in the class would most likely choose a slightly different topic. Below are five different topics concerned with some aspect of technology. For each topic, indicate what the writer's possible purpose (entertainment, information, or persuasion) could be.

Topic	Purpose
1. the cost of iPods	_____
2. my cell phone nightmare	_____
3. the meaning of *e-commerce*	_____
4. how to send a text message	_____
5. why our company should upgrade now	_____

Audience: The Writer's Intended Readers

Effective writers learn about their audience and use what they learn so that the audience will be receptive to their ideas. Several important questions need to be asked. For example, what do the readers already know about the subject? What are their attitudes toward the subject? Will they be in agreement with the writer's point of view? Will they be of similar age? Will they have a similar level of education? Will they have interests, tastes, or political points of view that agree?

Any number of factors could be important in determining how a writer chooses words and presents ideas. For example, if the readers are small children, the vocabulary and ideas of the piece will have to be age appropriate. On the other hand, if the readers are professionals who want to increase their knowledge in a certain field, the writer will be expected to know and use the terminology of that field. If the readers are likely to consider the subject a very sensitive one, the writer certainly will not want to treat the subject lightly.

ACTIVITY **Identifying an Audience and a Purpose**

Below are five possible writing subjects. In each case, choose a specific audience and imagine the writer's purpose. An example is done for you.

Subject	Audience	Purpose
Description of two history courses		

_____   _____

	Subject	Audience	Purpose
1.	Instructions for CPR (cardiopulmonary resuscitation)	_____	_____
2.	A proposal to set up a group home for emotionally disturbed adults in a neighborhood	_____	_____
3.	Description of features on a new-model computer	_____	_____
4.	A letter to a local newspaper arguing for a civilian police review board	_____	_____
5.	My so-called job	_____	_____

Voice: How the Writer's Attitude Is Revealed

It is very difficult for a writer to be objective; writing almost always reveals conscious and unconscious attitudes. The voice of the writer comes through the text in the words that are chosen and the strategies that are used. In general, we can think of voice as revealing two different attitudes:

1. **An attitude toward the subject matter.** A politician might speak *passionately* about a subject. A comic writer could be *humorous* or *sarcastic* about a subject. A critic could reveal a *lighthearted* or *judgmental* attitude.

2. **An attitude toward the audience.** The writer's attitude toward the audience ranges from very formal (such as the attitude of an expert presenting a research paper in an academic journal) to less formal (such as the attitude of a student writing a friendly and casual letter to a classmate).

The skilled writer learns how to choose an appropriate and consistent voice, depending on the purpose of the writing. Cooking instructions on a box of rice, for example, are probably almost completely voiceless, with no indication of the writer's personality. The reporting of a news event should also be without any apparent voice, although sometimes the writer's personal attitude sneaks in through choice of a word that carries a positive or negative connotation. Sometimes an attitude is revealed by the choice of facts to include or exclude. In general, writing that seeks to inform is usually more objective than writing that seeks to entertain or persuade.

Another way a writer expresses voice is by the choice of which personal pronoun to use in a piece. A writer chooses a pronoun that fits the subject and the audience. For a diary or a memoir, because you would most likely be talking about yourself, the first person (*I* or *we*) would be the obvious choice. In a book about how to arrange flowers, the author might want to address readers in the informal second person (*you*), the common choice for writing that gives directions or advice. For a business proposal that suggests how to market a new product, the third person (*he, she, it,* or *they*) would be the most appropriate. The third person is the most formal and objective. It is the expected voice for academic and professional writing. In short, the choice of personal pronoun is determined by the appropriate level of formality needed between the writer and the writer's audience.

Two additional points about voice need to be kept in mind. The first point is the importance of being consistent. Do not change your writing voice without a clear reason for doing so. In other words, if you begin by addressing your readers as *you*, do not switch to *we* later on in the same piece of writing. The second point is to be sincere. Do not try to be someone you are not. For instance, taking unfamiliar words from a thesaurus is not a good idea because these words could easily be used in the wrong way and will nearly always sound a little out of place compared to the rest of your writing. If English is your second language, you might have to be especially careful. You will most likely need a more complete understanding of words and their shades of meaning before you use them in your writing.

FORMAL WRITING IN THE THIRD PERSON (*HE, SHE, IT,* OR *THEY*)

In formal writing, where there is a distance between the writer and the reader, the *third person* is generally used. This is the voice you would use for most college-level work as well as job-related work. Read the paragraph that follows and study the writer's use of the third person. (Each use of a third-person pronoun has been italicized.)

> Many families feel lost trying to make sense of cyberspace. *They* become frustrated trying to find specific information such as the image of a skeleton for a child's science paper. *They* worry that a preteen daughter may not be safe when she is chatting online. Most parents are unsure how to navigate the web. The millions of pages of information on the net can make locating useful and enjoyable web pages seem more like work than play. How should families choose among them? Six exceptional web destinations will eliminate this uncertainty. As a group, these websites offer useful advice parents need and also provide fun features children want.

LESS FORMAL WRITING IN THE SECOND PERSON (*YOU, YOUR*)

Here is the same material, but written in a less formal voice, using the second person (*you*) and more casual language. This choice is effective when the writer is giving instructions or speaking directly to the reader. (Each use of the second person has been italicized.)

> Is *your* family lost in cyberspace? *You* know the feeling. Maybe it's the rush of frustration that comes after *your* son says he needs an image of a skeleton for a science paper but he can't find one on the Internet—and neither can *you*. Or perhaps it's that twinge of anxiety as *your* preteen daughter announces she wants to chat online, but *you* are not sure how she can do it safely. If *you* are unsure how to navigate the web, *you* are not alone. The millions of pages of information on the net can make locating useful and enjoyable web pages seem more like work than play. How can *you* choose among them? Consider six terrific web destinations. As a group, they offer the useful advice *you* need along with the fun features *your* children want.

ACTIVITY **4** **Voice: Rewriting a Paragraph Using First Person Singular (*I*)**

Compose a new paragraph using the same contents in the two paragraphs you have just read, but now use the first-person singular (*I*). Remember that using the first-person singular results in the most informal voice in writing. The result is a more personal and casual tone, such as used in a diary or a memoir.

_____

_____

_____

_____

_____

_____

_____

_____

_____

_____

_____

_____

ACTIVITY **5**   **Voice: Rewriting a Paragraph to Avoid the Second Person (_You_)**

In many college courses, one important objective is for students to learn the proper standards for writing academic and work-related assignments. This involves the use of the more formal voice (not the second person _you_) in written work. Rewrite the following paragraph to avoid the use of the second person _you_. For instance, the opening words "Your world" could be rewritten as "The world," "This world," or "Our world."

> Your world is getting smaller, and the pace of change is quickening. When you graduate you will change jobs as many as ten times over the course of your career, often moving in completely new directions. You will probably end up in a career that is fairly unrelated to what you studied in college and find yourself working with colleagues from many different nations and cultures. You will succeed if you think broadly. You should take courses that will give you the greatest range of opportunity. Your world has become much more interdependent. Health, law, business, and many other fields all operate in a world of permeable borders. You need an international outlook to prevent the spread of disease, to reduce the flow of illicit drugs, or to resolve environmental challenges. If you understand other societies and cultures, you will have a wider base of knowledge and have better communication skills than those who do not.

_____

_____

_____

_____

_____

_____

_____

_____

_____

_____

_____

_____

Unity: All Parts Relating to the Central Theme

In a good piece of writing, every sentence serves the central theme, with every detail directly related to the main idea. All of the parts go together to make up a whole. The result is a sense of oneness or wholeness, so that by the end of the piece, the writing feels complete and the reader has no trouble grasping the writer's main point.

ACTIVITY **6**   **Editing Student Writing for Unity**

The following paragraph lacks unity because some sentences do not contribute to the main idea. As you read the paragraph, cross out any sentences that do not contribute to the unity of the piece.

Many parents fear the time when their children reach adolescence. When that time does come, some parents are afraid to give their children freedom to make choices. These same parents do not admit that their children have any ideas or feelings that are valid. Many adults like to look back on their own childhoods. Pets are often remembered fondly. Conflicts between parents and children are bound to develop. Some conflicts, of course, are a sign of healthy development within the family. Psychologists say that parents should not be fearful when teenagers challenge authority. Challenging authority is a normal part of the maturing process. Adults without children have none of these concerns. The need for privacy is also normal during adolescence and should be respected and not feared. On the other hand, when the right moment comes along and a teenager wants to talk, parents should not miss the chance. Sometimes teenagers and their younger brothers and sisters fight continually over the most trivial things. Most important of all is the need for parents to be sensitive to the feelings of their teenagers. Remember, adolescence does not last for a lifetime, but a good relationship between parent and child can!

Coherence: Clear and Logical Progression of Thought

A piece of writing needs careful organization of all its parts so that one idea leads logically to the next. To help all the parts relate to one another, writers use three important techniques: *repetition of key words, careful pronoun reference,* and *transitional expressions.*

All writers must continually work to achieve coherence. Even professional writers work on more than one draft because they see room for improvement as they move from one idea, one sentence, or one paragraph to the next. If something is unclear or lacks logical sequence, they revise. You too will be working on coherence in many of the chapters of this book.

The following paragraph is taken from E. B. White's "The Eye of Edna," an essay in which the writer reflects on the consequences of a hurricane visiting the East Coast of the United States. The paragraph demonstrates how a master writer achieves coherence in his work.

°**Odysseus:** Hero of Homer's ancient Greek epic poem, who faced many obstacles during his many years of wandering before he could get home.

> Weather, of course, is an obsession with the television people. Our home now boasts a television set, and somebody is always telling me the temperature in Great Falls, Montana—which is like telling me that a man has just changed his shirt in Sicily. Moreover, the weather broadcasters have become emotionally involved with the natural scene, and feel personally responsible for inclemency. Odysseus° in all his seafaring never had such a sense of the gods at work, helping and hindering. Two rainy weekends in succession put an almost unbearable strain on weather announcers, and they begin using queer meteorological terms like "gloomy," "dreary," and "miserable." Soon we will have weather tips sent to us by satellites on the prowl in space, and heaven knows what kind of view they will take of disturbances. There is much to be said for a pretty girl and her mass of cold air sweeping down from Canada.

REPETITION OF KEY WORDS

When we study this paragraph, it soon becomes apparent that key words are repeated as the piece moves from sentence to sentence. The topic *weather* appears four times, beginning with the first word in the topic sentence. The other instances occur as adjectives: *weather broadcasters, weather announcers,* and *weather tips.*

USING PRONOUNS AND SYNONYMS TO REFER TO KEY WORDS

Notice how many other words or phrases E. B. White has found to substitute for the term *weather: temperature, the natural scene, inclemency* (bad weather), *rainy* (bad weather), *disturbances, meteorological* (having to do with weather conditions), and *mass of cold air* (bad weather). The paragraph would have been very tedious had the writer repeated the term *weather* in all these cases.

Coherence is also achieved through the careful use of pronouns. Look at sentences five and six in the White paragraph. The first pronoun *they* refers to *weather announcers* and the second pronoun *they* refers to *weather satellites.* In the seventh sentence, the pronoun *her* in *her mass of cold air* refers to *girl.* E. B. White brings more than a touch of humor to his paragraph when he contrasts the cold, mechanical weather satellites in space with the image of a pretty girl giving the weather report on television, *"her mass of cold air sweeping down from Canada"* becoming pleasantly confused with *"her mass of gold hair sweeping down."*

USE OF TRANSITIONAL EXPRESSIONS

Finally, coherence is achieved through the careful use of transitions, words and expressions that show how ideas relate to each other. If you turn to Appendix E at the back of this textbook, you will find a listing of several of these words and expressions. Each of the two transitions found in our paragraph clearly move the reader forward to the next idea. The first transitional word, *moreover,* signals that he is going to add another point. Not only do the media become overly *obsessed* with the weather (the controlling idea in the topic sentence) but the weather people also become too *emotionally involved.* The second transition, *soon,* is a transition of time. This transition signals something that happened or will happen later in time. We notice that since E. B. White wrote this essay more than fifty years ago, weather satellites have indeed become commonplace.

  ACTIVITY **7**   **Studying a Text for Coherence**

Read the following paragraph to discover the techniques used by the writer to achieve coherence. Find (1) two examples of the repetition of key words, (2) two examples of pronoun reference, and (3) one example of a transitional word or expression. Label each of the examples that you find. (If necessary, refer to Appendix E for a list of transitional words and expressions.)

There are, if you believe a study by Inktomi and the NEC Research Institute, more than one billion web pages currently online and accessible to the public. These pages are not numbered. They are not organized. They do not come with a table of contents or an index. It's as if people around the world took all their books and magazines, ripped out all the pages, and dumped them into one gigantic pile. And in the past five years, that pile has grown bigger and bigger and bigger. So how do you find your way through this maze of information? Search engines. As with any technology, some very smart people have devised new search engines for the Internet, based on the lessons of the previous generation. Names like Google, Yahoo!, and Alta Vista have become well known. They will likely be your best bet for quickly finding what you need on the web.

Exploring Online

Go to academic.cengage.com/devenglish/scarry to find the **Writer's Online Workplace,** a website designed for students using this book. You will find links to handouts, interactive quizzes, and other online resources as you explore the following topics:

- subject
- purpose
- audience
- voice, including use of the second person
- coherence
- transitional expressions

Working Together

Knowing Your Audience

Every writer should plan a piece of work by first narrowing the topic, knowing the target audience, and then keeping that audience in mind as the work progresses. The following paragraph is from Patricia T. O'Conner's book on writing, *Words Fail Me*. In the passage, the author addresses the issue of a writer's audience and the importance of our awareness of audience in the writing process.

All writing has an intended audience, even the telephone book (it may be monotonous, short on verbs, and heavy on numbers and proper nouns, but it sure knows its readers!). Your audience probably won't be as wide as your area code, but it could be almost anyone—your landlord, a garden club, the parole board, Internet jocks, a college admissions director, fiction readers, the editorial page editor, the Supreme Court. Someone is always on the receiving end, but who? It's a big world out there, and before you write you have to narrow it down. Once you've identified your audience, everything you do—every decision you make about vocabulary, tone, sentence structure, imagery, humor, and the rest—should be done with this target, your reader, in mind.

After reviewing the text, divide into groups. The members of each group work together to fill in the following chart showing the relationship between audience, topic, writer, and voice. For example, who would write to a landlord, what might be the topic of such a letter, and would the writer use the first person (*I, we*), second person (*you*), or third person (*he, she, it, they*)?

Audience	Possible Topic	Possible Writer	Choice of Voice
a landord			
an Internet chat room			
a college admissions director			
dear diary			
a parole board			
the editor of a newspaper			
fiction readers			
the Supreme Court			

If time permits, the class should come together to compare their charts. Choose one word that would describe the *tone* that should be set in each writing project.

Portfolio Suggestion

When writers for advertising agencies work up an ad campaign, they must know their target audience. These writers choose every word for their ads with the greatest care. Because we live in such a visual culture, they also make sure that the illustrations for their ads are compelling. Collect ads from magazines and newspapers that you find especially well-done. Study the words and pictures of these ads, noting the intended audience in each case. How does the ad target its audience? Preserve the ads and any notes for future writing projects that might interest you: audience in advertising, the careful choice of vocabulary in advertisement, the psychology of advertising.

PART

2

Creating Effective Sentences

Many students need to use their college writing classes to fill in gaps not addressed in previous school classes. When students have papers returned with sentence-level errors corrected, they realize the corrections are valuable, but they do not always understand exactly what is wrong with their word choice or structure. Without that understanding, the suggestions and corrections of the instructors are to no avail. If students are going to be able to revise, edit, and proofread their work, they will need to understand the basic grammatical terms and concepts. Learning these terms and understanding sentence structure will give every student the confidence needed to work with the written word. Part 2 of this book carefully presents the foundational sentence-level concepts in a sequence that begins very simply and builds on previous knowledge until a very thorough understanding is achieved. When student writers are in control of this material, revising and editing any paper, especially the paper that has been returned with correction symbols, will become a more meaningful activity.

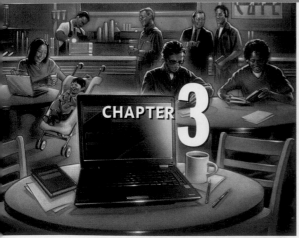

CHAPTER 3

Finding Subjects and Verbs in Simple Sentences

By the time you finish this chapter, you will understand what is essential in the construction of the most basic sentence, called the **simple sentence.** Your practice of the following skills will lay the foundation for the other chapters in Part 2:

CHAPTER OBJECTIVES

- finding the **subject** of a simple sentence, including sentences with **prepositional and appositive phrases**
- finding the **verb** of a simple sentence
- identifying six **parts of speech** in a simple sentence

We express our ideas in more than one way. When we respond to someone with a gesture such as shaking our head, we are expressing an idea. When we make a comment by saying a single word such as "cool," we are also expressing an idea, this time verbally. The shake of the head usually means either *yes* or *no;* the word *cool* is slang that conveys approval. When we speak informally with friends, we have the advantage of having our tones and gestures understood. When we express ourselves in written form, however, our words must be more deliberate and more precise.

What Is a Complete Sentence?

As writers, we need to express ourselves in complete sentences so that our ideas will be fully understood. This need for completeness means that every writing student must have a clear understanding as to what makes up a sentence.

> A **complete sentence** is a group of words that contains a subject and a verb and also expresses a complete thought.
>
> **Avon lifts weights.**

How Do You Find the Subject of a Sentence?

The most basic sentence is called the *simple sentence*. *Simple* in this case does not mean *easy*, but it does mean that the sentence has only one subject-verb group. For most simple sentences, you can find the subject by keeping in mind five generalizations. Use generalizations 1 and 2 to complete the practice exercise that follows.

GENERALIZATION 1 | **In a sentence, the subject usually answers the question "Who or what is the sentence about?"**

GENERALIZATION 2 | **The subject often occurs early in the sentence.**

PRACTICE

In the following sentences, find the subject by asking yourself, "Who or what is the sentence about?"

1. The gym seemed noisier than usual.
2. Our coach was shouting last-minute instructions.
3. He expected total concentration.
4. Six cheerleaders were warming up.
5. People were beginning to fill the bleachers.

GENERALIZATION 3 | **The subject of a sentence is usually a noun or a pronoun.**

FINDING NOUNS

> A **noun** is a word that names a person, place, or thing. A noun can function as a subject, an object, or a possessive in a sentence.
>
> **Subject:** *Avon* lifts weights.
> **Object:** The coach trained *Avon*.
> **Possessive:** *Avon's* coach always arrives early.

Nouns can be categorized in two different ways:

1. **Common nouns or proper nouns.** Most nouns in English are *common nouns*. They are not capitalized. *Proper nouns* name particular persons, places, or things. They are always capitalized.

Common nouns	Proper nouns
aunt	Aunt Meriam
country	Nigeria
watch	Timex

2. **Concrete nouns or abstract nouns.** A second way to categorize nouns is to identify them as concrete nouns or abstract nouns. *Concrete nouns* name all the things we can see or touch, such as *desk, car,* or *friend. Abstract nouns* name the things we cannot see or touch, such as *justice, honesty,* or *friendship.*

Concrete nouns	Abstract nouns
face	loneliness
people	patriotism
jewelry	beauty

PRACTICE

Underline every noun in each of the sentences below.

1. The morning of June 27 was clear and sunny.
2. The flowers were blossoming profusely, and the grass was richly green.
3. The people of the village began to gather in the square.
4. The lottery was conducted by Mr. Sommers.
5. The jovial man had time and energy to devote to civic activities.

FINDING PRONOUNS

A **pronoun** is a word that takes the place of a noun. Like a noun, a pronoun can be a subject or an object in a sentence. It can also be used to show possession.

Subject:	*He* lifts weights.
Object:	The coach trained *him.*
Possessive:	*His* coach always arrives early.

There are four different categories of pronouns. (To see the complete list of these pronouns, consult Appendix B, page A13.) The chart on the next page lists only those pronouns that function as the subjects of sentences.

PRACTICE

In each of the sentences below, replace the underlined word or words with a pronoun.

1. The crowd arrived early.   *They*
2. The gym was noisy.   *it*
3. People waited eagerly.   *They*
4. Coach Bradway had not lost a game yet this season.   *He*
5. Steven and I found the best seats in the front row.   *We*
6. Not one person could predict the outcome.   *No one*

Pronouns That Function as Subjects

PERSONAL PRONOUNS THAT CAN BE SUBJECTS

	Singular	**Plural**
1st person:	I	we
2nd person:	you	you
3rd person:	he / she / it	they

INDEFINITE PRONOUNS THAT CAN BE SUBJECTS

Singular

anyone	everyone	no one	someone
anybody	everybody	nobody	somebody
anything	everything	nothing	something
each	another	either (of)	neither (of)
one (of)	much	such (a)	

Plural

both	few	many	several

Singular or plural depending on meaning

all	more	none	some
any	most		

RELATIVE PRONOUNS THAT CAN BE SUBJECTS

who   what

DEMONSTRATIVE PRONOUNS THAT CAN BE SUBJECTS

this   these
that   those

GENERALIZATION 4   **Noun or pronoun subjects in a sentence can be modified by adjectives.**

An **adjective** is a word that modifies (describes or limits) a noun or a pronoun. Adjectives usually come directly in front of the nouns they modify, but they can also appear later in the sentence and refer back to the noun or pronoun.

young Avon   He is *young*.

PRACTICE   Underline the adjectives in each of the following sentences.

1.   The swimmer was confident.

2.   Her long and strenuous workouts would soon pay off.

3.   Several meters remained to reach the finish line.

4.   Suddenly, she felt a terrible cramp in one leg.

5.   A disappointing defeat would be the result.

GENERALIZATION 5   **The subject of a sentence can be compound.**

> A **compound subject** is made up of two or more nouns or pronouns joined by one of the following: *and, or, either/or, neither/nor.*
>
> *Avon* and *his coach* lift weights.

PRACTICE   Underline the compound subject in each of the following sentences.

1. Exercise and diet are the secrets to good health.

2. Mothers and fathers should help their children establish healthy lifestyles.

3. Unfortunately, biological factors or environmental factors could cause health problems.

PRACTICE   The following sentences illustrate the different kinds of subjects you will encounter in this chapter. Examine each sentence and decide who or what the sentence is about. Underline the subject of each sentence. Then, on the line to the right, write the kind of subject (for example, *concrete noun* or *personal pronoun*) you have underlined. Be as specific as possible.

1. The young child played.   _Common noun_

2. Young Helen Keller played.   _Concrete noun_

3. She played.   _Personal pronoun_

4. The park grew chilly.   _Concrete noun_

5. The leaves stirred.   _Concrete noun_

6. A thought suddenly struck her.   _Compound Subject_

7. Her parents and teacher would be waiting.   _Concrete noun_

> **NOTE:** Not every noun or pronoun in a sentence is necessarily the subject of a verb. Remember that nouns and pronouns function as subjects, objects, and possessives. In the following sentence, which noun is the subject and which noun is the object?
>
> Helen drank the water.
>
> If you chose *Helen* as the subject and *water* as the object, you were correct.

In the exercises that follow, you will have the opportunity to practice finding subjects. Refer to the definitions, charts, and previous examples as often as needed.

EXERCISE **Finding the Subject of a Sentence**

Underline the subject in each of the following sentences. An example is done for you.

The loudspeaker blared.

1. The train stopped.
2. Steven Laye had arrived.
3. He was afraid.
4. Everything looked so strange.
5. The fearful man held his bag tightly.
6. The tunnel led up to the street.
7. Buses and cars choked the avenues.
8. People rushed everywhere.
9. The noise gave him a headache.
10. Loneliness filled his heart.

EXERCISE   2   **Finding the Subject of a Sentence**

Underline the subject in each of the following sentences.

1. The road twisted and turned.
2. A young boy hurried along briskly.
3. He carried an important message.
4. A red-winged blackbird flew overhead.
5. Dark clouds and a sudden wind surprised him.
6. His family would be elated.
7. Someone was raking the leaves.
8. His father called out his name.
9. The old man tore open the envelope.
10. The message was brief.

EXERCISE   3   **Finding the Subject of a Sentence**

Underline the subject in each of the following sentences.

1. The Chicago World's Fair opened.
2. Americans had never seen anything like it.
3. Architects had designed a gleaming white city.
4. The buildings and grounds were unique.
5. George Ferris designed an enormous wheel 264 feet high.
6. It could carry sixty passengers per car.
7. The inventor George Westinghouse designed the fair's electric motors and even the electric lights.
8. Other fair inventors included Thomas Edison and Alexander Graham Bell.
9. All played an important part.
10. The future seemed bright.

EXERCISE   **Composing Your Own Sentences**

Create ten sentences using a variety of subjects. If you wish, you may use the suggested nouns and pronoun given below.

Proper noun:	John McCain
Common noun:	politician
Abstract noun:	patriotism
Compound subject:	Vietnam veteran and senator
Pronoun:	he

Exchange sentences with a classmate. For each sentence your classmate has written, underline and identify the subject to show that you understand the various terms.

FINDING THE SUBJECT IN SENTENCES WITH PREPOSITIONAL PHRASES

The sentences in Exercises 1 and 2 were short and basic. If we wrote only sentences of that type, our writing would sound choppy. Complex ideas would be difficult to express. One way to expand a simple sentence is to add one or more prepositional phrases.

He put his suitcase on the seat.

On is a preposition. *Seat* is a noun used as the object of the preposition. *On the seat* is a prepositional phrase.

> A **prepositional phrase** is a group of words containing a preposition and an object of the preposition along with any modifiers. Prepositional phrases contain nouns or pronouns, but these nouns or pronouns are *never* the subject of the sentence.
>
> on the train
>
> against the wall
>
> throughout his life

In sentences with prepositional phrases, the subject may be difficult to spot. What is the subject of the following sentence?

In the young man's apartment, books covered the walls.

In the sentence above, what is the prepositional phrase? Who or what is the sentence about? To avoid making the mistake of thinking that a noun in the prepositional phrase could be the subject, a good practice is to cross out the prepositional phrase.

~~In the young man's apartment~~, books covered the walls.

With the entire prepositional phrase crossed out, it becomes clear that the subject of the sentence has to be the noun *books*.

The subject of a sentence is *never* found within the prepositional phrase.

If you memorize the prepositions in the following list, you will be able to easily spot prepositional phrases in sentences.

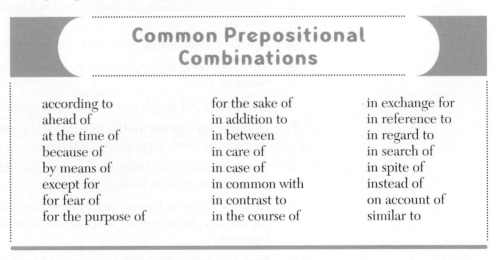

Common Prepositions

about	behind	except	onto	toward
above	below	for	out	under
across	beneath	from	outside	underneath
after	beside	in	over	unlike
against	between	inside	past	until
along	beyond	into	regarding	up
among	by	like	since	upon
around	concerning	near	through	with
as	despite	of	throughout	within
at	down	off	till	without
before	during	on	to	

In addition to these common one-word prepositions, many other prepositions are composed of two-word, three-word, and four-word combinations. The following list provides a sampling.

Common Prepositional Combinations

according to	for the sake of	in exchange for
ahead of	in addition to	in reference to
at the time of	in between	in regard to
because of	in care of	in search of
by means of	in case of	in spite of
except for	in common with	instead of
for fear of	in contrast to	on account of
for the purpose of	in the course of	similar to

EXERCISE **Recognizing Prepositions**

In the following paragraph, find ten different prepositions and circle them.

During the 1950s and 1960s, many young couples left the cities for greener places. A new study by the Brookings Institution claims these first suburbs are now struggling. Their problems are different from those of the inner cities or faster-growing newer cities. New housing projects and job opportunities within the older suburbs have slowed to a trickle. Meanwhile, the elderly population in these original suburbs has been growing at nearly double the national rate.

Much more attention has been lavished on fast-growing outer suburbs and Sunbelt communities.

 ### Recognizing Prepositional Phrases

In the following paragraph, find ten prepositions. Circle each preposition and underline the entire prepositional phrase.

People across the country are anxious about the high cost of heating. After the devastating Gulf Coast hurricanes of 2005, fuel prices spiked. On account of these higher fuel prices, many people are making changes to their homes. Some are turning their fears into actions. They have plugged cracks, insulated attics, enlisted energy specialists for advice, or invested in fleece socks.

 ### Finding Subjects in Sentences With Prepositional Phrases

Remember that you will never find the subject of a sentence within a prepositional phrase. In each of the following sentences, cross out prepositional phrases. Then underline the subject of each sentence. An example follows:

> <u>People</u> paid ~~for telegram messages by the word.~~

1. On Friday, January 27, 2006, Western Union sent its last telegram.
2. With the ascendancy of modern technology, the telegram is no longer needed.
3. In 1851 in Rochester, New York, Western Union had its beginnings.
4. Messages were transmitted by Morse code over the wires and delivered by couriers.
5. Eventually, telegraph service drove the pony express out of business.
6. Until the emergence of the telegraph, the average delivery time for a message by pony express took ten days.
7. At the height of the telegram business, in 1929, two hundred million telegrams were sent around the world.
8. Now for Western Union, money transfers, bill payment, and products such as telephone service and Internet access will form the core of their business.
9. In the past, families sent messages of births, deaths, birthdays, and weddings by telegram.
10. In the present era, e-mail and fax messages have taken the place of the telegram.

FINDING THE SUBJECT IN SENTENCES WITH APPOSITIVE PHRASES

An **appositive phrase** is a group of words within a sentence that gives us extra information about a noun or pronoun in that sentence. It is set off by commas.

Example:

Martin Johnson, *the retired salesman,* sat at his desk.

In this sentence, the words *the retired salesman* make up the appositive phrase. These words give extra information about Martin Johnson and are separated by commas from the rest of the sentence. If you were to leave out the appositive phrase, notice that what remained would still be a complete sentence with the main idea undisturbed:

Example:

Martin Johnson sat at his desk.

Now the subject is clear: *Martin Johnson*

The subject of a sentence is never found within an appositive phrase.

PRACTICE

In each of the following sentences, cross out the appositive phrase and then underline the subject.

1. Alex Harkavy, a high school senior, has an auditory-processing disorder.

2. Marcia Rubinstein, an educational consultant, can help him find the right college.

3. For instance, Landmark, a college in Putney, Vermont, specializes in programs for students with learning disabilities.

4. A new federal law, the Americans with Disabilities Act, was enacted in 1990.

5. Now many colleges, both public and private ones, offer support for learning-disabled students.

6. One particular guidebook, *Peterson's Colleges with Programs for Students with Learning Disabilities or Attention Deficit Disorder,* is especially helpful.

OTHER PROBLEMS IN FINDING SUBJECTS

Sentences with a Change in the Normal Subject Position

Some sentences begin with words that indicate that a question is being asked. Such words as *why, where, how,* and *when* are adverbs, and they signal to the reader that a question will follow. These opening words are not the subjects. The subjects occur later in these sentences. The following sentences begin with words that signal a question:

Why is *he* going away?

How did *he* find his sister in the city?

Where is her *office*?

Notice that in each case the subject is not in the opening part of the sentence. However, if you answer the question or change the question into a statement, the subject becomes easier to identify.

> *He* is going away because . . .
>
> *He* found his sister by . . .

Sentences Starting with *there* or *here*

Such words as *there* or *here* are adverbs. They cannot be the subjects of sentences.

> There is a new teacher in the department.
>
> Here comes the woman now.

Who or what is this first sentence about? This sentence is about a teacher. *Teacher* is the subject of the sentence. Who or what is the second sentence about? This sentence is about a woman. *Woman* is the subject of the second sentence.

Commands

Sometimes a sentence contains a verb that gives an order:

> Go to Chicago.
>
> Help your sister.

In sentences that give orders, *you* is not written down but is understood to be the subject. This is the only case where the subject of a sentence may be left out.

 PRACTICE　Underline the subject in each of the sentences below.

1.　Here in America the sale of human organs for transplant is against the law.

2.　Unfortunately, there is a disturbing illegal market in the sale of these organs.

3.　Where are some people desperately looking for kidneys?

4.　Why are so many donors exploited and unprotected?

5.　Get involved.

6.　Work toward a solution to this tragic social problem.

EXERCISE　8　**Finding Subjects in Simple Sentences**

In each of the following sentences, cross out prepositional phrases and appositive phrases. Then underline the subject. An example follows:

> ~~In every car of the crowded train,~~ <u>passengers</u> settled down ~~for the night~~.

1.　In the night train, the child slept.

2.　Here the motion of the railroad cars lulled the passengers.

3. The child's mother, a single parent, put a coat under the child's head for a pillow.

4. Outside the window, the lights from small towns and villages twinkled.

5. Sometimes passengers could look into people's windows.

6. There was a silence in the train.

7. Why do people travel in the middle of the night?

8. In most cases, children will rest quietly at night.

9. Will the woman with a young child and heavy suitcases have a difficult time at the end of the trip?

10. On the platform waits an elderly man, anxious for the first sight of his grandson.

EXERCISE **9**   **Finding Subjects in Simple Sentences**

In each of the following sentences, cross out prepositional phrases and appositive phrases. Then underline the subject. An example follows:

Where ~~in the United States~~ can we find Lake Okeechobee?

1. Where can you find the only subtropical preserve in North America?

2. Look on a map at the southern tip of Florida.

3. Here lies the Everglades, a natural treasure.

4. At one time, this Florida peninsula was not habitable.

5. Now, five million people live there.

6. The Everglades, a national park since 1947, has been in constant danger of destruction.

7. Marjory Stoneman Douglas, author of the book *The Everglades: River of Grass*, became a national crusader for the Everglades.

8. With the expansion of new development, these marshes are shrinking fast.

9. Do we have a responsibility to nature?

10. In 2000, Congress approved a bill for the restoration of the marshland.

EXERCISE **10**   **Finding Subjects in Simple Sentences**

In each of the following sentences, cross out prepositional phrases and appositive phrases. Then underline the subject. An example follows:

Spinach and broccoli are two well-known health foods.

1. Steven G. Pratt, ophthalmologist at Scripps Memorial Hospital in La Jolla, California, is an expert on the role of nutrition in health.

2. In his new book *Superfoods Healthstyle,* Dr. Pratt adds dark chocolate to his list of superfoods.

3. Here are some of the other superfoods: avocados, garlic, and honey.

4.   Why are apples so beneficial?

5.   They provide a great source of fiber, potassium, and disease-fighting antioxidants.

6.   Don't remove the peels.

7.   The concentration of antioxidants is in the apple's skin.

8.   Throw an avocado into your salad.

9.   It will increase the body's absorption of beta-carotene from foods like carrots and tomatoes.

10. With exercise and weight control, the foods on Dr. Pratt's list can extend your life.

How Do You Find the Verb of a Sentence?

Verbs tell time.

Because a verb tells time (past, present, or future), you can test which word in a sentence functions as the verb of that sentence. Use the sentences below as models.

Present tense: Today, the woman *dances*.

HINT: Change the time to the *past* by beginning the sentence with *yesterday*.

Past tense: Yesterday, the woman *danced*.

HINT: Change the time to the *future* by beginning the sentence with *tomorrow*.

Future tense: Tomorrow, the woman *will dance*.

PRACTICE

Test the sentences below to determine which word functions as the verb in the sentence. Try three versions of each sentence: one beginning with *today*, one beginning with *yesterday*, and the third beginning with *tomorrow*. Which is the word that changes? Circle that word. This is the word that functions as the verb in the sentence.

1.   The reason for his popularity is his foreign policy.

2.   She has little control over the decision.

3.   The test comes at a bad time.

Verbs fall into three classes: action verbs, linking verbs, and helping verbs.

ACTION VERBS

An **action verb** tells us what the subject is doing and when the action occurs.

For example:

The woman *studied* ballet.

What did the woman do? She *studied*. What is the time of the action? The action took place in the *past* (-*ed* is the past-tense ending).

Most verbs are *action verbs*. Here are a few examples.

Examples of Action Verbs

arrive	despise	help	write	watch	wait
leave	learn	make	speak	fly	
enjoy	forget	open	teach	catch	

EXERCISE **Finding Action Verbs**

Each of the following sentences contains an action verb. Cross out prepositional phrases and appositive phrases. Next, underline the subject. Finally, circle the action verb. Is the action in the present, past, or future? An example follows:

Many people begin hobbies in childhood.

1. Collectors enjoy the search for unusual items.

2. Some people collect very strange objects.

3. A collection, like odd rocks or unique automobiles, will give a person some individuality.

4. One man saved the fortunes from fortune cookies.

5. A group in Michigan often trades spark plugs.

6. In Texas members of a club gather many types of barbed wire.

7. One person in New York kept handouts from the street.

8. Arthur Fiedler, the late conductor of the Boston Peps Orchestra, hung hundreds of fire hats on pegs around his study.

9. Tom Bloom finds "inspected by" tickets in the pockets of new clothes.

10. Collections will entertain us from childhood to old age.

EXERCISE **Finding Action Verbs**

Each of the following sentences contains an action verb. Cross out preposi-tional phrases and appositive phrases. Next, underline the subject. Finally, circle the action verb. Note that each verb you circle has a tense. Is the action in the past, present, or future? An example follows:

With the rise of literacy, the demand for reading glasses increased.

1. Nero, an emperor of ancient Rome, gazed at gladiators in combat through a large emerald.

2.   The Chinese manufactured sunglasses seven hundred years ago.

3.   From quartz, monks carved the first magnifying glasses for reading.

4.   In the fourteenth century, with the rise of the Venetian glass industry, glass lenses replaced quartz lenses.

5.   In London in 1728, a man invented a pair of glasses with metal pieces and hinges.

6.   George Washington bought a pair of these new glasses.

7.   By 1939, movie producers in Hollywood devised colored contact lenses for special effects in horror movies.

8.   In 1948, an American technician developed the first pair of modern contact lenses.

9.   Now laser surgery repairs many eyesight problems.

10.   Perhaps in the future nobody will need glasses or contact lenses.

LINKING VERBS

> A **linking verb** is a verb that links the subject of a sentence to one or more words that describe or identify the subject.

The child (is) a constant dreamer.   She (seems) distracted.
We (feel) sympathetic.

In each of these examples, the verb links the subject to a word that identifies or describes the subject. In the first example, the verb *is* links *child* with *dreamer*. In the second example, the verb *seems* links the pronoun *she* with *distracted*. Finally, in the third example, the verb *feel* links the pronoun *we* with *sympathetic*.

Common Linking Verbs

act	become	look	sound
appear	feel	remain	taste
be (am, is, are, was, were,	get	seem	turn
has been, or have been)	grow	smell	

 EXERCISE 13   **Finding Linking Verbs**
Each of the following sentences contains a linking verb. Cross out prepositional phrases and appositive phrases. Underline the subject of the sentence.

Then draw an arrow to the word or words that identify or describe the subject. Finally, circle the linking verb. An example follows:

Dreams(are) very important in many cultures.

1. My dream last night was wonderful.

2. I had been transformed.

3. I looked young again.

4. The house was empty and quiet.

5. In a sunlit kitchen with a book in hand, I appeared relaxed and happy.

6. In the morning light, the kitchen felt cozy.

7. It seemed safe.

8. The brewing coffee smelled delicious.

9. The bacon, my usual Sunday morning treat, never tasted better.

10. In this dreamworld, life felt satisfying.

EXERCISE 14 **Finding Linking Verbs**

Each of the following sentences contains a linking verb. Cross out prepositional phrases and appositive phrases. Underline the subject of the sentence. Then draw an arrow to the word or words that identify or describe the subject. Finally, circle the linking verb. An example follows:

Surprises (can be) fun.

1. We were excited about the birthday party.

2. The apartment looked empty.

3. Everyone remained quiet.

4. Jasmine turned red at the sound of "Surprise!"

5. She seemed stunned.

6. The music sounds wonderful.

7. The food smells delicious.

8. All of her presents will be lovely.

9. The birthday party is a complete success.

10. Everyone appears pleased with the evening.

HELPING VERBS (ALSO CALLED AUXILIARY VERBS)

> A **helping verb** is a verb that combines with a main verb to form a verb phrase. It always comes before the main verb and expresses a special meaning or a particular time.

In the following examples, helping verbs indicate the time the action of the verb *sleep* takes place.

Helping verbs	Time expressed by helping verbs
He *is* sleeping.	right now
He *might* sleep.	maybe now or in the future
He *should* sleep.	ought to, now or in the future
He *could have been* sleeping.	maybe in the past

Common Helping Verbs

		Forms of *be*		Forms of *have*	Forms of *do*
can	shall	being	are	has	does
could	should	been	was	have	do
may	will	am	were	had	did
might	would	is			
must					

Remember that *be, do,* and *have* can also be used as the main verbs of sentences. In such cases, *be* is a linking verb and *do* and *have* are action verbs. The other helping verbs function only as helping verbs.

Be, do, and *have* used as helping verbs	*Be, do,* and *have* used as main verbs
I *am teaching* this class.	I *am* the teacher.
He *does work* hard.	He *does* the homework.
I *have borrowed* the money.	I *have* the money.

When we studied finding the subject of a sentence, we learned that *nouns* and *pronouns* could be subjects and that *adjectives* could modify these nouns and pronouns. In the same way, in finding the verb of a sentence, we learn that the adverb is the part of speech that modifies a verb.

> **Adverbs** are words that modify verbs, adjectives, or other adverbs.

An adverb modifying a verb:

Dreams **often** frighten young children.

An adverb modifying an adverb:

Dreams **very** often frighten young children.

An adverb modifying an adjective:

Dreams often frighten **very** young children.

Watch out for an adverb that comes between the helping verb and the main verb. In the following sentence, the word *often* is an adverb between the helping verb *can* and the main verb *frighten*.

Dreams (can) *often* (frighten) young children.

For more on adverbs see Chapter 10. For a list of common adverbs, see Appendix B (page **A16**).

EXERCISE 15   **Finding Helping Verbs**

Circle the complete verb in each sentence below. An example follows:

Why (has) this trip (been) so disappointing?

1. We have been driving in a snowstorm for several hours.

2. On Friday, we will have traveled two thousand miles.

3. The travel agent should have warned us about the trip.

4. I had always expected mild weather.

5. We cannot possibly arrive by dark.

6. According to my phone conversation with the hotel, they will hold our reservations.

7. During our stay, we could try the restaurant across the street from the hotel.

8. Shall we swim in the pool?

9. I might not have brought enough money.

10. I am making no promises about the rest of our trip.

EXERCISE 16   **Finding Helping Verbs**

Each of the following sentences contains a helping verb in addition to the main verb. In each sentence, cross out prepositional phrases and underline the subject. Then circle the complete verb. An example follows:

~~In this country~~, <u>daycare</u> (has become) an important issue.

1. How does a person start a daycare center?

2. First, notices can be put in local churches and supermarkets.

3. Then that person should also use word of mouth among friends.

4. Many parents will need infant care during the day, after-school care, or evening and weekend care.

5. With luck, a nearby doctor may be helpful with the local health laws and legal requirements.

6. Of course, the licensing laws of the state must be thoroughly researched.

7. Unfortunately, the director of a daycare center could have trouble finding an affordable place.

8. Any child daycare center will depend on its ever-widening good reputation.

9. In good daycare centers, parents are never excluded from meetings or planning sessions.

10. Finally, the center must be more interested in the character of its teachers than in the teachers' degrees.

How Do You Identify the Parts of Speech?

In this chapter, you have learned how most of the words in the English language function. These categories for words are called *parts of speech*. You have learned to recognize and understand the functioning of nouns, pronouns, adjectives, verbs, adverbs, and prepositions. (In later chapters, you will learn how the conjunction functions.) You can review your understanding of these parts of speech as you practice identifying them in the exercises provided here. You may also refer to Appendix B for a quick summary whenever you want to refresh your memory.

EXERCISE 17

Identifying Parts of Speech

In the sentences below, identify the part of speech for each underlined word. Choose from the following list:

a. noun   c. adjective   e. adverb
b. pronoun   d. verb   f. preposition

_____ 1. The people of the <u>country</u> of Mali, in Africa,

_____ 2. built a mosque out of <u>mud</u> bricks. The Great

_____ 3. Mosque <u>in</u> the town of Djenne was built

_____ 4. by the Mali people sometime <u>between</u> AD 1100 and

_____ 5. 1300. <u>Most</u> of the leaders of Mali at that time

_____ 6. were <u>Muslims</u>. Djenne became a center of Islamic

_____ 7. learning. When the leader Konboro <u>fervently</u> converted to

_____ 8. Islam, he <u>asked</u> a holy man, "How may I please God?"

_____ 9. The holy man said, "<u>Build</u> a mosque. The people

_____ 10. will bless your <u>name</u> for centuries."

EXERCISE ⑱   **Identifying Parts of Speech**

In the sentences below, identify the part of speech for each underlined word. Choose from the following list:

a. noun   c. adjective   e. adverb
b. pronoun   d. verb   f. preposition

_____   1. *The Grand Ole Opry* is a <u>famous</u> radio program.

_____   2. It began more than seventy <u>years</u> ago in Nashville, Tennessee.

_____   3. By the 1930s, the <u>program</u> was the best source of country music on the radio.

_____   4. In 1943, the program <u>could</u> be heard in every home in the nation.

_____   5. <u>Many</u> people traveled to Nashville.

_____   6. In Nashville, <u>they</u> could hear the performers for themselves.

_____   7. The existing old concert hall, <u>poorly</u> constructed in the nineteenth century, was not an <u>ideal</u> place for modern audiences.

_____   8. Television came in <u>during</u> the 1950s, and with it the demand for a new hall.

_____   9. Now the Nashville hall is <u>modern</u> and air-conditioned.

_____ 10. Three million people <u>visit</u> Nashville every year.

EXERCISE ⑲   **Identifying Parts of Speech**

In the sentences below, identify the part of speech for each underlined word. Choose from the following list:

a. noun   c. adjective   e. adverb
b. pronoun   d. verb   f. preposition

_____   1. Chubby Checker taught the <u>world</u> "The Twist."

_____   2. Dick Clark, host of *American Bandstand,* <u>decided</u> he liked "The Twist" and showcased it.

_____   3. The song shot up to number one <u>on</u> the pop charts in September 1960.

_____   4. Twisting became the biggest <u>teenage</u> fad.

_____   5. At first, <u>it</u> was considered strictly kid stuff.

_____   6. Then it became <u>respectable</u> among older groups.

_____   7. Liz Taylor and Richard Burton were seen twisting in the fashionable night spots of <u>Rome</u>.

_____   8. The dance set the pace <u>for</u> a decade.

_____   9. The "beautiful people" were seen <u>breathlessly</u> twisting at the Peppermint Lounge in New York.

_____ 10. The 1960s were a reckless and unruly <u>time</u>.

Mastery and Editing Tests

TEST   **Finding Subjects and Verbs in Simple Sentences**

In each of the following sentences, cross out prepositional phrases and appositive phrases. Then underline the subject and circle the complete verb. An example follows:

(Have) you (heard) ~~of the first cyber athlete~~?

1. Into this new century has burst the worldwide phenomenon of a new cyber sport.

2. Jonathan Wendell, a teenager from Kansas City, Missouri, spends eight to ten hours a day at the computer.

3. Is he doing his homework?

4. In fact, Jonathan (his game name is Fatal1ty) is playing video games.

5. Here in America, this young man has become the best video player.

6. Our first professional cyber athlete has won forty-one tournaments and has pocketed three hundred thousand dollars in tournament prizes.

7. Already, this teenager has become the world champion in five different video games.

8. Around the world, thousands of people find video games very addictive.

9. Now Jonathan "Fatal1ty" Wendell has launched his own Fatal1ty products.

10. Imagine his surprised parents!

TEST   **Finding Subjects and Verbs in Simple Sentences**

In each of the sentences in the following paragraph, cross out prepositional phrases and appositive phrases. Then underline the subject and circle the complete verb. An example follows:

~~In an unmarked grave at the edge of the woods~~ (lies) Marley.

Here is a true story about a very bad dog. In rural Pennsylvania, John Grogan, a columnist for the *Philadelphia Inquirer*, lived with his wife Jenny. Soon they would be ready for children. In preparation, this young couple bought a Labrador retriever puppy. Into their home came the wildly energetic, highly dysfunctional Marley. Marley could chew door frames to the studs and separate steel bars on his crate. Drool covered the legs of all visitors to the Grogan home. He was expelled from obedience school. In 2005, Marley's owner wrote a memoir about his dog. *Marley and Me* has now reached its twentieth printing. Why has this book become such a big success? Apparently, everyone loves a book about a bad but lovable dog.

TEST **3**   **Student Writing: Finding Subjects and Verbs in Simple Sentences**

In each of the sentences in the following paragraph, cross out prepositional phrases and appositive phrases. Then underline the subject and circle the complete verb.

(Has) anything strange ever (happened) ~~in your life~~?

In 1999, a young boy was playing baseball. Suddenly he was hit by a baseball bat. He could not breathe. In fact, his heart had stopped. Who would help? There was a nurse at the game. She acted quickly and performed CPR on the boy. The boy lived. Seven years later, this same nurse was eating dinner in a Buffalo restaurant. Unfortunately, a piece of food stuck in her throat. A worker at the restaurant did not hesitate. He had learned the Heimlich maneuver and successfully used the technique. Can you guess the young man's identity? The restaurant worker was the young baseball player from seven years ago. Imagine everyone's amazement! What are the chances of such a coincidence?

Exploring Online

Go to academic.cengage.com/devenglish/scarry to find the **Writer's Online Workplace,** a website designed for students using this book. You will find links to handouts, interactive quizzes, and other online resources as you explore the following topics:

- sentence subjects
- parts of speech
- action, linking, and helping verbs

Crossword Puzzle: Reviewing the Terms for Sentence Parts

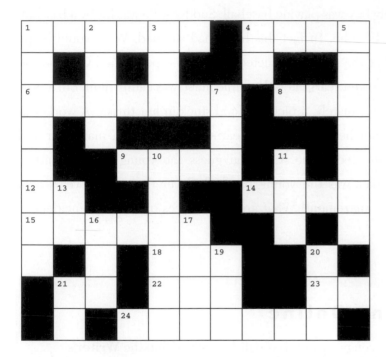

Review the names for sentence parts by doing this crossword puzzle. Feel free to work in pairs. If necessary, look back in the chapter for the answers.

Across

1. Verbs like *hop*, *sing*, and *play* are called ____ verbs.
4. Which of the following is a helping verb?
   hear, when, will, only
6. Every sentence has a ____ and a verb.
8. A helping verb
9. Which of the following is a preposition?
   must, upon, they, open
12. A preposition
14. *Word*, *witch*, *wall*, and *willow* are examples of the part of speech called a ____ .
15. Most nouns are ____ nouns. They are not capitalized.
18. In the following sentence, which word is used as an adjective?
    She has pet pigs for sale.
21. Which of the following is a preposition?
    he, be, by, if
22. In the following sentence, which word is an abstract noun?
    The era was not economically successful.
23. A preposition
24. A word that can take the place of a noun

Down

1. *Joy*, *confidence*, and *peace* are examples of this kind of noun (the opposite of a concrete noun).
2. Which word is the subject in the following sentence?
   Here is the tube of glue for Toby.
3. An indefinite pronoun
4. A plural pronoun
5. *Look*, *appear*, *feel*, and *seem* are examples of ____ verbs.
7. Which word is the object of the preposition in the following sentence?
   The car must weigh over a ton.
10. The opposite of a common noun is a ____ noun.
11. A personal pronoun
13. A preposition
16. In the following sentence, which word is a helping verb?
    She may pay the fee for her son.
17. Which of the following is a proper noun?
    king, Nero, hero, teen
19. In the following sentence, which word is an adjective?
    Nan quickly ran toward the tan man.
20. Which word is the verb in the following sentence?
    Run down to the car for our bag.
21. A common linking verb

CHAPTER 4

Making Subjects and Verbs Agree

In this chapter, you will practice making verbs agree with their subjects, especially in cases where subject-verb agreement is not immediately obvious.

CHAPTER OBJECTIVES

- Agreement when the subject is a personal pronoun
- Agreement when the verb is a form of *do* or *be*
- Agreement when the subject is hard to find
- Agreement when the subject is a collective noun
- Agreement when the subject is an indefinite pronoun
- Agreement when the subject is a compound subject
- Agreement when the subject has an unusual singular or plural form

What Is Subject-Verb Agreement?

Subject-verb agreement means that a verb must agree with its subject in *number* (singular or plural).

When the subject is a singular noun, the verb takes an -s (or -es) in the present tense.

The baby *sleeps*.
The baby *cries*.

When the subject is a plural noun, the verb does *not* take an -s (or -es) in the present tense.

The babies *sleep*.
The babies *cry*.

Notice that when you add *-s* or *-es* to an ordinary noun, you form the plural of that noun. However, when you add *-s* to a verb in the present tense, you are forming a singular verb. This rule causes a lot of confusion for student writers, especially those whose first language is not English. It may also be confusing to students who already speak and write English but whose local manner of speaking does not follow this rule. Although no one way of speaking is correct or incorrect, society does recognize a standard form that is acceptable in the worlds of school and business. Because we all must master this standard form, the material contained in this chapter is of the greatest importance to your success in college and beyond.

Subject-Verb Agreement with Personal Pronouns

The following chart shows personal pronouns used with the verb *sleep*. After you have studied the chart, what rule can you state about how a verb should end when the subject of that verb is a personal pronoun?

Personal Pronouns

	Singular	Plural
First person:	I *sleep*	we *sleep*
Second person:	you *sleep*	you *sleep*
Third person:	he she } *sleeps* it	they *sleep*

PRACTICE   Circle the correct verb in each of the following sentences.

1. The dog (bark, barks).
2. It (wake, wakes) up the neighborhood.
3. The neighbors (become, becomes) very angry.
4. They (deserve, deserves) a quiet Sunday morning.
5. I (throws, throw) an old shoe at the dog.

Subject-Verb Agreement with the Verbs *do* and *be*

Although you might have heard someone say, "It don't matter" or "We was working," these expressions are not considered standard English because the subjects do not agree with the verbs. Study the two charts that follow to learn which forms of *do* and *be* are singular and which forms are plural.

The Verb *do*

Singular	Plural
I *do*	we *do*
you *do*	you *do*
he she } *does* it	they *do*

(Never use *he don't, she don't,* or *it don't.*)

The Verb *be*

Present Tense			Past Tense		
Singular		**Plural**	**Singular**		**Plural**
I *am*		we *are*	I *was*		we *were*
you *are*		you *are*	you *were*		you *were*
he		they *are*	he		they *were*
she	*is*		she	*was*	
it			it		

(Never use *we was, you was,* or *they was.*)

PRACTICE

Circle the verb that agrees with the subject.

1. He (doesn't, don't) study in the library anymore.
2. We (was, were) hoping to find him there.
3. The library (doesn't, don't) close until eleven o'clock.
4. (Was, Were) you late tonight?
5. Irina (doesn't, don't) care if you stay until closing time.

EXERCISE **Making the Subject and Verb Agree**

In the blanks next to each sentence, write the subject of the sentence and the correct form of the verb.

	Subject	Verb
1. Mystery writers from around America (presents, present) an award called the Edgar, named after Edgar Allan Poe.	_____	_____
2. They (nominates, nominate) several writers each year for their award.	_____	_____
3. A successful mystery writer (lives, live) in our town.	_____	_____
4. He (doesn't, don't) live too far from me.	_____	_____
5. Sometimes we (sees, see) him out walking.	_____	_____
6. He always (wears, wear) an old wide-brimmed hat.	_____	_____
7. His books usually (centers, center) around a sports theme.	_____	_____
8. His latest book (is, are) about a murder at the U.S. Open Tennis Tournament.	_____	_____
9. He (was, were) nominated for the Edgar Award for best paperback of the year.	_____	_____
10. We (doesn't, don't) know yet if he will win the award.	_____	_____

EXERCISE **2**   **Making the Subject and Verb Agree**

In the blanks next to each sentence, write the subject of the sentence and the correct form of the verb.

	Subject	Verb
1. Many companies today (tests, test) their workers for drugs.		
2. To many people, it (seems, seem) an invasion of privacy.		
3. Employers (worries, worry) that bus and train drivers are using drugs on the job.		
4. They (doesn't, don't) want the lives of their passengers at risk.		
5. Even operators of rides in amusement parks (undergoes, undergo) tests.		
6. Professional athletes on a team (has, have) special problems because of unwelcome publicity.		
7. Some factories (installs, install) hidden video cameras for surveillance.		
8. The General Motors Company (hires, hire) undercover agents as workers.		
9. In Kansas City, drug-sniffing dogs (was, were) used in a newspaper office.		
10. (Has, Have) you ever taken a drug test?		

EXERCISE **3**   **Making the Subject and Verb Agree**

In the blanks next to each sentence, write the subject of the sentence and the correct form of the verb.

	Subject	Verb
1. My sister (works, work) for the school system.		
2. She (lives, live) with her dog and two cats.		
3. I (be, am, is) studying radiology.		
4. I (wants, want) medical coverage.		
5. Everyone (been, has been, have been) worried about the future.		
6. They (needs, need) job security.		
7. Oscar (am, be, is) in my biology class.		
8. Classes (is, are, be) canceled during the strike.		

	Subject	Verb
9. Our office (has, have) a new computer.	_____	_____
10. It (has, have) much greater capacity than our previous model.	_____	_____

Subject-Verb Agreement with Hard-to-Find Subjects

As you learned in Chapter 3, a verb does not always immediately follow the subject. Other words or groups of words called *phrases* (prepositional or appositive phrases, for example) can come between the subject and the verb. Furthermore, subjects and verbs can be inverted when they are used in questions or in sentences beginning with *there* or *here*.

When looking for subject-verb agreement in sentences where the subjects are difficult to find, keep two points in mind:

- Subjects are *not* found in prepositional phrases or appositive phrases.
- Subjects can be found after the verb in sentences that are questions and in sentences that begin with the word *there* or the word *here*.

EXERCISE **4**   **Agreement with Hidden Subjects**

In each sentence below, cross out prepositional phrases, appositive phrases, and the word *there* or the word *here*. Then underline the subject. Finally, circle the correct verb.

1. Here (is, are) a plan about time management.

2. Too much busywork in your day (prevents, prevent) efficiency.

3. A period of time without interruptions (is, are) crucial.

4. People usually (does, do) too many things at once.

5. Why (is, are) frequent breaks important?

6. Constant clutter on people's desks (causes, cause) frustration.

7. Why (does, do) perfectionists have so much difficulty?

8. The habit of procrastination (is, are) another area of time management.

9. There (is, are) several other distracting activities, from watching television to playing video games.

10. Children in a family (needs, need) to help with chores.

EXERCISE **5**   **Agreement with Hidden Subjects**

In each sentence below, cross out prepositional phrases, appositive phrases, and the word *there* or the word *here*. Then underline the subject. Finally, circle the correct verb.

1. Here (is, are) some basic medical supplies needed for every home.

2. A thermometer in the medicine chest (is, are) crucial.

3. There (is, are) a box of bandages on hand for minor injuries.

4. A vaporizer in the bedroom at night (relieves, relieve) bronchial congestion.

5. Pads of sterile gauze often (helps, help) dress wounds.

6. A small bottle of Coca-Cola syrup (proves, prove) helpful for treating stomach upsets.

7. A useful tool, a pair of tweezers, (removes, remove) splinters.

8. In a home ready for emergencies, a list of emergency phone numbers (sits, sit) next to the telephone.

9. Why (has, have) cold compresses been useful in treating sprains?

10. Every person with a sense of responsibility (needs, need) a resource book on first aid at hand.

Subject-Verb Agreement with Collective Nouns

Collective nouns name a group of people or things.

Frequently Used Collective Nouns

assembly	couple	orchestra
audience	crowd	panel
board	faculty	public
class	family	senate
club	group	team
committee	herd	tribe
council	jury	troop

A *collective noun* (also called a *group noun*) is considered singular unless the meaning is clearly plural.

Usually, a collective noun takes a singular verb or requires a singular pronoun to refer to that noun. The reasoning is that the group acts as a single unit.

The class *was waiting* for *its* turn to use the gym.

The Cub Scout troop *is holding its* jamboree in July.

The orchestra *performs* in Cincinnati next week.

Sometimes a collective noun takes a plural verb or requires a plural pronoun to refer to that noun because the members of the group are clearly acting as individuals, with separate actions as a result. One clue that a group noun will be considered plural is if the verb shows a difference of opinion: *disagree, argue, debate, differ.*

> The class *were putting* on their coats.
>
> *(Clearly, each member has his or her own coat.)*
>
> The Cub Scout troop *were having* difficulty with *their* tents.
>
> *(Here, the meaning is that each person is individually having trouble with his tent.)*
>
> The orchestra *are debating* whether or not to go on tour.
>
> *(Some individuals think they should go on tour; some think they should not.)*

NOTE: The word *number* is a collective noun that is governed by the following rule:

If the definite article (*the*) is used with *number*, the meaning is singular.

> *The number* of reality shows on television *has* increased.

If the indefinite article (*a, an*) is used with *number*, the meaning is plural.

> *A number* of reality shows on television *have* been canceled.

EXERCISE **Agreement with Collective Nouns**

Collective nouns can sometimes be singular or plural depending on the writer's intention. After each sentence of the following exercise, the words in parentheses indicate the writer's intended meaning. Underline the subject and circle the correct verb in each sentence.

1. The construction crew (is, are) being blamed for the accident. (*acting as a unit*)

2. In this case, the union (accuses, accuse) the crew. (*acting as a unit*)

3. A few days after the accident, the same group (files, file) charges. (*acting as a unit*)

4. The crew's legal team (is, are) uncertain about their strategy. (*acting as individuals*)

5. The public (voices, voice) their concerns to the media. (*acting as individuals*)

6. The crowd (grows, grow) more and more impatient. (*acting as a unit*)

7. The audience (interrupts, interrupt) the proceedings. (*acting as individuals*)

8. The jury (hears, hear) the evidence. (*acting as a unit*)

9. The group (has, have) very different opinions. (*acting as individuals*)

10. The crowd (sits, sit) on the edge of their seats to hear the verdict. (*acting as individuals*)

EXERCISE   **Agreement with Collective Nouns**

Use the following general rule for collective nouns: A collective noun is considered singular unless the members of the group are acting as individuals with different ideas or separate actions. In the following exercise, underline the subject and circle the correct verb in each sentence.

1.   The Spanish club (is, are) hiring a speaker for the meeting.

2.   The trio (performs, perform) mostly on weekends.

3.   The group (needs, need) a sponsor for its organization.

4.   The faculty (is, are) not in agreement about the new grading policy.

5.   The committee (was, were) undecided about who should be invited.

6.   The team (has, have) beaten its strongest opponent.

7.   A crowd usually (attends, attend) the competition.

8.   The board of directors (disagrees, disagree) about the proposed reorganization.

9.   The panel tonight (was, were) not all ready for the questions posed to them.

10. The junior class (is, are) choosing their class rings this week.

Subject-Verb Agreement with Indefinite Pronouns

Care should be taken to learn which indefinite pronouns are singular and which are plural.

Indefinite Pronouns

INDEFINITE PRONOUNS TAKING A SINGULAR VERB

everyone	someone	anyone	no one
everybody	somebody	anybody	nobody
everything	something	anything	nothing
each	another	either (of)	neither (of)
one (of)	much	such (a)	

Everyone *is* expecting a miracle.

INDEFINITE PRONOUNS TAKING A PLURAL VERB

both	few	many	several

The talks between the two countries failed. Both *were* to blame.

INDEFINITE PRONOUNS TAKING A SINGULAR OR PLURAL VERB
DEPENDING ON THE MEANING IN THE SENTENCE

all	any	more	most
none	some		

The books are gone. All of them *were* very popular.

The sugar is gone. All of it *was* spilled.

EXERCISE **Agreement with Indefinite Pronouns**

Underline the subject and circle the correct verb in each sentence.

HINT: When a prepositional phrase follows an indefinite pronoun, be sure that the verb agrees with the indefinite pronoun subject.

<u>Each</u> of my friends (wants, want) a degree.

1. Nobody (knows, know) how many drugs are contained in plants that grow in the rainforest.

2. Some (argues, argue) that wonderful drugs could be derived from many plants.

3. Most of the pharmaceutical experts (remains, remain) skeptical.

4. All of the research (is, are) expensive and often (proves, prove) fruitless.

5. Everybody (agrees, agree) that the tropical forest is a source of medicine.

6. One of the dangers (is, are) that if we wait, the tropical forest may disappear.

7. One of the two U.S. companies in Costa Rica (is, are) Merck and Company.

8. Each of the companies (has been, have been) paying the country for the right to search the rainforest.

9. Among scientists, some (recommends, recommend) that governments subsidize drug research.

10. Vincristine and vinblastine are two medicines found in the rainforest; both (is, are) used for cancer treatment.

EXERCISE **Agreement with Indefinite Pronouns**

Underline the subject and circle the correct verb in each sentence.

1. One of the classic Spanish colonial towns still existing today (is, are) St. Augustine, Florida.

2. Almost nobody (realizes, realize) the difference between the alligator of the Southern wetlands and the crocodile of southern Florida.

3. Most of the South's coast (is, are) lined with barrier islands.

4. Nobody (reaches, reach) Florida's Gulf Islands except by boat.

5. One of the special Southern treats (remains, remain) a bag of boiled peanuts.

6. Anyone visiting a Southern home (is, are) likely to be served iced tea, the "house wine" of the South.

7. (Doesn't, Don't) everybody love the music from Mississippi: rock 'n' roll, blues, and country and western?

8. Some of the country's most colorful folk art (is, are) found by driving on the back roads.

9. Not all of the plantation houses in the Old South (looks, look) like Tara in *Gone with the Wind*.

10. Southerners often have distinctive names; many of them (uses, use) double names such as Billie Jean, James Earl, or Peggy Sue.

Subject-Verb Agreement with Compound Subjects

> **If the parts of a compound subject are connected by the word *and*, the verb is usually plural.**

Alberto *and* Ramon *are* the winners.

The exception to this rule occurs when the two subjects are thought of as a single unit.

> **If the parts of a compound subject connected by *and* are thought of as a single unit, the verb is singular.**

Peanut butter *and* jelly *is* my favorite sandwich.

The rule becomes more complicated when the parts of the compound subject are connected by *or, nor, either, either/or, neither, neither/nor, not only/but also.*

> **When the parts of a compound subject are connected with *or, nor, either, either/or, neither, neither/nor, not only/but also*, use the following rules:**
>
> 1. **If both subjects are singular, the verb is singular.**
>
>   *Either* Alberto *or* Ramon *is* the winner.
>
> 2. **If both subjects are plural, the verb is plural.**
>
>   *Either* my friends *or* my two brothers *are* the winners.
>
> 3. **If one subject is singular and one subject is plural, the verb agrees with the subject closest to the verb.**
>
>   *Either* my friends *or* my brother *is* the winner.
>
>   *Either* my brother *or* my friends *are* the winner.

EXERCISE **Subject-Verb Agreement with Compound Subjects**

Underline the compound subject and circle the correct verb in each sentence.

1. Macaroni and cheese (is, are) my son's favorite supper.

2. This meal and others like it (has, have) too much fat.

3. My mother and father, on the other hand, often (enjoys, enjoy) a fruit salad for their main meal.

4. For many of us, our shopping habits or cooking routine (needs, need) to be changed.

5. Either a salad or a cooked vegetable with a sprinkling of cheese (is, are) a better choice than macaroni and cheese.

6. Adults and children (does, do) need to watch their diets.

7. Too many pizzas and sodas (is, are) a disaster for people's health.

8. Either the lack of exercise or the eating of fatty foods (causes, cause) more problems than just weight gain.

9. Neither potato chips nor buttered popcorn (is, are) a good snack choice.

10. An apple or grapes (makes, make) a better choice.

EXERCISE 11   Subject-Verb Agreement with Compound Subjects

In each sentence, underline the compound subject and circle the correct verb.

1. Students and their teacher (meets, meet) at the University of Indiana to do marriage research.

2. Either Robert Levenson or John Gollman (uses, use) the video to examine how couples interact during arguments.

3. Neither body language nor the spoken words (is, are) unimportant.

4. Criticism, whining, or withdrawal (reveals, reveal) potential trouble.

5. Sweating, blood flow, and heart rate (is, are) also monitored during arguments.

6. Positive moments or good memories (needs, need) to outnumber the negative moments.

7. A man or a woman marrying someone with a different fighting style (risks, risk) an unhappy marriage.

8. Courtrooms or a baseball field (provides, provide) structured times and places for people to fight.

9. A particular time and a particular place (needs, need) to be set aside for talking about marital problems.

10. A happy husband and wife (gives, give) each other support and friendship.

Subject-Verb Agreement with Unusual Nouns

Do not assume that every noun ending in -s is plural or that all nouns that do not end in -s are singular. There are some exceptions. Here are a few of the most common exceptions.

1. Some nouns are always singular in meaning but end in -s:

mathematics	diabetes	United States
economics	measles	Kansas

Mathematics *is* my major.

2. Some nouns are always plural in meaning.

clothes	tweezers	pants
scissors	fireworks	pliers

My blue pants *are* ripped.

3. Some nouns change internally rather than add -*s* at the end:

Singular	Plural
foot	feet
tooth	teeth
child	children
man	men
woman	women
mouse	mice
ox	oxen
goose	geese

4. Some nouns remain the same whether singular or plural:

Singular	Plural
deer	deer
elk	elk
fish	fish
moose	moose

5. When some foreign words are used in English, they continue to form the plural by following the rules of their original languages. For example, here are four Latin words that follow the Latin rule (-*um* changes to -*a* to form the plural):

Singular	Plural
bacterium	bacteria
datum	data
medium	media
stratum	strata

Mastery and Editing Tests

TEST **Making the Subject and Verb Agree**

In the blanks next to each sentence, write the subject of the sentence and the correct form of the verb. An example follows.

	Subject	Verb
The price of airline tickets to England (has, have) remained fairly reasonable.	price	has
1. Included in the price of the trip (was, were) five nights in a lovely hotel and all meals.	_____	_____
2. Nobody in the family (knows, know) how to swim.	_____	_____
3. Dimitry and Craig (works, work) well together.	_____	_____
4. The student senate (meets, meet) every Tuesday.	_____	_____

5. Where (is, are) the wrapping paper for these packages? _____ _____

6. In the entire building, there (is, are) only two windows. _____ _____

7. Either the fruit pies or that chocolate cake (looks, look) like the best choice for your picnic. _____ _____

8. Public performances (makes, make) me nervous. _____ _____

9. One of my most favorite television shows (is, are) *60 Minutes*. _____ _____

10. The town council (disagrees, disagree) on the planned expansion. _____ _____

TEST 2 **Making the Subject and Verb Agree**

Using your own words and ideas, complete each of the following sentences. Be sure the subject and verb agree. An example follows:

The best place for wedding receptions is a restaurant with a view.

1. Our team _____

2. The box of chocolates _____

3. Both of my sisters _____

4. The effects of a pay cut on a family _____

   _____

5. Where are _____

6. Not only the teacher but also the students _____

   _____

7. The jury _____

8. Each of the contestants _____

9. There is _____

10. The table of contents in that book _____

TEST 3 **Editing Student Writing: Making the Subject and Verb Agree**

The following paragraph contains seven errors in subject-verb agreement. For each sentence, cross out prepositional phrases and appositive phrases, underline the subject, and circle the verb. Place a check over errors in agreement. On the lines following, list the subject and the correct form of the verb for each sentence.

Bedbugs Are Back

[1]People in hotels and apartments around the country are complaining.

[2]Gradually more and more places, including college dormitories, has bedbugs.

³How does these pests get into a room? ⁴International travel has been largely to blame. ⁵Unfortunately, bedbugs have the ability to survive for over a year without a meal. ⁶Furthermore, insecticides from a local hardware store is no longer effective. ⁷Your new mattress sometimes arrive on a truck with an old mattress (filled with bedbugs) from another customer. ⁸Also, a bedbug easily rides unseen from one place to another in a pants cuff or a jacket. ⁹Either a crack in a wall or a ridge between the floor boards are enough room for a bedbug. ¹⁰These invisible vampires of the night traumatizes their victims. ¹¹The number of them often grows quickly from only a few into several thounsands. ¹²Unsightly, itchy red welts are left behind by this bloodsucking bug. ¹³Nobody in my circle of friends knowingly visit a home with these invisible and nearly indestructible pests.

	Subject	Correct form of verb
1.	_____	_____
2.	_____	_____
3.	_____	_____
4.	_____	_____
5.	_____	_____
6.	_____	_____
7.	_____	_____
8.	_____	_____
9.	_____	_____
10.	_____	_____
11.	_____	_____
12.	_____	_____
13.	_____	_____

TEST **Editing Student Writing: Using Correction Symbols**

Instructors often use commonly accepted symbols to mark corrections in student writing. The editing symbol for subject-verb agreement is **agr.** (See the inside back cover for a list of common editing symbols.) The paragraph below contains five subject-verb agreement errors. Write **agr** above each error you find, and then write the subject and the correct verb form on the lines provided below. (In sentence 9, consider *audience* as a collective noun that acts as a unit.)

¹Why don't everybody like a hair-raising horror movie? ²I don't see many of my college classmates at all the latest shows. ³My girlfriend doesn't like these

kinds of movies, and neither do any of her friends. [4]In fact, the theaters are filled almost exclusively with teenagers. [5]My friends and I pays our eight bucks and anticipate a nightmare. [6]Each of us hope for a thrill. [7]Emotions like love, friendship, or kindness go by the wayside. [8]The audience wants blood and guts! [9]It don't matter if the plot is ridiculous and the acting is terrible. [10]The typical horror movie with all its violent scenes appeal to our worst nature. [11]One of my favorite horror movies is *The Hills Have Eyes*. [12]Fortunately for my friends and me, a popular horror movie these days usually has a sequel. [13]We look forward to the next adrenaline rush.

Five subject-verb agreement corrections

	Subject	Correct form of the verb
1.	_____	_____
2.	_____	_____
3.	_____	_____
4.	_____	_____
5.	_____	_____

Exploring Online

Go to academic.cengage.com/devenglish/scarry to find the **Writer's Online Workplace,** a website designed for students using this book. You will find links to handouts, interactive quizzes, and other online resources as you explore the following topic:

- subject-verb agreement

Working Together

Focused Freewriting: Preserving Family History

Though it is more difficult to write about my father than about my mother, since I spent less time with him and knew him less well, it is equally as liberating. Partly this is because writing about people helps us to understand them, and understanding them helps us to accept them as part of ourselves. Since I share so many of my father's characteristics, physical and otherwise, coming to terms with what he has meant to my life is crucial to a full acceptance and love of myself.

Alice Walker, the well-known novelist and essay writer, expressed these thoughts in a journal that she kept for a time. She discovered that by writing down her thoughts and feelings about her father she felt liberated. We can all be liberated by a better understanding of the people who have shaped our lives. Obviously, we cannot know everything about another person, even a person with whom we have lived, but we can put together stories we have heard from relatives, along with memories that we have ourselves. When we write about family members, it is always good to remember that each person's perspective is colored by his or her own personality and by a memory that may not be entirely accurate. In this regard, you might want to create a portrait of a family member through the eyes of a person other than yourself, always keeping in mind that people's recollections can be distorted.

Questions for Class Discussion

1. On the basis of the Alice Walker quote above, can you explain why Alice Walker found writing about her father to be liberating?

2. To what extent should we feel that our family members are "part of ourselves"? What if we do not like or accept everything about a family member? In that case, what should we do about including that family member in a memoir?

3. What types of information might you be tempted to write in a journal entry about a family member? Are there any people who could provide you with stories that you would like to include in your entry?

4. What would you like your grandchildren to know about you?

5. What characteristics, both mental and physical, do you believe you have inherited? Do you like what you have inherited? What do you wish had been left out?

6. Think about a person who has been adopted. How is preserving family history made more complicated for such a person? What advice could you offer?

7. What are the most common obstacles people face that prevent them from accepting themselves?

Freewriting

Freewrite for fifteen minutes. Share a story, a memory of some kind, or a description of a family member that you find worthy of recording. You might tell a story about yourself, one that you would like your family to remember. Think of your piece of writing as the beginning of a memoir that future members of your family would like to have.

Portfolio Suggestion

Save the freewriting you have done on your family's history. This is a topic that you may want to return to again and again. Children will appreciate all the stories and memories you can gather about your relatives. This may be one of the greatest gifts you can give your family.

Understanding Fragments and Phrases

Groups of words that go together are not necessarily sentences. In this chapter, you will learn to recognize the different sentence parts and distinguish between a phrase and a sentence. Your focus will be on three skills.

CHAPTER OBJECTIVES

- Distinguish a fragment from a sentence when one of the following elements is missing:

    a subject

    a verb

    a complete thought

- Identify the six kinds of phrases in English:

    noun phrases (includes appositive phrases)

    prepositional phrases

    verb phrases

    infinitive phrases

    participial phrases

    gerund phrases

- Understand the three different functions of the present participle:

    as part of a verb phrase

    as an adjective

    as a noun

The fragment is a major problem for many student writers. A thought may be clear in a writer's mind, but on paper the expression of this idea may be incomplete because it does not include a subject, a verb, or a complete thought. In this section, you will improve your ability to spot fragments (incomplete sentences), and you will learn how to correct them. This practice will help you avoid fragments in your own writing.

Here, for example, is a typical conversation between two people at lunchtime. It is composed entirely of fragments, but the two people who are speaking have no trouble understanding each other.

Doug: Had any lunch?
Nelida: A sandwich.

Doug: What kind?

Nelida: Ham and swiss on rye.

Rewritten in complete sentences, this brief conversation might go as follows:

Doug: Did you have any lunch yet?

Nelida: Yes, I had a sandwich.

Doug: What kind of sandwich did you have?

Nelida: I had ham and swiss cheese on rye bread.

In the first conversation, misunderstanding is unlikely since the two speakers stand face to face. Seeing the other's gestures and hearing the intonations in the other's voice help each one grasp the other's meaning. These short phrases are enough for communication because the speakers are using more than just words to convey their thoughts. They understand each other because each one has no difficulty completing the thoughts in the other's mind.

In writing, however, readers cannot be present to observe tone of voice, gestures, or other signals for themselves. They cannot be expected to read the writer's mind. For a reader, only words grouped into sentences and sentences grouped into paragraphs can provide clues to the meaning. Because writing often involves thoughts that are abstract and even complex, fragments cause great difficulty and sometimes result in total confusion for the reader.

EXERCISE **Putting a Conversation into Complete Sentences**

The following conversation could have taken place between two students at the start of their English class. Rewrite the conversation in complete thoughts (or standard sentences). Remember the definition of a sentence:

> A **complete sentence** has a subject and a verb and expresses a complete thought.

Nick: Early again.

Chandra: Want to get a front row seat.

Nick: Your homework ready?

Chandra: Nearly.

Nick: Think he'll give a quiz today?

Chandra: Hope not.

Nick: Looks like rain any minute.

Chandra: Bad news.

Nick: Going to the game Saturday?

Chandra: Probably.

Conversation rewritten in standard sentences

Nick: _____

Chandra: _____

Nick: _____

Chandra: _____

Nick: _____

Chandra: _____

Nick: _____

Chandra: _____

Nick: _____

Chandra: _____

Remember that when you write in complete sentences, the results may differ from the way you would express the same ideas in everyday conversation with a friend.

Although you will occasionally spot incomplete sentences in professional writing, you may be sure the writer is using these fragments intentionally. In such cases, the fragment may be appropriate because it captures the way a person thinks or speaks or because it creates a special effect. A student developing his or her writing skills should be careful to use only standard-sentence form so that every thought will be communicated effectively. Nearly all the writing you will do in your life—business correspondence, papers in school, or reports in your job—will demand standard-sentence form. Fragments will be looked upon as a sign of ignorance rather than evidence of a creative style!

What Is a Fragment?

A **fragment** is a piece of a sentence.

A group of words may appear to be a sentence but if one of the following elements is missing, the result is a fragment.

a. The subject is missing:

> Brought the plans to my office.

b. The verb is missing:

> The architect to my office.

c. Both the subject and the verb are missing:

> To my office.

d. The subject and verb are present, but the group of words does not express a complete thought:

> The architect brought.

EXERCISE **Understanding Fragments**

Each of the following ten groups of words is a fragment. In the blank next to each fragment, identify the missing part that prevents it from being a complete sentence. Select one of the following possibilities for each answer.

a.   The subject is missing.

b.   The verb is missing.

c.   Both the subject and the verb are missing.

d.   The subject and verb are present, but the group of words does not express a complete thought.

An example follows:

Fragment	**What is missing?**
the red fox	**b** (verb)

1.   returned to the river   _____

2.   a bird on the oak branch   _____

3.   between the island and the mainland   _____

4.   the hawk in a soaring motion   _____

5.   the fishing boats on the lake   _____

6.   dropped like a stone into the water   _____

7.   the silence of the forest   _____

8.   carried the fish to the tree   _____

9.   the fisherman put   _____

10.   into the net   _____

How Do You Correct a Fragment?

1. **Add the missing part or parts.**

Fragment:	across the lake
To be added:	subject and verb
Complete sentence:	I swam across the lake.

    The prepositional phrase *across the lake* is a fragment because a prepositional phrase cannot function as the subject or the verb in a sentence. Furthermore, the words *across the lake* do not express a complete thought.

2. **Join the fragment to the sentence where it belongs.**

    If you look at the context in which a fragment occurs, you will often find that the complete thought is already present. The writer did not recognize that the fragment belonged to the sentence that came just before or to the sentence that immediately followed. Therefore, another way to correct a fragment is to join the fragment to the sentence that precedes it or to the sentence that immediately follows it. Which sentence you choose depends on where the information in the fragment belongs. Study the example below.

Incorrect:	In the middle of the night, I swam. Across the lake. The water was cool and inviting.
Correct:	In the middle of the night, I swam across the lake. The water was cool and inviting.

    Fragments can exist in a writer's work for a number of reasons. A writer may become careless for a moment or may not fully understand how all the parts of a sentence work. If the writer does not have a clear idea of what he or she is trying to say, fragments and other errors are more likely to occur. Sometimes another try at expressing the same idea may produce a better result.

EXERCISE **Making Fragments into Sentences**

Change the fragments of Exercise 2 into complete sentences by adding the missing part or parts that you have already identified.

1. returned to the river

    _____

2. a bird on the oak branch

    _____

3. between the island and the mainland

    _____

4. the hawk in a soaring motion

    _____

5. the fishing boats on the lake

    _____

6. dropped like a stone into the water

_____

7. the silence of the forest

_____

8. carried the fish to the tree

_____

9. the fisherman put

_____

10. into the net

_____

EXERCISE **4** **Finding Fragments That Belong to Other Sentences**

Each of the following passages contains two or more fragments. First, read each passage carefully. Then place a check in front of each fragment you find. Finally, draw an arrow to indicate the sentence to which the fragment belongs. An example follows:

Adelle assisted the dancers. She stood backstage during the performance. ✔ Between numbers. She helped the ballerinas change costumes.

1. Fishing is one of the oldest sports in the world. And can be one of the most relaxing. A person with a simple wooden pole and line can have as much fun as a sportsman. With expensive equipment. For busy executives, overworked teachers, and even presidents of nations. Fishing can be a good way to escape from the stress of demanding jobs.

2. The first electric car was built in 1887. It was sold commercially. Six years later. At the turn of the century, people had great faith in new technology. In fact, three hundred electric taxicabs were operating in New York City by 1900. However, electric cars soon lost their popularity. The new gasoline engine became more widely used. With our current concern over pollution. Perhaps electric cars will become desirable once again.

3. Tiger Woods is famous for his success as a championship golfer. He is also known for his work with children. In Anaheim, California, Tiger has recently opened a learning center. For fourth to twelfth graders. Children can apply for a wide range of classes. Including robotics, creative writing, forensics, and

photography. Eventually, the center will serve five thousand children. Tiger is planning the construction of other centers around the country. At a cost of five million dollars apiece. He is grateful for his loving and supportive family. And wants to help less-fortunate children.

What Is a Phrase and How Many Kinds of Phrases Are There?

> A **phrase** is a group of words belonging together but lacking one or more of the three elements necessary for a sentence.

Fragments are usually made up of phrases. These phrases are often mistaken for sentences because they are words that go together as a group. However, they do not fit the definition of a sentence. *Do not confuse a phrase with a sentence.*

The English language has six kinds of phrases, and you should learn to recognize each one. You have already studied three of these kinds of phrases in Chapter 3.

The Six Types of Phrases in English

1. **Noun phrase**   a noun with its modifiers:

   many large round stones

2. **Prepositional phrase**   a preposition with its object and modifiers:

   among the large round stones

3. **Verb phrase**   a main verb with its helping verbs and modifiers:

   were sweetly singing

   has slowly vanished

4. **Infinitive phrase**   the word *to* with the base form of the verb and any other words that complete the phrase:

   to move gracefully

5. **Participial phrase**   a present or past participle and the other words that complete the phrase:

   moving gracefully

   greatly encouraged

   The participial phrase functions as an **adjective.**

   Moving gracefully, the skater looked like a ballet dancer.

   Greatly encouraged, the coach decided she was ready for competition.

6.   **Gerund phrase**   a present participle and the other words that complete the phrase:

> moving gracefully

The gerund phrase functions as an **noun.**

> *Moving gracefully* was the skater's best quality.

Like the verb phrase, the infinitive phrase, the participial phrase, and the gerund phrase are all formed from verbs. However, these phrases do not function as verbs in sentences.

INFINITIVE PHRASE

An infinitive phrase usually functions as a noun.

Infinitive phrase as subject:

> *To continue this argument* would be useless.

Infinitive phrase as object:

> She began *to move gracefully.*

NOTE: The word *to* can also be used as a preposition, as in *I wrote to my son.*

PRACTICE

See whether you can distinguish between the infinitive phrases and the prepositional phrases. In each of the following sentences, label the italicized phrase as an infinitive phrase (**INF**) or prepositional phrase (**PP**).

_____   1.   I stopped by his office *to say goodbye.*

_____   2.   The trail of evidence led directly *to him.*

_____   3.   We were lucky *to have discovered* his fraudulent activities.

_____   4.   The manager had forced him *to tell the truth.*

_____   5.   His leaving will be a relief *to the staff.*

PARTICIPIAL PHRASE

How Is the Participle Formed?

The present and past participles are formed from the base verb:

Present participle: base verb + *-ing*

> running, looking, trying

Past participle: base verb + the regular past tense ending *-d* or *-ed*

> disappointed, folded, turned

or

base verb + irregular past tense form

> told, gone, given,

Below are the same participles given above, this time with words that might complete their phrases.

Examples of **present participial phrases:**

running home, looking very unhappy, trying hard

Examples of **past participial phrases:**

greatly disappointed, folded incorrectly, turned slightly

told tearfully, gone quickly, given gratefully

How Does a Participial Phrase Function?

A participial phrase functions as an **adjective** in a sentence. By studying the following sentences, you can observe how the above phrases can be used in complete sentences. These phrases function as adjectives for the noun or pronoun that follows them.

Running home, the worker lost her wallet.

Looking very unhappy, she retraced her steps.

Greatly disappointed, she could not find it.

Told tearfully, the story saddened her friends.

GERUND PHRASE

The gerund is formed from the present participle. Along with any words that go with it, the gerund phrase functions as a **noun.** As such, it can be the subject or the object of a sentence.

Gerund phrase as subject: *Long-distance running* is strenuous exercise.
Gerund phrase as object: I like *long-distance running.*

PRACTICE

See whether you can distinguish between participial phrases and gerund phrases. In each of the following sentences, label the italicized phrase as a participial phrase (P) or a gerund phrase (G). Remember, the participial phrase functions as an *adjective.* The gerund phrase functions as a *noun.*

_____ 1. *Standing totally still,* the child hoped the bee would fly away.

_____ 2. *Playing the violin* is not easy.

_____ 3. The athlete will try *deep-sea diving.*

_____ 4. *Waiting patiently,* we ordered something to drink.

_____ 5. *Edited slowly and carefully,* the essay was much improved.

EXERCISE **5**   **Identifying Phrases**

Identify each of the underlined phrases.

1. <u>Visiting New York</u> can be a nightmare or a thrill.   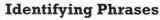

2. Many people love to see the Broadway shows. _____

3. Museums, restaurants, shopping, and the varied night life offer endless possibilities for the tourist. _____

4. Riding the subways, tourists see another side of New York. _____

5. My brother Don was pickpocketed on a hot and crowded subway last summer. _____

6. Coming from the country, he thought the prices were outrageous and the noise and traffic unbearable. _____

7. Finding a parking spot may have been his most frustrating experience. _____

8. In addition to these problems, the question of physical safety concerns most tourists. _____

9. The city has completed many projects to clean up the Times Square area. _____

10. New York's continual fascination is the rich mix of cultures and lifestyles from all over the world. _____

EXERCISE 6 **Identifying Phrases**

The following sentences come from a paragraph by John Steinbeck. Identify each of the underlined phrases.

1. At dawn Cannery Row seems _____

2. to hang suspended out of time _____

3. in a silvery light. _____

4. The splashing of the waves _____

5. can be heard. _____

6. Flapping their wings, the seagulls _____

7. come to sit on the roof peaks shoulder to shoulder. _____

8. Cats drip over the fences and slither like syrup over the ground to look for fishheads. _____

9. Silent early morning dogs parade majestically. _____

10. No automobiles are running then. _____

EXERCISE **7**   **Identifying Phrases**

Identify each of the underlined phrases.

1. For years scientists debated the existence of global warming.
   _____

2. In the last five years, the serious debate has ended.
   _____

3. Pouring more and more greenhouse gases into the atmosphere, humans are causing the earth to grow warmer.
   _____

4. Massive sections of ice are melting in the Arctic and Antarctic.
   _____

5. Sea levels are projected to rise gradually.
   _____

6. Warming a full degree Fahrenheit since 1970, the oceans are fueling more intense typhoons and hurricanes.
   _____

7. By the year 2050, more than a million animal species worldwide may be extinct.
   _____

8. We could be approaching the point of no return.
   _____

9. Curbing greenhouse gases is now a worldwide emergency.
   _____

10. Congress needs to regulate greenhouse gases.
    _____

The Three Functions of the Present Participle

The present participle causes problems for students working with sentence fragments. Because the participle is used sometimes as a verb (in a verb phrase), sometimes as an adjective (in a participial phrase), and sometimes as a noun (in a gerund phrase), it causes a good deal of confusion for students.

The present participle can function in three different ways.

1. The participle functions as a *verb* in a **verb phrase.**

   The student *was taking* an exam.

2. The participle functions as an *adjective* in a **participial phrase.**

   Taking an exam, the student felt stressed.

3. The participle functions as a *noun* in a **gerund phrase.**

   Taking an exam can be stressful.

In each of these cases, the present participle is part of a phrase. Remember, a phrase is not a sentence.

EXERCISE 8   **Using the Present Participle in a Verb Phrase**

Below are five present participles. Add a helping verb to each one and use this verb phrase to write a complete sentence of your own. An example follows:

Present participle:	sitting
Verb phrase:	is sitting
Sentence:	The couple is sitting on the balcony.

1. building _____

2. crying _____

3. traveling _____

4. writing _____

5. thinking _____

EXERCISE 9   **Using the Present Participle in a Participial Phrase**

Each of the following phrases contains a present participle. Use each participial phrase to compose a sentence in which the phrase functions as an adjective. An example follows:

Present participle:	sitting
Participial phrase:	sitting on the balcony
Participial phrase used as an adjective in a sentence:	Sitting on the balcony, the couple enjoyed the moonlight.

1. building a house

  _____

  _____

2. crying over the broken vase

  _____

  _____

3. traveling in Mexico

  _____

  _____

4. hastily writing the letter

  _____

  _____

5. thinking about the problem

  _____

  _____

EXERCISE 10   **Using the Present Participle in a Gerund Phrase**

Each of the following phrases contains a present participle. Use each gerund phrase to compose a sentence in which the phrase functions as a noun. An example follows:

Present participle:	sitting
Gerund phrase:	sitting on the balcony
Gerund phrase used as a noun in a sentence:	Sitting on the balcony is relaxing.

1. building a house

    _____

    _____

2. crying over the broken vase

    _____

    _____

3. traveling in Mexico

    _____

    _____

4. hastily writing the letter

    _____

    _____

5. thinking about the problem

    _____

    _____

How Do You Make a Complete Sentence from a Fragment That Contains a Participle?

When a participle is used incorrectly, the result is often a fragment. Here are three ways to turn a fragment containing a participle into a sentence.

Fragment: He *talking* in his sleep.

1. Correct the main verb of the sentence.

    a. Add a helping verb to the participle to form a verb phrase:

        He *was talking* in his sleep. (*The participle needs a helping verb.*)

    b. Change the participle to a different form of the verb (such as the past tense).

        He *talked* in his sleep.

2.   Use the participle as an adjective, being sure to provide a subject and verb for the sentence.

Talking in his sleep, he muttered something about his credit card bills.

3.   Use the participle as a noun in a gerund phrase.

Talking in his sleep revealed his innermost thoughts.

EXERCISE 11   **Correcting the Fragment That Contains a Participle**

Make four complete sentences from each of the following fragments. Use the following model as your guide.

Fragment: using the back stairway

a.   He is using the back stairway. (*verb phrase*)

b.   He uses the back stairway. (*simple present tense*)

c.   Using the back stairway, he got away without being seen. (*participial phrase used as an adjective*)

d.   Using the back stairway is not a good idea. (*gerund phrase used as a noun*)

1.   moving out of the house

a. _____

b. _____

c. _____

d. _____

2.   talking on the telephone

a. _____

b. _____

c. _____

d. _____

3.   driving the car down Highway 60

a. _____

b. _____

c. _____

d. _____

EXERCISE 12

Correcting the Fragment That Contains a Participle

The following passage is made up of fragments containing participles. Rewrite the passage, creating complete sentences. Use any of the three correction methods discussed on pages 86 and 87.

I walking through the deserted apartment building. Poking around in piles of junk. The brick walls crumbling. Two children playing in the dismal hallways. Waiting for someone to restore the house to its former glory.

_____

_____

_____

_____

_____

EXERCISE 13

Correcting the Fragment That Contains a Participle

The following passage has four fragments containing participles. Place a check in front of each fragment. Then rewrite the passage using complete sentences. Use any of the four correction methods discussed previously.

Finally at age 42 taking my driving test. I felt very nervous. My son was sitting in the back seat. All my papers sitting on the front seat. The inspector got into the car and sat on my insurance form. He looked rather sour and barely spoke to me. Trying not to hit the curb. I parallel parked surprisingly well. I managed to get through all the maneuvers. Now tensely waiting for the results.

_____

_____

_____

_____

_____

_____

_____

_____

_____

_____

_____

_____

_____

EXERCISE 14 **Correcting Fragments**

Rewrite each fragment so that it is a complete sentence.

1. early morning a time of peace in my neighborhood

   _____

   _____

2. the gray mist covering up all but the faint outlines of nearby houses

   _____

   _____

3. the shapes of cars in the streets and driveways

   _____

   _____

4. to sit and look out the window

   _____

   _____

5. holding a steaming cup of coffee

   _____

   _____

6. the only sound the rumbling of a truck

   _____

   _____

7. passing by on the highway a quarter mile away

   _____

   _____

8. children all in their beds

   _____

   _____

9. no barking dogs

   _____

   _____

10. in this soft, silent dreamworld

   _____

   _____

EXERCISE 15   **Correcting Fragments**

Each of the following groups of words is a phrase. First, name each phrase. Second, make each phrase into a complete sentence.

1. two champion boxers

    Name of phrase: _____

    Sentence: _____

    _____

2. to watch

    Name of phrase: _____

    Sentence: _____

    _____

3. in the ring

    Name of phrase: _____

    Sentence: _____

    _____

4. are hitting each other

    Name of phrase: _____

    Sentence: _____

    _____

5. at each sound of the bell

    Name of phrase: _____

    Sentence: _____

    _____

6. gratefully supported

    Name of phrase: _____

    Sentence: _____

    _____

7. to conduct the fight

    Name of phrase: _____

    Sentence: _____

    _____

8. the screaming fans

Name of phrase: _____

Sentence: _____

_____

9. by the second round

Name of phrase: _____

Sentence: _____

_____

10. knocked unconscious

Name of phrase: _____

Sentence: _____

_____

Mastery and Editing Tests

TEST **1**   ### Recognizing and Correcting the Fragment

The following description of people on a dance floor at the Peppermint Lounge appeared in The *New Yorker* in the 1960s. The description is made up entirely of fragments. Rewrite the description, making each fragment into a sentence.

Place always jammed. Huge line outside. Portals closely guarded. Finally made it last night, after hour's wait. Exhilarating experience! Feel ten years younger. Hit Peppermint close to midnight, in blue mood. Inside, found pandemonium. Dance floor packed and popping. Was battered by wild swinging of hips and elbows. . . . Garb of twisters seems to run gamut. Some couples in evening dress, others in T shirts and blue jeans. Young. Old. Businessmen. Crew Cuts. Beatniks.

_____

_____

_____

_____

_____

_____

_____

_____

_____

_____

_____

_____

_____

TEST **2** **Recognizing and Correcting the Fragment**

The following paragraph contains seven fragments. Read the paragraph and place a check in front of each fragment. Then rewrite the paragraph, being careful to use only complete sentences.

That afternoon the street was full of children. Taking a shower in the rain. Soaping themselves and rushing out into the storm. To wash off the suds. In a few minutes, it was all over. Including the rubdown. The younger children took their showers naked. Teetering on the tips of their toes and squealing to one another. The stately coconut palm in one corner of the patio. Thrashed its branches high over the dripping children bouncing on the cobblestones.

_____

_____

_____

_____

_____

_____

_____

_____

_____

_____

_____

TEST **3** **Editing Student Writing: Recognizing and Correcting the Fragment**

The following paragraph contains six fragments. Read the paragraph and place a check in front of each fragment. Then rewrite the paragraph, being careful to use only complete sentences.

We called it our house. It was only one room. With about as much space as a tent. Painted in a pastel color with a red-tiled roof. The front window reaching nearly from the sidewalk to the roof. We could look up and down the street. Sitting indoors on the window seat. Our kitchen was a small narrow area. With the brick stove and two benches to serve as shelves. Three steel bars and a short piece of lead pipe from a scrap heap to make a grate.

_____

_____

_____

_____

_____

_____

_____

_____

_____

_____

_____

TEST 4   **Editing Student Writing: Using Correction Symbols**

As you learned in Test 4 of Chapter 4 (page 70), instructors often use correction symbols to mark errors in student writing. The correction symbol for a fragment is **frag**. In the paragraph below, find five fragments (**frag**) and five errors in subject-verb agreement (**agr**). Mark each error with the commonly used correction symbol, and then correct the errors on the lines provided following the paragraph.

¹My younger brother is happy about his first job at McDonald's. ²The most popular fast food restaurant. ³His cousin and a friend also works here. ⁴His uniform, a blue and white striped shirt with blue pants, are provided for free. ⁵One of the employees show him the register. ⁶Everyone learn all the different jobs. ⁷Either the manager or the trainer tell him about the importance of patience. ⁸Getting along with other people, too. ⁹You start at the bottom. ¹⁰Work yourself up. ¹¹After six months, a supervisor reviews your work. ¹²Some workers in the group get a raise and become crew trainers. ¹³One big disadvantage. ¹⁴Low pay!

Five corrected fragments

1. _____

2. _____

3. _____

4. _____

5. _____

Five subject-verb agreement corrections

	Subject	Correct form of the verb
6.	_____	_____
7.	_____	_____
8.	_____	_____
9.	_____	_____
10.	_____	_____

Exploring Online

Go to academic.cengage.com/devenglish/scarry to find the **Writer's Online Workplace,** a website designed for students using this book. You will find links to handouts, interactive quizzes, and other online resources as you explore the following topics:

- sentence fragments
- verbal phrases (infinitive, participial, and gerund phrases)

Examining an Advertisement for Fragments

The key to Chinatown's future lies in its past.

Respect for its elders. Hope for its young. A strong sense of family. Even though these traditional values reach back to Chinatown's past, they also propel it forward into the future. Instilling the community with a spirit that's new. Fresh. And vital.

One example that reflects this spirit is Equality House. It provides 59 units of rehabilitated housing for both the elderly and homeless families. People of all nationalities. All backgrounds. Living together. Working together.

And who's responsible for this good work? The Asian Americans For Equality. A group that believes housing, along with other essential community services, helps to preserve Chinatown and its culture. So that its people will always be proud to live and work there. For more information, call Doris W. Koo, (212) 677-7210.

Bankers Trust Company
Community Development Group

1. Advertising companies devote a great deal of their time and attention to market research. This research helps the company target its message to the most likely audience for its product or service. Who is the advertiser in this newspaper ad? Who is the intended audience? What is the product or service being advertised?

2. Like many advertisements we see in magazines and newspapers, this Bankers Trust Company advertisement is made up of short, snappy constructions that are not always complete sentences. Advertisers write in this way because they want to attract our attention. However, when we write for school or for work, our compositions must be made up of only complete sentences. Review the advertisement at the left and identify all of the fragments you can find. If needed, review the two ways to correct a fragment (page 78). Then rewrite the ad, correcting all fragments.

Portfolio Suggestion

Choose a product or a service that particularly appeals to you. Clip newspaper or magazine ads, or both, that deal with this product or service. Take notes on television ads or billboard ads. Review them at a later time for possible use in comparison or contrast essays.

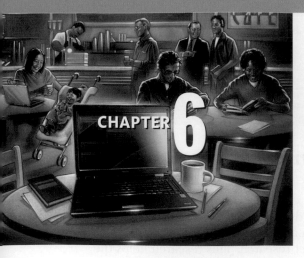

CHAPTER 6

Combining Sentences Using Three Options for Coordination

In this chapter, you will practice the three ways of creating a **compound sentence.** When you use any one of these three options to combine simple sentences into a single compound sentence, you are using **coordination.** You will learn these three options:

CHAPTER OBJECTIVES

- using a comma plus a coordinating conjunction

- using a semicolon, an adverbial conjunction, and a comma

- using only a semicolon (no conjunction)

What Is Coordination?

So far you have worked with the simple sentence. If you review some of these sentences (such as the practice sentences on page 35), you will see that writing only simple sentences results in a choppy style and also makes it difficult to express complicated ideas. You will need to learn how to combine simple sentences correctly by using *coordination.* To understand coordination, be sure you know the meaning of the following three terms.

A **clause** is a group of words that has a subject and a verb:

she spoke

when she spoke

NOTE: Of the two clauses above, only *she spoke* could be a sentence. The clause *when she spoke* could not stand alone as a sentence because it does not express a complete thought. (Chapter 7 will cover this second type of clause.)

An **independent clause** is a clause that can stand alone as a simple sentence:

She spoke.

A **compound sentence** is a sentence that is created when two or more independent clauses are correctly joined, using the rules of coordination:

She spoke, and we listened.

The three preceding terms are all part of the definition of coordination.

> **Coordination** is the combining of two or more related independent clauses (you may think of them as simple sentences) that contain ideas of equal importance. The result is a compound sentence.
>
> **Two independent clauses:**   She spoke. We listened.
> **Compound sentence:**   She spoke, and we listened.

First Option for Coordination: Using a Comma Plus a Coordinating Conjunction

The most common way to form a compound sentence is to combine independent clauses using a comma plus a coordinating conjunction.

First Option for Coordination

Independent clause	Comma and coordinating conjunction	Independent clause
I had worked hard	, so	I expected results.

You will need to memorize the list of coordinating conjunctions given below. By doing this now, you will avoid confusion later on when you will be using a different set of conjunctions to combine clauses.

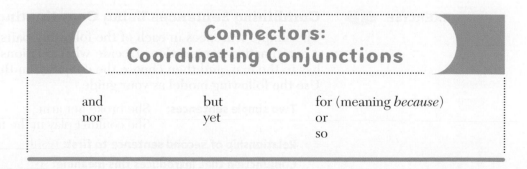

Connectors: Coordinating Conjunctions

and	but	for (meaning *because*)
nor	yet	or
		so

 In each of the following compound sentences, draw a single line under the subject and draw two lines under the verb for each independent clause. Then circle both the coordinating conjunction and the comma. An example follows:

The speaker <u>rose</u> to his feet**,** <u>and</u> the room <u>became</u> quiet.

1. The audience was packed for this was a man with an international reputation.

2. He could have told about all his successes but instead he spoke about his disappointments.

3. His words were electric so the crowd was attentive.

4. I should have brought a tape recorder or at least I should have taken notes.

Did you find a subject and verb for both independent clauses in each sentence? Now that you understand the structure of a compound sentence, you need to think about the meanings of the different coordinating conjunctions and how these conjunctions can be used to show the relationship between two ideas when each idea is given equal importance.

Coordinating Conjunctions and Their Meanings

Conjunction	Meaning	Example
and	to add an idea	He will call today, *and* he will call tomorrow.
nor	to add an idea when both clauses are in the negative	He will not call today, *nor* will he call tomorrow.
but	to contrast two opposing ideas	He will call today, *but* he might not call tomorrow.
yet	to emphasize the contrast between two opposing ideas (meaning *and despite this fact*)	He said he would call today, *yet* he did not.
for	to introduce a reason	He will call today, *for* he wants a loan.
or	to show a choice	He will call today, *or* he will call tomorrow.
so	to introduce a result	He will call today, *so* I must stay home.

EXERCISE 1   Combining Sentences Using Coordinating Conjunctions

The simple sentences in each of the following pairs could be combined with a coordinating conjunction. Decide what relationship the second sentence has to the first, and then choose the conjunction that makes the most sense. Use the following model as your guide.

Two simple sentences: She broke her arm.
                                          She couldn't play in the finals.

Relationship of second sentence to first: <u>result</u> _____

Conjunction that introduces this meaning: <u>so</u> _____

1.   Mr. Watson is kind and patient.
     His brother is sharp and nagging.

     Relationship of second sentence to first: _____

     Conjunction that introduces this meaning: _____

2.   The two adults are having great difficulty.
     They are trying to raise a teenager.

     Relationship of second sentence to first: _____

     Conjunction that introduces this meaning: _____

3.   Young Michael has no family of his own.
     He feels angry and alone.

     Relationship of second sentence to first: _____

     Conjunction that introduces this meaning: _____

4.   Michael hasn't been doing well in school.
     He isn't involved in any activities outside school.

     Relationship of second sentence to first: _____

     Conjunction that introduces this meaning: _____

5.   Mr. Watson encouraged Michael to do volunteer work at the hospital.
     This might give Michael the satisfaction of helping other people.

     Relationship of second sentence to first: _____

     Conjunction that introduces this meaning: _____

6.   Mr. Watson's brother wanted Michael to spend more time on his homework.
     He also wanted him to get a job after school to help with expenses.

     Relationship of second sentence to first: _____

     Conjunction that introduces this meaning: _____

7.   Michael liked going to the hospital.
     He was doing something important.

     Relationship of second sentence to first: _____

     Conjunction that introduces this meaning: _____

8.   He didn't earn any money.
     He liked helping people.

     Relationship of second sentence to first: _____

     Conjunction that introduces this meaning: _____

9.   Michael now wants to have a career working in a hospital.
     He will have a reason to work harder in school.

     Relationship of second sentence to first: _____

     Conjunction that introduces this meaning: _____

10. Mr. Watson thinks the hospital work was a good idea.
     His brother has to agree.

     Relationship of second sentence to first: _____

     Conjunction that introduces this meaning: _____

EXERCISE ❷   **Combining Sentences Using Coordinating Conjunctions**

Below are ten sentences. Some of them are compound sentences needing a comma and a coordinating conjunction. Some of them are simple sentences (with only compound subjects or compound verbs). These do not require a comma. Fill in each blank with a comma (if required) and a coordinating conjunction that best supports the meaning of the sentence.

1. The San Francisco Earthquake of 1906 may have shaken down hundreds of buildings _____ the fire that followed destroyed nearly everything left standing.

2. One hour after the earthquake smoke could be seen from one hundred miles away _____ for three days and nights the sky was filled with smoke.

3. Outside the city not a flicker of wind stirred _____ the heated air of the fire produced an enormous gale within the city.

4. This gale-force wind fed the flames _____ quickly spread the fire.

5. Firefighters tried valiantly to save buildings _____ before long the flames would reappear on all sides and destroy the structures.

6. The stories of many heroic deeds will never be told _____ will the number of dead ever be known.

7. The flames could not be stopped _____ people had no choice but to flee.

8. People pulling heavy trunks up and down the steep hills of the city eventually had to abandon them _____ their survival depended on moving more quickly.

9. Tens of thousands of refugees camped around the city _____ fled to surrounding cities.

10. Nothing much remained of San Francisco following the fire except for memories _____ a few homes on the outskirts of the city.

EXERCISE ❸   **Combining Sentences Using Coordinating Conjunctions**

For each of the following compound sentences, choose the coordinating conjunction that best supports the meaning of the sentence. Circle the letter corresponding to your choice.

1. The two detectives carefully checked the scene for fingerprints, _____ they could not find one clear print.

   a. so   b. but   c. nor   d. or

2. The safe was open, _____ a single bag of coins remained.

   a. but   b. and   c. or   d. for

3. There was no sign of forced entry, _____ they believed it was probably an inside job.

   a. so   b. nor   c. but   d. or

4. The restaurant owner could not be found, _____ could the two waiters be located.

   a. and   b. for   c. so   d. nor

5.   Suddenly they became interested in one of the tables, _____ the surface seemed splattered with blood.

   a.   and   b.   for   c.   yet   d.   so

6.   The missing tablecloth could also be significant, _____ they took photographs of the other tablecloths.

   a.   nor   b.   so   c.   but   d.   or

7.   One detective looked in the closets, _____ he decided they contained nothing significant.

   a.   or   b.   so   c.   but   d.   nor

8.   They might find another clue, _____ the blood stains may be their only evidence.

   a.   or   b.   yet   c.   nor   d.   but

9.   There were no witnesses, _____ maybe DNA would tell a story.

   a.   for   b.   nor   c.   or   d.   but

10.   Either they get a break in the case, _____ the mystery may never be solved.

   a.   and   b.   nor   c.   so   d.   or

Second Option for Coordination: Using a Semicolon, an Adverbial Conjunction, and a Comma

The second way to form a compound sentence is to combine independent clauses by using a semicolon, an adverbial conjunction, and a comma.

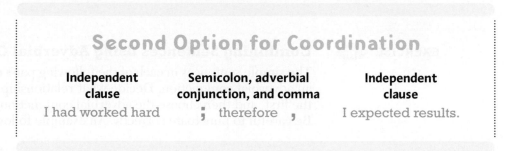

Second Option for Coordination

Independent clause	Semicolon, adverbial conjunction, and comma	Independent clause
I had worked hard	; therefore ,	I expected results.

The conjunctions used for this method are called **adverbial conjunctions** (or conjunctive adverbs). These conjunctions are similar in meaning to the common coordinating conjunctions, but they sound more formal than the shorter conjunctions such as *and* or *but*. Using these adverbial conjunctions gives more emphasis to the clause than using coordinating conjunctions.

Less emphasis: He was late, and he had the wrong documents.

More emphasis: He was late; furthermore, he had the wrong documents.

Just as you memorized the list of coordinating conjunctions on page 97, you should memorize the following list of adverbial conjunctions.

Connectors: Frequently Used Adverbial Conjunctions

Addition (*and*)	Contrast (*but*)	Alternative (*or*)	Result (*so*)	Likeness	Emphasis	To show time
in addition	however	instead	accordingly	likewise	indeed	meanwhile
also	nevertheless	on the other hand	hence	similarly	in fact	
besides	nonetheless	otherwise	therefore			
furthermore			thus			
moreover						

PRACTICE   In each of the following compound sentences, draw a single line under the subject and draw two lines under the verb for both independent clauses. Then circle the semicolon, adverbial conjunction, and comma. An example follows:

> The jet was the fastest way to get there; moreover, it was the most comfortable.

1. The restaurant is always too crowded on Saturdays; nevertheless, it serves the best food in town.
2. The land was not for sale; however, the house could be rented.
3. The lawsuit cost the company several million dollars; consequently, the company went out of business a short time later.
4. The doctor told him to lose weight; furthermore, she instructed him to stop smoking.

EXERCISE **Combining Sentences Using Adverbial Conjunctions**

The simple sentences in each of the following pairs could be combined by using an adverbial conjunction. Decide what relationship the second sentence has to the first, and then choose the adverbial conjunction that makes the most sense. Be careful to punctuate correctly. An example follows:

> Our family would like to purchase a computer/; in addition, _____
> w̶We would like to buy a fax machine.

1. In the past, people wrote with pen or pencil. _____
   The computer has now become the favorite writing tool.

2. Computers provide a powerful way to create documents. _____
   They are essential for storing large amounts of information efficiently.

3. At first, some feared the use of electronics for creating written work. _____
   Nearly all have now overcome their fears.

4. Computers have already revolutionized today's offices. _____
   No modern business can afford to be without them.

5.   Most students are using computers in the classroom. _____
     Many students are e-mailing homework to their teachers from home
     computers.

6.   The prices of many computers are coming down these days. _____
     Owning a computer is a real possibility for more people.

7.   Some children know more about computers than many adults.
     _____
     Some children are teaching the adults.

8.   Professional writers have become enthusiastic about the use of
     computers. _____
     Some writers still use yellow pads.

9.   The electronic revolution is barreling ahead. _____
     The nation faces a great challenge to keep up with it.

10. We have many technological aids to writing. _____
     The source for all our ideas remains the human brain.

EXERCISE 5   ## Combining Sentences Using Adverbial Conjunctions

The simple sentences in each of the following pairs could be combined by using an adverbial conjunction. Decide on the relationship between the two sentences, and circle the letter of the adverbial conjunction that makes the most sense.

1.   Women are supposed to talk more than men.
     This may not always be true.

     a. thus   b. moreover
     c. also   d. however

2.   The cell phone has become a part of everyday life.
     Researchers have become interested in this new area of study.

     a. furthermore   b. therefore
     c. on the other hand d. nonetheless

3.   Researchers began with a popular assumption about women and men.
     They found the results of the study led to an opposite conclusion.

     a. thus   b. nonetheless
     c. also   d. likewise

4.   Women use their wireless phones 377 minutes a month.
     Men, on average, use their wireless phones a good deal more—
     438 minutes a month.

     a. on the other hand b. therefore
     c. thus   d. likewise

5.   Men can be seen using their phones almost everywhere.
     Women use their phones mostly at home.

     a. similarly   b. in addition
     c. however   d. accordingly

6.   Men use their phones in very public places.
     They prefer to conduct a great deal of their business in this way.

     a. however   b. meanwhile
     c. indeed   d. otherwise

7. Women still rule the traditional phones at home.
    Women talk 544 minutes a month at home compared with men's use of just 314 minutes.

    a. however   b. in fact
    c. besides   d. meanwhile

8. Researchers counted the number of times men used their cell phones.
    They listened carefully to the male tone of voice.

    a. otherwise   b. similarly
    c. in addition   d. instead

9. The use of cell phones in public is annoying to many.
    The use of cell phones while driving can be dangerous.

    a. therefore   b. furthermore
    c. otherwise   d. nevertheless

10. The cell phone is relatively new technology.
    Companies are hopeful about people's increased use of the cell phone.

    a. likewise   b. in addition
    c. accordingly   d. meanwhile

EXERCISE 6   ## Combining Sentences Using Adverbial Conjunctions

Using the suggested adverbial conjunction, add another independent clause to each of the following independent clauses to create a compound sentence that makes sense. Remember to punctuate correctly.

1. (however) We were told not to leave the building ——————

2. (therefore) I hadn't done the homework very carefully ——————

3. (otherwise) She was happy to find a dress on sale ——————

4. (instead) Matthew doesn't like office work ——————

5. (in fact) The running shoes are expensive ——————

6. (furthermore) The windows were in poor condition ——————

7. (consequently) The hurricane struck last night ——————

8. (meanwhile) I worked feverishly for days on the report ——————

9.   (nevertheless) The young singer was nervous ⸺⸺⸺⸺⸺

⸺⸺⸺⸺⸺⸺⸺⸺⸺⸺⸺⸺⸺⸺⸺⸺

10.   (moreover) The car is the fastest way to get to work ⸺⸺⸺⸺

⸺⸺⸺⸺⸺⸺⸺⸺⸺⸺⸺⸺⸺⸺⸺⸺

Third Option for Coordination: Using a Semicolon

A third and less commonly used way to form a compound sentence is to combine two independent clauses by using only a semicolon.

Third Option for Coordination

Independent clause	Semicolon	Independent clause
I had worked hard	**;**	I expected results.

You might choose the semicolon if the grammatical structure of each independent clause is similar or if the ideas in each independent clause are very closely related. In the following sentence, the grammatical structure of each independent clause is similar:

The women pitched the tents; the men cooked the dinner.

In the following sentence, the two independent clauses contain closely related ideas:

The women pitched the tents; they were happy to set up camp before dark.

EXERCISE **Combining Sentences Using the Semicolon**

Read each of the following sentences. If the sentence is a compound sentence that requires a semicolon, insert the semicolon where needed. If the sentence requires no punctuation, leave it as is.

1.   The assistant wrote the speech the manager delivered it at the national meeting.

2.   The man stood in front of me blocking the way to my car.

3.   The apartment was light and airy the property was neat and clean.

4.   Shoppers were pushing grocery carts down the aisles workers were stocking the shelves.

5.   My sister plans to learn three foreign languages she already knows two.

6.   I worked in the stockroom counting inventory at least thirty-five hours a week.

7. He tried to explain nobody gave him a chance.

8. Many teenagers spend hours playing video games and listening to music.

9. Writing in my journal helps me think through problems I can relive an incident to think about it more clearly.

10. Ming-Na agreed to take the teaching position late on a Friday afternoon in August.

EXERCISE 8

Combining Sentences Using the Semicolon

Create a compound sentence by adding a semicolon and another independent clause to each of the following sentences. Both clauses in each compound sentence must have similar grammatical structures or have closely related ideas. Use the following example as your model.

Simple sentence:	The guests are putting on their coats.
Compound sentence:	The guests are putting on their coats; the cab is at the door.

1. The pickup truck was filled with old furniture.

   _____

   _____

2. Children played in the streets.

   _____

   _____

3. The union voted to strike.

   _____

   _____

4. The older men wore ties.

   _____

   _____

5. The judge dismissed the jurors.

   _____

   _____

Before taking the mastery tests at the end of this chapter, review the information presented in the chapter by studying the following chart. (The same information can also be found on the inside front cover of this textbook.)

Three Options for Coordination

OPTION 1

Independent clause + Comma and coordinating conjunction *(and, nor, but, yet, for, or, so)* + Independent clause

I had worked hard, *so* I expected results.

OPTION 2

Independent clause + Semicolon, adverbial conjunction, and comma *(also, besides, in addition, furthermore, moreover, instead, on the other hand, otherwise, however, nevertheless, nonetheless, accordingly, hence, therefore, thus, likewise, similarly, indeed, in fact, meanwhile)* + Independent clause

I had worked hard; *therefore,* I expected results.

OPTION 3

Independent clause + Semicolon + Independent clause

I had worked hard; I expected results.

Mastery and Editing Tests

TEST ①   **Combining Sentences Using Coordination**

In the blank to the left of each group of four sentences, write the letter of the sentence that is a correct example of coordination.

 1.
  a. The restaurant was busy at lunchtime, however everyone was patient.
  b. The restaurant was busy at lunchtime, but everyone was patient.
  c. The restaurant was busy at lunchtime; yet everyone was patient.
  d. The restaurant was busy at lunchtime, nonetheless, everyone was patient.

_C_ 2.
  a. The car had many extra features in fact the interior was custom designed.
  b. The car had many extra features; in fact the interior was custom designed.
  c. The car had many extra features; in fact, the interior was custom designed.
  d. The car had many extra features, in fact, the interior was custom designed.

3. a. It was the coldest winter in many years, accordingly, the heating bills were much higher.
     b. It was the coldest winter in many years so the heating bills were much higher.
     c. It was the coldest winter in many years; therefore, the heating bills were much higher.
     d. It was the coldest winter in many years the heating bills were much higher.

 4. a. The command center staff watched the monitors for the space capsule was landing.
     b. The command center staff watched the monitors; for the space capsule was landing.
     c. The command center staff watched the monitors, for the space capsule was landing.
     d. The command center staff watched the monitors; for, the space capsule was landing.

 5. a. The dinner was cold; the service was poor.
     b. The dinner was cold the service was poor.
     c. The dinner was cold, moreover the service was poor.
     d. The dinner was cold; moreover, the service was poor.

TEST 2   Combining Sentences Using Coordination

In the blank to the left of each group of four sentences, write the letter of the sentence that is a correct example of coordination.

 1. a. The theater was crowded, consequently, not everyone could get a good seat.
     b. The theater was crowded; consequently not everyone could get a good seat.
     c. The theater was crowded, so not everyone could get a good seat.
     d. The theater was crowded; so not everyone could get a good seat.

2. a. The first apartment had no bedroom but it had a large beautiful living room.
     b. The first apartment had no bedroom, however, it had a large beautiful living room.
     c. The first apartment had no bedroom; nevertheless, it had a large beautiful living room.
     d. The first apartment had no bedroom; yet it had a large beautiful living room.

 3. a. January had been bitterly cold; therefore, few people had attended the festival.
     b. January had been bitterly cold, however, few people had attended the festival.
     c. January had been bitterly cold also few people had attended the festival.
     d. January had been bitterly cold; in addition few people had attended the festival.

C ___ 4. a. The community waited for the news, nonetheless the crew kept digging.
   b. The community waited for the news; and the crew kept digging.
   c. The community waited for the news; meanwhile, the crew kept digging.
   d. The community waited for the news, yet, the crew kept digging.

b ___ 5. a. The village should balance its budget, likewise the taxes will have to be raised.
   b. The village should balance its budget; otherwise, the taxes will have to be raised.
   c. The village should balance its budget, besides the taxes will have to be raised.
   d. The village should balance its budget; or the taxes will have to be raised.

TEST 3 **Editing Student Writing: Combining Sentences Using Coordination**

After reading the following paragraph, find three places where you could combine two simple sentences into a compound sentence using coordination. Use each of the three options learned in this chapter to form new compound sentences. Write your new sentences on the lines provided after the paragraph.

My children were still in college. My old job with an accounting firm had ended. I needed to earn some money. The thought of a new job made me nervous. What would it be like? Then I saw an ad for openings with Old Navy. I decided to apply. They offered a salary plus a good discount for employees. At the interview, I was the only person over twenty-five. They must have liked me. They hired me the next day! I was sent to their largest downtown location. The first day on the job was scary. I was assigned to a "buddy." The young woman could have been one of my daughters. She explained how to be in control of the stockroom. She showed me how to use a scanner to find out the current price of an item. She advised me on how to keep items on hold for customers. She gave me a feeling of confidence. I never thought I would feel that way. My spirit was willing. I learned a lot. My feet hurt by the end of the first day. I spent half of my first month's salary on Old Navy clothes. I had wanted new clothes for a long time. Some of the clothes were for myself. Some of the clothes were for my daughters.

Option 1: _____

_____

_____

Option 2: _____

_____

_____

Option 3: _____

_____

_____

TEST 4   **Editing Student Writing: Using Correction Symbols**

The correction symbol for an error in coordination is **coord**. In the following paragraph, find five errors in coordination (**coord**), two fragments (**frag**), and three subject-verb agreement errors (**agr**). Mark the errors with the commonly used correction symbols, and then correct these errors on the lines provided after the paragraph.

[1]Sometimes hardships make a person stronger. [2]Even in childhood. [3]My mother has always been sickly so I have learned to be independent. [4]It has happened gradually. [5]The phone would ring I would answer it. [6]Here is some of my weekly duties. [7]I help my brothers with their homework and go to their baseball games. [8]I cook nightly dinners once a week I do the grocery shopping. [9]Friends of our family feels sorry for us but we are not unhappy. [10]Especially sitting around the fire at night in the family room. [11]During the last few years, my father and I have become very close. [12]I have learned from adversity in fact I have found strength for the future. [13]The knowledge of my father's love, kindness, and generosity remain my inspiration.

Five coordination corrections

1. _____

2. _____

3. _____

4. _____

5. _____

Two corrected fragments

6. _____

7. _____

Three subject-verb agreement corrections

Subject	Correct form of the verb
8.	
9.	
10.	

Exploring Online

Coordination and subordination are often studied together, and the skills needed for one are critical for the other. See the Exploring Online feature at the end of Chapter 7 for online work involving coordination and subordination.

Working Together

Summarizing a Class Discussion: What Is a Fair Salary?

We often hear people expressing outrage at the salaries some people earn. For instance, sports figures and entertainers enjoy multimillion-dollar salaries, whereas daycare employees and postal workers, who have serious responsibilities in their jobs, earn a small fraction of that money in their lifetimes.

Discuss this topic in class, making sure that each person has the opportunity to express an opinion. Choose one person to record the important points made during the class discussion. These points should be written on the board even though everyone is responsible for keeping his or her own notes. While discussing this topic, keep the following questions in mind:

Questions for Group Discussion

1. How are salaries set in our society? Give specific examples, based on your own experience and what you have learned from the media.

2. What is today's minimum wage? Is it possible for a person to live on a salary based on that minimum wage?

3. From time to time, there are discussions and disagreements among business and government leaders as to what the minimum wage should be—or even if there should be a minimum wage at all. What should be the minimum wage? In view of what entertainers and sports stars earn, should there be a *maximum* wage law?

4. How should society judge the value of some people's work over the work of others? In what kind of society could everyone receive the same salary, or is that not a desirable goal?

Following the class discussion, each student should use board notes and class notes to write a summary of the discussion. Remember that the summary must include all the important ideas that the discussion generated. If time permits, several students should read their summaries out loud. Did members of the class agree on the major points?

Portfolio Suggestion

Material such as the notes you have just taken on the class discussion can become part of the prewriting stage for an essay on this topic or a related topic. Save your notes and your summary in case you want to use the material for a future essay.

CHAPTER 7

Combining Sentences Using Subordination

In this chapter, you will learn how **subordination** is used to form **complex sentences.** This will involve the following skills.

CHAPTER OBJECTIVES

- Recognizing the difference between an independent clause and a dependent clause.
- Understanding the two options for combining an independent clause with a dependent clause that begins with a subordinating conjunction:

    begin with the dependent clause and use a comma

    begin with the independent clause and do not use a comma

- Understanding how to combine an independent clause with a dependent clause that begins with a relative pronoun:

    use commas in a sentence with a relative clause that is non-essential to the main idea

    do not use commas in a sentence with a relative clause that is essential to the main idea

    place the relative pronoun and its clause immediately following the word to which it is related

What Is Subordination?

In Chapter 6, when you studied *coordination*, you learned that both clauses in a *compound sentence* are independent clauses. In *subordination*, only one clause can be an independent clause. Any other clause must be a dependent clause. Such a dependent clause is dependent on (or subordinate to) the independent clause, and together these clauses make up a *complex sentence.*

> **Subordination** is the method of combining two clauses that contain ideas not equally important. The more important idea is in the **independent clause,** and the less important idea is in the **dependent clause.** The result is a **complex sentence.**

The Difference between an Independent Clause and a Dependent Clause

An *independent clause* stands alone as a complete thought; it could be a simple sentence.

Independent clause: I drank the water.

A *dependent clause* begins with a connecting word, and even though the clause contains a subject and a verb, it does not stand alone as a complete thought. The idea is not complete.

Dependent clause: When I drank the water, . . .

Before you write your own complex sentences, practice the following exercises to be sure you understand the difference between an independent clause and a dependent clause.

EXERCISE 1   **Identifying Dependent and Independent Clauses**

In the blank to the left of each group of words, write *IC* if the group of words is an independent clause (a complete thought) or *DC* if the group of words is a dependent clause (not a complete thought, even though it contains a subject and a verb).

_____   1.   before the show began

_____   2.   while Betty bought the tickets

_____   3.   I played some video games

_____   4.   the line at the concession stand was too long

_____   5.   seven movies were being shown at this cineplex

_____   6.   unless we sat up close to the screen

_____   7.   we had to split up

_____   8.   I had time to get myself a box of popcorn

_____   9.   because the previews took fifteen minutes

_____   10.   when the main feature started

EXERCISE 2   **Identifying Dependent and Independent Clauses**

In the blank to the left of each group of words, write *IC* if the group of words is an independent clause (a complete thought) or *DC* if the group of words is a dependent clause (not a complete thought, even though it contains a subject and a verb).

_____   1.   William Faulkner was a regional writer

_____   2.   he was born near Oxford, Mississippi

_____   3.   where he lived and died

_____   4.   even if he used the dialect of the area

_____   5.   some of his books share the same characters and themes

_____   6.   because Faulkner devoted many pages to greed, violence, and meanness

_____   7.   until the year he died

_____   8.   he won the Nobel Prize in 1950

_____   9.   when he was recognized as one of America's greatest writers

_____   10.   although Faulkner departed from the traditional style of prose

EXERCISE   **Identifying Dependent and Independent Clauses**

In the blank to the left of each group of words, write *IC* if the group of words is an independent clause (a complete thought) or *DC* if the group of words is a dependent clause (not a complete thought, even though it contains a subject and a verb).

_____ 1. Harry Potter mania continues to sweep the country

_____ 2. hundreds of children and parents wait in lines

_____ 3. because they want to purchase a copy of *Harry Potter and the Half-Blood Prince*, the sixth book in the series

_____ 4. as they count the minutes

_____ 5. until the stores open

_____ 6. J. K. Rowling wrote her first book in a cafe

_____ 7. while her infant daughter slept

_____ 8. in one day, the book sold seven million copies in the United States and United Kingdom

_____ 9. many are surprised at the book's length

_____ 10. since it is 652 pages

Using Subordinating Conjunctions

In *coordination*, you combined ideas by using connecting words called *coordinating conjunctions* and *adverbial conjunctions*. In *subordination*, you combine ideas by using two different sets of connecting words called *subordinating conjunctions* and *relative pronouns*. Begin this section by memorizing the list of subordinating conjunctions given in the chart below.

Connectors: Frequently Used Subordinating Conjunctions

after	in order that	unless
although	once	until
as, as if	provided that	when, whenever
as long as, as though	rather than	where, wherever
because	since	whereas
before	so that	whether
even though	though	while
if, even if		

We all went out for pizza *after the game was over*.

In the above sentence, the dependent clause *after the game was over* contains a subject (*game*) and a verb (*was*). The word *after* functions as a subordinating conjunction that joins the two clauses. The result is a *complex sentence* because the sentence contains an independent clause and a dependent clause.

However, many of the words in this chart may also function as prepositions.

We all went out for pizza *after the game*.

In the above sentence, *after* functions as a preposition that introduces the prepositional phrase *after the game*. The sentence is a *simple sentence* because it contains only one independent clause.

In the next practice, see whether you can spot the difference between a word used as a preposition in a prepositional phrase and a word used as a subordinating conjunction at the beginning of a dependent clause.

PRACTICE

Identify each of the following groups of words as a prepositional phrase (PP) or a dependent clause (DC).

_____   1.   before the dance began

_____   2.   before the dance

_____   3.   since the first of the month

_____   4.   since I started this journal

_____   5.   after the war

_____   6.   after my dad visited

The following chart contains the subordinating conjunctions grouped according to their meanings. When you use one of these conjunctions, you must be sure that the connection made between the independent clause and the dependent clause has the meaning you intend.

The Functions of Subordinating Conjunctions

To introduce a condition: *if, even if, as long as, provided that, unless* (usually after a negative independent clause)

I will go *as long as* you go with me.

I won't go *unless* you go with me.

To introduce a contrast: *although, even though, though, whereas, while*

I will go *even though* you won't go with me.

To introduce a cause: *as, because, since*

I will go *because* the meeting is very important.

To show time: *after, before, since, when, whenever, while, until* (usually after a negative independent clause)

I will go *when* it is time.

I won't go *until* it is time.

To show place: *where, wherever*

I will go *wherever* you send me.

To show purpose: *in order that, so that*

I will go *so that* I can hear the candidate for myself.

When you write a complex sentence, you can choose the order of the clauses. You can begin with the *independent clause*, or you can begin with the *dependent clause*.

Two Options for Subordination Using Subordinating Conjunctions

OPTION 1

Begin with the independent clause. Do not use a comma.

We can finish our homework if Tamika leaves.

OPTION 2

Begin with the dependent clause followed by a comma.

If Tamika leaves, we can finish our homework.

Notice that a comma is used only for the second option. Your ear will remind you to use the correct punctuation. Read aloud the sample sentence given above for option 2. Listen to the natural pause at the end of the dependent clause before continuing with the rest of the sentence. Where you pause is the place to put a comma.

PRACTICE

Use a subordinating conjunction to combine each of the following pairs of sentences.

1. Use the subordinating conjunction *after:*

> Calvin went out to celebrate.
> He won the wrestling match.

a. Begin with an independent clause:

_____

b. Begin with a dependent clause:

_____

2. Use the subordinating conjunction *when:*

> Carla returned from Venezuela this spring.
> The family was excited.

a. Begin with an independent clause:

_____

b. Begin with a dependent clause:

_____

EXERCISE 4   **Combining Sentences Using Subordination**

Use each of the following subordinating conjunctions to compose a complex sentence. An example has been done for you.

| **Subordinating conjunction:** | after |
| **Complex sentence:** | After the game was over**,** we all went out for pizza. |

1. as if

_____

_____

2. before

_____

_____

3. until

_____

_____

4. although

_____

_____

5. because

_____

_____

EXERCISE 5

Combining Sentences Using Subordination

Use subordination to combine each of the following pairs of sentences. Refer to the list of subordinating conjunctions if necessary.

1. He was eating breakfast.
   The results of the election came over the radio.

   _____

   _____

2. The town council voted against the plan.
   They believed the project was too expensive.

   _____

   _____

3. I will see Maya Angelou tonight.
   She is speaking at the university.

   _____

   _____

4. The worker hoped for a promotion.
   Not one person in the department had received a promotion last year.

   _____

   _____

5. The worker hoped for a promotion.
   All his work was done accurately and on time.

   _____

   _____

EXERCISE 6

Combining Sentences Using Subordination

Read the following paragraph. All the sentences are simple sentences. Find three places where you could effectively combine two sentences to create a complex sentence. On the lines provided below the paragraph, write the new complex sentences you have created.

At the present time, the United States recycles 10 percent of its trash. It burns another 10 percent. The remaining 80 percent goes to landfills. Over the next few years, many of our landfills will close. They are full. Some of them are leaking toxic wastes. Some parts of the Northeast already truck much of their trash to landfills in Pennsylvania, Ohio, Kentucky, and West Virginia. The garbage continues to pile up. The newspapers print stories about it every week. Trash is not a very glamorous subject. People in every town talk about the problem. One magazine, called *Garbage,* is printed on recycled paper. No town ever before gathered together information about garbage. The town of Lyndhurst, New Jersey, began what is the world's only garbage museum. One landfill now has a restaurant on its premises. Another landfill displays some of its unusual garbage. It displays these objects like trophies. We really want to solve the garbage problem. We must change our "buy more and throw everything old away" mentality.

1. _____

   _____

   _____

2. _____

   _____

   _____

3. _____

   _____

   _____

Using Relative Pronouns

Begin this section by studying the relative pronouns in the following box.

Relative Pronouns

who (whose, whom) *whoever (whomever)*	used if the pronoun refers to a person	*what* *whatever* *which* *whichever*	used if the pronoun refers to a thing
that	used most often to refer to things, but is sometimes used to refer to people	*where*	used if the pronoun refers to a place
		when	used if the pronoun refers to a time

Sentences can often be combined with a relative pronoun. These two simple sentences sound short and choppy:

The researcher had a breakthrough.

He was studying diabetes.

To avoid this choppiness, a writer might want to join the two related ideas by using a relative pronoun.
If the clause is put in the wrong place, the result will confuse the reader.

Incorrectly combined: The researcher had a breakthrough *who* was studying diabetes.

The relative pronoun *who* refers to *researcher*, so the clause *who was studying diabetes* must be placed immediately after *researcher.*

Correctly combined: The researcher *who* was studying diabetes had a breakthrough.

The relative pronoun and its clause must immediately follow the word to which it is related.

A sentence may have more than one relative clause. Study the following sentence, which contains two relative clauses. Notice that each relative pronoun immediately follows the word to which it is related.

The researcher *who* was studying diabetes had a breakthrough, *which* he reported to the press.

PRACTICE

Combining Sentences Using Relative Pronouns

Combine each pair of sentences into one complex sentence by using a relative pronoun. Do not use commas. An example follows:

Simple sentence: The florist created the flower arrangement.

Simple sentence: She called us last weekend.

Complex sentence: The florist *who* called us last weekend created the flower arrangement.

1.   The chemistry lab is two hours long.
     I attend that chemistry lab.

     Combined: _____

2.   The student assistant is very knowledgeable.
     The student assistant is standing by the door.

     Combined: _____

3. The equipment was purchased last year.
   The equipment will make possible some important new research.

   Combined: _____

   _____

PUNCTUATING RELATIVE CLAUSES

The following two sentences have dependent clauses that begin with relative pronouns (*that* and *which*). Punctuating these sentences correctly depends on understanding the difference between the functions of the two clauses.

> You should never eat fruit *that you haven't washed first.*

> Mother's fruit salad**,** *which she prepares every Sunday***,** is delicious.

1. A relative clause is said to be a *restrictive clause* if it is essential to the meaning of the sentence. It does not require commas, and the pronoun *that* is often used.

> You should never eat fruit *that you haven't washed first.*

The basic meaning of the sentence is not that you should never eat fruit. The relative clause is necessary to restrict the meaning to only fruit that is not washed. In this case, the relative clause is essential to the main idea of the sentence.

2. A relative clause is said to be a *nonrestrictive clause* if it is *not* essential to the meaning of the sentence. This clause does require commas to set it off, and the pronoun *which* is often used.

> Mother's fruit salad**,** *which she prepares every Sunday***,** is delicious.

In this sentence, the relative clause is not essential to the main idea. In fact, if the clause were omitted, the main idea would not be changed. The commas are used to show that the information contained in the relative clause is not essential to the meaning of the main idea.

Subordination Using Two Types of Relative Pronoun Clauses

RESTRICTIVE CLAUSE

The relative clause is essential to the meaning of the sentence. No commas are used.

> You should never eat fruit *that you haven't washed first.*

NONRESTRICTIVE CLAUSE

The relative clause in not essential to the meaning of the sentence. Commas must be used.

> Mother's fruit salad**,** *which she prepares every Sunday***,** is delicious.

PRACTICE

Punctuating Relative Clauses

Choose whether to insert commas in the sentences that follow. Use the following examples as your models.

> The man *who is wearing the Hawaiian shirt* is the bridegroom.

In the sentence above, the bridegroom can be identified only by his Hawaiian shirt. Therefore, the relative clause *who is wearing the Hawaiian shirt* is essential to the meaning. No commas are necessary.

> Al, *who was wearing a flannel shirt,* arrived late to the wedding.

In the sentence above, the main idea is that Al was late. What he was wearing is not essential to that main idea. Therefore, commas are needed to set off this nonessential information.

1. The poem that my classmate read in class was very powerful.

2. The teacher who guided our class today is my favorite college professor.

3. Her biology course which met four times a week for two hours each session was extremely demanding.

4. You seldom learn much in courses that are not demanding.

5. My own poetry which has improved over the semester has brought me much satisfaction.

Now you are ready to practice combining your own sentences by using relative pronouns. The following exercises ask you to insert a variety of relative clauses into simple sentences. Pay careful attention to the punctuation.

EXERCISE 7

Combining Sentences Using Relative Pronouns

Insert a relative clause into each of the following ten sentences. Use each of the possibilities (*who, whose, whom, which, that*) at least once. Be sure to punctuate correctly. An example has been done for you.

Simple sentence: The leader was barely five feet tall.

Complex sentence: The leader, who was always self-conscious about his height, was barely five feet tall.

1. The president _____
   asked his advisors for help.

2. His advisors _____
   met with him in his office.

3. The situation _____
   was at a critical point.

4. Even his vice president _____
   appeared visibly alarmed.

5. Stacked on the table, the plans _____
   looked impressive.

6. The meeting _____
   began at two o'clock.

7. Every idea _____
   was examined in great detail.

8. Several maps _____
    showed the area in question.

9. One advisor _____
    was vehemently opposed to the plan.

10. Finally, the group agreed on a plan of action _____

EXERCISE 8   **Combining Sentences Using Relative Pronouns**

Combine each of the following pairs of sentences by using a relative pronoun.

1. Stress can do a great deal of harm.
    We experience stress every day.

    _____

    _____

2. People often use food to help them cope.
    Some people's jobs are demanding.

    _____

    _____

3. The practice of eating to cope with stress is often automatic.
    The practice of eating to cope usually goes back to childhood.

    _____

    _____

4. Some foods can actually increase tension.
    People turn to foods in times of stress.

    _____

    _____

5. Sweet foods are actually not energy boosters.
    Sweet foods are popular with people who need a lift.

    _____

    _____

6. Another substance is caffeine.
    People use other substances to get an energy boost.

    _____

    _____

7. One of the biggest mistakes people make is to use alcohol as an aid to
    achieving calm.
    Alcohol is really a depressant.

    _____

    _____

8. People should eat three light meals a day and two small snacks.
   People want to feel a sense of calm.

   _____

   _____

9. Getting enough protein is also important in keeping an adequate energy
   level.
   An adequate energy level will get you through the day.

   _____

   _____

10. A person should eat regularly to avoid binges.
    Binges put on pounds and drain one's energy.

    _____

    _____

EXERCISE 9 **Combining Sentences Using Relative Pronouns**

Combine each of the following pairs of sentences by using a relative pronoun.

1. Murray, Kentucky, is a Norman Rockwell painting come to life.
   It is in the middle of America's heartland.

   _____

   _____

2. You will soon notice the blue, clean lakes.
   They are bustling with activity.

   _____

   _____

3. The town is surrounded by water.
   This water is perfect for sailing, waterskiing, fishing, and relaxing.

   _____

   _____

4. Scouting enthusiasts enjoy the National Scouting Museum.
   The museum has exhibits for hands-on experience.

   _____

   _____

5. The same museum has a large collection of paintings by Norman Rockwell.
   His work reflects the surrounding landscape.

   _____

   _____

6.   Murray State University is an important part of local life.
     The university often has inexpensive concerts and other activities.

     _____

     _____

7.   The Homestead is a working farm.
     It shows the way families lived a century ago.

     _____

     _____

8.   The Homestead also puts on old-fashioned weddings.
     The wedding parties are made up of actors and actresses in beautiful an-
     tique attire.

     _____

     _____

9.   People can see herds of buffalo.
     People like to see rare sights.

     _____

     _____

10. At the end of the day, you can enjoy the local cooking.
     Murray is famous for its local cooking.

     _____

     _____

Subordination

I: USE A SUBORDINATING CONJUNCTION.

a.   **Begin with the independent clause. Do not use a comma.**

     We can finish our homework if Tamika leaves.

b.   **Begin with the dependent clause followed by a comma.**

     If Tamika leaves, we can finish our homework.

II: USE A RELATIVE PRONOUN CLAUSE.

a.   **If the relative clause is essential information, the clause is restrictive. Do not use commas.**

     You should never eat fruit *that you haven't washed first.*

b.   **If the relative clause is not essential information, the clause is nonrestrictive. Use commas.**

     Mother's fruit salad, *which she prepares every Sunday,* is delicious.

Mastery and Editing Tests

TEST 1 **Combining Sentences with a Subordinating Conjunction or a Relative Pronoun**

Combine each of the following pairs of sentences by using either a subordinating conjunction or a relative pronoun.

1. Here is the apartment building.
   It will be torn down next year.

   _____

   _____

2. The police stood by the door.
   They blocked our entrance.

   _____

   _____

3. She wore high heels.
   They made marks in the wooden floor.

   _____

   _____

4. My aunt is a tyrant.
   Her name is Lena.

   _____

   _____

5. Her outfit was classy.
   Her hair was dirty and unattractive.

   _____

   _____

6. The interviewer did not smile.
   He discovered we had a friend in common.

   _____

   _____

7. I had a test the next day.
   I stayed up to watch a Bette Davis movie.

   _____

   _____

8. The skater fell and broke his arm.
   He was trying to skate backward.

   _____

   _____

9. For a moment her face glowed with pleasure.
Her face was usually serious.

_____

_____

10. I was thinking.
The toast burned.

_____

_____

TEST 2 **Combining Sentences Using Coordination and Subordination**

Now you are ready to have some fun! James Thurber, a famous American humorist, wrote a magazine article that included a portrait of a man named Doc Marlowe. Below are some simple sentences created from one of the paragraphs in that article. Read the entire paragraph and then choose three places where sentences could be combined to improve meaning and style. Do not hesitate to change the wording in the original to accomplish your revisions. Whether or not your instructor provides you with Thurber's own version, remember that there is always more than one way to revise a piece of writing.

I met Doc Marlowe at old Mrs. Willoughby's rooming house. She had been a nurse in our family. I used to go and visit her over weekends sometimes. I was very fond of her. I was about eleven years old then. Doc Marlowe wore scarred leather leggings and a bright-colored bead vest. He said he got the vest from the Indians. He wore a ten-gallon hat with kitchen matches stuck in the band, all the way around. He was about six feet four inches tall, with big shoulders, and a long, drooping mustache. He let his hair grow long, like General Custer's. He had a wonderful collection of Indian relics and six-shooters. He used to tell me stories of his adventures in the Far West. His favorite expressions were "Hay, boy!" and "Hay, boy-gie!" He used these the way some people now use "Hot dog!" or Doggone!" I thought he was the greatest man I had ever seen. He died. His son came in from New Jersey for the funeral. I found out something. He had never been in the Far West in his life. He had been born in Brooklyn.

1. _____

_____

_____

2. _____

_____

_____

3. _____

   _____

   _____

   _____

TEST 3   **Editing Student Writing: Combining Sentences
Using Coordination and Subordination**

Following is a student paragraph composed of mostly simple sentences. Read
the entire paragraph and then choose three places where sentences could be
combined to improve the meaning and style. Do not be afraid to change the
wording to accommodate the changes you want to make. You can combine
clauses using coordination and subordination.

In-line skating became widely popular during the 1980's. It is also known as
rollerblading. In-line skates are a cross between ice skates and roller skates. The
wheels are in a single row down the middle of the skate. They usually have only
one brake. The brake is on the heel of the right foot. This skate was developed
to help hockey players practice off the ice. This practice blossomed into a
multimillion-dollar industry, sport, and pastime. There were stunt teams, racing
teams, and skating clubs. It became a popular form of recreation and exercise.
You should be careful when attempting in-line skating. Skaters must wear the
proper protection. Protective pads should be worn over the elbows, wrists, and
knees in order to cover all joints. The head is particularly vulnerable. A helmet
should be worn at all times. Skaters can achieve speeds of five to twenty-five
miles per hour or more. Since 1996, the sport's trendy status has faded. Today,
children are more likely to be seen on scooters. Teenagers seem to prefer
skateboards.

1. _____

   _____

   _____

   _____

2. _____

   _____

   _____

   _____

3. _____

   _____

   _____

TEST **Editing Student Writing: Using Correction Symbols**

The correction symbol for an error in subordination is **subord.** In the paragraph below, find five errors in subordination (**subord**), two errors in coordination (**coord**), one fragment (**frag**), and two subject-verb agreement errors (**agr**). Mark the errors with the commonly used correction symbols and then correct these errors on the lines provided after the paragraph.

¹Fashion is always looking for a fresh idea. ²Are you tired yet of the low-rise pants with the cropped shirts that reveals the bellybutton? ³Have you seen too many young men, who walk along holding up their pants? ⁴Are you glad to see lime green become last season's popular color? ⁵And the wedding scene! ⁶Every young female guest wears a black dress every bride wears a strapless gown. ⁷One fact is for certain. ⁸Another fad will replace a fading one. ⁹Take, for example, shoe fashions. ¹⁰After a generation of women enjoyed wearing comfortable shoes to work now young women are once again wearing pointed toes and spiked heels. ¹¹This new generation of women will ruin their feet, if they wear such shoes for very long. ¹²While older people look for safety and comfort it seems younger people prefer being provocative and even dangerously shocking. ¹³Another purpose of fads, of course, are to keep up our spirits. ¹⁴After the tragedy of 9/11, several fashion ads were recalled, because they were in bad taste. ¹⁵The patriotic look was in with a lot of red, white, and blue. ¹⁶The fashion industry is likely to be responsive to our nation's sobering circumstances however it is unlikely to come up with anything bordering on dowdy. ¹⁷Too many teens want to express themselves by the clothes they wear.

Five subordination corrections

1. _____

   _____

2. _____

   _____

3. _____

   _____

4. _____

   _____

5. _____

   _____

Two coordination corrections

6. _____

_____

7. _____

_____

Corrected fragment

8. _____

Two subject-verb agreement corrections

Subject	Correct form of the verb
9. _____	_____
10. _____	_____

Exploring Online

Go to academic.cengage.com/devenglish/scarry to find the **Writer's Online Workplace,** a website designed for students using this book. You will find links to handouts, interactive quizzes, and other online resources as you explore the following topics:

- coordination and subordination
- combining sentences with the comma and semicolon

Working Together

Narrowing the Topic through Group Discussion: A Person's First Job

When you get your first job, you are not only earning your first paychecks but also learning your first lessons about the world of work. In this newspaper article, Anita Santiago, the owner of a Los Angeles advertising agency, writes about her first job in her native city of Caracas, Venezuela. After you have read the article, discuss the questions that follow. As you exchange ideas suggested by the article, you will find yourself concentrating on those aspects of the subject that interest you the most. These particular areas of interest would make good topics for your own writing.

Questions for Group Discussion

1. At first, Anita Santiago thought the job of selling encyclopedias would be perfect because she loved books. What job experiences have members of the class had that turned out differently than expected?

2. When the writer tells us that her company in Caracas "just sent me out into the streets . . . to sell books" without any preparation, she is reporting a common experience people have when they are hired for jobs but are not given any training. What experiences have students in the class had with jobs for which the employees were not properly trained? What were the results?

3. Anita Santiago remembers that when someone sold a set of encyclopedias, a gong sounded in the company's office. In jobs that members of the class have had, how were accomplishments recognized? Were they ignored? What were the results of this attention or neglect?

4. Anita Santiago concludes her essay by telling us that, although she did not know it at the time, her eventual business success began with that first job in Caracas. When have you learned something important from a job experience, but realized its value only later in life?

5. The writer admits that when she began her job she was very idealistic, but at some point she obviously became more realistic. When have you been idealistic about something in your life, but circumstances forced you to modify your thinking?

6. Anita Santiago believes, "You have to walk through unpleasantness to get to success." Based on your experience, do you agree or disagree?

7. Who is the hardest-working person you have ever known? Describe what this person did that makes you admire him or her so much.

8. The writer tells us that her Spanish-language advertising campaigns "come quite easily" to her because she knows the culture so well. When has something come easily to you because of your background or some other source of special knowledge or expertise?

Portfolio Suggestion

Save your notes from this discussion of a person's first job. From this general topic, narrow down the issues to three or four specific aspects that would be of interest to you for future writing projects.

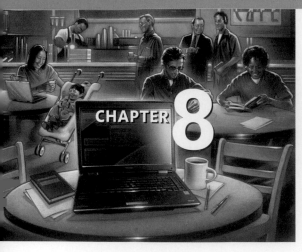

CHAPTER 8

Correcting Fragments and Run-Ons

As you work with the material of this chapter, you will understand the value of all your previous study on phrases and clauses. Here you will see more complicated fragments and several types of run-on sentences. You will learn how each one can be made into an acceptable sentence. Mastering the skills of this chapter will make editing your own work much easier.

CHAPTER OBJECTIVES

● Identify **three types of fragments:**

one or more phrases

one or more dependent clauses

a combination of phrases and dependent clauses

● Identify **three types of run-on sentences:**

the *and* run-on

the fused run-on

the comma splice

What Is a Fragment?

> A **fragment** is a piece of a sentence.

HOW MANY KINDS OF FRAGMENTS ARE THERE?

1. A fragment could be a phrase:

   I sat down. *In the school bus.* Howard, the school bully, came and sat down beside me.

   NOTE: The prepositional phrase *in the school bus* is a fragment, not a sentence.

2. A fragment could be a dependent clause:

   As I sat down. Howard, the school bully, came and sat down beside me.

   NOTE: The dependent clause *as I sat down* is a fragment, not a sentence.

3. A fragment could be a combination of phrases and dependent clauses:

   One Friday afternoon, as I sat down in the school bus that was filled with screaming kids.

NOTE: *On a recent Friday afternoon* is a prepositional phrase; *as I sat down* is a dependent clause; *in the school bus* is a prepositional phrase; *that was filled* is a dependent clause; and *with screaming kids* is a prepositional phrase. A combination of phrases and dependent clauses is not a sentence.

HOW DO YOU MAKE A COMPLETE SENTENCE FROM A FRAGMENT?

If the fragment is a phrase, you have two options for revising it. Option 1 is to attach it either to the sentence that comes before it or to the sentence that comes after it. Option 2 is to make the phrase into a sentence by adding an independent clause.

Fragment:	I sat down. *In the school bus.* Howard, the school bully, came and sat down beside me.
Revision Option 1:	I sat down in the school bus. Howard, the school bully, came and sat down beside me.
Revision Option 2:	I sat down. Forty screaming kids were in the school bus. Howard, the school bully, came and sat down beside me.

If the fragment has a combination of dependent clauses and phrases but has no independent clause, you again have two options for revising it. Option 1 is to make one of the dependent clauses into an independent clause by removing the conjunction. Option 2 is to add an independent clause.

Fragment:	*One Friday afternoon, as I sat down in the school bus that was filled with forty screaming kids.*
Revision Option 1:	One Friday afternoon, I sat down in the school bus that was filled with forty screaming kids.
Revision Option 2:	One Friday afternoon, as I sat down in the school bus that was filled with forty screaming kids, Howard, the school bully, came and sat down beside me.

EXERCISE **Recognizing Fragments**

Identify each of the examples below as one of the following:

a.   sentence
b.   fragment—phrase
c.   fragment—dependent clause
d.   fragment—combination of phrases and dependent clauses

_____   1.   At the bus stop.

_____   2.   While I was not looking.

_____   3.   Someone took my bookbag.

_____   4.   Because so many people were watching.

_____   5.   Although someone must have seen the theft when they were waiting for the bus around three o'clock.

_____   6.   Even though I asked everyone.

_____   7.   Nobody seemed to have noticed.

_____ 8. After I reported the theft to the police because I knew I should
          because it's important to document these kinds of incidents.

_____ 9. In the event of other similar thefts.

_____ 10. When I got home and called my husband who was really angry
          about the situation.

EXERCISE **2**   **Recognizing and Correcting Fragments**

Revise the ten examples from Exercise 1. Put your revised sentences into
paragraph form, correcting all fragments.

_____

_____

_____

_____

_____

_____

_____

_____

_____

_____

EXERCISE **3**   **Student Writing: Recognizing and Correcting Fragments**

Read the following paragraph carefully. Find the five fragments and underline them. Then fix each fragment (using the options for correcting fragments,
found on page 135), and write the new sentences on the lines below.

   Howard Crane the shortest kid in my entire seventh grade. He was always

getting into fights, and he used terrible language. If you've ever known a bully.

Howard was a prime example. One Friday afternoon as we sat in the school bus on our way home. Howard began taunting my younger brother. Because our parents had told us to ignore Howard. So my brother just looked straight ahead. Saying nothing. I was growing angrier and angrier. I had to do something.

1. _____

   _____

2. _____

   _____

3. _____

   _____

4. _____

   _____

5. _____

   _____

What Is a Run-On?

In conversation, when we retell events that have occurred, we often link our thoughts together in one long narrative. Here is what one person involved in a car accident reported to a police officer at the scene:

> I was driving along on Route 80 and my daughter asked my wife to change the radio station and my wife told my daughter to do it herself so she unhooked her seatbelt and reached over from the back seat to change the station but then her brother tickled her and she lost her balance and fell on the gear shift and that moved the gear into neutral so the car instantly lost power and that's when we were hit by the van behind us.

The man relating the accident ran all the parts of this entire event together without any separations. As a result, the account appears as a **run-on.** In formal writing, a run-on is considered a serious error.

> **Run-ons** are independent clauses that have been combined incorrectly.

HOW MANY KINDS OF RUN-ONS ARE THERE?

Run-ons may occur when the writer is unable to recognize where one complete thought ends and another thought begins. Run-ons also may occur if the writer is not sure of the standard ways of connecting ideas. Certain marks of punctuation are needed to show where two clauses join. Other punctuation signifies the end of a thought. Study the following three types of run-ons.

1. **The *and* run-on:** two or more relatively long independent clauses connected with a coordinating conjunction without any punctuation

   Incorrect: I met Charlyce in a yoga class at the YWCA and we liked each other immediately and we soon became friends.

2. **The fused run-on:** two or more independent clauses run together without any punctuation

> **Incorrect:** I met Charlyce in a yoga class at the YWCA we soon became friends.

3. **The comma splice:** two or more independent clauses run together with only a comma

> **Incorrect:** I met Charlyce in a yoga class at the YWCA, we soon became friends.

HOW DO YOU CORRECT A RUN-ON SENTENCE?

There are three basic ways to correct a run-on sentence.

1. Make two sentences with end punctuation.

> **Correct:** I met Charlyce in a yoga class at the YWCA. We soon became friends.

2. Make a compound sentence using one of the three methods of coordination.

> **Correct:** I met Charlyce in a yoga class at the YWCA, and we soon became friends.
>
> I met Charlyce in a yoga class at the YWCA; indeed, we soon became friends.
>
> I met Charlyce in a yoga class at the YWCA; we soon became friends.

3. Make a complex sentence using subordination.

> **Correct:** Soon after I met Charlyce in a yoga class at the YWCA; indeed, we became friends.
>
> Charlyce and I became friends soon after we met in a yoga class at the YWCA.

> **NOTE:** See the inside front cover for a quick review of coordination and subordination.

PRACTICE

Below are five run-on sentences. Correct them by using any of the three strategies given for correcting run-ons.

1. In recent years several celebrities, including Michael J. Fox, Lance Armstrong, and Melissa Etheridge, have shared their health situations with the public, this has had a beneficial effect.

2. In 1995, Christopher Reeve became a quadriplegic after a horse riding accident, he and his wife worked tirelessly until their untimely deaths to draw attention to the need for better treatments and cures for spinal cord injuries.

3. Katie Couric, the American media personality, lost her husband to colon cancer in 1998 after his death, Katie became a spokeswoman for colon cancer awareness.

4. In fact, Katie had a colonoscopy on the air in March of 2000 and she inspired many to follow her example.

5. Katie Couric's efforts have become known as the "Couric effect," we now know a celebrity can draw significant attention and support to worthwhile causes.

EXERCISE **Recognizing and Correcting Run-Ons**

Here is the same run-on sentence that you read earlier in this chapter. Rewrite the report correctly. Put a period at the end of each complete thought. You may have to omit some of the words that loosely connect the ideas, or you may want to use coordination and subordination. Remember to make each new sentence begin with a capital letter.

I was driving along on Route 80 and my daughter asked my wife to change the radio station and my wife told my daughter to do it herself so she unhooked her seatbelt and reached over from the back seat to change the station but then her brother tickled her and she lost her balance and fell on the gear shift and that moved the gear into neutral so the car instantly lost power and that's when we were hit by the van behind us.

_____

_____

_____

_____

_____

_____

_____

_____

_____

EXERCISE **Recognizing and Correcting Run-Ons**

The following story is written as one sentence. Rewrite the story correctly. Put a period at the end of each complete thought. You may have to omit some of the words that loosely connect the ideas, or you may want to use coordination and subordination. Remember to make each new sentence begin with a capital letter.

My best friend is accident-prone if you knew her you'd know that she's always limping, having to write with her left hand or wearing a bandage on her head or ankle, like last week for example she was walking down the street minding her own business when a shingle from someone's roof hit her on the head and she had to go to the emergency room for stitches, then this week one of her fingers is purple because someone slammed the car door on her hand sometimes I think it might be better if I didn't spend too much time with her you know her bad luck might be catching!

_____

_____

_____

_____

_____

_____

_____

_____

EXERCISE **Student Writing: Recognizing and Correcting Run-Ons**

The following story is written as one sentence. Rewrite the story correctly. Put a period at the end of each complete thought. You may have to omit some of the words that loosely connect the ideas, or you may want to use coordination and subordination. Remember to make each new sentence begin with a capital letter.

One morning, not too early, I will rise and slip downstairs to brew the coffee and no baby will wake me up and no alarm clock will rattle my nerves and the weather will be so warm that I will not have to put on my coat and hat to go out for the paper there will be no rush I will go to the refrigerator and take out eggs and sausage the bathroom will be free so I will be able to take a shower with no one knocking on the door and I will not have to run up and down the stairs first looking for someone's shoes and then for someone's car keys I will leisurely fix my hair and pick out a lovely suit to wear the phone might ring and it will be a friend who would like to have lunch and share the afternoon with me money will be no problem maybe we'll see a movie or drive to the nearby city to visit a museum and the countryside will be beautiful and unspoiled my life will seem fresh and promising.

_____

_____

_____

_____

_____

_____

_____

_____

_____

_____

_____

_____

Mastery and Editing Tests

TEST   **Editing for Fragments and Run-Ons**

On the lines provided below the paragraph, identify each numbered group of words as a sentence (S), fragment (F), or run-on (R). Then rewrite the paragraph, correcting any fragments and run-ons.

[1]In laboratory experiments, scientists have discovered a diet. [2]That extends the life of their animals up to 50 percent or more. [3]This diet prevents heart disease, diabetes, and kidney failure and it greatly retards all types of cancer. [4]Even slowing down the aging process of cataracts, gray hair, and feebleness. [5]Staying on this diet keeps the mind flexible and the body active to an almost biblical old age. [6]These rats, fish, and worms stay very slim, they are fed a diet of necessary vitamins and nutrients but only 65 percent of the calories of the animal's normal diet. [7]Every creature fed this restricted diet has had a greatly extended life span. [8]The results of caloric restriction are spectacular. [9]Says Richard Weindruch, a gerontologist at the National Institute on Aging in Bethesda, Maryland. [10]Gerontologists have tried many things to extend life but this is the only experiment that works every time in the lab. [11]Animals that received enough protein, vitamins, and minerals to prevent malnutrition. [12]They survived to a grand old age and it does not seem to matter whether they ate a diet composed largely of fats or carbohydrates. [13]Researchers warn against people undertaking this diet too hastily, it is very easy to become malnourished. [14]Dr. Roy Walford is a pioneer in the field from the University of California he believes humans could live to an extraordinarily advanced age. [15]If they were to limit their caloric intake.

1. _____   5. _____   9. _____   13. _____

2. _____   6. _____   10. _____   14. _____

3. _____   7. _____   11. _____   15. _____

4. _____   8. _____   12. _____

Your version:

_____

_____

_____

_____

_____

_____

_____

_____

_____

_____

_____

_____

_____

_____

_____

_____

_____

TEST **2**   **Editing for Fragments and Run-Ons**

On the lines provided below, identify each numbered group of words as a sentence (S), fragment (F), or run-on (R). Then rewrite the paragraph, correcting any fragments and run-ons.

[1]Recently, I watched a daytime show on laser peels and viewers watched a procedure that took less than two minutes. [2]In front of the television cameras and the live audience. [3]A guest had the wrinkles zapped away from around her eyes. [4]These high-energy laser beams which are said to be quick, painless, and safe. [5]Adding this technology to face-lifts, dermabrasion, collagen injections, and chemical peels! [6]Lasers were first used by dermatologists to remove port-wine stains in the 1970s. [7]Now these laser peels have become quite common. [8]For many people, this means they can now look as young as they feel but the healing process can be painful and messy. [9]Most physicians believe this is a much more precise method of rejuvenating the skin. [10]Because it's so much more accurate, so much more predictable, and so much safer than other methods. [11]One note of caution. [12]Any physician with little or no training can buy the equipment therefore a person should always check out the doctor's experience. [13]A practitioner

without experience could zap too deeply and cause tissue damage. [14]Following a laser zap, a person must scrupulously avoid the sun for several months, afterwards one must always wear sunscreen. [15]One bad point. [16]Laser technology is expensive full-face laser peels cost thousands of dollars. [17]Sorry, no long-term scientific studies to prove their safety.

1._____   6._____   11._____   16._____

2._____   7._____   12._____   17._____

3._____   8._____   13._____

4._____   9._____   14._____

5._____   10._____   15._____

Your version:

_____

_____

_____

_____

_____

_____

_____

_____

_____

_____

_____

_____

_____

_____

_____

_____

_____

_____

TEST **3** **Editing Student Writing: Correcting Fragments and Run-Ons**

On the lines provided below, identify each numbered group of words as a sentence (S), fragment (F), or run-on (R). Then rewrite the paragraph, correcting any fragments and run-ons.

[1]Many parents worry that their children are not reading enough others worry about what the children are reading. [2]In fact, most children are not reading

anything at all, houses are filled with the sounds from CD players, television sets, and video games. ³If children never see their parents reading or going to the library. ⁴They will most likely not develop good reading habits. ⁵Children who see their parents reading magazines, books, and newspapers. ⁶These children will grow up thinking that reading is a natural part of daily life. ⁷Parents can do many things to encourage reading. ⁸Like accompanying them to the library and helping them pick out books. ⁹Parents can encourage children to memorize poetry and they can show them how to read maps when they travel. ¹⁰Since most young people like children's magazines with pictures and short texts on current topics. ¹¹Parents could subscribe to these magazines for their children. ¹²Reading stories out loud as a family, with everybody participating, after the workday is over. ¹³That is the best idea of all.

1. _____   6. _____   11. _____

2. _____   7. _____   12. _____

3. _____   8. _____   13. _____

4. _____   9. _____

5. _____   10. _____

Your version:

_____

_____

_____

_____

_____

_____

_____

_____

_____

_____

_____

_____

_____

TEST 4 **Editing Student Writing: Using Correction Symbols**

The correction symbol for a run-on error is **ro.** In the paragraph below, find four run-ons (**ro**), three fragments (**frag**), two complex sentences with incorrect punctuation for subordinate clauses (**subord**), and one subject-verb agreement error (**agr**). Mark the errors with the commonly used correction symbols, and then correct the errors on the lines provided after the paragraph.

[1]If human development is to continue we will eventually have to develop forms of renewable energy. [2]In the 1980s and 1990s, the United States lagged behind Europe and Asia in the development of wind power in fact, many of our machines were inefficient, of poor design, and expensive to maintain. [3]Mostly only people living along coastal areas having high winds were attracted to investing in wind power. [4]Because the major technology to enable the commercial use of wind power improved dramatically starting in 1999 wind farms have begun springing up in much broader geographical areas. [5]Not only along the coastal areas. [6]Undoubtedly, many refinements and improvements in the years to come. [7]Wind power is extremely attractive, once the equipment is set up, nobody has to buy the wind that blows across the land. [8]Portland, Oregon, is planning a wind farm that will supply all of that city's energy needs. [9]And this would be the equivalent of taking 12,000 cars off the road every year. [10]One farmer in the Portland area has several windmills, he tells everyone that he cultivates three crops: wheat, cattle, and wind. [11]He has power for his own use and he sells the extra power to the region's power grid. [12]Each of his windmills bring in three to four thousand dollars a year in income.

Four corrected run-on sentences

1. _____
   _____
   _____

2. _____
   _____

3. _____
   _____

4. _____
   _____

Three corrected fragments

5. _____

6. _____
   _____

7. _____
   _____

Two subordination corrections

8. _____

_____

9. _____

_____

_____

Subject-verb agreement correction

Subject	Correct form of the verb
10. _____	_____

Exploring Online

Go to academic.cengage.com/devenglish/scarry to find the **Writer's Online Workplace,** a website designed for students using this book. You will find links to handouts, interactive quizzes, and other online resources as you explore the following topics:

- fragments and run-ons
- comma splice run-ons

Working Together

Discussion and Freewriting: First Impressions

Some modern approaches to dating are very different from those of years ago. When people date nowadays, they may use up-to-date technology to help ensure success in their personal lives. Some use chat rooms on the Internet, but others depend on services that match people according to their tastes and backgrounds. Still other people use a special face-to-face encounter. Following is an account of the phenomenon known as "speed dating."

Have you heard of the term speed dating? It's the latest trend for time-starved singles in major metropolitan areas. A host of new entrepreneurs have risen up to take advantage of the craze, forming companies with descriptive names such as 8 Minute Dating, Hurry Date, and PreDate. According to PreDate, speed dating "is a fun and efficient way for busy single professionals to meet. You'll meet other people in your age and interest group through a series of face-to-face, six-minute 'predates' in a private area at a local upscale restaurant/bar." Wow . . . twelve face-to-face dates or more in one night!

Wow indeed. Make a good impression in those first six minutes or the "relationship" is over. That's a lot of pressure. And even six minutes may be too many by a factor of two. According to communications professor Michael Sunnafrank, people tend to draw conclusions about someone within as little as three minutes of having met them. And researchers at Carleton University suggest that it takes as little as one-twentieth of a second for people to register likes and dislikes about another person. That's fast.

First impressions exist, and they are powerful. As a class, discuss the following questions. All students should take notes. Following the discussion, each student should choose one aspect of the subject that is of interest and freewrite on the topic for the time allotted by the instructor.

1. Is it a good thing to act on first impressions?
2. When did you have a first impression that proved correct (or incorrect?)
3. Do you know any people who made an impulsive decision based on "love at first sight" and then lived to regret it?
4. Do you consider yourself an impulsive person? Do you act on first impressions?
5. Would you participate in speed dating?
6. What characteristics would you be looking for in those first six minutes?
7. Advertisers count on consumers forming good first impressions when they read their ads. What are some of the techniques these advertisers use to ensure a good first impression of their products?
8. What could you do to ensure a good first impression (for a job interview, for a date, for starting in a new school)?

Portfolio Suggestion

Keep the notes and freewriting you have done on this topic in your portfolio. Your instructor may want you to return to this topic to develop your freewriting into a complete college essay.

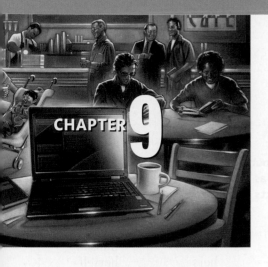

CHAPTER 9

Choosing Correct Pronouns

In this chapter, you will work on choosing the correct pronoun forms in constructions that tend to cause confusion. You will learn to do the following:

CHAPTER OBJECTIVES

● Use the correct pronoun **case**

with **comparisons**

with **compound constructions**

with **who/whom constructions**

● Understand the relationship between a pronoun and its **antecedent** in order to

choose a pronoun that agrees **in number** with its antecedent

choose a pronoun that agrees **in person** with its antecedent

make certain that the antecedent of a pronoun is not **missing, ambiguous,** or **repetitious**

Pronouns and Case

Most of us generally use the correct pronoun forms when we speak and write. However, the fact that pronouns have **case** (that is, they can change forms depending on their function in a particular sentence) causes confusion in three particular constructions: comparisons, compound constructions, and *who/whom* constructions.

> **Case** refers to the form a noun or pronoun takes, depending on how it is used in a sentence. Notice in the following examples how the pronoun *I* changes its form when it changes its function:
>
> **Subject:** *I* needed a car.
> **Object:** Dad bought a used Honda for *me*.
> **Possessive:** *My* commute to work will now be easier.
> The title to the car is *mine*.
> **Reflexive:** I've assumed all responsibility for the car *myself*.

The following chart provides a helpful listing of the different pronoun forms.

Pronoun Case

	Pronouns used as subjects	Pronouns used as objects	Pronouns used as possessives	Pronouns used as reflexives
Singular	I	me	my, mine	myself
	you	you	you, yours	yourself
	he	him	his	himself
	she	her	hers	herself
	it	it	its	itself
Plural	we	us	our, ours	ourselves
	you	you	your, yours	yourselves
	they	them	their, theirs	themselves
Singular or plural	who	whom	whose	

● Study the chart and notice there are no such forms as *hisself, themself,* or *theirselves.*
● Be careful not to confuse *whose* with *who's* (who is, who has) or *its* with *it's* (it is).

PRONOUN CASE WITH COMPARISONS

Choosing the correct pronoun for a comparison is easier if you complete the comparison in your own mind. For example, choose the correct pronoun in the following sentence:

The swimmer is much stronger than (he, him, his).

You might be tempted to choose the pronoun *him.* However, if you complete the comparison in your own mind, you will choose the correct pronoun:

The swimmer is much stronger than (*he,* him, his) *is.*

The second sentence shows that *he* is the correct answer because the pronoun *he* is used as the subject in the clause *he is.* Now you can clearly see that "The swimmer is much stronger than him is" would be the wrong choice.

PRACTICE   Circle the correct pronoun in each of the sentences below.

1. My brother did not enjoy the vacation as much as (I, me, mine).

   HINT: Before you choose, try adding *did* to complete the comparison:

   My brother did not enjoy the vacation as much as (*I, me, mine*) *did.*

2. The altitude in Quito affected my brother more than (I, me).

   HINT: Before you choose, try adding *it affected* to complete the comparison:

   The altitude in Quito affected my brother more than *it affected* (*I, me*).

3. The tour guide directed his speech to the travel agents rather than to my brother and (I, me)

HINT: Before you choose, try adding *to* after the *and*.

The tour guide directed his speech to the travel agents rather than to my brother and *to* (I, me)

EXERCISE **Choosing the Correct Pronoun with Comparisons**

Circle the correct pronoun in each of the sentences below. Remember to complete the comparison in your own mind.

1. I am as deeply involved in this proposal as (they, them).
2. Farida's research has been less extensive than (we, us, our, ours).
3. She did study the final proposal more than (I, me).
4. The attractiveness of the competing proposal troubled my coworkers more than (I, me).
5. Their company had acquired fewer clients than (we, us).
6. Our policies are much better than (them, theirs).
7. The contract was awarded to us rather than (they, them).
8. The results will matter more to the client than (she, her).
9. I will celebrate much longer tonight than (she, her).
10. An immediate vacation is more important for me than (he, him).

PRONOUN CASE IN COMPOUND CONSTRUCTIONS

In a sentence that has a compound subject or a compound object, choosing the correct pronoun will be easier if you read the sentence and leave out one of the pronouns.

Today, she and (I, me) should buy the tickets.

You might be tempted to choose the pronoun *me*. However, if you try reading this same sentence leaving out the first pronoun (*she*), you will choose the correct pronoun.

Today, (*I*, me) *should buy* the tickets.

The second sentence shows that *I* is the correct answer because the pronoun *I* is used as the subject for the verb *should buy*. Now you can clearly see that "Today, me should buy the tickets" is the wrong choice.

PRACTICE Circle the correct pronoun in each of the sentences below.

1. Developers and (he, him) hope to renovate that building.

HINT: Try the sentence without the words *developers and*.

(He, Him) hopes to renovate that building.

2. They spoke to the construction company and (I, me).

   HINT: Try the sentence without the words *the construction company and.*

   They spoke to (I, me).

EXERCISE **Choosing the Correct Pronoun in Compound Constructions**
In each of the following sentences, circle the correct pronoun.

1. Sara called from Washington to speak with Leslie and (I, me).
2. Both Damon and (I, me) keep a daily journal.
3. Today, we received the letters from you and (she, her).
4. Among Sasha, Jerry, and (I, me), Sasha is the best writer.
5. Mavis and (she, her) are hoping for good grades this term.
6. Because Sal and (she, her) decided to go, the group could no longer fit into one car.
7. (He, Him) and (I, me) handed our journals in to the professor.
8. When we were sick, my aunt ran lots of errands for Kathleen and (I, me).
9. The dinner gave Nelson and (he, him) the chance to be together.
10. The two men, (he, him) and Tyrone, were brothers.

PRONOUN CASE IN *WHO/WHOM* CONSTRUCTIONS

At times, most of us are confused by the use of the *who* and *whom* pronouns, partly because *whom* has become uncommon in spoken English. In written English, however, the difference in the ways these two words function in a sentence is still important.

Who is always used in the subject position in a sentence.

   Who is going with you to the performance?

Who is the subject of the verb phrase *is going.*

   Who did you say is going with you to the performance?

Who is the subject of the verb phrase *is going* (even though a second clause, *did you say,* interrupts the first clause).

   He is the person *who* is going with me.

Who is the subject of the verb phrase *is going* in the second clause, *who is going with me.*

Whom is always used in the object position in a sentence.

   Whom did the director choose for the part?

Whom is the direct object of the verb phrase *did choose*.

> To *whom* did the director give the part?

Whom is the object of the preposition *to*.

If there is more than one clause in the sentence, you will find it helpful to cross out all the words except the clause with the *who/whom* pronoun. Then you will better understand how *who/whom* functions within its own clause.

> ~~The scholarship will be given to~~ (whoever, whomever) wins the poetry contest.

In the clause (*whoever, whomever*) *wins the poetry contest*, the pronoun *whoever* is the correct choice. *Whoever* is the subject for the verb *wins*. (The entire clause is considered the object of the preposition *to*.)

PRACTICE

In each of the sentences below, cross out all the words except the clause containing the *who/whom* pronoun. Then decide whether the *who/whom* functions as a subject or as an object within that clause and circle the correct choice.

1. She is the friend (who, whom) I treasured.

   Look at: (who, whom) I treasured

2. She is the friend (who, whom) I knew could be trusted.

   Look at: (who, whom) could be trusted

3. They will award the prize to (whoever, whomever) is the best.

   Look at: (whoever, whomever) is the best.

4. I don't know (who, whom) should do the work.
5. That is the girl (who, whom) I hope will win.

EXERCISE 3

Choosing the Correct Pronoun Using *Who/Whom*

Circle the correct pronoun in each of the sentences below.

1. (Who, Whom) has the conductor chosen as the lead soloist at tonight's choral conert?
2. (Whoever, Whomever) sold us the tickets gave us the best seats in the house.
3. From (who, whom) can we obtain a program?
4. (Who, Whom) of these singers can you tell needs more practice?
5. The director gave the solo parts to (whoever, whomever) was qualified.
6. Our eyes were glued on (whoever, whomever) was singing the lead.
7. (Who's, Whose) solo did you think was performed with the most musicality?

8. We will enjoy the soloist (who, whom) music critics have praised.

9. (Who's, Whose) music was left on the piano?

10. Most of the singers (who, whom) I heard at the concert were impressive.

Remember that, to avoid confusion, you can always cross out other clauses in the sentence so you can concentrate on the clause in question.

~~I don't know~~ (who, whom) ~~I think~~ should do the work.

~~That is the girl~~ (who, whom) ~~I believe~~ was dancing.

EXERCISE

Choosing the Correct Pronoun Using *Who/Whom*

Circle the correct pronoun in each of the sentences below.

1. In relationships, the issue of (who, whom) is best suited to run the family's finances is always critical.

2. Everyone knows couples for (who, whom) money is the source of endless squabbles.

3. Most couples quickly decide (who, whom) is the right person to balance the checkbook.

4. (Who, Whom) should the couple trust for financial advice?

5. Another question is (who's, whose) responsible for the final decisions about making large purchases?

6. To (who, whom) do most people listen about long-range financial planning?

7. Researchers (who, whom) have studied this area of human behavior have reached some surprising conclusions.

8. Couples (who's, whose) weddings were costly like to remember those expenses.

9. However, these same couples (who, whom) have children to educate seldom want to talk about college costs.

10. A couple for (who, whom) future goals are very different need to listen to expert advice.

EXERCISE

Choosing Correct Pronoun Forms

Practice pronoun case with all three constructions. Circle the correct pronoun in each of the sentences below.

1. Jamel and (she, her) presented the project today.

2. Between you and (I, me), I think it was outstanding.

3. Their visual materials will help (whoever, whomever) will study the project later.

4. He is usually a better speaker than (she, her).

5. (Whoever, Whomever) heard them agreed that it was an impressive presentation.

6. (Who, Whom) do you think made the best points?

7.   I am not as deeply involved in my project as (they, them).

8.   Their research was much more detailed than (us, our, ours).

9.   The professor gave both Carolyn and (he, him) A's.

10. My partner and (I, me) will have to work harder to reach this standard.

EXERCISE **6**   **Student Writing: Choosing Correct Pronoun Forms**

Practice pronoun case with all three constructions. In the following paragraph, circle the correct pronoun wherever you have a choice.

When my mother and (I, me) decided to care for my very ill father at home, some of our friends objected. My sister and (they, them) said we would be exhausted and unable to handle the stress. The people (who, whom) we met at the hospital had the same opinion. To (who, whom) could we go for help in the middle of the night? My father, (who, whom) we believed would be happier at home, had been our first consideration. Of course, we would have benefited if either my mother or (I, me) had been a nurse. However, we did have a visiting nurse available at times. We were more confident than (they, them) that we could handle the situation. We were the only ones for (who, whom) this work would be a labor of love.

Pronoun-Antecedent Agreement

When you use a pronoun in your writing, that pronoun must refer to a word used previously in the text. This previously used word is called the *antecedent*.

> An **antecedent** is a word (or words) that is replaced by a pronoun later in a piece of writing.
>
> The *pool* was crowded. *It* was a popular place on a hot summer day.
>
> In this example, the pronoun *it* replaces the word *pool. Pool*, in this case, is referred to as the *antecedent* of the pronoun *it*.

The next three rules concerning pronouns are often troublesome to writers. Study each rule carefully, and complete the exercises that follow.

RULE 1   **A pronoun must agree in *number* (singular or plural) with any other word to which it refers.**

The following sentences illustrate a lack of pronoun-antecedent agreement in **number.**

Lacks agreement: The *pool* was crowded. *They* were popular places on a hot summer day.

In this example, *pool* is the antecedent of the pronoun *they*. However, *pool* is singular and *they* is plural. The pronoun *it* must be used to agree in number with the antecedent *pool*.

Pronoun-antecedent agreement can be particularly complicated if the pronoun is an indefinite pronoun. Words like *everyone* or *nobody* are singular. They require a singular pronoun.

Lacks agreement: *Everyone* worked on *their* final draft.

Even though you may hear people use the plural pronoun *their* to refer to a singular subject, this usage is not correct in formal writing. Here are two other approaches writers often take:

Sexist construction: *Everyone* worked on *his* final draft.

Awkward construction: *Everyone* worked on *his or her* final draft.

This last form is technically correct, but the continual use of the construction *his or her* will soon begin to sound awkward and repetitious. Often, the best solution to the problem is to revise the construction so that the pronoun and the antecedent are plural:

Pronouns agree: *All* the students worked on *their* final drafts.

Another way around the problem is to avoid the pronoun altogether or use the article:

Avoids the pronoun: Everyone worked on final drafts.

Everyone worked on the final drafts.

Another problem with pronoun-antecedent agreement in **number** occurs when a demonstrative pronoun (*this, that, these, those*) is used with a noun. In such a case, the pronoun must agree with the noun it modifies:

Singular: this kind, that kind; this type, that type
Incorrect: *These kind* of shoes hurt my feet.
Correct: *This kind* of shoe hurts my feet.

Plural: these kinds, those kinds; these types, those types
Incorrect: *Those type* of cars always need oil.
Correct: *Those types* of cars always need oil.

PRACTICE   Rewrite each of the following sentences so that the pronoun agrees with its antecedent in *number.* It may be helpful to draw an arrow from the pronoun to its antecedent.

1. Everyone should bring their suggestions to the meeting.

   _____

2. This sorts of clothes are popular now.

   _____

3. No one knew what they were doing.

   _____

4. If the bird watchers hope to see anything, one must get up early.

   _____

5. These type of book appeals to me.

   _____

RULE 2   **A pronoun must agree with its antecedent in *person.***

The following sentence lacks pronoun-antecedent agreement in **person:**

Lacks agreement: When mountain climbing, *one* must maintain *your* concentration at all times.

When you construct a piece of writing, you choose a "person" as the voice in that piece of writing. Your instructor may advise you which personal pronoun to use for a particular writing assignment. Whatever guidelines you are given, the important point is to be consistent and use the same **person.** Below are some examples in which the pronouns agree:

When mountain climbing, *you* must maintain *your* concentration at all times.

When mountain climbing, *I* must maintain *my* concentration at all times.

When mountain climbing, *we* must maintain *our* concentration at all times.

PRACTICE   Correct each of the following sentences so that the pronoun agrees with its antecedent in *person.*

1. I enjoy math exams because you can show what you know.
2. When I took geometry, we discovered that frequent review of past assignments helped make the course seem easy.
3. People always need to practice your skills to not forget them.
4. Math games can be fun for a student if you have a spirit of curiosity.
5. When studying math, you must remember that we have to "use it or lose it."

RULE 3   **The antecedent of a pronoun should not be *missing*, *ambiguous*, or *repetitious*.**

⬤ **Missing antecedent:**

In Florida, *they* have beautifully developed retirement areas.

In this sentence, we do not know to whom *they* refers. If the text has not told us that *they* refers to the Florida government, real estate developers, or some other group, then we must say that the antecedent is *missing*. The sentence should be rewritten to avoid *they*.

Acceptable revision: Many Florida communities have beautifully developed retirement areas.

⬤ **Ambiguous antecedent:**

Margaret told Lin that *she* needed to earn one thousand dollars during the summer.

In this sentence, *she* could refer to either Margaret or Lin. The sentence should be revised in a way that will avoid this confusion.

Acceptable revision: Margaret said that Lin needed to earn one thousand dollars during the summer.

⬤ **Repetitious pronoun and antecedent:**

The book, *it* describes the Great Depression.

The subject in this sentence should be either the noun *book* or, if there is already an antecedent, the pronoun *it*. Using both the noun and the pronoun results in needless repetition.

Acceptable revision: The book describes the Great Depression.

PRACTICE   Rewrite the following sentences so that the antecedents are not *missing*, *ambiguous*, or *repetitious*.

1. The biologist asked the director to bring back his microscope.

    _____

    _____

2. The report, it says that the number of science and engineering students seeking doctoral degrees has fallen 50 percent since the mid-1960s.

    _____

    _____

3. At the laboratory, they said the research had run into serious difficulties.

    _____

    _____

4. The testing equipment was accidentally dropped onto the aquarium, and it was badly damaged.

_____

_____

5. I don't watch the 10 o'clock news anymore because they have become too slick.

_____

_____

EXERCISE 7 **Making Pronouns and Antecedents Agree**

The following sentences contain errors with pronouns. Rewrite each sentence so that pronouns agree with their antecedents and so that there are no missing, ambiguous, or repetitious antecedents in the sentence.

1. His father mailed him his high school yearbook.

_____

2. No one wants their income reduced.

_____

3. When a company fails to update its equipment, they often pay a price in the long run.

_____

4. The woman today has many more options open to them than ever before.

_____

5. Everybody knows their own strengths best.

_____

6. Each of the workers anticipates their summer vacation.

_____

7. If the campers want to eat quickly, each one should help themselves.

_____

8. These sort of bathing suits look ridiculous on me.

_____

9. On the application, it says you must pay a registration fee of thirty-five dollars.

_____

10. The doctor said that those type of diseases are rare here.

_____

EXERCISE   **Making Pronouns and Antecedents Agree**

The following sentences may contain errors with pronouns. Rewrite the sentences so that pronouns agree with their antecedents and so that there are no missing, ambiguous, or repetitive antecedents. If a sentence is correct, mark a *C* on the line provided.

1. The teacher told the parent he needed the test results.

    _____

2. The county submitted their proposal for the bridge repairs.

    _____

3. We all rushed to our cars because you had to wait for the thunderstorm to stop.

    _____

    _____

4. Anyone who fails the final will be unlikely to get his or her diploma.

    _____

5. A young person does not receive enough advice on how they should choose their career.

    _____

    _____

6. These type of watches are very popular.

    _____

7. People were rescued from our homes.

    _____

8. No one brought their books today.

    _____

9. The college it is holding homecoming weekend on October 5.

    _____

10. They call Indiana the Hoosier state.

    _____

EXERCISE **9**   **Making Pronouns and Antecedents Agree**

Each of the following sentences contains an error in pronoun-antecedent agreement. Edit each sentence so that pronouns agree with their antecedents and so that there are no missing, ambiguous, or repetitive antecedents.

1. Everyone should go to a live concert once in their life.

2. Last month, Cynthia invited Vermell to a Mary J. Blige concert because she loves her music.

3. They said the tickets would be sold out quickly.

4. If you get up early enough, a person has a good chance to buy decent seats.

5. These type of events are very expensive.

6. The night of the concert, the arena it was jammed with young people.

7. The security guards told the fans that they must be careful about pushing and shoving.

8. People have been trampled in these sort of crowds.

9. Finally, you could hear the music begin; our long wait for tickets had been worth the trouble.

10. Her songs have positive lyrics; that's why I like it so much.

Mastery and Editing Tests

TEST **Using Pronouns Correctly**

Each of the following sentences contains pronouns. Edit each sentence to correct errors in pronoun case, pronouns that do not agree with their antecedents, and missing, ambiguous, or repetitive antecedents. If the sentence does not contain an error, mark it with a *C.*

1. One should plant flowers if you like improving your front yard.

2. A friend sent Mike his favorite coffee.

3. In the book, it said that fish oil is good to take for arthritis.

4. My mom and me have a great day planned for Saturday.

5. Whom do you think is coming to our art show?

6. They ought to fix these potholes outside our school.

7. The customer and she agreed on a price.

8. That athlete is much faster than me.

9. These sorts of chairs tend to be uncomfortable.

10. He did all the work on the house hisself.

TEST **2** **Using Pronouns Correctly**

Each of the following sentences contains pronouns. Edit each sentence to correct errors in pronoun case, pronouns that do not agree with their antecedents, and missing, ambiguous, or repetitive antecedents. If the sentence does not contain an error, mark it with a *C.*

1. In the ad it said you should send a résumé.

2. To who do you think we should send these bulletins?

3. A pharmacist must triple check every order he fills.

4. Just between you and I, the firm is in financial trouble.

5. Those lessons helped Karen more than him.

6. We always buy these type of coats.

7. The bank warns people that you should always balance your checkbooks.

8. Janelle's sister brought her plan to the council.

9. The assignments they are going to require library research.

10. Everyone did his part.

TEST **Editing Student Writing: Using Pronouns Correctly**

The following paragraph contains ten errors in pronoun usage. Edit the paragraph to correct all the errors.

Nobody wants their taxes increased. Last Tuesday, the tax assessor sent my father his statement. The letter reported a huge tax increase, so it was a shock. In the letter, they said the tax must be paid within five days. If one is not wealthy, you can have trouble paying such a bill on time. My father, who is generally calm in these kind of situations, was upset. This hardworking man, he marched to the town hall. He complained to them. They had nothing to say. One of them shook their head sympathetically, but he still had to pay the bill.

TEST **Editing Student Writing: Using Correction Symbols**

The correction symbol for an error in pronoun case is **pron ca.** The correction symbol for an error in pronoun-antecedent agreement is **pron ref.** In the paragraph below, find two pronoun case errors (**pron ca**), four pronoun-antecedent errors (**pron ref**), one fragment (**frag**), one run-on (**ro** or **coord**), one subordination error (**subord**), and one subject-verb agreement error (**agr**). Mark the errors with the commonly used correction symbols, and then correct the errors on the lines provided after the paragraph.

¹John Dickens, whom was the father of the great novelist Charles Dickens, was never able to handle their money successfully. ²The family had to move to smaller and smaller houses as the finances of the family became worse. ³Eventually, they found themself living in a small part of a house. ⁴Young Charles was sent to a pawnbroker's shop. ⁵To sell the family's books, silver teapots and spoons, and other family possessions. ⁶Little by little, even the family furniture had to be sold, and he was placed in debtor's prison. ⁷In those days, this is what they did to the head of the family if he or she could not pay debts. ⁸When Charles was twelve he suffered another traumatic event because of his family's situation. ⁹He was

taken out of school and his parents put him to work pasting labels on bottles of shoe polish. ¹⁰He never recovered from the psychological shock. ¹¹His formal education, it was over. ¹²As a result of these childhood traumas, Charles Dickens's numerous novels, which are filled with many a colorful character, portrays children trapped by circumstances they cannot control.

Two pronoun case corrections

	Incorrect pronoun form	Correct pronoun form
1.	_____	_____
2.	_____	_____

Four pronoun reference corrections

	Pronoun	Correction
3.	_____	_____
4.	_____	_____
5.	_____	_____
6.	_____	_____

Corrected fragment

7. _____

_____

_____

Corrected run-on sentence

8. _____

_____

_____

Subordination correction

9. _____

_____

_____

Subject-verb agreement correction

	Subject	Correct form of the verb
10.	_____	_____

Exploring Online

Go to academic.cengage.com/devenglish/scarry to find the **Writer's Online Workplace,** a website designed for students using this book. You will find links to handouts, interactive quizzes, and other online resources as you explore the following topics:

- choosing the correct pronoun
- pronoun-antecedent agreement

Discussion and Freewriting: Love or Duty?

Princess Must Face Immigration Charges

SAN DIEGO, July 17 (AP)—A princess who fled Bahrain with fake documents to marry an American marine must face charges of illegally entering the United States, an immigration judge said today.

The judge, Ignacio Fernandez, refused to dismiss the charges, a ruling that prevents the princess, Meriam Al Khalifa, from applying for permanent residency without seeking political asylum.

Ms. Al Khalifa, who is 19, plans to apply for asylum on the ground that she faces extreme persecution for marrying a non-Muslim if she returns to Bahrain, her lawyer said. She has up to a year to apply for political asylum.

A spokesman for the Bahraini Embassy in Washington said that the princess' family was eager for her to return and that she would not face persecution.

The hearing was closed to the public, but her lawyer provided an account of the ruling.

Ms. Al Khalifa lives with her husband, Lance Cpl. Jason Johnson, on Camp Pendleton, a Marine base 40 miles north of San Diego. They met last year in the Bahraini capital of Manama, where the 25-year-old marine was assigned to a security unit.

Ms. Al Khalifa's father is a cousin of Bahrain's head of state, Emir Hamad bin Isa Al Khalifa.

In July 2000, the news story of the princess from Bahrain who defied her parents and ran away with an American marine made international headlines. The story was of great interest to many readers and raised many complicated issues. Readers wanted to know more about the princess and what could have happened to her. For example, was the princess obliged to obey her parents? Did she have the right to follow her heart, leave her country without the proper papers, and then enter the United States illegally?

In addition to the conflict between romantic love and duty to one's parents, the story showed the clash between two cultures, each one with its distinct customs and values. In Bahrain, this nineteen-year-old Muslim princess had lived with servants and chauffeurs. In America, she would be adopting the modest lifestyle of her new husband and his family. She would no longer have the support of her mother and father. She would be among people who did not follow her customs and share her religious background.

Group Discussion

Brainstorm with your classmates to make a list of the various issues this princess would have to face after she made her decision to elope with the American marine. Once the list is completed, briefly discuss each item, keeping in mind that each item could be a writing opportunity.

Freewriting

Each student should respond to the facts and implications of this news event using the insights reached during the class discussion. Choose one aspect of the story that is of real interest and use the time given by your instructor to freewrite on this topic. Keep in mind that, as the work of the semester continues, some of these same issues are likely to resurface, and you will be able to continue your thinking about a theme that interests you as you approach other writing opportunities.

Portfolio Suggestion

You may want to pursue the topics of cross-cultural relationships or immigration raised here. Search the Internet for other articles and news stories relating to these topics. These issues are deeply relevant to most Americans today.

CHAPTER 10

Working with Adjectives, Adverbs, and Parallel Structure

Adjectives and adverbs are used to describe, limit, or qualify other words. In this chapter, you will study

CHAPTER OBJECTIVES

- **adjectives and adverbs used in comparisons,** especially irregular forms
- the most commonly **confused adjectives and adverbs,** including *good* and *well*
- **misplaced modifiers** and **dangling modifiers**
- the adverb *not* and the avoidance of **double negatives**

Items listed in a series need to be presented in a similar form. In this chapter, you will also learn how to use **parallel structure** by

- making **words in a series** the same parts of speech
- making **phrases in a series** the same kinds of phrases
- making certain that **clauses in a series** are not combined with words or phrases

What Is the Difference between an Adjective and an Adverb?

Adjectives modify nouns and pronouns.

Charlene is a *studious* person.

She is *studious*.

Adverbs modify verbs, adjectives, and other adverbs. They often end in *-ly*. They usually answer one of the following questions: *How? When? Where? Why?* or *To what extent?*

Charlene *happily* dreams about her vacation.

You cannot be *too* careful.

Charlene worked *very* quickly.

Since not all adverbs end in *-ly*, it is useful to learn some of these most common adverbs.

List of Common Adverbs

always	much	seldom
even	never	sometimes
ever	not	surely
hardly	now	tomorrow
just	often	too
later	only	very
more	quite	yesterday

Adjectives and Adverbs Used in Comparisons

For most adjectives and adverbs of *one syllable*, add *-er* for the comparative form and *-est* for the superlative form.

The following chart lists some one-syllable adjectives (adj) and adverbs (adv) along with their comparative and superlative forms.

Comparative Forms of One-Syllable Adjectives and Adverbs

Adjective or adverb	Comparative form (compares two things or groups)	Superlative form (compares three or more things or groups)
light (adj)	lighter	lightest
short (adj)	shorter	shortest
fast (adv)	faster	fastest
hard (adv)	harder	hardest

Some adjectives and adverbs of *two syllables* take *-er* and *-est*, while others use *more* (or *less*) and *most* (or *least*). When in doubt, consult a dictionary.

The following chart lists some two-syllable adjectives and adverbs along with their comparative and superlative forms.

Comparative Forms of Two-Syllable Adjectives and Adverbs

Adjective or adverb	Comparative form (compares two things or groups)	Superlative form (compares three or more things or groups)
easy (adj)	easier	easiest
funny (adj)	funnier	funniest
happy (adj)	happier	happiest
lovely (adj)	lovelier	loveliest
helpful (adj)	more helpful	most helpful
famous (adj)	more famous	most famous
quickly (adv)	more quickly	most quickly
slowly (adv)	more slowly	most slowly

For adjectives and adverbs of *three or more syllables,* use *more* (or *less*) for the comparative form and *most* (or *least*) for the superlative form.

The following chart lists some three-syllable adjectives and adverbs along with their comparative and superlative forms.

Comparative Forms of Three-Syllable Adjectives and Adverbs

Adjective or adverb	Comparative form (compares two things or groups)	Superlative form (compares three or more things or groups)
successful (adj)	more successful	most successful
delicious (adj)	more delicious	most delicious
easily (adv)	more easily	most easily
carefully (adv)	more carefully	most carefully

Some commonly used adjectives and adverbs have irregular forms. Study the following chart of commonly used adjectives and adverbs that have irregular comparative and superlative forms.

Irregular Comparative Forms

Adjective or adverb	Comparative form (compares two things or groups)	Superlative form (compares three or more things or groups)
bad (adj)	worse	worst
badly (adv)	worse	worst
good (adj)	better	best
well (adv or adj)	better	best
many (adj)	more	most
much (adj or adv)	more	most
more (adj or adv)	more	most
far (adj or adv)	farther or further	farthest or furthest
little (adj or adv)	less	least

farther/further

Use *farther* or *farthest* to indicate physical distance.

She could not walk any *farther*.

Use *further* or *furthest* to indicate mental distance.

The lawyer made a *further* argument.

little/few

Do not confuse *little* with *few*. Use *little* when you cannot easily count the item modified.

They had *little grain* for the cattle.

Use *fewer* when you can count the item modified.

They had *fewer cattle* this year than last year.

EXERCISE **Adjectives and Adverbs Used in Comparisons**

In the sentences below, fill in each blank with the correct form of the word given in parentheses.

1. This chapter is _____ than the last one.
   (easy)

2. She is the _____ woman in the police department.
   (tall)

3. That machine is _____ operated than the one in the other room.
   (easily)

4. He feels _____ today than he did yesterday.
   (good)

5. That woman is the _____ chef in San Francisco.
   (famous)

6. This paralegal is the _____ person in the office.
   (helpful)

7. Would you please drive _____ than your father?
   (slowly)

8. Unfortunately, this is the _____ business trip I have ever made.
   (bad)

9. His illness became _____ .
   (bad)

10. This lasagna is the _____ lasagna I have ever tasted.
    (delicious)

EXERCISE 2 **Adjectives and Adverbs Used in Comparisons**

In the sentences below, fill in each blank with the correct form of the word given in parentheses.

1. *Star Wars: Episode II* was _____ than *Star Wars: Episode I.*
   (exciting)

2. She was _____ than she had been in a long time.
   (healthy)

3. The _____ hamburger I ever ate was at a restaurant in Denver.
   (good)

4. The cheetah is the _____ animal in the world.
   (fast)

5. It is _____ to drive at night than during the day.
   (dangerous)

6. That new law seems _____ written than the previous one.
   (carefully)

7. My cat is the _____ pet I've ever had.
   (lazy)

8. Quitting her job was the _____ thing from her mind.
   (far)

9. Her second job was _____ than her first one.
   (bad)

10. She is the _____ worker in the entire company.
    (honest)

The Most Commonly Confused Adjectives and Adverbs

To strengthen your understanding of modifiers, study the list of adjectives and adverbs given below.

awful/awfully

awful (adj): She looks *awful.* (*Awful* is a predicate adjective after the linking verb *looks.*)

awfully (adv): She looks *awfully* tired. (*Awfully* is an adverb modifying the adjective *tired.*)

bad/badly

bad (adj):   The play was *bad*. (meaning *not good*)

He feels *bad*, even though the fever is down. (meaning *sick*)

He feels *bad* about losing the money. (meaning *sorry* or *upset*)

badly (adv):   He painted badly. (meaning *not well*)

The team *badly* needs a win. (meaning *very much*, with verbs such as *want* or *need*)

good/well

good (adj):   Alice Walker is a *good* writer.

The food tastes *good*.

He feels *good* about his work.

(Remember that *good* is always an adjective.)

well (adv):   He dances *well*. (meaning *skillfully*)

He behaved *well*. (meaning *in a proper manner*)

The praise for his book was *well* deserved. (meaning *fully*)

He gets along *well* with people. (meaning *successfully*)

well (adj):   He feels *well*. (*Well* is an adjective only when referring to *health*.)

poor/poorly

poor (adj):   The *poor* man was now homeless. (meaning pitiful or penniless)

poorly (adv):   She scored *poorly* on the exam.

quick/quickly

quick (adj):   She is *quick* at word games.

quickly (adv):   She works *quickly*.

quiet/quietly

quiet (adj):   After ten at night, the dorm has *quiet* hours.

quietly (adv):   Talk *quietly* after ten o'clock.

real/really

real (adj):   The medics responded to a *real* emergency. (meaning *genuine, not imaginary*)

really (adv):   The student is *really* determined to do well. (meaning *genuinely, truly*)

sure/surely

sure (adj):   I am *sure* she was the person driving the car.

(meaning *certain, confident, firm*)

surely (adv):   She was *surely* speeding.

(meaning *certainly, truly*)

NOTE: *Real* and *sure* are often used informally in everyday conversation as adverbs to mean *very* or *certainly*, as in "I'm real sorry about your illness," or "I'm sure sorry about your illness." However, this usage is not acceptable in formal writing.

PRACTICE   Choose the correct adjective or adverb in each of the following sentences. You may find it helpful to draw an arrow to the word that the adjective or adverb is modifying.

1. The child was (awful, awfully) sick.

2. The nurse felt (bad, badly) about the child.

3. The child didn't do (good, well) in class.

4. Let's act (quick, quickly) and try to help her.

5. The mother was (real, really) upset.

Misplaced and Dangling Modifiers

Study the following five sentences and discuss how the placement of the modifier *only* changes the meaning of each sentence.

Only Charlene telephoned my brother yesterday. (Nobody else telephoned.)

Charlene *only* telephoned my brother yesterday. (She did not e-mail or visit.)

Charlene telephoned *only* my brother yesterday. (She called no one else.)

Charlene telephoned my *only* brother yesterday. (The writer has only one brother.)

Charlene telephoned my brother *only* yesterday. (She didn't telephone until yesterday.)

A modifier is a word, phrase, or clause that functions as an adjective or an adverb.

my *only* brother

Only modifies the noun *brother;* therefore, *only* functions as an adjective.

the marine *who is my brother*

Who is my brother is a clause that modifies the noun *marine;* therefore, *who is my brother* functions as an adjective clause.

just yesterday

Just modifies the adverb *yesterday;* therefore, *just* functions as an adverb.

MISPLACED MODIFIERS

> A **misplaced modifier** is a modifier in a position that makes the meaning of the sentence confusing, awkward, or ambiguous.

Below is a list of modifiers that are often misplaced. When you use one of these words, be sure it immediately precedes the word or word group it modifies.

Modifiers Often Misplaced

almost	exactly	just	nearly	scarcely
even	hardly	merely	only	simply

1. The modifier is in a **confusing** position because it does not immediately precede the word it modifies.

    Confusing placement of a *word* modifier:

    > *Nearly* the salesperson sold the used car to the customer.

    Nearly, an adverb, cannot modify the noun *salesperson.*

    Revised: The salesperson *nearly* sold the used car to the customer.

    Nearly correctly modifies the verb *sold.*

    Confusing placement of a *phrase* modifier:

    > *With all the rusty spots,* the salesperson could not sell the car.

    Is it the salesperson who has rusty spots or the car?

    Revised: The salesperson could not sell the car *with all the rusty spots.*

    Confusing placement of a *clause* modifier:

    > The salesperson could not sell the used car to the customer *that needed extensive body work.*

    Is it the customer or the car that needs extensive body work?

    Revised: The salesperson could not sell the used car *that needed extensive body work* to the customer.

2. The modifier is in an **awkward** position, interrupting the flow of the sentence.

   Awkward placement:

   > We want *to* after the lunch hour *study* in the library.

   Revised: After the lunch hour, we want *to study* in the library.

Although the use of the infinitive that is interrupted (called a "split infinitive") has now become more accepted in standard English, the result is frequently awkward and often interrupts the flow of the sentence.

3. The modifier is in an **ambiguous** position (sometimes called a "squinting modifier").

   Ambiguous placement:

   > The used-car salesperson when questioned *seriously* doubted he could sell the rusty car.

Was the salesperson seriously questioned or did he seriously doubt? From the placement of *seriously*, it is impossible to know.

   Revised: When *seriously questioned,* the used-car salesperson doubted he could sell the rusty car.

   or, depending on the intended meaning,

   > When questioned, the used-car salesperson *seriously doubted* he could sell the rusty car.

EXERCISE 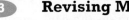 **3**   **Revising Misplaced Modifiers**

Revise each of the following sentences to avoid misplaced modifiers.

1. I gave the puppy to my sister with the white paws.

   _____

2. I am looking for the keys to the filing cabinets which are missing.

   _____

3. We decided to before the camping trip buy better sleeping bags.

   _____

4. As a pilot, passenger safety had always come first.

   _____

5. They need to immediately after the party go directly home.

   _____

6. The dance contestants waited eagerly watching the faces of the judges.

   _____

7.   The jeweler wanted to for his new customer design a special charm bracelet.

_____

8.   I took my daughter to my office who loved a day off from school.

_____

9.   The accountant forgot almost to tell his client about the change in the law.

_____

10. There are five tablets in this medicine bottle exactly.

_____

DANGLING MODIFIERS

> A **dangling modifier** is a modifier without a logical or identifiable word, phrase, or clause to modify in the sentence.

Sentence with a dangling modifier: Working on the car's engine, the dog barked all afternoon.

Who was working on the engine? According to the sentence, it is the dog who was working on the engine. _Working on the car's engine_ is a participial phrase that modifies the subject _dog_. As it stands, the sentence makes no sense.

TWO OPTIONS FOR REVISING A DANGLING MODIFIER

Option 1:   Create a new subject for the independent clause.

Working on the car's engine, _I_ heard the dog barking all afternoon.

Now the modifying phrase _working on the car's engine_ modifies the pronoun subject I.

Option 2:   Create a dependent clause (a dependent clause begins with a subordinating conjunction or relative pronoun and has a subject and a verb).

While I was working on the car's engine, the dog barked all afternoon.

Now the modifying phrase _working on the car's engine_ has been changed into a dependent clause.

EXERCISE 4   **Revising Dangling Modifiers**

Revise each of the following sentences to avoid misplaced or dangling modifiers.

1.   Victor fed the dog wearing his tuxedo.

_____

2.   Visiting Yellowstone National Park, Old Faithful entertained us by performing on schedule.

_____

_____

3.   Hoping to see the news, the television set was turned on at seven o'clock.

_____

_____

4.   Running up the stairs, the train had already left for Philadelphia.

_____

_____

5.   After running over the hill, the farm was visible in the valley below.

_____

_____

6.   Dressed in a Dracula costume, I thought my son looked perfect for Halloween.

_____

_____

7.   Hanging from the ceiling in her bedroom, she saw three spiders.

_____

8.   After wiping my glasses, the redbird flew away.

_____

9.   Howling without a stop, we listened to the neighbor's dog all evening.

_____

_____

10.   After painting my room all afternoon, my cat demanded her dinner.

_____

_____

EXERCISE 5   **Revising Misplaced or Dangling Modifiers**

Revise each of the following sentences to avoid misplaced or dangling modifiers.

1.   Leaping upstream, we fished most of the day for salmon.

_____

_____

2.   At the age of ten, my family took a trip to Washington, D.C.

_____

_____

3.   Skimming every chapter, my biology textbook made more sense.

_____

_____

4.   A woodpecker was found in Cuba that had been considered extinct.

_____

_____

5.   Working extra hours last week, my salary dramatically increased.

_____

_____

6.   We watched a movie in the theater that had won an Academy Award for best picture.

_____

_____

7.   The truck caused a traffic jam, which was broken down on the highway, for miles.

_____

_____

8.   Last week while shopping, my friend's purse was stolen.

_____

_____

9.   While eating lunch outdoors, our picnic table collapsed.

_____

_____

10. Our car is in the parking lot with two bags of groceries unlocked.

_____

Avoiding the Double Negative with the Adverb *not* and Other Negative Words

The adverb *not* is one of several words that carry a negative meaning. In standard English, having two negative words in the same sentence is not acceptable.

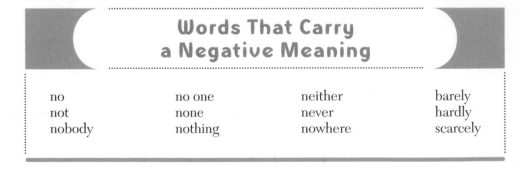

Words That Carry a Negative Meaning

no	no one	neither	barely
not	none	never	hardly
nobody	nothing	nowhere	scarcely

You can correct a sentence that contains a double negative by removing either one of the two negative words.

Incorrect: I *don't* have *no* food in my house.

Possible corrections: I *don't* have food in my house.

                            I have *no* food in my house.

PRACTICE   Revise each of the following sentences to correct the double negative.

1. A person shouldn't never go out with something cooking on the stove.
2. You haven't neither a bike nor a car.
3. I don't want nothing.
4. I won't never break my promise.
5. I can't hardly wait until summer.

Parallel Structure: Making a Series of Words, Phrases, or Clauses Balanced within the Sentence

Which one of the following sentences has the more balanced structure?

> His favorite hobbies are playing the trumpet, listening to jazz, and to go to concerts.

> His favorite hobbies are playing the trumpet, listening to jazz, and going to concerts.

If you selected the second sentence, you made the better choice. The second sentence uses parallel structure to balance the three phrases in the series (*playing the trumpet, listening to jazz, going to concerts*). Matching each of the items in the series with the same *-ing* structure makes the sentence easier to understand and more pleasant to read. Words, phrases, and even sentences in a series can be made parallel.

RULE 1   **Words in a series should be the same parts of speech.**

Not parallel: The town was small, friendly, and the atmosphere was peaceful.

The series is composed of two adjectives and one clause.

Parallel: The town was small, friendly, and peaceful.

The series is composed of three adjectives: *small*, *friendly*, and *peaceful*.

RULE 2   **Phrases in a series should be the same kind of phrases (*infinitive phrase, prepositional phrase, verb phrase, noun phrase, or participial phrase*).**

Not parallel: Her lost assignment is in her closet, on the floor, and a pile of clothes is hiding it.

The series is composed of two prepositional phrases and one clause.

Parallel: Her lost assignment is in her closet, on the floor, and under a pile of clothes.

The series is composed of three prepositional phrases beginning with *in, on,* and *under.*

RULE 3

Clauses in a series should not be mixed with phrases.

Not parallel: The street was narrow, the shops were charming, and crowds in the cafe.

The series is composed of two clauses and one phrase.

Parallel: The street was narrow, the shops were charming, and the cafe was crowded.

The series is composed of three clauses.

 PRACTICE

Each of the following sentences lacks parallel structure. In each sentence, revise the underlined section to make the series parallel.

1.   My favorite armchair is lumpy, worn out, and <u>has dirt spots everywhere.</u>

2.   She enjoys reading novels, studying the flute, and <u>sews her own clothes.</u>

3.   He admires teachers who make the classroom an exciting place and <u>willingly explaining the lesson more than once.</u>

EXERCISE 6   **Revising Sentences for Parallel Structure**

Each of the following sentences lacks parallel structure. Underline the word, phrase, or clause that is not parallel and revise it so that its structure balances with the other items in the pair or series. An example has been done for you.

Not parallel: The best leather comes from Italy, from Spain, and <u>is imported from Brazil.</u>

Parallel: The best leather comes from Italy, Spain, and Brazil.

1.   Winter in Chicago is very windy, extremely snowy, and has many bitterly cold days.

2.   I would prefer to fix an old car rather than watching television.

3.   Mr. Lee is a helpful neighbor, a loyal friend, and dedicated to his children.

4.   The apartment is crowded and without light.

5.   The dancer is slender, tall, and moves gracefully.

6.   The nursery was cheerful, large, and had a lot of sun.

7.   My friend loves to play chess, to read science fiction, and working out at the gym.

8.   For homework today I must read a chapter in history, do five exercises for Spanish class, and working on my term paper for political science.

9. The painting reveals the artist's talent and his imagination is revealed.

10. The cars race down the track, turn the corner at great speed, and then they are heading for the homestretch.

EXERCISE **Revising Sentences for Parallel Structure**

Each of the following sentences lacks parallel structure. Underline the word, phrase, or clause that is not parallel and revise it so that its structure balances with the other items in the pair or series.

1. The dog had to choose between jumping over the fence or he could have dug a hole underneath it.

2. She disliked going to the beach, hiking in the woods, and she didn't care for picnics, either.

3. As I looked down the city street, I could see the soft lights from restaurant windows, I could hear the mellow sounds of a nightclub band, and carefree moods of people walking by.

4. The singers have been on several road tours, have recorded for two record companies, and they would like to make a movie someday.

5. They would rather order a pizza than eating their sister's cooking.

6. I explained to the teacher that my car had broken down, my books had been stolen, and no assignment pad.

7. That night, the prisoner was sick, discouraged, and she was filled with loneliness.

8. As the truck rumbled down the street, it suddenly lurched out of control, smashed into a parked car, and then the truck hit the storefront of my uncle's hardware store.

9. The teacher is patient, intelligent, and demands a lot.

10. He was determined to pass the math course, not only to get his three credits but also for a sense of achievement.

EXERCISE **Revising Sentences for Parallel Structure**

Each of the following sentences lacks parallel structure. Underline the word, phrase, or clause that is not parallel and revise it so that its structure balances with the other items in the pair or series.

1. The first-grade teacher told us that our child was unruly, mischievous, and talked too much.

2. The dog's size, its coloring, and whenever it barked reminded me of a wolf.

3. Shabna is not only very talented but she is also acting kindly to everyone.

4. He dried the dishes; putting them away was the job of his wife.

5. Jordan would rather travel and see the world than staying home and reading about other places.

6. For weeks he tried to decide whether he should major in chemistry, continue with accounting, or to take a year off.

7. Her depression was a result of the loss of her job, the breakdown of her marriage, and a teenage daughter who was a problem.

8. She must either cut back on her expenses or selling her car.

9. His office is down a dark hallway, on the fourth floor, and having no windows.

10. He went through four years of college, one year of graduate school, and then doing one year teaching seventh-grade science.

Mastery and Editing Tests

TEST **1** ## Revising Sentences for Correct Use of Modifiers and Parallel Structure

Each sentence has an error in the use of a modifier or in parallel structure. Rewrite each sentence to correct the error you find.

1. He devoured the bone, tore up his new bed, and jumping up on the new sofa.

_____

_____

2. The student almost received enough money from his aunt to pay for his semester's tuition.

_____

_____

3. She returned from vacation rested, with a great deal of energy, and happy.

_____

_____

4. Joseph managed to find time to coach the team with two other day jobs.

_____

_____

5. I'm the most happy man alive.

_____

_____

6. Discovered by accident, the football fan took the diamond ring to the lost and found.

    _____

    _____

7. Books were piled on the reading tables, magazines were tossed on chairs, and scraps of paper everywhere.

    _____

    _____

8. Being nearly deaf, the whistle of the train did not warn him of the danger.

    _____

    _____

9. The audience was bored because he talked slow.

    _____

    _____

10. The bus, judging the fog was too thick, stopped by the side of the road.

    _____

    _____

TEST   2   **Revising Sentences for Correct Use of Modifiers and Parallel Structure**

Each sentence has an error in the use of a modifier or in parallel structure. Rewrite each sentence to correct the error you find.

1. The job demands computer skills, math ability, and with accounting background.

    _____

    _____

2. My sister is not only a talented musician, but she is also teaching with great success.

    _____

    _____

3. Raking the leaves this morning, more than one hundred geese flew overhead.

    _____

    _____

4. Follow the directions for writing the essay carefully.

    _____

5.   The astronomer completed the calculation at the observatory that he had been working on for nearly a decade.

_____

_____

6.   He's the baddest speaker I've ever heard.

_____

7.   My older brother is guilty of lecturing me instead of a good example.

_____

_____

8.   The new highway follows the river, bypasses the small towns, and you can save a lot of time.

_____

_____

9.   He only ordered an appetizer.

_____

_____

10. I don't want nothing to eat.

_____

_____

TEST 3   **Revising Sentences for Correct Use of Modifiers and Parallel Structure**

Each sentence has an error in the use of a modifier or parallel structure. Rewrite each sentence to correct the error you find.

1.   The car stopped quick to avoid the child.

_____

_____

2.   My friend is generous, hard-working, and a talker.

_____

_____

3.   The members of Congress would rather stonewall the proposal than to pass the new law.

_____

_____

4.   When covered with thin ice, you should not skate on the lake.

_____

_____

5. Last year, the citizen just paid half of his taxes.

6. From the airport, I will either take the bus or the shuttle to the hotel.

7. For the holidays, we plan to do some cooking, see a few good movies, and listening to jazz.

8. Working late into the night, the page numbering on my report kept printing out incorrectly.

9. I haven't seen nobody today.

10. The child behaved real good during the performance.

TEST 4   **Editing Student Writing: Using Correction Symbols**

The commonly used correction symbols for errors in modifiers are **adj** (adjective), **adv** (adverb), and **dm** (dangling modifier). The correction symbol for an error in parallel structure is **//**. In the paragraph below, find four errors with modifiers—two adjective forms (**adj**), one adverb form (**adv**), and one dangling modifier (**dm**); two errors in parallel structure (**//**); one incorrect pronoun reference (**pron ref**); one fragment (**frag**); and two subject-verb agreement errors (**agr**). Mark the errors with the commonly used correction symbols, and then correct the errors on the lines provided after the paragraph.

[1]The criminal justice system in the United States has changed dramatically in recent years. [2]We have come a long way since the nineteenth century, when the use of fingerprint evidence was all that an investigator had to help them. [3]The use of DNA has led to this real important change. [4]DNA testing is a scientific method of determining whether two samples of organic material comes from the same source. [5]Testing for DNA, an individual may be placed at a particular crime scene. [6]These scientific tests may contradict criminal convictions from the past.

⁷In such cases, this evidence becomes more strong than any jury finding. ⁸Just a few years ago, the discoveries made through the use of DNA testing in Illinois were so dramatic that the governor ordered all executions in that state canceled. ⁹Also, it appears that people elsewhere have been wrongfully convicted and jailed for many kinds of offenses, including first-degree murder, sexual assault, and people who were dealing drugs. ¹⁰People who have been in prison for years, in New York, in Ohio, and the state of California, have been found innocent and have been released. ¹¹One of the few problems with DNA evidence are the expense of running the tests. ¹²However, the most best news for the future is that problems of wrongful convictions by juries will occur a lot less often. ¹³Because DNA evidence will be presented whenever possible as part of courtroom evidence.

Four modifier corrections

1. _____
2. _____
3. _____
4. _____

Two parallel structure corrections

5. _____
_____
6. _____
_____

Pronoun reference correction

    Antecedent   **Pronoun**

7. _____   _____

Fragment corrected

8. _____
_____
_____
_____

Two subject-verb agreement corrections

    Subject   **Correct form of the verb**

9. _____   _____
10. _____   _____

Exploring Online

Go to academic.cengage.com/devenglish/scarry to find the **Writer's Online Workplace,** a website designed for students using this book. You will find links to handouts, interactive quizzes, and other online resources as you explore the following topics:

- misplaced and dangling modifiers
- humorous misplaced modifiers
- parallel structure

Working Together

Preparing and Editing a Résumé

Below is a draft of a résumé written by a college student who is looking for a summer job. This résumé covers many good points that are necessary for an effective résumé; however, it still needs editing before it can be presented to a possible employer. Study each entry on the résumé and then answer the questions that follow.

Gary Sommers
645 Franklin AVe.
Norman, Oklahoma
Home Telephone: 662-1919

Present Job Objective	A summer position as an assistant in ~~teh~~ *the* mayor's office
Education	High School Diploma, Kennedy High School, Norman, Oklahoma
	B.A., Business Administration, University of Oklahoma Expected date of graduation: june 2006
	Courses in Business and Computers: Principles of Accounting, Microeconomic Theory, Problem solving and Structured Programming, Computer Systems and Assembly

WORK EXPERIENCE

9/04 to present 2004–2006	Tutor, Math Lab, University of Oklahoma Summer Volunteer at Camp Sunshine, a day camp for disabled children
Special skills:	fluent in spanish

Computer Skills: familiar with Microsoft Word, EXCEL,

Interests: soccer, guitar

REFERENCES: Available on request

1. Can you find any typos, misspelled words, or errors in capitalization or punctuation?
2. Can you find anything inconsistent in the design or layout? (Look for places where parallel structures are needed.)
3. If Gary Sommers corrected even a single error by using an ink pen instead of printing out a corrected version of the entire résumé, what do you think a potential employer might conclude?
4. Is there any information that is missing from this sample résumé?
5. Why has Mr. Sommers not included such facts as date of birth and marital status?
6. When looking for a job, how does a person go about obtaining the necessary references? How many references does one need?
7. How could Mr. Sommers highlight his interest in the particular job for which he is applying?

Portfolio Suggestion

Using the same general headings as in this sample résumé, draft your own résumé. Copy it onto a disk or CD that you will keep. Remember to update the résumé regularly. You may want to have two or more versions emphasizing different experiences or skills.

CHAPTER 11

Practicing Irregular Verbs

In this chapter, you will learn the principal parts of fifty irregular verbs. These verbs are divided into the following groups:

CHAPTER OBJECTIVES

- eight verbs that do not change their forms
- two verbs with the same simple and past participle forms
- twenty verbs with the same past tense and past participle forms
- twenty verbs that differ in all three forms

What Are the Principal Parts of Irregular Verbs?

The English language has more than one hundred verbs that do not form the past tense or past participle with the usual *-ed* ending. Their forms are irregular. When you listen to children aged four or five, you often hear them use *-ed* to form the past tense of every verb, as in "Yesterday, I *goed* to my aunt's house." Later on, they will learn that the verb *to go* is unusual, and they will change to the irregular form, "Yesterday, I *went*. . . ." The best way to learn these verbs is to listen to how they sound. In Appendix C of this book, you will find an extensive list of the three principal parts of these verbs: the simple form (also called dictionary form, infinitive form, or basic form), the past tense, and the past participle (used with perfect tenses, after *has*, *have*, *had*, or *will have*, or with the passive voice, after the verb *to be*).

Practicing Fifty Irregular Verbs

Learn the three principal parts of all fifty irregular verbs given in this chapter. Pronounce them out loud until you have learned them. If you don't know the meaning of a particular verb or you cannot pronounce a verb and its forms, ask your instructor for help. Most irregular verbs are very common words that you will be using often in your writing and speaking. You will want to know them well.

Eight Verbs That Do Not Change Their Forms
(notice that they all end in *-t* or *-d*)

Simple form	Past tense	Past participle	Simple form	Past tense	Past participle
bet	bet	bet	hurt	hurt	hurt
cost	cost	cost	put	put	put
cut	cut	cut	quit	quit	quit
hit	hit	hit	spread	spread	spread

Two Verbs with the Same Simple and Past Participle Forms

Simple form	Past tense	Past participle
come	came	come
become	became	become

PRACTICE Using the verb given in parentheses, fill in the correct form in each of the following sentences.

1. Last year, the tuition for my education _____ 7 percent more than it
   (cost)
   did the year before.

2. I have _____ trying to guess my expenses for next year.
   (quit)

3. The message has _____ that college costs continue to spiral.
   (spread)

4. Most parents have been _____ with large tax increases.
   (hit)

5. Financing a child's higher education has _____ a difficult task.
   (become)

Twenty Verbs with the Same Past Tense and Past Participle Forms

Simple form	Past tense	Past participle	Simple form	Past tense	Past participle
bend	bent	bent	creep	crept	crept
lend	lent	lent	keep	kept	kept
send	sent	sent	sleep	slept	slept
spend	spent	spent	sweep	swept	swept
			weep	wept	wept
catch	caught	caught			
teach	taught	taught	bring	brought	brought
			buy	bought	bought
bleed	bled	bled	fight	fought	fought
feed	fed	fed	seek	sought	sought
lead	led	led	think	thought	thought
speed	sped	sped			

PRACTICE Using the verb given in parentheses, fill in the correct form in each of the following sentences.

1. Last year, the school district _____ new chemistry texts.
   (buy)

2. Some citizens felt the district had _____ too much money on these
    (spend)

    new books.

3. They claimed the taxpayers were being _____ dry.
    (bleed)

4. These citizens argued that the school should have _____ the old
    (keep)

    books.

5. The teachers _____ the old books were worn out.
    (think)

6. Parents, on the other hand, _____ to hire two new teachers.
    (seek)

7. They _____ for a smaller class size.
    (fight)

8. Most teachers _____ classes that were too large.
    (teach)

9. One father _____ a campaign to educate the community.
    (lead)

10. He _____ every citizen a letter to explain the problem.
    (send)

Twenty Verbs That Differ in All Three Forms

Simple tense	Past tense	Past participle	Simple tense	Past tense	Past participle
blow	blew	blown	begin	began	begun
fly	flew	flown	drink	drank	drunk
grow	grew	grown	ring	rang	rung
know	knew	known	shrink	shrank	shrunk
throw	threw	thrown	sing	sang	sung
			sink	sank	sunk
bite	bit	bitten (or bit)	spring	sprang	sprung
drive	drove	driven	swim	swam	swum
hide	hid	hidden (or hid)			
ride	rode	ridden			
rise	rose	risen			
stride	strode	stridden			
write	wrote	written			

PRACTICE   Using the verb given in parentheses, fill in the correct form in each of the following sentences.

1. We have _____ many country and western singers over the years,
    (know)

    but Patsy Cline remains a special figure.

2. She _____ her career near her small hometown in Virginia.
    (begin)

3. She _____ wherever she could find people to listen.
   (sing)

4. People immediately recognized the exceptional quality of her voice, and

   her audiences _____.
   (grow)

5. At sixteen, Patsy Cline auditioned for a local radio station and _____
   (drive)

   from town to town, singing in clubs and taverns.

6. During the early 1960s, her records _____ on popularity charts
   (rise)

   throughout the country.

7. After the worldwide success of "Walkin' after Midnight," Patsy Cline

   _____ her way to stardom.
   (ride)

8. In 1963, on her way back from Kansas City, the singer had _____
   (fly)

   as far as Tennessee when her plane crashed, and she was killed.

9. Other stars have _____ up in the last forty years, but Patsy Cline
   (spring)
   will remain one of the great legends of country music.

10. Much has been _____ about Patsy Cline, and a feature-length film
    (write)
    titled *Sweet Dreams* has been made about her life.

EXERCISE ❶ **Practicing Irregular Verb Forms**

For each verb given in parentheses, supply the past tense or the past participle.

Ever since people _____ to write, they have _____ about the
(begin)   (write)

great mysteries in nature. For instance, why did the dinosaurs disappear? In the

past, no one _____ why. Scientists now have _____ on one strong
(know)   (bet)

possibility. That possibility is that sixty-five million years ago, a six-mile-wide

chunk of rock _____ the earth and _____ up a thick cloud of dust.
(hit)   (throw)

The dust _____ the sunlight from the earth; therefore, certain life forms
(keep)

disappeared. Some scientists have _____ to the conclusion that this
(come)

could have _____ the earth's animal population by as much as 70 percent.
(shrink)

Other scientists are not so sure that this is true. They believe time has _____
(hide)

the real reason for the disappearance of the dinosaurs.

EXERCISE 2   **Practicing Irregular Verb Forms**

For each verb given in parentheses, supply the past tense or the past participle.

Nearly everyone has _____ a cold at some time or another. Medical
(catch)

researchers have long _____ a cure for the common cold, but so far they
(seek)

have had no success. The cold virus has _____ throughout the world,
(spread)

and the number of its victims has _____ every year. Past experience has
(rise)

_____ us that people who have _____ plenty of liquids and taken
(teach)   (drink)

aspirin have gotten over colds more quickly than those who have not, but this is not

a good enough remedy. People once believed that you _____ a fever and
(feed)

starved a cold, but recent research has _____ to a disclaimer of this belief.
(lead)

Other research, including the search for a vaccine, has _____ a lot of time
(cost)

and effort. So far, the new knowledge has not _____ a cure.
(bring)

EXERCISE 3   **Practicing Irregular Verb Forms**

The following paragraph is written in the present tense. Rewrite the paragraph using the past tense.

The jockey drives his pickup truck to the race track. He strides into the stalls where the horses are kept. His head swims with thoughts of the coming race. He springs into the saddle and rides to the starting gate. The bell rings, and the horses fly out of the gate. They speed around the first turn. The crowd grows tense, and excitement spreads as the horses sweep across the finish line.

_____

_____

_____

_____

_____

_____

_____

_____

More Irregular Verbs

Appendix C (page A19) gives an alphabetical listing of nearly every irregular verb. Use that list to supply the correct form for each verb in the following exercises.

EXERCISE 4   **Practicing More Irregular Verb Forms**

For each verb given in parentheses, supply the past tense or the past participle.

1. The photographer _____ several rolls of film.
(shoot)

2.   The contractor _____ two houses in the neighborhood.
(build)

3.   The audience _____ when the singer attempted the high notes.
(flee)

4.   The pipe _____ yesterday; we are waiting for a plumber.
(burst)

5.   He _____ the dog for a wolf.
(mistake)

6.   The firefighters _____ down the ladder.
(slide)

7.   Life _____ the family a cruel blow.
(deal)

8.   The artist had _____ two portraits of his wife.
(draw)

9.   The pond was _____ enough for ice skating.
(freeze)

10.   He had washed and _____ out all his clothes in the sink.
(wring)

EXERCISE **5**   **Practicing More Irregular Verb Forms**

Read the following paragraph. Find and circle the ten irregular verbs that are written incorrectly. In the spaces provided, write the correct forms of the ten irregular verbs.

Mr. Weeks, an alumnus of our university, had gave a large sum of money to the school just before he died. A committee was choosen to study how the money should be used. Each member thunk about the possibilities for several weeks before the meeting. Finally, the meeting begun in late November. Each member brung his or her ideas. One gentleman fealt the school should improve the graduate program by hiring two new teachers. Another committee member layed out a proposal for remodeling the oldest dormitory on campus. Janice Spaulding had writen a plan for increasing scholarships for deserving students. A citizen unexpectedly swang open the door and strode into the room. She pleaded with the school to provide more programs for the community. After everyone had spoke, the committee was asked to make a more thorough study of each project.

1. _____   6. _____

2. _____   7. _____

3. _____   8. _____

4. _____   9. _____

5. _____   10. _____

EXERCISE **6**   **Practicing More Irregular Verb Forms**

For each verb given in parentheses, supply the past tense or the past participle.

1.   We _____ in the sand for clams.
(dig)

2. The director _____ the script on the table.
   (fling)

3. The family had _____ the child's birthday.
   (forget)

4. The clerk _____ the clock before going home.
   (wind)

5. The door seemed to be _____.
   (stick)

6. The dog _____ itself as it came out of the water.
   (shake)

7. The youth _____ he was telling the truth.
   (swear)

8. Yesterday, the food had _____ on the table all day without being
   (lie)
   touched.

9. The bill has been _____.
   (pay)

10. The hosts _____ their guests to drink in their home.
    (forbid)

Mastery and Editing Tests

TEST 1   **Using Correct Irregular Verb Forms**

In each of the following sentences, underline the irregular verb. If the verb form is wrong, correct it. If the form is correct, mark it with a *C*.

1. She sung for a huge crowd Saturday night.

2. I was shook by the accident.

3. The ship sunk off the coast of Florida.

4. The large cat creeped up on its prey.

5. She lended him the money.

6. The volunteers had fed most of the people before the Red Cross arrived.

7. The athlete had swum the English Channel once before.

8. The winds blowed all through the night.

9. The letter was writen by candlelight.

10. Have you rode that horse before?

TEST 2   **Using Correct Irregular Verb Forms**

In each of the following sentences, underline the irregular verb. If the verb form is wrong, correct it. If the form is correct, mark it with a *C*.

1. The chef from Hawaii teached the students how to cook for a luau.

2. He had brung too many clothes with him on the trip.

3. People had knowed for many years that organic food was healthier.

4. The sweater shrunk in the dryer.

5. Lindbergh flied across the Atlantic nonstop in 1927.

6. In the years that followed, the population growed to 291 million.

7. The architect begun his plans for the new medical complex.

8. Several people in North America have catched the West Nile virus through mosquito bites.

9. When baseball spread across the country right after the Civil War, players who misbehaved were fined a nickel, a dime, or even a quarter by the umpires.

10. Some people have mistakenly thunk that animals could not feel pain.

TEST 3 **Using Correct Irregular Verb Forms**

In each of the following sentences, underline the irregular verb. If the verb form is wrong, correct it. If the form is correct, mark it with a *C*.

1. The salesperson strided into the room with the utmost confidence.

2. The fork was bended out of shape.

3. My mom sweeped the kitchen floor every night.

4. She was hurt by the unkind comments.

5. The patient drunk the quart of pink liquid.

6. She weeped when she heard the news.

7. The sisters seeked out their family's history.

8. Stan throwed the first pitch in the game.

9. My name was put on the list.

10. The pipe sprung a leak.

TEST 4 **Editing Student Writing: Using Correction Symbols**

The correction symbol for an error in verb form is **vb**. In the paragraph below, find six errors in irregular verbs (**vb**), one error in parallel structure (**//**), two fragments (**frag**), and one error in subject-verb agreement (**agr**). Mark the errors with the commonly used correction symbols, and then correct the errors on the lines provided after the paragraph.

[1]In 1903, Horatio Nelson Jackson made a bet of fifty dollars that he could drive across the country in less than three months. [2]No one at that time had ever drove an automobile from California to New York. [3]When he begun his trip, he had no worries about traffic problems. [4]Because there were hardly any cars. [5]However, there were other concerns. [6]One major problem a hundred years ago were the absence of service stations along the way. [7]When his car broke down, Horatio sleptin whistle-stop towns, waiting for parts to be delivered by train. [8]The roads were trails of mud or dust. [9]If they existed at all. [10]Furthermore, the cars at that time had no shock absorbers, power steering, air conditioning, seatbelts, and they had no radios either. [11]Despite these difficulties, Horatio won his bet.

¹²He rumbled down Fifth Avenue in New York with his mechanic and his bulldog named Bud. ¹³He become the first person to drive an automobile across the country. ¹⁴Recently, an Indiana dentist and his wife reenacted that trip of a century ago in a 1904 Winton, a car that is no longer produced. ¹⁵The century-old car speeded along at twenty-five or thirty miles an hour. ¹⁶The couple faced problems when a wheel fell off, the brakes catched fire, and a tire went flat. ¹⁷After the trip, the dentist commented, "By comparison, driving in a modern car is like riding on a magic carpet."

Six irregular verb form corrections

1. _____

2. _____

3. _____

4. _____

5. _____

6. _____

Parallel structure correction

7. _____

_____

Two corrected fragments

8. _____

_____

9. _____

_____

Subject-verb agreement correction

Subject	Correct form of the verb

10. _____   _____

Exploring Online

Go to academic.cengage.com/devenglish/scarry to find the **Writer's Online Workplace,** a website designed for students using this book. You will find links to handouts, interactive quizzes, and other online resources as you explore the following topic:

- irregular verbs

Working Together

Preparing for a Job Interview

Among the most important moments in our working lives are those times when we are searching for a first job or when we find ourselves moving from one job to another. Because a critical part of any job search is a successful interview, it is essential to be prepared to answer direct questions from the person who may hire you. Personnel officers of companies, along with counselors who help people get jobs in those companies, all agree that a job applicant should expect certain questions in an interview.

Here are five questions considered to be the most important:

1. What is your notion of the ideal job?

2. What image do you have in mind of the supervisor or manager you would like to work for?

3. What qualifications separate you from any other candidate for this job?

4. What is the most balanced portrait you can give of yourself?

5. What are your greatest strengths? What weaknesses about yourself have you recognized?

Experts say that the last two questions are especially tricky because they call for very personal answers. Also, when people respond to these questions, they tend either to talk too much about themselves or to give answers that are too brief.

The president of one counseling service suggests that an effective way to answer the question about a self-portrait is to ask another question, such as "Can you tell me about some problems you have had in your company, so I can focus my response?" In this way, you will have some good examples to use as part of your answer. Another counselor says that, when you are interviewed, you should "be honest, be yourself, and do your homework."

Working in Groups

Divide into five groups. Each group should take one of the five questions from the above list. Each student should devote ten minutes of freewriting to respond to his or her group's question. Following the freewriting, the group should then spend another ten minutes discussing the responses generated by its members. Sometimes groups like to exchange their freewriting so others can read their responses aloud or silently. One member of the group will then present a summary of the group's response to the rest of the class.

Portfolio Suggestion

Use this opportunity to work on your own answers to these job-interview questions. Write out your answers and save them for future reference. You may find them useful when you are preparing for an actual job interview.

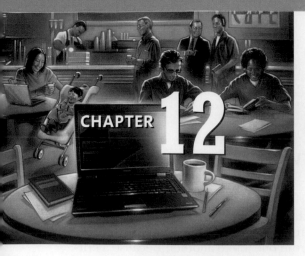

CHAPTER 12

Mastering Verb Tenses

Using verb tenses correctly is at the heart of understanding a language. In this chapter, you will learn to do the following:

CHAPTER OBJECTIVES

- Use the **present perfect** and **past perfect tenses** correctly.
- Understand the **sequence of tenses.**
- Avoid unnecessary **shifts in verb tense.**
- Understand when to choose the **active voice** and when to choose the **passive voice.**
- Recognize constructions that require the **subjunctive mood.**
- Know how to use should/would, used to/supposed to, can/could, and will/would.

How Many Verb Tenses Are There in English?

Not all languages express time by using exactly the same verb tenses. Students for whom English is a second language know that one of their major tasks in learning English is to understand how to use each of the tenses. Because the next sections of this chapter concern common problems with tense, a chart of the English verb tenses is provided below. You may want to refer to this list from time to time. Notice that the chart gives example sentences for each tense and continuous form.

The Six English Verb Tenses and Their Continuous Forms

THREE SIMPLE TENSES	SIMPLE CONTINUOUS FORMS	THREE PERFECT TENSES	PERFECT CONTINUOUS FORMS
1. Present	**Present continuous**	**4. Present perfect**	**Present perfect continuous**
you walk	you are walking	you have walked	you have been walking
I run	I am running	I have run	I have been running
2. Past	**Past continuous**	**5. Past perfect**	**Past perfect continuous**
you walked	you were walking	you had walked	you had been walking
I ran	I was running	I had run	I had been running
3. Future	**Future continuous**	**6. Future perfect**	**Future perfect continuous**
you will walk	you will be walking	you will have walked	you will have been walking
I will run	I will be running	I will have run	I will have been running

How Do You Use the Present Perfect and the Past Perfect Tenses?

The perfect tenses need special attention because they are generally not well understood or consistently used in the accepted way.

HOW DO YOU FORM THE PERFECT TENSES?

The **present perfect tense** consists of *has* or *have* plus the past participle of the main verb:

has worked

have worked

The **past perfect tense** consists of *had* plus the past participle of the main verb:

had worked

WHAT DO THESE TENSES MEAN?

> The **present perfect tense** can be used to describe an action that started in the past and continues to the present time.

Jennifer *has worked* at the hospital for ten years.

This sentence indicates that Jennifer began to work at the hospital ten years ago and is still working there now. The following time line shows that the action began ten years ago and continues up to the present time.

Study these other examples of sentences using the present perfect tense:
In each case, the action started in the past and continues up to the present time.

She *has studied* violin since 1980.

I *have* always *appreciated* his generosity.

> The **present perfect tense** can also be used to describe an action that has just taken place or an action that took place at an indefinite time in the past.

An action that has just taken place:

Has Jennifer *found* a job yet?

Jennifer *has* (just) *found* a new job in Kansas City.

An action that took place at an indefinite time:

Have you ever *been* to San Diego?

Yes, I *have been* there three times.

If the time were definite, you would use the simple past:

> Jennifer *found* a new job yesterday.
>
> Yes, I *was* in San Diego last week.

PRACTICE

Complete the following sentences by filling in the blanks with either the simple past tense or the present perfect tense.

1. I _____ to Mexico in 2002.
    (go)

2. I _____ deep-sea diving a few times.
    (go)

3. The drummer in the band _____ percussion since he was five.
    (study)

4. It _____ the jury two hours to reach their verdict yesterday.
    (take)

5. Washington, D.C., _____ the capital of our country for many years.
    (be)

> The **past perfect tense** describes an action completed in the past before another past action or a specific time.

> Jennifer *had worked* at the hospital for ten years before she *moved* away.

In this sentence, there are two past actions: Jennifer *worked* and Jennifer *moved*. The action that took place first is in the past perfect (*had worked*). The action that took place later, but was also completed in the past, is in the simple past (*moved*). The following time line shows that one past action (*had worked*) was completed before another past action (*moved*).

	moment of speaking		
first action in the past	**second action in the past**		
x	x		
PAST	**PRESENT**		**FUTURE**
had worked	moved		

Study these other examples of sentences using the past perfect tense:

> I *had* just *finished* when the bell *rang*.
>
> He *said* that Randall *had told* the class about the experiment.
>
> We *had provided* the information long before last week's meeting.
>
> He *had left* for work by 8 a.m.

NOTE: In informal speech and writing, the simple past tense is often used to express the past perfect tense.

Informal writing or speech:	The child *witnessed* the accident before he ran away.
Formal writing:	The child *had witnessed* the accident before he ran away.

PRACTICE   Complete the following sentences by filling in the blanks with either the present perfect tense or the past perfect tense of the verb given.

1. Mexico City ———————— visitors for many years.
    (fascinate)

2. This city ———————— the third-largest city in the world, and people
    (become)

    ———————— it grow larger every year.
    (watch)

3. The suburbs of the city ———————— old villages that ————————
    (replace)   (exist)

    peacefully since the days of the Aztecs.

4. Yolanda told us that she ———————— in Fort Worth before she moved to
    (live)

    Mexico City.

5. Today, Mexico City ———————— a computer-controlled subway system
    (build)

    to deal with its huge transportation problem.

What Is the Sequence of Tenses?

> The term **sequence of tenses** refers to the logical relationship of verb tenses in sentences that have more than one clause.

If the tense of the independent clause is in the **present** (he *knows*), here are the possibilities for the dependent clause:

Independent clause (IC)	Dependent clause (DC)	Time of the DC in relation to the IC
	that she studies.	same time
He knows	that she studied.	earlier
	that she *will* study.	later

If the tense of the independent clause is in the **past** (he *knew*), here are the possibilities for the dependent clause:

Independent clause (IC)	Dependent clause (DC)	Time of the DC in relation to the IC
	that she studied.	same time
He knew	that she *had* studied.	earlier
	that she *would* study.	later

If the independent clause is in the **future** (he *will know*), here are the possibilities for the dependent clause:

Independent clause (IC)	Dependent clause (DC)	Time of the DC in relation to the IC
	if she studies.	same time
He will know	if she *has* studied.	earlier
	if she *will* study.	later

EXERCISE ❶ **Practicing with Sequence of Tenses**

In each of the following sentences, the verb in the independent clause has been underlined. Choose the correct verb tense for the verb in the dependent clause. Use the examples above if you need help.

1. The program <u>will continue</u> only after the coughing and fidgeting

    _____.
    (stop)

2. Because he was poor and unappreciated by the music world when he

    died in 1791, Mozart <u>did not realize</u> the importance that his music

    _____ in the future.
    (have)

3. Dad <u>will tell</u> us tonight if he _____ a new car next month.
    (buy)

4. Albert Einstein <u>failed</u> the entrance exam at the Swiss Federal Institute

    of Technology because he _____ a very disciplined student.
    (be + never)

5. Einstein <u>studied</u> only subjects that he _____.
    (like)

6. Cancer researchers <u>think</u> it's likely that a cure for most cancers

    _____ found.
    (be + soon)

7. We <u>know</u> that science _____ now close to finding a cure for
    (be)

    leukemia.

8. The interviewer <u>felt</u> that the young woman _____ more than
    (know)

    she was telling him.

9. The doctor went into the operating room. She <u>hoped</u> that the operation

    _____ as planned.
    (go)

10. The doctor came out of the operating room. She <u>said</u> that the operation

    was over and _____ well.
    (go)

EXERCISE 2   **Practicing with Sequence of Tenses**

Complete each of the following sentences, by choosing the verb tense that makes the meaning clear. Circle the letter of the correct answer.

1. It was 2003 and the moment everyone _____ for.
   a. will wait   b. is waiting
   c. had been waiting   d. waits

2. With only a fifteen-second lead and less than a week to go, Lance Armstrong was sprinting up the mountain when his handlebar _____ tangled on a fan's knapsack.
   a. has become   b. became
   c. had become   d. becomes

3. Armstrong _____ on the asphalt and had to remount.
   a. fell   b. falls
   c. had fallen   d. would fall

4. His trainers knew that Armstrong was tired from the effects of a virus he _____ from his three-year-old son.
   a. is catching   b. has caught
   c. catches   d. had caught

5. At the time, Armstrong's coach thought, "This is going to be a good thing because Lance _____ better when he is angry and in pain."
   a. rode   b. is riding
   c. has ridden   d. rides

6. Armstrong's buddy Hamilton continued in the race, even though he _____ his collarbone and was in excruciating pain.
   a. had broken   b. broke
   c. has broken   d. was breaking

7. Because many factors such as illness, bad weather, crashes, and spectator interference _____ predictable, the Tour de France has been one of the world's greatest sporting challenges.
   a. were not   b. are not
   c. had not been   d. would not be

8. Armstrong had predicted that the race _____ tight.
   a. is   b. will be
   c. had been   d. would be

9. "So far," Armstrong says, "this past race _____ to be my most difficult one."
   a. will turn out   b. is turning out
   c. has turned out   d. had turned out

10. Armstrong says he will race again in 2004 if he _____ better prepared.
    a. feels   b. has felt
    c. had been feeling   d. would have felt

Avoiding Unnecessary Shifts in Verb Tense

Unless there is some reason to change tenses, inconsistent shifting from one tense to another should be avoided. Study the following examples:

Shifted tenses: The customer demanded (past tense) to see the manager. He *was* (past tense) angry because every jacket he *tries* on (Why present tense?) *has* (Why present tense?) something wrong with it. A button *was* (past tense) missing on the first, the lining *did* not *hang* (past tense) properly on the second, and the collar *had* (past tense) a stain on the third.

Revised: The customer demanded (past tense) to see the manager. He *was* (past tense) angry because every jacket he *tried* on (past tense) *had* (past tense) something wrong with it. A button *was* (past tense) missing on the first, the lining *did* not *hang* (past tense) properly on the second, and the collar *had* (past tense) a stain on the third.

NOTE: When the subject is a created work, such as a book, play, poem, or piece of music, be especially careful about the verb tense. Although the work was created in the past, it is still enjoyed in the present. In this case, the present tense is used.

Shakespeare's *Hamlet* <u>is</u> a great play. It <u>was written</u> four centuries ago.

EXERCISE **Correcting Unnecessary Shifts in Verb Tense**

Each sentence has an unnecessary shift in verb tense. Revise each sentence so that the tenses remain consistent.

1.   After I complete that writing course, I took the required history course.

2.   In the beginning of the movie, the action was slow; by the end, I am sitting on the edge of my seat.

3.   The textbook gives the rules for writing a bibliography, but it didn't explain how to do footnotes.

4.   While working on her report in the library, my best friend lost her note cards and comes to me for help.

5.   The encyclopedia gave several pages of information about astronomy, but it doesn't give any information about black holes.

6.   "Salvation" was written by Langston Hughes; he tells a powerful story.

7.   This is an exciting book, but it had too many characters.

8.   The senator was doing just fine until along comes a younger and more energetic politician.

9.   At the end of *Gulliver's Travels*, the main character rejects the company of people; he preferred the company of horses.

10.   My sister arrives late, as usual, and complained that her dinner was cold.

EXERCISE **Correcting Unnecessary Shifts in Verb Tense**

The following paragraph contains unnecessary shifts in verb tense. Change each incorrect verb to its proper form.

Charles Dickens was a nineteenth-century author whose work is well known today. One of the reasons Dickens remained so popular is that so many of his stories are available not only as books but also as movies, plays, and television productions. We all knew from our childhood the famous story of Uncle Scrooge and Tiny Tim. Often we saw a television version of *A Christmas Carol* at holiday time. If you have never read the story of Oliver Twist in book form, you might have seen the musical *Oliver!* Also, there was a movie version of *Great Expectations*. Many students still studied *A Tale of Two Cities* in high school. No matter how many adaptations of Dickens's books they see, people seem to agree that there was no substitute for the books themselves. At first, the vocabulary seemed difficult, but if you concentrate on the story and read a chapter or two every day, you will find yourself not only comprehending these wonderful stories but also loving the richness of Dickens's use of language.

EXERCISE **Editing Student Writing: Correcting Unnecessary Shifts in Verb Tense**

The following paragraph was part of an essay written by a first-year college student. It contains unnecessary shifts in verb tense. Revise the paragraph so that verb tenses are consistent.

I remember last year when I was trying to choose the right school and worrying about it a lot. One day, a friend says that, instead of talking about it all the time, I should visit a few places and actually see them. One afternoon, I decide to do just that. I take the bus, get off in the center of town, and from there walked to the campus. It's very clean, with no graffiti on any of the walls. Behind the visitor's desk stood two students passing out brochures on programs and majors. The student union looks inviting, so I went in to get a soda and check it out. I sit down and started listening to the students at the other tables. I was curious to hear bits of their conversations. Students seemed to be treating each other with respect. I did not hear one sarcastic remark, and no one is rude to anyone else. I went to the library and had the same experience. Everyone seems so helpful and friendly. I knew this was the kind of atmosphere I would like. On my way out, I pick up an application from the visitor's desk. Both of the students behind the desk are smiling at me as I leave.

What Is the Difference between the Passive Voice and the Active Voice?

In the **active voice,** the subject is doing something.

The committee made the decision.

> **In general, choose the active voice to achieve direct, economical, and forceful writing. Most writing should be in the active voice.**

In the **passive voice,** something is done to the subject.

The decision was made by the committee.

or

The decision was made.

The first passive sentence de-emphasizes the actor (*the committee*) by moving it out of the subject place. The second passive sentence omits the actor entirely.

> **Choose the passive voice to de-emphasize the actor or to avoid naming the actor altogether.**

Study the three sentences that follow. All three deal with President Kennedy's assassination. The first is in the active voice, and the other two are in the passive voice. Discuss with your classmates and instructor what would cause a writer to choose each of the following sentences to express the same basic fact.

1. Lee Harvey Oswald shot President John F. Kennedy in 1963.
2. President John F. Kennedy was shot by Lee Harvey Oswald in 1963.
3. President John F. Kennedy was shot in 1963.

HOW DO YOU FORM THE PASSIVE VOICE?

A sentence in the passive voice consists of the subject acted upon, followed by a form of the verb *to be* and the past participle. The actor may appear in a *by* phrase at the end.

Forming the Passive Voice

Subject acted upon	+ verb *to be*	+ past participle	+ *by* phrase (optional)
The race	was	won	(by the runner)
The meals	have been	cooked	(by the chef)
The books	are	illustrated	(by the artists)

EXERCISE **6**

Forming Active Voice and Passive Voice

Complete each of the following examples by supplying either the active or the passive voice. Then discuss with the rest of the class the reasons a writer would choose either the active or the passive voice to express each idea.

Active Voice	Passive Voice
1. _____	1. The wrong number was dialed (by the child).
2. _____	2. The sweater was crocheted very carefully (by my grandmother).
	3. _____
3. The tornado struck Cherry Creek last spring.	
4. The wind blew the leaves across the yard.	4. _____
5. _____	5. In the seventies, platform shoes were worn (by many fashionable young men and women).

EXERCISE **7**

Forming Active Voice and Passive Voice

Complete each of the following examples by supplying either the active or the passive voice. Then discuss with the rest of the class the reasons a writer would choose either the active or the passive voice to express each idea.

Active Voice	Passive Voice
1. The jury announced the verdict after five hours of deliberation.	1. _____
2. _____	2. "Blue Suede Shoes" was sung by Elvis Presley.
3. The sleet turned the old municipal building into an ice castle.	3. _____
4. _____	4. The priceless vase was smuggled (by someone) out of the country.
5. _____	5. More concern was shown (by television viewers) over the Super Bowl than over the outbreak of an international conflict.

What Is the Subjunctive Mood?

Verbs in the English language have three possible moods.

1. The **indicative mood** expresses statements of fact:

   He *drives* home every Sunday.

   Most sentences call for the indicative mood.

2. The **imperative mood** expresses commands:

> *Drive* home on Sunday!

3. The **subjunctive mood** expresses conditions contrary to fact:

> *If I were you,* I would drive home on Sunday.

or follows certain verbs of demand or urgency:

> *I insist that he drive* home on Sunday.

Of the three moods possible for verbs in English, the subjunctive mood has the most limited use.

> The **subjunctive mood,** the most limited of the three moods for English verbs, uses special verb forms to express statements contrary to fact or to express demand or urgency after certain verbs.

Below are three instances that call for the subjunctive. In each of these three instances, notice that the *-s* is *not* added in the third person singular present tense.

1. **For unreal conditions introduced with *if* or *wish*, use *were* if the verb is *be*.**

> If he were my teacher, I would be pleased.
>
> I wish he were my teacher.

2. **For clauses starting with *that* after verbs such as *ask, request, demand, suggest, order, insist,* or *command,* use the infinitive form of the verb.**

> I demand that she be on time.
>
> Sullivan insisted that Jones report on Tuesday.

3. **For clauses starting with *that* after adjectives expressing urgency, as in *it is necessary, it is imperative, it is urgent, it is important,* and *it is essential,* use the infinitive form of the verb.**

> It is necessary that she wear a net covering her hair.
>
> She insisted that Robert be ready by five a.m.

PRACTICE

In the following sentences, underline the word or phrase that determines the subjunctive and circle the subjunctive. An example has been done for you.

> Truman suggested that the country adopt the Marshall Plan in 1947.

1. When President Roosevelt died in 1945, the law required that

Vice President Truman take over immediately.

2. It was essential that President Truman act quickly and decisively.

3. Truman must have wished that he were able to avoid using the atomic bomb to bring an end to World War II.

4. He felt it was necessary that the United States help Europe recover from the destruction of World War II.

5. President Truman always insisted that other countries be economically strong.

Knowing How to Use *should | would, used to | supposed to, can | could,* and *will | would*

should/would

Do not use more than one modal auxiliary (*can, may, might, must, should, ought*) with the main verb.

Incorrect:	Joel *shouldn't ought* to sell his car.
Correct:	Joel *ought not* sell his car.
	or
	Joel *shouldn't* sell his car.

Do not use *should of, would of,* or *could of* to mean *should have, would have,* or *could have.*

| **Incorrect:** | Elana *would of* helped you if she *could of.* |
| **Correct:** | Elana *would have* helped you if she *could have.* |

can/could; will/would

Use *could* as the past tense of *can.*

I *see* that he *can do* the job.
I *saw* that he *could do* the job.

Use *would* as the past tense of *will.*

I *see* that he *will do* a good job.
I *saw* that he *would do* a good job.

used to/supposed to

Do not omit the final -*d* in the phrases *used to* and *supposed to.*

Incorrect:	I am *use to* walking to school.
Correct:	I am *used to* walking to school.
Incorrect:	We are *suppose to* meet him for dinner.
Correct:	We are *supposed to* meet him for dinner.

Mastery and Editing Tests

TEST **Using Correct Verb Forms**

Revise each of the following sentences to avoid problems with verbs.

1. He hadn't ought to drive so fast.

   _____

2. The officer said that the motorist drove through a red light.

   _____

HINT: Here two actions took place in the past, one of them preceding the other.

3. I wish I was a senior.

   _____

4. "Araby" was written by James Joyce; it told the story of a young boy's first love.

   _____

5. She is working on the project since 1997.

   _____

6. The map was studied by the motorist. (*Use active voice.*)

   _____

7. My father ask me last night to help him build a deck.

   _____

8. I should of kept the promise I made.

   _____

9. I insist that she keeps her clothes on her side of the room.

   _____

10. Someone washes the floor every Monday. (*Use passive voice.*)

    _____

TEST **Editing Student Writing: Using Correct Verb Forms**

In the following paragraph, change ten verb forms to the correct forms.

[1]When the day arrived, my mother was jubilant. [2]We drive to the synagogue. [3]My aunt Sophie and her daughters come with us. [4]Once in the temple, the women were separated from the men. [5]They sat upstairs in their assigned places. [6]I was ask to keep my hat on and was given a shawl to wear that I seen before. [7]I was suppose to wait for the rabbi to call me. [8]My turn finally comes. [9]I walked up to a table in the front. [10]There I read from the sacred scriptures in Hebrew. [11]My mother had told me that if I was to read the scriptures fluently, she would be very proud. [12]I knew I could of read louder, but I was nervous. [13]Afterward, I was taken by my family to a fine kosher restaurant for a celebration. (*Change to the active voice.*) [14]There I receive a beautiful gold charm bracelet.

TEST **3**   **Editing Student Writing: Using Correct Verb Forms**

In the following paragraph, change ten verb forms to the correct forms.

¹My semester of chemistry seemed ill-fated from the very start. ²When I lost my textbook the first week of classes, I should of known I was in for trouble. ³The second week, I had the flu and miss two classes. ⁴On the following Monday, when I finally start off for class again, the bus was so delayed that I walked into the classroom half an hour late. ⁵The teacher scowls at me and ask to speak to me after class. ⁶I always use to sit in the front row so I could see the board and hear the lectures. ⁷Because I am late, I will have to take a seat in the last row. ⁸I wish I was able to start this class over again the right way. ⁹No one had ought to have such an unlucky start in any class.

TEST **4**   **Editing Student Writing: Using Correction Symbols**

In the paragraph below, find four errors with verbs (**vb**), one error in parallel structure (**//**), one dangling modifier (**dm**), one fragment (**frag**), one error in subordination (**subord**), one run-on (**ro**), and one subject-verb agreement error (**agr**). Mark the errors with the commonly used correction symbols, and then correct the errors on the lines provided after the paragraph.

¹Our college professor was amazed last year when a man comes to our English class to deliver a pizza to a student. ²The student later explained that he missed lunch. ³The professor was surprised that the student seen no problem with this incident. ⁴The pizza was confiscated. ⁵Across America today, cell phones and other electronic gadgets in the classrooms are a cause for concern among teachers, administrators, and sometimes even students are getting upset. ⁶Going off in class, the lessons are disturbed by cell phones. ⁷Some students leave classes, they go out into the hallways to make calls. ⁸Others play video games or watch movies, that they have downloaded onto their laptops. ⁹Cheating with handheld organizers and cell phone messaging are also problematic for teachers. ¹⁰At the college I attend, many professors have made policies regarding electronic devices in their classrooms. ¹¹Banning these devices is suppose to result in a more controlled classroom. ¹²I am not convinced this is a good idea. ¹³Because a student may urgently need to communicate with someone.

Four verb corrections

1. _____

2. _____

3. _____

4. _____

Parallel structure correction

5. _____

_____

_____

Dangling modifier correction

6. _____

Corrected fragment

7. _____

_____

Subordination correction

8. _____

_____

Corrected run-on

9. _____

_____

Subject-verb agreement correction

      Subject   **Correct form of the verb**

10. _____   _____

Exploring Online

Go to academic.cengage.com/devenglish/scarry to find the **Writer's Online Workplace,** a website designed for students using this book. You will find links to handouts, interactive quizzes, and other online resources as you explore the following topics:

- verb tense consistency
- active and passive voice
- subjunctive mood

Working Together

Problem Solving: Integrity in the Workplace

Recently, a young office worker went to his superior and reported that a fellow worker was incorrectly reporting the company's profits. It was clear that the intention was to give the impression the company was doing better than it really was. His superior told the young worker not to worry about the situation, and that he himself would take care of it. Before long, this same worker was let go. He believed he was fired because of his honesty, and he began to suspect a conspiracy of dishonesty among the others in his company. The worker may have paid a high price for being a whistleblower: he lost his job.

The lack of integrity in today's workplace has reached the level of a national disgrace. Consider the following list of scandals that have reached the public's awareness in recent years.

- Enron deceives its shareholders by pretending it is profitable when it is not.
- The lobbyist Jack Abramoff defrauds Indian tribes by promising them favors he cannot or will not act upon.
- Red Cross workers steal money donated for the victims of Hurricane Katrina.
- Government officials attempt to silence a NASA scientist when he tries to publish his findings on global warming.
- Two New York City police officials are found guilty of secretly murdering people for the Mafia instead of protecting the lives of their citizens.

Working in Groups

Divide into groups. Each group should develop a presentation in which an account of dishonesty in the workplace is given. It may be an actual situation a member of the group has personally observed, or it may be a current scandal that has just made the news. Part of each group's presentation should include a list of the steps the employee should take. Do not forget to consider what precautions the employee should take to protect himself or herself.

Each member of the class should take notes during the presentations and jot down questions, along with any points of disagreement. After all the presentations have been given, determine if the class agrees or disagrees on the process that an employee should follow if he or she uncovers dishonesty in the workplace.

Portfolio Suggestion

All groups (charitable organizations, educational institutions, political institutions, and social institutions) are affected by dishonesty. Depending on your interests and job goals, you might want to study how a scandal or case of corruption has affected one of these institutions. A fascinating research paper could develop from the notes you save from the class presentations.

215

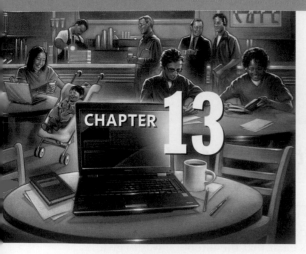

CHAPTER 13

Using Correct Capitalization and Punctuation

In this chapter, you will learn the basic rules of capitalization and punctuation that govern English. Many of these rules you undoubtedly know already:

CHAPTER OBJECTIVES

- ten basic rules for **capitalization**
- ten basic uses of the **comma**
- three uses for the **apostrophe**
- four uses for **quotation marks**
- three uses for the **semicolon**
- four uses for the **colon**
- use of the **dash** and **parentheses**

In college and at work, you will have to be in control of capitalization and punctuation. When is a word important enough to need a capital letter? Where are commas needed in a sentence? These and other questions will be answered when you know the fundamental rules and how to apply them. Carefully study the examples that are given under each rule. Notice that you will often learn how to capitalize and punctuate by learning what *not* to do.

Ten Basic Rules for Capitalization

RULE 1 | **Capitalize the first word of every sentence.**

Every building was old. Our house was the oldest.

RULE 2 | **Capitalize the names of specific things and places.**

Specific buildings:

I went to the Jamestown Post Office.
   but
I went to the post office.

Specific streets, cities, states, and countries:

She lives on Elam Avenue.
   but
She lives on the same street as my mom and dad.

Specific organizations:

He collected money for the March of Dimes.
> but
He collected money for his favorite charity.

Specific institutions:

The loan is from the First National Bank.
> but
The loan is from one of the banks in town.

Specific bodies of water:

My uncle fishes every summer on Lake Michigan.
> but
My uncle spends every summer at the lake.

RULE 3
Capitalize days of the week, months of the year, and holidays. Do not capitalize the names of seasons.

The last Thursday in November is Thanksgiving Day.
> but
I cannot wait until spring.

RULE 4
Capitalize the names of all languages, nationalities, races, religions, deities, and sacred terms.

My friend who is Ethiopian speaks very little English.
The Koran is the sacred book of Islam.

RULE 5
Capitalize the first word and every important word in a title. Do not capitalize articles, prepositions, or short connecting words unless they begin the title.

For Whom the Bell Tolls is a famous novel by Ernest Hemingway.
Her favorite short story is "A Rose for Emily."

RULE 6
Capitalize the first word of a direct quotation.

The teacher said, "You have been chosen for the part."
> but
"You have been chosen," she said, "for the part."

NOTE: In the second sentence, *for* is not capitalized because it is a continuation of the sentence in quotation marks.

RULE 7 **Capitalize historical events, periods, and documents.**

The American Revolution
The Colonial Period
The Bill of Rights

RULE 8 **Capitalize the words *north*, *south*, *east*, and *west* when they are used as places rather than as geographical directions.**

He comes from the Midwest.
> but
The farm is about twenty miles west of Omaha.

RULE 9 **Capitalize people's names.**

Proper names:

Charles Wong

Professional titles when they are used with the person's proper name:

Judge Lowry   but   the judge
Professor Shapiro but   the professor

Terms for relatives (mother, sister, nephew, uncle) when they are used in the place of proper names:

I told Grandfather I would meet him later.
> but
I told my grandfather I would meet him later.

NOTE: Terms for relatives are not capitalized if a pronoun, article, or adjective is used with the name.

RULE 10 **Capitalize brand names.**

Lipton's Noodle Soup but noodle soup
Velveeta Cheese   but cheese

EXERCISE ① **Capitalization**

In each of the following sentences correct any word that requires capitalization.

1. The italian student got a job in the school cafeteria.

2. Our train ride through the canadian rockies was fabulous.

3. The author often made references in his writing to the torah.

4.   A student at the university of delaware was chosen for the national award.

5.   My uncle's children always have a party on halloween.

6.   I met the president of american telephone and telegraph company last friday at a convention in portland, oregon.

7.   In 1863, president Lincoln wrote his famous emancipation proclamation.

8.   My niece asked, "why don't you consider moving farther south if you hate the winter so much?"

9.   The united auto workers voted not to go on strike over the new contract.

10. A very popular radio program in the east is called *a prairie home companion.*

EXERCISE **Capitalization**

In each of the following sentences correct any word that requires capitalization.

1.   Every tuesday, the general visits the hospital.

2.   On one level, the book *the lord of the rings* can be read as a fairy tale; on another level, the book can be read as a christian allegory.

3.   The golden gate bridge in san francisco may be the most beautiful bridge in the world.

4.   She is the sister of my french teacher.

5.   I've always wanted to take a trip to the far east in spring.

6.   The kremlin, located in moscow, once housed the soviet government.

7.   I needed to see dr. Ghavami, but the nurse told me the doctor would not be in until next week.

8.   He shouted angrily, "why don't you ever arrive at your history class on time?"

9.   The scholastic aptitude test will be given on january 18.

10. While yet a teenager growing up in harlem, james Baldwin became a baptist preacher.

EXERCISE **Capitalization**

In each of the following sentences correct any word that requires capitalization.

1.   The lawyer's office is located on south pleasant street.

2.   My uncle lives farther south than grandmother.

3.   I'd like to move to the south if I could find a job there.

4.   The well-known anthropologist Margaret Mead was for many years director of the museum of natural history in new york city.

5.   The constitution of the united states was signed in constitution hall on september 17, 1787.

6.   Sculptor John Wilson was commissioned to create a bust of rev. Martin Luther King jr.

7.   The project will be funded partly with money from the national endowment for the arts.

8.   I read the magazine article in *newsweek* while I was waiting in the dentist's office yesterday.

9.   The tour took the retired teachers above the arctic circle.

10. Many gerber baby foods no longer have sugar and salt.

Ten Basic Uses of the Comma

You may feel uncertain about when to use a comma. The starting point is to concentrate on a few basic rules. These rules will cover most of your needs.

The tendency now in English is to use fewer commas than in the past. There is no one complete set of rules on which everyone agrees. However, if you learn these ten basic uses, your common sense will help you figure out what to do in other cases. Remember that a comma usually signifies a pause in a sentence. As you read a sentence out loud, listen to where you pause within the sentence. A pause is often a clue that a comma is needed. Notice that in each of the examples for the following ten uses, you can pause where the comma is placed.

RULE 1

Use a comma to separate three or more items in a series.

No comma is used for only two items:

He was *silent and lonely.*

Commas are used to separate three or more items in a series. These items can be composed of words, phrases, or clauses.

Three words (in this case, adjectives) in a series:

He was *silent, lonely,* and *afraid.*

Three phrases (in this case, verb phrases) in a series:

He *ran in the race, finished among the top ten,* and *collapsed happily on the ground.*

NOTE: It is also considered acceptable to omit the comma before the *and* that introduces the last item in the series:

He was *silent, lonely* and *afraid.*

RULE 2

Use a comma to set off parts of dates, addresses, and geographical names.

I was born on August 18, 1965, in the middle of a hurricane.
I lived at 428 North Monroe Street, Madison, Wisconsin, for many years.
I dreamed of spending a semester in Quito, Ecuador, to study art.

RULE 3

Use a comma to set off a number of adjectives that modify a noun.

I carried my *favorite, old, green* coat.

Sometimes two adjectives in front of a noun go together to give a distinct meaning. In this case, they would not be separated by commas:

I carried my favorite, *dark green* coat.

The words *dark* and *green* belong together to give the meaning of a single color: *dark* modifies the color *green,* and the two words together describe the color of the coat.

PRACTICE

In each of the following sentences, insert commas wherever they are needed.

1. On November 14 1977 officials discovered a major body of polluted water in Oswego New York.

2. Problems with the water supply of the United States Europe Canada and other parts of the world are growing.

3. Water is colorless tasteless odorless and free of calories.

4. You will use on an average day twenty-four gallons of water for flushing thirty-two gallons for bathing and washing clothes and twenty-five gallons for other uses.

5. It took 120 gallons of water to create the eggs you ate for breakfast 3,500 gallons for the steak you might eat for dinner and more than 60,000 gallons to produce the steel used to make your car.

RULE 4

Use a comma along with a coordinating conjunction to combine two simple sentences (also called independent clauses) into a single compound sentence. (See Chapter 6 on coordination.)

The house was on fire, but I was determined not to leave my place of safety.

Be careful to use the comma with the conjunction only when you are combining sentences. When you are combining words or phrases, no comma is used.

My sister was safe but not happy.

My mother and father were searching for her.

She was neither in class nor at work.

PRACTICE

In each of the following sentences, insert commas wherever they are needed.

1. The most overused bodies of water are our rivers but they continue to serve us daily.

2. American cities often developed next to rivers and industries followed soon after in the same locations.

3. The people of the Industrial Age can try to clean the water they have used or they can watch pollution take over.

4. The Great Lakes are showing signs of renewal yet the struggle against pollution there must continue.

5. Many people have not yet been educated about the dangers to our water supply nor are all our legislators fully aware of the problem.

RULE 5 · **Use a comma to follow introductory words, expressions, phrases, or clauses.**

● introductory words (such as *yes, no, oh, well*):

> Oh, I never thought he would do it.

● introductory expressions (transitions such as *as a matter of fact, finally, secondly, furthermore, therefore*):

> Therefore, I will give you a second chance.

● introductory phrases:

Long prepositional phrase:	In the beginning of the course, I thought I would never be able to do the work.
Participial phrase:	Walking on tiptoe, the young mother quietly peeked into the nursery.
Infinitive phrase:	To be quite honest, I don't believe he's feeling well.

● introductory dependent clauses beginning with a subordinating conjunction:

> When the food arrived, we all grabbed for it.

(For more examples, see Chapter 7 on subordination.)

PRACTICE   In each of the following sentences, insert commas wherever they are needed.

1. To many people from the East the plans to supply more water to the western states seem unnecessary.

2. However people in the West know that they have no future without a good water supply.

3. When they entered Salt Lake Valley in 1847 the Mormons found dry soil that needed water before crops could be grown.

4. Confidently the new settlers dug ditches that brought the needed water.

5. Learning from the past modern farmers are trying to cooperate with nature.

RULE 6 · **Use commas surrounding a word, phrase, or clause when the word or group of words interrupts the main idea.**

● interrupting word:

> We will, however, take an X-ray.

- interrupting phrase:

    Prepositional phrase: I wanted, *of course,* to stay.

    Appositive phrase: Mariella, *the girl with the braids,* has a wicked sense of humor.

- interrupting clause:

    He won't, I think, try that again.

    Mariella, who wears braids, has a wicked sense of humor.

Sometimes the same word, phrase, or clause can be used in more than one way, and the way the word is used determines the rule for punctuation. For example, consider the word *however.* Use commas if the word interrupts in the middle of a clause:

We will, *however,* take an X-ray.

Use a semicolon and a comma if the word connects two independent clauses:

We will take an X-ray; *however,* the doctor cannot read it today.

Now consider the example of the relative clause *who wears braids.* Use commas if the clause interrupts and is not essential to the main idea:

My sister, *who wears braids,* has a wicked sense of humor.

Do not use commas if the clause is part of the identity, necessary to the main idea:

The girl *who wears braids* is my sister.

> **NOTE:** The clause *who wears braids* is necessary for identifying which girl is the sister.

PRACTICE

In each of the following sentences, insert commas wherever they are needed.

1. Some parts of our country I believe do not have ample supplies of water.
2. The rocky soil of Virginia for example cannot absorb much rainwater.
3. Johnstown, Pennsylvania an industrial city of forty-eight thousand is situated in one of the most flood-prone valleys of America.
4. It is not therefore a very safe place to live.
5. The Colorado which is one of our longest rivers gives up most of its water to farmers and cities before it reaches the sea.

RULE 7
Use commas around nouns in direct address. (A noun in direct address is the name or title used in speaking to someone.)

I thought, Rosa, that I saw your picture in the paper.

PRACTICE

In each of the following sentences, insert commas wherever they are needed.

1. Dear your tea is ready now.
2. I wonder Jason if the game has been canceled.
3. Dad could I borrow five dollars?

4. I insist sir on speaking with the manager.

5. Kim is that you?

RULE 8   **Use commas in numbers of one thousand or larger.**

1,999

1,999,999,999

PRACTICE   In each of the following numbers, insert commas wherever they are needed.

1. 4876454

2. 87602

3. 156439600

4. 187000

5. 10000000000000

RULE 9   **Use a comma to set off exact words spoken in dialogue.**

"Let them," she said, "eat cake."

NOTE: Commas (as well as periods) are placed inside the quotation marks.

PRACTICE   In each of the following sentences, insert commas wherever they are needed.

1. "I won't" he insisted "be a part of your scheme."

2. He mumbled "I plead the Fifth Amendment."

3. "I was told" the defendant explained "to answer every question."

4. "This court case" the judge announced "will be televised."

5. "The jury" said Al Tarvin of the press "was handpicked."

RULE 10   **Use a comma wherever it is necessary to prevent a misunderstanding.**

Before eating, the cat prowled through the barn.

PRACTICE   In each of the following sentences, insert commas wherever they are needed.

1. Kicking the child was carried off to bed.

2. To John Russell Baker is the best columnist.

3. When you can come and visit us.

4. We surveyed the students in the class; out of the twenty seven were married.

5. Some types of skin cancers can kill doctors say.

EXERCISE **Using the Comma Correctly**

In each of the following sentences, insert commas wherever they are needed.

1. In Weaverville California the local high school administrators made an interesting discovery.

2. At a cost of four hundred dollars a year per student a private company was offering college-level advanced placement courses on the web.

3. Because some students need these courses to get into more competitive colleges everyone thought this would be a perfect way to take advantage of the new technology.

4. The problems however soon became apparent when two students signed up for a government course.

5. Brian Jones a senior who wants to be a record producer and Jeremy Forbes a classmate who dreams of being a cartoonist found these problems very frustrating.

6. Their worst problems were long delays getting online many technical glitches and the absence of a teacher to encourage persistence.

7. Out of six hundred students who enrolled in one of the company's online courses last year two-thirds did not complete enough course work to take the final exam.

8. Government officials have praised the use of this electronic support for schools but others say online courses are a poor replacement for the 180000 new teachers the country really needs.

9. Still others worry that too many cyberspace offerings provide only supplemental services such as SAT training college counseling and virtual field trips.

10. Francisco J. Hernandez an educator at the University of California at Santa Cruz says "Our intent is not to be an alternative to a high-quality teacher and classroom but to be an alternative to nothing because that's what students are getting right now."

EXERCISE 5

Using the Comma Correctly

In each of the following sentences, insert commas wherever they are needed.

1. Abraham Lincoln was born on February 12 1809 in Kentucky.

2. In 1816 after selling most of their possessions the Lincoln family moved to Indiana.

3. During their first weeks in Indiana the family hunted for food drank melted snow and huddled together for warmth.

4. After a little formal education Lincoln worked on a ferryboat on the Ohio River.

5. The first large city that Lincoln visited was New Orleans an important center of trade in 1828.

6. Among the 40000 people living in New Orleans at the time of Lincoln's visit there were people from every state and several foreign countries.

7. New Orleans also showed Lincoln such city luxuries as fancy clothes gleaming silverware expensive furniture and imported china and glassware.

8. As a result of this visit Lincoln must have compared the log cabin of his childhood with the wealthy houses of the big city.

9. A few years later Lincoln became a merchant but his failure in business left him in debt for more than ten years.

10. We should be grateful that Lincoln who started off in a business career turned his attention to politics.

EXERCISE **6**   **Using the Comma Correctly**

In each of the following examples, insert commas wherever they are needed.

1. The Hope Diamond is one of the most famous if not *the* most famous gems in the world.

2. Mined in India the diamond reached Europe in 1668 along with the story that there was a curse on the stone.

3. The curse or so the legend goes is that bad fortune followed the diamond because it had been stolen from a temple in India.

4. Nearly all of its owners including Queen Marie Antoinette of France a French actress who was shot to death and an American woman whose children were killed in accidents have met with tragedy.

5. Well if we cannot share in the history of the Hope Diamond we can see it in the Smithsonian Institution in our nation's capital.

6. Other gems not as famous have served people throughout history as payments for ransom as bribes and as lavish wedding presents.

7. One of the most famous mines in South America is an emerald mine started in 1537 in Colombia.

8. As the earth's crust erodes rough stones may find their way into streams rivers and other bodies of water.

9. The greatest quantity of diamonds emeralds amethysts topazes and other precious and semiprecious stones is to be found in Africa and South America.

10. We could travel to these places if we had the time the money and the interest.

Three Uses for the Apostrophe

RULE 1   **Use an apostrophe to form the possessive.**

- Add *'s* to any singular noun:

    the pen of the teacher   = the teacher**'s** pen
    the strategy of the boss = the boss**'s** strategy
    the wheel of the car   = the car**'s** wheel

Be careful to choose the right noun when you form the possessive. Always ask yourself *who* or *what* possesses something. In the previous examples, the teacher possesses the pen, the boss possesses the strategy, and the car possesses the wheel. Note the following unusual possessives:

Hyphenated words: mother-in-law**'s** advice
Joint possession: Lucy and Desi**'s** children
Individual possession: John**'s** and Steve**'s** ideas

● Add *'s* to any irregular plural noun that does not end in *-s:*

the hats of the children = the children**'s** hats

the harness of the oxen = the oxen**'s** harness

● Add *'s* to most indefinite pronouns:

everyone**'s** responsibility

somebody**'s** wallet

another**'s** problem

> **NOTE:** A **possessive pronoun** (*his, hers, its, ours, yours, theirs, whose*) never takes an apostrophe.
>
> > *Whose* key is this?
> > The key is *his.*
> > The car is *theirs.*

● Add only an apostrophe (without *-s*) to a regular plural noun that ends in *-s:*

the coats of the ladies   = the ladies**'** coats

the store of the brothers = the brothers**'** store

● A few singular nouns ending in the *s* or *z* sound are awkward to pronounce if another *s* sound is added. In those cases, the final *-s* is optional. Let your ear help you make the decision.

Jesus' robe   or   Jesus's robe

Moses' law   or   Moses's law

RULE 2

Use *'s* to form certain plurals to prevent confusion.

● letters of the alphabet:

When he writes, all his *a***'s** look like *o***'s.**

● abbreviations with periods:

My sisters both have PhD**'s** from Berkeley.

● words referred to in a text:

He uses too many *you know***'s** when he speaks.

> **NOTE:** Never use an apostrophe to form any other plurals.

RULE 3

Use an apostrophe to show where one or more letters have been omitted in a contraction.

---

cannot   = can't

should not = shouldn't

will not   = won't (This is the only commonly used contraction that
                changes its spelling.)

I am   = I'm

she will   = she'll

EXERCISE **7**

Using the Apostrophe

Fill in each of the blanks below with the correct form of the word, following the rules for using the apostrophe.

1. rays of the sun   the _____ rays
2. the reputation of the press   the _____ reputation.
3. length of the room   the _____ length
4. the house of Anthony and Maria
   (*joint possession*)   _____ house
5. the idea of nobody   _____ idea
6. The book belongs to him.   The book is _____.
7. in the reign of Queen Elizabeth   in _____
8. That is her opinion. (*form a contraction*) _____ her opinion.
9. shirts for boys   _____ shirts
10. the cover of the book   the _____ cover

EXERCISE **8**

Using the Apostrophe

Fill in each of the blanks below with the correct form of the word, following the rules for using the apostrophe.

1. clarity of the diamond   the _____ clarity
2. the flight of the geese   the _____ flight
3. the work of Ann and Chris
   (*individual possession*)   _____ work
4. the plan of someone   _____ plan
5. The drums belong to her.   The drums are _____.
6. the testimony of the witness   the _____
7. We cannot leave yet. (*form a contraction*) We _____ leave yet.
8. the leaves of the tree   the _____ leaves
9. the cheese of the farmers   the _____ cheese
10. the lifestyle of my brother-in-law   my _____ lifestyle

EXERCISE **9**

Using the Apostrophe

Fill in each of the blanks below with the correct form of the word, following the rules for using the apostrophe.

1. the engine of the train   the _____ engine
2. the spirit of the class   the _____ spirit
3. the center for women   the _____ center
4. the wish of everybody   _____ wish
5. The toys belong to them.   The toys are _____.
6. The child mixes up *b* and *d*.
   (*use the plural*)   The child mixes up _____.

7. I will not leave this house. (*form a contraction*)   I _____ leave this house.

8. the grain of the wood   the _____ grain

9. the verdict of the jurors   the _____ verdict

10. the policies of Ridge School and
    Orchard School (*individual possession*)   _____ policies

Four Uses for Quotation Marks

RULE 1   **Use quotation marks for a direct quotation (a speaker's exact words).**

"Please," I begged, "go away."

Do not use quotation marks for an indirect quotation (reporting a speaker's words).

I begged her to go away.

RULE 2   **Use quotation marks for material copied word for word from a source.**

According to the *New York Times,* "The average adult body contains 40 to 50 quarts of water. Blood is 83 percent water; muscles are 75 percent water; the brain is 74 percent water; and even bone is 22 percent water."

RULE 3   **Use quotation marks for titles of shorter works such as short stories, one-act plays, poems, articles in magazines and newspapers, songs, essays, and chapters of books.**

"A Modest Proposal," an essay by Jonathan Swift, is a masterpiece of satire.

"The Lottery," a short story by Shirley Jackson, created a sensation when it first appeared in the *New Yorker.*

NOTE: The title of a full-length work (such as a book, a play of several acts, a magazine, or a newspaper) is italicized in print and underlined when handwritten.

| **In print:** | Many famous short stories have first appeared in the *New Yorker.* |
| **Handwritten form:** | *Many famous short stories have first appeared in the New Yorker.* |

RULE 4   **Use quotation marks for terms referred to in a special way.**

"Duckie" is a term of affection used by the British, in the same way we would use the word "honey."

PRACTICE

In each of the following sentences, insert quotation marks wherever they are needed.

1. The Gift of the Magi is one of the short stories in O. Henry's book *The Four Million*.

2. Franklin Delano Roosevelt said, We have nothing to fear but fear itself.

3. The president told his cabinet that they would have to settle the problem in the next few days.

4. The term punk refers to a particular form of rock music.

5. She read the article Trouble in Silicon Valley in a recent issue of *Newsweek*.

If these five sentences had been handwritten, which words would have been underlined?

Three Uses for the Semicolon

RULE 1	**Use a semicolon to join two independent clauses whose ideas or sentence structures are related.**

He decided to consult the map; she decided to ask a pedestrian.

RULE 2	**Use a semicolon in front of an adverbial conjunction used to combine two sentences.**

He decided to consult the map; however, she decided to ask a pedestrian.

RULE 3	**Use a semicolon to separate items in a series when the items themselves contain commas.**

I had lunch with Linda, my best friend; Mrs. Armstrong, my English teacher; and Jan, my sister-in-law.

NOTE: If the writer had used only commas to separate the items in this example, the reader might think five or six people had gone to lunch together.

PRACTICE

In each of the following sentences, insert a semicolon wherever needed.

1. One of the best ways to remember a vacation is to take numerous photos one of the best ways to recall the contents of a book is to take notes.

2. The problem of street crime must be solved otherwise, the number of vigilantes will increase.

3. The committee was made up of Kevin Corey, a writer Anita Poindexter, a professor and Jorge Rodriguez, a politician.

4. The bank president was very cordial however, he would not approve the loan.

5. The retailer wants higher profits the customer wants lower cost.

Four Uses for the Colon

RULE 1

Use a colon after an independent clause when the material that follows is a series of items, an illustration, or an explanation.

- a series of items:

    Please order the following items: five dozen pencils, twenty rulers, and five rolls of tape.

Notice that in the sentence below, no colon is used because there is not a complete sentence before the list.

    The courses I am taking this semester are Freshman Composition, Introduction to Psychology, Art Appreciation, and Survey of American Literature.

- an explanation or illustration:

    She was an exceptional child: at seven she was performing on the concert stage.

Do not use a colon directly after a verb; after the preposition *except* or *regarding;* or after the expression *such as, for example, especially,* or *including.*

RULE 2

Use a colon for the salutation of a business letter.

Dear Sales Office Manager:
Dear President Gonzalas:

RULE 3

Use a colon when using numerals to indicate time.

We will eat at 5:15.

RULE 4

Use a colon between the title and the subtitle of a book.

Plain English Please: A Rhetoric

PRACTICE

In each of the following sentences, insert colons wherever they are needed.

1. Three pianists played in New York on the same weekend André Watts, Claudio Arrau, and Jorge Bolet.
2. The official has one major flaw in his personality greed.
3. The restaurant has lovely homemade desserts such as German chocolate layer cake and baked Alaska.
4. The college offers four courses in English literature Romantic Poetry, Shakespeare's Plays, The British Short Story, and The Modern Novel.
5. Arriving at 6 15 in the morning, Marlene brought me a sausage and cheese pizza, soda, and a gallon of ice cream.

Use of the Dash and Parentheses

Commas, dashes, and parentheses can all be used to show an interruption of the main idea. The particular form of punctuation you choose depends on the degree of interruption.

RULE 1

Use dashes for a less formal and more emphatic interruption of the main idea. Dashes are seldom used in formal writing.

He came—I thought—by car.

She arrived—and I know this for a fact—in a pink Cadillac.

RULE 2

Use parentheses to insert extra information that some of your readers might want to know but that is not at all essential for the main idea. Such information is not emphasized.

Johann Sebastian Bach (1685–1750) composed the six Brandenburg Concertos.

Plea bargaining (see Section 4.3) was developed to speed court verdicts.

PRACTICE   Insert dashes or parentheses wherever needed.

1. Herbert Simon is and I don't think this is an exaggeration a genius.
2. George Eliot her real name was Mary Ann Evans wrote *Silas Marner.*
3. You should in fact, I insist see a doctor.
4. Unemployment brings with it a number of other problems see the study by Brody, 1982.
5. Mass media television, radio, movies, magazines, and newspapers are able to transmit information over a wide range and to a large number of people.

EXERCISE **Other Marks of Punctuation**

In each of the following sentences, insert marks of punctuation wherever they are needed. Choose from quotation marks, semicolon, colon, dashes, and parentheses.

1. To measure crime, sociologists have used three different techniques official statistics, victimization surveys, and self-report studies.
2. The Bells is one of the best-loved poems of Edgar Allan Poe.
3. The lake has one major disadvantage to swimmers this summer weeds.
4. E. B. White wrote numerous essays for adults however, he also wrote some very popular books for children.
5. Tuberculosis also known as consumption has once again become a serious health issue.
6. The Victorian Period 1837–1901 saw a rapid expansion of industry.

7. He promised me I know he promised that he would come to my graduation.

8. Do you know what the French expression déjà vu means?

9. She wanted to go to the movies he wanted to stay home and watch a movie on the DVD player.

10. She has the qualifications needed for the job a teaching degree, a pleasant personality, two years' experience, and a love of children.

EXERCISE **Other Marks of Punctuation**

In each of the following sentences, insert marks of punctuation wherever they are needed. Choose from quotation marks, semicolon, colon, dashes, and parentheses.

1. Many young people have two feelings about science and technology awe and fear.

2. The three people who helped work out the real estate transaction were Mr. Doyle, the realtor Mrs. White, the bank officer and Scott Castle, the lawyer.

3. The book was titled *English Literature The Victorian Age.*

4. I decided to walk to school, she said, because the bus fare has been raised again.

5. She brought the following items to the beach a bathing suit, towel, sunglasses, and several books.

6. The conference I believe it is scheduled for sometime in January will focus on the development of a new curriculum.

7. The song Memories comes from the Broadway show *Cats.*

8. The complex lab experiment has these two major problems too many difficult calculations and too many variables.

9. The mutt that is to say, my dog is smarter than he looks.

10. Violent crime cannot be reduced unless the society supports efforts such as strengthening the family structure, educating the young, and recruiting top-notch police.

EXERCISE **Other Marks of Punctuation**

In each of the following sentences, insert marks of punctuation wherever they are needed. Choose from quotation marks, semicolon, colon, dashes, and parentheses.

1. Star Wars is the popular term for the development of atomic weapons for use in space.

2. My father enjoyed spending money my mother was frugal.

3. The student's short story Ten Steps to Nowhere appeared in a collection titled *The Best of Student Writing.*

4. The report stated specifically that the company must if it wants to grow sell off at least 10 percent of its property.

5. The foreign countries she visited were Mexico, Israel, and Morocco.

6. Remember, the doctor told the patient, the next time I see you, I want to see an improvement in your condition.

7. These students made the high honor roll Luis Sanchez, Julie Carlson, and Tenesha Moore.

8. The scientist showed the students a glass of H_2O water and asked them to identify the liquid.

9. He said that he would give us an extension on our term papers.

10. The work was tedious nevertheless, the goal of finding the solution kept him motivated.

Mastery and Editing Tests

TEST **Editing for Correct Capitalization and Punctuation**

In the following sentences, each underlined portion may contain an error. If an error exists, circle the letter of the proper correction. If there is no error, circle the letter for "No change is necessary."

1. An <u>article</u> titled <u>"The Biker Question: To Roar or Not to Roar"</u> appeared in the *New York Times* on <u>Friday July 25, 2003.</u>

    a. Article
    b. "The biker question: To roar or not to roar"
    c. Friday, July 25, 2003.
    d. No change is necessary.

2. Motorcycle <u>enthusiasts have a choice, they can</u> have their engines run <u>quietly, or they can</u> replace the <u>exhaust systems and assault people</u> with the loud noise.

    a. enthusiasts have a choice: they can
    b. quietly or they can
    c. exhaust systems, and assault people
    d. No change is necessary.

3. <u>Wayne Doenges, a seventy-five-year-old retired engineer,</u> rides the roads of Indiana on his quietly running, chromed-out, six-cylinder <u>Honda Valkyrie.</u>

    a. Wayne Doenges, a seventy-five-year-old retired Engineer,
    b. Wayne Doenges a seventy-five-year-old retired engineer
    c. honda valkyrie
    d. No change is necessary.

4. <u>My bike attracts attention he boasts in a positive way.</u>

    a. "My bike attracts attention" He boasts "In a positive way."
    b. "My bike attracts attention," he boasts, "in a positive way."
    c. "My bike attracts attention, he boasts, in a positive way."
    d. No change is necessary.

5. <u>Other bikers however prefer</u> the thunderous noise from special exhaust systems that have no noise dampening system.

    a. Other bikers, however, prefer
    b. Other bikers; however, prefer
    c. Other Bikers however prefer
    d. No change is necessary.

6. Sometimes these two groups meet at the <u>American Motorcycle Rally</u> that is held <u>every Summer in June at Lake George, New York.</u>

   a. american motorcycle rally
   b. every Summer in june at Lake George, New York.
   c. every summer in June at Lake George, New York.
   d. No change is necessary.

7. For Rick <u>Gray, a lawyer from Lancaster, Pennsylvania,</u> riding a quiet motorcycle is like a form of <u>Buddhist meditation.</u>

   a. Gray, a Lawyer from Lancaster, Pennsylvania,
   b. Gray a lawyer from Lancaster Pennsylvania
   c. buddhist meditation
   d. No change is necessary.

8. <u>Mr. Gray, who is the Chairman of the American Motorcycle Association,</u> owns thirteen <u>motorcycles and rides 20,000 to 35,000 miles each year.</u>

   a. Mr. Gray, who is the chairman of the American Motorcycle Association,
   b. Mr. Gray, who is the Chairman of the American Motorcycle association,
   c. motorcycles, and rides 20000 to 35000 miles each year.
   d. No change is necessary.

9. <u>Vice President Pamela Amette</u> of the <u>Motorcycle Industry Council</u> says, "<u>it's illegal to install</u> an exhaust system that does not meet federal requirements."

   a. Vice president Pamela Amette
   b. motorcycle industry council
   c. "It's illegal to install
   d. No change is necessary.

10. Although some bikers think a loud level of noise will warn cars and trucks of their <u>presence, a study</u> done by <u>the university of California at Los Angeles</u> shows that the level of noise does not decrease the chance of accidents.

    a. presence; a study
    b. presence—a study
    c. the University of California at Los Angeles
    d. No change is necessary.

TEST 2 **Editing for Correct Capitalization and Punctuation**

Read the following paragraph and insert the correct capitalization and marks of punctuation wherever they are needed.

[1]The expression your name is mud has its origin in a person from history. [2]Samuel Mudd was a doctor in Maryland during the civil war. [3]About 4 a.m. on april 15 1865 at his home in charles county Maryland dr. Mudd was awakened by men who needed medical attention. [4]One was john wilkes booth who had just shot president Abraham Lincoln at ford's theatre in Washington, d.c. [5]Mudd set and bandaged booths broken leg before the assassin went on his way. [6]A few days later the doctor was arrested and charged with being part of the conspiracy to kill the president. [7]He was convicted by a military court and sentenced to life in

prison but in 1869 president Andrew Johnson commuted his sentence. [8] Since that time dr. Mudds descendants have tried without success to overturn that original conviction. [9] One politician united states representative Steny Hoyer introduced a bill the Samuel Mudd relief act that would have cleared the doctors name but it failed to pass. [10] Last march after another setback Richard Mudd the grandson of Samuel Mudd said to reporters as long as the United States lasts the story of my 31-year-old grandfather being put in prison for life for setting a broken leg is never going to end.

TEST 3

Editing for Correct Capitalization and Punctuation

Read the following paragraph and insert the correct capitalization and marks of punctuation wherever they are needed.

[1] valentines day is celebrated on february 14 as a festival of romance and affection. [2] People send their sweethearts greeting cards that ask won't you be my valentine? [3] Children like to make their own valentines from paper doilies, red construction paper bright foils and wallpaper samples. [4] These customs probably came from the ancient roman festival of lupercalia which took place every february 15. [5] The festival honored juno the roman goddess of women and marriage and pan the god of nature. [6] Young men and women chose partners for the festival by drawing names by chance from a box. [7] After exchanging gifts they often continued to enjoy each others company long after the festival and many were eventually married. [8] In the year 496 the church changed the lupercalia festival of february 15 to saint valentines day on February 14 but the sentimental meaning of the old festival has remained to the present time. [9] According to the book *popular antiquities,* which was written in 1877 people were observing this holiday in england as early as 1446. [10] One account tells of young men wearing the names of their ladies on their sleeves for several days. [11] The expression he wears his heart on his sleeve probably came from this custom. [12] In the united states valentines day became popular in the 1800s at the time of the civil war. [13] Many of the valentines of that period were hand-painted and today their beautiful decorative qualities make them collectors items.

TEST 4

Editing Student Writing: Using Correction Symbols

The correction symbol for errors in capitalization is **cap**, and for errors in punctuation it is **punc**. In the following paragraph, find three errors in capitalization (**cap**), four errors in punctuation (**punc**), one error in verb tense (**vb**), one error in pronoun reference (**pron ref**), and one fragment (**frag**). Mark the errors with the commonly used editing symbols, and then correct the errors on the lines provided after the paragraph.

[1]When I was growing up in Honduras, my Grandmother made me a delicious cup of hot chocolate every morning. [2]I've only recently learned about its interesting history. [3]Chocolate is made from the seeds of the fruit of the cacao tree which is an unusual plant that produces flowers and fruits on its trunk, not on its branches. [4]The story of chocolate goes back to its origins in central America more than 1,500 years ago. [5]Recently, they found a piece of chocolate in a tomb that dates back to 600 BC. [6]The ancient maya made the cacao into a drink but it was the foam, not the liquid, that they most enjoyed. [7]Scientists had always believe that the common people had not been allowed access to cacao plants, but this idea was proved wrong when cacao plants were found in the ashes of the ancient Salvadoran village of Ceren. [9]A village that was buried by a volcano in 590. [10]The people of Ceren made beautiful ceramics into which they mixed cacao paste vanilla chiles and other spices to concoct a delicious drink. [11]In some marketplaces in southern Mexico, it is still possible to buy a similar drink, referred to by the locals as popo. [12]You are lucky if you have the opportunity to sample a cup.

Three capitalization corrections

1. _____

2. _____

3. _____

Four sentences with corrected punctuation

4. _____

_____

5. _____

_____

6. _____

_____

_____

7. _____

_____

One verb tense correction

8. _____

One pronoun reference correction (a missing antecedent)

Pronoun	Correction
9. _____	_____

One fragment corrected

10. _____

_____

Exploring Online

Go to academic.cengage.com/devenglish/scarry to find the **Writer's Online Workplace,** a website designed for students using this book. You will find links to handouts, interactive quizzes, and other online resources as you explore the following topics:

- capitalization
- punctuation, including
  commas
  semicolons
  question marks
  quotation marks
  parentheses
  dashes
  apostrophes

Working Together

Writing a Review: Eating Out

Newspapers and magazines hire writers to review movies and plays, restaurants, concerts, art gallery openings, and other events. You might think that being paid to eat out would be the perfect way to earn a living!

Read the following newspaper review of a typical neighborhood restaurant. The review contains important information that a customer would need to know, such as location, days and hours of operation, menu, atmosphere, price, and other special features.

Eating Out

If you appreciate authentic Chinese food, you should go for lunch or dinner to the Golden Fortune Restaurant, located at 99 Elm Avenue in Ellington. It is just above the South Side Plaza, walking distance from the center of town. The Golden Fortune Restaurant is the kind of restaurant you will want to visit more than once. The food is expertly prepared, the prices are very moderate, and the service is always friendly. We particularly liked the warm and relaxed atmosphere, partly the result of soft classical music playing in the background.

Many of the lunch and dinner selections at the Golden Fortune are traditional, with a few surprises. All of the vegetables used are fresh, and there is a choice of white or brown rice. The appetizers are large enough to serve two people. On our first visit, we were delighted with the combination platter. It is the most popular appetizer on the menu because it allows diners to sample a half dozen of the house specialties.

One unique touch at this restaurant is the choice of 24 different teas. Instead of having an ordinary pot of green tea placed in front of you, as in most Chinese restaurants, at the Golden Fortune you can choose from a wide variety. These include green tea with passion fruit, peach tea, and even milk tea with oatmeal. Customers enjoy trying new combinations each time they visit. Our favorite is the black tea with plum. If you like, you may bring your own wine or beer, and the waiters will be happy to serve it.

Some of the most popular main courses are beef with garlic sauce, crispy honey chicken on a bed of rice and vegetables, and a variety of delicious stir-fry dishes. If you choose a stir-fry at the Golden Fortune, you may select a favorite sauce and type of noodle along with a meat or fish, and the kitchen will make up the dish you want.

The Golden Fortune is open for lunch from noon to 4 p.m. and for dinner from 5 p.m. until 11 p.m. every day of the week. No reservations are needed. For take-out orders, call 548-4407 after 11 a.m.

Divide into groups of five. Each group should decide on a restaurant or event to review and list the basic subjects that will be covered in that review. Each person in the group should then select one subject and write a paragraph of at least five sentences about it. Return to the group to listen to each other's paragraphs as they are read. Decide on the best order for the paragraphs, and together compose an introduction and conclusion for the piece. Then put these paragraphs together to construct a complete review.

Portfolio Suggestion

Keep this review in your portfolio. Whenever you go to a restaurant, musical event, or movie, keep in mind that these are all places where reviewers go and write down their reactions. You can too!

PART

3

Understanding the Power of Words

When some writers start work on a project, they first brain-storm or cluster their ideas. Other writers feel more comfort-able freewriting to produce their first drafts. No matter which approach a writer takes, making thoughtful word choices is one of the most important parts of the writing process. When writer and social activist Malcolm X set out to educate him-self in prison, he copied a complete dictionary by hand—certainly a systematic approach to the study of words! You too should concentrate on individual words. This unit focuses on aspects of the writing process that relate to words: word choice, word meanings, wordiness, appropriate words, and words often confused.

CHAPTER 14

Choosing Words That Work

When you write, your choice of words is always of critical importance. In this chapter, you will explore various issues related to words:

CHAPTER OBJECTIVES

- words rich in meaning
- denotations and connotations of words
- wordiness in the form of
  - redundant expressions
  - wordy phrases
  - overuse of the verb *to be*
  - unnecessary repetition of the same word
  - unnecessary use of *there is* or *there are*
  - flowery or pretentious language
  - apologetic, tentative expressions
- language inappropriate for formal writing, such as
  - slang
  - clipped language
  - sexist language
  - trite expressions (clichés)

Using Words Rich in Meaning

Writing involves a constant search to find the right words to express thoughts and feelings as accurately as possible. When a writer wants to be precise or wants to give a flavor to a piece of writing, the creative possibilities for word choice and sentence construction are almost endless. The creative writer looks for words that have rich and appropriate meanings and associations.

For instance, if you were describing a person under five years of age, you might choose one of these words:

imp	brat	preschooler	child
toddler	tot	youngster	

Some words have no associations beyond their strict dictionary meaning; these words are said to be neutral. Which word in the list is the most neutral, with the least negative or positive emotional associations?* A person writing a brochure

*Your answer should be *child*.

for a nursery school would probably choose the word *preschooler* because it identifies the age of the child. A person talking about a child who has just learned to walk might use the word *toddler* because it carries the association of a small child who is toddling along a bit unsteadily. What informal and unkind word might an angry older sibling shout when a younger brother or sister has just colored all over a favorite book?*

EXERCISE 1   **Using Words Rich in Meaning**

The five words in Column A all have the basic meaning of *thin*. However, an additional meaning makes each word richer and more specific. Match each word in Column A with the letter of the definition from Column B that best fits the word.

	Column A		Column B
_____	1. slender	a.	unattractively thin
_____	2. emaciated	b.	thin and bony with a haggard appearance
_____	3. lean	c.	gracefully long and slim
_____	4. skinny	d.	containing little fat, in shape, fit
_____	5. gaunt	e.	extremely thin, undernourished, and sickly

Most languages are rich with words that describe eating. Column A contains a few English words about eating. Match each word in Column A with the letter of the definition from Column B that best fits the word.

	Column A		Column B
_____	1. taste	a.	to eat with small quick bites
_____	2. devour	b.	to bite or chew on something persistently
_____	3. nibble	c.	to eat between meals
_____	4. gorge	d.	to test the flavor of a food
_____	5. gnaw	e.	to stuff oneself with food
_____	6. snack	f.	to eat up greedily

EXERCISE 2   **Using Words Rich in Meaning**

The words *eat, drink, song,* and *walk* are neutral words (having no positive or negative associations). Each neutral term is followed by four words, each one with its own precise meaning. In each case, give a definition for the word. Use your dictionary.

Example: crunch: <u>to eat with a noisy crackling sound</u>

to eat

1. gobble: _____

2. savor: _____

3. munch: _____

4. chomp: _____

*Your answer should be *brat*.

to drink

1. sip: _____

2. gulp: _____

3. slurp: _____

4. lap: _____

a song

1. aria: _____

2. lullaby: _____

3. ballad: _____

4. hymn: _____

to walk

1. lumber: _____

2. amble: _____

3. stride: _____

4. roam: _____

Understanding Loaded Words: Denotation/Connotation

The careful writer considers more than the dictionary meaning of a word. Some words have different meanings for different people.

> The **denotation** of a word is its strict dictionary meaning. The **connotation** of a word is the meaning (apart from the dictionary meaning) that a person attaches to a word because of that individual's personal experience with the word.
>
> | | |
> |---|---|
> | **Word:** | liberal (adj) |
> | **Denotation (political):** | favoring nonrevolutionary progress or reform |
> | **Possible connotations:** | socially active, freethinking, too generous, far left, favoring many costly government programs |

Politicians are usually experts in understanding the connotations of a word. They know, for instance, that if they want to get votes in a conservative area, they should not refer to their own views as liberal. The strict dictionary meaning of *liberal* is "favoring nonrevolutionary progress or reform," certainly an idea that most people would support. However, when most people hear the words *liberal* and *conservative,* they bring to the words many political biases and experiences from their past: their parents' attitudes, the political and social history of the area in which they live, and other factors that may correctly or incorrectly influence their understanding of the words.

Choosing words that are not neutral but that have more exact or appropriate meanings is a powerful skill for a writer, one that will help your reader better understand the ideas you want to communicate. As your vocabulary grows, your writing will become richer and deeper. Your work will reflect your understanding of the many shades of meaning that words can have.

EXERCISE **3**   **Denotation/Connotation**

In this exercise, you have the opportunity to think of words that are richer in associations than the neutral words underlined in the sentences below. Write your own word choice in the space to the right of each sentence. Discuss with others in your class the associations you make with the words you have chosen.

1.   I live in a <u>house</u> at the edge of town.   _____

2.   I <u>walk</u> home from work every night.   _____

3.   Usually the same <u>person</u> is always walking behind me.   _____

4.   She is always carrying a lot of <u>stuff</u>.   _____

5.   She looks as if she is <u>old</u>.   _____

6.   She has <u>marks</u> all over her face.   _____

7.   Sometimes I try to <u>talk</u> with her.   _____

8.   She has such an <u>unusual</u> look in her eyes.   _____

9.   Sometimes I can hear her <u>talking</u> to herself.   _____

10.   At night when I am <u>sitting</u> in my favorite armchair, I often think of her and wish she could tell me the story of her life.   _____

EXERCISE **4**   **Denotation/Connotation**

The following sentences contain words that may have positive or negative associations for you. Read each sentence and study the underlined word or phrase. Below each sentence, write the emotional meaning the underlined word or phrase has for you. Discuss your answers with your classmates. An example follows.

Sentence: Her <u>brother</u> went with her so that she would not have to drive <u>alone</u>.

Explanation: The word *brother* has a positive connotation. We expect a brother to be someone who is helpful and protective.

1.   The <u>dog</u> stood at the door; his size was quite astounding.

_____

_____

2.   The <u>foreigner</u> approached the ranch slowly.

_____

_____

3. His <u>pickup truck</u> was parked in front.

_____

_____

4. A woman and child were peering out from behind the <u>fence</u>.

_____

_____

5. The <u>stranger</u> carried a long object of some kind.

_____

_____

EXERCISE 5   **Denotation/Connotation**

When you write, you create a tone by the words you choose. Review the sentences you worked with in Exercise 4. For each sentence, create a more positive tone, either by changing the underlined word or phrase to a different word or phrase or by adding adjectives to modify the underlined word or phrase.

1. _____

_____

2. _____

_____

3. _____

_____

4. _____

_____

5. _____

_____

Wordiness: In Writing, Less Can Be More!

In his book *The Elements of Style*, the famous writer E. B. White quotes his old teacher William Strunk Jr., who said that a sentence "should contain no unnecessary words" and a paragraph "no unnecessary sentences." Strunk's philosophy of writing also includes the commandment he gave many times in his classes at Cornell University: "Omit needless words!" It was a lesson that E. B. White took to heart, with the wonderful results that we see in his own writing.

Following is a summary of some important ways you can cut the number of your words to strengthen the power of your ideas. Read each example of wordiness, and notice how the revision makes the idea more concise.

1. **Redundant expressions**	**Revisions**
circle around	circle
blue in color	blue
past history	history
connect together	connect
true fact	fact
surrounded on all sides	surrounded
very unique	unique

2. **Wordy phrases**	**Revisions**
in the event that	if
due to the fact that	because
for the stated reason that	because
in this day and age	today
at this point in time	now
in the neighborhood of	about

3. **Overuse of the verb *to be***	**Revisions**
The man is in need of help.	The man needs help.
They are of the opinion that a lawyer should be called.	They believe a lawyer should be called.

4. **Unnecessary repetition of the same word**	**Revision**
The book is on the table. The book is my favorite. I have read the book five times.	The book on the table is my favorite. I have read it five times.

5. **Unnecessary use of *there is* or *there are***	**Revisions**
There are two major disadvantages to the new proposal.	The new proposal has two major disadvantages.
There is no doubt but that the sun will rise tomorrow.	No doubt the sun will rise tomorrow.

6. **Flowery or pretentious language**	**Revision**
It is delightful to contemplate the culinary experience we will enjoy after the termination of this cinematic event.	I can't wait until we have pizza after the movie.

7. **Apologetic, tentative expressions**	**Revisions**
In my opinion, the grading policy for this course should be changed.	The grading policy for this course should be changed.
Right now, it seems to me that finding a job in my field is very difficult.	Right now, finding a job in my field is very difficult.
In this paper, I will try to explain my views on censorship of the campus newspaper.	Censoring the campus newspaper is a mistake.

EXERCISE **6**   **Revising Wordy Sentences**

Revise each of the following sentences to avoid wordiness.

1. The date for the final completion of your project is May 18.

    _____

2. The thought of the exam is causing her to be in a constant state of tension.

    _____

3. There is no better place to study than in our library.

    _____

4. Some people have the belief that astrology is a science.

    _____

5. We are all in need of better organizational skills.

    _____

6. As far as mechanical ability is concerned, Mike is very handy.

    _____

7. She is in the process of cooking dinner.

    _____

8. Due to the fact of the rain, the game will be canceled.

    _____

9. In my opinion, it would seem to me that the reasons for unemployment are complex.

    _____

10. The box had an oblong shape.

    _____

EXERCISE **7**   **Revising Wordy Sentences**

Revise each of the following sentences to avoid wordiness.

1. The gentleman is of a kindly nature.

    _____

2. I was told he is a male actor.

    _____

3. The price was in the neighborhood of fifty dollars.

    _____

4. In regard to the letter, it was sent to the wrong address.

    _____

5. It is everyone's duty to be in attendance at the meeting today. (Avoid the verb *to be*.)

    _____

6.   My best friend is above me in height.

_____

7.   I tiptoed down the stairs on my toes in order to surprise everyone.

_____

8.   They made the discovery that I was not upstairs.

_____

9.   A member of the teaching staff at this institution of higher learning failed to submit in a timely fashion the fruits of my endeavors for the course during this entire period from September to December.

_____

10. Even though I am not an expert, I think that more neighborhood health clinics are needed.

_____

Recognizing Language Appropriate for Formal Writing

In speaking or writing to family and friends, an informal style is always appropriate because it is relaxed and conversational. On the other hand, writing and speaking in school or at work require a more formal style, one that is less personal and more detached in tone. In formal writing situations, slang is not appropriate. Furthermore, sexist or disrespectful language is never acceptable.

> **Slang** is a term that refers to special words or expressions that a particular group of people use, often with the intention of keeping that meaning private. A characteristic of a slang word or expression is that it is often used only for a limited time and then forgotten. For example:
>
> The party was *swell.* (1940s)
> The party was *groovy.* (1960s)
> The party was *awesome.* (1980s)
> The party was *phat.* (1990s)
> The party was *hot.* (2000s)

Slang or informal words	Acceptable words
bucks	dollars
kids	children
cops	police
a bummer	a bad experience
off the wall	crazy
yummy	delicious
chow	food

Clipped language refers to the use of shortened words to make communication more relaxed and informal. Clipped language is not appropriate in more formal writing, which requires standard English.

Clipped language	Acceptable words
doc	doctor
fridge	refrigerator
pro	professional
TV	television

Sexist language refers to the use of single-gender nouns or pronouns to apply to both men and women. This was standard usage in the past, but writers and publishers today avoid such language.

Sexist language: Everyone must bring *his* project on Tuesday.

There are several options for revising sentences with sexist language:

1. Revise the sentence using plural pronouns and plural antecedents.

All students must bring *their* projects on Tuesday.

2. Change the pronoun to an article.

Everyone must bring *a* project on Tuesday.

3. Replace a single-gender term with an inclusive term.

Everyone must bring *his or her* project on Tuesday.

4. Change the sentence to the passive voice.

All projects must be brought to class on Tuesday.

Study the following example of the use of sexist language in a particular context. How could you correct it?

Sexist language: The teacher is an important *man. He* can influence the lives of many children in a community.

Nonsexist language: The teacher is an important person who can influence the lives of many children in the community.

The following partial list of sexist terms is accompanied by present-day acceptable forms.

Sexist terms	Acceptable terms
authoress	author
businessman	business executive, businessperson
chairman	chairperson
common man	average person
congressman	member of congress, legislator
fireman	firefighter
forefathers	ancestors
mailman	mail carrier, postal worker
mankind	humanity, people
salesman	sales associate, salesperson, sales representative
stewardess	flight attendant

Trite expressions (or clichés) are expressions that may have been fresh at one time but now have become stale from overuse.

Trite expressions	Acceptable expressions
cool as a cucumber	calm
mad as a hornet	angry
a golden opportunity	an exceptional opportunity
light as a feather	light
busy as a bee	busy
dead as a doornail	dead
slowly but surely	gradually
without rhyme or reason	senseless

EXERCISE 8

Recognizing Language Inappropriate for Formal Writing

The following sentences contain words that are informal, slang, sexist, or trite. Circle the word or phrase in each sentence that is inappropriate for formal writing, and on the line to the right of each sentence, provide a more formal word or expression to replace the inappropriate one.

1. I wish you would stop beating around the bush. _____

2. She told her friends to chill out. _____

3. The entire evening turned out to be a bummer. _____

4. The businessmen in the community support the science project. _____

5. The time has come to level with the director. _____

6. The first experiment turned out to be a downer. _____

7. The scientist has guts to continue the research. _____

8. The entire lab is a dump. _____

9. The guys often spend the night there. _____

10. They work until two or three in the morning and then crash. _____

EXERCISE 9

Recognizing Language Inappropriate for Formal Writing

The following sentences contain words that are informal, slang, sexist, or trite. Circle the word or phrase in each sentence that is inappropriate for formal writing, and on the line to the right of each sentence, provide a more formal word or expression to replace the inappropriate one.

1. Don't bug me about studying. _____

2. I aced the last French test. _____

3. Bring me some grub tonight. _____

4.   He's my buddy.   _____

5.   How lousy is the weather outside?   _____

6.   The bodybuilder is as strong as an ox.   _____

7.   I still have a crush on that intern.   _____

8.   The medical doctor is a well-respected
     person in most communities; he is
     considered a role model for our children.   _____

9.   I think it's gonna be nice tomorrow.   _____

10. I ain't seen the new neighbors yet.   _____

Studying a Student Essay for Word Choices

ACTIVITY 1   **Making Better Word Choices**

When Sandra Russell wrote an essay on the experience of living through a tornado, she composed more than one draft. Below are six sentences that she could have written when she worked on the first draft of her essay.

Rewrite each of the sentences, focusing particularly on revising the underlined words. Your revisions could include different word choices or additional words, phrases, and clauses that make the sentences more descriptive and interesting.

1.   All afternoon, <u>clouds were getting dark</u>. (*Add more descriptive detail.*)

_____

_____

2.   I could <u>see lightning</u> and <u>hear thunder</u>. (*Add more descriptive detail.*)

_____

_____

3.   She <u>took</u> my hand and <u>took</u> me to the storm cellar. (*Choose more descriptive verbs.*)

_____

_____

4.   We <u>sat</u> in the <u>cellar</u>. (*Choose more descriptive words.*)

_____

_____

5.   <u>Stuff</u> lay around our yard. (*Be more specific.*)

_____

_____

6.   <u>The storm</u> came through my neighborhood, <u>destroying lots of property</u>. (*Be more specific.*)

_____

_____

ACTIVITY 2   **Sharing Sentence Revisions**

Share your revised sentences with other members of your class. For each of the six sentences, choose three revised examples to write on the board for the class to review.

ACTIVITY 3   **Working with a Student Essay**

Read the complete student essay out loud. Following the reading, search the essay to discover how Sandra Russell expressed the six ideas you revised in Activity 1. Underline the six sentences as you find them. Discuss with class members how these ideas were successfully expressed by the student writer.

Bad Weather

I was born in Booneville, Arkansas, and grew up on a small farm about five miles south of Paris. Naturally, I grew up in an area where tornados are feared each spring. I didn't really understand this until one humid, still night in April of 1985.

All afternoon, dark threatening clouds had been building up in the west, blocking out the sun. I could see the lightning dance about the sky as the thunder responded by shaking the ground beneath my feet. The wind softly stirred the tree tops but then quickly died as it got darker and darker.

I walked outside and listened to the silence ringing in my ears. In the distance, I could hear a rumble, soft at first but slowly and steadily intensifying. My mom came outside and stood at my side and listened to the rumbling noise. Everything was still; nothing dared to move. Even my dog Moose lay quietly, as if punished, in his doghouse. It was almost as if he knew what was about to happen.

"Mama, what's that noise?" I asked her, but she didn't answer. She grabbed my hand and dragged me to the storm cellar. I didn't have time to argue with her before I heard the rumble nearly upon us. We huddled in the musty-smelling cellar. The roar was so loud it hurt my ears. I could hear the whistling of the wind above us. I cried and screamed for the awful noise of the whistle to stop, but no one could hear me above the ferocious noise. The rumble barreled on us, and it seemed as if it would never end. The air was still in the dark cellar, but I could hear it as it moved violently above our heads. I didn't think the thundering noise would ever end.

I hadn't realized that I had quit breathing until it finally stopped. I drew a quick breath and thanked God it was over and my mother and I were safe. We crawled out of the cellar and took the first real look at our home. Trees were uprooted. Glass and boards and even a stop sign lay scattered around our yard. The roof on our house was damaged and a few windows were broken out, but that was all. Even most of our animals had survived that day, including Moose.

That night is one that I'll never forget. A moderately sized tornado (about an F3 on the Fujita scale) ripped through my neighborhood, destroying ten houses and damaging fifty others. No tornado warnings were issued for that area until ten minutes after it was already over, but still no one was seriously injured. The local television station didn't even bother to comment on its mistake. Until that night I had never realized how an event could change the way you feel about something for the rest of your life. I look at the television and see tornado, hurricane, and even flood victims with new eyes. They are real, just like me.

by Sandra Russell

Mastery and Editing Tests

TEST **Student Writing: Editing for Wordiness**

Below is an introductory paragraph of six sentences, taken from a student essay. On the lines that follow, revise the paragraph so that wordiness in each sentence is eliminated.

In the paragraph that follows, I am going to make an attempt to name at least some of the earliest Spanish explorations in the New World. To take just the first example, it was in 1513 that an extraordinary event of considerable magnitude took place in what is now Florida when the Spanish explorer Ponce de Leon landed there. It was in the same area, and little more than a quarter of a century later, that the explorer Hernando de Soto, who later discovered the Mississippi River, also landed in Florida in 1539. Among historians and among those who are interested in cultural history, Florida has reached noteworthy status for another reason. In 1565, Pedro Menendez de Aviles landed in Florida and began building the city of St. Augustine, the oldest permanent settlement in the United States. We all know that explorers in every age and in every part of the world have to be of a courageous nature and personality, but in those days Spanish explorers were perhaps the bravest of their time because they dared to be among the very first to set foot in what was then known as the New World.

_____

_____

_____

_____

_____

_____

_____

_____

_____

_____

_____

_____

TEST **Student Writing: Editing for Inappropriate Language**

Each sentence in the following paragraph contains at least one example of inappropriate language. Underline the inappropriate words, and then rewrite the paragraph, revising any language that is not appropriate in formal writing.

When my sis was hired by a major electronics company last summer, we were a little worried about her. She had flunked math in school, so we wondered if she had chosen the right kind of company. The person who had the job before her was let go because he had an attitude. Imagine our surprise when she soon announced that she had been selected chairman of an important committee at work. She said that she really didn't want to be in a leadership position, but we all knew she was nuts about it.

_____

_____

_____

_____

_____

_____

_____

_____

_____

_____

_____

 TEST 3

Editing for Wordiness and Inappropriate Language

The following paragraph contains examples of wordiness as well as inappropriate language (slang, clipped words, and sexist terms). Underline each problem as you find it, and then revise the paragraph. (Hint: Fifteen words or phrases need revision. Find and revise at least ten.)

One of the most outstanding scientists in the U.S. today came from China in 1936. She is Chien-Hsiung Wu, and her story is the story of the development of physics in our century. When Miss Wu came to America in 1936, she intended to do grad work and hightail it back to China. However, World War II broke out, and she remained to teach at Smith College, where she enjoyed working with the Smithies. Very soon after that, she was employed by Princeton U. At that time, she was the only girl physicist hired by a top research university. Later, she became an important workman on Columbia University's Manhattan Project, the project that developed the A bomb. She hunkered down at Columbia for more than thirty years, her many scientific discoveries bringing her world recognition. In 1990, Chien-Hsiung Wu became the first living scientist to have an asteroid named in her honor. This celestial object whirling in the darkest corners of outer space is now carrying her name.

_____

_____

_____

_____

_____

_____

_____

_____

_____

_____

_____

_____

_____

_____

_____

_____

_____

_____

Exploring Online

Go to academic.cengage.com/devenglish/scarry to find the **Writer's Online Workplace,** a website designed for students using this book. You will find links to handouts, interactive quizzes, and other online resources as you explore the following topics:

- tone
- reducing wordiness
- avoiding sexist language

Being Tactful in the Workplace

Words are charged with meanings that can be encouraging and supportive or hurtful and wounding. Although workers in government offices and other public places are there to help the public, they often are so overworked that they do not always respond in positive ways. Below are seven comments and questions that might be heard in an office where a person has gone to get help. In each case, revise the language so that the comment or question is more encouraging.

1. I don't have any idea what you're talking about.

   _____

   _____

   _____

   _____

2. Why don't you learn to write so people can read it?

   _____

   _____

3. We don't accept sloppy applications.

   _____

   _____

4. How old are you anyway?

   _____

   _____

5. Can't you read directions?

   _____

   _____

6. What's the matter with you? Why can't you understand this simple procedure?

   _____

   _____

7. I don't have time today for people like you!

   _____

   _____

Share your revisions with each other. Then, as a class, discuss some individual experiences in which the use of language made you or someone you know feel hurt or upset. These experiences may have occurred at a campus office, a local bank, or a local shop. How could a change of language have improved each situation?

Portfolio Suggestion

Using the "Working Together" activity and class discussion, write on one of the following:

- Discuss the importance of using polite language in the workplace. (You can use the examples given during classroom discussion.)

- Give advice to employers on training their employees how to speak to people on the job.

- Describe the difficulty workers have when customers or clients are rude. (If you have had a job, you may have experienced such a situation. How did you deal with the situation?)

CHAPTER 15

Paying Attention to Look-Alikes and Sound-Alikes

In this chapter, you will focus on forty-eight sets of words that are frequently confused.

CHAPTER OBJECTIVES

- Group I: ten sets of words that sound alike
- Group II: ten additional sets of words that sound alike
- Group III: five sets of words including contractions that sound like other words
- Group IV: ten sets of words that sound or look almost alike
- Group V: ten additional sets of words that sound or look almost alike
- Group VI: three sets of verbs that are most often confused: *lie/lay*, *rise/raise*, and *sit/set*

Many words in English are confusing because they either sound alike or look alike but are spelled differently and have completely different meanings. Every student needs to watch out for these troublesome words, often called "look-alikes" and "sound-alikes." Students whose first language is not English will find this chapter especially helpful.

In this chapter, words that are often confused have been grouped into six manageable sections so that you can study each section in one sitting. Within each set of confused words, each word is defined and used in a sentence. After you have studied the spellings and definitions, fill in the blanks with the correct words. Master each group before you proceed to the next.

Group I: Words That Sound Alike

aural/oral

aural (adj): related to hearing
oral (adj): related to the mouth

The ear specialist gave the child an *aural* exam.

The dentist urged him to improve his *oral* hygiene.

The student dreaded giving _____ reports in class because a high fever

had caused _____ nerve damage and affected his hearing.

buy/by

buy (verb): to purchase
by (prep): [1]near; [2]past; [3]not later than

He hopes to *buy* a car.

Let's meet *by* the clock.

They drive *by* my house every morning.

Please arrive *by* six o'clock.

_____ the time they are ready to _____ a house, the market will

have passed them _____.

capital/capitol

capital (adj): [1]adding financial value; [2]fatal
capital (noun): [1]leading city; [2]money
capitol (noun): a legislative building

The new addition is a *capital* improvement on their home.

The governor opposes *capital* punishment.

The *capital* [leading city] of Wyoming is Cheyenne.

The retailer has *capital* to invest in remodeling.

The dome of the state *capitol* [legislative building] is gold.

She needed _____ to rebuild her home, but she first went to the

_____ [legislative building] to obtain needed permits.

close/clothes

close (verb): to shut
close (noun): end or conclusion
clothes (noun): garments

Please *close* the door.

Finally, the war came to a *close*.

The *clothes* were from the local women's store.

NOTE: **Cloth** is a piece of fabric, not to be confused with the word *clothes*, which as a noun is always plural.

The *cloth* for the table was my mother's.

Because she wanted to buy new _____, she shopped all day until the

_____ of business.

coarse/course

coarse (adj): rough; common or of inferior quality
course (noun): [1]direction; [2]part of a meal; [3]unit of study

The coat was made from a *coarse* fabric.

He told a *coarse* joke.

What is the *course* of the spaceship?

The main *course* of the meal was served.

English is a required *course* at my school.

A few students in that _____ made _____ comments during

every class meeting.

complement/compliment

complement (noun):	[1]what is required to make a thing complete; [2]something that completes
complement (verb):	to complete
compliment (noun):	an expression of praise
compliment (verb):	to praise

The kitchen has a full *complement* of pots and pans.

Her shoes *complement* the outfit.

The chef received a *compliment* on his dessert.

The food critic *complimented* the chef.

The library had such a full _____ of books in my field, I felt I had to

_____ the librarian.

forward/foreword

forward (verb):	to send a letter or a package to another address
forward (adj):	[1]bold or pushy; [2]going toward the front or the future
forward (adv):	toward the front or the future
foreword (noun):	introduction to a book, usually written by someone other than the author of the book

Please *forward* my mail.

She was so *forward;* she pushed her way in.

He took one step *forward.*

Read the *foreword* first.

Please excuse me for being so _____ as to offer advice to a stranger, but

be sure to read the book's _____ before you begin.

passed/past

passed (verb):	(past tense of *to pass*) to move ahead or by
past (noun):	the time before the present
past (prep):	beyond
past (adj):	no longer current

She *passed* the library.

Don't live in the *past.*

He walked *past* the house.

Her *past* failures have been forgotten.

When he walked _____ the professor's office, he found out that he had

_____ both tests he had taken during the _____ week.

plain/plane

plain (adj):	[1]ordinary; [2]clear
plain (noun):	flat land without trees
plane (noun):	[1]aircraft; [2]carpenter's tool for shaving wood; [3]level of development

We ate a *plain* meal of soup and bread.

The directions were given in *plain* English.

They crossed the *plain* by covered wagon.

The passengers were seated on the *plane*.

A carpenter's *plane* and drill are needed for the job.

A scientist's thoughts are on a different *plane* from most people's.

He wanted _____ directions on how to operate the jet _____.

presence/presents

presence (noun): [1]the state of being present; [2]a person's manner
presents (noun): gifts
presents (verb): (third person singular of *to present*) to introduce or offer

Your *presence* is needed in the dean's office.

She has a wonderful *presence*.

The child had many birthday *presents*.

The senator *presents* the award each year.

The singer showed great _____ as she accepted the _____ from

her fans.

EXERCISE **Group I Words**

Circle the words that correctly complete each of the following sentences.

1. When I telephoned the doctor, he warned me that the (aural, oral) medicine was to be used only in my child's ear; this medicine was not an (aural, oral) medicine.

2. (Buy, By) the time I arrived at the store, the sale was over and I could not (buy, by) what I needed.

3. The senators met in Athens, the (capital, capitol) of Greece, to discuss the question of (capital, capitol) punishment.

4. I hurried to take several yards of wool (close, clothes, cloth) to the tailor, who had agreed to make some new winter (close, clothes, cloth) for my family; I knew he would (close, clothes, cloth) at five o'clock.

5. Every (coarse, course) in the meal was delicious, but the bread was rather (coarse, course).

6. She always wears clothes that (complement, compliment) each other, but she never expects a (complement, compliment).

7. I so much looked (forward, foreword) to reading the new book that I read the (forward, foreword) the very first day.

8. I have spent the (passed, past) few days wondering if I (passed, past) the exam.

9. The storm had been raging over the (plain, plane) for hours when the (plain, plane) suddenly went down.

10. Each year, the mayor (presence, presents) an award as well as several lovely (presence, presents) to outstanding members of the community.

EXERCISE 2

Group I Words

Edit the following paragraph for word confusions. Circle the errors and write the correct words on the lines below the paragraph.

Wolfgang Mozart was a child star of the eighteenth century. At three years old, he could pick out chords and tunes on the piano. Buy age four, he was composing at the piano. As a musical genius, Mozart had an extremely well-developed oral sense. When Mozart was only six, he and his sister played before the emperor in Vienna, the capitol of Austria. The emperor paid Mozart a complement by having his portrait painted. Among other presence was an embroidered suit of cloths. In the coarse of his life, Mozart wrote church music, sonatas, operas, and chamber music. Like many great artists of the passed, he was ahead of his time and created on such a different plain from other composers of his day that his own era never fully appreciated him. Today, Mozart is recognized as one of music's greatest composers. You might be interested in reading a book of Mozart's letters. Be sure to read the forward.

_____   _____

_____   _____

_____   _____

_____   _____

_____   _____

Group II: Words That Sound Alike

principal/principle

principal (adj):	[1]most important; [2]main
principal (noun):	[1]head of a school; [2]sum of money invested or borrowed
principle (noun):	rule or standard

The *principal* dancer was superb.

What is the *principal* reason for your decision?

The *principal* of the school arrived late.

The *principal* and interest on the loan were due.

He is a man of *principle*.

The _____ reason the _____ resigned was a matter of

_____.

rain/reign/rein

rain (noun):	water falling to earth in drops
reign (noun):	period of a king or queen's rule
rein (noun):	strap attached to a bridle, used to control a horse

I'm singing in the *rain.*

When was the *reign* of Henry the Eighth?

I grabbed the pony's frayed *rein.*

The queen's _____ began on a day of heavy _____.

sight/site/cite

sight (noun):	[1]ability to see; [2]something seen
site (noun):	[1]plot of land where something is, was, or will be located; [2]place for an event
cite (verb):	to quote as an authority or example

His *sight* was limited.

The Grand Canyon is an awesome *sight.*

Here is the *site* for the new courthouse.

Please *cite* the correct law.

The ancient burial _____ was a very impressive _____. The

archaeologists _____ the old inscriptions when they published their

findings.

stationary/stationery

stationary (adj):	standing still
stationery (noun):	writing paper, usually with matching envelopes

He hit a *stationary* object.

She wrote the letter on her *stationery.*

She remained _____ as she read the letter written on the blue

_____.

to/too/two

to (prep):	in a direction toward
too (adv):	[1]also; [2]excessively
two (noun, adj):	2

We walked *to* the movies.

We walked home *too.*

The tickets were *too* expensive.

She has *two* children.

Billy and Maria are _____ movie fans who go _____ a show every

week; their daughter always goes _____.

vain/vane/vein

vain (adj):	[1]conceited; [2]unsuccessful
vane (noun):	ornament, often in the shape of a rooster, that turns in the wind (seen on tops of barns)
vein (noun):	[1]blood vessel; [2]branching framework of a leaf; [3]area in the earth where minerals such as gold or silver are found; [4]passing attitude

He was attractive but *vain*.

We made a *vain* attempt to contact his brother.

The weather *vane* pointed southwest.

The *veins* carry blood to the heart.

The miner found a *vein* of silver.

She spoke in a humorous *vein*.

Carla is so _____; she wears makeup to conceal every splotch and

_____ on her cheeks.

waist/waste

waist (noun):   middle portion of the body
waste (verb):   to use carelessly
waste (noun):   discarded objects

His *waist* is thirty-six inches around.

He *wasted* too much time watching television.

The *waste* was put into the garbage pail.

Jewel is concerned about the size of her _____, but she will not

_____ her money on diet pills.

weather/whether

weather (noun):   atmospheric conditions
whether (conj):   if it is the case that

The *weather* in Hawaii is gorgeous.

I'll go *whether* I'm ready or not.

I will go to the islands on vacation, _____ the _____ is good or not.

whole/hole

whole (adj):   complete
hole (noun):   opening

He ate the *whole* pie.

I found a *hole* in the sock.

Despite the _____ in the apple, he ate the _____ apple.

write/right/rite

write (verb):   [1]to form letters and words; [2]to compose
right (adj):   [1]correct; [2]conforming to justice, law, or morality
right (noun):   [1]power or privilege to which one is entitled; [2]direction opposite to left
rite (noun):   traditional, often religious, ceremony

I will *write* a poem for your birthday.

What is the *right* answer?

Trial by jury is a *right* under the law.

The senator's position is to the *right.*

A bridal shower is a *rite* of passage.

Each of the speakers wanted to _____ the _____ kind of speech

for the ceremony, a _____ that happens only once a year.

 EXERCISE 3

Group II Words

Circle the words that correctly complete each of the following sentences.

1. The (principal, principle) was respected because he would not compromise his one fundamental (principal, principle).

2. The museum had on display a horse's (rain, reign, rein) that dated from the (rain, reign, rein) of Queen Isabella.

3. You do not have to (sight, site, cite) statistics to convince me of the importance of caring for my (sight, site, cite).

4. He bought the (stationary, stationery) from a clerk who said nothing and remained (stationary, stationery) behind the counter the entire time.

5. I want (to, too, two) go (to, too, two) the movies, and I hope you do (to, too, two).

6. I could tell the actor was (vain, vane, vein) when she kept hiding a long blue (vain, vane, vein) on her leg.

7. It is a (waist, waste) of time to try to get him to admit the size of his (waist, waste).

8. We always listen to the (weather, whether) report, (weather, whether) it's right or wrong.

9. I am telling you the (whole, hole) story about the (whole, hole) in our new carpet.

10. Every American has the (write, right, rite) to participate in any religious (write, right, rite) of his or her own choosing.

 EXERCISE 4

Group II Words

Edit the following paragraph for word confusions. Circle the errors and write the correct words on the lines below the paragraph.

The company officials searched for years until they found the proper sight for their gem mine. First, they investigated legal records to make sure they had the rite to drill in the area. Then they drilled several wholes to see if there were any vanes worth exploring. They were surprised to learn they were in the area that had been the principle mining area for Spanish colonizers in the sixteenth century. No exploration had been done since the rein of King Philip IV. They even found stationary in the archives that had been sent from Spain. The modern explorers eventually determined that they were to late to find any more emeralds, but they did have a good chance of discovering semiprecious stones. They did not want to waist any more time. They began work right away. In all kinds of whether, the work progressed. The results were worth their efforts.

_____   _____

_____   _____

_____   _____

_____   _____

_____

Group III: Contractions That Sound Like Other Words

it's/its

it's: contraction of *it is*
its: possessive pronoun of *it*

> *It's* early.
> *Its* tail is short.

_____ too late now to put the space vehicle into _____ orbit.

they're/their/there

they're: contraction of *they are*
their: possessive pronoun of *they*
there: at that place

> *They're* happy.
> *Their* children are healthy.
> Look over *there*.

_____ excited about the new apartment; _____ is more light,

and _____ son will have his own room.

we're/were/where

we're: contraction of *we are*
were: past tense of *are*
where: at or in what place

> *We're* happy.
> The days *were* too short.
> *Where* are we?

We need to know _____ you were last night. _____ you safe?

After all, _____ your parents.

who's/whose

who's: contraction of *who is*
whose: possessive pronoun

> *Who's* the author of this book?
> *Whose* clothes are these?

_____ beach chair is this, and _____ to blame for breaking it?

you're: contraction of *you are*
your: possessive pronoun of *you*

You're the boss.

Your team has won.

When _____ diploma is in hand, _____ a happy graduate.

EXERCISE 5

Group III Words

Circle the words that correctly complete each of the following sentences.

1. (It's, Its) obvious that the car has lost (it's, its) muffler.

2. The pearl has lost (it's, its) luster, and (it's, its) impossible to restore it.

3. When (they're, their, there) in school, (they're, their, there) parents work in the restaurant (they're, their, there) on the corner.

4. Now that (they're, their, there) living in the country, (they're, their, there) expenses are not so great, so they might stay (they're, their, there).

5. (We're, Were, Where) hoping our friends (we're, were, where) not hurt at the place (we're, were, where) the accident occurred.

6. (We're, Were, Where) did the coupons go that (we're, were, where) saving?

7. (Who's, Whose) car is double-parked outside, and (who's, whose) going to move it?

8. (Who's, Whose) the pitcher at the game today, and (who's, whose) glove will he use?

9. When (you're, your) a father, (you're, your) free time is never guaranteed.

10. Please give me (you're, your) paper when (you're, your) finished writing.

EXERCISE 6

Group III Words

Edit the following paragraph for word confusions. Circle the errors and write the correct words on the lines below the paragraph.

Psychologists tell us that laughter is found only among human beings. Of all creatures, where the only ones who laugh. Psychologists are interested in what makes people laugh, but so far there best explanations are only theories. From a physical point of view, your healthier if you laugh often. Laughter is good for you're lungs, and its an outlet for extra energy. Among it's other effects are the release of anxieties and anger. The comedian, who's job depends on figuring out what makes people laugh, often pokes fun at the behavior of other people. However, a joke about a local town might not be funny in front of an audience of people who like living their. Were all familiar with jokes that are in bad taste. Its a good idea to recognize who your audience is.

_____   _____

_____   _____

_____   _____

_____   _____

_____   _____

Group IV: Words That Sound or Look Almost Alike

accept/except

accept (verb):   [1]to receive with consent; [2]to admit; [3]to regard as true or right
except (prep):   other than, but

> I *accept* the invitation with pleasure.
>
> I *accept* responsibility.
>
> I *accept* your explanation.
>
> Everyone *except* me was ready.

I will _____ all the applications _____ the late one.

advice/advise

advice (noun):   opinion as to what should be done
advise (verb):   [1]to suggest; [2]to counsel

> I need good *advice.*
>
> He *advised* me to take a different course.

I _____ you to get the best _____ possible.

affect/effect

affect (verb):   [1]to influence; [2]to change
effect (noun):   result
effect (verb):   to bring about

> Smoking will *affect* your health.
>
> The *effects* of the hurricane were evident.
>
> The hurricane *effected* devastating changes in the county.

The low grade will _____ his chances of getting into law school; this

could have a terrible _____ on his future.

breath/breathe

breath (noun):   [1]air that is inhaled or exhaled; [2]the act of inhaling or exhaling
breathe (verb):   to inhale or exhale

> You seem out of *breath.*
>
> Don't *breathe* in these fumes.

When they went mountain climbing, every _____ was difficult. By the

time they reached the top, they could hardly _____.

choose/chose

choose (verb):   to select
chose (verb):   past tense of *choose*

I *choose* a bagel for breakfast every day.

Yesterday I *chose* to sleep late.

This year I will try to _____ my clothes more carefully because last year

I _____ several items that didn't suit me.

conscience/conscious/conscientious

conscience (noun):   a person's recognition of right and wrong
conscious (adj):   [1]awake; [2]aware of one's own existence
conscientious (adj):   [1]careful; [2]thorough

His *conscience* bothered him.

The patient was *conscious* and able to talk.

The student was *conscientious* about doing her homework.

In the story of Pinocchio, Jiminy Cricket acts as the puppet's _____ be-

cause Pinocchio is not _____ of right and wrong. The cricket does a very

_____ job.

costume/custom

costume (noun):   special style of dress for a particular occasion
custom (noun):   common tradition

The child wore a clown *costume* for Halloween.

One *custom* at Thanksgiving is to serve turkey.

My cousin in New Orleans follows the _____ of wearing a special

_____ for Mardi Gras.

council/counsel/consul

council (noun):   group that governs
counsel (verb):   to give advice
counsel (noun):   [1]advice; [2]a lawyer
consul (noun):   government official in the foreign service

The student *council* meets every Tuesday.

Please *counsel* the elderly couple.

The patient needs legal *counsel*.

The prisoner has requested *counsel*.

He was appointed a *consul* by the president.

When I appeared before the _____, they gave me good _____,

advising me to meet with El Salvador's own _____.

desert/dessert

desert (verb):   to abandon
desert (noun):   barren land
dessert (noun): last part of a meal, often sweet

Don't *desert* me now.

The cactus flowers in the *desert* are beautiful.

We had apple pie for *dessert*.

When the caravan became lost in the _____, they did not think about a

full meal with _____. All they wanted was some water.

diner/dinner

diner (noun):   [1]person eating a meal; [2]restaurant with a long counter and booths
dinner (noun): main meal of the day

The *diner* waited for her check.

I prefer a booth at the *diner*.

What is for *dinner?*

That _____ is a good place for _____. You can tell by the number

of satisfied _____ there.

EXERCISE **7**

Group IV Words

Circle the words that correctly complete each of the following sentences.

1. The judge refused to (accept, except) most of the evidence (accept, except) for the testimony of one witness.

2. I need some good (advice, advise); is there anyone here who could (advice, advise) me?

3. How does the allergy medicine (affect, effect) you? Some medicine may have more than one adverse side (affect, effect).

4. The injured skier was told to (breath, breathe) deeply and exhale slowly; the doctor could see her (breath, breathe) in the chilly winter air.

5. Now we (choose, chose) fruit for a snack; in the past we usually (choose, chose) junk food.

6. The thief, when he became (conscience, conscientious, conscious), gave himself up to the police because his (conscience, conscientious, conscious) was bothering him.

7. Before you visit China, you should read about its (costumes, customs), including its New Year celebration at which colorful (costumes, customs) are worn.

8. The town (council, counsel, consul) needs its own legal (council, counsel, consul) to help interpret the law.

9. The chef made a chocolate layer cake for (desert, dessert); don't (desert, dessert) me before we eat it all.

10. All I want for (diner, dinner) is a salad; do you think I can get a good one at this local (diner, dinner)?

EXERCISE **8**   **Group IV Words**

Edit the following paragraph for word confusions. Circle the errors and write the correct words on the lines below the paragraph.

For thousands of years, it has been a costume to enjoy wine. Today, some people chose to drink wine with diner, while others wait until desert. There are wine clubs where people look for advise as to what they should drink; these people are very conscience about making the correct choice. Others look for council in magazines that tell them how to chose the correct wine for a food. They except the words of the experts on some wines whose prices would take your breathe away.

_____   _____

_____   _____

_____   _____

_____   _____

Group V: Words That Sound or Look Almost Alike

emigrate/immigrate
emigrant/immigrant

emigrate (verb):	to leave (a country or region)
immigrate (verb):	to come (into a country or region)
emigrant (noun):	person who leaves one country to settle in another country
immigrant (noun):	person who comes into a country to settle there

They *emigrated* from Europe.
Many people have *immigrated* to the United States.
Each *emigrant* left with memories.
Nearly every *immigrant* landed first at Ellis Island.

People who _____ from Eastern Europe often _____ to the United States. In the old country, the _____ are missed by their relatives; in the new country, they become valued _____.

farther/further

farther (adj, adv):	a greater distance (physically)
further (adj, adv):	a greater distance (mentally); additional
further (verb):	to help advance (a person or a cause)

They had to walk *farther* down the road.
The speaker made a *further* point.
The tutor will *further* my chances on the exam.

The judge made a _____ argument when he said the building should be _____ from the creek.

loose/lose

loose (adj):   not tightly fitted
lose (verb):   [1]to be unable to keep or find; [2]to fail to win

The dog's collar is *loose.*

Don't *lose* your keys.

Don't *lose* the game.

She warned him that his watch was _____ and he might _____ it.

personal/personnel

personal (adj):   [1]relating to an individual; [2]private
personnel (noun):   people employed by an organization

Is this your *personal* account or your corporate account?

He asked for his *personal* mail.

All *personnel* in the company were interviewed.

The manager took a _____ interest in the _____ in his department.

quiet/quit/quite

quiet (adj):   [1]free from noise; [2]calm
quit (verb):   [1]to give up; [2]to stop
quite (adv):   [1]completely; [2]rather

They loved the *quiet* village.

He *quit* smoking.

She is not *quite* alone.

She is coming *quite* soon.

Christina was _____ determined to find a _____ spot to study be-

fore she _____ for the day.

receipt/recipe

receipt (noun):   paper showing that a bill has been paid
recipe (noun):   formula for preparing a mixture, especially in cooking

No exchanges can be made without a *receipt.*

I found my *recipe* for caramel flan.

Here is your sales _____ for the cookbook; I hope you enjoy each

_____ in it.

special/especially

special (adj):   not ordinary
especially (adv):   particularly

We're planning a *special* weekend.

She is *especially* talented in art.

A sixteenth birthday party is a _____ event for a girl, _____ when

all of her friends can attend.

than/then

than (conj or prep):   used to make a comparison
then (adv):   ¹at that time; ²next

This cake is sweeter *than* that one.

I was at work *then*.

First he blamed his parents; *then* he blamed me.

Billy and Janice cook at home rather _____ eat out; _____ they

usually go to a movie.

thorough/though/thought/through/threw

thorough (adj):   accurate and complete
though (adv or conj):   despite the fact that
thought (verb):   past tense of *think*
through (prep):   from one end to the other
(Note: *thru* is not standard spelling.)
threw (verb):   past tense of *throw*

She always does a *thorough* job.

I worked even *though* I was exhausted.

I *thought* about my goals.

We drove *through* the tunnel.

He *threw* the ball to me.

We _____ she did a _____ job of cleaning the apartment, even

_____ she _____ out some papers that she should have looked

_____ more carefully.

use/used to

use (verb):   to employ for a purpose (past tense is *used*)
used to: ¹an expression indicating that an activity is no longer done in the present; ²accustomed to or familiar with

Yesterday, I *used* my father's car.

I *used to* take the bus to school, but now I ride my bike.

I am *used to* walking to school.

I _____ enjoy fixing my own car, but then I _____ my local

garage for the first time, and now I _____ that garage all the time.

EXERCISE ⑨   **Group V Words**

Circle the word that correctly completes each of the following sentences.

1.   My parents (emigrated, immigrated) from Greece.

2.   Let's not travel any (farther, further) tonight.

3.   Your belt is too (loose, lose).

4.   Most of the (personal, personnel) at this company are well trained.

5.   Please be (quiet, quit, quite) while she is performing.

6.   Keep this (receipt, recipe) for tax purposes.

7.   He made a (special, especially) trip to visit his daughter.

8.   I would rather read a good book (than, then) watch television.

9.   When she walked (thorough, though, thought, through, threw) the door, he didn't recognize her even (thorough, though, thought, through, threw) he had known her all his life.

10.   I am not (use, used) to staying up so late.

EXERCISE 10   **Group V Words**

Edit the following paragraph for word confusions. Circle the errors and write the correct words on the lines below the paragraph.

Advertising is very old: some advertisements on paper go back farther than three thousand years. In ancient Greece, it was quiet common to see signs advertising different kinds of services, but it was not until printing was invented that modern advertising was born. In Europe in the seventeenth century, people use to place ads in newspapers; some of these ads were personnel messages, but most were for business. When emigrants came to the United States, they used advertisements to find jobs; we can imagine them going thorough each newspaper very carefully. Today, advertising is all around us, special on television. If we are not careful, we can loose our focus when we watch advertising. For example, when a commercial interrupts a chef who is giving us a receipt for a complicated new dish, we are likely to remember the flashy commercial better then the chef's directions.

_____   _____

_____   _____

_____   _____

_____   _____

Group VI: *lie/lay, rise/raise,* and *sit/set*

These six verbs (*lie/lay, rise/raise,* and *sit/set*) are perhaps the most troublesome verbs in the English language. Not only are their principal parts irregular and easily confused with each other, but in addition, one set is reflexive and cannot take an object whereas the other set must always take a direct object. First learn the principal parts of the three reflexive verbs whose action is accomplished by the subject only.

VERBS REQUIRING NO OBJECT: *LIE, RISE,* AND *SIT*

The reflexive verbs *lie, rise,* and *sit* are used when the subject is doing the action without any help. No other person or object is needed to accomplish the action.

The verbs *lie, rise,* and *sit* do not require an object.

I *lie* down.

I *rise* up.

I *sit* down.

Principal Parts of *lie, rise,* and *sit*

Verb meaning	Present	Present participle	Past	Past participle
lie: to recline	lie	lying	lay	has lain or have lain
rise: to stand up or move upward	rise	rising	rose	has risen or have risen
sit: to take a sitting position	sit	sitting	sat	has set or have sat

Here are some additional sentences with reflexive verbs:

The *cat is lying* on the rug.

The *sun rose* in the east.

The *woman sat* on the sofa.

PRACTICE Fill in the blank in each of the following sentences with the correct form of the reflexive verb.

1. As I write this postcard, the sun is _____.
   (rise)

2. The new tools _____ on the workbench. (*Use present tense.*)
   (lie)

3. He was _____ at the breakfast table when the phone rang.
   (sit)

4. Last night, we _____ in bed watching a television show.
   (lie)

5. Last year, the workers _____ at five o'clock every morning.
   (rise)

6. The cat is always _____ on my favorite chair.
   (lie)

7. It was very late when they _____ down to dinner.
   (sit)

8. The price of cigarettes has _____ dramatically.
   (rise)

9. The newspapers have _____ in the driveway for days.
   (lie)

10. The child has _____ a long time in front of the camera.
    (sit)

VERBS REQUIRING A DIRECT OBJECT: *LAY, RAISE,* AND *SET*

The three verbs *lay*, *raise*, and *set* always require a direct object.

I *lay* the book down.

I *raise* the flag.

I *set* the table.

Principal Parts of Verbs
lay, raise, and *set*

Verb meaning	Present	Present participle	Past	Past participle
lay: to put something	lay	laying	laid	has laid or have laid
raise: to move something up	raise	raising	raised	has raised or have raised
set: to place something	set	setting	set	has set or have set

Here are some additional examples of these verbs. Notice that each verb takes a direct object.

The cat *laid her ball* on the rug.

The sunshine *raised our spirits.*

The woman *set her hat* on the sofa.

PRACTICE   Fill in the first blank in each of the following sentences with the correct form of the verb. Then choose a direct object for each verb and put it in the second blank.

1. The postal worker said he had _____ the _____ on the back porch.
   (lay)

2. The father _____ his _____ to be a caring person. (*Use past tense.*)
   (raise)

3. We always _____ the _____ on the counter.
   (set)

4. They are _____ down the new _____ today.
   (lay)

5. Every night, I _____ out my _____ for the following day.
   (lay)

6. The citizen _____ many _____ whenever the board meets.
    (raise)

7. She has _____ the _____ to record tonight's program.
    (set)

8. Last week, the coach _____ the _____ for the game.
    (lay)

9. We were _____ the _____ for dinner.
    (set)

10. He has _____ a substantial amount of _____ for the charity.
    (raise)

EXERCISE 11   **Group VI Words**

Fill in the blank in each of the following sentences with the correct form of the correct verb.

1. I have _____ the suitcases in your room.
    (lie, lay)

2. I am _____ in my favorite rocking chair.
    (sit, set)

3. She likes me to _____ by her bed and read to her in the evening.
    (sit, set)

4. Last spring, the manufacturers _____ the prices.
    (rise, raise)

5. Yesterday, the price of the magazine _____ by a dime.
    (rise, raise)

6. When I entered the room, the woman _____ to greet me.
    (rise, raise)

7. The woman _____ her head when I entered the room.
    (rise, raise)

8. I usually _____ down in the afternoon.
    (lie, lay)

9. The auto mechanic is _____ under the car.
    (lie, lay)

10. I can't remember where I _____ my keys.
    (lie, lay)

EXERCISE 12   **Group VI Words**

Fill in the blank in each of the following sentences with the correct form of the correct verb.

1. The cat has _____ in the sun all day.
    (lie, lay)

2. If you feel sick, _____ down on that bed.
    (lie, lay)

3. The elevator always _____ quickly to the tenth floor.
    (rise, raise)

4. The boss _____ her salary twice this year.
    (rise, raise)

5. His parents _____ down the law when he came home late.
    (lie, lay)

6. The carpenters _____ the roof when they remodeled the house.
    (rise, raise)

7. The dog _____ up every night and begs for food.
    (sit, set)

8. Last week, I _____ in front of my television set nearly every night.
    (sit, set)

9. I always watch the waiter _____ on a stool after his shift is done.
    (sit, set)

10. We have _____ out cookies and milk for Santa Claus
    (sit, set)

    every year since the children were born.

Mastery and Editing Tests

TEST **1**   **Choosing Correct Words**
Circle the words that correctly complete the sentences.

In the (past, passed), the major way to identify people was (thorough, though, thought, through, threw) the use of fingerprints. That technique was developed during the (rain, reign, rein) of Queen Victoria in England. With modern technology has come iris recognition, a method of identification that uses the information stored in the iris, the colored section of the eye that surrounds the pupil. The iris contains more information (than, then) any other part of the body; (it's, its) 266 features can be measured fully. In contrast, fingerprints contain only 30 features. Iris recognition was developed in 1994 by a computer scientist at Cambridge University in England, and now (it's, its) used to identify people at airport security checkpoints and in some banks. To scan a person's iris, a machine directs a beam of infrared light on the person from fourteen inches away. The (whole, hole) procedure takes about one minute. For thirty-five thousand dollars, a bank could (buy, by) a machine that would measure an iris, but (they're, their, there) is a problem: the bank's customers would not be able to use a different bank's ATM. So far, the questions about this new technology have concerned accuracy and cost, but (who's, whose) to judge the importance of safeguarding an individual's privacy?

TEST **2**   **Choosing Correct Words**
Circle the words that correctly complete the sentences.

Coffee has a long history and an interesting one. Long before it was brewed, coffee was enjoyed (plain, plane) or mixed with vegetables and eaten as food. The (sight, site, cite) of the first cultivated coffee was most likely Kaffa, a part of Ethiopia not far from the (capital, capitol) of that country. That is (we're, were, where) coffee most likely got (it's, its) name. (Than, Then) in the fourteenth century, merchants came across the (desert, dessert) from Arabia to Kaffa, obtained coffee seeds, and began to grow coffee in their own countries. The people of Arabia were (quiet, quite, quit) happy to enjoy coffee, (special, especially) because it took the place of alcohol, which they were not allowed to drink. The first (loose, lose) coffee beans came to Europe in 1615, and the drink has remained popular ever since.

TEST 3 Choosing Correct Words

Circle the words that correctly complete the sentences.

People have pierced their ears (thorough, though, thought, through, threw) every period of recorded history. Ancient Egyptians, Persians, Hebrews, and others would (sit, set) jewels, pearls, and other precious stones into gold and silver to make earrings. They even (use, used) to hang earrings from the statues of their gods and goddesses. When the Egyptians put mummies in their tombs, they would (lie, lay) earrings in the coffins as decorations for the people to wear in the afterlife. Centuries ago, both men and women wore earrings, but one Roman emperor thought his people were becoming (to, too, two) (vain, vane, vein). After speaking out against the use of earrings, he (farther, further) stated that men could not wear them. We do not know how people reacted to that announcement, but there would be an uproar today because people see wearing (they're, their, there) jewelry as a (right, write, rite). Hardly anyone would (accept, except) such a regulation today.

Exploring Online

Go to academic.cengage.com/devenglish/scarry to find the **Writer's Online Workplace,** a website designed for students using this book. You will find links to handouts, interactive quizzes, and other online resources as you explore the following topic:

- look-alikes and sound-alikes

Working Together

Examining the Issue of Plagiarism

Plagiarism is the unethical use of someone else's ideas or words as if they were your own. When your writing contains material from the work of another writer, you must give credit to the person who produced that material, or else you will be accused of plagiarism. All writers are expected to be responsible and clearly acknowledge the sources for their work. College students should be especially careful about plagiarism because they are often under stress to get assignments in on time and may be tempted to take the easy way out and copy from someone else's work. However, this lack of honesty in submitting someone else's work as your own is usually severely punished.

One professional writer who should have been aware of the seriousness of plagiarism is the American writer Alexander Theroux. Theroux, who has taught at Harvard and Yale, published a collection of essays titled *The Primary Colors.* A woman happened to be reading Theroux's book along with another work, *Song of the Sky* by Guy Murchie. The Guy Murchie book, published in 1954, was little known and had been out of print for some time. The reader noticed some remarkable similarities between some passages from the two books. Study one of these passages from Alexander Theroux's book and compare it to a passage from Guy Murchie's book.

Song of the Sky, page 29

"Blue water is salty, warm, and deep and speaks of the tropics where evaporation is great and dilution small—the Sulu Sea, the Indian Ocean, the Gulf Stream. Green water is cool, pale with particles, thin with river and rain, often shallow."

The Primary Colors, page 16

"Incidentally, blue water is invariably salty, warm, and deep and speaks of the tropics, where evaporation is great and dilution minimal—the Sulu Sea, the Indian Ocean, the Gulf Stream. Green water, on the other hand, is cool, pale with particles, thin with river and rain, often shallow."

Questions for Small-Group Discussion

1. Discuss the extent to which the two passages differ.

2. When asked about the striking similarities between his book and *Song of the Sky,* Alexander Theroux stated, "I just thought it was my own work. I can't always remember the source of where I found something." Discuss the writer's explanation. Is it satisfactory? Do you think there is a more likely explanation?

3. When this example of plagiarism was discovered, the publisher of the Theroux book announced that future editions would either leave out the plagiarized passages or give direct credit to *Song of the Sky.* Was this a good solution? In your opinion, is there anything else the publisher should do in such a case?

4. If a college student is found guilty of plagiarism, what should the penalty be?

5. It has been said that when students plagiarize material in school those students really cheat themselves because any benefit from learning is lost. Discuss.

6. What is the policy on plagiarism given in the catalogue of the educational institution you attend?

Portfolio Suggestion

A democracy depends on the integrity of its institutions and its individual citizens to function. Make a list of the ways college students you have observed reveal a lack of integrity. Have you observed cheating on tests, buying papers on the Internet, or copying of other students' assignments? You may want to write an essay in which you predict the effects this behavior will have when these same students graduate and assume leadership positions in their communities.

PART 4

Creating Effective Paragraphs

In many ways, Part 4 is the heart of your work in this course. After you have carefully focused on the importance of the topic sentence, you will study the different methods used to develop ideas, with particular emphasis on achieving coherence. You will then have several opportunities to write paragraphs of your own, using more than one approach: following a guided step-by-step approach or a more creative approach that first presents carefully chosen professional model paragraphs and then lists a number of related topics for writing assignments.

285

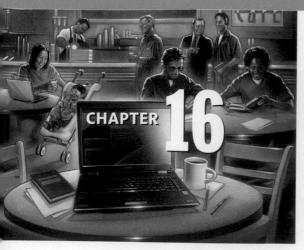

CHAPTER 16

Working with Paragraphs: Topic Sentences and Controlling Ideas

The well-developed paragraph almost always has a topic sentence. In this chapter, you will learn how to recognize and generate your own strong topic sentences. The following topics are presented:

CHAPTER OBJECTIVES

- identifying the characteristics of an acceptable paragraph
- finding the topic sentence of a paragraph
- distinguishing between a topic sentence and a title
- finding the topic in a topic sentence
- finding the controlling idea of a topic sentence
- choosing controlling ideas
- writing topic sentences

What Is a Paragraph?

> A **paragraph** is a group of sentences that develops one main idea. A paragraph may stand by itself as a complete piece of writing, or it may be a section of a longer piece of writing, such as an essay.

No single rule can prescribe how long a paragraph should be, but paragraphs that are too short make a reader feel that basic information is missing. On the other hand, if a paragraph is too long, the reader will become bored or confused. For a paragraph to be effective, the length must be sufficient to develop the main idea. An adequate paragraph is usually six or seven sentences long but no more than ten or twelve sentences. When you read newspapers or magazines, you will find paragraphs as short as one sentence, but unless a paragraph reports a dialogue, one sentence is seldom considered an acceptable paragraph in well-developed writing.

Your instructor may want a demonstration of your ability to use the computer before you begin writing and printing out your own paragraphs. You will need to follow the standard paragraph form, including consistent margins, an indented first sentence, capitalization of the first word of each sentence, and correct end punctuation for each complete sentence. There may be other requirements such as double spacing and where to place certain submission information including your name and the date. Although this may appear to be a very basic exercise, many students need guidance with some aspects of the work. While you are in college, you will need to be comfortable composing on the computer, so use this opportunity to learn something new. For example, you could learn how to set margins, how to use the spell-check feature, how to paginate, or how to make charts.

EXERCISE **Standard Paragraph Form**

Form the following sentences into a standard paragraph. Follow your instructor's requirements for margins and spacing. Then print out your work, being sure to check the page for typos and other errors.

1. The local high school became a haven for disaster victims.

2. In the large basement, thirty families huddled in little groups of four or five.

3. Volunteer workers were busy carrying in boxes of clothing and blankets.

4. Two Red Cross women stood at a long table sorting through boxes to find sweaters and blankets for the shivering flood victims.

5. One heavyset man in a red woolen hunting jacket stirred a huge pot of soup.

6. Men and women with tired faces sipped their steaming coffee and wondered if they would ever see their homes again.

7. Outside, the downpour continued.

What Is a Topic Sentence?

> A **topic sentence** states the main idea of a paragraph. It is the most general sentence of the paragraph. All the other sentences serve to explain, describe, extend, or support this main-idea sentence.

Most paragraphs you read will begin with the topic sentence. However, some topic sentences come in the middle of the paragraph; others come at the end. Some paragraphs have no stated topic sentence at all; in those cases, the main idea is implied. Students are usually advised to use topic sentences in all their work to be certain that the writing has a focus and develops a single idea at a time. Whether you are taking an essay exam in a history course, doing a research paper for a sociology course, or writing an essay in a composition course, thoughtful use of topic sentences will always bring better results. Good topic sentences help both the writer and the reader think clearly about the main points.

Below are two paragraphs. Each paragraph makes a separate point, which is stated in its topic sentence. In both of these paragraphs, the topic sentence happens to be first. Read the paragraphs and notice how the topic sentence is the most general sentence; it states the main idea of each paragraph. The other sentences explain, describe, extend, or support the topic sentence.

I went through a difficult period after my father died. I was moody and sullen at home. I spent most of the time in my bedroom listening to music on the radio, which made me feel even worse. I stopped playing soccer after school with my friends. My grades in school went down. I lost my appetite and seemed to get into arguments with everybody. My mom began to look worried, but I couldn't bring myself to participate in an activity with any spirit. It seemed life had lost its joy for me.

Fortunately, something happened that spring that brought me out of my depression. My uncle, who had been crippled in the Vietnam War, came to live with us. I learned many years later that my mother had asked him to come and live with us in the hope that he could bring me out of myself. I, on the other hand, was told that it was my responsibility to help my uncle feel at home. My mother's plan worked. My uncle and I were both lonely people. A friendship began that was to change both our lives for the better.

EXERCISE **Finding the Topic Sentence of a Paragraph**

Each of the following five paragraphs contains a topic sentence that states the main idea of the paragraph. Find the sentence that best states the main idea and underline it. Keep in mind that the topic sentence will not always be the first sentence of the paragraph.

1.   Mountains of disposable diapers are thrown into garbage cans every day. Tons of yogurt containers, soda cans, and other plastic items are discarded without so much as a stomp to flatten them out. If the old Chevy is not worth fixing, tow it off to sit with thousands of others on acres of fenced-in junkyards. Radios, televisions, and toasters get the same treatment because it is easier and often less expensive to buy a new product than to fix the old one. Who wants a comfortable old sweater if a new one can be bought on sale? No thought is given to the fact that the new one will look like the old one after two or three washings. We are the great "Let's junk it" society!

2.   Anyone who has been in the hospital with a serious illness can tell you that the sight of a good nurse is the most beautiful sight in the world. Today, the hospital nurse has one of the hardest jobs of all. Although a doctor may

direct the care and treatment of a patient, it is the nurse who must see to it that the care and treatment are carried out. A nurse must pay attention to everything, from the condition of the hospital bed to the scheduling of medication throughout the day and night. In addition to following a doctor's orders for the day, the nurse must respond to whatever the patient might need at any given moment. A sudden emergency requires the nurse to make an immediate judgment: can the situation be handled with or without the doctor being called in? More recently, nurses have become increasingly burdened by paperwork and other administrative duties. Many people worry that the increasing demands on nurses will take them away from what they do best—namely, taking care of people on a one-to-one basis.

3.   Anything can happen at a county agricultural fair. It is the perfect human occasion, the harvest of the fields and of the emotions. To the fair come the man and his cow, the boy and his girl, the wife and her green tomato pickles, each anticipating victory and the excitement of being separated from his or her money by familiar devices. It is at a fair that a man can be drunk forever on liquor, love, or fights; at a fair that your front pocket can be picked by a trotting horse looking for sugar, and your hind pocket by a thief looking for his fortune.

4.   This was one of the worst situations I had ever been in. There was a tube in my nose that went all the way to the pit of my stomach. I was being fed intravenously, and there was a drain in my side. Everybody came to visit me, mainly out of curiosity. The girls were all anxious to know where I had gotten shot. They had heard all kinds of tales about where the bullet struck. The bolder ones wouldn't even bother to ask: they just snatched the cover off me and looked for themselves. In a few days, the word got around that I was in one piece.

5.   On hot summer days, the only room of the house that was cool was the sunporch. My mother brought out all her books and papers and stacked them up on the card table. There she would sit for hours at a stretch with one hand on her forehead trying to concentrate. Baby Kathleen would often sit in her playpen, throwing all her toys out of the pen or screeching with such a piercing high pitch that someone would have to come and rescue Mom by giving the baby a cracker. Father would frequently bring in cups of tea for everyone and make Mother laugh with his Irish sense of humor. It was there I would

love to curl up on the wicker sofa (which was too short for my long legs even at twelve) and read one of the forty or fifty books I had bought for ten cents each at a local book fair. The sounds of neighborhood activities—muted voices, a back door slamming, a dog barking—all these were a background that was friendly yet distant. During those summer days, the sunporch was the center of our lives.

EXERCISE **Finding the Topic Sentence of a Paragraph**

Each of the following five paragraphs contains a topic sentence that states the main idea of the paragraph. Find the sentence that best states the main idea and underline it. Keep in mind that the topic sentence will not always be the first sentence of the paragraph.

1.   Last evening at a party, a complete stranger asked me, "Are you a Libra?" Astrology is enjoying increasing popularity all across the United States. My wife hurries every morning to read her horoscope in the paper. At the local stores, cards, books, T-shirts, and other useless astrological products bring fat profits to those who have manufactured them. Even some public officials, like the British royal family, are known to consider the "science" of astrology before scheduling an important event.

2.   Travelers to the United States have usually heard about the wonders of Niagara Falls and the Grand Canyon. These same tourists are not always so aware that an impressive variety of other sights awaits them in this country. The spectacular beauty of the Rocky Mountains and the wide majesty of the Mississippi River are sure to please the tourist. The green hills and valleys of the East are a contrast to the purple plains and dramatic skies of the West. The sandy beaches of the southern states are becoming increasingly popular. Even the area of the Great Lakes becomes a center of activity for boating, fishing, and swimming throughout the summer months.

3.   When we remember something, our brain uses more than one method to store the information. Short-term memory helps recall recent events; long-term memory brings back items that are further in the past; and deep retrieval gives access to long-buried information that is sometimes difficult to recall. Whether these processes are chemical or electrical, we do not yet know, and much research remains to be done before we can say with any certainty. The brain is one of the most remarkable organs, a part of the body that we have only begun to investigate. It will be years before we even begin to understand all its complex processes.

4.   Some of the homes were small with whitewashed walls and thatched roofs. We were eager to see how they were furnished. The living rooms were simple, often with only a plain wooden table and some chairs. The tiny bedrooms usually had room for only a single bed and a small table. Occasionally, a bedroom would be large enough to have a stove made of richly decorated tiles. Visiting these houses was an experience that would always stay in our memory. All of the windows held boxes for flowers so that even in the dark of winter there was the promise of a blaze of colors in the spring.

5.   Advertisements that claim you can lose five pounds overnight are not to be trusted. Nor are claims that your luck will change if you send money to a certain post office box in a distant state. You should also avoid chain letters you receive in the mail that promise you large amounts of money if you will cooperate and keep the chain going. Many people are suspicious of the well-publicized million-dollar giveaway promotions that seem to offer enormous cash prizes, even if you do not try the company's product. We should always be suspicious of offers that promise us something for little or no effort or money.

EXERCISE   **Finding the Topic Sentence of a Paragraph**

The topic sentence is missing in each of the following four paragraphs. Read each paragraph carefully and circle the letter of the best topic sentence for that paragraph.

1.   Ninety-five percent of the population in China had been illiterate. He knew that American public schools would take care of our English, but he had to be the watchdog to nurture our Chinese knowledge. Only the Cantonese tongue was ever spoken by him or my mother. When the two oldest girls arrived from China, the schools of Chinatown received only boys. My father tutored his daughters each morning before breakfast. In the midst of a foreign environment, he clung to a combination of the familiar old standards and what was permissible in the newly learned Christian ideals.

  a.   Education was always a priority in our family.

  b.   My father made sure that his sons received a proper education.

  c.   Learning Cantonese was an essential part of my education.

  d.   My father believed that the girls deserved educational opportunities just as much as the boys in the family.

2.   How to hold a pair of chopsticks (palm up, not down); how to hold a bowl of rice (one thumb on top, not resting in an open palm); how to pass something to elders (with both hands, never one); how to pour tea into the tiny, handleless porcelain cups (seven-eighths full so that the top edge would be cool enough to hold); how to eat from a center serving dish (only the piece in front of your place; never pick around); not to talk at table; not to show up outside of one's room without being fully dressed; not to be late,

ever; not to be too playful—in a hundred and one ways, we were molded to be trouble-free, unobtrusive, quiescent, cooperative.

    a.   From a very young age, I was taught proper table manners.

    b.   Very early in my life, I was taught the manners of a Chinese lady.

    c.   Many Chinese customs differ from American customs.

    d.   Learning manners in a Chinese American household.

3.   I was never hungry. Though we had no milk, there was all the rice we wanted. We had hot and cold running water—a rarity in Chinatown—as well as our own bathtub. Others in the community used the YWCA or YMCA facilities, where for twenty-five cents, a family could draw six baths. Our sheets were pieced from dishtowels, but we had sheets. I was never neglected, for my mother and father were always at home. During school vacation periods, I was taught to operate many types of machines—tacking (for pockets), overlocking (for the raw edges of seams), buttonhole, double seaming; and I learned all the stages in producing a pair of jeans to its final inspection, folding, and tying in bundles of a dozen pairs by size, ready for pickup. Denim jeans are heavy—my shoulders ached often. My father set up a modest nickel-and-dime piecework reward for me, which he recorded in my own notebook, and he paid me regularly.

    a.   Learning the family trade.

    b.   Life in Chinatown for most people was very hard.

    c.   Learning how to sew was an important part of my upbringing.

    d.   Life was often hard, but there was little reason for unhappiness.

4.   Mother would clean our living quarters thoroughly, decorate the sitting room with flowering branches and fresh oranges, and arrange candied fruits or salty melon seeds for callers. All of us would be dressed in bright new clothes, and relatives or close friends who came to call would give each of us a red paper packet containing a good luck coin—usually a quarter. I remember how my classmates would gleefully talk of their receipts. But my mother made us give our money to her, for she said that she needed it to reciprocate to others.

    a.   I always enjoyed dressing up for Chinese holidays.

    b.   Every holiday was unique and had its own special blend of traditions and festivities.

    c.   The Chinese New Year, which would fall sometime in late January or early February, was the most special time of the year.

    d.   There was much work to be done during times of celebration.

DISTINGUISHING A TOPIC SENTENCE FROM A TITLE

The topic sentence works like a title by announcing to the reader what the paragraph is about. However, keep in mind that the title of an essay or book is usually a single word or short phrase, whereas the topic sentence of a paragraph must *always* be a complete sentence.

Title:	Backpacking in the mountains
Topic sentence:	Backpacking in the mountains last year was an exciting experience.

Title:	The stress of college registration
Topic sentence:	College registration can be stressful.

EXERCISE 5

Distinguishing a Topic Sentence from a Title

Tell whether each of the following examples is a title (T) or a topic sentence (TS) by writing *T* or *TS* in the space provided.

_____ 1. The benefits of a college education

_____ 2. The outstanding achievements of aviator Charles Lindbergh

_____ 3. The president's cabinet faced two major problems

_____ 4. The basis of the Arab-Israeli conflict

_____ 5. The Mediterranean diet is perhaps the healthiest diet in the world

_____ 6. The astounding beauty of the Rocky Mountains at dusk

_____ 7. The finest sports car on the market

_____ 8. Fast-food restaurants are popular with families having small children

_____ 9. The expense of maintaining a car

_____ 10. Maintaining a car is expensive

EXERCISE 6

Distinguishing a Topic Sentence from a Title

Tell whether each of the following examples is a title (T) or a topic sentence (TS) by writing *T* or *TS* in the space provided.

_____ 1. Dreams can be frightening

_____ 2. The advantages of getting a job after high school

_____ 3. *Frida* tells the tragic story of a famous Mexican artist

_____ 4. The home of my dreams

_____ 5. Walking on the beach at sunset calms me down after a stressful day at work

_____ 6. Sewing requires great patience as well as skill

_____ 7. Selecting the right camera for an amateur

_____ 8. Finding the right place to study was my most difficult problem at college

_____ 9. The worst bargain of my life

_____ 10. The old car I bought from my friend's father turned out to be a real bargain

EXERCISE 7

Distinguishing a Topic Sentence from a Title

Tell whether each of the following examples is a title (T) or a topic sentence (TS) by writing *T* or *TS* in the space provided.

_____ 1. How to make friends at college and still have time to study

_____ 2. With the widespread use of computers, word-processing skills are needed for many jobs

_____ 3. The disadvantages of living alone

_____ 4. The fight to keep our neighborhood park

_____ 5. The peacefulness of a solitary weekend at the beach

_____ 6. Our investigation into the mysterious death of Walter D.

_____ 7.   The flea market looked promising

_____ 8.   The two main reasons divorce is common

_____ 9.   The single life did not turn out to be as glamorous as I had hoped

_____ 10. The increasing popularity of board games

FINDING THE TOPIC IN A TOPIC SENTENCE

To find the topic in a topic sentence, ask yourself what subject the writer is going to discuss. In the first sentence that follows, the topic is underlined. Underline the topic in the second example.

Backpacking in the mountains last year was an exciting experience.

College registration can be stressful.

Note that a topic sentence may have a two-part topic:

The differences between softball and baseball may not be readily apparent to the person who is unfamiliar with the games.

EXERCISE 8

Finding the Topic in a Topic Sentence

Find the topic in each of the following topic sentences. For each sentence, ask yourself this question: What topic is the writer going to discuss? Then underline the topic.

1.   Remodeling an old house can be frustrating.

2.   College work demands more independence than high school work.

3.   A well-made suit has three easily identified characteristics.

4.   Growing up near a museum had a profound influence on my life.

5.   My favorite room in the house would seem ugly to most people.

6.   A student who goes to school full-time and also works part-time has to make careful use of every hour.

7.   One of the disadvantages of skiing is the expense.

8.   Spanking is the least successful way to discipline a child.

9.   An attractive wardrobe does not have to be expensive.

10. Of all the years in college, the first year is usually the most demanding.

EXERCISE 9

Finding the Topic in a Topic Sentence

Find the topic in each of the following topic sentences. For each sentence, ask yourself this question: What topic is the writer going to discuss? Then underline the topic.

1.   Taking care of a house can easily be a full-time job.

2.   Many television news programs are more interested in entertaining than providing newsworthy information.

3. One of the undisputed goals in teaching is to be able to offer individualized instruction.

4. Whether it's a car, a house, or a college, bigger isn't always better.

5. Violence on television is disturbing to most child psychologists.

6. In today's economy, carrying at least one credit card is probably advisable.

7. Much highway advertising is not only ugly but also distracting for the driver.

8. Figuring out a semester course schedule can be a complicated process.

9. In recent years, we have seen a dramatic revival of interest in quilting.

10. The grading system of the state university is quite different from that of the small liberal arts college in my hometown.

EXERCISE **Finding the Topic in the Topic Sentence**

Find the topic in each of the following topic sentences. For each sentence, ask yourself this question: What topic is the writer going to discuss? Then underline the topic.

1. To my surprise, the basement had been converted into a small studio apartment.

2. Of all the presidents, Abraham Lincoln probably enjoys the greatest popularity.

3. Nature versus nurture is a controversial issue in child psychology.

4. If you don't have a car in the United States, you have undoubtedly discovered that public transportation is in a state of decay.

5. When we met for dinner that night, I was shocked at the change that had come over my friend.

6. According to the report, current tax laws greatly benefit those who own real estate.

7. Marian Anderson, the famous singer, began her career in a church choir.

8. As we rode into town, the streets seemed unusually empty.

9. The United Parcel Service offers its employees many long-term benefits.

10. Many people claim that clipping coupons can save them as much as 30 percent of their food bill.

What Is a Controlling Idea?

A topic sentence should contain not only the topic but also a controlling idea.

> The **controlling idea** of a topic sentence is the point the writer makes about the topic.
>
> **Backpacking trips are *exhausting*.**

A particular topic could have any number of possible controlling ideas, depending on the writer's focus. On the same topic of *backpacking*, three writers might make different points:

A family backpacking trip can be much more *satisfying* than a trip to an amusement park.

or

Our recent backpacking trip was a *disaster.*

or

A backpacking trip *should be a part of every teenager's experience.*

FINDING THE CONTROLLING IDEA OF A TOPIC SENTENCE

When you look for the controlling idea of a topic sentence, ask yourself this question: What is the point the writer is making about the topic?

In each of the following examples, underline the topic and circle the controlling idea.

Sealfon's Department Store is my favorite store in town.

The writer of this topic sentence announces that the focus will be on what makes the store a favorite.

Sealfon's Department Store is too expensive for my budget.

The writer of this topic sentence announces that the focus will be on the store's high prices.

EXERCISE 11

Finding the Controlling Idea

Below are ten topic sentences. For each sentence, underline the topic and circle the controlling idea.

1. Vigorous exercise is a good way to reduce the effects of stress on the body.

2. Buffalo and Toronto differ in four major ways.

3. Television violence causes aggressive behavior in children.

4. Athletic scholarships available to women are increasing.

5. Caffeine has several adverse effects on the body.

6. Serena Williams and her sister Venus have dominated the world of women's tennis.

7. Training a parakeet to talk takes great patience.

8. Babysitting for a family with four preschool children was the most difficult job I've ever had.

9. The hours between five and seven in the morning are my most productive.

10. The foggy night was spooky.

EXERCISE   **Finding the Controlling Idea**

Below are ten topic sentences. For each sentence, underline the topic and circle the controlling idea.

1. Piano lessons turned out to be an unexpected delight.

2. The training of Japanese policemen is quite different from American police training.

3. An Olympic champion has five distinctive characteristics.

4. The candidate's unethical financial dealings will have a negative impact on this campaign.

5. A bicycle ride along the coast is a breathtaking trip.

6. The grocery store is another place where people waste a significant amount of money every week.

7. Being an only child is not as bad as people think.

8. Rewarding children with candy or desserts is an unfortunate habit of many parents.

9. A childhood hobby often develops into a promising career.

10. The writing of a dictionary is an incredibly detailed process.

EXERCISE 13   **Finding the Controlling Idea**

Below are ten topic sentences. For each sentence, underline the topic and circle the controlling idea.

1. Learning to type takes more practice than talent.

2. Shakespeare's plays are difficult for today's students.

3. Atlanta, Georgia, is one of the cities in the Sunbelt that is experiencing significant population growth.

4. Half a dozen new health magazines are enjoying popularity.

5. The importance of good preschool programs for children has been sadly underestimated.

6. The disposal of toxic wastes has caused problems for many manufacturers.

7. Censorship of school textbooks is a controversial issue in most towns.

8. Finding an inexpensive method to make saltwater drinkable has been a difficult problem for decades.

9. Developing color film is more complicated than developing black and white.

10. The cloudberry is one of the rare berries of the world.

CHOOSING CONTROLLING IDEAS

Teachers often assign one general topic on which all students must write. Likewise, when writing contests are announced, the topic is often the same for all contestants. Since very few people have exactly the same view or attitude toward a topic, it is likely that no two papers will have the same controlling idea. There could be as many controlling ideas as there are people to write them. The secret to writing a successful topic sentence is to find the controlling idea that is right for you.

EXERCISE **Choosing Controlling Ideas to Write Topic Sentences**

Below are two topics. For each topic, think of three possible controlling ideas, and then write a topic sentence for each of these controlling ideas. An example is done for you.

Topic: My mother

Three possible controlling ideas:
1. Unusual childhood
2. Silent woman
3. Definite ideas about alcohol

Three different topic sentences:
1. My mother had a most unusual childhood.
2. My mother is a very silent woman.
3. My mother has definite ideas about alcohol.

1. **Topic:** My grandmother

First controlling idea: _____

First topic sentence: _____

_____

Second controlling idea: _____

Second topic sentence: _____

_____

Third controlling idea: _____

Third topic sentence: _____

_____

2. **Topic:** California (or another state)

First controlling idea: _____

First topic sentence: _____

_____

Second controlling idea: _____

Second topic sentence: _____

_____

Third controlling idea: _____

Third topic sentence: _____

_____

EXERCISE **15** **Choosing Controlling Ideas to Write Topic Sentences**

Below are two topics. For each topic, think of three possible controlling ideas, and then write a topic sentence for each of these controlling ideas. An example is done for you.

> **Topic:** The movie *Apollo 13*
>
> **Three possible controlling ideas:**
> 1. Filled with suspense
> 2. Reveals the bravery of the astronauts
> 3. Explores the importance of teamwork
>
> **Three different topic sentences:**
> 1. *Apollo 13* is a movie filled with suspense.
> 2. *Apollo 13* is a movie that reveals the bravery of the astronauts when faced with a life or death situation.
> 3. *Apollo 13* is a movie that explores the importance of teamwork.

1. **Topic:** Reality television shows

    First controlling idea: _____

    First topic sentence: _____

    _____

    Second controlling idea: _____

    Second topic sentence: _____

    _____

    Third controlling idea: _____

    Third topic sentence: _____

    _____

2. **Topic:** Working in a nursing home

    First controlling idea: _____

    First topic sentence: _____

    _____

    Second controlling idea: _____

    Second topic sentence: _____

    _____

    Third controlling idea: _____

    Third topic sentence: _____

    _____

EXERCISE **Choosing Controlling Ideas to Write Topic Sentences**

Below are two topics. For each topic, think of three possible controlling ideas, and then write a topic sentence for each of these controlling ideas. An example is done for you.

Topic: Fitness and health

Three possible controlling ideas:
1. The growth of new lines of products
2. Increased popularity of health clubs
3. Use of exercise DVDs and equipment at home

Three different topic sentences:
1. Recent years have seen the creation of entire lines of products devoted to fitness and health.
2. The high level of interest in physical fitness and health has resulted in a widespread growth of health clubs across the country.
3. A person can improve his or her health by exercising at home with a professional on DVD or working out on one of the many pieces of equipment available for private use.

1. **Topic:** Rap music

   First controlling idea: _____

   First topic sentence: _____

   _____

   Second controlling idea: _____

   Second topic sentence: _____

   _____

   Third controlling idea: _____

   Third topic sentence: _____

   _____

2. **Topic:** Junk food

   First controlling idea: _____

   First topic sentence: _____

   _____

   Second controlling idea: _____

   Second topic sentence: _____

   _____

   Third controlling idea: _____

   Third topic sentence: _____

   _____

Mastery and Editing Tests

TEST **1**   **Further Practice Writing Topic Sentences**

Develop each of the following topics into a topic sentence. In each case, the controlling idea is missing. Decide on the point you wish to make about the topic. Then include this controlling idea as part of your topic sentence. When you are finished, underline the topic and circle your controlling idea. Be sure your topic sentence is a complete sentence and not a fragment. An example has been done for you.

Topic: My brother's car accident

Controlling idea: Tragic results

Topic sentence: My brother's car accident had (tragic results) for the entire family.

1. **Topic:** Teaching a child good manners

    Controlling idea: _____

    Topic sentence: _____

    _____

2. **Topic:** Two years in the military

    Controlling idea: _____

    Topic sentence: _____

    _____

3. **Topic:** Living with your in-laws

    Controlling idea: _____

    Topic sentence: _____

    _____

4. **Topic:** Moving to a new location

    Controlling idea: _____

    Topic sentence: _____

    _____

5. **Topic:** Going on a diet

    Controlling idea: _____

    Topic sentence: _____

    _____

TEST **2**   **Further Practice Writing Topic Sentences**

Develop each of the following topics into a topic sentence. In each case, the controlling idea is missing. Decide on the point you wish to make about the topic. Then include this controlling idea as part of your topic sentence. When you are finished, underline the topic and circle your controlling idea. Be sure your topic sentence is a complete sentence and not a fragment.

1. **Topic:** Camping

   Controlling idea: _____

   Topic sentence: _____

   _____

2. **Topic:** Vegetarians

   Controlling idea: _____

   Topic sentence: _____

   _____

3. **Topic:** Noisy neighbors

   Controlling idea: _____

   Topic sentence: _____

   _____

4. **Topic:** Driving lessons

   Controlling idea: _____

   Topic sentence: _____

   _____

5. **Topic:** Subways

   Controlling idea: _____

   Topic sentence: _____

   _____

TEST **3**

Further Practice Writing Topic Sentences

Develop each of the following topics into a topic sentence. In each case, the controlling idea is missing. Decide on the point you wish to make about the topic. Then include this controlling idea as part of your topic sentence. When you are finished, underline the topic and circle your controlling idea. Be sure your topic sentence is a complete sentence and not a fragment.

1. **Topic:** Computer programming

   Controlling idea: _____

   Topic sentence: _____

   _____

2. **Topic:** Body piercing

   Controlling idea: _____

   Topic sentence: _____

   _____

3. **Topic:** Allergies

   Controlling idea: _____

   Topic sentence: _____

   _____

4. **Topic:** Motorcycles

   Controlling idea: _____

   Topic sentence: _____

   _____

5. **Topic:** Eating out

   Controlling idea: _____

   Topic sentence: _____

   _____

Exploring Online

Go to academic.cengage.com/devenglish/scarry to find the **Writer's Online Workplace,** a website designed for students using this book. You will find links to handouts, interactive quizzes, and other online resources as you explore the following topics:

- paragraphs and topic sentences
- paragraph development
- finding the topic sentence

Working Together

Exploring Controlling Ideas: A Person's Lifestyle

In developing an essay on any given topic, a writer has an almost endless number of possible controlling ideas from which to choose. Student writers often express amazement when they discover how another writer has approached a given topic. "I never thought of doing that," they say. Let's explore some of these possible approaches to a topic as we brainstorm for different controlling ideas on the topic of *a person's lifestyle.*

What follows is an example of just one controlling idea on a person's lifestyle, which uses comparison and contrast as a method of development.

My parents' lifestyle is a completely different arrangement from my own.

Begin by dividing into groups. Each person in each group should provide at least two controlling ideas for possible use in a piece of writing on a person's lifestyle. One person in the group should bring all the controlling ideas together into a single list that will be shared with the entire class. Finally, all the groups should come together and share their lists. How many different controlling ideas have come out of the work of all the groups? Do these controlling ideas cover all the different methods for developing ideas discussed in this textbook?

Portfolio Suggestion

Each student in the class should copy the list of controlling ideas developed by the class. Organize the ideas into groups according to most obvious method of development: description, example, narration, process, classification, cause and effect, definition, comparison and contrast, or argument. Save this list in your portfolio as a reminder of the ways you could develop your own thinking on a given topic. Your instructor may ask you to choose the controlling idea that is most interesting to you for an essay on this aspect of a person's lifestyle.

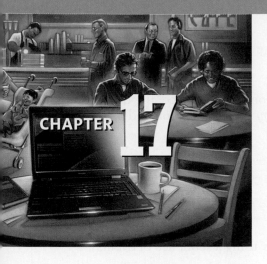

CHAPTER 17

Working with Paragraphs: Supporting Details

To develop a paragraph successfully, you must use appropriate details to support the main idea of that paragraph. In this chapter, you will learn several skills related to supporting details:

CHAPTER OBJECTIVES

- identifying supporting details
- choosing supporting details based on the method of paragraph development
- avoiding restatement of the topic sentence
- making supporting details specific

What Is a Supporting Detail?

Once you have constructed a topic sentence made up of the topic and its controlling idea, you are ready to support your statement with details. The quality and number of these details will largely determine the effectiveness of your writing. You can hold your readers spellbound with your choice of details, or you can lose your readers' interest because your details are not compelling.

A **supporting detail** is a piece of evidence used by a writer to make the controlling idea of the topic sentence convincing and interesting to the reader. A piece of evidence might be a descriptive image, an example taken from history or personal experience, a reason, a fact (such as a statistic), a quotation from an expert, or an anecdote used to illustrate a point.

Poor supporting details:	Many people died of the flu in the 1960s.
Effective supporting details:	In 1968 in the United States, seventy thousand people died of the Hong Kong flu.

How Do You Choose Supporting Details?

For a paragraph to be well developed, the main idea must be supported with several details. As you work through the chapters in this section, you will have opportunities to use many types of supporting details. In the chart on the next page, you can see the different methods of paragraph development. A writer chooses supporting details according to what best fits the method of development. For instance, if the writer is describing someone's appearance, the details are made up of sensory images (for example, *a raspy voice, olive skin,* and *the scent of Old Spice cologne*).

Methods of Paragraph Development

Narration:	telling a story using a sequence of events
Description:	using sensory images to create a picture with words
Process:	using steps explaining how to do something or explaining how something works
Example:	giving instances or illustrations of the main idea
Comparison/contrast:	showing similarities or differences
Cause and effect:	examining reasons or outcomes
Extended definition:	analyzing at some length the meaning of a word or concept
Classification:	dividing a subject into groups or parts

As you choose your supporting details, keep in mind that the readers do not necessarily have to agree with your point of view. However, your supporting details must be good enough to make your readers at least respect your attitude. Your goal should be to educate your readers. Try to give them some understanding of your subject. Don't assume they know about your topic or are interested in it. If you provide enough specific details, your readers will feel they have learned something new about the subject, and this alone is a satisfying experience for most people. Effective supporting details will encourage readers to keep on reading. They will make your points more memorable, and they will give pleasure to those who are learning new material or trying to picture the images you have created.

Read the following paragraph and observe how it provides effective details that support the controlling idea of the topic sentence.

> Everyone has heard of surefire formulas to prevent getting a cold. Popular home methods include a cold shower, regular exercise, and a hot rum toddy. Some people swear by cod-liver oil, tea with honey, citrus fruit juices, or keeping one's feet dry. Americans spent billions last year for cold and cough remedies. Advertisers have claimed preventive and curative virtues for vitamins, alkalizers, lemon drinks, antihistamines, decongestants, timed-release capsules, antibiotics, antiseptic gargles, bioflavonoids, nose drops and sprays, and a variety of other products. There are at least three hundred over-the-counter products, most of which are a combination of ingredients sold for the treatment of symptoms of the common cold. Many of these drugs neither benefit nor harm the cold victim, but there is no doubt that they benefit the drug manufacturers! Now—just as fifty years ago—Americans on average will suffer two to three colds a year, with the infectious stages lasting about a week, regardless of any physical measure, diet, or drug used. U.S. Public Health Service studies show that, during the winter quarter of the year, 50 percent of the population experiences

a common cold; during the summer quarter, the figure drops to 20 percent. The increased incidence of colds in winter reflects the fact that people spend more time indoors, thereby allowing the viruses to travel from person to person. In fact, one is less likely to catch a cold after exposure to the elements than after mixing with a convivial group of snifflers and sneezers at a fireside gathering.

PRACTICE

Using the lines provided, copy the topic sentence from the previous paragraph. Then answer the questions about the details that support the topic sentence.

Topic sentence: _____

_____

What are some examples of home remedies?

_____

_____

What are some examples of over-the-counter remedies?

_____

_____

What fact is given?

_____

_____

What expert is named? What is the statistic given by that source?

_____

_____

EXERCISE 　**Finding the Topic Sentence and Supporting Details**

Read each paragraph below. On the lines that follow, write the topic sentence and identify the supporting details.

1.　　　Saturday afternoon was a blessed time on the farm. First of all, there would now be no mail in till Monday afternoon, so that no distressing business letters could reach us till then, and this fact in itself seemed to close the whole place in. Secondly, everybody was looking forward to the day of Sunday, when they would rest or play all the day, and the Squatters could work on their own land. The thought of the oxen on Saturday pleased me more than all other things. I used to walk down to their paddock at six o'clock, when they were coming in after the day's work and a few hours' grazing. Tomorrow, I thought, they would do nothing but graze all day.

FROM ISAK DINESEN,
Out of Africa

Topic sentence: _____

First reason: _____

_____

Second reason: _____

_____

Third reason: _____

2.　　　More people watched the Super Bowl than watched Neil Armstrong's walk on the moon. Fifteen percent of all television programs produced are sports programs. Professional football games have a yearly attendance of over ten million spectators, and both baseball leagues together draw over three million spectators every year. In one year, North American spectators spent over $3 million for tickets to sports events. There probably is not a person in the United States who does not recognize a picture of Muhammad Ali, and who cannot identify a picture of the soccer star Pelé? The popularity of sports is enormous.

ADAPTED FROM RONALD W. SMITH AND ANDREA FONTANA,
Social Problems (1972)

Topic sentence: _____

First statistical fact: _____

_____

Second statistical fact: _____

_____

_____

Examples of recognizable sports stars: _____

EXERCISE **2**   **Finding the Topic Sentence and Supporting Details**

Read each paragraph below. On the lines that follow, write the topic sentence and identify the supporting details.

1.   Hilda takes an enormous amount of space, though so little time, in my adolescence. Even today, her memory stirs me; I long to see her again. She was three years older than I, and for a short while all I wanted was to look like, sound like, and dress like her. She was the only girl I knew who told me I wrote excellent letters. She made a plaster cast of my face. She had opinions on everything. She took a picture of me, at sixteen, which I have still. She and I were nearly killed, falling off a hillside road in her small car. Hilda was so full of life, I cannot believe her dead.

FROM HAN SUYIN,
A Mortal Flower

Topic sentence: _____

_____

First example: _____

_____

Second example: _____

Third example: _____

Fourth example: _____

Fifth example: _____

Sixth example: _____

2.   A steadily accumulating body of evidence supports the view that cancers are caused by things that we eat, drink, breathe, or are otherwise exposed to. That evidence is of three kinds. First, the incidence of many types of cancers differs greatly from one geographic region of the world to another. Second, when groups of people permanently move from one country to another, the incidence of some types of cancer changes in their offspring. For example, when Japanese move to this country, the relatively high rate of occurrence of stomach cancer they experience in Japan falls so that their children experience such cancer only a fifth as frequently, the same incidence as other Americans. Asians have low incidence of breast cancer, but when they come to the United States, it increases sixfold. Third, we are becoming aware of an increasing number of chemical pollutants in air and water and food that have proven to be cancer-producing.

FROM MAHLON B. HOAGLAND,
The Roots of Life

Topic sentence: _____

_____

First piece of evidence: _____

_____

Second piece of evidence (and example): _____

_____

_____

Third piece of evidence: _____

_____

Finding the Topic Sentence and Supporting Details

Read each paragraph below. On the lines that follow, write the topic sentence and identify the supporting details.

1.　　　Transportation was simple then. Two good horses and a sturdy wagon met most needs of a villager. Only five or six individuals possessed an automobile in the Pueblo of 300. A flatbed truck fixed with wooden rails and a canvas top made a regular Saturday trip to Sante Fe. It was always loaded beyond capacity with Cochitis taking their wares to town for a few staples. With an escort of a dozen barking dogs, the straining truck made a noisy exit, northbound from the village.

FROM JOSEPH H. SUINA,
And Then I Went to School

Topic sentence: _____

First example: _____

Second example: _____

_____

Third example: _____

_____

Fourth example: _____

_____

2.　　　Fairness is the ability to see more than one side in a situation, and sometimes it even means having the ability to decide against your own interests. For example, in San Antonio, Texas, a woman was locked in a bitter custody dispute that involved her thirteen-year-old son. The mother loved her son and wanted custody of him, even though she had a major health problem. She listened patiently while her ex-husband argued for full custody of the child. The woman felt that she had presented a good case before the judge, but when the boy was asked for his feelings in the matter, the mother found herself faced with a difficult situation: her son wanted to live with his father. Fairness to the child led the mother to give up her fight. Fairness, she discovered, is often painful because it means recognizing what is right instead of insisting on your own personal bias.

Topic sentence: _____

_____

Anecdote: _____

_____

_____

_____

_____

_____

_____

Avoiding Restatement of the Topic Sentence

You should be able to recognize the difference between a genuine supporting detail and a simple restatement of the topic sentence. The following is a poor paragraph because all its sentences merely restate the topic sentence.

> The wedding day was the highest point in a girl's life—a day to which she looked forward all her unmarried days and to which she looked back for the rest of her life. All the events of the day were unlike those of any other day in her life before or after. Everyone would remember this day. Each event was unforgettable. The memories would last a lifetime. A wedding was the beginning of living "happily ever after."

By contrast, this paragraph, from Margaret Mead's "From Popping the Question to Popping the Pill," has excellent supporting details:

> The wedding day was the highest point in a girl's life—a day to which she looked forward all her unmarried days and to which she looked back for the rest of her life. The splendor of her wedding, the elegance of dress and veil, the cutting of the cake, the departure amid a shower of rice and confetti, gave her an accolade of which no subsequent event could completely rob her. Today people over fifty years of age still treat their daughter's wedding this way, prominently displaying the photographs of the occasion. Until very recently, all brides' books prescribed exactly the same ritual they had prescribed fifty years before. The etiquette governing wedding presents—gifts that were or were not appropriate, the bride's maiden initials on her linen—was also specified. For the bridegroom the wedding represented the end of his free, bachelor days, and the bachelor dinner the night before the wedding symbolized this loss of freedom. A woman who did not marry—even if she had the alibi of a fiancé who had been killed in war or had abilities and charm and money of her own—was always at a social disadvantage while an eligible bachelor was sought after by hostess after hostess.

EXERCISE **Distinguishing a Supporting Detail from a Restatement of the Main Idea**

Each topic sentence below is followed by four additional sentences. Three of these additional sentences contain acceptable supporting details, but one of the sentences is simply a restatement of the topic sentence. In the space provided, identify each sentence as *SD,* for supporting detail, or *R,* for restatement.

1. I am surprised when I think how neat I used to be before school started.

    _____ a. In my closet, I had my clothes arranged in matching outfits with shoes, hats, and even jewelry to go with them.

    _____ b. I have always taken great pride in having all my things in order.

    _____ c. If I opened my desk drawer, compartments of paper clips, erasers, staples, pens, pencils, stamps, and rulers greeted me, without a penny or safety pin out of place.

    _____ d. On top of my chest of drawers sat a comb and brush and two oval frames with pictures of my best friends; that was all.

2. Iceland has a very barren landscape.

    _____ a. One-tenth of the island is covered by ice.

    _____ b. There is not a single forest on the entire island.

    _____ c. Nearly everywhere you look in Iceland, you see vast desolate areas.

    _____ d. Three-fourths of the island is uninhabitable.

3. Until recently, books have been the most important method of preserving knowledge.

    _____ a. Without books, much of the knowledge of past centuries would have been lost.

    _____ b. Leonardo da Vinci kept notebooks of his amazing inventions and discoveries.

    _____ c. During the Middle Ages, monks spent their entire lives copying books by hand.

    _____ d. The Library of Congress in Washington, D.C., is given a copy of every book published in the United States.

4. Most adults no longer wonder whether cigarette smoking is bad for their health.

    _____ a. Based on the evidence from more than thirty thousand studies, a federal law requires that cigarette manufacturers place a health warning on their packages.

    _____ b. Studies have shown that smoking causes nearly 80 percent of lung cancer deaths in this country.

    _____ c. Few people today have any doubts about the connection between cigarette smoking and poor health.

    _____ d. We know that 30 percent of the deaths from coronary heart disease can be attributed to smoking.

5. When the Mexican earthquake struck in 1985, scientists and city planners learned a great deal about the kinds of buildings that can survive an earthquake.

    _____ a. Buildings that had foundations resting on giant rollers suffered very little damage.

    _____ b. Buildings that were made only of adobe material simply fell apart when the earthquake struck.

_____ c. Many modern buildings were designed to vibrate in an earthquake, and these received the least amount of shock.

_____ d. After the 1985 Mexican earthquake was over, officials realized why some buildings were destroyed and others suffered hardly any damage at all.

EXERCISE 5   **Distinguishing a Supporting Detail from a Restatement of the Main Idea**

Each topic sentence below is followed by four additional sentences. Three of these additional sentences contain acceptable supporting details, but one of the sentences is simply a restatement of the topic sentence. In the space provided, identify each sentence as *SD*, for supporting detail, or *R*, for restatement.

1. In the last thirty years, the number of people living alone in the United States has increased by 400 percent.

   _____ a. People are living alone because the number of divorces has dramatically increased.

   _____ b. Many young people are putting off marriage until they are financially more secure or emotionally ready.

   _____ c. More and more Americans are finding themselves living alone.

   _____ d. An increasing percentage of our population is in the age group over sixty-five, among whom are many widows and widowers.

2. Today, people are realizing the disadvantages of using credit cards too often.

   _____ a. People should think twice before borrowing money on credit.

   _____ b. Interest rates on credit cards can reach alarming rates.

   _____ c. Credit cards encourage buying on impulse, rather than planning a budget carefully.

   _____ d. Many credit card companies charge an annual fee for the privilege of using cards.

3. In medicine, prevention is just as important as treatment.

   _____ a. A good way for a person to keep in touch with his or her health is to have an annual physical.

   _____ b. To stay healthy, people should watch their weight.

   _____ c. Some researchers claim that taking an aspirin every day thins the blood, which prevents clotting.

   _____ d. Where health is concerned, warding off a disease is as critical as curing it.

4. Since World War II, the status of women in Japan has changed.

   _____ a. In 1947, women won the right to vote.

   _____ b. Women's position in Japanese society has altered over the past forty-five years.

   _____ c. Many Japanese women now go on to get a higher education.

   _____ d. Women can now own property in their own name and seek divorce.

5. Certain factors that cannot be changed have been shown to contribute to heart attacks and stroke.

    _____ a. Three out of four heart attacks and six out of seven strokes occur after the age of sixty-five, so age is definitely a factor.

    _____ b. Heart attacks and strokes have many causes, some of which we can do nothing about.

    _____ c. African Americans have nearly a 45 percent greater risk of having high blood pressure, a major cause of heart attacks and strokes.

    _____ d. Men are at greater risk than women in their chance of suffering from cardiovascular disease.

How Do You Make Supporting Details Specific?

Students often write paragraphs that are made up of too many general statements. With such paragraphs, the author's knowledge is in doubt, and you may suspect that the point being made has no basis in fact. Here is one such paragraph that never rises beyond generalities.

> Doctors are terrible. They cause more problems than they solve. I don't believe most of their treatments are necessary. History is full of the mistakes doctors have made. We don't need all those operations. We should never ingest all those drugs doctors prescribe. We shouldn't allow them to give us all those unnecessary tests. I've heard plenty of stories that prove my point. Doctors' ideas can kill you.

Here is another paragraph on the same topic. It is much more interesting and convincing because the writer has made use of supporting details rather than relying on general statements.

> Evidence shows that "medical progress" has been the cause of tragic consequences and even death for thousands of people. X-ray therapy was thought to help patients with tonsillitis. Now many of these people are found to have developed cancer from these X-rays. Not so long ago, women were kept in bed for several weeks following childbirth. Unfortunately, this cost many women their lives because they developed fatal blood clots from being kept in bed day after day. One recent poll estimates that thirty thousand people each year die from the side effects of drugs that were prescribed by doctors. Recently, the Centers for Disease Control and Prevention reported that 25 percent of the tests done by clinical laboratories were done poorly. All this is not to belittle the good done by the medical profession, but to impress on readers that it would be foolish to rely totally on the medical profession to solve all our health problems.

This paragraph is much more likely to be of real interest. Even if you wanted to disprove the author's point, it would be very hard to dismiss these supporting details, which are based on facts and information that can be verified. Because the author sounds reasonable, you have respect for the presentation of specific facts, even if you have a different position on the topic.

In writing effectively, the ability to go beyond the general statement and get to the accurate pieces of information is what counts. A good writer tries to make his or her reader an expert on the subject. Readers should go away excited to share with the next person they meet the surprising information they have just learned. A writer who has a statistic, a quotation, an anecdote, a historical example, or a descriptive detail has the advantage over all other writers, no matter how impressive these writers' styles may be.

Good writing, therefore, is filled with supporting details that are specific, correct, and appropriate for the subject. Poor writing is filled with generalizations, stereotypes, vagueness, untruths, and sometimes even sarcasm and insults.

EXERCISE **Creating Supporting Details**

Below are five topic sentences. Supply three supporting details for each one (inventing, when necessary). Be sure each detail is specific, not general or vague.

1. The first semester in college can be overwhelming.

   a. _____

   b. _____

   c. _____

2. Designer clothing is a bad investment.

   a. _____

   b. _____

   c. _____

3. Dr. Kline is a dedicated teacher.

   a. _____

   b. _____

   c. _____

4. It is difficult to stop snacking between meals.

   a. _____

   b. _____

   c. _____

5. My sister is the sloppiest person I know.

   a. _____

   b. _____

   c. _____

EXERCISE **Creating Supporting Details**

Below are five topic sentences. Supply three supporting details for each one (inventing, when necessary). Be sure each detail is specific, not general or vague.

1. December has become a frantic time at our house.

   a. _____

   b. _____

   c. _____

2. My best friend can often be very immature.

   a. _____

   b. _____

   c. _____

3. Each sport has its own peculiar injuries associated with it.

   a. _____

   b. _____

   c. _____

4. My car is on its "last wheel."

   a. _____

   b. _____

   c. _____

5. Watching too much television has serious effects on family life.

   a. _____

   b. _____

   c. _____

EXERCISE 8   **Creating Supporting Details**

Below are five topic sentences. Supply three supporting details for each one (inventing, when necessary). Be sure each detail is specific, not general or vague.

1. Maintaining a car is a continual drain on one's budget.

   a. _____

   b. _____

   c. _____

2. Climate can affect a person's mood.

   a. _____

   b. _____

   c. _____

3. Last year, I redecorated my bedroom.

   a. _____

   b. _____

   c. _____

4. Washington, D.C., is the best city for a family vacation.

   a. _____

   b. _____

   c. _____

5.   The amateur photographer needs to consider several points when
     selecting a camera.

     a. _____

     b. _____

     c. _____

Exploring Online

Go to academic.cengage.com/devenglish/scarry to find the **Writer's
Online Workplace,** a website designed for students using this book.
You will find links to handouts, interactive quizzes, and other online
resources as you explore the following topics:

- supporting details
- using specific and concrete details

Working Together

Peer Editing: Recording National, Community, or Family Traditions

Celebrations are important milestones in the living traditions of individuals, groups, and even entire nations. Traditional celebrations affirm people's lives and help them feel connected to each other. Celebrations also support a country's need to preserve a sense of its own history. The photograph to the left shows a Native American community sharing an important celebration together.

Divide into groups. Make a list of celebrations (such as birthdays or Thanksgiving) observed by the members of the group. Next, consider what makes each celebration special. If you were to write about a particular holiday, what supporting details would you use? In the case of Thanksgiving, for example, the details would probably center around the meal that would be served. How many other celebrations have the same emphasis on food?

Each person should then write a paragraph describing a chosen celebration. Be sure to have a topic sentence and at least eight more sentences that support the topic sentence. Be sure that these eight sentences provide details that will help the reader construct a picture of the event.

Exchange papers. After you have read the paper you have been given, mark it in the following ways:

1. Underline the topic sentence.
2. Make a ✔ in front of the sentence you believe contains the most effective supporting detail.
3. Make an **X** in front of the sentence you believe has the weakest supporting detail.
4. Using the editing symbols from the inside back cover of your book, mark any errors that you find.
5. The following sentences could have been found in student essays on the subject of *Thanksgiving*. Each of the sentences has been rated on a scale from one to four (one being the best). Use the rating guide to judge the paper you are reading. In the upper right corner of the paper, rate the overall quality of the details by giving the essay a score of one to four.

Rating 1: The details are very specific. For example,

Mamma always ordered her fresh Thanksgiving turkey three weeks in advance from Ike at Goldfinger's Meat Market on Fourth Street.

Rating 2: The details are often specific. For example,

> Mamma ordered our Thanksgiving turkey from the local meat market.

Rating 3: The details are often too general. For example,

> Mamma fixed a turkey every Thanksgiving.

Rating 4: The details are almost always too general. For example,

> Thanksgiving dinner was always great.

6. Select a sentence you believe is too general. Rewrite it with more specific details that you think would make the sentence more interesting. Write your new version at the bottom of the student's paper.

Portfolio Suggestion

When your paragraph has been returned to you, identify it as your first draft. Write a second version in which you make your details more specific. Label this version as your second draft. Be sure to show both versions to someone who can comment on your changes. Are you happier with the second version? Save both versions in your portfolio.

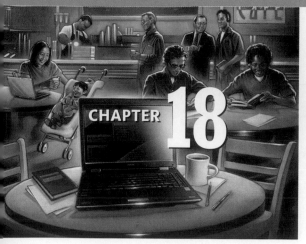

18

Developing Paragraphs: Illustration

To give clarity to a general idea or an abstract notion, every writer needs to use **illustration** or **example.** This method of development is the focus of this chapter. The following topics are presented:

CHAPTER OBJECTIVES

- three ways to illustrate a point
- four sources of examples
- transitions to introduce examples
- analyzing paragraphs with examples
- taking a step-by-step approach to create paragraphs that use illustration
- studying models to create paragraphs that use illustration

What Is Illustration?

A main idea must be supported by details. Using an illustration is one of the best ways to do this.

> **Illustration** (often called **example** or **exemplification**) is a method of developing an idea by providing one or more instances of that idea. Illustrations or examples serve to clarify the idea, make the idea more convincing, or make an abstract idea more concrete.
>
> **One example of American craftsmanship is the Tiffany lamp.**

Writers use illustration in three basic ways.

1. To provide a list of brief examples, given without any particular grouping:

   Topic sentence

   <u>As a child, I had pen pals from all over the world</u>. These included my cousin Britt-Marie from Sweden, Ying from Hong Kong, Simone from France, Etsuko from Japan, and several children from Kenya.

2. To provide a list of brief examples arranged into groups:

   Topic sentence

   <u>As a child, I had pen pals from all over the world</u>. From Europe were my Swedish cousin Britt-Marie and a pretty French girl named Simone. From the Pacific came the beautiful monthly letters of Etsuko and an occasional postcard from Ying in Hong Kong. Finally, from Africa came a number of charming letters from several school-children in Kenya.

3. To select one item from a possible list and develop it more fully into a longer and more developed example, called an **extended example** (possibly consisting of an **anecdote** based on the principles of narration):

Topic sentence

> <u>As a child, I had pen pals from all over the world</u>. It all started when my cousin Britt-Marie in Sweden sent me a funny little letter in crazy English. Sitting on our front porch swatting flies one morning in August, I was considering walking the two miles uptown to the library when the mailman handed me an envelope with colorful stamps on it. It was probably the first piece of mail I had ever received. I barely knew I had a cousin Britt-Marie. But there she was—a young girl writing just to me from across the Atlantic Ocean. I was hooked from that very day. Although I eventually had pen pals from many other countries, Britt-Marie remained my favorite. In fact, we still communicate, now by e-mail, at least once every few weeks.

Always remember that the anecdote must support the larger point contained in the topic sentence—namely, the writer had pen pals from all over the world.

Where Does the Writer Find Examples?

Writers draw on four main sources for examples.

1. **Personal experience and knowledge of the world.** Writers find supporting examples for their work everywhere, beginning with their own experience. What you have observed and what has happened to you are two excellent sources of examples for your writing. You have gained a great deal of knowledge either formally or informally, and you can call upon that knowledge when you look for examples to illustrate your points.

2. **Imagination.** When writers need examples for their work, they often find it useful to create imaginary examples or situations that provide specific details. Humorous writers do this all the time when they tell jokes. You, too, can use your imagination to generate examples when your writing does not require strictly factual information. A hypothetical example is particularly useful to illustrate a point, and it often begins with a phrase such as "Imagine the following situation" or "Consider this hypothetical case" or "Ask yourself what would happen if. . . ."

3. **Interviews and surveys.** Obtaining examples through interviews and informal surveys can enrich your writing by allowing you to present very specific information and facts about your main idea. We see and hear interviews on television and radio every day, as people from all walks of life tell their stories on every topic imaginable. We are accustomed to seeing professional interviewers ask questions, but you can also gain examples in this way by talking to your friends and classmates and learning from them.

4. **Outside research.** Printed or electronic material from outside sources provides specific examples for your work. This research usually involves going to a library and finding information in books and magazines as well as using the Internet. This kind of research is necessary for term papers and many other kinds of college work, and it always requires a careful listing of the sources used.

EXERCISE   **The Sources for Illustrations**

Each of the following three paragraphs develops an idea by using illustration. Read each paragraph and decide what source the writer used to obtain the illustration. Choose from the following list:

- example from personal experience or knowledge
- imaginary or hypothetical example
- information from an interview or survey conducted by the writer
- outside research (material found in books, in articles, or on the Internet)

Topic sentence   1.   <u>Most students today believe they must learn how to use a computer if they are to be competitive in the job market.</u> A case in point is my first-year writing class. Out of the twenty-three students surveyed, all but two felt they must be computer literate before they leave college or they might not be able to get the jobs they want. Fifteen of the students currently own their own computers and claim they are able to get their college work done more easily. Two of these fifteen students actually have part-time jobs, one in the library and one in the history department, where they both enter data on computers. This seems to show that these students already are at an advantage over the rest of the students who are still learning to use a computer.

Type of illustration: _____

Topic sentence   2.   <u>Most students today believe they must learn how to use a computer if they are to be competitive in the job market.</u> Just to illustrate, if a person wants a career in auto mechanics and thinks he or she has no need to learn how to use a computer, that person is likely to be surprised. What if the auto mechanic needs to operate a sophisticated computer to determine malfunctions in cars? What if the staff expects the mechanic to understand how to enter data on the office computer and also expects the person to know how to read the computer printouts? What if he or she must go to school to learn the newest technology, and instead of working with actual cars, everyone works on computer simulations?

Type of illustration: _____

Topic sentence   3.   <u>Most students today realize they must learn how to use computers to compete in the job market.</u> Last semester, I took my first computer course. To my great pleasure, I found that my new skills helped me not only write compositions but also practice my math. I also discovered that I could go online and talk with people all over the world who have interests similar to my own. In addition, I was able to use the computer to access information from the school library. I plan to become a teacher, and I will be able to use my computer skills to make tests and worksheets, research information for class, and help students make discoveries for themselves.

Type of illustration: _____

EXERCISE   **The Sources for Illustrations**

Below is a topic sentence. Write a paragraph in which you support the idea of the topic sentence by using one or more illustrations. Identify the source of your illustration as one of the following:

- example from personal experience or knowledge
- imaginary or hypothetical example

- information from an interview or survey you have conducted yourself
- outside research (material found in books, in articles, or on the Internet)

Topic sentence: *Many advertising claims are deceptive.*

Your paragraph:

_____

_____

_____

_____

_____

_____

_____

_____

_____

Source of illustration: _____

EXERCISE   3

The Sources for Illustrations

Below is a topic sentence. Write a paragraph in which you support the idea by using one or more illustrations. Identify the source of your illustration as one of the following:

- example from personal experience or knowledge
- imaginary or hypothetical example
- information from an interview or survey you have conducted yourself
- outside research (material found in books, in articles, or on the Internet)

Topic sentence: *Taste in music is very personal.* (Consider doing a survey of several class members.)

Your paragraph:

_____

_____

_____

_____

_____

_____

_____

_____

_____

Source of illustration: _____

Achieving Coherence

CHOOSING AN ORDER DEPENDING ON THE TYPE OF ILLUSTRATION

1. If the illustration is a *story* or an *anecdote,* the author usually uses *time order.*
2. If the illustration is made up of *several descriptive examples*, the author might use *spatial order* (top to bottom, right to left, etc.).
3. If the illustration calls for a *logical order,* this logic will determine the sequence.
4. If no special order seems necessary, the author often places the *strongest or most important example last*, because this is what the reader is likely to remember best.

USING TRANSITIONS

Writers often signal the beginning of an illustration by using a key phrase. Below is a list of phrases commonly used to signal the beginning of an illustration.

Transitions Commonly Used in Illustration

For example, . . .	Take the case of . . .
Another example is . . .	For instance, . . .
To illustrate, . . .	A personal anecdote will illustrate
An illustration of this is . . .	this point.
A case in point is . . .	To be specific . . .

EXERCISE   **Analyzing Paragraphs That Use Examples**

Read the following paragraph by Suzanne Britt, and then answer the questions about it.

Topic sentence   Being a connoisseur of junk has wonderfully mucked up my entire life. You know the song about favorite things like raindrops on roses and whiskers on kittens? Well, I've got my own list of favorite things: I like the insides of filthy bus stations, unsavory characters, a Dr Pepper can floating on the sun-flecked water, Jujubes, the greasy tug and tang of beef jerky wrapped in cellophane, the kitchen drawer beside the phone, the Sunday clutter around the house, the noble whiff of manure, the sweaty odor of a person I love, the smoke-filled room in which I get to inhale the equivalent of eleven cigarettes without breaking my promise to quit, the pigeon droppings in the square, the grease under the fingernails of a gas station attendant (if I can still find one), the rusty Brillo on the sink, the bathroom glass placidly growing bacteria for the whole family, *People* magazine, a dog-eared paperback, a cold pork chop eaten at the refrigerator door.

1. State the topic sentence in your own words._____

   _____

2. How many examples are given in the paragraph? _____

3. Underline the examples in the paragraph.

4. Does the author use any words or phrases to signal any of the examples? If so, circle each one. _____

5. If there is more than one example, can you suggest any order for them?

   _____

EXERCISE 5 **Analyzing Paragraphs That Use Examples**
Read the following paragraph and then answer the questions about it.

Dr. George Gallup and his American Institute of Public Opinion conducted surveys for two years on the reading habits of Americans in all walks of life and different sections of the land; one of the striking facts "that is scored and under-scored in these studies is the tremendous influence of Hollywood on reading tastes." Gallup points out that Hollywood boosts the classics of literature into new and extraordinary popularity. When the movie *David Copperfield* was being publicized, the Cleveland library system ordered more than 125 extra copies of the book to meet the probable rise in demand; and although the system had 500 copies of the book, library shelves were bare of *David Copperfield* and other Dickens novels for weeks. The film *Wuthering Heights* served as a remarkable boomerang to that book's popularity. Four publishing houses sold out all their editions of the work in a short time, and bookstores and public libraries could not cope with demand after the rediscovery of the Brontë masterpiece.

Topic sentence

1. State the topic sentence in your own words. _____

   _____

2. How many examples are given in the paragraph? _____

3. Underline the examples in the paragraph.

4. Does the author use any words or phrases to signal any of the examples? If so, circle each one. _____

5. If there is more than one example, can you suggest any order for the examples?

_____

_____

_____

_____

_____

EXERCISE **6**

Analyzing Paragraphs That Use Examples

Read the following paragraph and then answer the questions about it.

Topic sentence

     One of the most wonderful aspects of Sabatini's teaching was his desire to give encouragement. Even if the student did not have a great voice or did not show true promise, Sabatini would find something to praise, some little ray of hope that might help the student continue in the right direction. Let me relate an anecdote that will demonstrate this man's positive approach. One day, I was called in to Sabatini's studio to play the piano for a new pupil. This young man had come many miles to study with Sabatini, and I could see at once that he was very nervous. That he knew just a few words of Italian only made him more apprehensive. I started to play the music for the test aria. As usual, Sabatini sat in his chair with his eyes closed, listening. The young man's voice floated through the room, small and shaky at first, but growing a little more confident as he went on. Finally, after it was over, we all waited for the great man's judgment. Sabatini looked up and spoke through me. "I cannot do much for this young man," he said slowly, "because God has already done so much for him." When I translated this for the student, his face gained a new color and he smiled for the first time. That day started his period of study with Sabatini, and three years later he made his first appearance in the opera house. I have always known that his great career really began with those first words of encouragement from his teacher.

1. State the topic sentence in your own words. _____

_____

2. How many examples are given in the paragraph? _____

3. Mark the example (or examples) in the paragraph.

4. Does the author use any words or phrases to signal the use of an illustration? If so, circle each one. _____

5. If there is more than one example, can you suggest any order for the examples?

_____

Writing a Paragraph Using a Step-by-Step Approach to Illustration

Mastering any skill, including writing, requires a disciplined attitude. One way to master the skill of creating a piece of writing is to take a step-by-step approach, focusing on one issue at a time. This approach results in a minimum of stress. Another advantage is that the writer does not miss important points or misunderstand any part of the process. Of course, there are other ways to build effective paragraphs through illustration, but here is one logical method you can use that will always achieve good results.

Step-by-Step Approach to Writing a Paragraph Using Illustration

1. Compose your topic sentence, being sure to consider carefully your choice of controlling idea.

2. When using examples, consider the options: personal experience, hypothetical examples, interviews or surveys, and research. What type of example will fit your idea best? At this stage, brainstorming with a group of classmates is usually helpful.

3. Decide how many examples you will provide to develop your paragraph: one extended example with several sentences or several brief examples of one sentence each.

4. If you have more than one example, decide on the order to present them. Many writers start with the least important example and end with the most important.

5. Write down each example, using complete sentences. Does each example support your main idea? If not, the example should be deleted; otherwise, your paragraph will lack unity.

6. Write a final sentence that concludes what you want to say about this idea.

7. Copy your sentences into standard paragraph form. Indent five spaces to begin the paragraph and be sure to double-space.

8. Always make a final check for spelling errors and other mistakes such as omitted words.

NOTE: When you use a computer spell-check feature, keep in mind that this feature will alert you only to spellings that do not match words in its dictionary. If you type *there* when you mean *their*, the spell-checker will see an acceptable word. When it comes to a final editing, there is no substitute for your own careful reading.

EXERCISE **7** ## Writing a Paragraph Using a Step-by-Step Approach to Illustration

This exercise will guide you through the construction of a paragraph using illustration. Start with the topic suggested below. Use the eight steps to help you work through the stages of the writing process.

Topic: Animals that make good pets

People have many reasons for enjoying pets, ranging from the desire for simple companionship to a need for protection. In recent years, the list of animals has expanded beyond the traditional animals we all know—dogs, cats, fish, and birds—as people have chosen some very exotic animals to keep as pets. People have been known to keep deadly snakes in their homes, and in New York City a man was discovered to have a dangerous Bengal tiger in his small apartment. Keeping in mind the subject of traditional and nontraditional pets, choose a controlling idea about keeping a pet, an idea that will give you the opportunity to use several specific examples of pets people like to have. For instance, you might write about whether society should outlaw certain pets as inappropriate or even dangerous or, if you could choose two or three pets for yourself, which ones you would choose and why.

1. Topic sentence:

_____

_____

2. Which type of example (or types of examples) will you use?

_____

_____

3. How many examples will you give? _____

4. List your examples in order. (One good example may be enough. Probably no more than three or four brief examples would fit in one paragraph.)

a. _____

b. _____

c. _____

d. _____

5. Write down each example.

6. Write the sentence that will conclude your paragraph.

_____

_____

7. On a separate piece of paper or on the computer, copy your sentences into standard paragraph form.

8. Do a final reading to check for errors and omissions.

EXERCISE 8

Writing a Paragraph Using a Step-by-Step Approach to Illustration

This exercise will guide you through the construction of a paragraph using illustration. Start with the topic suggested below. Use the eight steps to help you work through the stages of the writing process.

Topic: Bad habits people have

Good habits are often difficult to maintain, but bad habits seem to come easily into our lives and stay there without much effort. In your view, what are some of the worst habits people have, habits you wish you could convince them to eliminate? As you write on this topic and give several examples of bad habits, you may (or may not) want to include yourself as one of the individuals illustrating this subject.

1. Topic sentence:

_____

2. Which type of example (or types of examples) will you use?

_____

_____

3. How many examples will you give? _____

4. List your examples in order. (One good example may be enough. Probably no more than three or four brief examples would fit in one paragraph.)

a. _____

b. _____

c. _____

d. _____

5. Write down each example.

_____

_____

_____

_____

_____

_____

_____

_____

_____

6. Write the sentence that will conclude your paragraph.

_____

_____

7. On a separate piece of paper or the computer, copy your sentences into standard paragraph form.

8. Do a final reading to check for errors and omissions.

EXERCISE 9

Writing a Paragraph Using a Step-by-Step Approach to Illustration

This exercise will guide you through the construction of a paragraph using illustration. Start with the topic suggested below. Use the eight steps to help you work through the stages of the writing process.

Topic: Examples of art in our daily lives

We often think of *art* as something far removed from our lives, intended only for galleries and museums. However, if we think about the items we use every day (our dishes, our clothes, the colors we choose to paint our walls), we realize that our choices of these items represent our individual attempts to make our lives more beautiful and more satisfying. What examples can you give that show your own artistic taste or style? In what ways have you tried to make your own world include things of beauty or artistic value?

1. Topic sentence:

_____

2. Which type of example (or types of examples) will you use?

_____

_____

3. How many examples will you give? _____

4. List your examples in order. (One good example may be enough. Probably no more than three or four brief examples would fit in one paragraph.)

a. _____

b. _____

c. _____

d. _____

5. Write down each example.

_____

_____

_____

_____

_____

_____

_____

_____

_____

_____

_____

_____

_____

6. Write the sentence that will conclude your paragraph.

_____

_____

7. On a separate piece of paper or on the computer, copy your sentences into standard paragraph form.

8. Do a final reading to check for errors and omissions.

Studying Model Paragraphs to Create Paragraphs Using Illustration

ASSIGNMENT 1: THINGS ARE NOT ALWAYS WHAT THEY SEEM

Write a paragraph about something that at first glance seems positive and appealing but appears very different when you take a second look. The following paragraph is taken from *Grand Canyon*, a book by the naturalist and essayist Joseph Wood Krutch.

> ## Model Paragraph:
> ## Appearances Can Be Deceiving
>
> Topic sentence
>
> Quite frequently it is the "cute" animals who create problems under even the slightly unnatural conditions of a park. Take, for instance, the chipmunks and the ground squirrels. No creature is more endearing, and the fact that some species eat the flower stalks of the agave, a spectacularly beautiful flowering plant, is not serious so long as the ground squirrel population is kept down by foxes. But once the fox has been exterminated, the agave also is threatened with extinction. Even the trays of seed put out to attract birds for the benefit of visitors mean that the chipmunks who come uninvited multiply so alarmingly that they, like the beggar deer, have to be periodically transported to remoter areas where artificial overpopulation is not a problem.

Ten suggested topics

Things (or people) that may not be what they seem:

1. Politicians
2. Promising jobs
3. Friendly neighbors
4. Expensive clothing
5. Sweet-talking boyfriend or girlfriend
6. Winning the lottery
7. An adorable pet
8. A great-looking used car
9. A relationship established online
10. Sleeping pills

ASSIGNMENT 2: SHOPPING

Most people have very strong feelings about having to do certain shopping tasks. Write a paragraph that gives one or more examples of your worst or favorite shopping tasks. The following paragraph is taken from Phyllis Rose's essay "Shopping and Other Spiritual Adventures in America Today."

Model Paragraph: Shopping for Blue Jeans

Topic sentence

Try to think of a kind of shopping in which the object is all-important and the pleasure of shopping is at a minimum. For example, consider the purchase of blue jeans. I buy new blue jeans as seldom as possible because the experience is so humiliating. For every pair that looks good on me, fifteen look grotesque. But even shopping for blue jeans at Bob's Surplus on Main Street—no frills, bare-bones shopping—is an event in the life of the spirit. Once again I have to come to terms with the fact that I will never look good in Levi's. Much as I want to be mainstream, I never will be.

Ten suggested topics

Shopping

1. For weekly groceries
2. For a bathing suit
3. For an outfit to wear to a party
4. For a gift for a very fussy relative
5. By catalogue
6. On the Home Shopping Network
7. For a used car
8. For bargains
9. For a gift for a child
10. For something an elderly person needs

ASSIGNMENT 3: WHAT DO WE HAVE A RIGHT TO EXPECT FROM OTHERS?

We enter into relationships believing that people will behave in an expected way. Often we are sadly disappointed. Write a paragraph in which you give one or more examples of how you expect people to act when they are in certain relationships. The following paragraph is from a piece of advice written by the famous columnist Ann Landers.

Model Paragraph: Advice to Parents

Topic sentence

Parents have the right to expect their children to pick up after themselves and perform simple household chores. For example, every member of the family over six years of age should clean the bathtub and the sink so they will be in respectable condition for the next person. He or she should also run errands and help in the kitchen if asked—in other words, carry a share of the load without feeling persecuted. The days of "hired help" are, for the most part, gone. And this is good. Boys as well as girls should be taught to cook and clean, do laundry, and sew on buttons. This is not "sissy stuff." It makes for independence and self-reliance.

Ten suggested topics

Expectations of

1. Domestic partners
2. Grandparents
3. Teachers
4. Students
5. Waiters
6. Customers
7. Patients
8. Employers
9. Coworkers
10. Friends

ASSIGNMENT 4: REMEDIES TO CURE WHAT AILS US

Health food stores are enjoying great popularity, partly because so many people believe that natural products can alleviate a wide range of complaints. Write a paragraph in which you give examples of popular trends for solving an everyday problem. In the following paragraph, the author provides several examples of currently available remedies that people are using in place of traditional medicine.

Model Paragraph: The Popularity of Natural Remedies

Topic sentence

Many stores today are selling newly accepted natural remedies for all types of human ailments. For instance, people with AIDS use the herb astragalus as a natural way to boost their immune systems. Other people concerned about their immune systems but only worried about colds or flu use echinacea, a plant extract, to help them resist sickness. People who want to lose weight also are seeking out help from natural remedies. One of the most popular examples of remedies for overweight people is the Chinese herb ma huang. This is a powerful substance and can be dangerous for some because it can cause heart attacks or strokes, especially if it is used with caffeine. One of the cures most sought after is the cure for cancer, and again natural substances hold out some promise of relief. For example, shark cartilage is believed by many to stop the growth of cancerous tumors or even eliminate them altogether. Many users of herbs and other natural healing substances take these supplements to improve their general health. For instance, ginseng is used throughout the world as a revitalizing tonic, and garlic has been said to combat infections, prevent blood clots, and lower blood pressure. Although many claims are made for natural remedies, we do not always have proof that they work as well as some people say they do.

Ten suggested topics

Remedies for

1. Stress
2. The common cold
3. The "blues"
4. The hiccups
5. Thumbsucking
6. Smoking
7. Shyness
8. Writer's block
9. Insomnia
10. Boredom

Exploring Online

Go to academic.cengage.com/devenglish/scarry to find the **Writer's Online Workplace,** a website designed for students using this book. You will find links to handouts, interactive quizzes, and other online resources as you explore the following topic:

- using examples in paragraphs

Working Together

Researching Examples: Phobias

Roberto has a serious problem. His job involves a significant amount of travel, but he has an abnormal fear of flying. He may have to change jobs if he can't find a way to deal with his fear.

A phobia is an abnormal fear of a particular thing or situation. All of us fear one thing or another, but when that fear is abnormally deep and does not have any logical basis, we call it a phobia. People who suffer from phobias often realize that their fears are unreasonable, but they are not able to control them. It does not matter that the phobia is not logical; the person suffering from it has very real physical reactions, including a pounding of the blood, a sinking feeling in the stomach, trembling, and a feeling of faintness. Very often, a traumatic childhood experience leads to a phobia later in life.

Working in Groups

Working in groups of three or so, locate information on at least three phobias. Common ones include claustrophobia, agoraphobia, acrophobia, and zenophobia. Find enough information about these phobias so that you would be able to write a well-developed paragraph on each one in an essay on the subject. You will want to define each phobia, and you will also want to explain how the phobia complicates the life of the person who has to deal with it.

Portfolio Suggestion

When your group finds an article or some other source of information on one of the selected phobias, print out or make copies of the material. Each group member will then have information to use in an essay devoted to the subject.

CHAPTER 19

Developing Paragraphs: Narration

If you are an effective storyteller or if you like to have a good story told to you, you will enjoy this chapter on narration. You will improve your writing skills by focusing on these narrative elements:

CHAPTER OBJECTIVES

- making a point
- ordering details according to time sequence
- using transitions to show a shift in time
- taking a step-by-step approach to create narrative paragraphs
- studying model paragraphs to create narrative paragraphs

What Is Narration?

> **Narration** is the oldest and best-known form of verbal communication. It is, quite simply, the telling of a story.

Every culture in the world, past and present, has used narration to provide entertainment as well as information for the people of that culture. Because everyone likes a good story, the many forms of narration, such as novels, short stories, soap operas, and full-length movies, are always popular.

The following narrative paragraph, taken from Helen Keller's autobiography, tells the story of her realization that every object has a name. The paragraph shows the enormous difficulties faced by a seven-year-old girl who was unable to see, hear, or speak.

The morning after my teacher came, she led me into her room and gave me a doll. The little blind children at the Perkins Institution had sent it and Laura Bridgman had dressed it; but I did not know this until afterward. When I had played with it a little while, Miss Sullivan slowly spelled into my hand the word "d-o-l-l." I was at once interested in this finger play and tried to imitate it. When I finally succeeded in making the letters correctly, I was flushed with childish pleasure and pride. Running downstairs to my mother I held up my hand and made the letters for doll. I did not know that I was spelling a word or even that words existed; I was simply making my fingers go in monkey-like imitation. In the days that followed I learned to spell in this uncomprehending way a great many words, among them *pin, hat, cup* and a few verbs like *sit, stand,* and *walk.* <u>But my teacher had been with me several weeks before I understood that everything has a name.</u>

Topic sentence

Using Narration to Make a Point

At one time or another, you have probably met a person who loves to talk on and on without making any real point. This person is likely to tell you everything that happened during the day, including every sight and every sound. Your reaction to the unnecessary and seemingly endless supply of details is probably one of fatigue and hope for a quick getaway. This is not narration at its best! A good story is almost always told to make a point: it can make us laugh, it can make us understand, or it can change our attitudes.

When Helen Keller tells the story of her early experiences with her teacher, she is careful to use only those details that are relevant to her story. For example, the doll her teacher gave her is an important part of the story. This doll reveals not only something about Helen Keller's teacher but also the astounding fact that Helen did not know that objects have names. With this story, we see the beginning of Helen's long struggle to communicate with other people.

EXERCISE **Using Narration to Make a Point**

Each of the following is the beginning of a topic sentence for a narrative paragraph. Complete each sentence by providing a controlling idea that could serve as the point for the story.

1. Because my family is so large (or small), I have had to learn to _____

   _____

2. When I couldn't get a job, I realized _____

   _____

3. After going to the movies every Saturday for many years, I discovered

   _____

   _____

4. When I arrived at the room where my business class was to meet, I found

   _____

   _____

5. When my best friend got married, I began to see _____

   _____

EXERCISE **Using Narration to Make a Point**

Each of the following is the beginning of a topic sentence for a narrative paragraph. Complete each sentence by providing a controlling idea that could serve as the point for the story.

1. When I looked more closely at the man, I realized _____

   _____

2. When the president finished his speech, I concluded _____

   _____

3.   By the end of the movie, I had decided _____

_____

4.   After I changed the course as well as the teacher, I felt _____

_____

5.   When I could not get past the office secretary, I realized _____

_____

EXERCISE 3   Using Narration to Make a Point

Each of the following is the beginning of a topic sentence for a narrative paragraph. Complete each sentence by providing a controlling idea that could serve as the point for the story.

1.   When the art teacher tore up my sketches in front of the class, I decided

_____

_____

2.   When there were no responses to my ad, I concluded _____

_____

3.   After two days of trying to sell magazine subscriptions, I knew _____

_____

4.   After I had actually performed my first experiment in the lab, I understood

_____

_____

5.   The first time I tried to cook dinner for a group of people, I found out

_____

_____

Achieving Coherence

PLACING DETAILS IN ORDER OF TIME SEQUENCE

When you write a narrative paragraph, the details given are usually ordered according to time sequence. That is, you tell what happened first, then what happened next, and next, until finally you get to the end of the story. In your narrative, you could be describing events that took place in a matter of minutes or over a period of many years.

In the following paragraph, the story takes place in a single day. The six events that made the day a disaster are given in the order they happened. Although some stories flash back to the past or forward to the future, most use the chronological order of the events.

Topic sentence   <u>My day was a disaster</u>. First, it had snowed during the night, which meant I had to shovel before I could leave for work. I was mad that I hadn't gotten up earlier. Then I had trouble starting my car, and to make matters worse, my daughter wasn't feeling well and said she didn't think she should go to school. When I eventually did arrive at work, I was twenty minutes late. Soon I found out my assistant had forgotten to make copies of a report I needed at nine o'clock. I quickly had to make another plan. By five o'clock, I was looking forward to getting my paycheck. Foolish woman! When I went to pick it up, the office assistant told me that something had gone wrong with the computers. I would not be able to get my check until Tuesday. Disappointed, I walked down the hill to the parking lot. There I met my final defeat. In my hurry to park the car in the morning, I had left my parking lights on. Now my battery was dead. Even an optimist like me had the right to be discouraged!

EXERCISE **Placing Details in Order of Time Sequence**

The topic below is followed by supporting details. These supporting details are not in any particular order. Put the events in order according to time sequence by placing the appropriate number in the space provided.

An emergency in an apartment building

_____ He ran to the corner and pulled the fire alarm.

_____ The fire began around six o'clock.

_____ When the firefighters came, they found flames leaping out of the third-floor windows.

_____ A man walking his dog spotted smoke coming from the building.

_____ Official orders were given to evacuate the building.

EXERCISE 5 **Placing Details in Order of Time Sequence**

The topic below is followed by supporting details. These supporting details are not in any particular order. Put the events in order according to time sequence by placing the appropriate number in the space provided.

From the life of Amelia Earhart, pioneer aviator and writer

_____ Amelia Earhart was born in Atchison, Kansas, in 1897.

_____ Before 1920, she worked as a nurse's aide.

_____ When she was sixteen, her family moved to St. Paul, Minnesota.

_____ Four years after her history-making flight across the Atlantic, she made her solo flight across that same ocean.

_____ After learning to fly in the early 1920s, she became, in 1928, the first woman to cross the Atlantic, although on that trip she was a passenger and not a pilot.

_____ Three years after her solo Atlantic flight, she became the first person to fly from Hawaii to California.

_____ On her last flight, in 1937, she was lost at sea; no trace of her was ever found.

EXERCISE **Placing Details in Order of Time Sequence**

The topic below is followed by supporting details. These supporting details are not in any particular order. Put the events in order according to time sequence by placing the appropriate number in the space provided.

From the life of Sojourner Truth, crusader, preacher, and the first African American woman to speak out against slavery

_____ She was received by Abraham Lincoln in the White House the year before that president was assassinated at the end of the Civil War.

_____ She was forty-six when she took the name of Sojourner Truth.

_____ Sojourner Truth began life as a slave when she was born in 1797, but she was set free in 1827.

_____ She spent her final years giving lectures throughout the North.

_____ In 1850, she traveled to the West, where her speeches against slavery and for women's rights drew large crowds.

_____ At the beginning of the Civil War, she was active in gathering supplies for the black regiments that were fighting in the war.

_____ Not long after her first trip west, she settled in Battle Creek, Michigan.

USING TRANSITIONS THAT SHOW A SHIFT IN TIME

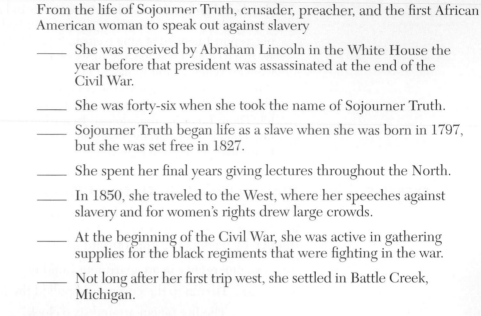

Transitions are words and phrases that help a reader move smoothly from one idea to another and make the proper connection between those ideas.

Although transitions must not be overused, they are important tools for every writer. Here is the Helen Keller paragraph you studied earlier, this time with each of the transitional words and phrases printed in boldface.

> **The morning after** my teacher came, she led me into her room and gave me a doll. The little blind children at the Perkins Institution had sent it and Laura Bridgman had dressed it; but I did not know this **until afterward.** When I had played with it **a little while,** Miss Sullivan slowly spelled into my hand the word "d-o-l-l." I was **at once** interested in this finger play and tried to imitate it. When I **finally** succeeded in making the letters correctly, I was flushed with childish pleasure and pride. Running downstairs to my mother I held up my hand and made the letters for doll. I did not know that I was spelling a word or even that words existed; I was simply making my fingers go in monkey-like imitation. **In the days that followed** I learned to spell in this uncomprehending way a great many words, among them _pin, hat, cup_ and a few verbs like _sit, stand,_ and _walk._ But my teacher had been with me **several weeks** before I understood that everything has a name.

Notice how the time transitions used in this paragraph make the order of events clear. _"The morning after_ my teacher came" gives the reader the sense that the action of the story is being told day by day. In the second sentence, Helen Keller gives information she learned later—_afterward._ The writer then tells us that when she had played with the doll _a little while,_ she suddenly—_at once_—became interested in the connection between an object and the word for that object. This realization was one of the central lessons in young Helen

Keller's education, and it became the starting point for all of her later learning. She uses two more transitional phrases to tell us about the beginning of this education: *In the days that followed,* we learn, she mastered a great many words, although it took her *several weeks* before she learned the even more important concept that everything has a name. Much of the meaning of this paragraph would not have been clear without the careful use of these time transitions.

As you write your own narrative paragraphs, you will find yourself using your own transitional words and expressions. However, as a reminder and a guide, the following chart will serve as a helpful reference.

Transitions Commonly Used in Narration to Show a Shift in Time

recently	now; by now	within a few minutes	several weeks later
previously	at once	soon; soon afterward	the following month
earlier	suddenly	later; later on	finally
in the past	immediately	after a little while	eventually
a few days ago	meanwhile	then	in the end
a hundred years ago	at the same time	next; the next day	

EXERCISE **7** **Working with Transitions**

Below is the beginning of an essay by John McMurtry about the violence of football. Fill in each of the blanks with a transition of time that might have been the author's choice.

¹_____ my neck got a hard crick in it. I couldn't turn my head;

to look left or right I'd have to turn my whole body. ²But I'd had cricks in my neck

since I started playing grade-school football and hockey, so I just ignored it.

³_____ I began to notice that when I reached for any sort of large

book (which I do pretty often as a philosophy teacher at the University of

Guelph) I had trouble lifting it with one hand. ⁴I was losing the strength in my

left arm, and I had such a steady pain in my back I often had to stretch out on the

floor of the room I was in to relieve the pressure. ⁵_____ I men-

tioned to my brother, an orthopedic surgeon, that I'd lost the power in my arm

since my neck began to hurt. ⁶_____ I was in a Toronto hospital not

sure whether I might end up with a wasted upper limb. ⁷Apparently the steady

pounding I had received playing college and professional football in the late

1950s and early 1960s had driven my head into my backbone so that the discs had crumpled together at the neck—"acute herniation"—and had cut the nerves to my left arm like a pinched telephone wire (without nerve stimulation, of course, the muscles atrophy, leaving the arm crippled). [8]So I spent my Christmas holidays in the hospital in heavy traction and for much of ——————— my neck was in a brace. [9]——————— most of the pain has gone, and I've recovered most of the strength in my arm. [10]But ——————— I still have to don the brace, and surgery remains a possibility.

EXERCISE

Working with Transitions

Below is a narrative paragraph. On the lines provided, list all the transitions of time that give order to the paragraph.

By now, Jason was skating along feeling in the best of moods. He was aware every moment that he was wearing his new pair of roller blades, and several times he even smiled from so much inner pleasure. He hardly noticed when suddenly he found himself skating down his own street. Immediately, neighborhood children spotted him and ran up to him, calling to him by name, "Jason, Jason, where did you get those skates?" In a short time, Jason found himself surrounded by nine or ten children who were running alongside him. Finally, with a flair, he turned, stopped dead, and blurted out happily, "It's my birthday today!"

_____   _____

_____   _____

_____   _____

_____

EXERCISE

Working with Transitions

Below is a narrative paragraph from a story by the Russian writer Ivan Turgenev. Note all the transitions of time that give order to the paragraph and copy them on the lines provided.

I went to the right through the bushes. Meantime the night had crept close and grown up like a storm cloud; it seemed as though, with the mists of evening, darkness was rising up on all sides and flowing down from overhead. I had come upon some sort of little, untrodden, overgrown path; I walked along it, gazing intently before me. Soon all was blackness and silence around—only the quail's cry was heard from time to time. Some small nightbird, flitting noiselessly near the ground on its soft wings, almost flapped against me and scurried away in alarm. I came out on the farther side of the bushes, and made my way along a field by the hedge. By now I could hardly make out distant objects; the field showed dimly white around; beyond it rose up a sullen darkness, which seemed to be moving up closer in huge masses every instant. My steps gave a muffled sound in the air that grew colder and colder. The pale sky began again to grow blue—but it was the blue of night. The tiny stars glimmered and twinkled in it.

_____   _____

_____   _____

_____

Writing a Narrative Paragraph Using a Step-by-Step Approach

Mastering any skill, including writing, requires a disciplined attitude. One way to master the skill of creating a piece of writing is to take a step-by-step approach, focusing on one issue at a time. This approach results in a minimum of stress. Another advantage is that the writer does not miss important points or misunderstand any part of the process. Of course, there are other ways to build effective narrative paragraphs, but here is one logical method you can use that will always achieve good results.

Step-by-Step Approach to Writing a Narrative Paragraph

1. Study the given topic, and then plan your topic sentence with its controlling idea.

2. List all the events that come to your mind when you think about the story you have chosen.

3. Choose the important events, dropping any that do not directly relate to your controlling idea.

4. Put your list in the correct time sequence.

5. Write one complete sentence for each of the events you have chosen from your list, adding any significant details.

6. Write a concluding statement that gives some point to the events of the story.

7. Copy your sentences into standard paragraph form.

8. Always make a final check for spelling errors and other mistakes such as omitted words.

NOTE: When you use a computer spell-check feature, keep in mind that this feature will alert you only to spellings that do not match words in its dictionary. If you type _there_ when you mean _their_, the spell-checker will see an acceptable word. When it comes to a final editing, there is no substitute for your own careful reading.

EXERCISE **10**   **Writing a Narrative Paragraph
Using a Step-by-Step Approach**

This exercise will guide you through the construction of a complete narrative paragraph. Start with the suggested topic. Use the eight steps to help you work through the stages of the writing process.

Topic: Nearly every family has a favorite story they like to tell about one of their members, often a humorous incident that happened to one of them. There are also crises and tragic moments in the life of every family. Choose a story, funny or tragic, from the life of a family you know.

1.   Topic sentence: _____

_____

_____

_____

_____

2.   Make a list of the events that took place.

a. _____

_____

b. _____

_____

c. _____

d. _____

e. _____

f. _____

g. _____

h. _____

i. _____

j. _____

3.   Circle the five or six events you believe are the most important for the point of the story.

4.   Put your final choices in order by numbering each of them.

5.   Using your final list, write at least one sentence for each event you have chosen.

a. _____

_____

b. _____

_____

c. _____

_____

d. _____

_____

e. _____

_____

f. _____

_____

6. Write a concluding statement. _____

_____

_____

7. On a separate piece of paper or on the computer, copy your sentences into standard paragraph form.

8. Do a final reading to check for errors and omissions.

EXERCISE 11 **Writing a Narrative Paragraph Using a Step-by-Step Approach**

This exercise will guide you through the construction of a complete narrative paragraph. Start with the suggested topic. Use the eight steps to help you work through the stages of the writing process.

Topic: Tell the story of an incident you witnessed that revealed an unfortunate lack of sensitivity (or even cruelty) on someone's part. What did you observe the person doing? How did other people react? What did you do or wish you had done in response to this incident?

1. Topic sentence: _____

_____

2. Make a list of the events that took place.

a. _____

b. _____

c. _____

d. _____

e. _____

f. _____

g. _____

h. _____

i. _____

j. _____

3. Circle the five or six events you believe are the most important for the point of the story.

4. Put your final choices in order by numbering each of them.

5. Using your final list, write at least one sentence for each event you have chosen.

   a. _____

   _____

   b. _____

   _____

   c. _____

   _____

   d. _____

   _____

   e. _____

   _____

   f. _____

   _____

6. Write a concluding statement. _____

   _____

   _____

7. On a separate piece of paper or on the computer, copy your sentences into standard paragraph form.

8. Do a final reading to check for errors and omissions.

Studying Model Paragraphs to Create Paragraphs Using Narration

ASSIGNMENT 1: THE STORY OF HOW YOU FACED A NEW CHALLENGE

Write a paragraph telling the story of a day when you faced an important challenge of some kind. It could have been a challenge in school, at home, or on the job. The following paragraph by journalist Betty Rollin provides an example of such an experience.

Model Paragraph: Deadline

Topic sentence

<u>When I awoke that morning I hit the floor running</u>. I washed my face, brushed my teeth, got a pot of coffee going, tightened the sash on my bathrobe, snapped my typewriter out of its case, placed it on the kitchen table, retrieved my notes from the floor where they were stacked in manila folders, unwrapped a pack of bond paper, put the top sheet in the typewriter, looked at it, put my head on the keys, wrapped my arms around its base and cried.

Ten suggested topics

1. The day I started a new job
2. My first day in a difficult course
3. The day I began my first term paper
4. The day I organized my room
5. The day of an important job interview
6. The day I faced a large debt
7. The day I had to end a relationship
8. The day I started driving lessons
9. The day I was faced with a death in the family
10. The day I met a deadline

ASSIGNMENT 2: THE STORY OF A FIGHT OR ARGUMENT

Write a paragraph in which you tell the story of a fight or confrontation you were involved in or witnessed. What are the important details of the incident that remain most clearly in your mind? The following paragraph, from Albert Halper's short story "Prelude," tells the story of a street fight.

Model Paragraph: The Fight

Topic sentence

But the people just stood there afraid to do a thing. Then while a few guys held me, Gooley and about four others went for the stand, turning it over and mussing and stamping on all the newspapers they could find. Syl started to scratch them, so they hit her. Then I broke away to help her, and then they started socking me too. My father tried to reach me, but three guys kept him away. Four guys got me down and started kicking me and all the time my father was begging them to let me up and Syl was screaming at the people to help. And while I was down, my face was squeezed against some papers on the sidewalk telling about Austria and I guess I went nuts while they kept hitting me, and I kept seeing the headlines against my nose.

Ten suggested topics

A confrontation between

1. A police officer and a guilty motorist
2. Two neighbors
3. An angry customer and a store clerk
4. A frustrated parent and a child
5. A manager and an unhappy employee
6. A judge and an unwilling witness
7. A museum guard and a careless tourist
8. A politician and an angry citizen
9. A mugger and a frightened victim
10. An engaged couple about to break up

ASSIGNMENT 3: THE BEGINNING OF A SPECIAL RELATIONSHIP

Write a paragraph that tells the story of how you became close to another person. Select one particular moment when the relationship changed from casual friendliness to something deeper and more lasting. Perhaps you shared an experience that brought you together. The following paragraph, taken from Morley Callaghan's short story "One Spring Night," tells of a young man who is falling in love.

Model Paragraph: Falling in Love

Topic sentence

<u>Bob had taken her out a few times when he had felt like having some girl to talk to who knew him and liked him</u>. And tonight he was leaning back good-humoredly, telling her one thing and then another with the wise self-assurance he usually had when with her; but gradually, as he watched her, he found himself talking more slowly, his voice grew serious and much softer, and then finally he leaned across the table toward her as though he had just discovered that her neck was full and soft with her spring coat thrown open, and that her face under her little black straw hat tilted back on her head had a new, eager beauty. Her warm, smiling softness was so close to him that he smiled a bit shyly.

Ten suggested topics

1. A moment when my relationship with a parent changed
2. The day my relationship with a fellow student changed
3. A moment when I understood my child in a new way
4. When I learned something new about a neighborhood merchant
5. When I shared an experience with a fellow worker
6. When I made friends with someone older or younger than myself
7. When my relationship with my brother or sister changed
8. The moment when my attitude about a grandparent changed
9. When a stranger became a friend
10. When a relationship deepened

ASSIGNMENT 4: YOU WON'T BELIEVE WHAT HAPPENED TO ME TODAY!

Tell the story of a day you found yourself facing a difficult or frustrating situation. The following paragraph, from Berton Roueche's short story "Phone Call," describes a day in the life of a young man, a day when nothing seemed to go right.

Model Paragraph: The Truck Breaks Down

I got out of the truck and got down on my knees and twisted my neck and looked underneath. Everything looked O.K. There wasn't anything hanging down or anything. I got up and opened the hood and looked at the engine. I don't know too much about engines—only what I picked up working around Lindy's Service Station the summer before last. But the engine looked O.K., too. I slammed down the hood and lighted a cigarette. It really had me beat. A school bus from that convent over in Sag Harbor came piling around the bend, and all the girls leaned out the windows and yelled. I just waved. They didn't mean anything by it—just a bunch of kids going home. The bus went on up the road and into the woods and out of sight. I got back in the truck and started it up again. It sounded fine. I put it in gear and let out the clutch and gave it the gas, and nothing happened. The bastard just sat there. So it was probably the transmission. I shut it off and got out. There was nothing to do but call the store. I still had three or four deliveries that had to be made and it was getting kind of late. I knew what Mr. Lester would say, but this was one time when he couldn't blame me. <u>It wasn't my fault</u>. It was him himself that told me to take this truck.

Topic sentence

Ten suggested topics

1. When I ran out of money
2. When I ran out of gas
3. When I was accused of something I didn't do
4. When I was stopped by the police (or by some other authority)
5. When I was guilty of . . .
6. When something terrible happened just as everything seemed to be going so well
7. When the weather didn't cooperate
8. When I locked myself out of the house
9. When I couldn't reach my family by phone
10. When my entire report was deleted by mistake

ASSIGNMENT 5: A MEMORABLE EXPERIENCE FROM CHILDHOOD

Write a paragraph in which you remember a special moment from your childhood. The following childhood memory is from George Orwell's novel *Coming Up for Air.*

Model Paragraph: The Forgotten Pool

Topic sentence

It was an enormous fish. I don't exaggerate when I say it was enormous. It was almost the length of my arm. It glided across the pool, deep under water, and then became a shadow and disappeared into the darker water on the other side. I felt as if a sword had gone through me. It was by far the biggest fish I'd ever seen, dead or alive. I stood there without breathing, and in a moment another huge thick shape glided through the water, and then another and then two more close together. The pool was full of them. They were carp, I suppose. Just possibly they were bream or tench, but more probably carp. Bream or tench wouldn't grow so huge. I knew what had happened. At some time this pool had been connected with the other, and then the stream had dried up and the woods had closed round the small pool and it had just been forgotten. It's a thing that happens occasionally. A pool gets forgotten somehow, nobody fishes in it for years and decades, and the fish grow to monstrous sizes. The brutes that I was watching might be a hundred years old. And not a soul in the world knew about them except me.

Ten suggested topics

1. The first time I went swimming
2. My first time on a roller coaster (or on another ride)
3. A frightening experience when I was home alone
4. My most memorable Halloween (or other holiday)
5. The best birthday party I ever had
6. My first bicycle (or car)
7. The greatest present I ever received
8. A memorable visit to a favorite relative
9. My first time traveling alone
10. The first time I went camping

Exploring Online

Go to academic.cengage.com/devenglish/scarry to find the **Writer's Online Workplace,** a website designed for students using this book. You will find links to handouts, interactive quizzes, and other online resources as you explore the following topics:

- writing a narrative composition
- the importance of sentence order

Working Together

Telling Stories That Make a Point

Aesop is believed to have been a Greek slave who lived about 2,500 years ago. He created over two hundred fables, many of which have become part of our international literary heritage. The following example of his work is a classic fable, one that has a timeless moral.

> A farmer realized he was dying. He did not want to leave this world without being sure that all of his sons knew how to be good farmers. He called them to his bedside and said, "My sons, I am about to depart from this world. After I go, however, I want you to search for what I have hidden in the vineyard. When you find it, you will possess all that I am able to leave you."
>
> The young men were convinced their father had buried some great treasure on the property. After he died, they all took their shovels and dug up every part of the vineyard. They found no trea-sure at all, but their digging helped the grapevines so much that the next year's harvest saw the best crop of grapes in many years.
>
> **Moral:** Our greatest treasure is what comes from our own hard work.

Group Discussion

Wouldn't all of us like to get something for nothing? Share with your classmates a recent story of someone you know or have heard about who, like the sons of the farmer in the fable, wanted to get something for nothing. (Do you know people who gamble? Do you know people who expect their relatives to keep supporting them? Do you know anyone who has inherited money?)

Then share with your classmates a story about someone you know or have heard about who achieved something by working very hard. Do you think Aesop's moral is true—namely, that what we achieve by our own hard work is the greatest treasure?

Portfolio Suggestion

Write a true story or a fictional tale about one of the following:

1. What happened to someone who wanted to get something for nothing
2. What happened to someone who, by his or her own hard work, achieved something significant

Give your story the same one-sentence moral that Aesop gave to his fable or, using the same one-sentence model, make up your own moral.

CHAPTER 20

Developing Paragraphs: Description

To create effective paragraphs of description, a writer must call upon the five senses. This chapter focuses on several skills important to descriptive writing:

CHAPTER OBJECTIVES

- creating a topic sentence containing a **dominant impression**
- avoiding vague dominant impressions
- supporting the topic sentence with details that evoke **sensory images**
- putting the details in a logical order, usually a **spatial order** of some kind
- taking a step-by-step approach to create descriptive paragraphs
- studying model paragraphs to create descriptive paragraphs

What Is Description?

One method of developing a paragraph is to use descriptive details. Almost any novel you pick up will begin with one or more paragraphs of description because the author needs to set the stage for the story.

> **Description** uses sensory images to create a picture with words.

The following example comes from a personal essay written by Joseph H. Suina. In this paragraph, he describes his childhood home. As you study this description, look for the details that make this paragraph effective.

Topic sentence

During those years, Grandmother and I lived beside the plaza in a humble one-room house. It consisted of a traditional fireplace, a makeshift cabinet for our few tin cups and dishes, and a wooden crate that held our two buckets of all-purpose water. At the far end of the room were two rolls of bedding we used as comfortable sitting "couches." Consisting of thick quilts, sheepskin, and assorted blankets, these bed rolls were undone each night. A wooden pole the length of one side of the room was suspended about 10 inches from the ceiling beams. A modest collection of colorful shawls, blankets, and sashes draped over the pole making this part of the room most interesting. In one corner was a bulky metal trunk for our ceremonial wear and few valuables. A dresser, which was traded for some of my grandmother's well-known pottery, held the few articles of clothing we owned and the "goody bag." Grandmother always had a flour sack filled with candy, store bought cookies, and Fig Newtons. These were saturated with a sharp odor of moth balls. Nevertheless, they made a fine snack with coffee before we turned in for the night. Tucked securely in my blankets, I listened to one of her stories or accounts of how it was when she was a little girl. These accounts seemed so old fashioned compared to the way we lived. Sometimes she softly sang a song from a ceremony. In this way I fell asleep each night.

When you use effective sensory images in your writing, the descriptive details that result will be memorable and convincing to your reader. Such details will make a tremendous difference in how well your reader is able to imagine what you are describing. You can demonstrate this to yourself by answering the following questions about the descriptive paragraph above on Suina's childhood home.

1. What do you see? _____

_____

_____

2. What do you hear? _____

3. What suggests how something would feel to the touch? _____

_____

4. What can you smell? _____

5. What can you taste? _____

Working with Description

SELECTING THE DOMINANT IMPRESSION

It is not enough to give random pieces of information about the particular person, object, or place you are describing. The overall effect of a piece of descriptive writing should be to create a *dominant impression.* Each individual sentence that you write should be part of a picture that becomes clear when the reader finishes the paragraph.

> The **dominant impression** is the overall impression created by a descriptive piece of writing. This impression is often summed up by one word or phrase in the topic sentence.
>
> **Topic sentence:** My childhood home was humble.

When you write a descriptive paragraph, you should know what impression you are trying to achieve with your supporting details. For example, when you describe a place, the dominant impression you want to create could be one of *comfort* or it could be one of *elegance.* When you write a description of a person, you might want to present the impression of an outgoing, gregarious person or perhaps the very opposite, that of a *shy, withdrawing* sort of person. Often it is useful to incorporate the dominant impression into the topic sentence. This will help you focus as you write and will leave no doubt in the reader's mind as to the direction of your thinking. All the other sentences should support this impression you are working to create.

The following charts contain two short lists of possible dominant impressions. Use them as a guide while you work through this chapter.

Dominant Impressions for Descriptions of Place

crowded	cozy	inviting	cheerful	dazzling
romantic	restful	dreary	drab	uncomfortable
cluttered	ugly	tasteless	unfriendly	gaudy
stuffy	eerie	depressing	spacious	sunny

Dominant Impressions for Descriptions of People

creative	angry	independent	proud	dependable
tense	shy	aggressive	generous	sullen
silent	witty	pessimistic	responsible	efficient
snobbish	placid	bumbling	bitter	easygoing

EXERCISE   **Selecting the Dominant Impression**

Each of the following places could be the topic for a descriptive paragraph. Fill in the blank to the right of each topic with an appropriate dominant impression. Use the list in the box if you need help. Remember that there is no single right answer; the word you choose should represent the impression you want to create.

Topic	Dominant impression
A hotel lobby	spacious
1. A high school gym on prom night	
2. Your barber or hairdresser's shop	
3. The room where you are now sitting	
4. The grocery store nearest you	
5. A hardware store	
6. The post office on Saturday morning	
7. A waiting room	
8. A sports stadium	
9. The home of your best friend	
10. The kitchen in the morning	

EXERCISE **2**   **Selecting the Dominant Impression**

Each of the following people could be the topic for a descriptive paragraph. Fill in the blank to the right of each topic with an appropriate dominant impression. Use the list in the box if you need help. Remember that there is no single right answer; the word you choose should represent the impression you want to create.

Topic   **Dominant impression**

1.   An actor being interviewed on television   _____

2.   An old woman in a nursing home   _____

3.   A librarian   _____

4.   A bank clerk on a busy day   _____

5.   A farmer   _____

6.   A politician running for office   _____

7.   A cab driver   _____

8.   A shoe salesperson   _____

9.   A bride   _____

10. A soldier just discharged from the service   _____

REVISING VAGUE DOMINANT IMPRESSIONS

Certain words have become so overused that they no longer have any specific meaning for a reader. Careful writers avoid these words because they are almost useless in descriptive writing. Here is a list of the most commonly overused words:

Vague and Overused Words

good	fine	typical
bad	okay	interesting
nice	normal	beautiful

The following paragraph is an example of the kind of writing that suffers from the continued use of vague words:

> I had a typical day. The weather was nice and my job was interesting. The food for lunch was okay; supper was good. After supper I saw my girl-friend, who is beautiful. That's when my day really became fun.

Notice that all of the details in the paragraph are vague. The writer has told us what happened, but we cannot really see any of the details that are mentioned.

This is because the writer has made the mistake of using words that have lost much of their meaning.

The next group of exercises will give you practice in recognizing and eliminating overused words.

EXERCISE 3

Revising Vague Dominant Impressions

In each of the spaces provided, write a word or phrase that creates a more specific dominant impression than the underlined word. An example has been done for you. You might want to work in groups to think of words and phrases that are more specific.

> **Vague:**   The tablecloth was <u>beautiful</u>.
>
> **Revised:**   The tablecloth was <u>of white linen with delicate blue embroidery</u>.

1. The sky was <u>beautiful</u>. _____

2. The water felt <u>nice</u>. _____

3. Walking along the beach was <u>fun</u>. _____

4. The storm was <u>bad</u>. _____

5. The parking lot was <u>typical</u>. _____

6. The main street is <u>interesting</u>. _____

7. The dessert tasted <u>good</u>. _____

8. My brother seems <u>normal</u>. _____

9. Our house is <u>fine</u>. _____

10. My job is <u>okay</u>. _____

EXERCISE 4

Revising Vague Dominant Impressions

In each of the spaces provided, write a word or phrase that creates a more specific dominant impression than the underlined word. Working in groups may be helpful.

1. It turned out to be a really <u>nice</u> date. _____

2. The window display was <u>beautiful</u>. _____

3. The boat ride was <u>fine</u>. _____

4. The circus was <u>fun</u>. _____

5. The lemonade tasted <u>awful</u>. _____

6. The play was <u>bad</u>. _____

7. His new suit looked <u>okay</u>. _____

8. The dance class was <u>fine</u>. _____

9. Her new watch was <u>nice</u>. _____

10. It was a <u>good</u> lecture. _____

EXERCISE **5** **Revising Vague Words**

Below is the paragraph from page 359 that is filled with vague words. Rewrite the paragraph, replacing the vague words with more specific details.

> I had a typical day. The weather was nice and my job was interesting. The food for lunch was okay; supper was good. After supper I saw my girlfriend, who is beautiful. That's when my day really became fun.

_____

_____

_____

_____

_____

_____

_____

RECOGNIZING AND CREATING SENSORY IMAGES

One of the basic ways all good writers communicate experiences to their readers is by using sensory images. We respond to writing that makes us *see* an object, *hear* a sound, *touch* a surface, *smell* an odor, or *taste* a flavor. When a writer uses one or more sensory images in a piece of writing, we tend to pay more attention to what the writer is saying, and we tend to remember the details of what we have read.

For example, if you came across the word *door* in a sentence, you might or might not pay attention to it. However, if the writer told you it was a *heavy wooden door, rough to the touch and creaking loudly when it opened,* you would not be as likely to forget it. The door would stay in your mind because the writer used sensory images.

> **Sensory images** are those details that relate to our senses: sight, sound, touch, smell, and taste.
>
> The floors were of black and white tile, the walls cream-colored with huge casement windows that opened onto a long veranda where the strains of violin music, soft voices, and the clink of glasses could be heard.

PRACTICE

The following sentences are taken from a description of a delicatessen. Notice how in each sentence the writer uses at least one sensory image to make the details of that sentence remain in your mind. As you read each of the sentences, identify the physical sense the writer appeals to when a sensory image is used.

1. A large refrigerator case against one wall was always humming loudly from the effort of keeping milk, cream, and several cases of soda and beer cool at all times.

   Physical senses: _____

   _____

   _____

2. Stacked on top of the counter were baskets of fresh rolls and breads that gave off an aroma containing a mixture of onion, caraway seed, and pumpernickel.

   Physical senses: _____

   _____

3. Mr. Rubino was always ready with a sample piece of cheese or smoked meat as a friendly gesture.

   Physical senses: _____

   _____

When you use sensory images, you will stimulate readers' interest, and these images will stay in their minds.

EXERCISE 6

Recognizing Sensory Images

The following paragraph contains examples of sensory images. Find the images and list them in the spaces provided.

Topic sentence

<u>I knew how a newspaper office should look and sound and smell—I worked in one for thirteen years.</u> The paper was the *New York Herald Tribune,* and its city room, wide as a city block, was dirty and disheveled. Reporters wrote on ancient typewriters that filled the air with clatter; copy editors labored on coffee-stained desks over what the reporters had written. Crumpled balls of paper littered the floor and filled the wastebaskets— failed efforts to write a good lead or a decent sentence. The walls were grimy—every few years they were painted over in a less restful shade of eye-rest green—and the atmosphere was hazy with the smoke of cigarettes and cigars. At the very center the city editor, a giant named L. L. Engelking, bellowed his displeasure with the day's work, his voice a rumbling volcano in our lives. I thought it was the most beautiful place in the world.

FROM WILLIAM ZINSSER,
Writing with a Word Processor

Sensory images

Sight: _____

_____

Sound: _____

_____

Smell: _____

_____

EXERCISE 7

Recognizing Sensory Images

The following paragraph contains examples of sensory images. Find the images and list them in the spaces provided.

The lake ice split with a sound like the crack of a rifle. Thick slabs of ice broke apart, moving ponderously, edge grinding against edge, up-thrusting in jagged peaks, the green-gray water swirling over half-submerged floes. In an agony of rebirth, the splitting and booming of the ice reverberated across the thawing land. Streams raced toward the lake, their swift currents carrying fallen branches and undermining overhanging banks of earth and softened snow. Roads became mires of muck and slush, and the meadows of dried, matted grass oozed mud.

FROM NAN SALERNO,
Shaman's Daughter

Sensory images

Sight: _____

_____

Sound: _____

_____

Touch: _____

_____

EXERCISE **8**   **Recognizing Sensory Images**

The following paragraph contains examples of sensory images. Find the images and list them in the spaces provided.

Topic sentence

In the waiting room there were several kerosene stoves, placed about to warm the shivering crowd. The stoves were small black chimneys with nickel handles. We stood around them rubbing hands and watching our clothes steam. An American lady, in a slicker, like the men, and rubber boots up to her knees, kept bringing bowls of soup and shiny tin cups with hot coffee. Whatever she said to us and whatever we said to her neither understood, but she was talking the language of hot soup and coffee and kindness and there was perfect communication.

FROM ERNESTO GALARZA,
Barrio Boy

Sensory images

Sight: _____

_____

Sound: _____

_____

Touch: _____

_____

Taste: _____

_____

Smell: _____

EXERCISE **9**   **Creating Sensory Images**

Each of the following topic sentences contains an underlined word that identifies a physical sense. For each topic sentence, write three sentences that give examples of sensory images. For example, in the first sentence the sensory image of *sound* in the vicinity of a hospital could be illustrated by writing sentences that describe ambulance sirens, doctors being called over loudspeaker systems, and the voices of people in the waiting room.

1. As the nurse entered the hospital intensive care unit, she recognized the usual <u>sounds</u>.

    Write three sentences with sensory images:

    a. _____

    _____

    b. _____

    _____

    c. _____

    _____

2. I can't help stopping in the bakery every Sunday morning because the <u>smells</u> are so tempting.

    Write three sentences with sensory images:

    a. _____

    _____

    b. _____

    _____

    c. _____

    _____

3. I wasn't prepared for the <u>sight</u> that greeted me when I walked off the plane.

    Write three sentences with sensory images:

    a. _____

    _____

    b. _____

    _____

    c. _____

    _____

EXERCISE **Creating Sensory Images**

Each of the following topic sentences contains an underlined word that identifies a physical sense. For each topic sentence, write three sentences that give examples of sensory images.

1. Being pelted with snowballs was not a pleasant <u>feeling</u>.

   Write three sentences with sensory images:

   a. _____

   _____

   b. _____

   _____

   c. _____

   _____

2. They knew the garbage strike had gone on for a long time when they had to <u>hold their noses</u> walking down some streets.

   Write three sentences with sensory images:

   a. _____

   _____

   b. _____

   _____

   c. _____

   _____

3. Sitting on the cabin porch early in the morning, I hear the <u>sounds</u> of a world waking up.

   Write three sentences with sensory images:

   a. _____

   _____

   b. _____

   _____

   c. _____

EXERCISE 11 **Creating Sensory Images**

Each of the following topic sentences contains an underlined word that identifies a physical sense. For each topic sentence, write three sentences that give examples of sensory images.

1. Going to a dance club can be an overwhelming experience because of the many different <u>sounds</u> you hear there.

   Write three sentences with sensory images:

   a. _____

   _____

   b. _____

   _____

   c. _____

   _____

2. My friend Bill says he loves the <u>taste and texture</u> of the chocolate, the nuts, and the coconut when he eats that candy bar.

   Write three sentences with sensory images:

   a. _____

   _____

   b. _____

   _____

   c. _____

   _____

3. I could <u>see</u> that the tourist standing on the corner was confused.

   Write three sentences with sensory images:

   a. _____

   _____

   b. _____

   _____

   c. _____

   _____

Achieving Coherence: Putting Details in Spatial Order

In descriptive writing, supporting details are usually arranged according to **spatial order.** The writer describes items in much the same way as a camera might move across a scene. Items could be ordered from top to bottom, from left to right, from outside to inside, from nearby to farther away, or even around in a circle. Sometimes the most important image is saved for last to give the greatest impact to that image.

Here is a description of a hotel room in Bogota, Colombia, written by Virginia Paxton:

> The room was about the size of New York's Grand Central Station. It had been painted a fiendish dark green. A single light bulb hung from the thirteen-foot-high ceiling. The bed was oversized. The desk was gigantic, and the leather-covered chairs engulfed us. Although hot water ran from the cold faucet and cold from the hot, we were delighted.

Notice how the writer begins with a general description of the room, including its size and color, the height of the ceiling, and the light. Then the writer moves on to give details about the furniture. The final detail is one that is meant to be humorous (the mix-up with the hot and cold water); the writer wants to amuse us and convince us that she enjoyed the adventure of staying in an unusual hotel room. You might also say the order of details here goes from the outer edges of the room to the center. When writing a descriptive paragraph, no matter which method of spatial order you choose, the details should be in a sequence that will allow your reader to visualize the scene in a logical order. Can you explain why the dominant impression is the last word of the paragraph?

EXERCISE 12   **Using Spatial Order**

Each of the following topic sentences is followed by four or more descriptive sentences that are not in any particular order. Put these descriptive sentences in order by placing the appropriate number in the space provided.

1. The Statue of Liberty, now completely restored, is a marvel to visitors from all over the world.

    (*Order the material from bottom to top.*)

    _____ With current restoration finished, the crown continues to be used as a place where visitors can get a good view of New York Harbor.

    _____ The granite for the base of the statue was quarried and cut many miles from New York City and then taken by boat to Bedloe's Island, where the statue was built.

    _____ The torch has been repaired and will now be illuminated by outside lights, not lights from inside the torch itself.

    _____ The seven spikes that rise above the crown represent the seven seas of the world.

    _____ The body was covered with copper that was originally mined on an island off the coast of Norway.

2. The runway models in the designer's winter fashion show presented a classic look.

    (*Order the material from top to bottom.*)

    _____ The skirts were beautifully designed and made of quality fabrics.

    _____ The shoes were all high-heeled basic black pumps.

    _____ Exquisite silk scarves flowed as the models walked past the audience.

    _____ Meticulous attention was paid to hairstyles and makeup.

    _____ The sweaters were all made of cashmere in vibrant colors.

3. My aunt's kitchen is an orderly place.

(Order the material from near to far.)

_____ As usual, in the center of the table sits a vase with a fresh yellow daffodil.

_____ Nearby on the refrigerator, a magnet holds the week's menu.

_____ Sitting at the kitchen table, I am struck by the freshly pressed linen tablecloth.

_____ Looking across the room through the stained glass doors of her kitchen cupboards, I can see neat rows of dishes, exactly eight each, matching the colors of the tablecloth and wallpaper.

EXERCISE 13   **Using Spatial Order**

Each of the following topic sentences could be expanded into a fully developed paragraph. In the spaces provided, give four appropriate sensory images for the topic sentence. Be sure to give your images in a particular order. That is, the images should go from top to bottom, from outside to inside, from close to far, or around the area you are describing.

1. The airport terminal was as busy inside as it was outside.

a. _____

_____

b. _____

_____

c. _____

_____

d. _____

_____

2. The student lounge is a quiet and relaxing place in our school.

a. _____

_____

b. _____

_____

c. _____

_____

d. _____

3. The motel lobby had once been beautiful, but now it was beginning to look shabby.

a. _____

_____

b. _____

c. _____

_____

d. _____

_____

EXERCISE 14 **Using Spatial Order**

Each of the following topic sentences could be expanded into a fully developed paragraph. In the spaces provided, give four appropriate sensory images for the topic sentence. Be sure to give your images in a particular order. That is, the images should go from top to bottom, from outside to inside, from close to far, or around the area you are describing.

1. The shopping mall was supposed to be enjoyable, but the experience gave me a headache.

a. _____

_____

b. _____

_____

c. _____

_____

d. _____

_____

2. The pizza shop is so tiny that people are not likely to stay and eat.

a. _____

_____

b. _____

_____

c. _____

_____

d. _____

_____

3. The bus was filled with a strange assortment of people.

a. _____

_____

b. _____

_____

c. _____

_____

d. _____

_____

Writing a Descriptive Paragraph Using a Step-by-Step Approach

Mastering any skill, including writing, requires a disciplined attitude. One way to master the skill of creating a piece of writing is to take a step-by-step approach, focusing on one issue at a time. This approach results in a minimum of stress. Another advantage is that the writer does not miss important points or misunderstand any part of the process. Of course, there are other ways to build effective descriptive paragraphs, but here is one logical method you can use that will always achieve good results.

Step-by-Step Approach to Writing a Descriptive Paragraph

1. Study the given topic, and then plan your topic sentence, especially the dominant impression.
2. List at least ten sensory images that come to your mind when you think about the topic you have chosen.
3. Choose the five or six most important images from your list. Be sure these details support the dominant impression.
4. Put your list in order.
5. Write at least one complete sentence for each of the images you have chosen from your list.
6. Write a concluding statement that offers some reason for describing this topic.
7. Copy your sentences into standard paragraph form.
8. Always make a final check for spelling errors and other mistakes, such as omitted words.

NOTE: When you use a computer spell-check feature, keep in mind that this feature will only alert you to spellings that do not match words in its dictionary. If you type *there* when you mean *their*, the spell-checker will see an acceptable word. When it comes to a final editing, there is no substitute for your own careful reading.

EXERCISE **Writing a Descriptive Paragraph Using a Step-by-Step Approach**

The following exercise will guide you through the construction of a descriptive paragraph. Start with the suggested topic. Use the eight steps to help you work through the stages of the writing process.

Topic: A place you have lived

1.   Topic sentence (including a dominant impression): _____

_____

2. Make a list of possible sensory images.

    a. _____

    _____

    b. _____

    _____

    c. _____

    _____

    d. _____

    _____

    e. _____

    _____

    f. _____

    _____

    g. _____

    _____

    h. _____

    _____

    i. _____

    j. _____

3. Check the five or six images you believe are the most important for the description.

4. Put your selected details in order by numbering them.

5. Using your final list, write at least one sentence for each image you have chosen.

    a. _____

    _____

    b. _____

    _____

    c. _____

    _____

    d. _____

    _____

e. _____

_____

f. _____

_____

6. Write a concluding statement. _____

_____

7. On a separate piece of paper or on the computer, copy your sentences into standard paragraph form.

8. Do a final reading to check for errors and omissions.

EXERCISE 16

Writing a Descriptive Paragraph Using a Step-by-Step Approach

The following exercise will guide you through the construction of a descriptive paragraph. Start with the suggested topic. Use the eight steps to help you work through the stages of the writing process.

Topic: A person you admire

1. Topic sentence (including a dominant impression): _____

_____

2. Make a list of possible sensory images.

a. _____

b. _____

c. _____

d. _____

e. _____

f. _____

g. _____

h. _____

i. _____

j. _____

3. Check the five or six images you believe are the most important for the description.

4. Put your selected details in order by numbering them.

5. Using your final list, write at least one sentence for each image you have chosen.

a. _____

_____

b. _____

_____

c. _____

_____

d. _____

_____

e. _____

_____

f. _____

_____

6. Write a concluding statement. _____

_____

7. On a separate piece of paper or on the computer, copy your sentences into standard paragraph form.

8. Do a final reading to check for errors and omissions.

EXERCISE 17   **Writing a Descriptive Paragraph Using a Step-by-Step Approach**

The following exercise will guide you through the construction of a descriptive paragraph. Start with the suggested topic. Use the eight steps to help you work through the stages of the writing process.

Topic: The junk drawer in your kitchen

1. Topic sentence (including a dominant impression): _____

_____

2. Make a list of possible sensory images.

a. _____

b. _____

c. _____

d. _____

e. _____

f. _____

g. _____

h. _____

i. _____

j. _____

3. Check the five or six images you believe are the most important for the description.

4. Put your selected details in order by numbering them.

5. Using your final list, write at least one sentence for each image you have chosen.

   a. _____

   _____

   b. _____

   _____

   c. _____

   _____

   d. _____

   _____

   e. _____

   _____

   f. _____

   _____

6. Write a concluding statement. _____

   _____

7. On a separate piece of paper or on the computer, copy your sentences into standard paragraph form.

8. Do a final reading to check for errors and omissions.

Studying Model Paragraphs to Create Descriptive Paragraphs

ASSIGNMENT 1: A DESCRIPTION OF A HOME

Write a paragraph in which you describe a house or room that you remember clearly. Choose your dominant impression carefully and then select your sensory images to support that impression. In your description you may want to include the person who lives in the house or room. In the following model paragraph from Charles Chaplin's *My Autobiography*, notice the importance of the last sentence, in which the writer gives added impact to his paragraph by identifying the person who lives in the house he has described.

Model Paragraph: The Bungalow

Topic sentence

It was dark when we entered his bungalow, and when we switched on the light I was shocked. The place was empty and drab. In his room was an old iron bed with a light bulb hanging over the head of it. A rickety old table and one chair were the other furnishings. Near the bed was a wooden box upon which was a brass ashtray filled with cigarette butts. The room allotted to me was almost the same, only it was minus a grocery box. Nothing worked. The bathroom was unspeakable. One had to take a jug and fill it from the bath tap and empty it down the flush to make the toilet work. This was the home of G. M. Anderson, the multimillionaire cowboy.

Ten suggested topics

1. A student's apartment

2. A vacation cottage

3. A dormitory

4. The house of your dreams

5. Your bedroom

6. A kitchen

7. The messiest room you ever saw

8. The strangest room you ever saw

9. A house you will never forget

10. A house that did not fit the character of the person living there

ASSIGNMENT 2: A DESCRIPTION OF A PERSON

Describe a person whose appearance made a deep impression on you. You might recall someone you have personally known, or you might choose a familiar public figure. Brainstorm by making make a list of the images you remember when you think of this person, images that will create a vivid picture for your readers. What dominant impression do you want to leave with the reader? Is there a single word that conveys this impression? Remember that your supporting details should all support your choice of dominant impression. In the model paragraph that follows, Scott Russell Sanders remembers workingmen from his childhood in rural Tennessee.

Model Paragraph: Workingmen

Topic sentence   <u>The bodies of the men I knew were twisted and maimed in ways visible and invisible.</u> The nails of their hands were black and split, the hands tattooed with scars. Some had lost fingers. Heavy lifting had given many of them finicky backs and guts weak from hernias. Racing against conveyor belts had given them ulcers. Their ankles and knees ached from years of standing on concrete. Anyone who had worked for long around machines was hard of hearing. They squinted, and the skin of their faces was creased like the leather of old work gloves. There were times, studying them, when I dreaded growing up. Most of them coughed, from dust or cigarettes, and most of them drank cheap wine or whiskey, so their eyes looked bloodshot and bruised. The fathers of my friends always seemed older than the mothers. Men wore out sooner. Only women lived into old age.

Ten suggested topics

1. An elderly relative
2. A hard-working student
3. An outstanding athlete
4. A loyal friend
5. An overworked waitress
6. A cab driver
7. A fashion model
8. A gossipy neighbor
9. A street vendor
10. A rude salesperson

ASSIGNMENT 3: A DESCRIPTION OF A TIME OF DAY

Write a paragraph in which you describe the sights, sounds, and events of a particular time of day in a place you know well. In the model paragraph that follows, the writer has chosen to describe an especially busy time of day, the morning, when activity can be frantic in a large household.

Model Paragraph: Growing Up in Cleveland

Topic sentence

<u>I remember the turmoil of mornings in our house.</u> My brothers and sisters rushed about upstairs and down trying to get ready for school. Mom would repeatedly tell them to hurry up. Molly would usually scream down from her bedroom, "What am I going to do? I don't have any clean underwear!" Amy, often in tears, sat at the kitchen table still in her pajamas trying to do her math. Paul paced back and forth in front of the mirror angrily combing his unruly hair which stuck up in all directions while Roland threatened to punch him if he didn't find the pen he had borrowed the night before. Mother was stuffing sandwiches into bags while she sighed, "I'm afraid there isn't anything for dessert today." No one heard her. Then came the yelling up the stairs, "You should have left ten minutes ago." One by one, these unwilling victims were packed up and pushed out the door. Mother wasn't safe yet. Somebody always came back frantic and desperate. "My flute, Mom, where's my flute, quick! I'll get killed if I don't have it today." Every crisis apparently meant the difference between life and death. Morning at our house was like watching a troop preparing for battle. When they had finally gone, I was left in complete silence while my mother slumped on a chair at the kitchen table. She paid no attention to me.

Ten suggested topics

1. A Saturday afternoon filled with errands
2. The dinner hour at my house
3. Lunchtime in a cafeteria
4. A midnight raid on the refrigerator
5. New Year's Eve
6. TGIF (thank God it's Friday)
7. Getting ready to go out on a Friday night
8. My Sunday morning routine
9. Coming home from school or work
10. Watching late-night movies

ASSIGNMENT 4: A DESCRIPTION OF A PUBLIC PLACE

Write a paragraph in which you describe a place you know well or remember clearly. The model paragraph that follows is from *The Airtight Cage*, a classic study by Joseph Lyford of an urban neighborhood in a state of change.

Model Paragraph: A Condemned Building

Supply a topic sentence for this paragraph.

The wreckers would put a one-story scaffold in front of the building to protect automobiles and pedestrians, then begin at the top, working down story by story, gutting the rooms, ripping out woodwork, electrical wiring, plumbing, and fixtures. Once this was done, the men would hammer the shell of the house with sledges. Sections of brick wall would shudder, undulate for a second and dissolve into fragments that fell in slow motion. When the fragments hit the ground, the dust rocketed several feet into the air. The heaps of brick and plaster, coils and stems of rusty pipe attracted children from all over the area. On weekends and after 4 p.m. on weekdays, they would scamper from building to building, dancing in the second-, third-, and fourth-story rooms where fronts and backs had been knocked out, bombing each other with bricks and bits of concrete. Sometimes when they were dashing in and out of clouds of smoke and dust, with ruined buildings in the background, the children looked as if they were taking a town over under heavy artillery fire. The city eventually assigned a guard to stop the children but apparently there were too many of them to handle and the pandemonium continued.

Ten suggested topics

1. A large department store
2. A sports stadium
3. A coffee shop
4. A pizza parlor
5. A shoe store
6. A nightspot
7. A lively street corner
8. A college bookstore
9. A gymnasium
10. A medical clinic

ASSIGNMENT 5: A DESCRIPTION OF A TIME OF YEAR

Write a paragraph in which you describe a particular time of year. Make sure that all of the details you choose relate specifically to that time of year. In the model paragraph that follows, from "Boyhood in Jamaica" by Claude McKay, the writer remembers springtime on his native island.

> # Model Paragraph:
> # Seasons in Jamaica

Topic sentence

Most of the time there was hardly any way of telling the seasons. To us in Jamaica, as elsewhere in the tropics, there were only two seasons—the rainy season and the dry season. We had no idea of spring, summer, autumn, and winter like the peoples of northern lands. Springtime, however, we did know by the new and lush burgeoning of grasses and the blossoming of trees, although we had blooms all the year round. The mango tree was especially significant of spring, because it was one of the few trees that used to shed its leaves. Then, in springtime, the new leaves sprouted—very tender, a kind of sulphur brown, as if they had been singed by fire. Soon afterwards the white blossoms came out and we knew that we would be eating juicy mangoes by August.

Ten suggested topics

1. A winter storm
2. A summer picnic
3. Summer in the city
4. A winter walk
5. Jogging in the spring rain
6. Sunbathing on a beach
7. Signs of spring in my neighborhood
8. The woods in autumn
9. Ice skating in winter
10. Halloween night

Exploring Online

Go to academic.cengage.com/devenglish/scarry to find the **Writer's Online Workplace,** a website designed for students using this book. You will find links to handouts, interactive quizzes, and other online resources as you explore the following topics:

- principles, conventions, and strategies of writing description
- generating sensory details

Writing a Character Sketch

The following personal advertisement appeared in a newspaper:

> Young man seeks neat, responsible roommate to share off-campus apartment for next academic year. Person must be a nonsmoker and respect a vegetarian who cooks at home. Furniture not needed, but microwave and computer would be welcome!

Personal habits have a way of causing friction between people who share the same living space. For this reason, finding the right roommate in a college dormitory, finding the right person with whom to share an apartment, or finding the right long-term companion can be very difficult.

Divide into groups. Develop a random list of habits that can become problems when people share living space. Then, working together, group the items on your list into categories with general headings. For instance, one general heading might be *eating patterns*.

Portfolio Suggestions

1. Write a paragraph or two in which you provide a character description of yourself for an agency that will match you up with a roommate. As you write, be sure to include information about your interests, habits, attitudes, and other personal characteristics that could make a difference in the kind of person the agency will select for you.

2. Write a paragraph or two in which you provide a character sketch of the roommate you would like the agency to find for you.

3. Write your own description of what you imagine would be the "roommate from hell."

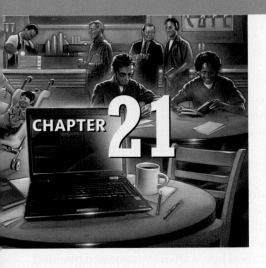

CHAPTER 21

Developing Paragraphs: Process Analysis

Giving instructions or explaining how something is done involves careful reconstruction of a sequence of steps. With a careless omission, an entire process can be misunderstood. In this chapter, you will learn the elements of writing good process paragraphs:

CHAPTER OBJECTIVES

- distinguishing between **directional** and **informational** process writing
- understanding the importance of **completeness**
- achieving coherence through **logical sequence** and the use of **transitions**
- taking a step-by-step approach to create process paragraphs
- studying model paragraphs to create process paragraphs

What Is Process Analysis?

> **Process analysis** is a method of development that provides a step-by-step explanation of how something is done or how something works.

A paragraph using process analysis may be **directional;** that is, the paragraph may be intended for a reader who needs to follow the directions to perform a task. Read the following example of a **directional** process paragraph:

Directional process paragraph

Tick Bites

Remove the tick with a pair of tweezers. Never try to remove a tick by burning it or applying kerosene or other substances. Gently grasp the tick with the tweezers as close to the skin as possible. Slowly pull the insect straight out. Do not twist as you pull, or the tick's body will separate from its head, leaving the head buried under your skin. As you pull, do not squeeze the body of the tick. Squeezing can inject infectious fluids from the tick to you. After removing the tick, thoroughly clean the bite area and your hands, preferably with an antiseptic such as rubbing alcohol. If the tick came from an area with a high incidence of Lyme disease, save the tick and consult a doctor. Otherwise, monitor the bite area. If small raised bumps appear at the bite site or if you develop a rash around the bite or flu-like symptoms, see your doctor. In the case of a tick bite, time is critical because the longer the tick is attached to a person's body, the greater the risk of contracting Lyme disease.

Topic sentence

Your daily life is filled with activities that involve the need for directional process. Instructions on a test, directions on how to get to a wedding reception, and your favorite spaghetti recipe are a few examples of the kinds of process writing you see and use regularly. You can find examples of directional process writing everywhere you look—in newspapers, magazines, and books, as well as on the containers and packages of products you use every day.

The other type of process writing is **informational.** In this case, you explain how something works or how something worked in the past. There is no expectation or even possibility that the reader will or could act upon it. The purpose of describing the process is purely to provide information. History books are filled with such writing. For instance, if you described how a Civil War general planned his battle strategy, this would be informational process writing. The following example tells how the writer and social activist Malcolm X accomplished his self-education. In the paragraph, the transitional words that signal the steps or stages of the process have been italicized.

Topic sentence

Informational process paragraph

> <u>When Malcolm X was in prison, he became very frustrated because</u> <u>he could not express his thoughts in letters written to his family and</u> <u>friends.</u> Nor could he read well enough to get the meaning from a book. He decided to change this situation. *First,* he got hold of a dictionary along with some paper and pencils. He was astounded at how many words there were. Not knowing what else to do, he turned to the first page and *began* by copying words from the page. It took him the entire day. *Next,* he read what he had written aloud, over and over again. He was excited to be learning words he never knew existed. *The next morning,* he reviewed what he had forgotten and *then* copied the next page. He found he was learning about people, places, and events from history. This process *continued until* he had filled a tablet with all the A's and *then* all the B's. *Eventually,* Malcolm X copied the entire dictionary!

Making Sure All the Steps Are Included

All of us have been given directions that seemed very clear at first but that did not produce the result we expected. Perhaps we misunderstood one of the steps in the process, or perhaps a step was missing. Maybe the person giving the information assumed that we already knew certain parts of the process or didn't think the process through carefully enough to identify all the steps. Directions must always be accurate and complete, even down to any special equipment needed to carry out the process.

The writer who presents a process is almost always more of an authority on the subject than the reader. In providing information or giving directions on how to do something, it is easy to leave out steps because they seem too obvious to be worth mentioning. However, a writer should never assume that the reader will be able to fill in any missing steps. An important part of process writing is always being aware of the audience.

EXERCISE **Is the Process Complete?**

Read the steps in the following set of instructions. Imagine yourself carrying out the process using only the information provided. Has any information been left out, or have any needed steps been omitted? (Although recipes are generally not presented in paragraph or essay form, they are good examples of process writing in which the order and completeness of the step-by-step procedure are of critical importance.)

How to make a Swedish spice cake

1. Butter an 8-inch tube pan and sprinkle with 2 tbsp. of fine dry bread crumbs.
2. Cream ½ cup of butter; add 1 cup firmly packed brown sugar and cream until light and fluffy.
3. In a small bowl, beat 2 egg yolks until light and add to the creamed mixture.
4. Sift together 1½ cups all-purpose flour, 1 tsp. baking power, 2 tsp. ground cardamon, and 2 tsp. ground cinnamon.
5. Add the dry ingredients to the creamed ingredients, mixing alternately with ½ cup light cream.
6. Beat egg whites until stiff and fold into batter.
7. Turn into prepared pan, bake, and serve unfrosted.

Missing step or steps: _____

_____

_____

EXERCISE 2

Is the Process Complete?

Read the steps in the following set of instructions. Imagine carrying out the process using only the information provided. Has any information been left out? Have any needed steps been omitted?

How to write a term paper

1. The student carefully considers the choices of topics, often taken from a list provided by the instructor.
2. The next step is perhaps the most important: searching for relevant information on the topic.
3. Once the student has reviewed all the available information, the topic may need to be further limited or modified.
4. Using a systemized approach, the student takes notes and documents sources and page numbers for each fact or quotation that she or he intends to use.
5. At this point, the student is often required to make an outline of the paper's major points. This helps the student organize the material gathered.
6. The student writes a first draft, including the citations.
7. Finally, the student checks that the paper follows the precise format (as well as any other directions) given by the instructor.
8. The paper is submitted on time.

Missing step or steps: _____

_____

_____

EXERCISE **Is the Process Complete?**

In the following process, decide whether any important steps have been omitted. Imagine yourself going through the process using only the information provided.

How to prepare for an essay exam

1. All of the assigned reading should be read, well in advance of the date of the test.

2. Throughout the semester, notes should be taken in class from the instructor's lessons.

3. Several days before the exam, the instructor usually explains what material will be covered on the exam. Students should ask whether the exam will be made up of one main essay question or several shorter essay questions.

4. A good night's sleep before the day of the test will ensure clear thinking.

5. At least two pens should be brought to the test, to avoid the problem of having a pen break or run out of ink.

6. To maintain a sense of calm, students should arrive at the test site a few minutes early so they have plenty of time to relax and get settled.

Missing step or steps: _____

_____

_____

_____

_____

Achieving Coherence

ORDERING IN LOGICAL SEQUENCE

When you are working with a process, it is important not only to make sure that the steps in the process are complete but also to present the steps in the right sequence. For example, if you are describing the process of cleaning an electric mixer, it is important to point out that you must first unplug the appliance before you remove the blades. A person could lose a finger if this part of the process were missing. Improperly written instructions have caused serious injuries and even death.

EXERCISE **Ordering in Logical Sequence**

The following steps describe the process of refinishing hardwood floors. Put the steps into their proper sequence.

_____ Sanding continues until the hardwood is exposed.

_____ A coat of polyurethane finish is applied.

_____ When the sanding is done, the floor is thoroughly cleaned with a vacuum sweeper to remove all the sawdust.

_____ The finish must then dry for three days before waxing and buffing.

_____ All furnishings are removed from the room.

_____ The initial sanding is done with a coarse sandpaper on the sanding machine.

_____ The edger and hand sander are used after the machine sanding to get to hard-to-reach places.

_____ A second coat of polyurethane finish is applied on the following day, using a brush or a roller.

_____ The coarse sandpaper on the machine is changed to a fine sandpaper for the final sanding.

_____ Nails sticking out from the floor should be either pulled out or set below the surface of the boards before starting the sanding.

EXERCISE 5   Ordering in Logical Sequence

The following steps describe the process of devising a filing system. Put the steps into their proper sequence.

_____ Filing of additional items should stop when mental fatigue sets in.

_____ Now the file folder is labeled, and the piece of paper is slipped in.

_____ All the pages to be filed should be gathered in one area, perhaps in the room where the filing cabinet is located.

_____ The file folders are alphabetized and put away in the file drawer. Your session for that time is finished.

_____ In addition, a wastebasket, file folders, labels, and a pen will be needed.

_____ The same procedure should be repeated with the next piece of paper, keeping in mind that this piece of paper might have a place in an existing file rather than a new one.

_____ Any page can be picked up at random to be studied. Does the item need to be saved? If the item has no value, it should be thrown away. If the item has value, the process moves to the next step.

_____ Once the filing system has been established, it's easy to maintain if, every time a particular file is consulted, the complete file is scanned quickly to identify any items that are no longer useful and need to be discarded.

_____ When the item seems worth saving, the question should be asked, What is this item about? That subject will be the title for the label on the file folder.

USING TRANSITIONS

Like writers of narration, writers who analyze a process usually order their material by time sequence. Although it would be tiresome to use the words *and then* for each new step, some transitions are necessary for the process to read smoothly and coherently. Here is a list of transitions frequently used in a process paragraph.

Transitions Commonly Used in Process Analysis

the first step	while you are . . .	the last step
in the beginning	as you are . . .	the final step
to start with	next	finally
to begin with	then	at last
first of all	the second step	eventually
	after you have . . .	

EXERCISE **Using Transitions to Go from a List to a Paragraph**

Select one of the three processes presented on pages 383–384. Use the list of steps, including missing steps that you supplied, to write a process paragraph. Be sure to include transitional devices to make the paragraph read smoothly and coherently.

_____

_____

_____

_____

_____

_____

_____

_____

_____

_____

_____

_____

_____

_____

_____

_____

_____

_____

_____

_____

Writing a Process Paragraph Using a Step-by-Step Approach

Mastering any skill, including writing, requires a disciplined attitude. One way to master the skill of creating a piece of writing is to take a step-by-step approach, focusing on one issue at a time. This approach results in a minimum of stress. Another advantage is that the writer does not miss important points or misunderstand any part of the process. Of course, there are other ways to build effective process paragraphs, but here is one logical method you can use that will always achieve good results.

Step-by-Step Approach to Writing a Process Paragraph

1. After you have chosen your topic and controlling idea, plan your topic sentence.

2. List as many steps or stages in the process as you can.

3. Eliminate irrelevant steps, add any equipment or materials needed, and explain any special circumstances of the process.

4. Put the steps in order.

5. Write at least one complete sentence for each of the steps you have chosen from your list.

6. Write a concluding statement that says something about the results of completing the process.

7. Copy your sentences into standard paragraph form.

8. Make a final check for spelling errors and other mistakes, such as omitted words.

NOTE: When you use a computer spell-check feature, keep in mind that this feature will alert you only to spellings that do not match words in its dictionary. If you type *there* when you mean *their,* the spell-checker will see an acceptable word. When it comes to a final editing, there is no substitute for your own careful reading.

EXERCISE **Writing a Process Paragraph Using a Step-by-Step Approach**

This exercise will guide you through the construction of a complete process paragraph. Start with the topic suggested below. Use the eight steps to take you through the stages of the writing process.

Topic: How to lose weight

Perhaps no topic has filled more book and magazine pages than the "lose five pounds in one week" promise. The wide variety of diet plans boggles the mind. Here is your chance to add your own version.

1. Topic sentence: _____

   _____

   _____

2. Make a list of all necessary steps.

   a. _____

   _____

   _____

b. _____

c. _____

d. _____

e. _____

f. _____

g. _____

h. _____

i. _____

j. _____

3. Eliminate irrelevant steps, add any equipment or materials needed, and explain any special circumstances.

4. Put your steps in order by numbering them.

5. Using your final list, write at least one sentence for each step you have chosen.

a. _____
_____

b. _____
_____

c. _____
_____

d. _____
_____

e. _____
_____

f. _____
_____

g. _____
_____

6. Write a concluding statement. _____
_____
_____

7. On a separate piece of paper or on the computer, copy your sentences into standard paragraph form.

8. Do a final reading to check for errors and omissions.

EXERCISE **8**   **Writing a Process Paragraph Using a Step-by-Step Approach**

This exercise will guide you through the construction of a complete process paragraph. Start with the topic suggested below. Use the eight steps to take you through the stages of the writing process.

Topic: How to choose a college (or other school for career training)

The factors that go into selecting a college can be extremely complicated. Sometimes an individual goes through an agonizing process before he or she is finally seated in a college classroom. Give advice to a prospective college student on how to go about finding the right college.

1. Topic sentence: _____

    _____

2. Make a list of all necessary steps.

    a. _____

    b. _____

    c. _____

    d. _____

    e. _____

    f. _____

    g. _____

    h. _____

    i. _____

    j. _____

3. Eliminate irrelevant steps, add any materials needed, and explain any special circumstances.

4. Put your steps in order by numbering them.

5. Using your final list, write at least one sentence for each step you have chosen.

    a. _____

    _____

    b. _____

    _____

    c. _____

    _____

    d. _____

    _____

    e. _____

    _____

f. _____

_____

g. _____

_____

6. Write a concluding statement. _____

_____

_____

7. On a separate piece of paper or on the computer, copy your sentences into standard paragraph form.

8. Do a final reading to check for errors and omissions.

EXERCISE 9   Writing a Process Paragraph Using a Step-by-Step Approach

This exercise will guide you through the construction of a complete process paragraph. Start with the topic suggested below. Use the eight steps to take you through the stages of the writing process.

Topic: How to set up a budget

Imagine you are the expert who has been hired by a couple to help them sort out their money problems. Together they bring in a reasonable salary, but despite this, they are always spending more than they earn.

1. Topic sentence: _____

_____

2. Make a list of all necessary steps.

a. _____

b. _____

c. _____

d. _____

e. _____

f. _____

g. _____

h. _____

i. _____

j. _____

3. Eliminate irrelevant steps, add any materials needed, and explain any special circumstances.

4. Put your steps in order by numbering them.

5. Using your final list, write at least one sentence for each step you have chosen.

a. _____

_____

b. _____

_____

c. _____

_____

d. _____

_____

e. _____

_____

f. _____

_____

g. _____

_____

6. Write a concluding statement. _____

_____

_____

7. On a separate piece of paper or on the computer, copy your sentences into standard paragraph form.

8. Do a final reading to check for errors and omissions.

Studying Model Paragraphs to Create Process Paragraphs

ASSIGNMENT 1 (DIRECTIONAL): HOW TO ACCOMPLISH A DAILY TASK

Write a paragraph in which you describe the process of carrying out a task. For example, you might write about how to learn to drive a car, how to play a musical instrument, or how to set up a new computer. The following paragraph describes a process for making a common beverage used by millions of people every day: an ordinary cup of tea.

Model Paragraph: How to Make a Good Cup of Tea

Topic sentence

Making a good cup of tea is exquisitely simple. First, the teapot is heated by filling it with water that has just come to a boil. This water is then discarded, and one teaspoon of loose tea per cup is placed in the teapot (the exact amount may vary according to taste). Fresh water that has just come to a boil is poured into the pot. A good calculation is six ounces of water for each cup of tea. The tea must now steep for three to five minutes; then it is poured through a strainer into a cup or mug. A pound of loose tea will yield about two hundred cups of brewed tea. Using a tea bag eliminates the strainer, but it is still best to make the tea in a teapot so that the water stays sufficiently hot. The typical restaurant service—a cup of hot water with the tea bag on the side—will not produce the best cup of tea because the water is never hot enough when it reaches the table and because the tea should not be dunked in the water; the water should be poured over the tea. Although tea in a pot often becomes too strong, that problem can be dealt with very easily by adding more boiling water.

Ten suggested topics

1. How to plan a move from one home to another
2. How to program a new cell phone
3. How to rewire a lamp
4. How to change the oil in your car
5. How to make the best . . . (choose your favorite dish)
6. How to prepare a package for mailing
7. How to pack a suitcase
8. How to inexpensively furnish an apartment
9. How to wallpaper or paint a room
10. How to plan a barbeque

ASSIGNMENT 2 (DIRECTIONAL): HOW TO CARE FOR YOUR HEALTH

Awareness of the importance of health and physical fitness has increased, bringing in big profits to health-related magazines, health clubs, health-food producers, and sports equipment manufacturers. Write a paragraph in which you show steps you could take for your mental or physical health. The following paragraph tells how to get a good night's sleep.

Model Paragraph: How to Get a Good Night's Sleep

Topic sentence

Getting a good night's sleep depends on following several important steps. First, the conditions in the bedroom must be correct. The temperature should be around sixty-five degrees, and the room should be as quiet as possible. Next, an important consideration is the bed itself. A good-quality mattress goes a long way toward preventing aches, which often wake people up when they turn over during the night. Using natural fabrics such as cotton and wool is a much better choice than using sheets and blankets made of synthetic materials that do not breathe. In addition, pillows that are either too soft or too hard can cause stiffness of the neck and lead to a poor night's sleep. Once the room is prepared, sleep is still not ensured. The next requirement is that the person going to bed feel relaxed and tired enough to sleep. This will not happen if the person has been lying around all day napping and, in general, leading a very inactive life. People who have trouble sleeping should try to keep an active schedule. Then, as bedtime nears, activities should become less stimulating and more relaxing. Finally, people often forget the importance of what they eat in the hours preceding bedtime. People should not go to bed hungry, nor should they overeat. Foods such as candy bars or cookies are full of sugar and act as stimulants. Such foods should be avoided, along with all caffeinated beverages. When these steps are followed, nearly everyone can look forward to a good night's sleep.

Ten suggested topics

1. How to plan a healthful diet
2. How to care for someone who is ill
3. How to plan a daily exercise program
4. How to choose a sport that is suitable for you
5. How to live to be one hundred
6. How to pick a doctor
7. How to make exercise and diet foods fun
8. How to stop eating junk food
9. How to deal with depression
10. How to find a spiritual side to life

ASSIGNMENT 3 (DIRECTIONAL): HOW TO WRITE SCHOOL ASSIGNMENTS

Your writing in school takes many forms. Write a paragraph in which you describe the process of a specific writing assignment. The following paragraph, adapted from Donald Murray's *Write to Learn,* shows the several steps you need to follow in the writing of a term paper.

Model Paragraph: Writing a Term Paper

Topic sentence

Doing a term paper involves both careful research on a topic and a methodical approach to writing up the results of that research. First, consult the important and up-to-date books and articles related to the topic. Next, find out the style of writing that the instructor wants. What are the requirements for the paper's length, organization, citation, and bibliography? Then write a draft of the paper as quickly as possible, without consulting notes or bibliography; this will help your ideas take form and will suggest how these ideas should be more fully developed. Before going any further, review your draft to see if a point of view or an attitude toward the topic is emerging. Finally, write a second draft that includes all the important information about the topic. This draft will include citations and a bibliography.

Ten suggested topics

1. How to prepare an oral report
2. How to write a résumé
3. How to write a letter of application (for a school or for a job)
4. How to report a science experiment
5. How to write a book review
6. How to revise an essay
7. How to take classroom notes
8. How to take notes from a textbook
9. How to write a letter home, asking for money
10. How to write a story for the school newspaper

ASSIGNMENT 4 (INFORMATIONAL): HOW TEAMWORK ACCOMPLISHES A TASK

Write a paragraph in which you describe the process used by an agency or group of people to achieve some important goal. The following paragraph, describing how wildfires are presently fought, is an example of informational process writing.

Model Paragraph: Fighting Wildfires

Topic sentence

When a wildfire starts, a process to protect lives and property is set in motion. At first, the fire is watched. Many fires do not go beyond the initial burn. If the fire appears to be spreading, the next step is to call on weather forecasters to study the weather patterns to predict where the fire will spread next. Firefighters called "hot shots" may hike into the area to begin their work of scraping, cutting, and clearing the brush that gives fuel to the fire. The first goal of the hot shots is to cut a containment perimeter around the fire rather than put it out. If it is too far to hike into an area, parachutists called "smoke jumpers" will go in to do the work. If the fire is moving too fast or in extremely rugged terrain, helicopter pilots drop chemicals or water on the fire to retard it. Although some fires are set by Mother Nature during lightning storms, the sad fact is that most fires are set by humans who carelessly toss away cigarette butts that have not been completely extinguished.

Ten suggested topics

1. How the relay race works
2. How lab experiments use teamwork
3. How a band requires teamwork
4. How a community garden or beautification project is organized
5. How a neighborhood crime-watch group functions
6. How an ambulance crew works together
7. How a town council operates
8. How an office should be run
9. How a school yearbook depends on team effort
10. How a student newspaper demands a dedicated team

Exploring Online

Go to academic.cengage.com/devenglish/scarry to find the **Writer's Online Workplace,** a website designed for students using this book. You will find links to handouts, interactive quizzes, and other online resources as you explore the following topics:

- writing a process composition
- looking at examples of process paragraphs and essays

Working Together

Building a Team

Either in school or in business, being able to work well with a group is of vital importance. If a team member does not understand or respect how groups should function, the experience may be frustrating at best and a failure at worst. Below are several questions for a discussion on teamwork. Select one student in the class to direct the discussion, while another student writes the main points of the discussion on the board.

Class discussion

1. When a group meets to work, what procedure should be followed?
2. How important is it that everybody first understand the task?
3. How can a group avoid the situation where only one person seems to be doing all the work?
4. What should be done about a person who tends to dominate all the discussions?
5. What can be done for a person who is very shy?
6. What can be done about a person who has an "attitude"?
7. How can the group be sure that the meeting does not end up with people chatting instead of focusing on the task?
8. How can personality conflicts be avoided?
9. How should disagreements be handled?

Use the material from the classroom discussion to write a process essay. In your essay, describe the procedure that should be followed when a group of people meets to work on a project. It might be helpful to use as an example a group of workers doing a particular job: teachers getting together to design a series of courses; magazine editors meeting to decide on a theme for their next issue; or a school's coaches planning their strategies for the upcoming season.

Portfolio Suggestion

Record some of the comments that you heard during the group discussion, making special note of two or three points you found especially interesting. Write at least one or two sentences for each of these special points, concentrating on some aspect about which you feel strongly. Place these completed sentences in your portfolio for possible use in future writing assignments. As you record the general comments and as you generate your own sentences, keep in mind that your notes may apply directly to your work in other college courses. The idea of building team spirit or learning to work with others has many direct applications, including the fields of sports, science, psychology, and sociology.

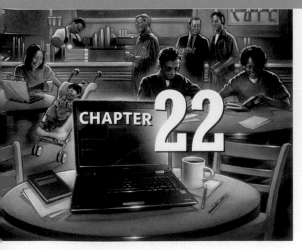

CHAPTER 22

Developing Paragraphs: Comparison/Contrast

Writing a paragraph using comparison or contrast requires the development of two topics at the same time. In this chapter, you will concentrate on the special needs of this challenging rhetorical form:

CHAPTER OBJECTIVES

- choosing a two-part topic
- ordering material using the point-by-point method or the block method
- improving coherence by using transitional phrases common to comparison/contrast writing
- taking a step-by-step approach to create comparison/contrast paragraphs
- studying model paragraphs to create comparison/contrast paragraphs

What Is Comparison/Contrast?

We use comparison and contrast every day. In the grocery store, we judge similar products before we decide to buy one of them; we listen to two politicians on television and think about the differences between their positions before we vote for one of them; and we read college catalogues and talk to our friends before we make a final choice as to which school we should attend.

When we compare or contrast two items, we need to consider exactly which points should be compared. We usually have a purpose or a need for making our decision as to which item is better or worse. For instance, if we are making an expensive purchase, a person who has not analyzed the situation might be tempted to rely on a clever salesperson, who may want to make an easy sale. A person might also be swayed by the price alone or make the decision based on impulse. We have all experienced the sad consequences of making such a decision without thinking it through. Comparison or contrast involves using a logical process.

Consider a common experience that involves making a decision that will directly affect a person's budget: finding the best apartment to rent. It is not often that a person finds an apartment perfect in all respects. Many factors will have to go into the decision of choosing among the apartments available. Will the monthly rent include utilities? If not, what are those costs likely to be? Is there a lease to be signed, or is the apartment available on a month-to-month basis? Do you have to put down an extra month's rent? How soon is the apartment available? Are pets allowed?

When the building and the apartment itself are considered, other basic questions come to mind. On what floor is the apartment located? Is there an elevator? What is the level of maintenance in the building? What type of security does the owner provide? Is the apartment furnished or unfurnished? How many bedrooms does it have? What is the condition of the rooms, the kitchen and bathroom in particular? Finally, the location of the apartment is a factor in a person's decision. Is the building close to needed transportation? Is it close to schools and shopping?

If you were writing about your choice of an apartment, these are some of the issues that would make your piece of writing fall into the category of *comparison or contrast*. With such an important decision as choosing the right apartment, we can see that comparison or contrast is not just a useful tool but an essential one.

> **Comparison or contrast,** as a method of development, involves examining similarities or differences between people, objects, or ideas to arrive at a judgment or conclusion.

A comparison tends to emphasize the similarities, whereas a contrast focuses more on the differences.

Choosing a Two-Part Topic

When writing a comparison/contrast paragraph, most problems are caused by the two-part topic. Therefore, very careful attention must be paid to the topic sentence. While you must be careful to choose two subjects that have enough in common to make them comparable, you must not choose two things having so much in common that you cannot possibly handle all the relevant points in a single paragraph. For example, a student trying to compare the Spanish word *río* with the English word *river* might be able to come up with only two sentences of material. With only a dictionary to consult, it is unlikely that the student would find enough material for several points of comparison. On the other hand, contrasting the United States with Europe would present such an endless supply of points that the tendency would be to give only general facts that the reader would already know. When the subject is too broad, the writing is often too general. A better two-part topic might be to compare traveling by train in Europe with traveling by train in the United States.

Once you have chosen a two-part topic that you feel is not too limiting and not too broad, you must remember that a good comparison/contrast paragraph devotes an equal or nearly equal amount of space to each of the two parts. If the writer is interested in only one of the topics, the danger is that the paragraph will end up being one-sided.

Here's an example of a one-sided contrast:

> American trains go to only a few towns, are infrequent, and are often shabby and uncomfortable. In contrast, European trains are much nicer.

The following example is a better-written contrast, which gives attention to both topics:

> American trains go to only a few large cities, run infrequently, and are often shabby and uncomfortable. In contrast, European trains go to virtually every small town, are always dependable, and are clean and attractive.

EXERCISE **1**   **Evaluating the Two-Part Topic**

Study the following topics. Decide whether each topic is *too broad* or *suitable* for a paragraph of comparison or contrast. Mark your choice in the appropriate space to the right of each topic given.

Topic	Too broad	Suitable
1. Australia and England	_____	_____
2. Indian elephants and African elephants	_____	_____
3. California champagne and French champagne	_____	_____
4. Wooden furniture and plastic furniture	_____	_____
5. Wood and plastic	_____	_____
6. Paperback books and hardcover books	_____	_____
7. Mothers and fathers	_____	_____
8. Taking photographs with a flash and taking photographs using available light	_____	_____
9. Doctors and lawyers	_____	_____
10. Trains and airplanes	_____	_____

EXERCISE **2**   **Working with Comparison or Contrast**

For each comparison or contrast, supply your own two parts of the topic. Each two-part topic should be one that you could develop as an example of comparison or contrast.

1. Compare/contrast two friends:

   My friend _____ with my friend _____

2. Compare/contrast two kinds of coats:

   _____ coats with _____ coats

3. Compare/contrast two kinds of diets:

   The _____ diet and the _____ diet

4. Compare/contrast two kinds of floors:

   _____ floors with _____ floors

5. Compare/contrast two kinds of entertainment:

   Watching _____ with looking at _____

6. Compare/contrast two kinds of rice:

   _____ rice with _____ rice

7. Compare/contrast two places where you can study:

   Studying in the _____ with studying in the _____

8. Compare/contrast the wedding customs of two groups:

   What _____ do at a wedding with what _____ do at a wedding

9. Compare/contrast two textbooks:

A textbook that has _____ with a textbook that contains

_____

10. Compare/contrast two politicians:

A local politician who _____ with a national politician

who _____

EXERCISE 3 **Working with Comparison or Contrast**

For each comparison or contrast, supply your own two parts of the topic. Each two-part topic should be one that you could develop as an example of comparison or contrast.

1. Compare/contrast two kinds of popular board games people play:

Playing _____ with playing _____

2. Compare/contrast two ways of looking at movies:

Watching movies on _____ with going to _____

3. Compare/contrast two careers:

A career in _____ with a career as a _____

4. Compare/contrast two ways of paying for a purchase:

Using _____ to buy something with using _____ to buy something

5. Compare/contrast two different lifestyles:

Living the life of a _____ with living as a _____

6. Compare/contrast two places to go swimming:

Swimming in a _____ with swimming in a _____

7. Compare/contrast a no-frills product with the same product sold under a standard brand name (such as no-frills corn flakes with Kellogg's corn flakes):

A no-frills _____ with _____

8. Compare/contrast two popular magazines:

_____ with _____

9. Compare/contrast two leisure activities:

Collecting _____ with _____

10. Compare/contrast two kinds of tests given in school:

The _____ kind of test with the _____ kind of test

Achieving Coherence: Two Approaches to Ordering Material

POINT-BY-POINT METHOD

One method for ordering material in a paragraph of comparison or contrast is known as the **point-by-point method.** When you use this method, you compare or contrast one part of the topic with the other, first on one point and then on the next, until you have covered all the points. For example, here is a paragraph from Julius Lester's *All Is Well*. In the paragraph, the writer uses the point-by-point method to compare the difficulties of being a boy with the difficulties of being a girl:

Topic sentence

> <u>Now, of course, I know that it was as difficult being a girl as it was a boy, if not more so.</u> While I stood paralyzed at one end of a dance floor trying to find the courage to ask a girl for a dance, most of the girls waited in terror at the other, afraid that no one, not even I, would ask them. And while I resented having to ask a girl for a date, wasn't it also horrible to be the one who waited for the phone to ring? And how many of those girls who laughed at me making a fool of myself on the baseball diamond would have gladly given up their places on the sidelines for mine on the field?

Notice how, after the opening topic sentence, the writer uses half of each sentence to describe a boy's situation growing up and the other half to describe a girl's experience. This technique is effective in such a paragraph, and it is most often used in longer pieces of writing in which many points of comparison are made. This method helps the reader keep the comparison or contrast carefully in mind at each point.

If the paragraph is broken down into its parts, this is how the point-by-point method appears:

Topic sentence: Now, of course, I know that it was as difficult being a girl as it was a boy, if not more so.

First point, first topic: While I stood paralyzed at one end of a dance floor trying to find the courage to ask a girl for a dance, . . .

First point, second topic: . . . most of the girls waited in terror at the other, afraid that no one, not even I, would ask them.

Second point, first topic: And while I resented having to ask a girl for a date, . . .

Second point, second topic: . . . wasn't it also horrible to be the one who waited for the phone to ring?

Third point, first topic: And how many of those girls who laughed at me making a fool of myself on the baseball diamond . . .

Third point, second topic: . . . would have gladly given up their places on the sidelines for mine on the field?

BLOCK METHOD

The other method for ordering material in a paragraph of comparison or contrast is known as the **block method.** When you use this approach, you present all of the facts and supporting details about one part of your topic, and then you give all of the facts and supporting details about the other part. Here, for example, is another version of the paragraph by Julius Lester, this time written according to the block method:

Topic sentence

> <u>Now, of course, I know that it was as difficult being a girl as it was being a boy, if not more so.</u> I stood paralyzed at one end of the dance floor trying to find the courage to ask a girl for a dance. I resented having to ask a girl for a date, just as I often felt foolish on the baseball diamond. On the other hand, most of the girls waited in terror at the other end of the dance floor, afraid that no one, not even I, would ask them to dance. In addition, it was a horrible

situation for the girls who had to wait for the phone to ring. And how many of those girls who stood on the sidelines would have gladly traded places with me on the baseball diamond?

Notice how the first half of this version presents all of the details about the boy, and the second part of the paragraph presents all of the information about the girls. This method is often used in shorter pieces of writing because with a shorter piece it is possible for the reader to keep the blocks of information in mind.

If the paragraph is broken down into its parts, this is how the block method appears:

Topic sentence: Now, of course, I know that it was as difficult being a girl as it was being a boy, if not more so.

First topic, points 1, 2, and 3: I stood paralyzed at one end of the dance floor trying to find the courage to ask a girl for a dance. I resented having to ask a girl for a date, just as I often felt foolish on the baseball diamond.

Second topic, points 1, 2, and 3: On the other hand, most of the girls waited in terror at the other end of the dance floor, afraid that no one, not even I, would ask them to dance. In addition, it was a horrible situation for the girls who had to wait for the phone to ring. And how many of those girls who stood on the sidelines would have gladly traded places with me on the baseball diamond?

You will want to choose one of these methods before you write a comparison or contrast assignment. Keep in mind that although the block method is most often used in shorter writing assignments, such as a paragraph, you can effectively employ the point-by-point method as well.

EXERCISE **4**   **Recognizing the Two Approaches to Ordering Material**

Each of the following passages is an example of comparison or contrast. Read each paragraph carefully and decide whether the writer has used the point-by-point method or the block method. Also decide whether the piece emphasizes similarities or differences. Indicate your choices in the spaces provided after each passage.

Topic sentence   1.   <u>Female infants speak sooner, have larger vocabularies, and rarely demonstrate speech defects.</u> (Stuttering, for instance, occurs almost exclusively among boys.) Girls exceed boys in language abilities, and this early linguistic bias often prevails throughout life. Girls read sooner, learn foreign languages more easily, and, as a result, are more likely to enter occupations involving language mastery. Boys, in contrast, show an early visual superiority. They are also clumsier, performing poorly at something like arranging a row of beads, but excel at other activities calling on total body coordination. Their attentional mechanisms are also different. A boy will react to an inanimate object as quickly as he will to a person. A male baby will often ignore the mother and babble to a blinking light, fixate on a geometric figure, and at a later point, manipulate it and attempt to take it apart.

_____ Point-by-point   _____ Block

_____ Similarities   _____ Differences

Topic sentence

2.   <u>Each man had, to begin with, the great virtue of utter tenacity and fidelity.</u> Grant fought his way down the Mississippi Valley despite acute personal discouragement and profound military handicaps. Lee hung on in the trenches at Petersburg after hope itself had died. In each man there was an indomitable quality . . . the born fighter's refusal to give up as long as he can still remain on his feet and lift his two fists. Daring and resourcefulness they had, too; the ability to think faster and move faster than the enemy. These were the qualities that gave Lee the dazzling campaigns of Second Manassas and Chancellorsville and won Vicksburg for Grant.

_____ Point-by-point   _____ Block

_____ Similarities   _____ Differences

Topic sentence

3.   <u>I first realized that the act of writing was about to enter a new era five years ago when I went to see an editor at the *New York Times.*</u> As I was ushered through the vast city room I felt that I had strayed into the wrong office. The place was clean and carpeted and quiet. As I passed long rows of desks, I saw that almost every desk had its own computer terminal and its own solemn occupant—a man or a woman typing at the computer keyboard or reading what was on the terminal screen. I saw no typewriters, no paper, no mess. It was a cool and sterile environment; the drones at their machines could have been processing insurance claims or tracking a spacecraft in orbit. What they didn't look like were newspaper people, and what the place didn't look like was a newspaper office. I knew how a newspaper office should look and sound and smell—I worked in one for thirteen years. The paper was the *New York Herald Tribune,* and its city room, wide as a city block, was dirty and disheveled. Reporters wrote on ancient typewriters that filled the air with clatter; copy editors labored on coffee-stained desks over what the reporters had written. Crumpled balls of paper littered the floor and filled the wastebaskets—failed efforts to write a good lead or a decent sentence. The walls were grimy—every few years they were painted over in a less restful shade of eye-rest green—and the atmosphere was hazy with the smoke of cigarettes and cigars. At the very center the city editor, a giant named L. L. Engelking, bellowed his displeasure with the day's work, his voice a rumbling volcano in our lives. I thought it was the most beautiful place in the world.

_____ Point-by-point   _____ Block

_____ Similarities   _____ Differences

Topic sentence

4.   <u>We went fishing the first morning.</u> I felt the same damp moss covering the worms in the bait can, and saw the dragonfly alight on the tip of my rod as it hovered a few inches from the surface of the water. It was the arrival of this fly that convinced me beyond any doubt that everything was as it always had been, that the years were a mirage and there had been no years. The small waves were the same, chucking the rowboat under the chin as we fished at anchor, and the boat was the same boat, the same color green and the ribs broken in the same places, and under the floorboards the same freshwater leavings and debris—the dead helgramite, the wisps of moss, the rusty discarded fishhook, the dried blood from yesterday's catch. We stared silently at the tips of our rods, at the dragonflies that came and went. I lowered the tip of mine into the water, tentatively, pensively dislodging the fly, which darted two feet away, poised, darted two feet back,

and came to rest again a little farther up the rod. There had been no years between the ducking of this dragonfly and the other one—the one that was part of memory. I looked at the boy, who was silently watching his fly, and it was my hands that held his rod, my eyes watching. I felt dizzy and didn't know which rod I was at the end of.

_____ Point-by-point   _____ Block

_____ Similarities   _____ Differences

5.   The streets are littered with cigarette and cigar butts, paper wrappings, particles of food, and dog droppings. How long before they become indistinguishable from the gutters of medieval towns when slop pails were emptied from the second-story windows? Thousands of New York women no longer attend evening services in their churches. They fear assault as they walk the few steps from bus or subway station to their apartment houses. The era of the medieval footpad° has returned, and as in the Dark Ages, the cry for help brings no assistance, for even grown men know they would be cut down before the police could arrive.

°**footpad**
(obsolete): a mugger
Topic sentence

_____ Point-by-point   _____ Block

_____ Similarities   _____ Differences

EXERCISE 5

Using the Point-by-Point Method for Contrast

Passage 3 on page 404 uses the block method to make its points of contrast. Rewrite the passage using the point-by-point approach.

EXERCISE 6

Using the Point-by-Point and Block Methods for Comparison or Contrast

Use the lists below to write a paragraph comparing or contrasting life in the city with life in a suburban area. First review the lists provided, adding your own ideas and omitting any you do not wish to use. Then, selecting either the block method or the point-by-point method, write a comparison or contrast paragraph.

Topic sentence: If I could move back to the city from the suburbs, I know I would be happy.

The following lists provide details that relate to living in the city and living in a suburban community:

Topic I **Advantages of the city**	**Topic II** **Disadvantages of the suburbs**
a. A short ride on the bus or subway gets you to work.	a. Commuting to work from the suburbs to the city is often time-consuming and exhausting.
b. Men are as visible as women in the neighborhood.	b. Because most men in the suburbs work in the city, few of them are active in the suburban community.
c. The architecture and ethnic diversity are stimulating.	c. The sameness of people and streets is monotonous.

d. Shopping for nearly everything can be done on foot.

d. Shopping requires a car.

c. People walk in their neighborhoods.

e. People use cars to go everywhere.

Notice that the writer who created this list emphasized the disadvantages of the suburbs, in contrast to the advantages of the city. No mention was made, for example, of overcrowding in the city. Another list could be created from the point of view of a person who prefers the suburbs.

Achieving Coherence: Using Transitions

The transitions in the following chart are useful to keep in mind when writing a comparison or contrast paragraph. Some of them are used in phrases, some in clauses. For example, notice the difference between *like* and *as*. *Like* is used as a preposition in a prepositional phrase:

My sister is just *like* me.

As is used as a subordinating conjunction to begin a clause:

My sister reads every evening in bed, *as does her older daughter*.

Transitions Commonly Used in Comparison/Contrast

Transitions for comparison		Transitions for contrast	
again	like	although	instead
also	likewise	and yet	nevertheless
as well as	moreover	but	on the contrary
both	the same as	despite	on the other hand
equally	similar to	different from	otherwise
furthermore	similarly	even though	still
just as	so	except for	though
just like	too	however	unlike
		in contrast with	whereas

EXERCISE **Using Transitions in Comparisons and Contrasts**

Read each of the following pairs of sentences and decide whether the idea being expressed is a comparison or a contrast. Next, combine the two sentences by using a transition you have chosen from the list above. Then write your new sentence on the lines provided. You may reword your new sentence slightly to make it grammatically correct. An example has been done for you.

Mr. Costello is a teacher.
His wife is a teacher.

First you decide that the two sentences show a comparison. Then you combine the two by using an appropriate transition:

> Mr. Costello is a teacher, just like his wife.
>
> or
>
> Mr. Costello is a teacher; his wife is too.

1. Dr. Rappole has a reputation for having an excellent bedside manner.

   Dr. Connolly is very withdrawn and speaks so softly we can hardly understand him.

   Your combined sentence: _____

   _____

   _____

2. In the United States, interest in soccer has become apparent only in recent years.

   Soccer has always been immensely popular in Brazil.

   Your combined sentence: _____

   _____

   _____

3. The French Revolution was directed by the common people.

   The Russian Revolution was directed by an elite group of thinkers.

   Your combined sentence: _____

   _____

   _____

4. Amy is carefree and fun loving, with little interest in school.

   Noreen, Amy's sister, is so studious and hardworking that she is always on the honor roll.

   Your combined sentence: _____

   _____

   _____

5. The apartment had almost no furniture, was badly in need of painting, and felt chilly even though I was wearing a coat.

   The other apartment was attractively furnished, had been freshly painted, and was so warm that I had to take off my coat.

   Your combined sentence: _____

   _____

   _____

EXERCISE 8

Using Transitions in Comparisons and Contrasts

First, identify each of the following pairs of sentences as a comparison or a contrast. Then combine the two sentences by using a transition from the list on page 406. Finally, write your new sentence on the lines provided.

1. Oprah Winfrey's daytime talk show deals with current controversial issues that are of importance to society.

    David Letterman's program gives people light entertainment in the evening.

    Your combined sentence: _____

    _____

    _____

2. Shakespeare's *Romeo and Juliet* is a famous love story that takes place in Italy.

    West Side Story is a modern-day version of Shakespeare's love story that takes place in New York City.

    Your combined sentence: _____

    _____

    _____

3. Hemingway's book *Death in the Afternoon* deals with the theme of man against nature.

    The same writer's novel *The Old Man and the Sea* deals with the theme of man against nature.

    Your combined sentence: _____

    _____

    _____

4. Some scientists believe that dinosaurs became extinct because they ran out of food.

    Some scientists think that dinosaurs were victims of a climate change induced by dust clouds thrown up by a meteor hitting earth.

    Your combined sentence: _____

    _____

    _____

    _____

5. The Museum of Modern Art in New York City shows paintings, photographs, movies, and many other forms of twentieth-century art.

    The Metropolitan Museum of Art in New York City contains sculptures, paintings, and other forms of art that date from the beginning of recorded history.

    Your combined sentence: _____

    _____

    _____

    _____

EXERCISE 9   **Using Transitions in Comparisons and Contrasts**

First, identify each of the following pairs of sentences as a comparison or a contrast. Then combine the two by using a transition from the list on page 406. Finally, write your new sentence on the lines provided.

1. A ballet dancer trains for years to master all aspects of dancing.

    A football player puts in years of practice to learn the game from every angle.

    Your combined sentence: _____

    _____

    _____

2. The University of Chicago is a large urban university that has the resources of a big city as part of its attraction for faculty and students.

    Fredonia State College is a small rural college that has beautiful surroundings as part of its attraction.

    Your combined sentence: _____

    _____

    _____

3. Ice cream, a popular dessert for many years, has many calories and added chemicals to give it more flavor.

    Tofutti is a dessert made of processed soybeans that is low in calories and contains no harmful additives.

    Your combined sentence: _____

    _____

    _____

4. Nelson Rockefeller gave much of his time and money for education and the arts.

    Andrew Carnegie set up a famous foundation to support learning and artistic achievement.

    Your combined sentence: _____

    _____

    _____

5. *A Soldier's Play* is a play that has a single setting for all of its action.

    A Soldier's Story, a film based on the play, is a movie that is able to use many different settings to present all of its action.

    Your combined sentence: _____

    _____

    _____

Writing a Comparison/Contrast Paragraph Using a Step-by-Step Approach

Mastering any skill, including writing, requires a disciplined attitude. One way to master the skill of creating a piece of writing is to take a step-by-step approach, focusing on one issue at a time. This approach results in a minimum of stress. Another advantage is that the writer does not miss important points or misunderstand any part of the process. Of course, there are other ways to build effective comparison or contrast paragraphs, but here is one logical method you can use that will always achieve good results.

Step-by-Step Approach to Writing a Comparison/Contrast Paragraph

1. After you have chosen your two-part topic, plan your topic sentence.

2. List all your ideas for points that could be compared or contrasted.

3. Choose the three or four most important points from your list.

4. Decide whether you want to use the point-by-point method or the block method of organizing your paragraph.

5. Write at least one complete sentence for each of the points you have chosen from your list.

6. Write a concluding statement that summarizes the main points, makes a judgment, or emphasizes what you believe is the most important point.

7. Copy your sentences into standard paragraph form.

8. Always make a final check for spelling errors and other mistakes, such as omitted words.

NOTE: When you use a computer spell-check feature, keep in mind that this feature will alert you only to spellings that do not match words in its dictionary. If you type *there* when you mean *their*, the spell-checker will see an acceptable word. When it comes to a final editing, there is no substitute for your own careful reading.

EXERCISE **Writing a Comparison or Contrast Paragraph Using a Step-by-Step Approach**

This exercise will guide you through the construction of a comparison or contrast paragraph. Start with the suggested topic. Use the eight steps as a guide.

Topic: Compare or contrast how you spend your leisure time with how your parents or friends spend leisure time.

1. Topic sentence: _____

   _____

   _____

2. Make a list of possible comparisons or contrasts.

   a. _____

   _____

   b. _____

   _____

   c. _____

   _____

   d. _____

   _____

   e. _____

   f. _____

   g. _____

   h. _____

   i. _____

   j. _____

3. Circle the three or four comparisons or contrasts that you believe are most important and put them in order.

4. Choose either the point-by-point method or the block method.

5. Using your final list, write at least one sentence for each comparison or contrast you have chosen.

   a. _____

   _____

   b. _____

   _____

   c. _____

   _____

   d. _____

   _____

   e. _____

   _____

   f. _____

   _____

   g. _____

   _____

6. Write a concluding statement. _____

_____

_____

7. On a separate piece of paper or on the computer, copy your sentences into standard paragraph form.

8. Do a final reading to check for errors and omissions.

EXERCISE ⑪ **Writing a Comparison or Contrast Paragraph Using a Step-by-Step Approach**

This exercise will guide you through the construction of a comparison or contrast paragraph. Start with the suggested topic. Use the eight steps as a guide.

Topic: Compare or contrast going to work right after high school with going on to further education after high school.

1. Topic sentence: _____

_____

2. Make a list of possible comparisons or contrasts.

a. _____

b. _____

c. _____

d. _____

e. _____

f. _____

g. _____

h. _____

i. _____

j. _____

3. Circle the three or four comparisons or contrasts that you believe are most important and put them in order.

4. Choose either the point-by-point method or the block method.

5. Using your final list, write at least one sentence for each comparison or contrast you have chosen.

a. _____

_____

b. _____

_____

c. _____

_____

d. _____

_____

e. _____

_____

f. _____

_____

g. _____

_____

6. Write a concluding statement. _____

_____

_____

7. On a separate piece of paper or on the computer, copy your sentences into standard paragraph form.

8. Do a final reading to check for errors and omissions.

EXERCISE 12 **Writing a Comparison or Contrast Paragraph Using a Step-by-Step Approach**

This exercise will guide you through the construction of a comparison or contrast paragraph. Start with the suggested topic. Use the eight steps as a guide.

Topic: Compare or contrast the styles of two television personalities (or two other public figures often in the news).

1. Topic sentence: _____

_____

2. Make a list of possible comparisons or contrasts.

a. _____

b. _____

c. _____

d. _____

e. _____

f. _____

g. _____

h. _____

i. _____

j. _____

3. Circle the three or four comparisons or contrasts that you believe are most important and put them in order.

4. Choose either the point-by-point method or the block method.

5. Using your final list, write at least one sentence for each comparison or contrast you have chosen.

   a. _____

   _____

   b. _____

   _____

   c. _____

   _____

   d. _____

   _____

   e. _____

   _____

   f. _____

   _____

   g. _____

   _____

6. Write a concluding statement. _____

   _____

   _____

7. On a separate piece of paper or on the computer, copy your sentences into standard paragraph form.

8. Do a final reading to check for errors and omissions.

Studying Model Paragraphs to Create Comparison or Contrast Paragraphs

ASSIGNMENT 1: CONTRASTING TWO VERSIONS OF REALITY

Write a paragraph in which you compare or contrast two versions of a topic. The following paragraph contrasts the Disney film depiction of the Pocahontas story with what we know to be more historically correct about the real Pocahontas.

Model Paragraph: Two Versions of the Pocahontas Story

Topic sentence

The Disney version of the Pocahontas story is not an accurate portrayal of what we know to be true. A seventeenth-century portrait of Pocahontas reveals her to be buxom, full-faced, and strong, not the Barbie-like glamour girl of Disney. John Smith, too, is portrayed inaccurately in the film. Far from the young blond heroic figure shown in the movie, John Smith was in actuality a bearded and weathered-looking man of thirty when he met Pocahontas. The dramatic version of romance and rescue is another historical inaccuracy of the Disney film. Most historians contend that the supposed "rescue" of John Smith was in fact a farce. The Powhatans, historians claim, may have been adopting Smith into their tribe through a ritual that required a little playacting. So, although Pocahontas may have rescued Smith, the circumstances of that rescue may have been very different from the film's depiction. Furthermore, there is no historical evidence to support a romance between Pocahontas and John Smith as the movie shows. The unfortunate reality was that Pocahontas was taken captive by the English and forced to marry an English tobacco planter named John Rolfe. The ending of the film is certainly the final blow to what we know to be fact. Pocahontas did not, as Disney suggests, stay in North America while John Smith sailed into the distance toward his native England. Instead, she traveled to England with Rolfe, her new husband. On the return trip to her native North America, at the young age of twenty-two, Pocahontas fell ill, probably with smallpox, and died.

Choose one of the topics suggested below or a topic you think of yourself, and compare or contrast the two versions of reality.

Ten suggested topics

1. A sports figure's public image with details of his or her private life exposed by the media

2. A politician's promises before an election with what he or she did after the election

3. A "friend" before and after you come into a large sum of money

4. Today's attitudes toward smoking compared to attitudes of your parents' generation

5. A celebrity's reputation in the past with his or her reputation today

6. A person who sees life as a glass that is half empty with a person who sees the same glass as half full

7. Baseball years ago with baseball now

8. Attitudes toward AIDS when the virus was first discovered with attitudes toward the disease today

9. Traditional portrayals of Native Americans (in old films, for example) with portrayals today

10. How a member of your family acts at home with how that same person acts in public

ASSIGNMENT 2: CONTRASTING TWO CULTURES

Write a paragraph in which you compare or contrast two cultures or an aspect of culture that may be observed in two societies. The following paragraph was written by Brenda David, an American teacher who worked with schoolchildren in Milan, Italy, for several years.

Model Paragraph: Children of Two Nations

Topic sentence

All young children, whatever their culture, are alike in their charm and innocence—in being a clean slate on which the wonders and ways of the world are yet to be written. <u>But during the three years I worked in a school in Milan, I learned that American and Italian children are different in several ways.</u> First, young American children tend to be active, enthusiastic, and inquisitive. Italian children, on the other hand, tend to be passive, quiet, and not particularly inquisitive. They usually depend on their parents to tell them what to do. Second, American children show their independence while their Italian counterparts are still looking to their parents and grandparents to tell them what to do or not do. Third, and most important to those who question the influence of environment on a child, the American children generally surpass their Italian schoolmates in math, mechanical, and scientific abilities. But American children are overshadowed by their Italian counterparts in their language, literature, art, and music courses. Perhaps the differences, which those of us at the school confirmed in an informal study, were to be expected. After all, what priority do Americans give to the technological skills? And what value do Italians—with the literature of poets and authors like Boccaccio, the works of Michelangelo, and the music of the world-famous La Scala opera at Milan—place on the cultural arts?

Ten suggested topics

Compare or contrast:

1. Two cuisines
2. Courtship in two cultures
3. Attitudes toward women's roles in two societies
4. Folk dancing in two countries
5. Raising children in two countries
6. Urban people with small-town people
7. Care for the elderly in two cultures
8. The culture of your neighborhood with the general culture of our society
9. The culture you live in now with the culture in which your parents were raised
10. Medical care in our society with the medical care of another society

ASSIGNMENT 3: COMPARING A PLACE THEN AND NOW

Write a paragraph in which you compare or contrast the appearance of a place when you were growing up with the appearance of that same place now. The following paragraph contrasts the way a small city was some years ago with how it appeared to the writer on a recent visit.

Model Paragraph: Thirty Years Later

Topic sentence

As I drove up Swede Hill, I realized that the picture I had in my mind all these years was largely a romantic one. It was here that my father had boarded, as a young man of eighteen, with a widow who rented rooms in her house. Now the large old wooden frame houses were mostly two-family homes; no single family could afford to heat them in the winter. The porches, which had once been beautiful and where people had passed their summer evenings, had peeling paint and were in poor condition. No one now stopped to talk; the only sounds to be heard were those of cars whizzing past. The immigrants who had come to this country and worked hard to put their children through school were now elderly and mostly alone, since their educated children could find no jobs in the small upstate city. From the top of the hill I looked down fondly on the town built on the hills and noticed that a new and wider highway now went through the town. My father would have liked that; he would not have had to complain about Sunday drives on Foote Avenue. In the distance I could see the large shopping mall, which now had most of the business in the surrounding area and which had forced several local businesses to close. Now the center of town no longer hummed with activity, as it once had. My town was not the same place I had known, and I could see that changes would eventually transform the entire area.

Ten suggested topics

Compare or contrast the way a place appears now with how it appeared some years ago:

1. A barber shop or beauty salon
2. A house of worship
3. A local "corner store"
4. A friend's home
5. Your elementary school
6. A local bank
7. A downtown shopping area
8. A restaurant or diner
9. An undeveloped place such as an open field or wooded area
10. A favorite local gathering place

ASSIGNMENT 4: COMPARING TWO APPROACHES TO A SUBJECT

Write a paragraph in which you compare or contrast two ways of considering a particular topic. The following paragraph contrasts two approaches to the art of healing—the traditional medical approach and the approach that involves less dependence on chemicals and more reliance on the body's natural defense system.

Model Paragraph: The Medical Profession and Natural Healing

Topic sentence

Natural healing is basically a much more conservative approach to health care than traditional medical practice. Traditional medical practice aims for the quick cure by means of introducing substances or instruments into the body that are highly antagonistic to whatever is causing the disease. A doctor wants to see results, and he or she wants you to appreciate that traditional medicine is what is delivering those results to you. Because of this desire for swift, decisive victories over disease, traditional medicine tends to be dramatic, risky, and expensive. Natural healing takes a slower, more organic approach to the problem of disease. It first recognizes that the human body is superbly equipped to resist disease and heal injuries. But when disease takes hold or an injury occurs, the first instinct in natural healing is to see what might be done to strengthen that natural resistance and those natural healing agents so that they can act against the disease more effectively. Results are not expected to occur overnight, but neither are they expected to occur at the expense of the body, which may experience side effects or dangerous complications.

Ten suggested topics

Compare or contrast:

1. Retiring and working after age sixty-five
2. Owning your own business and working for someone else
3. Two views on abortion
4. Two attitudes toward divorce
5. Two political viewpoints
6. Your lifestyle today and five years ago
7. Mothers who work at home and those who work away from home
8. Buying U.S.-made products and buying foreign-made goods
9. Two attitudes on the "right to die" issue
10. Two attitudes toward religion

ASSIGNMENT 5: COMPARING MALE ATTITUDES AND FEMALE ATTITUDES

Some observers believe that males tend to think one way about certain subjects and females tend to think another way. Other observers believe that such conclusions are nothing more than stereotypes and that people should not be divided in this fashion. The following paragraph reports that recent studies indicate a possible biological basis for some differences between males and females.

Model Paragraph: Differences between Boys and Girls

Topic sentence

<u>Recent scientific research has shown that differences in behavior between males and females may have their origins in biological differences in the brain.</u> Shortly after birth, females are more sensitive than males to some types of sounds, and by the age of five months a female baby can recognize photographs of familiar people, whereas a boy of that age can rarely accomplish this. Researchers also found that girls tend to speak sooner than boys, read sooner than they do, and learn foreign languages more easily than boys do. On the other hand, boys show an early visual superiority over girls and they are better than girls at working with three-dimensional space. When preschool girls and boys are asked to mentally work with an object, the girls are not as successful as the boys. In this case, as in several others, the girls are likely to give verbal descriptions while the boys are able to do the actual work in their minds.

Ten suggested topics

In a paragraph, compare or contrast what you believe are male and female attitudes toward one of the following topics:

1. Cooking
2. Sports
3. The nursing profession
4. Child care
5. The construction trade
6. Military careers
7. A career in science
8. Hobbies
9. Friendship
10. Clothing

Exploring Online

Go to academic.cengage.com/devenglish/scarry to find the **Writer's Online Workplace,** a website designed for students using this book. You will find links to handouts, interactive quizzes, and other online resources as you explore the following topics:

- paragraph development using comparison/contrast
- an interactive quiz about comparison/contrast
- examples of comparison/contrast paragraphs

Working Together

A Before and After Story

Below is an account of a radical change in one man's life. When you have read this before and after report (which uses the block method), share with your classmates some stories of changes in the lives of people you have known. Then write a before and after story of your own. Use the chart provided on the next page to help you plan your approach to the two-part topic.

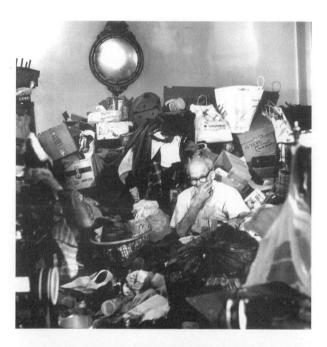

Before

Since I was fifteen, I've saved all kinds of stuff: bureau handles, small bottles, marbles, mirrors, nuts, screws, wire, cord, bathtub stoppers, mothballs, empty cigarette packs, frying pans, pencils that say different things on them, trusses, parking tickets. In 1997, my brother Harry, with whom I lived, slipped on some of my papers and got brought to a nursing home. The social worker wouldn't let him come back unless I got rid of my collections. So I bought a bus pass and visited him once a week. He died last year at eighty-five. If he'd had a hobby like me, he might have lived longer. I liked living in my junk, and I always knew where everything was. In the living room, the junk came up to about my chest. In the bedroom, it wasn't too bad; it just came up to my knees. I made paths to get around. It made me feel important. But I guess I overdid it. The landlord wanted me to get rid of my junk. A third of my neighbors wouldn't talk to me. I suspected I might get evicted. So this summer I had to let my junk go.

After

My nephew cleaned it out with some friends of his. It took ten days. I wasn't there. When I came back, I was disappointed. I thought more stuff would be saved. I had an empty feeling, like I was robbed. I lost memories of my four brothers and my mother. But things happen—what can you do? I'm too old to worry anymore. All that's left is my necktie collection and my cat, Wagging. The emptiness is a little hard to get used to. For one thing, the traffic noise is very loud now. And I feel hollow. My junk was sort of a freedom. I put so much work into saving—years and years—and it's suddenly gone. It's like somebody had died, a fire or an earthquake. It's like the change from hot to cold water. I may start saving certain things, like books, but I don't go out as much as I used to, so I can't collect as much. From now on, I'll have fewer hobbies.

Preparing to write a comparison or contrast paragraph involves noting points of comparison or contrast. Use the chart provided below.

POINTS TO COMPARE OR CONTRAST	BEFORE	AFTER
Point 1		
Point 2		
Point 3		
Point 4		
Point 5		

Portfolio Suggestion

You might find it fascinating to research one of the most bizarre examples of people, known as pack rats, who fill their homes with useless stuff. Go online and locate historical information on the Collyer brothers, two hermit hoarders who died in New York City shortly after World War II. Use the information you find on Homer and Langley Collyer to write an essay about people who cannot bring themselves to throw anything away.

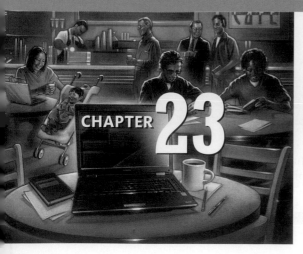

CHAPTER 23

Developing Paragraphs: Cause and Effect

In our daily lives, we often look for connections between two actions or events. We wonder if events are accidental, coincidental, or connected in some more causal way. When writers consider cause and effect, they use their writing to examine such relationships. This chapter focuses on important considerations for developing this rhetorical form:

CHAPTER OBJECTIVES

- avoiding errors in **logic**
- if the connection is causal, identifying the **immediate causes** and **underlying causes** or the **immediate effects** and **long-term effects**
- improving coherence by using transitional phrases common to cause and effect
- taking a step-by-step approach to create cause or effect paragraphs
- studying model paragraphs to create cause or effect paragraphs

What Is Cause and Effect?

> **Cause and effect,** as a method of development, is the search for the relationship between two actions or two events, one of which we conclude is the reason for the other action or event.

People have always looked at the world and asked, "Why did this happen?" or "What will be the result?" Ancient societies created beautiful myths and legends to explain the origin of the universe and our place in it, but modern civilization has emphasized the use of scientific methods of observation to find the cause of a disease or to determine why the planet Mars appears to be covered by canals. When we examine the spiritual or physical mysteries of our world, we are trying to discover the connections or links between events. In this chapter, we will refer to such connections between events as **causal relationships.**

Not everything that happens to us is due to luck or chance. For instance, a magic trick may appear to have no logical explanation to the child who watches, but the person performing that trick knows the secret of the connection between the rabbit and the hat. The search for causes or effects is a bit like detective work. A person looks for clues that will explain what might at first seem unexplainable. Learning to recognize causal relationships can help us better understand some of the events that happen to us over the course of our lives. This search for connections can be complex. Often the logical analysis of a problem reveals more than one possible explanation. Sometimes the best one can do is find **possible causes** or **probable effects.**

Writers who examine the causal relationship between two events are likely to use one or more of the terms in the following chart. Study the chart to become familiar with these terms associated most often with cause and effect.

Cause and Effect Terms

Causes: explaining **why**

giving **reasons**

understanding **problems**

determining **immediate causes** and **underlying causes**

Effects: predicting **results**

understanding **consequences**

providing **solutions**

determining **immediate effects** and **long-term effects**

Following are some examples of how a writer could signal causal relationships.

1. *If . . . , then . . .*

    If the school budget is defeated, **then** several teachers will have to be dismissed.

2. *The cause/reason/result/consequence/effect . . . was that . . .*

    The reason several teachers were dismissed **was that** the school budget was defeated.

    The result of the school budget defeat **was that** several teachers were dismissed.

3. *The problem . . . could be solved . . .*

    The problem of funding the school's wrestling team **could be solved** if enough people in the community would get together to raise the needed money.

PRACTICE   Use the above patterns to create sentences of your own on the topic of *study habits.*

1. If _____,

    then _____

2. The reason _____

    was that _____

3. The cause for _____

    was that _____

4. The consequence of _____
   was that _____
5. The problem of _____
   could be solved _____

EXERCISE **Finding Causes and Effects in Paragraphs**

Below are two paragraphs about a single topic: headaches. One paragraph considers the causes of a headache, and the other looks at some of the effects that recurring headaches have on people's lives. In each case, list the causal relationships given in the paragraph.

Cause: explaining why, giving reasons, understanding problems

Topic sentence
    <u>Headaches can have several causes.</u> Many people think that the major cause of headache is nervous tension, but strong evidence suggests diet and environment as possible factors. Some people get headaches because they are dependent on caffeine. Other people may be allergic to salt, or they may have low blood sugar. Still other people are allergic to household chemicals, including polishes, waxes, bug killers, and paint. If they can manage to avoid these substances, their headaches tend to go away. When a person has recurring headaches, it is important to look for the underlying cause, especially if the result of that search is freedom from pain.

What causes a headache?

1. _____
2. _____
      a. _____
      b. _____
      c. _____
3. _____
      a. _____
      b. _____
      c. _____
      d. _____

Effect: predicting results, understanding consequences, suggesting solutions

Topic sentence
    <u>Recurring headaches can have several disruptive effects on a person's life.</u> Severe headaches are more than temporary inconveniences. In many cases, these headaches make a person nauseated to the point that he or she must go to bed. Sleep is often interrupted because of the pain. This worsens the physical and emotional state of the sufferer. Those who try to maintain a normal lifestyle often rely on drugs to get through the day. Such drugs, of course, can have negative side effects. Productivity on a job can certainly be reduced, even to the point of regular absences. Finally, perhaps the most distressing aspect of all this is the seemingly unpredictable occurrence of these headaches. The interruption to a person's family life is enormous: plans canceled at the last minute and relationships with friends and family strained. It is no wonder that many of these people feel discouraged and even depressed.

What are some of the effects of headaches?

1. _____
2. _____
3. _____
4. _____
5. _____

EXERCISE **2**   ## Separating the Cause from the Effect

In each sentence, separate the *cause* (reasons or problems) from the *effect* (results, consequences, or solutions). Remember that the cause is not necessarily given first.

1. More than half of the mothers with children under one year of age work outside the home, which has resulted in the unprecedented need for daycare in this country.

   Cause _____

   _____

   Effect _____

2. Today, more than two-thirds of all preschool children have mothers who work, and four out of five school-age children have working mothers, which has led to increased strains on the daycare system.

   Cause _____

   _____

   Effect _____

3. In one national survey, more than half the working mothers reported that they had either changed jobs or cut back on their hours to be more available for their children.

   Problem _____

   _____

   Solution _____

4. Because they feel their children need the supervision of a parent, many mothers who work do so only when their children are in school and other mothers work only occasionally during the school year.

   Cause _____

   _____

   Effect _____

5. Many mothers experience deep emotional crises as a result of the conflict between the financial obligations of their home and their own emotional needs as parents.

   Problem _____

   _____

   Result _____

Avoiding Errors in Logic

Here is an example of a possible error in logic:

> Every time I try to write an essay in the evening, I have trouble getting to sleep. Therefore, writing must prevent me from sleeping.

In this case, the act of writing may indeed stimulate the person and prevent that person from getting to sleep. However, if the person is serious about finding the cause of the insomnia, he or she must find out whether other *factors* are to blame. For instance, if the person is drinking several cups of coffee while writing each evening, this could cause the person's sleep problems.

> ### Avoid These Common Errors in Logic
>
> 1. Do not confuse coincidence or chronological sequence with evidence of a causal relationship.
>
> 2. Look for underlying causes beneath the obvious ones and for far-reaching effects beyond the ones that first come to mind. Often what appears to be a single cause or a single effect is part of a much more complex relationship.

EXERCISE **Looking for the Causal Relationship**

Study each of the following situations. If the sequence of events is merely coincidental or the conclusion is unfounded, write *U* (unfounded) in the space provided. If the relationship is most likely causal, write *C*. Be prepared to explain your answers in class.

_____ 1. Every time I carry my umbrella, it doesn't rain. I am carrying my umbrella today; therefore, it won't rain.

_____ 2. We put fertilizer on the grass. A week later, the grass had grown two inches and turned a deeper green.

_____ 3. On Tuesday morning, I walked under a ladder. On Wednesday morning, I walked into my office and was told I had lost my job.

_____ 4. The child grew up helping her mother cook. In adulthood, she became a famous chef.

_____ 5. Tar and nicotine from cigarettes damage the lungs. People who smoke cigarettes increase their chances of dying from lung cancer.

_____ 6. A political scandal was exposed in the city on Friday. On Saturday night, only twenty-four hours later, a power blackout occurred in the city.

_____ 7. Increasing numbers of tourists came to the island last year. The economy of the island reached new heights.

_____ 8. Many natural disasters have occurred this year. The world must be coming to an end.

_____ 9. The biggest factory in a nearby town decided to relocate to another country. The town officials invited different industries to consider moving to the town.

_____ 10. That woman sings beautifully. She must have an equally beautiful personality.

EXERCISE 4   **Underlying Causes**

Below are five topics. For each topic, give a possible immediate or direct cause and then give a possible underlying cause. Discuss your answers in class. An example has been done for you.

Causes of a particular disease, such as tuberculosis

Immediate cause: contact with a carrier of the disease

Underlying cause: immune system weakened by poor nutrition

1. Causes for being selected out of several candidates for a position

   Immediate cause _____

   Underlying cause _____

2. Causes for immigration to the United States

   Immediate cause _____

   Underlying cause _____

3. Causes for spanking a child

   Immediate cause _____

   Underlying cause _____

4. Causes of an unreasonable fear you have

   Immediate cause _____

   Underlying cause _____

5. Causes of a bad habit you have

   Immediate cause _____

   Underlying cause _____

EXERCISE 5   **Immediate or Long-Term Effects**

Below are five topics. For each topic, give an immediate effect and then give a possible long-term effect. Discuss your answers in class. An example has been done for you.

Effects of using credit cards

Immediate effect: money available on the spot for purchases

Long-term effect: greater cost because of interest payments

1. Effects of horror movies on young children

   Immediate effect _____

   Long-term effect _____

2. Effects of tuition increases at four-year colleges

   Immediate effect _____

   Long-term effect _____

3. Effects on family life when both parents work outside the home

    Immediate effect _____

    Long-term effect _____

4. Effects of an after-school tutoring program

    Immediate effect _____

    Long-term effect _____

5. Effects of having a family member with special needs

    Immediate effect _____

    Long-term effect _____

Achieving Coherence: Using Transitions

Several transitional words and expressions are particularly useful in writing about causes or effects. You will need to feel comfortable using these words and expressions, and you will need to know what punctuation is required.

Transitions Commonly Used in Cause and Effect Writing

Common transitions for cause

because	He missed the opportunity *because* he was ill.
caused by	The missed opportunity was *caused by* illness.
the reason . . . is that	*The reason* he missed the opportunity *was that* he became ill.
results from	The missed opportunity *resulted from* his illness.

Common transitions for effect

accordingly	He was ill; *accordingly*, he missed the opportunity.
as a result	He was ill; *as a result*, he missed the opportunity.
resulted in	His illness *resulted in* his missing the opportunity.
consequently	He was ill; *consequently*, he missed the opportunity.
for this reason	He was ill. *For this reason* he missed the opportunity.
so	He was ill, *so* he missed the opportunity.
therefore	He was ill; *therefore*, he missed the opportunity.
thus	He was ill; *thus*, he missed the opportunity.

EXERCISE 6

Using Transitional Words and Expressions for Cause

Use each of the following words or phrases in a complete sentence that demonstrates you understand how to use the given term to express a causal relationship.

1. to be caused by

   _____

   _____

2. because (of)

   _____

   _____

3. resulted from

   _____

   _____

4. the reason is that (followed by an independent clause)

   _____

   _____

EXERCISE 7

Using Transitional Words and Expressions for Effect

Use each of the following words or phrases in a complete sentence that demonstrates you understand how to use the given term to point to an effect.

1. accordingly

   _____

   _____

2. as a result

   _____

   _____

3. results in

   _____

   _____

4. consequently

   _____

   _____

5. for this reason

   _____

   _____

6. so

   _____

   _____

7. therefore

   _____

   _____

Writing a Cause or Effect Paragraph Using a Step-by-Step Approach

Mastering any skill, including writing, requires a disciplined attitude. One way to master the skill of creating a piece of writing is to take a step-by-step approach, focusing on one issue at a time. This approach results in a minimum of stress. Another advantage is that the writer does not miss important points or misunderstand any part of the process. Of course, other ways build effective cause or effect paragraphs, but here is one logical method you can use that will always achieve good results.

Step-by-Step Approach to Writing a Cause or Effect Paragraph

1. After you have chosen your topic, plan your topic sentence.

2. Brainstorm by jotting down all possible causes or effects. Ask others for their thoughts. Do research if necessary. Consider long-range effects or underlying causes.

3. Choose the three or four best points from your list.

4. Decide on the best order for these points. (One way to organize them is from least important to most important.)

5. Write at least one complete sentence for each of the causes or effects you have chosen from your list.

6. Write a concluding statement.

7. On a separate piece of paper or on the computer, copy your sentences into standard paragraph form.

8. Always make a final check for spelling errors and other mistakes, such as omitted words.

NOTE: When you use a computer spell-check feature, keep in mind that this feature will alert you only to spellings that do not match words in its dictionary. If you type *there* when you mean *their*, the spell-checker will see an acceptable word. When it comes to a final editing, there is no substitute for your own careful reading.

EXERCISE **Writing a Causal Paragraph Using a Step-by-Step Approach**

This exercise will guide you through writing a paragraph using *cause* as the method of development. Start with the suggested topic. Use the eight steps to help you work through the stages of the writing process.

Topic: Why do so few Americans learn a second language?

1. Topic sentence: _____

_____

2. Make a list of possible causes. (*Consider underlying causes.*)

    a. _____

    b. _____

    c. _____

    d. _____

    e. _____

3. Cross out any points that may be illogical or merely coincidental.

4. Put your list in order.

5. Using your final list, write at least one sentence for each of the causes you have found.

    a. _____

    _____

    b. _____

    _____

    c. _____

    _____

    d. _____

    _____

    e. _____

6. Write a concluding statement. _____

    _____

    _____

7. On a separate piece of paper or on the computer, copy your sentences into standard paragraph form.

8. Do a final reading to check for errors and omissions.

EXERCISE 9   **Writing an Effect Paragraph Using a Step-by-Step Approach**

This exercise will guide you through writing a paragraph using *effect* as the method of development. Start with the suggested topic. Use the eight steps to help you work through the stages of the writing process.

Topic: What are the effects on college students of having a part-time job?

1. Topic sentence: _____

    _____

2. Make a list of possible effects. (*Consider long-range effects.*)

    a. _____

    b. _____

    c. _____

    d. _____

    e. _____

3. Cross out points that are illogical or merely the result of coincidence or time sequence.

4. Put your list in order.

5. Using your final list, write at least one sentence for each of the effects you have found.

    a. _____

    _____

    _____

    b. _____

    _____

    _____

    c. _____

    _____

    _____

    d. _____

    _____

    _____

    e. _____

    _____

6. Write a concluding statement. _____

    _____

    _____

7. On a separate piece of paper or on the computer, copy your sentences into standard paragraph form.

8. Do a final reading to check for errors and omissions.

Studying Model Paragraphs to Create Cause or Effect Paragraphs

ASSIGNMENT 1: THE CAUSES OF A SOCIAL PROBLEM

Write a paragraph about the causes of a social problem that is of concern to you. The following paragraph looks at possible causes for placing an elderly relative in a nursing home.

Model Paragraph: Old Age in Modern Society

Topic sentence

Industrialized societies have developed homes for elderly who are unable to care for themselves. Despite much criticism, these homes care for a growing percentage of our nation's elderly. Why do some people feel forced into placing parents in a nursing home? The most immediate cause is that, following serious illness, there is often no place for the elderly person to go where he or she can be cared for. In the family of today, it is often the case that both partners work outside the home, so no one is home during the day to care for the person. Hiring a nurse to be in the home every day is beyond the budget of nearly every family. Even when a family member can be home to care for the elderly person, the problems can be overwhelming. The older person can be too heavy for one or even two to manage. Bathing, particularly, can be dangerous in these circumstances. In addition, many elderly people have to be watched very carefully because of their medical condition. Many families do not have the proper training to meet these needs. Finally, elderly people who are senile and difficult can often intrude on a family's life to the point that a caregiver may never be able to leave the house or get a proper night's rest. Perhaps a better system of visiting nursing care could help some families keep their loved ones in their homes longer.

Ten suggested topics

1. The causes of homelessness
2. The causes of prostitution
3. The causes of teenage runaways
4. The causes of high school dropout rates
5. The causes of divorce
6. The causes of child abuse
7. The causes of white-collar crime
8. The causes of high stress among college students
9. The causes of road rage
10. The causes of the increase in childless couples

ASSIGNMENT 2: THE CAUSES THAT LED TO A PARTICULAR HISTORICAL EVENT

Write a paragraph about the causes that led to a particular event in history. This assignment will require some research. The following model paragraph looks at the causes for the loss of life when a supposedly unsinkable ship sank on its maiden voyage nearly one hundred years ago.

Model Paragraph: The Sinking of the *Titanic*

Topic sentence

> <u>After the British ship *Titanic* sank in the Atlantic Ocean on April 15, 1912, with the loss of more than 1,500 lives, investigators began an exhaustive search for the causes of the tragedy.</u> The immediate cause of this terrible loss of life was a large iceberg that tore a three-hundred-foot gash in the side of the ship, flooding five of its watertight compartments. Some believe that the tragedy took place because the crew members did not see the iceberg in time, but others see a chain of different events that contributed to the tragedy. First was the fact that the ship was not carrying enough lifeboats for all of its passengers: It had enough boats for only about half of the people on board. Furthermore, the ship's crew showed a clear lack of caring about the third-class, or "steerage," passengers, who were left in their cramped quarters below decks with little or no help as the ship went down. It has often been said that this social attitude of helping the wealthy and neglecting the poor was one of the real causes of the loss of life that night. Indeed, some of the lifeboats were not filled to capacity when the rescue ships eventually found them. Finally, the tragedy of the *Titanic* was magnified by the fact that some ships nearby did not have a radio crew on duty and therefore missed the distress signals sent by the *Titanic*. Out of all this, the need to reform safety regulations on passenger ships became obvious.

Ten suggested topics

1. Causes for the decline of the Roman Empire
2. Causes for the growth of the civil rights movement in the 1960s in the United States
3. Causes for the Vietnam War
4. Causes for the fall of communism in Europe
5. Causes for the victory (or loss) of a particular political candidate in a recent election
6. Causes for the enormous loss of life in the New York Triangle Shirtwaist Factory fire in 1911
7. Causes for the growth of the feminist movement during the 1970s in the United States
8. Causes for the Depression of 1929
9. Causes for the rise to power of Adolf Hitler
10. Causes for the repeal of Prohibition in 1932

ASSIGNMENT 3: THE EFFECTS OF A SUBSTANCE OR ACTIVITY ON THE HUMAN BODY

Write a paragraph about what happens to the human body when it uses a substance or engages in some activity. The following model paragraph is adapted from Norman Taylor's *Plant Drugs That Changed the World*.

Model Paragraph: Effects of Caffeine

Topic sentence

How much caffeine is too much? The ordinary cup of coffee, of the usual breakfast strength, contains about 1½ grains of caffeine (100 mg). That "second cup of coffee" hence means just about three grains of caffeine at one sitting. Its effects upon the nervous system, the increased capacity for thinking, its stimulating effects on circulation and muscular activity, not to speak of its sparking greater fluency—these are attributes of the beverage that few will give up. If it has any dangers, most of us are inclined to ignore them. But there is no doubt that excessive intake of caffeine at one time, say up to seven or eight grains (that is, 5 or 6 cups), has harmful effects such as restlessness, nervous irritability, insomnia, and muscular tremor. The lethal dose in humans is unknown, for there are no records of it. Experimental animals die in convulsions after overdoses, and from such studies it is assumed that a fatal dose of caffeine in humans may be about 150 grains (that is, ½ ounce). That would mean about one hundred cups of coffee!

Ten suggested topics

1. The effects of alcohol on the body
2. The effects of regular exercise
3. The effects of overeating
4. The effects of a strict diet
5. The effects of fasting
6. The effects of drug abuse
7. The effects of smoking
8. The effects of allergies
9. The effects of a sedentary lifestyle
10. The effects of vitamins

ASSIGNMENT 4: THE EFFECTS OF A COMMUNITY EMERGENCY OR DISASTER

Think of an emergency or disaster that took place in or around your community. This could be an event that you witnessed or that you heard about in the media. Describe the effects this disaster had on you or the people who were involved. The following model paragraph describes the effects that a large power outage had on the communities of the Northeast.

Model Paragraph: The Blackout of 2003

Topic sentence

On Thursday, August 14, 2003, a large area of the northeastern United States was plunged into darkness because of a power failure, resulting in what has become known as the Blackout of 2003. This unprecedented power failure, which affected several states and parts of Canada, struck in an instant and without warning. The result was a near paralysis of normal activity. Most seriously affected, of course, were those individuals, businesses, and institutions caught in a variety of dangerous situations. For example, many people were stuck in elevators; others were underground in dark, hot, crowded subways. In hospitals, patients requiring life support depended on emergency equipment to work properly. Apart from these dangerous aspects of the blackout, the financial loss to certain businesses was considerable. Restaurants and other food-related industries were forced to throw away much of their food. In such states as Michigan and Ohio, the National Guard had to distribute water. Sewage treatment plants that could not operate had to release raw sewage into their waterways. Transportation became another major problem. People who needed gasoline for their cars found that most gasoline pumps depended on electricity. The absence of working traffic lights made for huge traffic nightmares, and many airline flights were canceled. Even farmers needed generators rushed to them so they could operate their milking machines. Sadly, one effect of the emergency was that a few greedy individuals took advantage of the situation and overcharged people for items or services they needed. Reports surfaced of people paying forty dollars for simple nine-dollar flashlights. Luckily the power returned for most people within twenty-four hours and ended their discomfort. A more lasting effect, however, was the emerging realization that our electrical infrastructure is much more vulnerable than the general public had ever realized. In fact, the first thought on everyone's mind when the blackout occurred was that terrorists might have caused it. Some experts fear that even if terrorists did not initiate the blackout, the event will become a model or case study for future terrorist plans and activities. As soon as the

(continued)

emergency had passed, blame was placed on power company officials for not paying attention to the longstanding needs of the electrical system. People now must face the truth that creating a better system is going to involve huge amounts of money. Without any question, we can expect an increase in the cost of electricity. Surprisingly, not all of the long-term effects may be negative: officials may now be forced to plan and execute improvements that will lead to improved monitoring and maintenance of our power supply.

Ten suggested topics

1. The effects of a hurricane
2. The effects of an unexpected outbreak of a disease
3. The effects of a flood or other extensive water damage on a home or community
4. The effects of a prolonged heat wave
5. The effects of a bus, train, or taxi strike on a community
6. The effects of a major fire in a downtown block
7. The effects of the loss of small businesses in a community
8. The effects of the loss of an important community leader
9. The effects of decreased (or increased) services in communities
10. The effects of civil unrest in a city neighborhood

Exploring Online

Go to academic.cengage.com/devenglish/scarry to find the **Writer's Online Workplace,** a website designed for students using this book. You will find links to handouts, interactive quizzes, and other online resources as you explore the following topic:

- writing a cause and effect composition

Looking at Immediate and Long-Term Effects: The Story of Rosa Parks

Rosa Parks (1913–2005), who refused to give up her seat on an Alabama bus, set off a spark that inflamed the civil rights movement of that era. Her action is the subject of the following article. The instructor or a member of the class should read the excerpt aloud while the rest of the class listens, noting immediate or long-term effects and marking the text where each effect is given.

1   The incident that changed Parks's life occurred on Thursday, December 1, 1955, as she was riding home on the Cleveland Avenue bus from her job at Montgomery Fair, a downtown department store where she worked as an assistant tailor. The first ten seats on the city buses, which were always reserved for whites, soon filled up. She sat down next to a man in the front of the section designated for blacks, when a white male got on and looked for a seat. In such situations, the black section was made smaller. The driver, who was white, requested that the four blacks move. The others complied, but Parks refused to surrender her seat, so the driver called the police. Parks had been evicted from a bus twelve years earlier by the same driver, but this time it was different. In a *Black Women Oral History Project* interview, she said, "I didn't consider myself breaking any

(continued)

segregation laws . . . because he was extending what we considered our section of the bus." And in *Black Women* she explained, "I felt just resigned to give what I could to protest against the way I was being treated."

2   At this time there had been fruitless meetings with the bus company about the rudeness of the drivers and other issues—including trying to get the bus line extended farther into the black community, because three-quarters of the bus riders were from there. In the previous year three black women, two of them teenagers, had been arrested for defying the seating laws on the Montgomery buses. The community had talked many times about a citywide demonstration, such as boycotting the bus line, but it never developed. The Women's Political Council already had a network of volunteers in place and had preprinted flyers; they needed only a time and place for a meeting.

3   About six o'clock that evening, Parks was arrested and sent to jail. She was later released on a one-hundred-dollar bond, and her trial was scheduled for December 5. Parks agreed to allow her case to become the focus for a struggle against the system of segregation. On December 2, the Women's Political Council distributed more than fifty-two thousand flyers throughout Montgomery calling for a one-day bus boycott on the day of Parks's trial. There was a mass meeting of more than seven thousand blacks at the Holt Street Baptist Church. The black community formed the Montgomery Improvement Association and elected Martin Luther King Jr. president. The success of the bus boycott on December 5 led to its continuation. In the second month it was almost 100 percent effective, involving thirty thousand black riders. When Parks was tried, she was found guilty and fined ten dollars plus court costs of four dollars. She refused to pay and appealed the case to the Montgomery Circuit Court.

4   Following her release from jail, Parks went back to work but later lost her job, as did her husband. At home, the couple had to deal with threatening telephone calls. Rosa Parks devoted her time to arranging rides in support of the boycott. Blacks were harassed and intimidated by the authorities in Montgomery, and there was an attempt to break up their carpools. Parks served for a time on the board of directors of the Montgomery Improvement Association and often was invited elsewhere to speak about the boycott.

5   On February 1, 1956, in an attempt to have the Alabama segregation laws declared unconstitutional, the Montgomery Improvement Association filed a suit in the United States District Court in the names of four women and on behalf of all who had suffered indignities on the buses. On June 2 the lower court declared segregated seating on the buses unconstitutional. The Supreme Court upheld the lower court order that Montgomery buses must be integrated, and on December 20, 1956, the order was served on Montgomery officials. After 381 days of boycotting, resulting in extreme financial loss to the bus company, segregation and other discriminatory practices were outlawed on the city buses. Parks's refusal to give up her seat on a bus was the beginning of the civil rights movement of the 1950s and 1960s. Her action marked the beginning of a time of struggle by black Americans and their supporters as they sought to become an integral part of America.

6   With the notoriety surrounding her name, Parks was unable to find employment in Montgomery. Her husband became ill and could not work, so Parks, her husband, and her mother moved to Detroit in 1957 to join Parks's brother. Although her husband did not have a Michigan barber's license, he found work in a training school for barbers. In 1958 Parks accepted a position at Hampton Institute in Virginia for one year, after which she returned to Detroit and worked as a seamstress. She continued her efforts to improve life for the black community, working with the Southern Christian Leadership Conference in Detroit. In 1965 Parks became a staff assistant in the Detroit office of United States Representative John Conyers; she retired in 1988.

Working in Groups

After the excerpt has been read, the class should divide into groups. Each group should work up two lists: the immediate effects and the long-term effects of Rosa Parks's decision, as presented in the article. Come together again as a class and compare the lists. Has each group agreed on which effects were immediate and which effects were long-term?

Since the day in 1955 when Rosa Parks took her historic stand, many changes have taken place in civil rights in our society. Your instructor may want you to choose another area of civil rights (such as one of those listed below) to study the causes of that particular group's discontent or to study the effects of that group's struggle to obtain legal rights.

- rights of the dying
- rights of the unborn
- gay rights
- immigrants' rights

Portfolio Suggestion

Because civil rights is constantly evolving in our society, and because many different groups are continuing to press for their rights, we need to understand the underlying causes and the long-term effects of those struggles. Investigate newspapers, magazines, and the Internet for material on current civil rights struggles. You may have a particular struggle that you are deeply interested in. Keep the results in your portfolio. The material you collect could well be useful later when you might be asked to write about some aspect of this important topic.

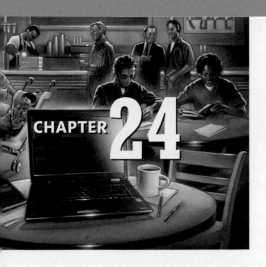

CHAPTER 24

Developing Paragraphs: Definition and Classification

Definition and classification are two more methods you can use to develop ideas. This chapter will give you an overview of both of these methods and suggest topics for writing.

CHAPTER OBJECTIVES

● Steps for using **definition** as a method of paragraph development:

    placing the term in a larger class

    identifying the term's characteristics

    providing examples

    using negation

    using extended definition or analysis

● Steps for using **classification** as a method of paragraph development:

    finding a basis for classifying

    making distinct categories

    checking for completeness

    checking for usefulness

What Is Definition?

> **Definition,** as a method of development, involves exploring the meaning or significance of a term.

The starting point for any good definition is to place the word into a larger **category** or **class.** For example, a *trout* is a kind of fish; a *doll* is a kind of toy; a *shirt* is an article of clothing. Here are the first four meanings of a dictionary entry for the word *family.*

> **family** (fam´e -le, fam´le) *n., pl.* **-lies.** *Abbr.* **fam.** 1. The most instinctive fundamental social or mating group, traditionally consisting of two parents rearing their children. 2. One's spouse and children. 3. A group of persons sharing a common ancestry: relatives, kinfolk, clan. 4. All the members of a household; those who share one's domestic home.

To what larger category does the word *family* belong? According to this dictionary entry, the *family* is the most basic of *social groups.*

Once a word has been put into a larger class, the next step is to provide the **identifying characteristics** that make the word different from other members in that class. What makes a *trout* different from a *bass*, a *doll* different from a *puppet*, a *shirt* different from a *sweater?* Here a definition can give examples. The dictionary definition of *family* identifies the family as, usually, two parents and their children. Three additional meanings provide suggestions for some variations.

When you write a paragraph or an essay that uses definition, the dictionary entry is only the beginning. It is not the function of a dictionary to go into great depth. A dictionary can provide only the basic meanings and synonyms. To help your reader understand a difficult term or idea, you will need to expand this definition into what is called an **extended definition.** With an *extended definition,* you seek to analyze a concept so that the reader will have a more complete understanding of it. For instance, you might include a historical perspective. When or how did the concept begin? How did the term change or evolve over the years, or how do different cultures understand the term? You become involved in the word's *connotations.* An extended definition, or *analysis* as it is sometimes called, draws on more than one method to arrive at an understanding of a term.

> An **extended definition** is an expanded definition, or analysis, of a concept or term, giving additional information that conveys a fuller meaning.

Working with Definition

The following paragraph, taken from *Sociology: An Introduction* by John E. Conklin, is the beginning of a chapter on the family. The author's starting point is very similar to the dictionary entry seen above.

Topic sentence
>   In every society, social norms define a variety of relationships among people, and some of these relationships are socially recognized as family or kinship ties. A *family* is a socially defined set of relationships between at least two people who are related by birth, marriage, or adoption. We can think of a family as including several possible relationships, the most common being between husband and wife, between parents and children, and between people who are related to each other by birth (siblings, for example) or by marriage (a woman and her mother-in-law, perhaps). Family relationships are often defined by custom, such as the relationship between an infant and godparents, or by law, such as the adoption of a child.

The author begins this definition by putting the term into a larger class. *Family* is one type of social relationship among people. The writer then identifies the people who are members of this group. Family relationships can be formed by marriage, birth, adoption, or custom. The author does not stop here. The extended definition explores the functions of the family, conflicts in the family, the structure of the family, and the special characteristics of the family.

The writer could also have defined *family* by **negation.** That is, he could have described what a family is *not:*

A family is not a corporation.

A family is not a formal school.

A family is not a religion.

When a writer defines a concept using negation, the definition should be completed by stating what the subject *is*:

A family is not a corporation, but it is an economic unit of production and consumption.

A family is not a formal school, but it is a major center for learning.

A family is not a religion, but it is where children learn their moral values.

EXERCISE   **Defining by Class**

Define each of the following terms by placing it in a larger class. Keep in mind that when you define something by class, you are placing it in a larger category so that the reader can see where it belongs. Use the dictionary if you need help. An example has been done for you.

Chemistry is <u>one of the branches of science.</u>

1. Mythology is _____

2. Nylon is _____

3. An amoeba is _____

4. A tricycle is _____

5. Cabbage is _____

6. Democracy is _____

7. Asbestos is _____

8. A piccolo is _____

9. Poetry is _____

10. A university is _____

EXERCISE   **Identifying Characteristics**

Using the same terms as in Exercise 1, give one or two identifying characteristics that differentiate your term from other terms in the same class. Use a dictionary. An example is done for you.

Chemistry is <u>the study of the structure, properties, and reactions of matter.</u>

1. Mythology _____

_____

2.   Nylon _____

_____

3.   An amoeba _____

_____

4.   A tricycle _____

_____

5.   Cabbage _____

_____

6.   Democracy _____

_____

7.   Asbestos _____

_____

8.   A piccolo _____

_____

9.   Poetry _____

_____

10. A university _____

_____

EXERCISE 3

Providing Examples

Examples make a concept more concrete. For each of the following terms, provide one good example that would help make a stronger definition. You may
need to consult an encyclopedia. An example has been done for you.

> **Term:**   Chemistry
>
> **Example:** Chemistry teaches us that hydrogen has the simplest structure
> of all the elements, with only one electron and one proton. It
> is colorless, highly flammable, the lightest of all gases, and the
> most abundant element in the universe.

1.   Mythology _____

_____

2.   Friendship _____

_____

3.   Philanthropist _____

_____

4.   Planet _____

_____

5.   Gland _____

_____

6. Greed _____

_____

7. Volcano _____

_____

8. Patriotism _____

_____

9. Terrorism _____

_____

_____

10. Equality _____

_____

EXERCISE 4   Defining by Negation

Define each of the following terms, using negation to construct your definition. Keep in mind that such a definition is not complete until you have also included a positive statement about the topic that you are defining. You may want to work in groups to arrive at your answers.

1. A *disability* does not mean _____

but it may mean _____

2. The *perfect car* need not be _____

but it should be _____

3. *Drugs* are not _____

but they are _____

4. *Freedom* is not _____

but it is _____

5. A *good job* does not have to _____

but it should _____

6. *Exercise* should not _____

but it should _____

7. A *university* is not _____

it is _____

8. A *legislator* should not _____

but he or she should _____

9. The *ideal pet* is not _____

it _____

10. A *boring person* is not _____

but he or she is _____

Transitions Commonly Used for Definition

is defined as
is understood to be
means that
is sometimes thought to be
signifies

WRITING A PARAGRAPH USING DEFINITION

Here is a list of possible topics for paragraphs. For each topic that you choose to write about, develop a complete paragraph of definition by using more than one of the techniques you have studied—*class, identifying characteristics, example,* and *negation*—as well as any further analysis, historical or cultural, that would help the reader.

Ten suggested topics
1. Panic
2. Ecology
3. A symphony
4. Football
5. Paranoia
6. Courage
7. Algebra
8. Democracy
9. Masculinity or femininity
10. Justice

What Is Classification?

Classification places items into separate categories to help people think about these items more clearly. Classification can be extremely useful and even necessary when large numbers of items are being considered.

To classify items properly, we must find *distinct categories* into which these items will fit. Each item must belong to only one category. For example, classifying motorcycles into three categories—imported motorcycles, U.S.-made motorcycles, and used motorcycles—would not be an effective use of classification because an *imported* motorcycle could also be a *used* motorcycle. The categories would therefore not be distinct.

A classification must also be *complete.* For example, if you classified motorcycles into the two categories of *new* and *used,* your classification would be complete because all motorcycles have to be either *new* or *used.* There is no other possibility. Depending on your purpose, other ways to classify motorcycles could be distinct and complete.

Finally, a classification should serve some *useful purpose.* For a person thinking of buying a motorcycle, classifying motorcycles into the categories of *new* or *used* to consider the advantages or disadvantages of each is clearly helpful for a decision on the better purchase.

Working with Classification

The following paragraph, taken from Judith Viorst's essay "Friends, Good Friends—and Such Good Friends," shows the writer classifying different kinds of friends.

Topic sentence

> There are medium friends, and pretty good friends, and very good friends indeed, and these friendships are defined by their level of intimacy. And what we'll reveal at each of these levels of intimacy is calibrated with care. We might tell a medium friend, for example, that yesterday we had a fight with our husband. And we might tell a pretty good friend that this fight with our husband made us so mad that we slept on the couch. And we might tell a very good friend that the reason we got so mad in that fight that we slept on the couch had something to do with that girl who works in his office. But it's only to our very best friends that we're willing to tell all, to tell what's going on with that girl in his office.

In this paragraph, the writer gives us four distinct types of friends, beginning with "medium friends," going on to "pretty good friends" and "very good friends," and ending with "very best friends." Her classification is complete because it covers a full range of friendships, and it is useful because people are naturally interested in the types of friends others have.

EXERCISE 5 **Finding the Basis for a Classification**

For each of the following topics, pick three different ways the topic could be classified. You may find the following example helpful.

Topic:	Vacation spots
Ways to divide the topic:	By price (first class, second class, economy), By special attractions (the beach, the mountains, the desert, and so on), By accommodations (motel, cabin, trailer)

1. Topic: Cars
   Ways to divide the topic: _____

   _____

2. Topic: Houses
   Ways to divide the topic: _____

   _____

3. Topic: Neighborhoods
   Ways to divide the topic: _____

   _____

4. Topic: Religions
   Ways to divide the topic: _____

   _____

5.   Topic: Soft drinks

Ways to divide the topic: _____

_____

6.   Topic: Dating

Ways to divide the topic: _____

_____

7.   Topic: Floor coverings

Ways to divide the topic: _____

_____

8.   Topic: Medicines

Ways to divide the topic: _____

_____

9.   Topic: Snack foods

Ways to divide the topic: _____

_____

10.   Topic: Relatives

Ways to divide the topic: _____

_____

EXERCISE 6   ## Making Distinct Categories

For each of the following topics, choose a basis for classification. Then divide the topic into as many distinct categories as you think the classification requires, and write the categories on the lines provided.

Keep in mind that, when you divide your topic, each item must belong to only one category. For example, if you were to classify cars by type, you would not want to make *sports cars* and *imported cars* two of your categories because several kinds of sports cars are also imported cars.

1.   Clothing stores

Distinct categories:

_____   _____   _____

_____   _____   _____

2.   Television commercials

Distinct categories:

_____   _____   _____

_____   _____   _____

3.   College sports

Distinct categories:

_____   _____   _____

_____   _____   _____

4. Doctors

Distinct categories:

_____   _____   _____

5. Hats

Distinct categories:

_____   _____   _____

_____   _____   _____

6. Courses in the English department of your college

Distinct categories:

_____   _____   _____

_____   _____   _____

7. Pens

Distinct categories:

_____   _____   _____

8. Dances

Distinct categories:

_____   _____   _____

_____   _____   _____

9. Mail

Distinct categories:

_____   _____   _____

_____   _____   _____

10. Music

Distinct categories:

_____   _____   _____

_____   _____   _____

Transitions Commonly Used for Classification

areas	kinds
categories; categorized by	parts
divisions; divided into	sections
fields	types
groups; groupings; grouped into	

WRITING A PARAGRAPH USING CLASSIFICATION

Here is a list of possible topics for paragraphs using classification. As you plan your paragraph, ask yourself the following questions: Does the classification help to organize the material? Are you sure that the classification is complete and that no item could belong to more than one category? Is there some purpose for classifying the items as you did? (For example, will it help someone make a decision or understand a concept?)

Ten suggested topics

1. Movies
2. Governments
3. Dogs
4. Careers
5. Celebrations
6. Summer jobs
7. Parents
8. Classmates
9. Coworkers
10. Restaurants

Exploring Online

Go to academic.cengage.com/devenglish/scarry to find the **Writer's Online Workplace,** a website designed for students using this book. You will find links to handouts, interactive quizzes, and other online resources as you explore the following topics:

- writing definition
- looking at examples of definition paragraphs
- classification techniques

Working Together

Who Is a Hero?

Some words or ideas are hard to define, either because they are complicated or because they are controversial. One such idea is the concept of heroism. The following paragraph, from Nicholas Thompson's essay "Hero Inflation," gives us a useful review of the changing definition of *heroism* in our society today.

> Roughly speaking, American heroes first needed bravery. But bravery is not sufficient because evil people can be brave, too. So, the second trait in American historical lore is nobility. Heroes must work toward goals that we approve of. Heroes must show ingenuity. Lastly, they should be successful. Rosa Parks wouldn't have been nearly as much of a hero if she hadn't sparked a boycott that then sparked a movement. Charles Lindbergh wouldn't have been nearly as heroized if the *Spirit of St. Louis* had crashed into the Atlantic, or if scores of people had made the flight before. Recently, though, a fourth trait—victimhood—seems to have become as important as anything else in determining heroic status. Today heroes don't have to do anything: they just need to be noble victims.

Working in Groups

Working together as a class, discuss the following Americans. Would you consider each one of them a hero? Why or why not?

- Krista McAuliffe, who risked and lost her life as an astronaut
- Hollywood celebrity Angelina Jolie, who adopts children from other lands
- Bill Gates, a wealthy businessman who gives away millions of dollars
- a bone marrow donor
- a firefighter killed in the World Trade Center attacks
- Muhammad Ali, known for his political courage as well as his athletic skills
- a man who jumped into the icy Potomac River in Washington, D.C., in January 1982 to save a stranger from drowning but who himself drowned in the attempt.

Work together to define *heroism* in a single sentence. Then look up the dictionary definition. How close are the two definitions?

Portfolio Suggestion

Using the above list, look up some of the more famous figures in an encyclopedia or on the Internet. Examine these people's lives and then make judgments about them. Are these people true heroes?

PART

5

Structuring the College Essay

In previous parts of this book, you focused on sentence mechanics and the construction of strong, well-developed paragraphs. As you worked on those paragraphs, you were also sharpening many of the same skills you will need to develop full-length college essays. Part 5 will take you through the additional requirements for expanding a single developed paragraph into a multiparagraph essay. This expansion includes careful construction of an inviting introductory paragraph with its important thesis statement, along with the construction of a concluding paragraph that is needed for a logical and satisfying ending. You will continue to practice the different methods for the development of body paragraphs. You will be organizing a greater amount of material than before, and you will be giving even greater attention to the careful use of transitions, so important in longer pieces of writing. Finally, in the last two chapters of Part 5, you will focus on three very challenging skills: writing an essay of persuasion or argument, writing a college research paper, and preparing for an essay examination. These final skills are intended to prepare you for the demands of additional college course work and for the needs of the workplace beyond.

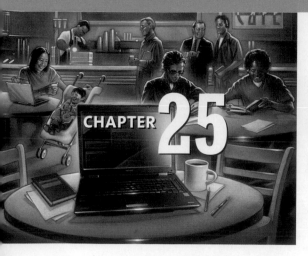

25

Moving from the Paragraph to the Essay

Before you begin writing fully developed college essays, your work in this chapter will focus on the essential parts of the essay form:

CHAPTER OBJECTIVES

- recognizing and writing a thesis statement
- writing an effective introductory paragraph
- using transitions between body paragraphs to achieve coherence
- writing an effective concluding paragraph
- composing titles

What Is a College Essay?

No matter what major a student chooses in college, developing skill as a writer is an important part of that student's growth and progress. Skill in the writing of college essays (also called *compositions*, *themes*, or simply *papers*) is necessary for nearly every college course, not only English Composition.

A paragraph, with its topic sentence and supporting details, must have a unified and coherent organization. The full-length essay must have the same characteristics. Because topics are developed at greater length and depth in essays than in paragraphs, making all the parts work together is a greater challenge.

> A **college essay** is a piece of nonfiction writing in which five or more paragraphs are used to develop a single topic. The essay usually includes an introductory paragraph that states the thesis, three or more supporting paragraphs that develop the topic, and a concluding paragraph.

The essay has three kinds of paragraphs:

1. The **introductory paragraph** is the first paragraph of the essay. Its purpose is to be so inviting that the reader will want to continue reading. In most essays, this introduction contains a **thesis statement.**

2. **Support paragraphs** (sometimes called **body paragraphs**) provide evidence that your thesis is valid. An essay must have at least three well-developed support paragraphs. (You studied these kinds of paragraphs in Part 4.) One paragraph must flow logically into the next. This is accomplished by the careful use of transitional expressions.

3. The **concluding paragraph** is the last paragraph of the essay. Its purpose is to give the reader a sense of having come to a satisfying conclusion. By

this point the reader should have the feeling that everything has been said that needed to be said.

What Is a Thesis Statement?

> A **thesis statement** gives the main idea of an essay.

The thesis statement tells what you are going to explain, defend, or prove about your topic. It is usually placed at the end of the introductory paragraph. A thesis statement is always a complete sentence, and it usually presents a viewpoint about a topic that can be defended or explained in the essay that follows.

Be careful not to confuse a title or a simple fact with a thesis statement. Remember that a **title** is usually a phrase, not a complete sentence. A **fact** is something known for certain—something that can be verified. A fact does not give a personal viewpoint.

Thesis statement:	Most children at five years of age should not be in school more than half the day.
	or
	Kindergarten children would benefit from all-day programs.
Title:	The Disadvantages of All-Day Kindergarten
	or
	The Advantages of All-Day Kindergarten
Fact:	Nearly all kindergartens in the United States offer only a half day of instruction.

PRACTICE Read each of the following statements. If you think the statement is a thesis, mark *TH* on the blank line. If you think the statement is a title, mark *T*. If you think the statement is a fact, mark *F*.

_____ 1. In the United States, kindergarten is not compulsory

_____ 2. Children should begin learning to read in kindergarten

_____ 3. Putting a child into kindergarten before he or she is ready can have several unfortunate effects on that child

_____ 4. Learning to read in kindergarten

_____ 5. In some European countries, children do not begin formal schooling until the age of seven

EXERCISE **Recognizing a Thesis Statement**

Identify each of the following as a *title* (T), a *thesis* (TH), or a *fact* (F).

_____ 1. The personal interview is the most important step in the employment process

_____ 2. Looking for a job

_____ 3. Sixty percent of all jobs are obtained through newspaper advertisements

_____ 4. The best time to begin a foreign language is in grade school

_____ 5. The importance of learning a foreign language

_____ 6. In the 1970s, the number of students studying foreign languages declined dramatically

_____ 7. Most Americans doing business with Japan do not know a word of Japanese

_____ 8. Working and studying at the same time

_____ 9. Many students in community colleges have part-time jobs while they are going to school

_____ 10. Working a part-time job while going to school puts an enormous strain on a person

EXERCISE 2   **Recognizing a Thesis Statement**
Identify each of the following as a *title* (T), a *thesis* (TH), or a *fact* (F).

_____ 1. It is estimated that two hundred grizzly bears live in Yellowstone National Park

_____ 2. The survival of grizzly bears in our country should be a top priority

_____ 3. When bears are young cubs, there are twice as many males as females

_____ 4. Only about 60 percent of bear cubs survive the first few years of life

_____ 5. Bears, a precious natural resource

_____ 6. The average life span of a bear today is only five or six years

_____ 7. The sad plight of the American grizzly bear

_____ 8. Five actions need to be taken to save the grizzly bear from extinction

_____ 9. To save the grizzly bear, we need laws from Congress, the cooperation of hunters and campers, and an educated general public

_____ 10. A decision to save the grizzly bear

EXERCISE 3   **Recognizing a Thesis Statement**
Identify each of the following as a *title* (T), a *thesis* (TH), or a *fact* (F).

_____ 1. Tons of ancient material have been taken out of Russell Cave

_____ 2. The opening of the cave is 107 feet wide and 26 feet high

_____ 3. People lived in this cave more than nine thousand years ago

_____   4.   Russell Cave in Jackson County, Alabama, should be preserved as an important source of information about the ancient people of North America

_____   5.   The way ancient people lived

_____   6.   All kinds of articles, from fish hooks to human skeletons, have been found in Russell Cave

_____   7.   Learning about the diet of an ancient people of North America

_____   8.   An archaeologist's discovery of Russell Cave

_____   9.   Some of the theories previously held about life in North America thousands of years ago must now be changed because of the discoveries made in Russell Cave

_____   10.   Russell Cave is the oldest known home of human beings in the southeastern United States

Writing an Effective Thesis Statement

An effective thesis statement has the following characteristics:

1. **A topic that is not too general.** A general topic must be narrowed in scope either by *limiting the topic* (changing the term to cover a smaller part of the topic) or *qualifying the topic* (adding phrases or words to the general term to narrow the topic).

General topic:	Swimming
Limited topic:	Floating (The term *floating*, which describes a kind of swimming, is more specialized than the term *swimming*.)
Qualified topic:	Swimming for health two hours a week (The addition of the phrase *for health two hours a week* narrows the topic considerably. Now the topic concentrates on the fact that the *time spent* and the *reason for swimming* are important parts of the topic.)

    A writer narrows a topic so that the material will fit the length of an essay (which is only a few paragraphs long) and so that the material will also fit the writer's knowledge and experience.

2. **A controlling idea that you can defend.** The controlling idea is what you want to show or prove about your topic; it is your point of view about that topic. Often the controlling idea is expressed by an adjective such as *beneficial, difficult,* or *unfair.*

    Learning to float at the age of twenty was a *terrifying* experience.

    Swimming two hours a week brought about a *dramatic* change in my health.

3. **An indication of what strategy of development is to be used.** Often the strategy is indicated by words such as the following: *description, steps,*

stages, examples, comparison, contrast, causes, effects, reasons, advantages, disadvantages, definition, analysis, or *argument.* Although not all writers state the strategy in the thesis statement, they must always have in mind what major strategy they plan to use to prove their thesis. Professional writers often use more than one strategy to prove their thesis. However, in this book you are asked to develop your essays by using one major strategy at a time. By working in this way, you can concentrate on understanding and developing the skills needed for each specific strategy.

Study the following thesis statement:

Although studying alone can be very effective, studying in a group can have many advantages.

Now look back and examine the characteristics of this thesis statement.

General topic:	Studying
Qualified topic:	Studying in a group (as opposed to studying alone)
Controlling idea:	To give the advantages of studying in a group
Strategy of development:	Contrast studying alone with studying in a group

EXERCISE **Writing Thesis Statements**

Below are four topics. For each one, develop a thesis statement by (a) limiting or qualifying the general topic, (b) choosing a controlling idea (what you want to explain or prove about the topic), and (c) selecting a strategy that you could use to develop that topic. An example is done for you.

General topic: Senior citizens

a. Limited or qualified topic:

Community services available to the senior citizens in Ann Arbor

b. Controlling idea:

To show the great variety of programs

c. Strategy for development (narration, examples, description, process analysis, cause and effect, definition, comparison/contrast, classification, or persuasion):

Classify the services into major groups

Thesis statement:

The senior citizens of Ann Arbor, Michigan, are fortunate to have three major kinds of programs available to help them deal with health, housing, and leisure time.

1. **General topic:** Miami (or another city with which you are familiar)

a. Limited or qualified topic:

_____

b. Controlling idea:

_____

c. Strategy for development (narration, examples, description, process analysis, cause and effect, definition, comparison/contrast, classification, or persuasion):

_____

Thesis statement:

_____

_____

_____

2. **General topic:** Female vocalist

a. Limited or qualified topic:

_____

b. Controlling idea:

_____

c. Strategy for development (narration, examples, description, process analysis, cause and effect, definition, comparison/contrast, classification, or persuasion):

_____

Thesis statement:

_____

_____

_____

3. **General topic:** Shopping

a. Limited or qualified topic:

_____

b. Controlling idea:

_____

c. Strategy for development (narration, examples, description, process analysis, cause and effect, definition, comparison/contrast, classification, or persuasion):

_____

Thesis statement:

_____

_____

_____

4. **General topic:** The library

a. Limited or qualified topic:

_____

b. Controlling idea:

_____

c. Strategy for development (narration, examples, description, process analysis, cause and effect, definition, comparison/contrast, classification, or persuasion):

_____

Thesis statement:

_____

_____

_____

EXERCISE **5**   **Writing Thesis Statements**

Below are five topics. For each one, develop a thesis statement by (a) limiting or qualifying the general topic, (b) choosing a controlling idea (what you want to explain or prove about the topic), and (c) selecting a strategy that you could use to develop that topic. Review the example in Exercise 4.

1. **General topic:** Television

a. Limited or qualified topic:

_____

b. Controlling idea:

_____

c. Strategy for development (narration, examples, description, process analysis, cause and effect, definition, comparison/contrast, classification, or persuasion):

_____

Thesis statement:

_____

_____

_____

2. **General topic:** Math (or another field of study)

a. Limited or qualified topic:

_____

b. Controlling idea:

_____

c. Strategy for development (narration, examples, description, process analysis, cause and effect, definition, comparison/contrast, classification, or persuasion):

_____

Thesis statement:

_____

_____

_____

3. **General topic:** Games

a. Limited or qualified topic:

_____

b. Controlling idea:

_____

c. Strategy for development (narration, examples, description, process analysis, cause and effect, definition, comparison/contrast, classification, or persuasion):

_____

Thesis statement:

_____

_____

_____

4. **General topic:** Clubs

a. Limited or qualified topic:

_____

b. Controlling idea:

_____

c. Strategy for development (narration, examples, description, process analysis, cause and effect, definition, comparison/contrast, classification, or persuasion):

_____

Thesis statement:

_____

_____

_____

Writing an Effective Introductory Paragraph

> An **introduction** has one main purpose: to grab your readers' interest so that they will keep reading.

There is no single way to write an introduction. However, because many good introductions follow a pattern, you may find it helpful to look at a few examples of patterns. When you are ready to create your own introductions, you can consider trying out some of these patterns.

1. **Begin with a general subject that can be narrowed down into the specific topic of your essay.** Here is an introduction to an essay about a family making cider on their farm:

The number of children who eagerly help around a farm is rather small. Willing helpers do exist, but many more of them are five years old than fifteen. In fact, there seems to be a general law that says as long as a kid is too little to help effectively, he or she is dying to. Then, just as they reach the age when they really could drive a fence post or empty a sap bucket without spilling half of it, they lose interest. Now it's cars they want to drive, or else they want to stay in the house and listen for four straight hours to The Who. There is one exception to this rule. Almost no kid that I have ever met outgrows an interest in cidering.

FROM NOEL PERRIN,
"Falling for Apples"

2. **Begin with specifics (a brief anecdote, a specific example or fact) that will broaden into the more general topic of your essay.** Here is the introduction to an essay on the place of news programs in our lives:

Let me begin with a confession. I am a news addict. Upon awakening I flip on the *Today* show to learn what events transpired during the night. On the commuter train which takes me to work, I scour the *New York Times*, and find myself absorbed in tales of earthquakes, diplomacy and economics. I read the newspaper as religiously as my grandparents read their prayerbooks. The sacramental character of the news extends into the evening. The length of my workday is determined precisely by my need to get home in time for Walter Cronkite. My children understand that my communion with Cronkite is something serious and cannot be interrupted for light and transient causes. What is news, and why does it occupy a place of special significance for so many people?

FROM STANLEY MILGRAM,
"Confessions of a News Addict"

3. **Give a definition of the concept that will be discussed.** Here is the introduction to an essay about the public's common use of two addictive drugs, alcohol and cigarettes:

Our attitude toward the word "drug" depends on whether we are talking about penicillin or heroin or something in-between. The unabridged three-volume Webster's says a drug is "a chemical substance administered to prevent or cure disease or enhance physical and mental welfare" or "a substance affecting the structure or function of the body." Webster's should have added "mind," but they probably thought that was part of the body. Some substances that aren't drugs, like placebos, affect "the structure or function of the body," but they work because we *think* they're drugs.

FROM ADAM SMITH,
"Some American Drugs Familiar to Everybody"

4. **Make a startling statement:**

Man will never conquer space. Such a statement may sound ludicrous, now that our rockets are already 1 million miles beyond the moon and the first human travelers are preparing to leave the atmosphere. Yet it expresses a truth which our forefathers knew, one we have forgotten—and our descendants must learn again, in heart-break and loneliness.

FROM ARTHUR C. CLARKE,
"We'll Never Conquer Space"

5.   **Start with an idea or statement that is a widely held point of view, and then surprise the reader by stating that this idea is false or that you hold a different point of view:**

Tom Wolfe has christened today's young adults as the "me" generation, and the 1970s—obsessed with things like consciousness expansion and self-awareness—have been described as the decade of the new narcissism. The cult of "I," in fact, has taken hold with the strength and impetus of a new religion. But the joker in the pack is that it is all based on a false idea.

FROM MARGARET HALSEY,
"What's Wrong with 'Me, Me, Me'?"

6.   **Start with a familiar quotation or a quotation by a famous person:**

"The very hairs of your head," says Matthew 10:30, "are all numbered." There is little reason to doubt it. Increasingly, everything tends to get numbered one way or another, everything that can be counted, measured, averaged, estimated or quantified. Intelligence is gauged by a quotient, the humidity by a ratio, pollen by its count, and the trends of birth, death, marriage, and divorce by rates. In this epoch of runaway demographics, society is as often described and analyzed with statistics as with words. Politics seems more and more a game played with percentages turned up by pollsters, and economics a learned babble of ciphers and indexes that few people can translate and apparently nobody can control. Modern civilization, in sum, has begun to resemble an interminable arithmetic class in which, as Carl Sandburg put it, "numbers fly like pigeons in and out of your head."

FROM FRANK TRIPPETT,
"Getting Dizzy by the Numbers"

7.   **Give a number of descriptive images that will lead to the thesis of your essay.** Here is the opening of a lengthy essay about the importance of sports in our lives:

I cannot remember when I was not surrounded by sports, when talk of sports was not in the air, when I did not care passionately about sports. As a boy in Chicago in the late Forties, I lived in the same building as the sister and brother-in-law of Barney Ross, the welterweight champion. Half a block away, down near the lake, the Sullivan High School football team worked out in the spring and autumn. Summers the same field was given over to baseball and men's softball on Sundays. A few blocks to the north was the Touhy Avenue Fieldhouse, where basketball was played, and lifeguards trained, and behind which, in a softball field frozen over in winter, crack-the-whip, hockey, and speed skating took over. To the west, a block or so up Morse Avenue, was the Morse Avenue "L" Recreations, a combined pool hall and bowling alley. Life, in short, was games.

FROM JOSEPH EPSTEIN,
"Obsessed with Sport: On the Interpretation of a Fan's Dreams"

8. **Ask a question that you intend to answer.** Many essays in magazines and newspapers use a question in the introductory paragraph to make the reader curious about the author's viewpoint. Some writing instructors prefer that students not use this method. Check with your instructor for his or her viewpoint. Here is an example of such an introduction:

> Suppose there were no critics to tell us how to react to a picture, a play, or a new composition of music. Suppose we wandered innocent as the dawn into an art exhibition of unsigned paintings. By what standards, by what values would we decide whether they were good or bad, talented or untalented, successes or failures? How can we ever know that what we think is right?

> FROM MARYA MANNES,
> "How Do You Know It's Good?"

9. **Use classification to indicate how your topic fits into the larger class to which it belongs or how your topic can be divided into categories that you are going to discuss.** Here is how the American composer Aaron Copland began an essay on listening to music:

> We all listen to music according to our separate capacities. But, for the sake of analysis, the whole listening process may become clearer if we break it up into its component parts, so to speak. In a certain sense we all listen to music on three separate planes. For lack of a better terminology, one might name these: the sensuous plane, the expressive plane, the sheerly musical plane. The only advantage to be gained from mechanically splitting up the listening process into these hypothetical planes is the clearer view to be had of the way in which we listen.

> FROM AARON COPLAND,
> "What to Listen For in Music"

What *Not* to Say in Your Introduction

1. Avoid telling your reader that you are beginning your essay:

   In this essay I will discuss . . .
   I will talk about . . .
   I am going to prove . . .

2. Do not apologize:

   Although I am not an expert . . .
   In my humble opinion . . .

3. Do not refer to later parts of your essay:

   By the end of this essay you will agree . . .
   In the next paragraph you will see . . .

4. Do not use trite expressions. Because these expressions have been overused, they have lost all interest and effectiveness. Using such expressions shows that you have not taken the time to come up with your own words to express your ideas. The following are some examples of trite expressions:

busy as a bee

you can't tell a book by its cover

haste makes waste

EXERCISE **6**   **Composing an Introductory Paragraph**

Compose your own introductory paragraph using one of the nine patterns that you have just studied. You may want to use one of the topics that were provided in Exercises 4 and 5 and for which you have already written a thesis statement. On the line below, write the number from the list of given patterns you have chosen to use. When you have finished, underline your thesis statement.

Pattern number _____

_____

_____

_____

_____

_____

_____

_____

_____

_____

_____

Achieving Coherence by Using Transitions

Successful essays use transitional expressions to help the reader understand the logic of the writer's thinking. Usually they occur when the writer is moving from one point to the next. They can also occur whenever an idea is complicated. The writer may need to summarize the points so far, emphasize a point already made, or repeat an important point. The transition may be a word, a phrase, a sentence, or even a paragraph.

Here are some transitional expressions that might be used to help the reader make the right connections.

1.   To make your points stand out clearly:

the first reason	second, secondly	finally
first of all	another example	most important
in the first place	even more important	all in all
	also, next	in conclusion
	then	to summarize

2.   To provide an example of what has just been said:

for example

for instance

3. To show the consequence of what has just been said:

> therefore
> as a result
> then

4. To make a contrasting point clear:

> on the other hand
> but
> contrary to current thinking
> however

5. To admit a point:

> of course
> granted

6. To resume your argument after admitting a point:

> nevertheless
> even though
> nonetheless
> still

7. To call the reader's attention to your organization:

> Before attempting to answer these questions, let me . . .
> In our discussions so far, we have seen that . . .
> At this point, it is necessary to . . .
> It is beyond the scope of this paper to . . .

A more subtle way to link one idea to another in an essay is to repeat a word or phrase from the preceding sentence. Sometimes a pronoun can take the place of the actual word.

Repeating a word from a preceding sentence:

I have many memories of my childhood in Cuba. These *memories* include the aunts, uncles, grandparents, and friends I had to leave behind.

Using a pronoun to refer to a phrase from a preceding sentence:

Like all immigrants, my family and I have had to build a new life from almost nothing. *It* was often difficult, but I believe the struggle made us strong.

EXERCISE **7**   **Finding Transitional Expressions**

Following are four paragraphs from a selection titled "Politics and the World," written by Kathryn and Ross Petras. Find the words that give this selection its coherence. Circle all the transitional expressions, underline pronouns that refer to antecedents, and box key terms that are repeated.

Some world problems have a way of lingering and festering. They appear, disappear, then reappear again in the daily newspapers of the world. Usually they're based on land: who controls it, who gets to live on it.

In the past the U.S. and the Soviet Union usually took opposing sides in these conflicts. Sometimes there were very real moral reasons for backing one side or another, but many times the reasons were said to be "geopolitical," which really meant if the Soviets were on one side, we decided to join the other—and vice versa.

All this could get pretty cynical. For one thing, almost every obscure corner of the world was declared "geopolitically strategic" at one point or another. For another, the morality could get very dicey. For example, during the 1970s we supported Ethiopia and the Soviets supported Somalia in their dispute over the Ogaden, a dry and remote desert region populated by Somali nomads but controlled by Ethiopia. Naturally, we set up military posts in our ally Ethiopia and the Soviets put in military bases in their ally Somalia, and each superpower talked of its love of and historic ties to its ally. Then local Marxists seized control in Ethiopia—and after a short while the U.S. and the Soviets calmly switched client states. The U.S. moved into the former Soviet bases in Somalia, the Soviets moved into Ethiopia, and both sides started talking about their *real* ties to their new ally.

Of course, once the Cold War was over, no one cared about either nation anymore, and they both degenerated into anarchy, aided by mounds of heavy weapons and automatic rifles helpfully supplied by both sides. Finally we moved in to save Somalia from itself and our legacy of arms sales—and congratulated ourselves on our humanity.

Writing an Effective Concluding Paragraph

A concluding paragraph has one main purpose: to give the reader the sense of having reached a satisfying ending to the topic discussed. Students often feel they have nothing to say at the end. A look at how professional writers frequently end their essays may ease your anxiety about writing an effective conclusion. You have more than one possibility. Here are some of the most frequently used patterns for ending an essay:

1. **Come full circle—that is, return to the material in your introduction.** Finish what you started there. Remind the reader of the thesis. Be

sure to restate the main idea using different wording. Here is the conclusion to the essay "Confessions of a News Addict." (The introductory paragraph appears on page 464.)

> Living in the modern world, I cannot help but be shaped by it, suckered by the influence and impact of our great institutions. The *New York Times*, CBS, and *Newsweek* have made me into a news addict. In daily life I have come to accept the supposition that if the *New York Times* places a story on the front page, it deserves my attention. I feel obligated to know what is going on. But sometimes, in quieter moments, another voice asks: If the news went away, would the world be any worse for it?

2. **Summarize by repeating the main points.** This example is the concluding paragraph to an essay on African art.

> In summary, African art explains the past, describes values and a way of life, helps man relate to supernatural forces, mediates his social relations, expresses emotions, and enhances man's present life as an embellishment denoting pride or status as well as providing entertainment such as with dance and music.

3. **Show the significance of your thesis by making predictions, giving a warning, giving advice, offering a solution, suggesting an alternative, or telling the results.** This example is the concluding paragraph to "Falling for Apples." (The introductory paragraph appears on page 464.)

> This pleasure goes on and on. In an average year we start making cider the second week of September, and we continue until early November. We make all we can drink ourselves, and quite a lot to give away. We have supplied whole church suppers. One year the girls sold about ten gallons to the village store, which made them some pocket money they were prouder of than any they ever earned from baby-sitting. Best of all, there are two months each year when all of us are running the farm together, just like a pioneer family.

4. **End with an anecdote that illustrates your thesis.** This example is the concluding paragraph to the essay "Obsessed with Sport." (The introductory paragraph appears on page 465.)

> When I was a boy I had a neighbor, a man who, after retirement, had a number of strokes. An old man and a young boy, we had in common a love of sports, which, when we met on the street, was our only topic of conversation. He once inspected a new glove of mine, and instructed me to rub it down with neat's-foot-oil, place a ball firmly in the pocket, wrap string tightly around the glove, and leave it like that for the winter. I did, and it worked. After his last stroke but one, he seldom left his house. Afternoons he spent in a chair in his bedroom, a blanket over his lap, listening to Cub games over the radio. It was while listening to a ball game that he quietly died. I cannot imagine a better way.

What *Not* to Say in Your Conclusion

1. Do not introduce a new point.
2. Do not apologize.
3. Do not end up in the air, leaving the reader feeling unsatisfied. This sometimes happens if the very last sentence is not strong enough.

A Note about Titles

Be sure to follow the standard procedure for writing your title.

1.   Capitalize the first and last words and all other words except articles (*the, a, an*), conjunctions, and prepositions.

2.   Do not underline the title or put quotation marks around it.

3.   Think of a short and catchy phrase (three to six words). Often writers wait until they have written a first draft before working on a title. A phrase taken from the essay might be perfect. If you still cannot think of a clever title after you have written a draft, choose some key words from your thesis statement.

4.   Center the title at the top of the page, and remember to leave about an inch of space between the title and the beginning of the first paragraph.

Exploring Online

Go to academic.cengage.com/devenglish/scarry to find the **Writer's Online Workplace,** a website designed for students using this book. You will find links to handouts, interactive quizzes, and other online resources as you explore the following topics:

- parts of the essay
- the thesis statement
- how to write an introduction
- how *not* to write an introduction
- body of the essay
- transitions
- writing a conclusion

Working Together

Planning the Parts of an Essay

The cartoon above uses the technique of a multiple-choice quiz to suggest some possible reasons education in America is in trouble. As a class, discuss each of the four areas of concern raised by the cartoonist. What do you think is the *thesis* for this cartoon?

Break into groups of five or six. Work together to produce a five- or six-paragraph essay using the organization and content suggested by Tom Toles. Include ideas that were presented in the class discussion or in your group. Assign each person in your group to one of the following paragraphs:

Introductory paragraph

Four paragraphs of support:

1. Learning versus sports
2. Reading versus television
3. A new idea versus a new car
4. Studying versus shopping

Concluding paragraph

Before you write, review the basic content for each paragraph so that each group member understands what should be in his or her paragraph.

Portfolio Suggestion

Keep this group essay in your portfolio. How well did the members of your group succeed in helping each other build one unified essay? Many people in their jobs are expected to work with colleagues to produce annual reports, write-ups of experiments, or brochures that advertise their products or services. Seek to improve your ability to work with others in school and on the job.

CHAPTER 26

Following the Progress of a Student Essay

Students will develop an essay of their own as they follow the progress of a student essay written by a woman named Raluca, whose second language is English. Working along with Raluca, students will do the following:

CHAPTER OBJECTIVES

- use the prewriting techniques of brainstorming and freewriting
- find a controlling idea for the thesis
- write an introductory paragraph
- decide on the topic sentences for three or more body paragraphs
- study the student essay for the development of the body paragraphs
- put the draft into essay form, adding the conclusion
- revise the draft using peer evaluation
- proofread the final essay for errors and omissions

Step 1: Approaching the Assignment: Using Prewriting Techniques

THE ASSIGNMENT

Write an essay describing a school you have attended. In many writing courses, topics are often assigned. At other times, a greater degree of flexibility is allowed. For greater benefit in the discussions in this chapter, all students will be working on the same general topic. Even though every student will begin with the same general topic, each essay will obviously have a very different result.

Raluca's topic: The school she attended as a child in Romania

Your topic: _____

Your topic could deal with a grade school, middle school, high school, driving school, summer school, institute, or college. In other words, you are free to select any educational institution that you have attended.

Notice that the instructor has narrowed this general topic on education to a more narrow focus: describing a specific school that the student has attended. In this way, the writing will not be limited to generalities, an attempt that would be doomed to failure. While the instructor has specified the method of development (description), every student will have to choose his or her own controlling idea. Therefore, every student's thesis will be different, depending on the controlling idea chosen. As in every essay, the controlling idea will remind the student to stay on track and produce a unified piece of writing.

BRAINSTORMING: DISCOVERING WHAT YOU KNOW AND THINK ABOUT A TOPIC

You can brainstorm in a number of ways: listing, clustering, mapping, or webbing. Whichever approach you choose, the purpose of the brainstorming stage is to allow your mind to wander freely on the topic.

Raluca Lists All the Items She Can Think of on Her Topic

Here is the list Raluca jotted down (in no particular order) when she thought about her school in Romania in the 1970s:

communism	testing and grading
uniforms	humiliation and shame
red scarves, blue jumpers	map
soap	fear
bring your own lunch	teachers enjoyed power
president's portrait	not much fun
blackboard	dreary room
memorization of poems	

ACTIVITY   **Constructing Your Brainstorming List**

Make a list of words or phrases that come to mind when you think about a specific school you attended. Put the name of your school at the top of your brainstorming list to identify your topic.

School: _____

_____   _____

_____   _____

_____   _____

_____   _____

_____   _____

_____   _____

_____   _____

FREEWRITING

Freewriting is another way to focus on the topic before you consciously organize the material. Raluca sat down and wrote the following piece in one session, not worrying about grammar errors, sentence errors, or organization. A member of the class should read Raluca's freewriting piece out loud.

Raluca's Freewriting

It's hard to explain what life in an communist country was like. Besides the fears, the unfulfilled needs and the constant untrust, life continued to be lived. School in Romania was mandatory and free. We had uniforms, this was a way of making all of us equal, we wore red scarfs, white socks and blue jumpers. The classrooms were very austere, with 15 double-desks, a blackboard and a map on the wall. The framed portrait of our president was present in the middle of the wall, above the blackboard, in every classroom. One teacher was teaching more subjects, and the day was divided in hours, with a 10 minutes break between hours. We didn't have to switch classrooms and we didn't spent a lot of time in school. Every day we had 4 or 5 hours, every hour with another subject. In literature, a lot of emphasis was placed on memorization, poems of the important Romanian authors, and during the vacations, mandatory lecture. We had to bring every day a soap and a towel, to wash our hands before eating. Food was brought from home and eaten in the classroom. The teachers were tough. Communist education is based on humiliation, it was a shame if you didn't give the right answer to a question or if you got bad grades. Sometimes the teachers enjoyed their power. It was like a sort of social stratification, based on how good your grades were. The results of the tests and the grades were communicated in front of the class. The grades were from 1-10. there were no multiple-choice tests; you had to memorize and give the answers, written, on the paper.

Freewriting is never a finished essay. Raluca has recalled several memories from her school days without worrying about mistakes or the order of her details. Since English is her second language, she has several phrases that are not idiomatic. She also has some errors with spelling and punctuation. However, this should not be a concern at this stage in the process. Often during the freewriting session, new ideas will emerge that the writer was not conscious of when beginning to write, ideas that were not in the brainstorming list. The flow of writing itself might move the mind in a new or different direction. Does Raluca have any new ideas that were not in her initial brainstorming list? Are there any details in the brainstorming list that she did not include in the freewriting?

ACTIVITY **Your Freewriting**

Your freewriting may be shorter or longer than Raluca's, but at this point, length is not important. Do not allow fear of making mistakes slow you down.

_____

_____

_____

_____

_____

_____

_____

_____

_____

_____

_____

_____

_____

_____

_____

_____

_____

_____

_____

_____

_____

_____

_____

_____

_____

_____

_____

_____

_____

_____

_____

_____

_____

_____

_____

_____

_____

_____

_____

_____

_____

_____

_____

_____

_____

_____

_____

_____

Step 2: Finding the Controlling Idea

A piece of freewriting differs from a more finished piece of writing. Freewriting may have no title, no introduction, and no carefully planned paragraphs with topic sentences. It might even be repetitious or hard to follow. A carefully constructed essay needs conscious organization both in its form (carefully developed paragraphs) and in its ideas (appropriate details that make sense). It must feel whole, the entire piece having a sense of unity. Therefore, the student should look at the freewriting not as a nearly completed essay but as a preliminary effort to generate some ideas and details for the essay that will eventually emerge. The organized essay might well look totally different from the freewriting. With the material generated in the brainstorming list and the freewriting, a writer must now consciously focus on the thesis and the organization of material.

Raluca Works on Her Controlling Idea for the Thesis Statement

The freewriting Raluca has done gives many details, but no single thesis statement gives unity to her work. Raluca needs to figure out what controlling idea will unify all this information about Romanian education. She needs to express this controlling idea in a thesis statement. Here are some of the thesis statements that Raluca considered as possibilities:

1. Life for a schoolchild in Romania was regimented.
2. The Romanian schoolroom was austere.
3. Life under communism was filled with fear.
4. The experience of schoolchildren in Romania in the 1970s was harsh.
5. Most teachers in Romanian schools during the 1970s discouraged questions or discussion.

Look over Raluca's thesis statements. Which thesis statement is too general and off the topic of the assignment? Which thesis statements seem too narrow and would provide only enough material for one or two paragraphs?

ACTIVITY **Determining the Controlling Idea for Your Thesis Statement**

Thinking about a thesis statement is a much more important step than most student writers realize. The success of an entire essay often depends on taking the time to determine the best controlling idea for that piece of writing. If the thesis statement is not clear in the writer's mind, the work is not likely to develop into a unified piece.

In writing about a school you have attended, here are some possible controlling ideas you might consider for the thesis:

technologically up to date	not well equipped
supportive	unsupportive
lacked discipline	disciplined
academically solid	academically weak
well run	not well run
carefully maintained	run-down
a happy place	an unhappy place

Remember, it is your *controlling idea* that will unify the essay. All the body paragraphs will have to fit under the heading of that controlling idea.

Keeping in mind the material from both of your prewriting activities (your brainstorming list and your freewriting), think of three controlling ideas that could be used for your essay. Form a thesis statement for each of them.

1. Controlling idea: _____

   Thesis statement: _____

2. Controlling idea: _____

   Thesis statement: _____

3. Controlling idea: _____

   Thesis statement: _____

Make a check beside the thesis statement you intend to use.

Step 3: Writing the Introductory Paragraph

Raluca Composes the Introductory Paragraph, Ending with the Thesis Statement

Raluca's freewriting lacks an introductory paragraph that ends with a thesis statement, one that will unify the entire piece of writing. She needs to rewrite the introduction, perhaps starting with the same general remarks she made in her freewriting. These general remarks can lead to the more narrowed focus of her thesis statement.

Below is the introductory paragraph that Raluca used in her final draft. The thesis statement is boldface. Compare this introduction to the first two sentences of Raluca's freewriting. How do they differ? Circle her controlling idea.

> Thirty-five years ago, life in a Communist country such as Romania was filled with fears, unfulfilled needs, and the constant distrust of others who might be spying on their neighbors. To a person born in the West, on this side of the Iron Curtain, it is hard to imagine what schoolchildren faced. Nevertheless, life had to be lived, and children went off to school every day. Remembering my childhood school days does not bring back many happy memories. **The experience of a schoolchild in Romania in the 1970s was harsh.**

ACTIVITY 3   **Composing Your Introductory Paragraph**

Write a possible introductory paragraph for your own essay. You might do as Raluca did by starting with a general idea that will lead to your more specific thesis statement with its controlling idea. Aim for at least four to five sentences, ending with the thesis statement. Underline the thesis statement.

_____

_____

_____

_____

_____

_____

_____

_____

Step 4: Deciding on the Topic Sentences for Three or More Body Paragraphs

Raluca Plans the Main Divisions of Her Essay and Writes a Topic Sentence for Each of These Divisions

When Raluca did her freewriting, she was not thinking about how to divide her material into body paragraphs. Now she must invest her time doing a better job of organizing the material. Thinking about all of the material she has generated, she decides on possible major divisions. Each of these main divisions could become a developed paragraph, each one beginning with a topic sentence. Here is the list she initially considered:

What the classroom looked like

How teachers treated students

How students were dressed

What a day was like

What subjects were studied

The communist approach to education

How students felt about school

Notice how this list differs from her brainstorming list. Here Raluca is working on ideas that will form the sections of her essay. The details she uses will all have to fall within these divisions. She decides on four areas and composes a topic sentence for each one:

1. How the classroom looked: The classroom was *stark*.
2. How the students were treated: Students were expected to be *obedient*.
3. What a class day was like: The school day was very *rigid*.
4. The communist approach to education   Communist education was based on *humiliation*.

Notice that each topic sentence has the topic and a controlling idea (in italics). Now she realizes exactly which details to place in each of these paragraphs. She will use only details that will support the controlling idea of each topic sentence.

ACTIVITY **Composing the Topic Sentences for Your Body Paragraphs**

Think about your material. What are three or four main divisions you could make, each to be developed into a paragraph? Write a topic sentence for each one of these. Circle the controlling idea in each sentence.

1. _____
2. _____
3. _____
4. _____

Step 5: Studying the Student Essay for Paragraph Development

Before you work on developing your body paragraphs, read Raluca's essay and discuss her body paragraphs. What are the strengths and weaknesses of each paragraph? Are there any additional details you would like to have known?

Raluca's Final Draft

Going to School behind the Iron Curtain

Life in a Communist country such as Romania in the 1970s was filled with fears, unfulfilled needs, and the constant distrust of others who might be spying on their neighbors. To a person born in the West, on this side of the Iron Curtain, it is hard to imagine what school-children faced. Nevertheless, life had to be lived, and children went off to school every day. Remembering my childhood school days does not bring back many happy memories. **The experience of a schoolchild in Romania in the 1970s was harsh.**

The classroom was stark. The only furniture in the room were the fifteen double desks for students and the teacher's desk at the front. A blackboard was on the front wall. The room was often quite cold and only on very dark days were the old ceiling lights turned on. When you entered the room, the only object to look at was the framed portrait of the country's president dominating the front wall above the blackboard. His unsmiling face and somber eyes looked down on everything we did. All across the country his face was at the head of every classroom. We were never allowed to forget who controlled our lives.

Students were expected to be obedient. We all wore uniforms: blue jumpers or blue pants, white blouses or shirts, red scarves or ties and white socks. This dress code kept us all looking the same. No one should look different or special in any way. I cannot remember that anyone complained. Each child brought his or her own lunch and soap. We ate our lunch in the classroom. We accepted our situation and did not expect anyone to provide us with any food or supplies. We understood our teachers would not have tolerated any complaints or unwillingness to follow orders.

The school day was very rigid. One teacher taught us all the subjects. The school day was divided into four or five hour-long classes, each one with a different subject. There was a ten-minute break between hours. We did not have to change rooms, and we were finished by early afternoon, sent home with lessons to do. Subjects were taught largely by memorization of facts. The individual teacher had no say in what material to cover. The curriculum was set by the authorities and rigidly adhered to. For instance, in literature classes, most of the emphasis was placed on memorizing poems by important Romanian authors. Children were not encouraged to ask questions, and discussions were most uncommon. When it was test time, we were given blank sheets of paper. There was no such thing as multiple-choice tests. Answers were right or wrong. Grading was from one to ten, with ten being the best.

Communist education was based on humiliation. It was shameful if we did not give the right answer to a question or if we got bad grades. Sometimes we could see that the teachers enjoyed their power. When test results were returned, our grades were shared in front of the entire class. Everyone knew that the only way to get ahead was to do well on the tests. There was no misbehaving. Bad behavior was not tolerated. Corporal punishment was allowed.

My memory of school in Romania is of days of dutiful work. There was little room for the joy of learning or the freedom of expression. If I were to pick a color to describe my school time, it would be gray. Education was memorizing and repeating what we were told—that was all.

ACTIVITY **Developing Your Body Paragraphs**

On the computer or on the lines provided below, develop each of your body paragraphs using just the details that support the controlling idea in the topic sentence you have chosen for each paragraph. Underline your topic sentences.

Body Paragraph 1

_____

_____

_____

_____
_____
_____
_____
_____
_____
_____
_____
_____
_____
_____
_____
_____
_____
_____
_____

Body Paragraph 2

_____
_____
_____
_____
_____
_____
_____
_____
_____
_____
_____
_____
_____
_____
_____
_____

Body Paragraph 3

_____
_____
_____

_____

_____

_____

_____

_____

_____

_____

_____

_____

_____

_____

_____

_____

_____

Step 6: Putting the Draft into Essay Form, Adding a Conclusion

Here is Raluca's conclusion again. Do any key words that were in her introduction recur here? Notice how Raluca has summed up the points of her essay in a creative way. Review Raluca's conclusion as a possible model for your own approach to an ending for your essay.

> My memory of school in Romania is of days of dutiful work. There was little room for the joy of learning or the freedom of expression. If I were to pick a color to describe my school time, it would be gray. Education was memorizing and repeating what we were told—that was all.

ACTIVITY **Putting Your Paragraphs into Essay Form, Adding a Conclusion**

On the computer, follow your instructor's specifications and copy your introduction and body paragraphs. Add a concluding paragraph that will bring the essay to a satisfying end.

Step 7: Revising the Draft Using Peer Evaluation

In the revision process you must think, rethink, and think again about all the parts that should make up the whole. One of the most helpful ways to begin thinking about your revision is to have others read your work and make suggestions. The peer evaluation form that follows will help others analyze your work.

ACTIVITY   **Using a Peer Evaluation Form**

Ask an individual or a group of individuals to use the following form to evaluate your work. With the feedback you receive, you will be ready to revise your draft.

Peer Evaluation Form

1. Introductory paragraph

   a. Is the introduction interesting? Could you make any suggestions for improvement?

   b. Underline the thesis. Circle the controlling idea.

2. Body paragraphs

   a. Has the writer used description as the method of development?

   b. Does each body paragraph have a topic sentence? Draw a wavy line under each topic sentence.

   c. Do the topic sentences all support the controlling idea of the thesis?

   d. Does the material in each body paragraph relate to its topic sentence? Put a check next to any sentence that should be dropped.

3. Details

   a. What is the overall quality of the details? Are they specific enough? Does the writer give names, dates, titles, places, colors, shapes, etc.? In the margin, suggest better details wherever they occur to you.

   b. You might be able to count the number of details in each paragraph. Do you believe there are enough details? Indicate in the margin where you believe additional details would improve the essay.

4. Coherence

   a. Does the essay follow a logical progression? If not, draw an arrow where you begin to feel confused.

   b. Has the writer used transitional words or phrases at any point to move from one idea to another? If so, put a box around these expressions. Can you suggest a spot where a transitional word or phrase would be an improvement?

   c. Has the writer used synonyms or pronouns to replace key words? If so, put a box around these words. If the writer repeats certain words too often, can you suggest in the margin any other synonyms, substitutions, or pronouns that would be an improvement?

5. What detail or idea did you like best about this essay?

Step 8: Proofreading the Final Essay for Errors and Omissions

Below are four sentences taken from Raluca's freewriting. Can you find any errors that need to be corrected?

1.   It's hard to explain what life in an communist country was like.

2.   Besides the fears, the unfulfilled needs and the constant untrust, life continued to be lived.

3.   We didn't spent a lot of time in school.

4.   Communist education is based on humiliation, it was a shame if you didn't give the right answer to a question or if you got bad grades.

ACTIVITY **8**   **Proofread Your Essay**

After your revisions are complete, you will need to proofread your essay. Look up in your dictionary any word that you suspect might have been misspelled. Run the spell-check program on your computer. Read each sentence aloud to check for omitted words, typos, or other corrections that might have to be made. Sometimes hearing a sentence read out loud helps to show where a better word choice or a punctuation mark is needed.

Exploring Online

Go to academic.cengage.com/devenglish/scarry to find the **Writer's Online Workplace,** a website designed for students using this book. You will find links to handouts, interactive quizzes, and other online resources as you explore the following topic:

- sample student essays

Working Together

Peer Editing: The Revision Stage

Below are four paragraphs taken from a student essay titled "How Students Are Managing the High Costs of a College Education."

PARAGRAPH 1

¹Going to college is now a big investment for many students and their families. ²Total costs average thirty-two thousand dollars at private schools and roughly half that amount at state universities. ³To make matters worse, the interest rates on educational loans have increased another 1.5 percentage points.

PARAGRAPH 2

¹In fact, 74 percent of full-time students now must combine school with work. ²This is much higher than in the past. ³And nearly half of those students work more than twenty-five hours a week. ⁴It is hard to believe. ⁵Of those who work more than twenty-five hours a week, 20 percent work full time and go to school full time. ⁶Students who work twenty-five hours or more a week are more likely to earn lower grades and often have to drop out of courses.

PARAGRAPH 3

¹Perhaps the best jobs are the ones that are right on campus. ²Work-study programs are popular at most schools, and some jobs such as designing websites or maintaining websites can be well paid. ³If a school offers a co-operative education program, it is usually a good thing. ⁴Real-world work experience can give a student the experience they need to qualify for good paying jobs as soon as they graduate and they are also building up their résumés for future job hunting. Some professional services charge a lot of money to help students polish their résumés.

PARAGRAPH 4

¹There are some ways to afford an education even when your family cannot help you. ²There are some young people who go to work for companies like UPS, who help their workers go to college by providing two thousand to three thousand dollars for their school costs. ³There are others who join the military so they can receive a free education. ⁴Some people feel that a soldier's free education comes with another sort of high price. ⁵More students are going to community colleges and living at home, cutting down on costs. ⁶And you can always work during the summer saving money for the next semester's courses.

Each of the paragraphs has at least one major need for revision. The introductory paragraph is lacking a thesis statement. Another paragraph needs a topic sentence. More than one paragraph contains repetition that needs revising. A fourth problem is unity. Look for any sentence that does not belong. Finally, see if you can catch several problems with pronouns and look for a run-on sentence that needs punctuation. Each group should decide on what revision is needed for each paragraph and be prepared to present the revision to the class.

Portfolio Suggestion

Remember that when you are preparing a manuscript on a computer, you must frequently save your file, giving each draft a different name. Keep your earlier drafts until you have made a last review of your final draft and you are certain you will have no further need to consult your old drafts again. Be sure to keep a disc as well as hard copy of papers submitted to your instructors. These safety measures help avoid lost or misplaced submissions.

CHAPTER 27

Writing an Essay Using Examples, Illustrations, or Anecdotes

This chapter will take you through the process of writing an essay using examples:

CHAPTER OBJECTIVES

● Explore the topic: Living with a Disability.

● Read and analyze a model essay: "Darkness at Noon," by Harold Krents.

● Follow the writing process to develop your own essay using examples.

Exploring the Topic: Living with a Disability

Many of us have to live with some disadvantage in our lives, thus the notion that most people have a disability of some kind. Society's view of people with disabilities has changed a great deal over the years. In the past, disabled people tended to avoid being in public and often did not try to join the rest of society in seeking an education or job advancement. Today, the situation is very different, as laws have been passed to protect the rights of people who have limitations. Being disabled should no longer mean being disadvantaged in our society.

1. What in your judgment are the most serious disabilites? What disabilities are less obvious than others?

   _____

   _____

   _____

   _____

2. Despite the more open and supportive atmosphere in our society today, many people do not know how to interact with disabled people. What are some of the misconceptions people have about those with disabilities? What mistakes do people often make when they encounter a disabled person?

   _____

   _____

   _____

   _____

3. Recently, an American man who had lost the use of both legs reached the top of Japan's Mount Fuji by riding a bicycle with a central hand

crank. What are some other remarkable accomplishments of people with serious disabilities?

_____

_____

_____

_____

4. What are some special considerations provided in schools and at work to help people with disabilities? In your opinion, what more could be done?

_____

_____

_____

_____

Reading a Model Essay with Examples, Illustrations, or Anecdotes

Darkness at Noon

Harold Krents

In the following essay, which appeared in the *New York Times,* the lawyer Harold Krents gives us a frank picture of his daily life as a sightless person, trying to retain his dignity in a world that is not always supportive.

1   Blind from birth, I have never had the opportunity to see myself and have been completely dependent on the image I create in the eye of the observer. To date, it has not been narcissistic.°

°**narcissistic**
characterized by excessive admiration of oneself

2   There are those who assume that since I can't see, I obviously cannot hear. Very often people will converse with me at the top of their lungs, enunciating° each word very carefully. Conversely,° people will also often whisper, assuming that since my eyes don't work, my ears don't either.

°**enunciating**
clearly pronouncing

°**conversely**
in the opposite or reverse way

3   For example, when I go to the airport and ask the ticket agent for assistance to the plane, he or she will invariably pick up the phone, call a ground hostess and whisper: "Hi, Jane, we've got a 76 here." I have concluded that the word "blind" is not used for one of two reasons: Either they fear that if the dread word is spoken, the ticket agent's retina will immediately detach, or they are reluctant to inform me of my condition of which I may not have been previously aware.

4   On the other hand, others know that of course I can hear, but believe that I can't talk. Often, therefore, when my wife and I go out to dinner, a waiter or waitress will ask Kit if *"he* would like a drink" to which I respond that "indeed *he* would."

°**graphically**
in sharp and vivid detail

5   This point was graphically° driven home to me while we were in England. I had been given a year's leave of absence from my Washington law firm to study for a diploma-in-law degree at Oxford University. During the year I became ill and was hospitalized. Immediately after admission, I was wheeled down to the X-ray room. Just at the door sat an elderly woman—elderly I would judge from the sound of her voice. "What is his name?" the woman asked the orderly who had been wheeling me.

6   "What's your name?" the orderly repeated to me.

7   "Harold Krents," I replied.

8   "Harold Krents," he repeated.

9   "When was he born?"

10   "When were you born?"

11   "November 5, 1944," I responded.

°**intoned**
said in a monotone

12   "November 5, 1944," the orderly intoned.°

13   This procedure continued for approximately five minutes, at which point even my saint-like disposition deserted me. "Look," I finally blurted out, "this is absolutely ridiculous. Okay, granted I can't see, but it's got to have become pretty clear to both of you that I don't need an interpreter."

14   "He says he doesn't need an interpreter," the orderly reported to the woman.

°**cum laude**
"with honors," a distinction
bestowed at graduation from a
college or university

15   The toughest misconception of all is the view that because I can't see, I can't work. I was turned down by over forty law firms because of my blindness, even though my qualifications included a cum laude° degree from Harvard College and a good ranking in my Harvard Law School class.

16   The attempt to find employment, the continuous frustration of being told that it was impossible for a blind person to practice law, the rejection letters, not based on my lack of ability but rather on my disability, will always remain one of the most disillusioning experiences of my life.

17   I therefore look forward to the day, with the expectation that it is certain to come, when employers will view their handicapped workers as a little child did me years ago when my family still lived in Scarsdale.

18   I was playing basketball with my father in our backyard according to procedures we had developed. My father would stand beneath the hoop, shout, and I would shoot over his head at the basket attached to our garage. Our next-door neighbor, aged five, wandered over into our yard with a playmate. "He's blind," our neighbor whispered to her friend in a voice that could be heard distinctly by Dad and me. Dad shot and missed; I did the same. Dad hit the rim; I missed entirely; Dad shot and missed the garage entirely. "Which one is blind?" whispered back the little friend.

19   I would hope that in the near future when a plant manager is touring the factory with the foreman and comes upon a handicapped and nonhandicapped person working together, his comment after watching them work will be, "Which one is disabled?"

Analyzing the Writer's Strategies

1.   In the opening paragraph, the writer establishes the situation that his blindness has placed him in: to form an image of himself, he must depend on others who can see him. Explain what the writer means when he tells us that, up until now, this image "has not been narcissistic."

2. What are the three misconceptions people have about the writer when they realize he is blind? Identify the paragraph that introduces each misconception. Mark these three paragraphs in the essay.

3. Each misconception the writer reports is followed by an anecdote in which quotation or dialogue is used. Study the three anecdotes the writer gives. In each case, why is the use of a quotation or a piece of dialogue an effective device for the essay?

4. Despite the essentially serious nature of the subject, Harold Krents is able to maintain his sense of humor. Where in the essay do you see him demonstrating this sense of humor?

Writing an Essay Using Examples, Illustrations, or Anecdotes

Of the many ways writers choose to support their ideas, none is more useful or appreciated than the example. All of us have ideas in our minds, but these ideas will not become real for our readers until we use examples to make our concepts clear, concrete, and convincing. Writers who use good examples will be able to hold the attention of their readers.

> **Illustration** or **example** is a method of developing ideas by providing one or more instances of the idea, making the abstract idea more concrete, clarifying the idea, or making the idea more convincing.

The following terms are closely related:

Example: a specific instance of something being discussed

Extended example: an example that is developed at some length, often taking up one or more complete paragraphs

Illustration: an example used to clarify or explain

Anecdote: a brief story used to illustrate a point

CHOOSING A TOPIC AND CONTROLLING IDEA FOR THE THESIS STATEMENT

Here is a list of possible topics that could lead to an essay in which *example* is used as the main method of development. The rest of this chapter will help you work through the various stages of the writing process.

1. Doctors I have encountered
2. The five greatest inventions of all time
3. Crises children face
4. What makes a class exciting
5. Features to look for when buying a . . .
6. The world's worst habits
7. The lifestyles of college students today
8. Superstitions
9. Poor role models
10. The five best recording artists today

Using this list or ideas of your own, jot down two or three topics that appeal to you.

_____

_____

_____

From these topics, select the one you think will give you the best opportunity for writing. About which one do you feel strongest? Which one are you the most expert about? Which one is most likely to interest your readers? Which one is best suited to being developed into a college essay containing examples?

Selected Topic: _____

Your next step is to decide what your controlling idea will be. What is the point you want to make about the topic you have chosen? For instance, if you chose to write about "Doctors I Have Encountered," your controlling idea might be "compassionate" or it might be "egotistical."

Controlling idea: _____

Now put your topic and controlling idea together into your thesis statement.

Thesis statement: _____

_____

GATHERING INFORMATION USING BRAINSTORMING TECHNIQUES

Take at least fifteen minutes to jot down every example you can think of that you could use in your essay. If your topic is not of a personal nature, you might form a group to help each other think of examples, anecdotes, and illustrations. Later, you may want to refer to material from magazines or newspapers if you feel your examples need to be improved. If you do use outside sources, be sure to take notes, checking the correct spelling of names and the accuracy of dates and facts.

_____

_____

_____

_____

_____

_____

_____

_____

_____

_____

SELECTING AND ORGANIZING THE MATERIAL

Review your list of examples, crossing out any ideas that are not useful. Do you have enough material to develop three body paragraphs? This might mean using three extended examples, some anecdotes, or several smaller examples that could be organized into three different groups. Decide on the order in which you want to present your examples. Do you have any ideas for how you might want to write the introduction? On the lines that follow, show your plan for organizing your essay. You may want to make an outline that shows major points and supporting details under each major point.

_____

_____

_____

_____

_____

_____

_____

_____

_____

_____

_____

_____

_____

_____

_____

WRITING THE ROUGH DRAFT

Now you are ready to write your rough draft. Approach the writing with the attitude that you are going to write down all your thoughts on the subject without worrying about mistakes of any kind. It is important that your mind be relaxed enough to allow your thoughts to flow freely. You do not need to follow your plan exactly. Just get your thoughts on paper. You are free to add ideas, drop others, or rearrange the order of your details at any point. Sometimes a period of freewriting leads to new ideas that are better than the ones you had in your brainstorming session. Once a writer has something on paper, he or she usually feels a great sense of relief, even though it is obvious revisions lie ahead.

Keep in mind that, in a paragraph with several examples, you will achieve coherence when the order of these examples follows some logical progression. You could start with the less serious and then move to the more serious, or you might start with the simpler one and move to the more complicated. If your examples consist of events, you might begin with examples from the more distant past and move forward to examples from the present day. Whatever logical progression you choose, you will find it helpful to signal your examples by using some of the transitional expressions that follow.

Transitions Commonly Used in Examples

an example of this is	for example	a typical case	the following illustration
to illustrate this	for instance	such as	To illustrate my point, let me tell you a story.
as an illustration	specifically	one such case	Let me prove my point with a story.

REVISING THE ROUGH DRAFT

You may revise your rough draft alone, with a group, with a peer tutor, or directly with your instructor. Here are some of the basic questions you should consider at this most important stage of your work.

Guidelines for Revision

1. Does the rough draft satisfy the conditions for the essay form? Is there an introductory paragraph? Are there at least three well-developed paragraphs in the body of the essay? Does each of these paragraphs have at least one example? Is there a concluding paragraph? Remember that one sentence is not usually considered an acceptable paragraph. (Many journalistic pieces do not follow this general rule because they often have a space limitation and are not expected to develop every idea.)

2. Have you used *example* as your major method of development? Could you make your examples even better by being more specific or by looking up statistics or facts that would lend more authority to your point of view? Could you quote an expert on the subject?

3. What is the basis for the ordering of your examples? Whenever appropriate, did you use transitions to signal the beginning of an example?

4. Is any important part missing? Are there any parts that seem irrelevant or out of place?

5. Are there words or expressions that could have been better chosen? Is there any place where you have been repetitious?

6. Find at least two verbs (usually some form of the verb *to be*) that could be replaced with more descriptive verbs. Add at least two adjectives that will provide better sensory images for the reader.

7. Find at least one place in the draft where you can add a sentence or two that will make an example better.

8. Can you think of a more effective way to begin or end?

9. Show your draft to two other readers and ask each one to give you at least one suggestion for improvement.

PREPARING THE FINAL COPY, PRINTING, AND PROOFREADING

The typing of the final version should follow the traditional rules for an acceptable submission.

Checklist for the Final Copy

Use only 8½-by-11–inch paper (never paper torn out of a spiral-bound notebook).

Type on only one side of the paper.

Double-space.

Leave approximately a 1½-inch margin on each side of the paper.

Put your name, the date, the title of your paper, and any other relevant information either on a separate title page or at the top of the first page. (Ask your instructor for specific advice on what information to include.)

Center the title. Do not put quotation marks around the title and do not underline it.

Do not hyphenate a word at the end of a line unless you are willing to consult a dictionary to check on the acceptable division of the word into syllables.

Indent each paragraph five spaces.

If your paper is more than one page, number the pages and staple the pages together so they will not get lost.

Do not forget to make a copy before you submit the paper.

NOTE: In most cases, college instructors will not accept handwritten work. However, if you are submitting handwritten work, you must be sure to write on every other line and have legible handwriting. Begin today to learn to type on a computer. You will be at a disadvantage if you cannot use the current technology.

Once you have typed your final version and printed it out, an important step still remains. This step can often mean the difference of an entire letter grade. You must *proofread* your paper. Even if you have used a spell-check feature available on your word-processing program, errors could remain in your paper. The spell-check feature finds only groupings of letters that are not words. For example, if you typed the word *form* when you meant to type *from*, the spell-checker would not catch this error. The secret of good proofreading is to look at each word and sentence construction by itself without thinking about the paper's content.

Checklist for Proofreading

Study each sentence: One way to proofread is to read backwards, starting with the last sentence and examining every sentence, one at a time. First, check that the sentence is really complete and not a fragment or a run-on. Then check the punctuation. Go on to the next sentence and do the same. In this way, you will develop a critical eye for spotting any problems with sentence-level errors.

Study each word: Read the paper again, this time studying each word in every sentence. Look at the letters of the word. Have you transposed any letters, or have you left off an ending such as *-ed* or *-s*? If there are any words you are not sure how to spell, do not forget to check the correct spelling. Are there any words you have omitted?

Exploring Online

Go to academic.cengage.com/devenglish/scarry to find the **Writer's Online Workplace,** a website designed for students using this book. You will find links to handouts, interactive quizzes, and other online resources as you explore the following topics:

- organizing the illustration essay
- things to watch for when writing the illustration essay

Brainstorming for Examples: Job Advancement

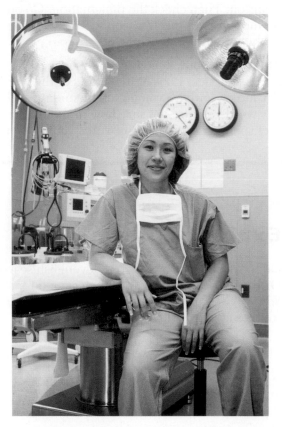

Many people think that, to keep a good job, they need to demonstrate that they are especially clever or smart, they are in with the boss, or they are special in some other way. However, when employers have been surveyed, their responses show that the first item on their list of priorities is a surprisingly simple one: they just want their workers to show up!

Assume that a worker is dependable and does show up every day. How does that worker obtain good performance evaluations that will lead to a more permanent position, earn a salary increase, or eventually lead to a job promotion?

Working in Groups

Sometimes, without being aware of it, people act in ways at work that harm their chance for job advancement. Bad evaluations can even result in a person being fired. Develop a list of examples of actions or attitudes that keep workers from moving ahead in their careers. Then come together as a class and make a composite list of examples on the board. Do any class members recall an actual incident they observed that would illustrate one of the examples?

Portfolio Suggestion

Keep your list of examples in your portfolio for a possible essay on the topic of job advancement. Following are a few other work-related topics that you might want to consider for longer research papers:

> globalization
>
> the declining influence of labor unions
>
> workers' loss of medical benefits and pension plans
>
> the Wal-Mart controversy
>
> whistleblowers (John Dean, Erin Brockovich, Mary McCarthy)

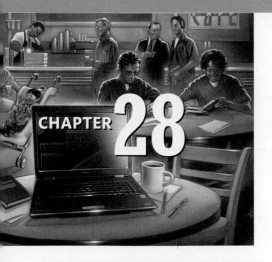

CHAPTER 28

Writing an Essay Using Narration

This chapter will take you through the process of writing an essay using narration:

CHAPTER OBJECTIVES

- Explore the topic: A Lasting Childhood Memory.
- Read and analyze a model essay: "Salvation," by Langston Hughes.
- Follow the writing process to develop your own essay using narration.

Exploring the Topic: A Lasting Childhood Memory

For most of us, childhood holds a mixture of happy and painful memories. Some memories are so lasting that they become part of our permanent consciousness. The recollection that the writer Langston Hughes preserves in the following selection is one of these lasting memories, in which a child finds his perceptions to be in conflict with those of the adults around him. The essay you will write in this chapter will be a narrative based on a childhood experience that made a lasting impression on you. As you answer the following questions, think about what childhood experience you might want to recall.

1. What roles should adults play at the different stages in a child's life?

_____

_____

_____

2. What are some of the adult demands that children typically resist?

_____

_____

_____

_____

3. What are some of the experiences common to most childhoods?

_____

_____

_____

4. What are some examples of painful experiences that often occur in childhood?

_____

_____

_____

_____

Reading a Model Essay with Narrative Elements

Salvation

Langston Hughes

Langston Hughes (1902–1967) was one of the most important writers of the twentieth century, bringing to his poetry, fiction, and essays profound commentary on the black experience in America. He was a leader of the Harlem Renaissance, a period during the 1920s when African American arts flourished in New York. Although Langston Hughes is perhaps best known for his poetry, the following selection, from his 1940 autobiography *The Big Sea,* has become famous. In it, he looks back on a central event of his youth, an event he realizes changed his vision of himself and his world.

1   I was saved from sin when I was going on thirteen. But not really saved. It happened like this. There was a big revival° at my Auntie Reed's church. Every night for weeks there had been much preaching, singing, praying, and shouting, and some very hardened sinners had been brought to Christ, and the membership of the church had grown by leaps and bounds. Then just before the revival ended, they held a special meeting for children, "to bring the young lambs to the fold." My aunt spoke of it for days ahead. That night I was escorted to the front row and placed on the mourners' bench° with all the other young sinners, who had not yet been brought to Jesus.

2   My aunt told me that when you were saved you saw a light, and something happened to you inside! And Jesus came into your life! And God was with you from then on! She said you could see and hear and feel Jesus in your soul. I believed her. I had heard a great many old people say the same thing and it seemed to me they ought to know. So I sat there calmly in the hot, crowded church, waiting for Jesus to come to me.

3   The preacher preached a wonderful rhythmical sermon, all moans and shouts and lonely cries and dire° pictures of hell, and then he sang a song about the ninety and nine safe in the fold,° but one little lamb was left out in the cold. Then he said: "Won't you come? Won't you come to Jesus? Young lambs, won't you come?" And he held out his arms to all us young sinners there on the mourners' bench. And the little girls cried. And some of them jumped up and went to Jesus right away. But most of us just sat there.

°**revival**
meeting for the purpose of bringing people into the faith

°**mourners' bench**
first pew in a church, where those who have not been saved await conversion

°**dire**
terrible

°**fold**
fenced enclosure for animals

°**work-gnarled**
misshapen from hard work

4   A great many old people came and knelt around us and prayed, old women· with jet-black faces and braided hair, old men with work-gnarled° hands. And the church sang a song about the lower lights are burning, some poor sinners to be saved. And the whole building rocked with prayer and song.

5   Still I kept waiting to *see* Jesus.

°**rounder**
someone who makes rounds, such as a security guard or a policeman

°**deacons**
members of the church chosen to help the minister

6   Finally all the young people had gone to the altar and were saved, but one boy and me. He was a rounder's° son named Westley. Westley and I were surrounded by sisters and deacons° praying. It was very hot in the church, and getting late now. Finally Westley said to me in a whisper: "God damn! I'm tired o' sitting here. Let's get up and be saved." So he got up and was saved.

7   Then I was left all alone on the mourners' bench. My aunt came and knelt at my knees and cried, while prayers and songs swirled all around me in the little church. The whole congregation prayed for me alone, in a mighty wail of moans and voices. And I kept waiting serenely° for Jesus, waiting, waiting—but he didn't come. I wanted to see him, but nothing happened to me. Nothing! I wanted something to happen to me but nothing happened.

°**serenely**
calmly

8   I heard the songs and the minister saying: "Why don't you come? My dear child, why don't you come to Jesus? Jesus is waiting for you. He wants you. Why don't you come? Sister Reed, what is this child's name?"

9   "Langston," my aunt sobbed.

10   "Langston, why don't you come? Why don't you come and be saved? Oh, Lamb of God! Why don't you come?"

°**knickerbockered**
dressed in short pants gathered below the knees

11   Now it was really getting late. I began to be ashamed of myself, holding everything up so long. I began to wonder what God thought about Westley, who certainly hadn't seen Jesus either, but who was now sitting proudly on the platform, swinging his knickerbockered° legs and grinning down at me, surrounded by deacons and old women on their knees praying. God had not struck Westley dead for taking his name in vain or for lying in the temple. So I decided that maybe to save further trouble, I'd better lie, too, and say that Jesus had come, and get up and be saved.

12   So I got up.

13   Suddenly the whole room broke into a sea of shouting, as they saw me rise. Waves of rejoicing swept the place. Women leaped in the air. My aunt threw her arms around me. The minister took me by the hand and led me to the platform.

14   When things quieted down, in a hushed silence, punctuated by a few ecstatic "Amens," all the new young lambs were blessed in the name of God. Then joyous singing filled the room.

15   That night, for the last time in my life but one—for I was a big boy of twelve years old—I cried. I cried, in bed alone, and couldn't stop. I buried my head under the quilts, but my aunt heard me. She woke up and told my uncle I was crying because the Holy Ghost had come into my life, and because I had seen Jesus. But I was really crying because I couldn't bear to tell her that I had lied, that I had deceived everybody in the church, that I hadn't seen Jesus, and that now I didn't believe there was a Jesus any more, since he didn't come to help me.

Analyzing the Writer's Strategies

1. A narration is a story, usually set in a particular time, place, and culture. Many of the references in "Salvation" are to specific religious terms that may not be familiar to every reader of the piece. Go through the essay and make a list of those words or expressions that refer to religious concepts or ideas. Learn their meanings through discussion with your classmates.

2. A narration achieves coherence when the details are placed in order of time sequence. Review the essay and underline the transitional words and expressions that indicate time, starting with "every night for weeks" in paragraph 1.

3. What do you believe is Hughes's purpose in telling this story? (See Chapter 2 for a review of the three purposes for writing.)

4. Mark five sentences in the story that provide descriptive details that capture the sights or sounds of a particular moment.

5. Throughout the piece, three people are quoted directly, but we never hear the narrator speaking directly to anyone. What effect does hearing others but never hearing the storyteller himself speak have on us as we read the story?

6. Irony is the gap between what might be expected and what actually takes place. Why is the ending of this story ironic?

Writing an Essay Using Narration

> **Narration** is the oldest and best-known form of verbal communication. It is, quite simply, the telling of a story.

CHOOSING A STORY AND THE POINT YOU WISH TO MAKE WITH THAT STORY

Here is a list of possible topics that could lead to an essay in which *narration* is the main method of development.

1. The experience (positive or negative) of moving to a new neighborhood

2. Surviving a separation or divorce

3. A lesson learned from the mistake (or success) of an older brother or sister (or other relative)

4. A spiritual experience

5. When I stood alone against others

6. An experience that made me feel alone

7. An experience that made me more confident in myself

8. The story of someone whose change in values or beliefs led that person to reject a culture or group, or the story of someone whose commitment to a value or belief led that person to remain faithful to a culture or group

9. A memorable classroom experience

10. An accident that affected my childhood

Using the above list of suggested topics to start you thinking, jot down two or three powerful memories you have from your own childhood. These are possible topics for your writing.

_____

_____

_____

From these topics, select the one you think will give you the best opportunity for writing an interesting story. Which one do you feel strongest about? Which one is most likely to interest your readers? Which topic is most suitable for a college essay?

Selected topic: _____

Good narration has a point. Think about your story. What point could you make by telling this story? In a story, a writer does not always come right out and state the point, but the reader should understand the point by the time he or she reaches the end.

Point of your story: _____

_____

_____

_____

The introductory paragraph for a story usually sets the scene. What time (time of year, time of day), place, and mood would you like to set in your introductory paragraph?

Time: _____

Place: _____

Mood: _____

GATHERING INFORMATION USING BRAINSTORMING TECHNIQUES

Take at least fifteen minutes to jot down the sequence of events for your story as you remember it. Try to remember the way things looked at the time, how people reacted (what they did, what they said), and what you thought as the events were happening. If you can go to the actual spot where the events took place, you might go there and take notes on the details of the place. Later on, you can sort through the material and pick out what you want to use.

SELECTING AND ORGANIZING THE MATERIAL

Review your brainstorming list, crossing out any details that are not appropriate. Prepare to build on the ideas that you like. Put these remaining ideas into an order that will serve as your temporary guide, such as an outline.

WRITING THE ROUGH DRAFT

Find a quiet place where you will not be interrupted for at least one hour. With the plan for your essay in front of you, sit down and write the story that is in your mind. Do not try to judge what you are putting down as right or wrong. What is important is that you let your mind relax and allow the words to flow freely. Do not worry if you find yourself not following your plan exactly. Keep in mind that you are free to add parts, drop sections of the story, or rearrange details at any point. Sometimes, if you just allow your thoughts to take you wherever they lead, new ideas will result. You may like these inspirations better than your original plan. Writing a rough draft is a little like setting out on an expedition; there are limitless possibilities, so it is important to be flexible. Keep in mind that in a narrative essay you will achieve coherence when the details are ordered according to a time sequence. One way to make the time sequence clear is to use transitional words that signal a time change. Here are some examples of carefully chosen transitional words that will help the reader move smoothly from one part of a story to the next.

Transitions Commonly Used in Narration

in December of 2007 . . .	suddenly	after a little while	several weeks passed
the following month	now; by now	then	later; later on
soon afterward	immediately	meanwhile	at the same time
at once	in the next month	next; the next day	finally

REVISING THE ROUGH DRAFT

You may revise your rough draft alone, with a group, with a peer tutor, or directly with your instructor. If you are working on a computer, making changes is so easy that you will feel encouraged to explore alternatives. Unlike making changes using traditional pen and paper, inserting or deleting material is a simple matter on a computer. Here are some of the basic questions you should consider when the time comes to revise your narration.

Guidelines for Revision

1. Does the rough draft satisfy the conditions for the essay form? Is there an introductory paragraph? Are there at least three well-developed paragraphs in the body of the essay? Is there a concluding paragraph? Remember that a single sentence is not a developed paragraph. One exception to this rule is when you use dialogue. When you write a story, you often include conversation between people. In this case, you start a new paragraph each time a different person speaks. This often means that one sentence is a separate paragraph.

2. Is your essay a narration? Does it tell the story of one particular incident that takes place at a specific time and location? Sometimes writers make the mistake of talking about incidents in a general way and commenting on the meaning of the incidents. Be careful. This would not be considered a narration. You must be a storyteller. Where does the action take place? Can the reader see it? What time of day, week, or year is it? What is the main character in the story doing?

3. Have you put the events of the story in a time order? Find the expressions you have used to show the time sequence.

4. Can you think of any part of the story that is missing and should be added? Is there any material that is irrelevant and should be omitted?

5. Are there sentences or paragraphs that seem to be repetitious?

6. Find several places where you can substitute stronger verbs or nouns. Add adjectives to give the reader better sensory images.

7. Find at least three places in your draft where you could add details. Perhaps you might add an entire paragraph that will more fully describe the person or place that is central to your story.

8. Can you think of a more effective way to begin or end?

9. Does your story have a point? If a person just told you everything he did on a certain day, that would not be a good story. A good story has a point.

10. Show your rough draft to at least two other readers and ask for suggestions.

PREPARING THE FINAL COPY, PRINTING, AND PROOFREADING

The typing of the final version should follow the traditional rules for an acceptable submission.

Checklist for the Final Copy

Use only 8½-by-11–inch paper (never paper torn out of a spiral-bound notebook).

Type on only one side of the paper.

Double-space.

Leave approximately a 1½-inch margin on each side of the paper.

Put your name, the date, the title of your paper, and any other relevant information either on a separate title page or at the top of the first page. (Ask your instructor for specific advice on what information to include.)

Center the title. Do not put quotation marks around the title and do not underline it.

Do not hyphenate a word at the end of a line unless you are willing to consult a dictionary to check on the acceptable division of the word into syllables.

Indent each paragraph five spaces.

If your paper is more than one page, number the pages and staple the pages together so they will not get lost.

Do not forget to make a copy before you submit the paper.

NOTE: In most cases, college instructors will not accept handwritten work. However, if you are submitting handwritten work, be sure to write on every other line and have legible handwriting. Begin today to learn to type on a computer. You will be at a disadvantage if you cannot use the current technology.

Once you have typed your final version and printed it out, an important step still remains. This step can often mean the difference of an entire letter grade. You must *proofread* your paper. Even if you have used a spell-check feature available on your word-processing program, errors could remain in your paper. The spell-check feature finds only groupings of letters that are not words. For example, if you typed the word *there* when you meant to type *their*, the spell-checker would not catch this error. The secret of good proofreading is to look at each word and sentence construction by itself without thinking about the paper's content.

Checklist for Proofreading

Study each sentence: One way to proofread is to read backwards, starting with the last sentence and examining every sentence, one at a time. First, check that the sentence is really complete and not a fragment or a run-on. Then check the punctuation. Go on to the next sentence and do the same. In this way, you will develop a critical eye for spotting any problems with sentence-level errors.

Study each word: Read the paper again, this time studying each word in every sentence. Look at the letters of the word. Have you transposed any letters, or have you left off an ending such as *-ed* or *-s*? If there are any words you are not sure how to spell, do not forget to check the correct spelling. Are there any words you have omitted?

Exploring Online

Go to academic.cengage.com/devenglish/scarry to find the **Writer's Online Workplace**, a website designed for students using this book. You will find links to handouts, interactive quizzes, and other online resources as you explore the following topics:

- writing the narrative essay
- principles and conventions of the narrative essay

Sharing Our Narratives

Everyone loves a good story, and children are especially fond of being read to by an older person. In connection with this chapter, everyone has written at least one piece that could be called a narrative or a story. Divide into groups of five or six students and have each person read his or her narrative out loud to the others. As you listen to the narratives, give each person the same careful attention you would want to have devoted to your work.

After everyone has had a turn reading, use a paper clip to attach a full-sized sheet of paper to each essay. Pass the essays around. Each person in the group will now respond to the essays by writing a few sentences on the sheet of paper. Use these questions as your guide:

1. What part of the story did you find most interesting?
2. Was there any part or detail that you found confusing?
3. What is one part you would have liked the writer to explain in more detail?
4. What do you think was the point of the story?

Portfolio Suggestion

Keep all the narratives you have worked on in this chapter in your portfolio. These could be the beginning of a series of stories written to capture the memories of your own childhood. You will be surprised how much you can recall when you focus on writing about these past events.

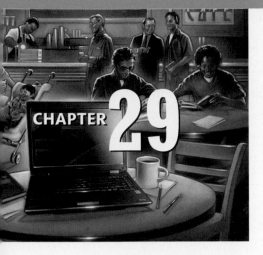

CHAPTER 29

Writing an Essay Using Process Analysis

This chapter will take you through the process of writing an essay using process analysis:

CHAPTER OBJECTIVES

- Explore the topic: Preparing for a Job Interview.
- Read and analyze a model essay: "How to Ace a Job Interview," by Richard Koonce.
- Follow the writing process to develop your own essay explaining to your readers how to do something.

Exploring the Topic: Preparing for a Job Interview

You are in the market for a job. You have read the newspaper ads, asked your friends for suggestions, made phone calls, and sent out résumés. Now you have a very promising interview coming up next week. What can you do to prepare for this important interview?

Everyone who works or who is looking for work has been in this situation. Whether getting ready for an interview or having already gone through the experience, everyone is interested in the all-important process of obtaining a satisfying work situation.

1. If you have ever gone through a job interview, share your experience with the class. What was the best (or worst) aspect of the interview? What questions were you asked? Were you prepared? Did you get the job?

_____

_____

_____

2. Imagine you are the person conducting a job interview. What would you be looking for in a prospective employee?

_____

_____

_____

3. What have you heard that people have done during interviews? What should a person *never* do in a job interview?

_____

_____

_____

4. What are some of the other important events in our lives that could benefit from careful planning?

_____

_____

_____

Reading a Model Essay with Steps in a Process

How to Ace a Job Interview

Richard Koonce

In the following essay, Richard Koonce takes us through the stages of the interview process, giving valuable pointers to job seekers. Whether we are heading toward an interview ourselves or advising a friend who is looking for a job, the following essay is filled with practical wisdom about what it takes to have a successful job interview.

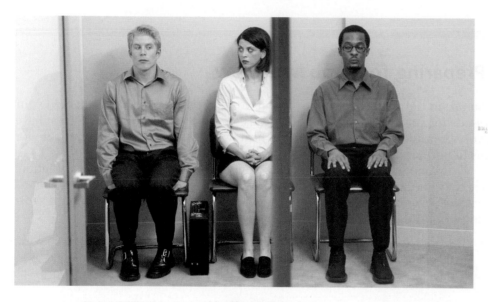

°**navigate the terrain**
make one's way
through the area

1   Next to public speaking, most people think that enduring a job interview is one of the most stressful human experiences.

2   I wouldn't quibble with that. However, a lot of people not only manage to master the art of effective interviewing as they go about job searches, but actually grow to enjoy the interview experience.

3   Good thing! Job interviews are something we all have to deal with from time to time in our careers. So, it pays to know how to handle yourself effectively when you're sitting across the desk from a prospective employer. Indeed, knowing how to navigate the terrain° of job interviews can pay off big time for your career, land you a better job than the one you initially interview for, and position you for the job success and satisfaction you deserve.

4   How do you ace a job interview? Here are some tips.

5   Recognize that when you interview for a job, employers are looking for evidence of four things: your ability to do the job, your motivation, your compatibility with the rest of the organization, and your self-confidence. If you understand how all those things play into an interviewer's questions (and an employer's hiring decisions), you'll have a better chance of getting hired.

6   Often the first thing an employer wants to know is, "Will you fit in?" Presuming a company has seen your résumé ahead of time and invited you for an interview, it may assume you have certain skills. Now they want to know, "Will you be compatible with everyone else that works here?"

7   Fitting in is a real hot button for employers. That's because it's expensive to go through the rehiring process if someone doesn't work out.

8   Along with determining compatibility, employers want to know that you're motivated to do a job. And, they want to know why you want to work for their organization. So be ready with career highlights that illustrate why hiring you would be a good decision for the organization. Showcase your talents as an instructional designer for example, or tell the interviewer about the process improvement efforts you've put in place in your current job that ensure continuous refinement of training courses. Concise oral vignettes° like these can make a great impression on interviewers.

°**vignettes**
short descriptive accounts

9   Throughout the interview, breathe deeply, speak slowly, and focus on projecting yourself confidently. This is important. Employers want to see self-confidence in job seekers. A lot of job seekers are too modest. They downplay their accomplishments. Don't embellish or exaggerate, but don't be a shrinking violet either. Rehearse ahead of time the answers to key questions that you expect to be asked, especially that all-time favorite: "Tell me about yourself."

10   Some other points to keep in mind:

11   Before the interview, do some research on the company you're interviewing with. That will enable you to demonstrate knowledge of the company when you meet the interviewer. It may also prompt questions that you'll want to get answers to, even as questions are being asked of you.

12   There are lots of research options. You can tap into the Internet and pull down everything from company profiles to *Dun and Bradstreet* financial reports. You can talk to friends or coworkers that may know something about the organization. And don't forget to watch the paper for late-breaking developments about the company. (If you read in the paper the day of your interview that your prospective employer is about to file Chapter 11,° you may want to think twice about working there!)

°**file Chapter 11**
apply for bankruptcy

13   Arrive for the interview early enough to go to the restroom to check yourself out. The last thing you want is to arrive for your interview beaded with sweat, having just sprinted there from the subway stop two blocks away.

14   Once in the interview, concentrate on making a pleasant and strong first impression. Eighty percent of the first impression an interviewer gets of you is visual—and it's formed in the first two minutes of the meeting! So, men, wear a well-made suit, crisply starched white or blue shirt, and polished shoes. Women, you can get away with more color than men, but dress conservatively in dresses, or jacket and skirt combinations. Wearing a colorful scarf is a good way to weave in color, but keep jewelry to a minimum.

15   As you answer questions, be sure to emphasize as often as you can the reasons why your skills, background, and experience make you a good fit for the job that you're interviewing for.

16   After the interview, immediately send a thank-you note to the interviewer. This is a critical point of interview etiquette. Many job candidates eliminate themselves from competition for a job because they don't do this.

17   Finally, learn from every job interview you have. Don't be hard on yourself if things don't go your way. Even job interviews that don't go well can be great learning experiences. And in my own life, I can look back on interviews where I'm glad I didn't get the job!

Analyzing the Writer's Strategies

1. How many paragraphs comprise the introduction?

2. According to the author, what are the four pieces of information employers want to know about a prospective employee?

3. The stages in this process consist of the following: (a) what you should know before the interview, (b) how you should prepare for the interview, (c) what you should do upon arrival at the interview, (d) how you should conduct yourself during the interview, and (e) what you should do after the interview. What is the author's advice at each of these stages?

4. From your own experience, can you think of any other advice that should have been included?

5. How does the writer's last paragraph provide a useful conclusion to the essay?

Writing an Essay Using Process Analysis (How to . . .)

> **Process analysis,** as a method of developing ideas, involves giving a step-by-step explanation of how to do something (called *directional process*) or how something works (called *informational process*).

The "how to" section of a library or bookstore is usually a busy area. People come to find books that will help them perform thousands of different tasks—from plumbing to flower arranging. If you want to learn how to cook Chinese dishes, assemble a child's bicycle, start your own business, or remodel your bathroom, you can find a book that will tell you how to do it. Thousands of books and articles have been written that promise to help people accomplish their goals in life. What do you think are the best-selling "how to" books in America? Perhaps you have guessed the answer: books on how to lose weight! For the essay that you write, be sure to choose a process with which you are already familiar.

CHOOSING A TOPIC AND CONTROLLING IDEA FOR THE THESIS STATEMENT

Here is a list of possible topics for an essay in which process analysis is the main method of development.

1. How to get good grades in college
2. How to prepare for a driver's test
3. How to plan a budget
4. How to buy a used car
5. How to study for a test
6. How to change a tire
7. How to redecorate a room
8. How to buy clothes on a limited budget
9. How to find the right place to live
10. How to make new friends

Using the above list of topics or ideas of your own, jot down two or three processes with which you are familiar.

_____

_____

_____

_____

From these topics, select the one you think will give you the best opportunity for writing. Which process do you feel strongest about? Which one is most likely to interest your readers? For which topic do you have the most first-hand experience?

Selected topic: _____

Your next step is to decide on your purpose in writing. Which of the two types of process writing will you be doing? Do you want to give directions on how to carry out each step in a process so that your readers can do this process themselves? For instance, will you provide directions on how to change a tire, perhaps suggesting that your readers keep these directions in the glove compartments of their cars? Or do you want to provide information on how a process works because you think your readers might find it interesting? For instance, you might explain the process involved in getting an airplane off the ground. Not many of us understand how this works, and very few of us will ever pilot a plane. Perhaps you know a lot about an unusual process that might amuse or entertain readers.

Directional _____ or informational _____

Now put your topic and controlling idea together into a thesis statement.

Thesis statement: _____

_____

GATHERING INFORMATION USING BRAINSTORMING TECHNIQUES

Take at least fifteen minutes to list as many steps or stages in the process as you can. If the process is one that others in your class or at home already know, consult with them about additional steps that you may have overlooked. You may also need to think of the precise vocabulary words associated with the process (such as the names of tools used for building or repairing something). The more specific you are, the more helpful and interesting the process analysis will be for your readers. List the steps or stages in the process:

_____

_____

_____

_____

_____

_____

_____

_____

_____

_____

_____

SELECTING AND ORGANIZING THE MATERIAL

Review your brainstorming list, asking yourself whether you now have a complete list. Have you left out any step that someone who is unfamiliar with this process might need to know? Is there some extra information you could provide along the way that would be helpful and encouraging? Do you have a special warning about something that the reader should *not* do? You might consider telling your readers exactly where in the process people are most likely to make mistakes.

Make an outline, giving each stage a heading. Underneath each heading, list all of the different ideas and vocabulary words that you should keep in mind as you begin to write. In a process essay, the most essential elements are the order, the accuracy, and the completeness of all the steps.

_____

_____

_____

_____

_____

_____

_____

_____

_____

_____

_____

_____

_____

WRITING THE ROUGH DRAFT

Write your rough draft, keeping in mind that your outline is only a guide. As you write, you will find yourself reevaluating the logic of your ideas, a perfectly natural step that may involve making some changes to your outline. You may think of some special advice that would help the reader; if you do, feel free to add the details. Your main goal is to get the process down on paper as completely and accurately as possible.

When you buy a product, the instructions that go with it usually take the form of a list of numbered items, each telling you what to do. In an essay, you do not usually number the steps. Instead, you signal the movement from one step to another by changing to a new paragraph, by using a transitional expression, or both. Like other methods for developing ideas, *process analysis* has its own special words and expressions that can be used to signal movement from one step to the next.

Transitions Commonly Used in Process Analysis

the first step	first of all	then	the last step
in the beginning	while you are	the second step	the final step
to start with	as you are	after you have	finally
to begin with	next	at last	eventually

REVISING THE ROUGH DRAFT

If you can leave some time between the writing of the rough draft and your revision of it, you will be able to look at your work with more objectivity. Under the best circumstances, you should put your first draft aside for a day or two before you return to it for revision.

You may revise alone, with a group, with a peer tutor, or directly with your instructor. The following guidelines contain basic questions you should consider when you approach this most important stage of your work.

Guidelines for Revision

1. Does the rough draft satisfy all the conditions for the essay form? Is there an introductory paragraph? Are there at least three well-developed paragraphs in the body of the essay? Have you written a concluding paragraph? Remember that a single sentence is not a developed paragraph.

2. Does the essay describe the process, in either a directional or an informational way?

3. Are the steps in the process in the correct order? In a process essay, the sequence of the steps is crucial. Placing a step out of order could result in a disaster of major proportions.

4. Are the directions accurate and complete? Check more than once that no important piece of information has been left out. Have you considered the points where some special advice might be helpful? Are there any special tools that would be useful?

5. Is any of the material not relevant?

6. Are there sentences or words that seem to be repetitious?

7. Find several places where you can substitute more specific verbs, nouns, or adjectives. Always try to use vocabulary that is appropriate for the process being described.

8. Can you think of a more effective way to begin or end?

9. Does the essay flow logically from one idea to the next? Could you improve this flow with better use of transitional expressions?

10. Show your draft to at least two other readers and ask for suggestions.

PREPARING THE FINAL COPY, PRINTING, AND PROOFREADING

The typing of the final version should follow the traditional rules for an acceptable submission.

Checklist for the Final Copy

Use only 8½-by-11–inch paper (never paper torn out of a spiral-bound notebook).

Type on only one side of the paper.

Double-space.

Leave approximately a 1½-inch margin on each side of the paper.

Put your name, the date, the title of your paper, and any other relevant information either on a separate title page or at the top of the first page. (Ask your instructor for specific advice on what information to include.)

Center the title. Do not put quotation marks around the title and do not underline it.

Do not hyphenate a word at the end of a line unless you are willing to consult a dictionary to check on the acceptable division of the word into syllables.

Indent each paragraph five spaces.

If your paper is more than one page, number the pages and staple the pages together so they will not get lost.

Do not forget to make a copy before you submit the paper.

NOTE: In most cases, college instructors will not accept handwritten work. However, if you are submitting handwritten work, you must be sure to write on every other line and have legible handwriting. Begin today to learn to type on a computer. You will be at a disadvantage if you cannot use the current technology.

Once you have typed your final version and printed it out, an important step still remains. This step can often mean the difference of an entire letter grade. You must *proofread* your paper. Even if you have used a spell-check feature available on your word-processing program, errors could remain in your paper. The spell-check feature finds only groupings of letters that are not words. For example, if you typed the word *then* when you meant to type *than*, the spell-checker would not catch this error. The secret of good proofreading is to look at each word and sentence construction by itself without thinking about the paper's content.

Checklist for Proofreading

Study each sentence: One way to proofread is to read backwards, starting with the last sentence and examining every sentence, one at a time. First, check that the sentence is really complete and not a fragment or a run-on. Then check the punctuation. Go on to the next sentence and do the same. In this way, you will develop a critical eye for spotting any problems with sentence-level errors.

Study each word: Read the paper again, this time studying each word in every sentence. Look at the letters of the word. Have you transposed any letters, or have you left off an ending such as *-ed* or *-s*? If there are any words you are not sure how to spell, do not forget to check the correct spelling. Are there any words you have omitted?

Exploring Online

Go to academic.cengage.com/devenglish/scarry to find the **Writer's Online Workplace,** a website designed for students using this book. You will find links to handouts, interactive quizzes, and other online resources as you explore the following topics:

- writing the process essay
- issues to consider when writing a process essay

Working Together

Deciding on a Logical Order: Sexual Harassment in the Workplace

The following letter was sent to the advice column of a local newspaper:

> Dear Dr. Karen: I have been with a bank for more than five years now, and at meetings every month or so I find myself working with one of the regional managers. He has always been polite at these meetings, but a few weeks ago, he started sending me e-mail that is very suggestive. He has even left inappropriate messages on my home telephone.
>
> I live alone, and these messages have upset me and have even frightened me. What should I do? Should I report this to my supervisor, who will probably think I am just overreacting? Everybody likes this man.
>
> Running Scared

Being harassed at work can create very complicated issues on the job. In many cases, the situation comes down to one person's word against that of another. Often, the person in the less powerful position is afraid to report a more powerful person to outside authorities. Fear of losing one's job is a strong incentive to remain silent. However, a person should not have to endure unacceptable behavior.

Consider the specific example described in the letter to Dr. Karen. Divide into groups and discuss the following questions concerning the woman who wrote the letter. Decide on the most logical order for the steps this person should take.

1. Should she confront the man who is harassing her?

2. Should she go to her supervisor? Should she tell her coworkers about the problem?

3. Should she share her problem with her friends?

4. Should she avoid the problem by quitting her job?

518

5. How important is evidence for a person in this situation? How and when should she gather documentation for a possible formal action?

6. Does she need a lawyer? Does she need to consider the consequences of a formal action?

Portfolio Suggestion

Write a process essay in which you outline the steps a person should take if he or she is being harassed on the job.

Discussion of this issue may remind you of other problems that arise in the workplace. If so, you may want to start gathering ideas on some of these other problems that are of interest to you. Your examination of these issues could relate directly to other subject areas you might study, such as psychology, sociology, business ethics, or business management.

CHAPTER 30

Writing an Essay Using Comparison/Contrast

This chapter will take you through the process of writing an essay using comparison/contrast:

CHAPTER OBJECTIVES

- Explore the two-part topic: Men and Women Look at Beauty.
- Read and analyze a model essay: "The Ugly Truth about Beauty," by Dave Barry.
- Follow the writing process to develop your own essay using comparison/contrast.

Exploring the Topic: Men and Women Look at Beauty

Standards of beauty may change, but the search for beauty is a continual one in our lives. Whether we accept society's definition of beauty or have our own ideas on the subject, the question of how we see ourselves in the context of our culture is of genuine interest to most people.

1. When you look at another person, what is the first thing you notice about that person? Is this the feature or quality you always find most attractive about someone else?

   _____

   _____

   _____

   _____

2. To what extent do you judge someone's appearance? Are you critical of people who do not pay a great deal of attention to how they look?

   _____

   _____

   _____

   _____

3. All of us have met people who are very attractive, and our first tendency is to admire such people. However, are there some possible disadvantages to being very handsome or very beautiful?

4. What are some of the more extreme measures people take to make themselves more attractive? Do you think these attempts are the result of pressures from society, the media, and the fashion and makeup industries, or do they result from inborn desires that people have?

5. What public figure (entertainer, politician, sports figure, and so on) do you consider to be especially handsome or beautiful? Why?

6. Is there too much of an emphasis in the media today on impossible standards of beauty?

Reading a Model Essay That Uses Comparison/Contrast

The Ugly Truth about Beauty

Dave Barry The writer Dave Barry has been called "the funniest man in America." His career has been largely devoted to pointing out the lighter side of life. After graduating from college, he worked as a newspaper reporter before discovering his true talent as a writer of humorous essays. The wry observations about modern life that filled his columns earned Barry a Pulitzer Prize in 1988. In the following essay, which first appeared in the *Philadelphia Inquirer* in 1998, the writer gives us an amusing look at how both sexes view the questions of what is beauty and who is beautiful.

1 If you're a man, at some point a woman will ask you how she looks.

2 "How do I look?" she'll ask.

3 You must be careful how you answer this question. The best technique is to form an honest yet sensitive opinion, then collapse on the floor with some kind of fatal seizure. Trust me, this is the easiest way out. Because you will never come up with the right answer.

4 The problem is that women generally do not think of their looks in the same way that men do. Most men form an opinion of how they look in seventh grade, and they stick to it for the rest of their lives. Some men form the opinion that they are irresistible stud muffins, and they do not change this opinion even when their

faces sag or their noses bloat to the size of eggplants and their eyebrows grow together to form what appears to be a giant forehead-dwelling tropical caterpillar.

5   Most men, I believe, think of themselves as average-looking. Men will think this even if their faces cause heart failure in cattle at a range of 300 yards. Being average does not bother them; average is fine, for men. This is why men never ask anybody how they look. Their primary form of beauty care is to shave themselves, which is essentially the same form of beauty care that they give to their lawns. If, at the end of his four-minute daily beauty regimen, a man has managed to wipe most of the shaving cream out of his hair and is not bleeding too badly, he feels that he has done all he can, so he stops thinking about his appearance and devotes his mind to more critical issues, such as the Super Bowl.

6   Women do not look at themselves this way. If I had to express, in three words, what I believe most women think about their appearance, those words would be: "not good enough." No matter how attractive a woman may appear to be to others, when she looks at herself in the mirror, she thinks: woof. She thinks that at any moment a municipal animal-control officer is going to throw a net over her and haul her off to the shelter.

7   Why do women have such low self-esteem? There are many complex psychological and societal reasons, by which I mean Barbie. Girls grow up playing with a doll proportioned such that, if it were a human, it would be seven feet tall and weigh 81 pounds, of which 53 pounds would be bosoms. This is a difficult appearance standard to live up to, especially when you contrast it with the standard set for little boys by their dolls . . . excuse me, by their action figures. Most of the action figures that my son played with when he was little were hideous-looking. For example, he was very fond of an action figure (part of the He-Man series) called "Buzz-Off," who was part human, part flying insect. Buzz-Off was not a looker. But he was extremely self-confident. You could not imagine Buzz-Off saying to the other action figures: "Do you think these wings make my hips look big?"

8   But women grow up thinking they need to look like Barbie, which for most women is impossible, although there is a multibillion-dollar beauty industry devoted to convincing women that they must try. I once saw an Oprah show wherein supermodel Cindy Crawford dispensed makeup tips to the studio audience. Cindy had all these middle-aged women applying beauty products to their faces; she stressed how important it was to apply them in a certain way, using the tips of their fingers. All the women dutifully did this, even though it was obvious to any sane observer that, no matter how carefully they applied these products, they would never look remotely like Cindy Crawford, who is some kind of genetic mutation.

9   I'm not saying that men are superior. I'm just saying that you're not going to get a group of middle-aged men to sit in a room and apply cosmetics to themselves under the instruction of Brad Pitt, in hopes of looking more like him. Men would realize that this task was pointless and demeaning.° They would find some way to bolster° their self-esteem that did not require looking like Brad Pitt. They would say to Brad: "Oh YEAH? Well what do you know about LAWN CARE, pretty boy?"

10   Of course many women will argue that the reason they become obsessed with trying to look like Cindy Crawford is that men, being as shallow as a drop of spit, WANT women to look that way. To which I have two responses:

11   1. Hey, just because WE'RE idiots, that does not mean YOU have to be; and

°**demeaning**
degrading

°**bolster**
support or buoy up

12   2. Men don't even notice 97 percent of the beauty efforts you make anyway. Take fingernails. The average woman spends 5,000 hours per year worrying about her fingernails; I have never once, in more than 40 years of listening to men talk about women, heard a man say, "She has a nice set of fingernails!" Many men would not notice if a woman had upward of four hands.

13   Anyway, to get back to my original point: If you're a man, and a woman asks you how she looks, you're in big trouble. Obviously, you can't say she looks bad. But you also can't say that she looks great, because she'll think you're lying, because she has spent countless hours, with the help of the multibillion-dollar beauty industry, obsessing about the differences between herself and Cindy Crawford. Also, she suspects that you're not qualified to judge anybody's appearance. This is because you have shaving cream in your hair.

Analyzing the Writer's Strategies

1. Underline the thesis of Barry's essay.
2. Read the introduction (paragraphs 1–3) and the conclusion (paragraph 13) of the essay and explain how Barry's conclusion echoes what he wrote in the introduction.
3. Find three sentences in the essay that you find humorous and explain what makes these sentences funny for you.
4. Dave Barry uses informal language. Find five examples of informal language or slang.
5. Find an example of Barry's use of simile (a comparison using *like* or *as*).
6. Summarize how Barry contrasts each of the following:
    a.   a man's daily regimen and a woman's daily regimen
    b.   a man's attitude about himself and a woman's attitude about herself
    c.   a Barbie doll and an action figure called Buzz-Off
    d.   a woman's attitude toward Cindy Crawford and a man's attitude toward Brad Pitt

Writing an Essay Using Comparison/Contrast

> **Comparison/contrast,** as a method for developing ideas, involves the careful examination of similarities and differences between people, objects, or ideas to arrive at a judgment or conclusion.

CHOOSING A TOPIC AND CONTROLLING IDEA FOR THE THESIS STATEMENT

Here is a list of possible topics for an essay in which comparison/contrast is the main method of development.

1.   High school classes and college classes
2.   Studying with a friend and studying alone
3.   Male and female stereotypes

4.   Your best friend in childhood and your best friend now
5.   Using public transportation and driving a car
6.   Our current president and any previous chief executive
7.   Two items you have compared when shopping
8.   Two apartments or houses where you have lived
9.   Cooking dinner at home and eating out
10.   Watching television and reading a book

Using the above list of topics or ideas of your own, jot down a few two-part topics that appeal to you.

_____

_____

_____

_____

From your list of two-part topics, select the one you think will give you the best opportunity for writing. Which one do you feel strongest about? Which one is most likely to interest your readers? For which topic do you have the most first-hand experience?

Selected topic: _____

Your next step is to decide what your controlling idea should be. What is your main purpose in comparing or contrasting these two topics? Do you want to show that although people think the two topics are similar, they actually differ in important ways? Do you want to show that one topic is better in some ways than the other? Do you want to analyze how something has changed over the years (a "then and now" essay)?

Controlling idea: _____

At this point, combine your two-part topic and controlling idea into one thesis statement.

Thesis statement: _____

_____

GATHERING INFORMATION USING BRAINSTORMING TECHNIQUES

Take at least fifteen minutes to brainstorm (using listing or clustering) as many points of comparison or contrast as you can on your chosen topic. You will probably want to think of at least three or four points. Under each point, brainstorm as many details as come to mind. For instance, if you are comparing two friends and the first point concerns the interests you have in common, recall as much as you can about the activities you share together. If you are brainstorming on a topic that other classmates or family members might know something about, ask them to help you think of additional points to compare. If special vocabulary comes to mind, jot that down as well. The more specific you are, the more helpful and interesting your comparison or contrast will be for your readers.

Points to Compare or Contrast

	Topic One	Topic Two
Point 1		
Point 2		
Point 3		
Point 4		
Point 5		

SELECTING AND ORGANIZING THE MATERIAL

Comparison/contrast always involves a two-part topic. For instance, you might compare the school you attend now with a school you attended in the past. Often we need to make choices or judgments, and we can make better decisions if we compare or contrast the two items in front of us. Because of the two-part topic, you have a choice in organizing the essay:

1. **The block method.** With this method, you write everything you have to say about one topic or idea, and then in a later paragraph or paragraphs you write entirely about the other topic. If you choose this method, when you discuss the second topic, you must be sure to bring up the same points and keep the same order as when you discussed the first topic.

2. **The point-by-point method.** With this method, you discuss one point and show how both topics relate to this point in one paragraph. Then, in a new paragraph, you discuss the second point and relate it to both topics, and so forth.

Which method will be better for the topic you have selected—the block method or the point-by-point method?

At this stage, review your brainstorming list, asking yourself if you have a complete list. Have you left out any point that might need to be considered? Do you have at least three points, and do you have enough material to develop both parts of the topic? You do not want the comparison or contrast to end up one-sided, with most of the content focused on only one part of the topic.

Make an outline, choosing one of the formats below, depending on whether you selected the block method or the point-by-point method. The example shown contrasts high school classes and college classes.

Outline for Block Method

   I. Topic 1   High school classes
- A. First Point   meet five days a week
- B. Second Point   daily homework
- C. Third Point   seldom require research papers
- D. Fourth Point   discipline problems

 II. Topic 2   College classes
- A. First Point   meet only two or three days a week
- B. Second Point   long-term assignments
- C. Third Point   often require research papers
- D. Fourth Point   no discipline problems

Outline for Point-by-Point Method

   I. First Point   How often classes meet
- A. Topic 1   high school classes meet five days a week
- B. Topic 2   college classes meet only two or three days a week

 II. Second Point   Homework
- A. Topic 1   high school classes have daily homework
- B. Topic 2   college classes have long-term assignments

III. Third Point   Research papers
- A. Topic 1   high school classes seldom require research papers
- B. Topic 2   college classes often require research papers

IV. Fourth Point   Discipline
- A. Topic 1   high school classes often have discipline problems
- B. Topic 2   college classes have no discipline problems

_____

_____

_____

_____

_____

_____

_____

_____

_____

_____

_____

_____

_____

_____

_____

_____

_____

_____

WRITING THE ROUGH DRAFT

Write your rough draft. Remember that your outline is only a guide. Most writers find that new ideas occur to them at this time. If you have new thoughts, you should feel free to explore them along the way. As you write, you will be constantly reevaluating the logic of your ideas.

Like other methods of developing ideas, comparison/contrast has its particular words and expressions that can be used to signal movement from one point to the next.

Transitions Commonly Used in Comparison/Contrast

Transitions for comparison		Transitions for contrast	
again	like	although	instead
also	likewise	and yet	nevertheless
as well as	moreover	but	on the contrary
both	the same as	despite	on the other hand
equally	similar to	different from	otherwise
furthermore	similarly	even though	still
just as	so	except for	though
just like	too	however	unlike
		in contrast with	whereas
		in spite of	while

REVISING THE ROUGH DRAFT

If you can leave an interval of time between the writing of the rough draft and your work on revising it, you will be able to look at your work with greater objectivity. Ideally, you should put your first draft aside for a day or two before you approach it again for revision.

When you revise, you may work alone, with a group, with a peer tutor, or directly with your instructor. Here are some of the basic questions you should consider during this most important stage of your work.

Guidelines for Revision

1. Does the rough draft satisfy the conditions for the essay form? Is there an introductory paragraph? Are there at least three well-developed paragraphs in the body of the essay? Is there a concluding paragraph? Remember, a single sentence is not a developed paragraph.

2. Does the essay compare or contrast a two-part topic and come to some conclusion about the comparison or contrast?

3. Did you use either the point-by-point method or the block method to organize the essay?

4. Have important points been omitted? Is any of the material irrelevant?

5. Are there repetitious sentences or paragraphs?

6. Find several places where you can substitute more specific verbs, nouns, or adjectives. Use vocabulary that is appropriate for the topic being discussed.

7. Can you think of a more effective way to begin or end?

8. Does the essay flow logically from one idea to the next? Would using any transitional expressions improve this flow?

9. Show your draft to at least two other readers and ask for suggestions.

PREPARING THE FINAL COPY, PRINTING, AND PROOFREADING

The typing of the final version should follow the traditional rules for an acceptable submission.

Checklist for the Final Copy

Use only 8½-by-11–inch paper (never paper torn out of a spiral-bound notebook).

Type on only one side of the paper.

Double-space.

Leave approximately a 1½-inch margin on each side of the paper.

Put your name, the date, the title of your paper, and any other relevant information either on a separate title page or at the top of the first page. (Ask your instructor for specific advice on what information to include.)

Center the title. Do not put quotation marks around the title and do not underline it.

Do not hyphenate a word at the end of a line unless you are willing to consult a dictionary to check on the acceptable division of the word into syllables.

Indent each paragraph five spaces.

If your paper is more than one page, number the pages and staple the pages together so they will not get lost.

Do not forget to make a copy before you submit the paper.

NOTE: In most cases, college instructors will not accept handwritten work. However, if you are submitting handwritten work, you must be sure to write on every other line and have legible handwriting. Begin today to learn to type on a computer. You will be at a disadvantage if you cannot use the current technology.

Once you have typed your final version and printed it out, an important step still remains. This step can often mean the difference of an entire letter grade. You must *proofread* your paper. Even if you have used a spell-check feature available on your word-processing program, errors could remain in your paper. The spell-check feature finds only groupings of letters that are not words. For example, if you typed the word *van* when you meant to type *ban,* the spell-checker would not catch this error. The secret of good proofreading is to look at each word and sentence construction by itself without thinking about the paper's content.

Checklist for Proofreading

Study each sentence: One way to proofread is to read backwards, starting with the last sentence and examining every sentence, one at a time. First, check that the sentence is really complete and not a fragment or a run-on. Then check the punctuation. Go on to the next sentence and do the same. In this way, you will develop a critical eye for spotting any problems with sentence-level errors.

Study each word: Read the paper again, this time studying each word in every sentence. Look at the letters of the word. Have you transposed any letters, or have you left off an ending such as *-ed* or *-s*? If there are any words you are not sure how to spell, do not forget to check the correct spelling. Are there any words you have omitted?

Exploring Online

Go to academic.cengage.com/devenglish/scarry to find the **Writer's Online Workplace,** a website designed for students using this book. You will find links to handouts, interactive quizzes, and other online resources as you explore the following topics:

- writing the comparison/contrast essay
- block method versus point-by-point method

Using Outside Sources: Comparing the Ideal Diet with an Actual Diet

The chart to the right shows where most Americans get their calories. Anyone who is aware of nutrition can quickly see that a diet made up mostly of these foods cannot be healthy.

Working in Groups

Make an outline of the foods you have eaten during the past week. Be sure to include snacks. Compare your outline with those of others in your group. Now go to the government website MyPyramid.gov to create a chart outlining the balance of foods you should eat to have a healthy lifestyle. Print out the chart. Discuss with your group whether your diet is closer to the average American diet or closer to the ideal diet as described on the government website.

MyPyramid.gov
STEPS TO A HEALTHIER YOU

**The Top Ten Sources
of Calories in the
American Diet**

Whole Milk

Cola

Margarine

White Bread

Rolls
(commercial ready-to-serve)

Sugar

2% Milk

Ground Beef
(broiled medium)

Wheat Flour

Pasteurized Process
American Cheese

SOURCE:
U.S. DEPARTMENT OF
AGRICULTURE

Portfolio Suggestion

Keep the materials you have gathered for an essay you might write on American eating habits (or your individual eating habits) compared to the ideal diet as described by MyPyramid.gov. Will you use the block method or the point-by-point method? Of course, there are always new diets being popularized in current magazines. You could also pick two diets that have been widely publicized (such as the South Beach diet and the Atkins diet) and compare them.

31

Writing an Essay Using Persuasion

In this chapter, you will learn to write persuasive essays by making use of the following aids:

CHAPTER OBJECTIVES

- a list of guidelines for writing an effective persuasive essay
- a list of common transitions to help achieve coherence
- two model persuasive essays, followed by related topics for writing your own essays
- two lists of factual material for use in writing persuasive essays
- additional topics for writing persuasive essays

What Is Persuasion?

From one point of view, all writing is persuasion because the main goal of any writer is to convince a reader to see, think, or believe in a certain way. There is, however, a more formal definition of persuasive writing. Anyone who has ever been a member of a high school debate team knows there are techniques that the effective speaker or writer uses to present a case successfully. Learning how to recognize these techniques of persuasion and how to use them in your own writing is the subject of this chapter.

> An essay of **persuasion** presents evidence intended to convince the reader that the writer's viewpoint is valid.

Guidelines for Writing a Persuasive Essay

Following are some basic guidelines for writing an effective persuasive essay.

1. **State a clear thesis.** Use words such as *must, ought,* or *should.* Study the following three sample thesis statements:

    The United States must reform its prison system.

    All states ought to have the same legal drinking age.

    We should not ban all handguns.

2. **Give evidence or reasons for your beliefs.** Your evidence is the heart of the essay. You must show the wisdom of your logic by providing the best evidence available.

3. **Use examples.** Well-chosen examples are among the best evidence for an argument. People can identify with a specific example from real life in a way that they cannot with an abstract idea. Without examples, essays of persuasion would be flat, lifeless, and unconvincing.

4. **Use opinions from recognized authorities to support your points.** One of the oldest methods of supporting an argument is to use one or more persons of authority to support your position. People will usually believe what well-known experts claim. However, be sure that your expert is someone who is respected in the area you are discussing. For example, if you are arguing that we must address the problem of global warming, your argument will be stronger if you quote a respected scientist who has studied the serious implications of global warming. A famous movie star giving the same information might be more glamorous and get more attention, but he or she would not be as great an authority as the scientist.

5. **Be careful to avoid faulty logic.**

    a. Do not appeal to fear or pity.

        Example: If we don't double the police force, innocent children will die.

    b. Do not make sweeping or false generalizations.

        Example: All women belong in the kitchen.

    c. Do not oversimplify with an either-or presentation.

        Example: A woman should either stay home and take care of her children or go to work but have no children.

    d. Do not give misleading or irrelevant support to your argument.

        Example: Don't hire that man; he has six children.

6. **Answer your critics in advance.** When you point out, beforehand, what your opposition is likely to say in answer to your argument, you are writing from a position of strength. You are letting your reader know that there is another side to the argument you are making. By pointing out this other side and then answering its objections in advance, you strengthen your own position.

7. **In your conclusion, point out the results, make predictions, or suggest a solution.** Here, you help your reader see what will happen if your argument is (or is not) believed or acted upon as you think it should be. You should be very specific and very rational when you point out results, making sure that you avoid exaggeration. For example, if you were arguing against the possession of handguns, it would be an exaggeration to say that if we don't ban handguns, "everyone will be murdered."

Achieving Coherence

Like other methods of developing an essay, persuasion has its own special words that signal parts of the argument. The following chart can help you find transitional expressions that will move you from one part of your argument to the next.

Transitions Commonly Used to Signal the Parts of a Persuasive Essay

To signal the thesis of an argument

I agree (disagree) that . . .
I support (do not support) the idea that . . .
I am in favor (not in favor) of . . .
I propose . . .
_____ must (must not) be changed
_____ should (should not) be adopted

To signal a reason

The first reason is . . .	because
An additional reason is . . .	can be shown
Another reason is . . .	for (meaning *because*)
The most convincing piece of evidence is . . .	in the first place
	in view of
	just because

To admit an opponent's point of view

Most people assume that . . .
One would think that . . .
We have been told that . . .
Popular thought is that . . .
Some may claim . . .
The opposition would have you believe . . .

To signal a conclusion

We can conclude that . . .	as a result
This proves that . . .	consequently
This shows that . . .	so
This demonstrates that . . .	therefore
This suggests that . . .	thus
This leads to the conclusion that . . .	
It follows that . . .	

Reading and Responding to Model Persuasive Essays

It's Time We Helped Patients Die

Dr. Howard Caplan

Howard Caplan is a medical doctor who specializes in geriatrics, the branch of medicine that deals with the care of older people. He is also the medical director of three nursing homes in Los Angeles, California.

As you read Dr. Caplan's essay, look for all of the elements of an effective argument. Where does the writer give his thesis statement? Where are his major examples? At what point does he use authorities to support his point of view? In addition, look for the paragraphs where he answers those who do not agree with him, and be sure to find that section of the essay where he predicts the future of euthanasia, commonly known as "mercy killing." As you read the essay, do you see any weaknesses in the writer's argument?

°aneurysm
sac formed by the swelling of a vein or artery

°astrocytoma
tumor made up of nerve cells

°nasogastric tube
tube inserted through the nose and into the stomach

1   For three years, the husband of one of my elderly patients watched helplessly as she deteriorated. She'd burst an aneurysm° and later had an astrocytoma° removed from her brain. Early in the ordeal, realizing that she'd never recover from a vegetative state, he'd pleaded with me to pull her nasogastric tube.°

2   I'd refused, citing the policy of the convalescent hospital. I told him I could do it only if he got a court order. But he couldn't bring himself to start such proceedings, although the months dragged by with no signs of improvements in his wife's condition. He grieved as her skin broke down and she developed terrible bedsores. She had to have several courses of antibiotics to treat the infections in them, as well as in her bladder, which had an indwelling catheter.

3   Finally I got a call from a lawyer who said he'd been retained by the family to force me to comply with the husband's wishes.

4   "I'm on your side," I assured him. "But you'll have to get that court order just the same."

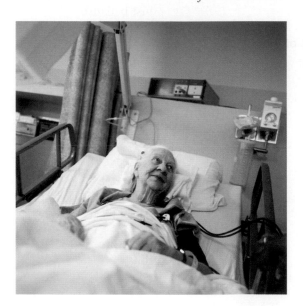

5   I went on to suggest—though none too hopefully—that we ask the court to do more than just let the patient starve to death. "If the judge will agree to let her die slowly, why won't he admit that he wants death to happen? Let's ask for permission to give her an injection and end her life in a truly humane manner."

6   The lawyer had no answer except to say, "Aw, come on, Doc—that's euthanasia!"

7   Frankly, I'd have been surprised at any other reaction. Although most states have enacted living-will laws in the past decade, none has yet taken the next logical step—legalizing euthanasia. But I believe it's time they did. Ten years of practice in geriatrics have convinced me that a proper death is a humane death, either in your sleep or being *put* to sleep.

8   I see appropriate patients every day in the extended-care facilities at which I practice. About 50 of the 350 people under my care have already ended their biographical lives. They've reached the stage in life at which there's no more learning, communicating, or experiencing pleasure. They're now simply existing in what is left of their biological lives.

°demented
people who have lost normal brain function

9   Most of these patients are the elderly demented.° A typical case is that of a woman in her 80s or 90s, who speaks only in gibberish and doesn't recognize her family. She has forgotten how to eat, so she has a feeding tube coming from her nose. She is incontinent, so she has an indwelling catheter. She can no longer walk, so she is tied into a wheelchair. She's easily agitated, so she gets daily doses of a major tranquilizer. Why shouldn't I, with the concurrence of her family and an independent medical panel, be allowed to quickly and painlessly end her suffering?

10   I think of another patient, a woman in her 50s, with end-stage multiple sclerosis, unable to move a muscle except for her eyeballs and her tongue. And

°**aphasic triplegic**
a person who has lost the
ability to express or comprehend
language and who has paralysis
of three limbs

younger patients: I have on my census a man in his early 40s, left an aphasic triplegic° by a motorcycle accident when he was 19. For nearly a quarter of a century, while most of us were working, raising children, traveling, reading, and otherwise going about our lives, he's been vegetating. His biographical life ended with that crash. He can't articulate—only make sounds to convey that he's hungry or wet. If he were to become acutely ill, I would prefer not to try saving him. I'd want to let pneumonia end it for him.

11   Of my remaining 300 patients, there are perhaps 50 to 100 borderline functional people who are nearing the end of their biographical lives and—were euthanasia legal—would probably tell me: "I'm ready to go. My bags are packed. Help me."

12   Anyone who's had front-line responsibility for the elderly has been asked if there wasn't "something you can give me" to end life. Such requests are made by patients who clearly see the inevitability of their deterioration and dread having to suffer through it. For these people, there is no more pleasure, let alone joy—merely misery. They want out.

13   What is their fate? Chances are they'll be referred for psychiatric consultation on the grounds that they must be seriously depressed. The psychiatrist, usually decades younger than the patient, does indeed diagnose depression and recommends an antidepressant.

14   But if such patients lived in the Netherlands, odds are they'd get assistance in obtaining a release from the slow dying process to which our modern technology condemns them. While euthanasia is not yet legal there, it's openly practiced. On a segment of the CBS show "60 Minutes" not long ago, I heard a Dutch anesthesiologist° describe how doctors in his country help 5,000 terminal patients slip away peacefully each year. Isn't that a promising indication of how well euthanasia would work in this country?

°**anesthesiologist**
a medical specialist who
administers anesthesia, or pain
killers, to people about to
undergo operations

15   I realize that there are those who vigorously oppose the idea. And there are moral issues to confront—how much suffering is too much, the one-in-several-million chance that a person given no hope of improving will beat the odds. But it's time for society to seriously reconsider whether it is immoral to take the life of someone whose existence is nothing but irreversible suffering. Euthanasia ought to be treated the same way the abortion issue has been treated: People who believe it a sin to take a life even for merciful reasons would not be forced to do so. What I'm pleading for is that doctors and their patients at least have the choice.

16   I doubt that we'll get congressional action on such an emotionally charged issue during my lifetime. Action may have to come at the state level. Ideally, legislatures should permit each hospital and each nursing home to have a panel that would approve candidates for euthanasia. Or it might be more practical to have one panel serve several hospitals and nursing homes in a geographic area. Made up of one or two physicians and a lawyer or judge, plus the attending doctor, the panel would assess the attending's findings and recommendations, the patient's wishes, and those of the immediate family. This would ensure that getting a heart-stopping injection was truly in the patient's best interests, and that there was no ulterior motive—for example, trying to hasten an insurance payout. Needless to say, members of the board would be protected by law from liability claims.

17   Then, if the patient had made it known while of sound mind that under certain circumstances he wanted a deadly substance administered, the process would be easy for everyone. But in most cases, it would be up to the attending to raise the question of euthanasia with the patient's relatives.

18   I'd start with those who've been part of the patient's recent life. If there are relatives who haven't seen the patient for years, it really shouldn't be any of their business. For instance, I'd try involving a son who's just kept in touch by phone. I'd say to him, "If you really want to stop this from happening, then you'd better come out here to see firsthand what's going on."

19   However, if he said, "Well, I can't really get away, Doctor, but I violently disagree," my answer would be, "Well, not violently enough. Everyone here can see what shape your mother's in. We're quite sure what she'd want if she could tell us, and we're going to help her."

20   Before any of this can happen, though, there's going to have to be widespread public education. The media will have to do a better job of discussing the issues than it has with living wills. Among my patients who are nearing death, there aren't more than a half-dozen with living wills attached to their charts. Patients' families often haven't even heard of them, and even when large institutions encourage families to get these things taken care of while the patient is still alert, it's hardly ever done.

21   Not knowing about living wills, unaware of no-code options, many families plunge their loved ones—and themselves—into unwanted misery. How many rapidly deteriorating patients are rushed from a nursing home to a hospital to be intubated, simply because that's the facility's rigid policy? How many families impoverish themselves to keep alive someone who's unaware of himself and his surroundings?

22   For that matter, how many people themselves suffer heart attacks or ulcers—not to mention divorces or bankruptcies—from the stresses involved in working to pay where Medicare and Medicaid leave off?

23   Every day in my professional life, I encounter illogical, irrational, and inhumane regulations that prevent me, and those with whom I work, from doing what we know in our souls to be the right thing. Before high technology, much of this debate was irrelevant. There was little we could do, for example, when a patient arrested.° And what we could do rarely worked.

°**arrested**
suffered cardiac arrest, in which the heartbeat stops

24   But times have changed. Now we have decisions to make. It helps to understand that many of the elderly infirm have accepted the inevitability—and, indeed, the desirability—of death. We who are younger must not mistake this philosophical position for depression. We need to understand the natural acceptance of death when life has lost its meaning.

25   About 28 percent of our huge Medicare budget is spent providing care during the last year of life. Far too little of that money goes to ensure that dying patients' last months are pain-free and comfortable. Far too much is wasted on heroic, pain-inducing measures that can make no difference. It's time to turn that ratio around—and to fight for the right to provide the ultimate assistance to patients who know their own fight to prolong life is a losing one.

Analyzing the Writer's Strategies

Because Dr. Caplan deals with a sensitive subject, many people might find his position to be dangerous and even frightening. Even before we examine his essay, the title of the piece and the writer's medical background gain our attention. When a doctor writes on matters of life and death, we tend to pay more attention than we otherwise might; the fact that Dr. Caplan works so closely with older people gives his views even more authority. For example, the facts and figures he gives in paragraphs 8 and 11 go a long way toward strengthening his point of view. In addition, the writer uses both his own experience and his observation of people in another country to convince us that his stand on this controversial topic is a valid one.

The writer's position is also supported by his precision in paragraphs 3–7, when he deals with the law; almost from the beginning, Dr. Caplan is seen as a careful and caring professional. We notice too that in paragraphs 12 and 13 he points out what happens under our present system, and in paragraphs 16–18 he gives practical suggestions that would help put his own system into operation. Finally, we see that in paragraph 15 he pays attention to the other side's arguments and then answers those arguments.

It is clear that Dr. Caplan's argument is carefully written and complete; it has all of the parts needed for a good persuasive essay. After you have studied each part of the essay, are you able to find any weaknesses in the writer's presentation?

Responding to the Writer's Argument

Take a position either for or against one of the following topics and write a persuasive essay supporting your position. Use the guidelines for writing a persuasive essay (pages 533–534) to help you construct the essay. Be sure to include all of the important parts needed for a good argument.

1. All medical care should be free in our society.
2. Doctors should not be burdened by outrageously high malpractice insurance payments.
3. If a person wishes to commit suicide for any reason, society should not try to interfere with that decision.
4. Doctors should always work to preserve life; they must never cooperate in any effort to end a life.
5. New medical technology has created more problems than it has solved.
6. Permitting euthanasia would create a dangerous precedent that could easily lead to government-sponsored murder of people it considers "undesirable."
7. People should always leave instructions (a living will) telling what should be done if they are terminally ill and are unable to respond to their surroundings.
8. A person's family has the responsibility to support decisions for life, not death, when a person is gravely ill, no matter how much money and effort it might cost that family.
9. In the case of a hopeless medical situation, no human being—including the person who is ill—has the right to make decisions that would lead to immediate death (euthanasia).
10. A husband or wife who helps a terminally ill spouse die should not be prosecuted by the law.

Censorship or Common Sense?

Roxana Robinson

Roxana Robinson, a professional writer, produced the following essay as a response to a controversial issue. Advocates of free speech objected when some libraries blocked unlimited Internet access for children. The writer's position is unmistakable: children are not adults, and we should shield our children from material that is clearly inappropriate. As you read the essay, note each section where the writer reports her position and each section where she reports the opposing point of view.

1   A 5-year-old is not ready to confront the world. This should be obvious, but it doesn't seem that way to many free-speech advocates, who are angry that some libraries around the country have installed software on their computers to block out Internet material that's unsuitable for children.

2   The objections are coming from some usual sources: the American Civil Liberties Union, for example, and Web publishers. But even the American Library Association has opposed the use of filtering software.

3   Traditionally, the library has been a safe place for children. And librarians have long been the guardians of public virtue. While they have been firm supporters of the First Amendment, they haven't generally interpreted it to mean that they should acquire large holdings of published pornography and make such materials available to children.

4   Librarians have always acquired books according to their own discrimination and their sense of what is appropriate to their neighborhoods. They generally refuse to buy, among other things, pornography. This isn't censorship; it's common sense.

5   If a library were to have a section of pornographic books, would we want these to be printed in large, colorfully illustrated, lightweight volumes, shelved near the floor where they were easily available to children? Probably not. But we have gone to a great deal of trouble to insure that computers are user friendly, with brightly colored graphics and easily accessible information.

6   Material on the Internet is not only uncensored but also unedited. Adults can be expected to make their own evaluations of what they find. Children, who lack experience and knowledge, cannot.

7   The debate over the filtering of the Internet is a bit like the debate over grants given out by the National Endowment for the Arts. It's all tangled up in false cries of censorship. Censorship is a legal term; it refers to government action prohibiting material from being circulated. This is very different from a situation in which a museum or an arts panel decides not to use public money to finance an exhibition or an artist.

8   Commendably, our society defends freedom of speech with great vigor. But there is a difference between allowing everything to be said and allowing everyone to hear it. We should know this by now, having seen the effects that exposure to television and movie violence has on children.

9   The A.C.L.U. and the American Library Association say that the use of filtering software in computers is censorship because it blocks access to constitutionally protected speech. But these cries are baffling and unfounded. The only control libraries are asserting is over a small portion of the audience, not over the material itself. Moreover, this control has a powerful historical precedent: parental guidance is even older than the Constitution.

10   The protection of children should be instinctive. A man may have the right to stand on the street and spew obscenities at passers-by, but he would be ordered to leave a kindergarten classroom.

11   It is absurd to pretend that adults and children are the same audience, and it is shameful to protect the child pornographer instead of the child.

Analyzing the Writer's Strategies

The use of the Internet in our schools, libraries, and homes brings us a world of knowledge and information. It also brings in such abuses as pornography, and many observers were alarmed when it became clear that children had almost unlimited access to this inappropriate material.

Roxana Robinson begins her essay by considering the position of those who argue for unlimited information directed at children; these are the groups that oppose censorship of any kind. The writer's own position is almost immediately apparent, as she comes down on the side of what she calls "common sense." She refers to a lesson from history when she observes in paragraph 3 that librarians have traditionally been the ones to keep sensitive material away from children—actions that were considered common sense, not censorship.

This is the writer's own approach for the rest of the essay, as she judges the difference between what adults should be able to absorb and what children are exposed to every day, thanks to modern technology. Children, the author claims, are in a special situation when it comes to these sensitive materials. In fact, she concludes, it is wrong for a society to be more concerned about the rights of a pornographer than about the protection of its children.

As you study the essay, decide whether the writer indulges in any faulty logic in making her case. In what paragraph is her thesis statement? What are the opposing groups she names in her essay?

Responding to the Writer's Argument

Take a position either for or against one of the following topics and write a persuasive essay supporting your position. Use the guidelines for writing a persuasive essay (pages 533–534) to help you construct your essay. Be sure to include all of the important parts needed for a good argument.

1.   Dictionaries should (or should not) be banned from elementary schools because some of the definitions include sexually explicit information.
2.   A Nazi should be permitted (or denied) the right to speak at a public meeting.
3.   The government of a country should (or should not) have the right to investigate what websites its citizens are looking at on the Internet.
4.   Anyone who wants to view pornography should (or should not) be allowed to do so.
5.   Violent video games should (or should not) be banned.

Constructing Persuasive Essays from Research Material

EXERCISE   1

Using Research Material to Construct a Persuasive Essay on Violence in the Media

The following pieces of information are on the controversial topic of *violence in movies, on television, and in videos.* To what extent do you believe the violence we see in the media is responsible for the level of violence in our so-ciety? You may select any number of the following items for your supporting evidence, or you may do research on your own to obtain other evidence for your point of view.

1.   More than nine hundred research studies on violent entertainment give overwhelming evidence that violent films and other programs are having a harmful effect on the American people.

2.   In some years, more than half of the films produced by Hollywood have intensely violent content.

3.   The National Coalition on Television Violence estimates that up to half of all violence in our country comes from the violent entertainment we are exposed to every day.

4.   In June 1999, shortly after the school massacre in Littleton, Colorado, legislation was proposed in Congress that would have made it a felony to expose children to books, movies, and video games that contain explicit sex or violence. The legislation failed to pass.

5.   Three surgeons general of the United States have publicly declared that violent entertainment is a serious health problem that contributes to the level of violence and number of rapes in our society.

6.   On television, 55 percent of the characters in prime-time programs are involved in violent confrontations at least once a week.

7.   Cartoons on television have become increasingly violent, averaging forty-eight acts of violence per hour.

8.   In a single year, the average child between four and eight will see more than 250 war-related cartoons and more than 1,000 commercials for war toys, time equal to more than three weeks of school.

9.   Lt. Col. Dave Grossman, a psychologist and army ranger, claims that video games function like firing ranges. These games use the same type of conditioning that was used to train soldiers to kill during the Vietnam War.

10. The National Coalition on Television Violence claims that children in homes with cable television or a VCR will have viewed thirty-two thousand murders and forty thousand attempted murders by the time they reach eighteen years of age.

EXERCISE   **Using Research Material to Construct a Persuasive Essay on Homeland Security**

Since the destruction of the World Trade Center, *homeland security* has be-come one of the most critical and controversial topics of our time. The safety of the entire nation is at stake, a situation that must be balanced by the need to preserve people's rights, as defined in the Bill of Rights. Following are pieces of information that could be used to make an argument for or against the need for greater emphasis on domestic security. Consider two questions. First, how much power should any government have to monitor the activities of its citizens? Second, is there a limit to the amount of money that should be spent on homeland security? You may select any number of the following items for your supporting evidence, or you may do research on your own to obtain other evidence for your point of view.

1.   In 1918, the Sedition Act made it a crime to criticize, in speech or in writing, the government or the Constitution. Under this legislation, more

than fifteen hundred people were arrested for disloyalty, among them the prominent labor leader Eugene Debs.

2. In 1920, the United States Department of Justice pursued suspected Communist Party members. After using agents and spies in thirty-three cities in twenty-three states, the government arrested ten thousand alleged radicals.

3. In 1976, the Senate imposed guidelines on the Federal Bureau of Investigation (FBI) that crippled that agency's preventive and peacekeeping functions. It could no longer investigate someone unless there was evidence of criminal activity. By 1982, the number of investigations had dropped from 4,868 to 38. As a result, in February 1995, when a citizen visited the FBI with a warning that Timothy McVeigh and two others planned to blow up public buildings, the FBI was not interested because its hands were tied. We all know the tragedy that resulted: the Oklahoma bombing.

4. In 1978, a Maryland state police officer infiltrated the Ku Klux Klan and gave the FBI reports on this group's plan for a series of bombings, including one at the home of an African American congressman. Following the guidelines that had been imposed on the FBI, it closed its files after ninety days. Luckily the police kept their informer in place and were able to prevent these actions from taking place.

5. After the Cold War, Americans felt less need to win the battle for hearts and minds around the world. Support for international broadcasting programs like Radio Free Europe and Voice of America decreased 40 percent. Meanwhile, extremist Islamic centers and schools were multiplying in the Middle East.

6. Under the provisions of the 1995 Counterterrorism Act, citizens can be fined and imprisoned for supporting the lawful activities of any organization identified as terrorist by the president; noncitizens can be deported for the same perceived offense.

7. Before 9/11, private boats could approach cruise ships unhindered. Only 2 percent of cargo containers were inspected at seaports. Now there is a one-hundred-yard security zone around cruise ships, and U.S. customs officers inspect high-risk cargo containers. Many argue, however, that the small budget for these inspections means the seaports are still vulnerable.

8. Those who argue for greater government surveillance believe that the most important need is the prevention of terrorist acts. This means authorities must have enough power to identify sympathizers who are providing support such as medical help, places to hide, money, and intelligence to would-be terrorists. The infamous Leon Trotsky (one of the founders of the Communist movement in Russia) once said, "No terrorist group can function without a screen of sympathizers."

9. Two months after 9/11, Congress passed the Aviation and Transportation Security Act, which federalized airport security. Sixty thousand people were employed to screen travelers at airports. Bulletproof cockpit doors were installed in airliners. Pilots could go through training to carry arms in the cockpit. By February 2002, screeners had seized 49,331 box cutters from passengers. However, many people criticize the screening of little old ladies and point out that there is very little screening of cargo. Furthermore, airliners are still vulnerable to missile attack.

10. After 9/11, the FBI, the Pentagon, the Central Intelligence Agency (CIA), and the National Security Agency realized they must find better ways to share their information. A new organization called the Government Terrorist Threat Integration Center, organized in 2003, meets every day to discuss the daily fiteen- to twenty-page report on the latest information on plots and threats against the United States. The Center has one hundred terrorist analysts and plans to increase that number.

Writing a Persuasive Essay

Choose one of the fifteen topics listed below and write an essay of at least five paragraphs. Use the seven points discussed on pages 533–534 as a guide for your writing.

Essay topics   Argue for or against:

1. Legalized prostitution
2. Gambling casinos
3. Stricter immigration laws
4. Prayer in the public schools
5. Abortion
6. Tax exemption for religious organizations
7. Capital punishment
8. Single-parent adoption
9. The right to same-sex marriage
10. Offensive song lyrics
11. Required courses in college
12. Stricter gun laws
13. School uniforms
14. Suspending a driver's license for drunk driving
15. Random drug testing in the workplace

Exploring Online

Go to academic.cengage.com/devenglish/scarry to find the **Writer's Online Workplace,** a website designed for students using this book. You will find links to handouts, interactive quizzes, and other online resources as you explore the following topics:

- three strategies of persuasion
- writing the persuasive essay

Working Together

Analyzing a Newspaper Editorial

The following editorial appeared in the *New York Times* on March 20, 2006. Read the piece out loud. Then divide into groups and discuss the questions that follow.

The Road to Nowhere

1 It seems insane that the National Park Service would even think of spending $600 million on a road that few people want and nobody needs—especially when the service has barely enough money to keep up appearances. But that could happen unless the Interior Department musters° the courage to resist Representative Charles Taylor of North Carolina.

2 Mr. Taylor, who says a new road would stimulate the local economy, runs the subcommittee that controls the Interior Department's budget. For that reason, neither the park service nor Interior's outgoing secretary, Gale Norton, has publicly criticized the idea. But there is more at stake here than pleasing one's paymaster. The road would not only blow a hole in the department's budget; it would also leave a scar on one of the most popular national parks.

3 At issue is a 30-mile road proposed for the north side of Fontana Lake on the eastern edge of the Great Smoky Mountains National Park in North Carolina. The road was promised to the residents of Swain County in 1943 when the Tennessee Valley Authority built a major hydroelectric dam, creating the lake and flooding out an existing road. After a fitful start in the 1960's, the road was abandoned for environmental and budgetary reasons.

4 Those reasons still apply. The road, including three big bridges, each the length of the Brooklyn Bridge, would breach° an unbroken tract of national forest, destroy wildlife habitat and poison hundreds of miles of streams. Its estimated cost of $604 million—up 40 percent from only a year ago—is three times the annual roads budget for the entire national park system, which is already suffering from a big repair backlog.

5 There is no pressing need for the project. Swain County has other roads. The road's opponents include Bill Frist, the Senate majority leader, and Swain County's own commissioners. There is broad agreement that restitution of some sort is due the residents of the region, and that the spirit if not the letter of the original agreement should be honored. A cash settlement of $52 million has been proposed.

6 As Mr. Taylor has noted, this will not generate the jobs and income that the road project would. But it's fair, and it won't do lasting damage. Interior should endorse the settlement. The department's neutrality serves only to keep alive an idea that makes even less sense now than it did in 1943.

°**musters**
summons up, gathers

°**breach**
disrupt

Questions for Group Discussion

1. What is the thesis of the editorial?
2. What supporting evidence, including historical facts and current statistics, are given in the editorial?
3. Does the editorial present the opinions of the other side of the argument?
4. Does the editorial say what will happen if nothing is done to stop the proposed road?
5. Does the editorial propose any solution to the problem?
6. Does the editorial seem reasonable to you?
7. Are you persuaded by the position the editorial takes? Why or why not?

Following the group discussion, your instructor may require each student to write his or her own analysis of the editorial using the above discussion as the basis for the analysis.

Portfolio Suggestion

For many readers, the editorial page is the best part of the newspaper. It is on this page that writers argue, passionately at times, about issues that are of great importance to them. Look at the editorial section of a newspaper at least once a week and clip editorials that are about subjects that interest you. This is one way to gradually develop a feeling for argumentative or persuasive writing. You can learn from editorials that are outrageous in their points of view, as well as from those that are logical and convincing.

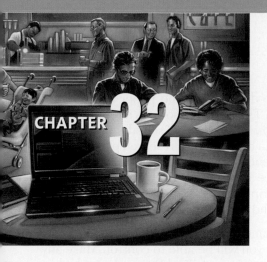

CHAPTER 32

Other College Writing: The Research Paper and the Essay Exam

In this chapter you will learn two critical skills needed for success in college:

CHAPTER OBJECTIVES

● How to write a research paper

    setting up a timetable

    choosing a topic

    looking for sources

    researching the topic

    taking notes

    incorporating sources into the paper

    avoiding plagiarism

    documenting sources

● How to take an essay exam

    coming to the exam well prepared

    forming a strategy

    recognizing frequently used terms

    using a thesis statement

How to Write a Research Paper

Of the skills you should be learning at this stage in your college career, mastering the research paper, or term paper, is one of the most important. The ability to write a well-researched and well-documented term paper has been called the single most useful tool any student can possess in college. Because writing a term paper calls for a number of closely related skills, it is not an easy task; because it is called for in so many college situations, it is a crucial one. These related skills include setting up a timetable, choosing a topic, looking for sources of relevant information, doing research and taking notes, incorporating sources into the draft, avoiding plagiarism, and documenting the sources that have been used.

SETTING UP A TIMETABLE

In school or work situations, effective use of time is critical to success. The writer of a college research paper is working under very real time pressures. The paper is due by a certain date, and the grade may well suffer if that deadline is not met. Given that the student is usually taking several other courses as well and must pay attention to their requirements, the demands of the paper are such that the student may easily feel overwhelmed. Therefore, as soon as a research paper assignment is given, a student should begin to plan a work schedule. Keeping on target during each stage is a key element in completing a research paper on time. The following schedule is intended as a general guide for a student who has been given a typical five-week period to produce a finished paper. The breakdown that follows is not a rigid week-by-week prescription but a series of pointers that may be adapted to individual circumstances and specific needs.

> **Week 1.** Make sure that you understand the instructor's requirements and that the topic you have chosen is one you will be able to control. Make any modifications needed to the topic, obtaining approval for any individual changes to the assignment. Start gathering relevant information.
>
> **Week 2.** Gather materials that are immediately available, including standard books and articles and information that can be downloaded. Highlight the important sections in these sources, write summaries of material, and take notes.
>
> **Week 3.** Continue to look for additional sources of material. Write an outline containing your thesis and main points. If you are in doubt regarding these points, talk to your instructor immediately. Changing direction after this point could be disastrous. Write a first draft to give yourself an overview of your entire paper.
>
> **Week 4.** Continue to review your collected materials, revising summaries and refining your choices of quotes. Review the first draft of your paper, adding sections as needed and inserting quoted material.
>
> **Week 5.** Place a halt on looking for new sources to work on the final draft and make a complete bibliography of sources (works cited). Edit all of the written parts and do a final review of the bibliography. Check quotations for accuracy. Do a final editing.

CHOOSING A TOPIC

You may be given a topic or list of topics by your instructor, or your instructor may allow you to select your own topic. If you are free to come up with your own subject, it is always a good idea to make certain your instructor gives approval to your choice. Similarly, if you choose a topic from a list you have been given and wish to modify that topic in any way, you should make sure that your instructor approves of the approach you intend to take. The time to discuss these issues is shortly after the topics have been handed out. If you attempt to modify a topic long after the period for research has begun, the delay could be damaging to your work and could seriously affect the grade you earn in the course.

LOOKING FOR SOURCES

Once your topic has been established, your next step is to find sources to draw on for facts and information. Sources are all around you, from your daily newspaper and weekly newsmagazine to articles in journals, entire books and reference works, and the vast resources of the Internet. Library research used to be a laborious process, often involving typed or even handwritten catalogue cards and slow searches for material. Today, what used to take hours or even days can be accomplished in minutes. An online search can tell you what exists, what is available, and how you can obtain it. Virtually every school library is connected to one or more of the computerized databases that serve colleges and universities throughout the country. Be sure to join an orientation tour of your college library and listen carefully to the procedures for doing research there. The success of your paper will depend on your perseverance in locating pertinent information.

Most instructors will want you to use a variety of sources. Some will specify the number of books and articles that must be used; others will allow you to choose your own combination of sources. No matter how many sources are called for, it is always a good idea to seek out a variety of research materials. A term paper containing material from an array of sources always gains strength and authority from the rich combination of information, and such a paper will almost certainly obtain a higher grade for you.

RESEARCHING THE TOPIC

Having selected your topic and paid attention to your instructor's requirements, you are now ready to consult the books, articles, and other sources you will be working with as you develop the different sections of your paper. The library will be your first and probably richest resource for material. Books on your subject will be among the most obvious sources close at hand. Current magazines should also be available on open racks, and encyclopedias and other standard reference works should be accessible on the open shelves for you to examine. Additional sources, in the form of articles and such, may be found on microfilm or microfiche. One of the most accessible locations for articles on virtually any subject is InfoTrac® College Edition found on the Internet. InfoTrac College Edition can provide you with the complete texts of articles that relate to your subject; you can print out the articles you need and file the hard copy in your folder of materials. If a resource such as *InfoTrac* is not available, the *Reader's Guide to Periodical Literature* is a trustworthy compilation of the subjects of magazine and newspaper articles.

When you have made notes from books, reference works, and other full-length sources, and when you have downloaded articles from Internet-related sources and have those articles in printed form, you are ready to review everything you have gathered. Underline or highlight paragraphs and larger sections of selections that contain material you believe will be useful to you.

TAKING NOTES

In doing research, whether conducting an interview, listening to a lecture, reading an article in a library periodical, or searching on the Internet, a student needs to be good at taking notes. Taking notes is not always a simple task because it involves making a judgment about what will be needed later on (for a research paper or for a test). Some people try to write down everything; others do not write down enough. Still others have trouble distinguishing between major points and minor details. Learning to take good notes is one of the most important skills a college student can master. Depending on how the information is going to be used, note taking can be done by quoting (direct or indirect), paraphrasing, or summarizing, or any combination of these.

INCORPORATING SOURCES INTO THE RESEARCH PAPER

The following paragraphs appear in the book *Fatherless America: Confronting Our Most Urgent Social Problem,* by David Blankenhorn. These paragraphs will be used to demonstrate how a student can incorporate sources into a research paper.

> The United States is becoming an increasingly
> fatherless society. A generation ago, a child could
> reasonably expect to grow up with his or her father.
> Today, a child can reasonably expect not to.
> Fatherlessness is approaching a rough parity with
> fatherhood as a defining feature of childhood.
>
> This astonishing fact is reflected in many statistics,
> but here are the two most important: Tonight, about
> 40 percent of U.S. children will go to sleep in homes
> in which their fathers do not live. More than half of
> our children are likely to spend a significant portion
> of childhood living apart from their fathers. Never
> before in this country have so many children been
> voluntarily abandoned by their fathers. Never before
> have so many children grown up without knowing what
> it means to have a father.
>
> Fatherlessness is the most harmful demographic
> trend of this generation. It is the leading cause of
> the decline in the well-being of children. It is also
> the engine driving our most urgent social problems,
> from crime to adolescent pregnancy to domestic violence.
> Yet, despite its scale and social consequences,
> fatherlessness is frequently ignored or denied.

USING DIRECT AND INDIRECT QUOTATION

A large part of writing a research paper is knowing how to incorporate the ideas of others into your text. This involves using a combination of carefully chosen direct and indirect quotations that will appear throughout the research paper. These quotations will lend authority to the points you are making. You must, however, be selective in using quotations. Students are sometimes tempted to include too many quotations or use quotations that are too long. Another common problem is the use of quotations that are not justified in the context of the material being presented. Unless every part of the quotation relates directly to the content of your paper, the quotation will seem out of place. Also, don't assume that your reader will see the relevance of a quotation. Always use the quotation in such a way that your reader will understand how the quotation relates to the point you are making.

> **Direct quotation** reproduces the exact words of another writer, using quotation marks.

The example below shows how a student could incorporate a **direct quotation** from the second paragraph of the Blankenhorn excerpt into a research paper.

> According to David Blankenhorn, "Tonight, about 40 percent of U.S. children will go to sleep in homes in which their fathers do not live."

> **Indirect quotation** uses one's own words to report on what another person has spoken or written.

The example below shows how the direct quotation above can be changed into an **indirect quotation.** Notice that the information is the same, but in the case of the indirect quotation, the writer uses his or her own words to express the ideas. No quotation marks are used.

> **David Blankenhorn claims that approximately 40 percent of American children live without fathers in their homes.**

> **NOTE:** If a direct quotation is four or more lines long, it is usually set off by indenting the quotation and not using quotation marks.

Paraphrasing

A second method of using the words or ideas of another writer is called *paraphrasing.* You use paraphrasing when you want to retain all the information a source offers, from a paragraph to a full page of material. When you paraphrase, you are required to pay close attention to your source because you must restate every idea contained in that source. Your paraphrase will be almost the same length as the original material. When you paraphrase, you cannot leave out any part of the original piece of writing, nor can you add any ideas of your own as you incorporate the material into your research paper. Paraphrasing demands a great deal of skill because a writer has to have extensive control of language to be able to restate ideas using different words and different sentence structures.

> **Paraphrasing** uses one's own words to restate each and every idea of a passage from another's work and results in a new passage that is virtually the same length as the original.

Here is how the first paragraph in the original text by David Blankenhorn might have been incorporated into a research paper using **paraphrase.**

> **Our country is turning into a society without fathers. Twenty-five years ago, children could look forward to being raised by their fathers, but that is no longer true. We are reaching the point when childhood is just as accurately described as growing up without a father as growing up with a father.**

Note that the paraphrase has fifty-two words and the original has only forty-seven words. It is difficult to be as succinct as a very good writer. Your own paraphrases may well be slightly longer than the originals.

Summarizing

A final method of incorporating the ideas of another writer into your research paper is *summarizing.* A summary includes only the main ideas of a published source; it is therefore a reduced version of the original. To write a summary, you will probably need to review the original material more than once to separate the main ideas from the details and specific examples. Although a summary should be significantly shorter than the text you are working from, you must not leave out any of that text's main ideas. Also, you may not add any ideas of your own. Writing successful summaries is a skill that is often used by writers as they research material for their own work. Extracting the main ideas from the works of others is at the heart of education itself.

> **Summarizing** uses one's own words to provide a condensed restatement of the main ideas of another person's work.

Below is a writer's **summary** of the first paragraph of the David Blankenhorn excerpt. Compare it to the paraphrase given above of the same material.

> American children today are as likely to grow up without a father as those of a generation ago were likely to be raised with one.

EXERCISE **Using Note-Taking Techniques**

The third paragraph from the David Blankenhorn excerpt is reproduced below.

> Fatherlessness is the most harmful demographic trend of this generation. It is the leading cause of the decline in the well-being of children. It is also the engine driving our most urgent social problems, from crime to adolescent pregnancy to domestic violence. Yet, despite its scale and social consequences, fatherlessness is frequently ignored or denied.

Demonstrate your skill at note-taking techniques by using material from the paragraph to write direct and indirect quotations, a paraphrase, and a summary.

1. Show how you could incorporate a *direct quotation* of the first sentence into a research paper.

    _____

    _____

2. Show how you could incorporate an *indirect quotation* of the first sentence into a research paper.

    _____

    _____

3. Write a *paraphrase* of the paragraph.

    _____

    _____

    _____

    _____

    _____

    _____

    _____

    _____

    _____

    _____

4. Write a *summary* of the paragraph.

_____

_____

_____

_____

AVOIDING PLAGIARISM

Plagiarism is the use of another person's work without acknowledging the source.

Whenever exact words, ideas, facts, or opinions from the works of other writers are used in a research paper and the sources are not specifically identified, the writer of the research paper is guilty of inappropriate use, known as *plagiarism*. Plagiarism is a very serious academic offense, which often results in receiving a failing grade for a course and in extreme cases results in expulsion from a school. However, as long as you quote sources correctly and cite your sources properly, the integrity of your own work will be assured.

DOCUMENTING SOURCES

Whether you use direct quotation, indirect quotation, paraphrase, or summary, you must acknowledge your sources in a consistent format. This format can vary, depending on the style your instructor wants you to use. The most commonly accepted authorities are the Modern Language Association (MLA style) and the American Psychological Association (APA style). MLA style is often used in the humanities, and APA style is recommended for use in scientific writing. Because so many combinations of sources and authorship are possible, you will need to have on hand some guidelines on the style your instructor requires so that you can prepare the documentation properly.

Documentation within the Body of the Paper

Documentation is required in two places. The first place is in the body of the paper itself, directly after a quotation or use of a source. In-text citations are brief (usually the last name of the author followed by a page reference in parentheses), providing just enough information so that the reader can find the full documentation at the end of the paper.

Documentation at the End of the Paper

Full documentation must be provided at the end of the paper, on a page usually titled "Works Cited." Below are examples of how some typical sources would be documented using MLA style. A citation in MLA style has three basic parts: the author's name (followed by a period), the title of the work (followed by a period), and the publishing information (followed by a period). Keep these additional rules in mind as well:

1. The citations are given in alphabetical order, according to the author's last name.

2. Titles follow the standard rules. Titles of full-length works such as books are italicized or underlined, and titles of shorter works such as chapters, essays, short stories, and articles are placed within quotation marks.

3. If the place of publication is a well-known city such as Boston or New York, the state need not be given. If the place is less well known, however, both city and state should be given.

4. If the citation takes more than one line, additional lines are indented five spaces.

SAMPLE ENTRIES FOR A WORKS-CITED PAGE IN MLA STYLE

Books

A book by a single author

Garbarino, James. <u>Lost Boys: Why Our Sons Turn Violent</u> <u>and How We Can Save Them</u>. New York: Free Press, 1999.

A book by two or three authors

Maxym, Carol, and Leslie York. <u>Teens in Turmoil</u>. New York: Penguin Books, 2001.

A book by four or more authors

Newman, Katherine S., et al. <u>Rampage: The Social Roots of</u> <u>School Shootings</u>. New York: Basic Books, 2004.

> **NOTE:** *et al.* means "and others."

A book with a corporate author (authored by an organization)

Opposing Viewpoints Resource Center. <u>Teen Violence:</u> <u>Opposing Viewpoints Digest</u>. Farmington Hills, MI: Gale Group, 2003.

An anthology of writings with one or more editors rather than an author

Howell, James C., et al., eds. <u>Sourcebook on Serious,</u> <u>Violent, and Chronic Juvenile Offenders</u>. Thousand Oaks, CA: Sage, 1995.

An encyclopedia or dictionary entry with an author

Gartner, Rosemary. "Violent Crime." <u>Encyclopedia of</u> <u>Sociology</u>. Ed. Edgar F. Borgatta et al. 4 vols. New York: Macmillan, 1992.

CHAPTER 32

A chapter or essay from a book

> Blankenhorn, David. "Fatherless Society." <u>Fatherless</u>
>   <u>America: Confronting Our Most Urgent Social</u>
>   <u>Problem.</u> New York: HarperCollins, 1995. 25-48.

Periodicals

Periodicals include newspapers, magazines, and journals.

Article in a newspaper

> Roth, Alex. "Dad Says Bullying Drove Son to Act." <u>San</u>
>   <u>Diego Union Tribune</u> 6 September 2001: A1.

> **NOTE:** Often a newspaper article does not give the name of the author. If the author is unknown, begin with the title of the article. Also, be sure to give the section in the newspaper where the article is found. (In the example above, the article was found in Section A, page 1.)

Article in a magazine

> Lyons, Gene. "The Media Is the Message: Notes on
>   Our Decadent Press." <u>Harper's</u> Oct. 2003: 77-82.

Article in a scholarly journal

> Wilkinson, Diane L., and Jeffrey Fagan. "What We Know
>   About Gun Use Among Adolescents." <u>Clinical Child and</u>
>   <u>Family Psychology Review</u> 4.2 (2001): 109-132.

> **NOTE:** If the journal is identified by its volume number, not by month or season, provide the volume and issue—in this case, volume 4, issue 2. Then give the year of publication in parentheses so as not to confuse the two sets of numbers.

Article from a periodical found online

> Magner, Carolyn. "When They Were Bad." <u>Salon.com</u> 9 Octo-
>   ber 2000 <http://www.salon.com/mwt/feature/2000/
>   10/09/freeze_out>.

> **NOTE:** Source information from the Internet is often incomplete. You will need to discuss with your instructor how complete the documentation must be. For example, you may need to go to the library and find the periodical article you wish to use on microfiche to retrieve the page numbers or other necessary information for the works cited page. For material found online,

your instructor will probably require you to add the Internet address (called the URL, or universal resource locator) and the date of retrieval as well.

Miscellaneous printed material

This material might include speeches, lectures, letters, interviews, studies, reports, pamphlets, conference presentations, music, works of art, and government documents, including charts and graphs.

Government document

United States. Department of Health and Human Services.

The Course of Life, Vol. 2: Latency, Adolescence and

Youth. Washington: GPO, 1980.

Interview

Lightburn, Anita. Personal interview. 1 Oct. 2005.

Study

National Television Violence Study, 1994-1995.

"Summary of Findings and Recommendations." 1 Oct.

1994. Online posting. Mediascope. 2 March 2004

<http://www.mediascope.org/pubs/ntvs.htm>.

Work of art

Matisse, Henri. Asia. Kimbell Art Museum, Fort Worth, TX.

Music

Beethoven, Ludwig van. Symphony no. 4 in B-flat major, op. 60.

How to Take an Essay Exam: Writing Well under Pressure

The first rule for doing well on any test is to come to the test well rested and well prepared. Research has shown that reviewing notes and reading assignments systematically throughout the semester is much more effective than cramming for a test the night before. You'll be greatly rewarded if you learn to use your time efficiently and wisely.

COMING TO THE EXAM WELL PREPARED

1. **Study the textbook chapters and your notes.** In your textbook, review headings and words in boldface type, as well as information you have highlighted or underlined. Look for both chapter reviews and summaries at the ends of chapters. If you have already made an outline, study that too.

2. **Avoid having to face any surprises when the exam is distributed.** When the test is first announced in class, ask whether it will include material from the textbook in addition to material covered in class. Also, find out the format of the test: how many essay questions there will be and how many points each question will be worth. Ask how much time you will have to complete the test.

3. **Form a study group if you can.** One way a study group can work is as follows: Each person comes to the study group prepared to present at least one major question that he or she thinks the instructor will ask and then to provide the information needed for answering that question. Each person in turn presents a different question along with the information needed for the answer. The other students take notes and add whatever additional information they can. Members of the group can also quiz each other on the information that is to be covered by the exam.

   If you are unable to be part of a study group, you should still try to predict what questions will be on the exam. Prepare an outline for study and then memorize your outline.

Remember that an essay test, unlike a multiple-choice test, requires more than simply recognizing information. In an essay exam, you must be able to recall ideas and specific details and present them quickly in your own words. Thus, for an essay exam, some material needs to be memorized. Memorizing both concepts and factual information is quite a demanding task.

FORMING A STRATEGY

The smart test taker does not begin to answer the first question immediately. Instead, he or she takes a few moments to look over the test and form a strategy for tackling it. The following pointers will help you become "test smart."

1. **When you receive the exam, read over each essay question twice.** How many points is each question worth? A well-written test will give you this information. How you budget your time should depend heavily on the importance of each question. If, for example, one essay question is worth fifty points, you should spend approximately half your time planning and answering that question. However, if the test consists of ten shorter essay questions and you have a class period of one hundred minutes, you should spend no more than ten minutes on each question, keeping a careful watch on your time. Students often write too much for the first four or five questions and then panic because they have very little time left to answer the final questions.

2. **When you read an essay question, ask yourself what method of development is being asked for.** We all know stories of people who failed tests because they misunderstood the question.

3. **Use key words from the test question itself to compose your thesis statement.** In a test, the thesis statement should be the first sentence. Don't try to be too clever on a test. State your points as directly and clearly as possible.

4. **Answer the question by stating your basic point and then including as many specific details as you have time or knowledge to give.** The more specific names, dates, and places (all spelled correctly) you can provide, the more points will be added to your grade.

5. **If a question has more than one part, be sure you answer all the parts.** Check over the question to be sure your answer covers all the parts.

Study the following question to determine exactly what is being asked for:

Sample essay question

What were the social changes that contributed to the rise of the feminist movement in the 1960s in the United States? Be specific.

If the question were one of ten short essay questions on a ninety-minute final examination, the following answer would probably be adequate:

Sample essay question answer

> The feminist movement grew out of many social changes happening in the 1960s in the United States. In 1961, the President's Commission on the Status of Women documented discrimination against women in the workforce. The result of the Commission's report was a growing public awareness, which soon led to the enactment of two pieces of legislation: the Equal Pay Act of 1963 and the Civil Rights Act of 1964. In addition, the development of the birth-control pill brought the discussion of sexuality out into the open. It also lowered the birthrate, leaving more women looking to the world of work. A high divorce rate, as well as delayed marriages, further contributed to more women being concerned with feminist issues. Finally, in 1966 the National Organization for Women was formed, which encouraged women to share their experiences with each other and to organize in an effort to lobby for legislative change.

Notice that the first sentence uses the key words from the question to state the thesis. The answer gives not one but four examples of the changes that were taking place in the 1960s. Moreover, the answer is very specific, naming legislation and an organization and giving dates whenever significant. Can you spot the transitional expressions the writer used to signal the movement from one example to the next?

RECOGNIZING FREQUENTLY USED TERMS

Sometimes terms in the question indicate which method of development the instructor is looking for in your answer.

Definition or Analysis: A definition should give the precise meaning of a word or term. When you define something in an essay, you usually write an *extended definition* or *analysis,* in which you explain the significance of the term in the context of your work.

Comparison/Contrast: When you *compare* two people or things, you focus on the similarities between them. When you *contrast* two items, you point out the differences. Often you may find yourself using both comparison and contrast in an essay.

Narration: Narration is the telling of a story through the careful use of a sequence of events. The events are usually (but not always) presented in chronological order.

Summary: When you write a summary, you supply the main ideas of a longer piece of writing.

Discussion: The general term *discuss* is meant to encourage you to analyze a subject at length. Inviting students to discuss some aspect of a topic is a widely used method of constructing examination questions.

Classification: When you *classify* items of any kind, you place them into separate groups so that large amounts of material can be more easily understood.

Cause and Effect: When you deal with causes, you answer the question *why;* when you deal with effects, you show *results* or *consequences.*

Process Analysis: You are using process analysis when you give a step-by-step explanation of how something works or how something is (or was) done.

EXERCISE **Methods of Development**

All of the following college essay questions deal with the topic of computers. Use the previous list of terms to decide which method of development is being called for in each case.

1. Trace the development of the computer, beginning in 1937. Be sure to include all significant developments discussed in class.

    Method of development: _____

2. Choose two of the word-processing programs practiced in class and discuss the similarities and differences you encountered. What in your opinion were the advantages and disadvantages of each?

    Method of development: _____

3. Explain the meaning of each of the following terms: *hard disk, memory, directory, menu,* and *software.*

    Method of development: _____

4. We have discussed many of the common business applications for the computer. Select ten applications and group them according to the functions they perform.

    Method of development: _____

5. Discuss the problems that have resulted in the typical office as a result of computer technology.

    Method of development: _____

EXERCISE **Methods of Development/Parts of a Question**

Each of the following is an example of an essay question that could be asked in a college course. In the spaces provided after each question, indicate (a) what method of development (definition, comparison/contrast, narration, summary, discussion, classification, cause and effect, or process analysis) is being called for and (b) how many parts there are to the question and what they consist of. This dictates how many parts there will be in your answer.

1. What does the term *sociology* mean? Include in your answer at least four different meanings the term *sociology* has had since this area of study began.

    Method of development: _____

    The different parts of the question: _____

    _____

    _____

2. Compare and contrast the reasons the United States entered the Korean War with the reasons it entered the Vietnam War.

    Method of development: ————————————————————————

    The different parts of the question: ——————————————

    ——

    ——

3. Trace the history of our knowledge of the planet Jupiter from the time it was first discovered until the present day. Include in your answer at least one nineteenth-century discovery and three of the most recent discoveries that have been made about Jupiter through the use of unmanned space vehicles sent near that planet.

    Method of development: ————————————————————————

    The different parts of the question: ——————————————

    ——

    ——

4. In view of the dramatic increase in cases of contagious diseases, describe the types of precautions now required for medical personnel. What changes are likely to be required in the future?

    Method of development: ————————————————————————

    The different parts of the question: ——————————————

    ——

    ——

5. Explain the three effects of high temperatures on space vehicles as they reenter the earth's atmosphere.

    Method of development: ————————————————————————

    The different parts of the question: ——————————————

    ——

    ——

6. What was the complete process of restoring the Statue of Liberty to its original condition? Include in your answer six different aspects of the restoration, from the rebuilding of the inside supports to the treatment of the metal surface.

    Method of development: ————————————————————————

    The different parts of the question: ——————————————

    ——

    ——

7. Trace the history of the English language from its beginning to the present day. Divide the history of the language into at least three different parts, using Old English, Middle English, and Modern English as your main divisions.

Method of development: _____

The different parts of the question: _____

_____

_____

8. Discuss the events that led up to World War II. Be sure to include the political and social problems of the time that directly and indirectly led to the war.

Method of development: _____

The different parts of the question: _____

_____

_____

9. Summarize the four theories that have been proposed as to why dinosaurs became extinct sixty-five million years ago.

Method of development: _____

The different parts of the question: _____

_____

_____

10. Define the term *monarchy* and discuss the relevance or irrelevance of this form of government in today's world.

Method of development: _____

The different parts of the question: _____

_____

_____

USING A THESIS STATEMENT

One of the most effective ways to begin an essay answer is to write a thesis statement. Your thesis statement should include the important parts of the question and should give a clear indication of the approach you intend to take in your answer. Writing your opening sentence in this way gives you a real advantage: as your professor begins to read your work, it is clear what you are going to write about and how you are going to treat your subject.

For example, suppose you had decided to write an essay answer to the following question:

Agree or disagree that doctors should be allowed to use germ-line gene therapy to alter a woman's egg, a man's sperm, or an embryo just a few days old to eliminate inherited diseases.

An effective way to begin your essay would be to write the following thesis sentence:

A strong argument exists to support the view that doctors should be allowed to use germ-line therapy to alter the egg, the sperm, or the embryo if the purpose is to eliminate an inherited disease.

The instructor would know that this was indeed the topic you had chosen and would also know how you intended to approach that topic.

EXERCISE **Writing Thesis Statements**

Rewrite each of the following essay questions in thesis-statement form. Read each question carefully and underline the word or phrase that indicates the method of development called for. An example has been done for you.

> **Essay question:** How does one learn another language?
>
> **Thesis statement:** The process of learning another language is complicated but usually follows four distinct stages.

1.   Essay question: Discuss Thorstein Veblen's theory of the leisure class.

Thesis statement: _____

_____

2.   Essay question: What are the effects of television violence on children?

Thesis statement: _____

_____

3.   Essay question: Trace the development of portrait painting from the Middle Ages to today.

Thesis statement: _____

_____

4.   Essay question: What are the major causes for the economic crisis facing the African nations today?

Thesis statement: _____

_____

5.   Essay question: What have been the most significant results of space exploration since the first moon landing?

Thesis statement: _____

_____

6.   Essay question: What are the problems when a couple adopts a child from one culture and raises that child in another culture?

Thesis statement: _____

_____

7.   Essay question: In what ways does the new Japan differ from the old Japan?

Thesis statement: _____

_____

8.   Essay question: What four countries depend on tourism for the major part of their national income, and why is this so?

Thesis statement: _____

_____

_____

9. Essay question: What factors should a college use when judging the merits of a particular student for admission?

   Thesis statement: _____

   _____

   _____

10. Essay question: Discuss the generally accepted definition of Alzheimer's disease, its sequence of characteristic symptoms, and the current methods of treatment.

    Thesis statement: _____

    _____

    _____

Exploring Online

Go to academic.cengage.com/devenglish/scarry to find the **Writer's Online Workplace,** a website designed for students using this book. You will find links to handouts, interactive quizzes, and other online resources as you explore the following topics:

- note-taking skills, including
    direct quotation
    paraphrasing
    summarizing
- the research paper
- key aspects of the research paper
- finding research topics
- research paper tutorial
- essay exam tutorial

Working Together

Incorporating Sources: Using Direct and Indirect Quotation, Paraphrasing, and Summarizing

Many Americans believe the number of drunk drivers in America is a national disgrace. The following excerpt from a report by the National Transportation Safety Board gives these observations on the subject:

> Nationally, the confidence of the drunk driver remains almost unshaken. Amazingly, four out of every ten drivers admit to driving while under the influence of alcohol, while 10 percent of all drivers on weekend nights can be legally defined as intoxicated. There are good reasons for this, one of which is brought out by a recent report from the National Transportation Safety Board. It found that only one in 2,000 who drive while intoxicated will be pulled over. And even with the most thorough police control and rigorous administration, it doesn't rise to more than one in 200. Yet, all too often, those who do escape arrest do not live to get home. Every year, about 25,000 do not, including 4,000 teens.

Working in Groups

Students should answer each question individually. Then together in your group, discuss the answers and agree on a single response for each question. Your instructor may expect the results to be submitted at the end of the class session.

1. Write a sentence of your own in which you give a *direct quote* from the second sentence of the excerpt above.

   _____

   _____

   _____

   _____

   _____

   _____

   _____

   _____

   _____

2. Write a sentence of your own in which you give an *indirect quote* from the second sentence of the excerpt above.

_____

_____

_____

_____

_____

_____

3. Write a *summary* for the paragraph. Remember that when you do this, you will be reducing the paragraph to one or two sentences that focus on the main ideas.

_____

_____

_____

_____

_____

_____

4. *Paraphrase* the last two sentences.

_____

_____

_____

_____

_____

_____

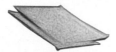

Portfolio Suggestion

- Be careful to save all the copies of the articles and other materials you have used to write your research paper. You could be asked to refer to your sources again to make changes, or you might expand on your topic in the future.

- Study your own research papers to see if you are overusing quotations out of a fear of writing paraphrases and making summaries of the source material. It is impossible to paraphrase or summarize material that you do not understand.

Further Readings for the College Writer

These selections show how professional writers have constructed their essays using the various methods of development studied throughout this textbook. Sometimes a writer uses more than one method of development in a single piece of writing. For instance, when Barbara Mujica presents her argument in favor of a single official language for our country, she also employs narration to tell a story based on her family's school experiences.

Each reading includes a background note that introduces the selection and tells something about the author. Glosses are provided in the margins to explain words or usages that might be unfamiliar. Following each reading is a section titled "Questions for Critical Thinking" that directs your attention to how each piece was constructed. Finally, the section "Writing in Response" invites you to generate essays of your own, based on themes suggested by each particular selection.

As you approach these readings, be sure to follow the suggestions of the next section, "Strategies for the Active Reader." Following these strategies in your college reading assignments will ensure your becoming a more critical reader, one of the basic goals for an educated person.

Strategies for the Active Reader

Becoming an active and involved reader is the key to success in college. The ability to absorb what you read relates directly to the ability to create effective college essays and term papers. Willingness to be an active reader will give you a definite advantage in school—and beyond. An active reader learns more and learns it more efficiently, throughout the weeks and months of required coursework. Increased awareness of the elements of reading and the requirements of writing will allow you to more quickly absorb the material contained in the books and essays you read. In fact, when you study closely the writing models contained in this book, you are doing what all the great writers of our literary past have done: they mastered their craft by turning to the best models they could find and using those models as their constant guides. This is how Shakespeare and Dickens learned, and you can also benefit from studying a wide variety of excellent models.

PREVIEWING

Before you begin to read a selection, you should examine the title. What announcement is the writer making? Are there key words in the title that should be noted? Read the introductory paragraph and the concluding paragraph and then skim through the other paragraphs. Keep in mind that this first look at the various paragraphs is not to be thought of as speed reading—an approach college students should not take. Speed reading is a technique that helps busy executives and other people who are under pressure to quickly scan newspaper and magazine articles. Are there any headings (usually in boldface type) announcing the different parts of the selection? In addition, you should note whether boxed features (often found in textbook chapters) give definitions of terms or other information in concise form. Also, look for key words or terms in boldface type, in addition to any sentences that are printed in italics. Words, headings, or sentences are presented in this way to emphasize their importance.

Another previewing technique is to read the first sentence of each paragraph. In many—but not all—cases, the first sentence is the topic sentence. Observing these key sentences before reading the entire piece is one of the best ways to get an overview of the material you are about to study.

ANNOTATING/TAKING NOTES

> Why is marking up a book indispensable to reading? First, it keeps you awake. (And I don't mean merely conscious; I mean wide awake.) In the second place, reading, if it is active, is thinking, and thinking tends to express itself in words, spoken or written. The marked book is usually the thought-through book. Finally, writing helps you remember the thoughts you had, or the thoughts the author expressed.
>
> MORTIMER ADLER

Once you have previewed the text, you are ready to begin a careful reading. Being an active reader means interacting with the text you are studying. This involves some or all of the following activities:

- **Underlining key points.** Key points include the thesis, topic sentences, and major divisions of the essay.
- **Highlighting significant portions of the text.** Highlighting should be used to mark portions of the text that have enduring value for you or that

you want to return to and remember. Some students make the mistake of highlighting too much material because they do not have enough experience distinguishing main ideas from less critical points.

- **Making brief marginal comments.** Marginal comments might be as brief as a question mark to indicate a word or idea you don't understand, an X to indicate an important comment, or an exclamation mark to emphasize a statement you find surprising. Sometimes you will want to make longer notations about the contents or the author's point of view. You might also find yourself disagreeing with the author, or you might have a comment on how the writer's ideas do not agree with your own experience.

- **Using the dictionary.** If you cannot figure out the meaning of a word from its context or from a gloss that has been provided, you should look up the meaning in a dictionary.

After reading a selection, you should be able to answer these basic questions:

1. What was the author's **purpose** in creating the piece of writing? Was it written to entertain, inform, or persuade?
2. Who is the intended **audience** for the selection?
3. What is the **structure** of the selection? How many paragraphs make up the introduction? How has the author developed the points?
4. How does the author achieve **coherence**? For example, where does the author use transitions, repetition, and pronouns?
5. Does the writer present both **facts** and **opinions**? Do you find yourself agreeing or disagreeing with the writer's point of view?

AN ANNOTATED TEXT

Below are a few paragraphs taken from the essay found on pages 625–628. Notice how the student has annotated the text.

Controlling idea

The (Changing) (American Family) — *Topic*

Thesis The American family is not dying. It is diversifying. This is the "secret" to understanding what is happening to ourselves, our children, and our society. Millions of people today are frightened about the future of the family. (Dire) predictions pour from the pulpit, the press, even from the White House. Emotional oratory about the need to "restore" the family is echoing through the nation.

why use quotation marks?

?

Examples

. . . .

Topic sentence   Because the economic and other conditions that made the (nuclear) family popular are changing, the nuclear family itself is less and less popular. America is no longer a nation of poorly educated blue-collar workers. Most of us work in service occupations or spend our time processing information. And today only some 7 percent of Americans *statistic hard to believe!* still live in classical nuclear families. The nuclear family is simply no longer the norm—and it is not likely to become the norm again, no matter how much pulpit-pounding or breast-beating we do about it. In its place, a new family system is emerging.

What does "nuclear" mean here?

part 3 of the essay   The Third Wave family: This new system is harder to describe because it is not based on a single dominant family form but on a dazzling diversity of household structures.

paragraph of example

use of statistics

For example, look at what is happening to single life. Between 1970 and 1978 alone, the number of people aged 14 to 34 who live alone nearly tripled in the United States. Today fully one-fifth of all households are live-alones. Some are alone out of necessity, others prefer it. Then there are the child-free couples. As James Ramey of the Center for Policy Research *use of authority* has pointed out, we are seeing a massive shift from "child-centered" to *why quotes?* "adult-centered" homes. The number of couples who deliberately decide not to have children—whether for economic, psychological, or ecological reasons—has increased dramatically.

why quotes?

Next come the single-parent households. Divorce rates may be level-ing out in this country, depending upon how they are measured, but broken nuclear households are so widespread that today as many as one out of seven children are raised by a single parent. In big cities that may run as high as one in four.

When was this essay written? Are these statistics still accurate?

Although I was raised in a single-parent household, I hope to marry and raise several children. Am I unusual?

REREADING

The pieces of writing we read as part of our day-to-day activities are generally read only once. For example, when we read an article in a newspaper or magazine to be informed or entertained, we seldom return to it. Reading in college is very different. As a college student under pressure to read a great deal for your coursework, you may be grateful to be able to get to your required reading even once, but you should try to find a chance to return to that material, if possible. For example, if you are studying difficult literary works, several readings may be necessary before the writer's meaning becomes clear. In most college courses, you will find it beneficial to read notes and textbook material more than once. The primary reason for this is that you will eventually be tested on that material. No matter what your reasons are for approaching written material, required or otherwise, if you are thoughtful in your reading, one of the great avenues to pleasure and meaning in life will be open to you.

Summer Reading

Michael Dorris

Important events from childhood never fade from our minds, and if we are able to write them down, they acquire an even greater reality. In writing the following essay, Michael Dorris achieved this greater reality. Long after this memorable summer from his adolescence, the late Native American professor and writer looked back on a debt that was repaid in an unexpected way, one that profoundly changed his life.

°**clientele**
group of customers

1   When I was fourteen, I earned money in the summer by mowing lawns, and within a few weeks I had built up a regular clientele.° I got to know people by the flowers they planted that I had to remember not to cut down, by the things they lost in the grass or stuck in the ground on purpose. I reached the point with most of them when I knew in advance what complaint was about to be spoken, which particular request was most important. And I learned something about the measure of my neighbors by their preferred method of payment: by the job, by the month—or not at all.

2   Mr. Ballou fell into the last category, and he always had a reason why. On one day he had no change for a fifty, on another he was flat out of checks, on another, he was simply out when I knocked on his door. Still, except for the money part, he was a nice enough old guy, always waving or tipping his hat when he'd see me from a distance. I figured him for a thin retirement check, maybe a work-related injury that kept him from doing his own yard work. Sure, I kept a running total, but I didn't worry about the amount too much. Grass was grass, and the little that Mr. Ballou's property comprised didn't take long to trim.

°**muted**
soft

3   Then, one late afternoon in mid-July, the hottest time of the year, I was walking by his house and he opened the door, motioned me to come inside. The hall was cool, shaded, and it took my eyes a minute to adjust to the muted° light.

4   "I owe you," Mr. Ballou began, "but . . ."

5   I thought I'd save him the trouble of thinking up a new excuse. "No problem. Don't worry about it."

6   "The bank made a mistake in my account," he continued, ignoring my words. "It will be cleared up in a day or two. But in the meantime I thought perhaps you could choose one or two volumes for a down payment."

7   He gestured toward the walls and I saw that books were stacked everywhere. It was like a library, except with no order to the arrangement.

8   "Take your time," Mr. Ballou encouraged. "Read, borrow, keep. Find something you like. What do you read?"

9   "I don't know." And I didn't. I generally read what was in front of me, what I could snag from the paperback rack at the drugstore, what I found at the library, magazines, the back of cereal boxes, comics. The idea of consciously seeking out a special title was new to me, but, I realized, not without appeal—so I browsed through the piles of books.

10   "You actually read all of these?"

11   "This isn't much," Mr. Ballou said. "This is nothing, just what I've kept, the ones worth looking at a second time."

12 "Pick for me, then."

13 He raised his eyebrows, cocked his head, regarded me appraisingly° as though measuring me for a suit. After a moment, he nodded, searched through a stack, and handed me a dark red hard-bound book, fairly thick.

14 *"The Last of the Just,"* I read. "By André Schwarz-Bart. What's it about?"

15 "You tell me," he said. "Next week."

16 I started after supper, sitting outdoors on an uncomfortable kitchen chair. Within a few pages, the yard, the summer, disappeared, the bright oblivion° of adolescence temporarily lifted, and I was plunged into the aching tragedy of the Holocaust, the extraordinary clash of good, represented by one decent man, and evil. Translated from French, the language was elegant, simple, overwhelming. When the evening light finally failed I moved inside, read all through the night.

17 To this day, thirty years later, I vividly remember the experience. It was my first voluntary encounter with world literature, and I was stunned by the undiluted power a novel could contain. I lacked the vocabulary, however, to translate my feelings into words, so the next week, when Mr. Ballou asked, "Well?" I only replied, "It was good."

18 "Keep it, then," he said. "Shall I suggest another?"

19 I nodded, and was presented with the paperback edition of Margaret Mead's *Coming of Age in Samoa.*°

20 To make two long stories short, Mr. Ballou never paid me a dime for cutting his grass that year or the next, but for fifteen years I taught anthropology at Dartmouth College. Summer reading was not the innocent pastime I had assumed it to be, not a breezy, instantly forgettable escape in a hammock (though I've since enjoyed many of those, too). A book, if it arrives before you at the right moment, in the proper season, at a point of intermission° in the daily business of things, will change the course of all that follows.

°**appraisingly** with the intention of making a judgment

°**oblivion** total forgetfulness of the world around

°*Coming of Age in Samoa* groundbreaking 1925 study of adolescent behavior in the South Pacific

°**intermission** a period between events

Questions **for Critical Thinking**

1. The author uses narration as his method of developing ideas about the importance of reading. He orders the material by presenting a sequence of events. Summarize this narrative by listing the sequence of events. (Do not quote the conversations in the essay.)

2. Review paragraphs 2 through 6 of the essay and decide why Mr. Ballou could not (or would not) pay Michael Dorris. Do you think he did not have enough money, or was he unwilling to spend money on something other than books?

3. What were the author's reading habits before his encounter with Mr. Ballou? What do you think his reading habits were after this summer experience?

4. The second book Mr. Ballou gave the author was the anthropologist Margaret Mead's *Coming of Age in Samoa,* a book often assigned in college anthropology courses. In the next sentence, Michael Dorris tells us that "for fifteen years I taught anthropology at Dartmouth College." What connection does the writer want us to make?

5. When is it appropriate or acceptable for a person to repay a financial debt not with money but with some other form of repayment, either in goods or in services? When is it not a good idea to try to settle a debt in this way?

6. In the first paragraph, the writer relates how he received no payment from some of his customers, and in the concluding paragraph returns to the idea that Mr. Ballou never gave him any money for mowing his lawn. The writer did, nevertheless, get paid. Explain.

Writing **in Response**

1. In this story an adolescent has a summer job that turns out to change his life. Write an essay in which you tell the story of yourself or someone else you know who had a part-time job while going to school. What happened? Were any lessons learned? You may want to use dialogue as part of your narration.

2. Write an essay in which you tell a story about a person in your neighborhood, a friend, or a relative. Remember that you will be relating a specific incident or a series of events to make a point. Your point might be what you learned from observing what happened to the person.

3. Michael Dorris concludes his essay by noting that if you come across a book "at the right moment," it could change the direction of your life. Write a narrative essay in which you tell the story of a life-changing event.

My Daughter Smokes

Alice Walker

Not everything passed down in a family from one generation to another is a positive inheritance. Alice Walker, the prize-winning author of *The Color Purple* and many other fiction and nonfiction works, deals with a deadly tradition in her family in the following autobiographical essay. Alice Walker was born in Georgia in 1944, the youngest of eight children. Her parents were sharecroppers. This essay not only draws on her Georgia childhood but also focuses on the next generation of her family. It shows us the writer's profound worldview and historical insights.

1   My daughter smokes. While she is doing her homework, her feet on the bench in front of her and her calculator clicking out answers to her algebra problems. I am looking at the half-empty package of Camels tossed carelessly close at hand. Camels. I pick them up, take them into the kitchen, where the light is better, and study them—they're filtered, for which I am grateful. My heart feels terrible. I want to weep. In fact, I do weep a little, standing there by the stove holding one of the instruments, so white, so precisely rolled, that could cause my daughter's death. When she smoked Marlboros and Players I hardened myself against feeling so bad; nobody I knew ever smoked these brands.

2   She doesn't know this, but it was Camels that my father, her grandfather, smoked. But before he smoked "ready-mades"—when he was very young and very poor, with eyes like lanterns—he smoked Prince Albert tobacco in cigarettes he rolled himself. I remember the bright-red tobacco tin, with a picture of Queen Victoria's° consort,° Prince Albert, dressed in a black frock coat and carrying a cane.

°**Queen Victoria**
queen of England, 1837–1901

°**consort**
the spouse of a king or queen

3   The tobacco was dark brown, pungent,° slightly bitter. I tasted it more than once as a child, and the discarded tins could be used for a number of things: to keep buttons and shoelaces in, to store seeds, and best of all, to hold worms for the rare times my father took us fishing.

°**pungent**
sharp and penetrating

4   By the late forties and early fifties no one rolled his own anymore (and few women smoked) in my hometown, Eatonton, Georgia. The tobacco industry, coupled with Hollywood movies in which both hero and heroine smoked like chimneys, won over completely people like my father, who were hopelessly addicted to cigarettes. He never looked as dapper° as Prince Albert, though; he continued to look like a poor, overweight, overworked colored man with too large a family; black, with a very white cigarette stuck in his mouth.

°**dapper**
stylish

5   I do not remember when he started to cough. Perhaps it was unnoticeable at first. A little hacking in the morning as he lit his first cigarette upon getting out of bed. By the time I was my daughter's age, his breath was a wheeze, embarrassing to hear; he could not climb stairs without resting every third or fourth step. It was not unusual for him to cough for an hour.

6   It is hard to believe there was a time when people did not understand that cigarette smoking is an addiction. I wondered aloud once to my sister—who is perennially° trying to quit—whether our father realized this. I wondered how she, a smoker since high school, viewed her own habit.

°**perennially**
continually; regularly

7   It was our father who gave her her first cigarette, one day when she had taken water to him in the fields.

8   "I always wondered why he did that," she said, puzzled, and with some bitterness.

9   "What did he say?" I asked.

10   "That he didn't want me to go to anyone else for them," she said, "which never really crossed my mind."

11   So he was aware it was addictive, I thought, though as annoyed as she that he assumed she would be interested.

12   I began smoking in eleventh grade, also the year I drank numerous bottles of terrible sweet, very cheap wine. My friends and I, all boys for this venture, bought our supplies from a man who ran a segregated bar and liquor store on the outskirts of town. Over the entrance there was a large sign that said colored. We were not permitted to drink there, only to buy. I smoked Kools, because my sister did. By then I thought her toxic darkened lips and gums glamorous. However, my body simply would not tolerate smoke. After six months I had a chronic° sore throat. I gave up smoking, gladly. Because it was a ritual with my buddies—Murl, Leon, and "Dog" Farley—I continued to drink wine.

°**chronic**
lasting a long time

13   My father died from "the poor man's friend," pneumonia, one hard winter when his bronchitis and emphysema had left him low. I doubt he had much lung left at all, after coughing for so many years. He had so little breath that, during his last years, he was always leaning on something. I remember once, at a family reunion, when my daughter was two, that my father picked her up for a minute—long enough for me to photograph them—but the effort was obvious. Near the very end of his life, and largely because he had no more lungs, he quit smoking. He gained a couple of pounds, but by then he was so emaciated° no one noticed.

°**emaciated**
unhealthily thin

14   When I travel to Third World countries I see many people like my father and daughter. There are large billboards directed at them both: the tough, "take-charge," or dapper older man, the glamorous, "worldly" young woman, both puffing away. In these poor countries, as in American ghettos and on reservations, money that should be spent for food goes instead to the tobacco companies; over time, people starve themselves of both food and air, effectively weakening and addicting their children, eventually eradicating° themselves. I read in the newspaper and in my gardening magazine that cigarette butts are so toxic that if a baby swallows one, it is likely to die, and that the boiled water from a bunch of them makes an effective insecticide.

°**eradicating**
getting rid of completely

15   My daughter would like to quit, she says. We both know the statistics are against her; most people who try to quit smoking do not succeed.*

16   There is a deep hurt that I feel as a mother. Some days it is a feeling of futility.° I remember how carefully I ate when I was pregnant, how patiently I taught my daughter how to cross a street safely. For what, I sometimes wonder; so that she can wheeze through most of her life feeling half her strength, and then die of self-poisoning, as her grandfather did?

°**futility**
uselessness

17   But, finally, one must feel empathy for° the tobacco plant itself. For thousands of years, it has been venerated° by Native Americans as a sacred medicine. They have used it extensively—its juice, its leaves, its roots, its (holy) smoke—to heal wounds and cure diseases, and in ceremonies of prayer and peace. And though the plant as most of us know it has been poisoned by chemicals and denatured° by intensive mono-cropping° and is therefore hardly the plant it was,

°**empathy for**
identification with

°**venerated**
treated with deep respect

°**denatured**
having its natural
qualities changed

°**mono-cropping**
raising only one crop

*Three months after reading this essay my daughter stopped smoking.

still, to some modern Indians it remains a plant of positive power. I learned this when my Native American friends, Bill Wahpepah and his family, visited with me for a few days and the first thing he did was sow a few tobacco seeds in my garden.

18 Perhaps we can liberate tobacco from those who have captured and abused it, enslaving the plant on large plantations, keeping it from freedom and its kin, and forcing it to enslave the world. Its true nature suppressed, no wonder it has become deadly. Maybe by sowing a few seeds of tobacco in our gardens and treating the plant with the reverence it deserves, we can redeem tobacco's soul and restore its self-respect.

19 Besides, how grim, if one is a smoker, to realize one is smoking a slave.

20 There is a slogan from a battered women's shelter that I especially like: "Peace on earth begins at home." I believe everything does. I think of a slogan for people trying to stop smoking: "Every home a smoke-free zone." Smoking is a form of self-battering that also batters those who must sit by, occasionally cajole° or complain, and helplessly watch. I realize now that as a child I sat by, through the years, and literally watched my father kill himself; surely one such victory in my family, for the rich white men who own the tobacco companies, is enough.

°**cajole**
to gently urge

Questions for Critical Thinking

1. On the basis of the first paragraph of the essay, construct a sentence that could be the thesis for this essay. Although Alice Walker does not directly provide her thesis in one sentence, you can find her controlling idea by reviewing her introductory paragraph. What do you think is implied by the title and the first sentence?

2. Review the essay and determine how many members of Alice Walker's family figure in this story of their lives.

3. The art of narration usually includes a sequence of events to tell a story. What is the sequence of events in Alice Walker's story?

4. To achieve coherence in narrative pieces, writers need to use transitions of time. Review the essay and underline all the transitional expressions you can find.

5. In the final paragraph of her essay, Alice Walker quotes the slogan "Peace on earth begins at home," and she adds, "I believe everything does." With your classmates, make a list of the kinds of problems that are best solved in the home. What problems cannot be solved in the home and require outside intervention?

6. When Alice Walker remembers the Prince Albert tobacco tin, with its picture of the elegant royal prince, she observes that her father "never looked as dapper as Prince Albert." Examine advertisements for widely used products that you consider harmful or dangerous. In your view, how far from these advertising images are the facts about the product?

Writing in Response

1. Alice Walker describes a bad habit that has linked the generations of her family. Think about your own family. Looking back on your parents or grandparents and then considering yourself or your own children, can you find a habit (bad or good) that goes through more than one

generation? If so, write an essay in which you trace how a habit has been passed down from one generation to another. These might include eating habits, work habits, sleep habits, or leisure-time habits.

2. Alice Walker tells us in a footnote that three months after reading her mother's essay, the daughter stopped smoking. How might Alice Walker's essay have played a part in that daughter's decision to quit smoking? Write an essay in which you deal with one of the following:

   - What would it take to break a bad habit of your own?
   - What are the ways to help someone break a bad habit?
   - Why do so many people persist in behaviors they know to be self-destructive?

3. Write an essay in which you discuss the possibility that some products on the market today are later found harmful. Your essay could include discussions of several products, or you could concentrate on one product and discuss your reservations about its safety.

4. Alice Walker gave up cigarettes because her throat hurt, but she continued to drink wine as a "ritual" with her "buddies." We all know that teenagers are likely to engage in harmful activities as a result of peer pressure. Tell a story from your experience that relates how one person you have known handled peer pressure.

The Paterson Public Library

Judith Ortiz Cofer

Places and events that shape our childhoods can create mixed memories for us as adults. For Judith Ortiz Cofer her experiences growing up in Paterson, New Jersey, made for both positive and negative recollections. Born in Hormigueros, Puerto Rico, in 1952, the young girl moved with her family to Paterson four years later; she would divide her time between the United States and Puerto Rico for the rest of her childhood. Eventually she attended college in Georgia and obtained an MA degree from Florida Atlantic University. The following essay shows the writer using her personal experience in her work. As one commentator has noted, "There is a strong island presence in her narratives, and the authenticity with which she captures life on the island is as powerful as her descriptions of the harsh realities of the Paterson community."

1   It was a Greek temple in the ruins of an American city. To get to it I had to walk through neighborhoods where not even the carcasses of rusted cars on blocks nor the death traps of discarded appliances were parted with, so that the yards of the borderline poor, people who lived not in a huge building, as I did, but in their own decrepit little houses, looked like a reversed archaeological site, **incongruous**° next to the pillared palace of the Paterson Public Library.

°**incongruous**
not fitting in; not in harmony

2   The library must have been built during Paterson's boom years as the model industrial city of the North. Enough marble was used in its construction to have kept several Michelangelos busily satisfied for a lifetime. Two roaring lions, taller than a grammar school girl, greeted those brave enough to seek answers there. Another memorable detail about the **façade**° of this important place to me was the phrases carved deeply into the walls—perhaps the immortal words of Greek philosophers—I could not tell, since I was developing **astigmatism**° at that time and could only make out the lovely geometric designs they made.

°**façade**
the face of a building

°**astigmatism**
a defect of the eye, resulting in blurred vision

3   All during the school week I both anticipated and feared the long walk to the library because it took me through enemy territory. The black girl Lorraine, who had chosen me to hate and terrorize with threats at school, lived in one of the gloomy little houses that circled the library like beggars. Lorraine would eventually carry out her violence against me by beating me up in a confrontation formally announced through the school grapevine so that for days I lived with a panic that has rarely been equaled in my adult life, since now I can get grown-ups to listen to me, and at that time disasters had to be a **fait accompli**° for a teacher or a parent to get involved. Why did Lorraine hate me? For reasons neither one of us fully understood at the time. All I remember was that our sixth grade teacher seemed to favor me, and her way of showing it was by having me tutor "slow" students in spelling and grammar. Lorraine, older and bigger than myself, since she was repeating the grade, was subjected to this ritual humiliation, which involved sitting in the hallway, obviously separated from the class— one of us for being smart, the other for the opposite reason. Lorraine resisted my efforts to teach her the basic rules of spelling. She would hiss her threats at me, addressing me as *You little spic*. Her hostility sent shudders through me. But baffling as it was, I also accepted it as inevitable. She would beat me up. I told my mother and the teacher, and they both reassured me in vague adult terms that a girl like Lorraine would not dare get in trouble again. She had a history of problems that made her a likely candidate for reform school. But Lorraine and I knew that the violence she **harbored**° had found a target: me—the skinny Puerto Rican girl whose father was away with the navy most of the time and whose mother did not speak English; I was the perfect choice.

°**fait accompli**
something already done

°**harbored**
held as a feeling

4   Thoughts like these occupied my mind as I walked to the library on Saturday mornings. But my need for books was strong enough to propel me down the dreary streets with their slush-covered sidewalks and the skinny trees of winter looking like dark figures from a distance: angry black girls waiting to attack me.

°**sanctuary**
a place of safety

5   But the sight of the building was enough to reassure me that sanctuary° was within reach. Inside the glass doors was the inexhaustible treasure of books, and I made my way through the stacks like the beggar invited to the wedding feast. I remember the musty, organic smell of the library, so different from the air outside. It was the smell of an ancient forest, and since the first books that I read for pleasure were fairy tales, the aroma of transforming wood suited me as a prop.

6   With my pink library card I was allowed to check out two books from the first floor—the children's section. I would take the full hour my mother had given me (generously adding fifteen minutes to get home before she sent my brother after me) to choose the books I would take home for the week. I made my way first through the world's fairy tales. Here I discovered that there is a Cinderella in every culture, that she didn't necessarily have the white skin and rosy cheeks Walt Disney had given her, and that the prince they all waited for could appear in any color, shape, or form. The prince didn't even have to be a man.

7   It was the way I absorbed fantasy in those days that gave me the sense of inner freedom, a feeling of power and the ability to fly that is the main reward of the writer. As I read those stories I became not only the characters but their creator. I am still fascinated by the idea that fairy tales and fables are part of humankind's collective unconscious°—a familiar theory that acquires concreteness in my own writing today, when I discover over and over that the character I create or the themes that recur in my poems and in my fiction are my own versions of the "types" I learned to recognize very early in my life in fairy tales.

°**collective unconscious**
according to Carl Jung,
a part of the human
memory all people share

°**decapitated**
beheaded

8   There was also violence in these stories: villains decapitated° in honorable battle, goblins and witches pursued, beaten, and burned at the stake by heroes with magic weapons, possessing the supernatural strength granted to the self-righteous in folklore. I understood those black-and-white duels between evil and justice. But Lorraine's blind hatred of my person and my knee-liquefying fear of her were not so clear to me at that time. It would be many years before I learned about the politics of race, before I internalized the awful reality of the struggle for territory that underscored the lives of blacks and Puerto Ricans in Paterson during my childhood. Each job given to a light-skinned Hispanic was one less job for a black man; every apartment leased to a Puerto Rican family was one less place available to blacks. Worst of all, though the Puerto Rican children had to master a new language in the schools and were often subjected to the scorn and impatience of teachers burdened with too many students making too many demands in a classroom, the blacks were obviously the ones singled out for "special" treatment. In other words, whenever possible they were assigned to special education classes in order to relieve the teacher's workload, mainly because their black English dialect sounded "ungrammatical" and "illiterate" to our white Seton Hall University and City College-educated instructors. I have on occasion become angry at being treated like I'm mentally deficient by persons who make that prejudgment upon hearing an unfamiliar accent. I can only imagine what it must have been like for children like Lorraine, whose skin color alone put her in a pigeonhole she felt she had to fight her way out of every day of her life.

9   I was one of the lucky ones; as an insatiable reader I quickly became more than adept at the use of the English language. My life as a navy brat, moving with my family from Paterson to Puerto Rico every few months as my father's tours of duty demanded, taught me to depend on knowledge as my main source of security. What I learned from books borrowed from the Greek temple among the ruins of the city I carried with me as the lightest of carry-on luggage. My teachers in both countries treated me well in general. The easiest way to become a teacher's pet, or *la favorita,* is to ask the teacher for books to read—and I was always looking for reading material. Even my mother's romantic novels by Corín Tellado and her *Buenhogar* (Spanish *Good Housekeeping* magazine) were not safe from my insatiable word hunger.

10   Since the days when I was stalked by Lorraine, libraries have always been an adventure for me. Fear of an ambush is no longer the reason why I feel my pulse quicken a little when I approach a library building, when I enter the stacks and inhale the familiar smell of old leather and paper. It may be the memory of the danger that heightens my senses, but it is really the expectation that I felt then and that I still feel now about books. They contained most of the information I needed to survive in two languages and in two worlds. When adults were too busy to answer my endless questions, I could always *look it up;* when I felt unbearably lonely, as I often did during those early gypsy years traveling with my family, I read to escape and also to connect: you can come back to a book as you cannot always to a person or place you miss. I read and reread favorite books until the characters seemed like relatives or friends I could see when I wanted or needed to see them.

11   I still feel that way about books. They represent my spiritual life. A library is my sanctuary, and I am always at home in one. It is not surprising that in recalling my first library, the Paterson Public Library, I have always described it as a temple.

12   Lorraine carried out her threat. One day after school, as several of our classmates, Puerto Rican and black, circled us to watch, Lorraine grabbed a handful of my long hair and forced me to my knees. Then she slapped my face hard enough that the sound echoed off the brick walls of the school building and ran off while I screamed at the sight of blood on my white knee socks and felt the throbbing on my scalp where I would have a bald spot advertising my shame for weeks to come.

13   No one intervened. To this crowd, it was one of many such violent scenes taking place among the adults and the children of people fighting over a rapidly shrinking territory. It happens in the jungle and it happens in the city. But another course of action other than "fight or flight" is open to those of us lucky enough to discover it, and that is channeling one's anger and energy into the development of a mental life. It requires something like obsessiveness for a young person growing up in an environment where physical labor and physical endurance are the marks of a survivor—as is the case with minority peoples living in large cities. But many of us do manage to discover books. In my case, it may have been what anthropologists call a cultural adaptation. Being physically small, non-English-speaking, and always the new kid on the block, I was forced to look for an alternative mode to survival in Paterson. Reading books empowered me.

14   Even now, a visit to the library recharges the batteries in my brain. Looking through the card catalog reassures me that there is no subject that I cannot investigate, no world I cannot explore. Everything that is is mine for the asking. Because I can read about it.

Questions **for Critical Thinking**

1. The essay begins with two paragraphs of description that are filled with sensory images. Review both paragraphs and underline each sensory image you can find. As you mark each image, note how the writer's description makes the neighborhood appear in sharp contrast to the library itself.

2. Although the writer clearly sees Lorraine as her enemy, she also shows a great deal of sympathy for her. In paragraph 8, what understanding does Judith Ortiz come to years later, as she looks back and remembers how Lorraine acted and what could have motivated her?

3. The author devotes much of her essay to an analysis of how much the love of reading has meant to her through the years. She describes it as her spiritual life. Review the essay and mark each place where the writer indicates a benefit that comes from reading. Why did she read as a child? What does reading mean to her now? How is it that some children develop a great interest in reading while others do not?

4. Narration usually includes a sequence of events with transitional expressions of time that help the reader move through the narrative. Review the essay and underline all the transitional expressions of *time* that you find.

5. In the essay, Lorraine clearly acts like a bully. Many children experience the terror of being bullied inside and outside of school. What should be done about a neighborhood (or school) bully? What are the dangers of not dealing with these children while they are still little?

Writing **in Response**

1. Write an essay in which you look back on your childhood experiences. Describe places that felt safe and secure and then describe the places that made you feel uncomfortable or even frightened.

2. The writer tells us that books enabled her to survive her childhood, and that exploring the library and learning to read independently empowered her. Discuss the importance that a book, a poem, a story, or even a short quotation or verse from a special book has had in your own life. How has this memorable reading empowered you or helped you survive a difficult situation?

3. Many Americans have a complex identity; that is, they must sometimes live in two worlds, moving between two cultures and two languages. Write an essay in which you discuss the advantages and disadvantages of living in more than one culture.

4. Write an essay that examines the reasons why some children become bullies or that examines the effects that bullying has on school children. Do you find any evidence of bullying in the actions of some adults?

Unforgettable Miss Bessie

Carl T. Rowan

Carl T. Rowan (1925–2000) enjoyed a long and distinguished career as a journalist, commentator, and high government official. Born in Tennessee, he attended college and graduate school before starting to work at the *Minneapolis Tribune* in 1948. He worked in the U.S. Department of State under presidents Kennedy and Johnson, serving as ambassador to Finland and later as director of the United States Information Agency. In 1965 he returned to newspaper work and broadcast journalism, where he was seen and heard on national television and radio. In 1991, he published his autobiography, *Breaking Barriers: A Memoir.*

°Beowulf
early English epic poem

1   She was only about five feet tall and probably never weighed more than 110 pounds, but Miss Bessie was a towering presence in the classroom. She was the only woman tough enough to make me read *Beowulf*° and think for a few foolish days that I liked it. From 1938 to 1942, when I attended Bernard High School in McMinnville, Tenn., she taught me English, history, civics—and a lot more than I realized.

2   I shall never forget the day she scolded me into reading *Beowulf.*

3   "But Miss Bessie," I complained, "I ain't much interested in it."

4   Her large brown eyes became daggerish slits. "Boy," she said, "how dare you say 'ain't' to me! I've taught you better than that."

5   "Miss Bessie," I pleaded, "I'm trying to make first-string end on the football team, and if I go around saying 'it isn't' and 'they aren't,' the guys are gonna laugh me off the squad."

6   "Boy," she responded, "you'll play football because you have guts. But do you know what *really* takes guts? Refusing to lower your standards to those of the crowd. It takes guts to say you've got to live and be somebody fifty years after all the football games are over."

7   I started saying "it isn't" and "they aren't," and I still made first-string end—and class valedictorian—without losing my buddies' respect.

8   During her remarkable 44-year career, Mrs. Bessie Taylor Gwynn taught hundreds of economically deprived black youngsters—including my mother, my brother, my sisters and me. I remember her now with gratitude and affection—especially in this era when Americans are so wrought-up about a "rising tide of mediocrity" in public education and the problems of finding competent, caring teachers. Miss Bessie was an example of an informed, dedicated teacher, a blessing to children and an asset to the nation.

9   Born in 1895, in poverty, she grew up in Athens, Ala., where there was no public school for blacks. She attended Trinity School, a private institution for blacks run by the American Missionary Association, and in 1911 graduated from the Normal School (a "super" high school) at Fisk University in Nashville. Mrs. Gwynn, the essence of pride and privacy, never talked about her years in Athens; only in the months before her death did she reveal that she had never attended Fisk University itself because she could not afford the four-year course.

10   At Normal School she learned a lot about Shakespeare, but most of all about the profound importance of education—especially for a people trying to move up from slavery. "What you put in your head, boy," she once said, "can never be pulled out by the Ku Klux Klan, the Congress or anybody."

°**Battle of Hastings**
important English battle of 1066
that established William of
Normandy as king

°**Magna Carta**
an English charter of political
rights, from 1215

°**Voltaire**
French writer and philosopher
(1694–1778)

°**Booker T. Washington**
African American educator
(1856–1915)

°**W. E. B. DuBois**
African American civil rights
leader, founder of the National
Association for the Advancement
of Colored People (NAACP)

°**prodded**
urged

°**vital**
essential

°**fret**
worry

°**Henry David Thoreau**
American writer (1817–1862)

°**Samuel Pepys**
famous English diary writer
(1633–1703)

°**William Cullen Bryant**
American poet (1794–1878)

°**immersed**
completely involved

°**simile**
a figure of speech that compares
two dissimilar things using the
words *like* or *as*

°**metaphor**
a figure of speech that compares
two dissimilar things

11 Miss Bessie's bearing of dignity told anyone who met her that she was "educated" in the best sense of the word. There was never a discipline problem in her classes. We didn't dare mess with a woman who knew about the Battle of Hastings,° the Magna Carta° and the Bill of Rights—and who could also play the piano.

12 This frail-looking woman could make sense of Shakespeare, Milton, Voltaire,° and bring to life Booker T. Washington° and W. E. B. DuBois.° Believing that it was important to know who the officials were that spent taxpayers' money and made public policy, she made us memorize the names of everyone on the Supreme Courts and in the President's Cabinet. It could be embarrassing to be unprepared when Miss Bessie said, "Get up and tell the class who Frances Perkins is and what you think about her."

13 Miss Bessie knew that my family, like so many others during the Depression, couldn't afford to subscribe to a newspaper. She knew we didn't even own a radio. Still, she prodded° me to "look out for your future and find some way to keep up with what's going on in the world." So I became a delivery boy for the Chattanooga *Times*. I rarely made a dollar a week, but I got to read a newspaper every day.

14 Miss Bessie noticed things that had nothing to do with schoolwork, but were vital° to a youngster's development. Once a few classmates made fun of my frayed, hand-me-down overcoat, calling me "Strings." As I was leaving school, Miss Bessie patted me on the back of that old overcoat and said, "Carl, never fret° about what you *don't* have. Just make the most of what you *do* have—a brain."

15 Among the things that I did not have was electricity in the little frame house that my father had built for $400 with his World War I bonus. But because of her inspiration, I spent many hours squinting beside a kerosene lamp reading Shakespeare and Thoreau,° Samuel Pepys° and William Cullen Bryant.°

16 No one in my family had ever graduated from high school, so there was no tradition of commitment to learning for me to lean on. Like millions of youngsters in today's ghettos and barrios, I needed the push and stimulation of a teacher who truly cared. Miss Bessie gave plenty of both, as she immersed° me in a wonderful world of similes,° metaphors° and even onomatopoeia.° She led me to believe that I could write sonnets as well as Shakespeare, or iambic-pentameter verse° to put Alexander Pope° to shame.

17 In those days the McMinnville school system was rigidly "Jim Crow," and poor black children had to struggle to put anything in their heads. Our high school was only slightly larger than the once-typical little red schoolhouse, and its library was outrageously inadequate—so small, I like to say, that if two students were in it and one wanted to turn a page, the other one had to step outside.

18 Negroes, as we were called then, were not allowed in the town library, except to mop floors or dust tables. But through one of those secret Old South arrangements between whites of conscience and blacks of stature, Miss Bessie kept getting books smuggled out of the white library. That is how she introduced me to the Brontës,° Byron, Coleridge, Keats° and Tennyson.° "If you don't read, you can't write, and if you can't write, you might as well stop dreaming," Miss Bessie once told me.

19 So I read whatever Miss Bessie told me to, and tried to remember the things she insisted that I store away. Forty-five years later, I can still recite her "truths to live by," such as Henry Wadsworth Longfellow's° lines from "The Ladder of Augustine":

°**onomatopoeia**
the sound of a word suggesting
its meaning as in *hiss* or *sizzle*

°**iambic-pentameter verse**
poetry of a particular meter

°**Alexander Pope**
English poet (1688–1744)

°**the Brontës**
family of 19th century British
novelists

°**Byron, Coleridge, Keats**
19th century British
Romantic poets

°**Tennyson**
British poet (1809–1892)

°**Henry Wadsworth
Longfellow**
American poet (1824–1884)

°**osmotic**
absorbing

°**rippled**
flowed out in little waves

The heights by great men reached and kept
Were not attained by sudden flight.
But they, while their companions slept,
Were toiling upward in the night.

20 Years later, her inspiration, prodding, anger, cajoling and almost osmotic° infusion of learning finally led to that lovely day when Miss Bessie dropped me a note saying, "I'm so proud to read your column in the Nashville *Tennessean*."

21 Miss Bessie was a spry 80 when I went back to McMinnville and visited her in a senior citizens' apartment building. Pointing out proudly that her building was racially integrated, she reached for two glasses and a pint of bourbon. I was momentarily shocked, because it would have been scandalous in the 1930s and '40s for word to get out that a teacher drank, and nobody had ever raised a rumor that Miss Bessie did.

22 I felt a new sense of equality as she lifted her glass to mine. Then she revealed a softness and compassion that I had never known as a student.

23 "I've never forgotten that examination day," she said, "when Buster Martin held up seven fingers, obviously asking you for help with question number seven, 'Name a common carrier.' I can still picture you looking at your exam paper and humming a few bars of 'Chattanooga Choo Choo.' I was so tickled, I couldn't punish either of you."

24 Miss Bessie was telling me, with bourbon-laced grace, that I never fooled her for a moment.

25 When Miss Bessie died in 1980, at age 85, hundreds of her former students mourned. They knew the measure of a great teacher: love and motivation. Her wisdom and influence had rippled° out across generations.

26 Some of her students who might normally have been doomed to poverty went on to become doctors, dentists and college professors. Many, guided by Miss Bessie's example, became public-school teachers.

27 "The memory of Miss Bessie and how she conducted her classroom did more for me than anything I learned in college," recalls Gladys Wood of Knoxville, Tenn., a highly respected English teacher who spent 43 years in the state's school system. "So many times, when I faced a difficult classroom problem, I asked myself, *How would Miss Bessie deal with this?* And I'd remember how she could handle it with laughter and love.

28 No child can get all the necessary support at home, and millions of poor children get *no* support at all. This is what makes a wise, educated, warm-hearted teacher like Miss Bessie so vital to the minds, hearts and souls of this country's children.

Questions for Critical Thinking

1. Carl Rowan's description of his beloved teacher Miss Bessie includes only a few physical descriptions of Miss Bessie. How many can you find? Why are these few details significant?

2. The picture we form of Miss Bessie is also created by the words that she spoke. Carl Rowan quotes Miss Bessie in several places in the essay. Find the important quotes that Carl Rowan remembers even now that he is an older man. Underline them. How might these quotes affect a person's life?

3. Carl Rowan uses many specific examples of the information he learned in Miss Bessie's class. Make a check beside the references he makes to historical people and events. Why do you think the writer included all this information?

4. When Miss Bessie pressured Carl Rowan into reading the ancient English poem *Beowulf,* she used her student's mistake in grammar to teach him another lesson. What was the lesson she taught him? What might one learn from reading literature or poetry from another time in history? In your opinion, was the lesson more important than what he could have learned from reading *Beowulf?*

5. In paragraph 5, Carl Rowan admits to his teacher that if he used proper grammar in front of other football players, they would laugh him off the team. To what extent is this a current attitude? In what circumstances is it not fashionable to be enthusiastic about learning?

Writing in Response

1. Speaking of the time in which he was raised, Carl Rowan tells us that his family could not afford "to subscribe to a newspaper" and "didn't even own a radio." Still, Miss Bessie urged him to "find some way to keep up with what's going on in the world." She was not a person to give up. What was Carl Rowan's solution to his inability to afford what he needed?

   In today's society, what are the best ways to keep up with "what's going on in the world"? If a person cannot afford to own the latest technology, what are the best ways to obtain the information that is available?

   Write an essay in which you give examples of several specific obstacles and how it is possible to overcome each one.

2. Write an essay of description in which your sensory images reveal the character of someone you have known. How did that person's character touch your life?

3. Our society is very concerned with acquiring money and possessions. Miss Bessie told Carl Rowan not to worry about "what you don't have. Just make the most of what you do have." Write an essay in which you describe three "things" you do have and how you intend to make the most of these talents or assets.

4. Carl Rowan observes that no child "can get all the necessary support at home." How much support should we expect a child to get at home? What kind of support should a child receive outside the home? Where can a child find such support? Write an essay in which you describe the support systems for children that already do or should exist in your community. How can we be assured that the children in a community are having their basic needs met?

5. In paragraph 6, Miss Bessie points to what should be most important to a person—to "be somebody fifty years after all the football games are over." Miss Bessie is taking the long view on the subject of "being somebody." How difficult is it for a young person to take such a long-term view? Is it asking too much to expect a young person to plan for the future? Write an essay that points out the reasons why so many youth do not plan for their futures.

A Day at the Theme Park

W. Bruce Cameron

W. Bruce Cameron began an Internet-based humor column in 1995, and within a year, he was the most widely read humorist on the World Wide Web. Four years later, he began his newspaper columns for the Denver, Colorado, *Rocky Mountain News.* His pieces had such wide appeal that he expanded some of them into a book, *8 Simple Rules for Dating My Teenage Daughter.* The book quickly became a bestseller and later became the basis of a television show, *8 Simple Rules.*

When the writer deals with problems that parents encounter while raising their children, he speaks from authority: W. Bruce Cameron is the father of three teenagers, two girls and a boy. The following essay, which originally appeared in the *Rocky Mountain News,* is clearly based on the author's personal experience. While his humor makes us smile, the essay carries with it an element of truth about how parents will make great sacrifices for the sake of their children.

°**endearing**
giving affection

°**utter**
complete

1   One of the most endearing° traits of children is their utter° trust that their parents provide them with all life's necessities, meaning food, shelter, and a weekend at a theme park.

2   A theme park is a sort of artificial vacation, a place where you can enjoy all your favorite pastimes at once, such as motion sickness and heat exhaustion. Adult tolerance for theme parks peaks at about an hour, which is how long it takes to walk from the parking lot to the front gate. You fork over an obscene amount of money to gain entrance to a theme park, though it costs nothing to leave (which is odd because you'd pay anything to escape). The two main activities in a theme park are (a) standing in line, and (b) sweating. The sun reflects off the concrete with a fiendish° lack of mercy. You're about to learn the boiling point of tennis shoes. Your hair is sunburned, and when a small child in front of you gestures with her hand she smacks you in the face with her cotton candy; now it feels like your cheeks are covered with carnivorous° sand.

°**fiendish**
cruel

°**carnivorous**
flesh eating

3   The ride your children have selected for you is a corkscrewing, stomach compressing roller coaster built by the same folks who manufactured the baggage delivery system at DIA.° Apparently the theme of this particular park is "Nausea." You sit down and are strapped in so tightly you can feel your shoulders grinding against your pelvis. Once the ride begins you are thrown about with such violence it reminds you of your teenager's driving. When the ride is over your children want to get something to eat, but first the ride attendants have to pry your fingers off the safety bar. "Open your eyes, please sir," they keep shouting. They finally persuade you to let go, though it seems a bit discourteous of them to have used pepper spray. Staggering, you follow your children to the Hot Dog Palace for some breakfast.

°**DIA**
Denver International Airport

4   Food at a theme park is so expensive it would be cheaper to just eat your own money. Your son's meal costs a day's pay and consists of items manufactured of corn syrup, which is sugar; sucrose, which is sugar; fructose, which is sugar; and sugar, which is sugar. He also consumes large quantities of what in dog food would be called "meat byproducts." When, after a couple of rides, he announces that he feels like he is going to throw up, you're very alarmed. Having seen this meal once, you're in no mood to see it again.

°**pummeling**
a beating

5   With the exception of that first pummeling,° you manage to stay off the rides all day, explaining to your children that it isn't good for you when your internal organs are forcibly rearranged. Now, though, they coax you back in line, promis-

°**acrophobia**
fear of heights

ing a ride that doesn't twist, doesn't hang you upside down like a bat, doesn't cause your brain to flop around inside your skull; it just goes up and then comes back down. That's it, Dad, no big deal. What they don't tell you is HOW it comes back down. You're strapped into a seat and pulled gently up into acrophobia,° the city falling away from you. Okay, not so bad, and in the conversation you're having with God you explain that you're thankful for the wonderful view but would really like to get down now.

6   And that's just how you descend: NOW. Without warning, you plummet to the ground in an uncontrolled free fall. You must be moving faster than the speed of sound because when you open your mouth, nothing comes out. Your life passes before your eyes, and your one regret is that you will not have an opportunity to punish your children for bringing you to this hellish place. Brakes cut in and you slam to a stop. You gingerly touch your face to confirm it has fallen off. "Wasn't that fun, Dad?" your kids ask. "Why are you kissing the ground?"

°**impervious**
unaffected

7   At the end of the day, you let your teenager drive home. (After the theme park, you are impervious° to fear.)

Questions for Critical Thinking

1. Is the purpose of this essay to inform, to persuade, or to entertain?

2. Explain what part of the one-sentence introduction is the topic.

3. What word could the writer have used for his controlling idea if he had wanted to reveal it in the beginning?

4. What one word in the two-sentence conclusion gives you the author's attitude toward theme parks and thus his controlling idea for this essay?

5. Choose a sensory image from each of the five body paragraphs (paragraphs 2–6) that you find especially humorous. Although humor is hard to analyze, try to explain why each image you have chosen caused you to be amused.

6. Underline the topic sentences of the body paragraphs.

Writing in Response

1. Many people have a dream to do something like go across the country on a motorcycle, visit Paris, or see the pyramids before they die. Write an essay that describes, either seriously or humorously, an activity that you want to do sometime during your lifetime.

2. In paragraph 2, the writer describes going to a theme park as "a sort of artificial vacation." Describe your idea of a "real" vacation.

3. We live in a permissive society. Write an essay that describes several situations in which a parent should say no.

4. Write an essay that describes a form of entertainment that you believe has become too expensive for the average person or family to enjoy.

5. Describe what you believe to be the best amusement or entertainment for children.

6. If you enjoy amusement parks, describe the three best rides you have ever been on.

My Heroes

Elizabeth Berg

Before she devoted herself to full-time writing, Elizabeth Berg worked in a number of professions, including that of a registered nurse. However, she came to the conclusion that writing was the most rewarding and creative outlet for her. Her success with fiction and nonfiction confirmed her choice. Her novel *Durable Goods,* published in 1993, was followed in 1997 by *Joy School.* Another novel, *Range of Motion,* appeared in 1995 and a television movie based on that story was produced five years later. A major theme in much of Elizabeth Berg's writing is the importance of celebrating the small things in life. As the author expresses it, "A lesson I learned from being a nurse is how important seemingly ordinary life is." Personal relationships are also at the center of much of this writer's fiction. The following essay shows her sensitivity to relationships among people and her focus on the common things of everyday life.

1   My eight-year-old daughter, Jenny, was given a school assignment not too long ago to write about a hero. "So who did you pick?" I asked her. I was imagining some possibilities: Rosa Parks, Christa McAuliffe, Sara Lee. But Jenny answered, "Laura."

2   "Who?" I asked.

3   "Laura," she said again.

4   "You mean your friend from across the street?" I asked.

5   "Yeah!" she said.

6   I was a little mystified. "How come you picked her?" I asked. "Because," Jenny answered in the ultrapatient° voice of Instructor of the Hopeless, "she is my hero."

°**ultrapatient**
extremely patient

7   "Oh," I said. "I see."

8   I must confess that at first I was disappointed. I thought that if her hero was only her friend, she had failed to appreciate the magnificent contributions that real heroes have made to the world. I thought I'd better go out that afternoon and buy some books about famous scientists, artists, athletes, world leaders. That would wise her up. Also, I'd have a look at what they were teaching her in school—didn't she have an appreciation for Martin Luther King?

9   But then I thought about who I would say my heroes are, and I realized that if I told the truth, they wouldn't be famous, either. For although it is undeniable that there have been outstanding people in history who have set glorious examples and inspired me mightily, the people who inspire me most tend to be those who touch me personally, and in quiet ways.

10   For example, I had an eighth-grade English teacher named Mrs. Zinz. She was demanding and rather straight-laced, I thought, but she taught us certain critical skills for reading and writing. She was concerned not only with what we learned but also with what we were becoming: She put a premium on honesty and tried to get us to understand why it was important. She insisted that we always do our best, and in her class, we almost always did. She told me that I was a terrific creative writer and encouraged my every effort.

11   As payment for all her good work, I, along with my evil best friend, tortured her. We laughed at her in class, tried to pit our other teachers against her by telling them how unfairly she graded, and once, in a moment of extreme obnoxiousness,° called her on the telephone over and over, only to hang up when she

°**obnoxiousness**
being very offensive

answered. Mrs. Zinz was no dummy. She knew who was calling her. In turn she called my mother, who insisted that I call Mrs. Zinz and apologize. With my face aflame, and between clenched teeth, I muttered a grossly insincere "Sorry." She accepted my apology warmly and with a style so graceful that I was infuriated all the more. And though I sulked every day in her class for the rest of the year, she never bowed by reacting to it. I got an A for the term. I moved soon after and lost track of Mrs. Zinz. I never did apologize in any legitimate way to her. Ironically, she is still an inspiration to me, a lesson in how not to lower yourself to someone else's level, even when that person is doing everything she can to make you crazy. She is, in that way, a hero.

12   My grandfather, known to me as "Papa," was also a hero of mine. For one thing, he made all of us grandchildren laugh all of the time. He told riddles that were viewed by us as the essence° of sophisticated humor. When he greeted us, he shook our hands enthusiastically and at great length, shouting, "How do! How do!" We used to line up and sit on his lap and watch him pop his dentures in and out of his mouth, an astounding feat that thrilled and terrified us—especially before we realized that the teeth were false. He was unfailingly warm and kind and knew how to make a friend out of a stranger; he loved people. I saw him as a man who felt light inside, happy; and feeling that way is no small task in a world that often seems intent on taking two back for every one you get.

°**essence**
the fundamental quality

13   Then there is my mother-in-law, Sylvia, who at the age of retirement went back to school to pursue a lifetime dream: getting a college diploma. She bumped her bifocals into microscopes, suffered verbal abuse at the hands of an insensitive computer instructor, got used to being the last one to finish every exam, and worried about homework on weekends when she could have been luxuriating° in the fact that she had nothing to do. She says that she learned an awful lot, but if you ask me, it's she who did the teaching. I am honored that our family has her love of learning to inspire us.

°**luxuriating**
enjoying with great pleasure

14   Beyond that, there are people who are heroes to me because of what they do: mail carriers, who, on days when I stay inside hiding from the cold or heat, subject themselves to hours of it; nurses, who care for those who can't care for themselves every second of every day. I admire stay-at-home mothers for their patience and their creativity in the face of almost no thanks or recognition, and working mothers for the way they juggle an awesome load of responsibilities.

15   There are people with chronic illness, for whom getting through each day is heroic. There are people who have married for sixty years, who have lessons to teach us all. There are those who are strong enough in heart and in spirit to speak up when something feels wrong to them, to go against the majority, and oftentimes to risk themselves for the sake of others. And then there are those whom I admire most: people who seem to have found the secret of calm and can relinquish° the race for the pleasure of seeing what's around them, right here, right now.

°**relinquish**
give up

16   I was thinking about all this when I saw Jenny and Laura come into the house. I wanted to know a little more about what had precipitated° Jenny's calling Laura a hero. Was it her sharing her brand-new toys? Being there to listen, to soothe, to make better a bad situation in the way that only good friends can? Well, as it happens, no. Jenny told me that Laura was her hero because Laura had saved her from drowning in a creek. "*What?*" I yelled.

°**precipitated**
made to happen

17   Laura rolled her eyes. "Jenny, the water was only about an inch deep." Jenny shrugged and said, "So? You still saved me."

18   Laura and I let pass a certain look between us. Then she and Jenny went outside again to play.

19   If you're smart, I thought, you gratefully take your heroes where you find them. As it happens, they are everywhere. So what if the water was only an inch deep? Someone was there, caring about Jenny and showing that she did, a safe hand stretched out to another who was in trouble. This seemed heroic indeed, and later that night when I was tucking her in, I told Jenny that I thought her choice was perfect. "I know," she yawned. "Good night."

Questions **for Critical Thinking**

1.   You have to read more than one paragraph of this piece to find the writer's thesis statement. Underline what you believe is the thesis statement.

2.   Choose one of the following introductory patterns as the best description of the introductory pattern used for this essay:
   a.   a general subject is narrowed down into a more specific topic
   b.   a well-known expression or familiar quotation is used
   c.   a definition of the concept to be discussed is given
   d.   a brief anecdote introduces the topic
   e.   classification indicates how the topic fits into a larger class

3.   In which paragraph does the author list several examples in a single sentence?

4.   In this essay of illustration, mark each example provided by the author. Circle transitions that signal an example.

5.   Explain how the essay comes full circle. Where does the conclusion begin?

Writing **in Response**

1.   One of the author's heroes was a grade school teacher, Mrs. Zinz, who showed the young student how to act with dignity. Write an essay giving examples of lessons you have learned from teachers who provided more than academic instruction.

2.   In paragraph 13, the author describes how her mother-in-law returns to school at a time in her life when she did not have to do so. Write an essay that gives examples of how some people continue to learn (whether they go back to school or not).

3.   Write an essay that gives examples of how retired people can still be productive and useful to society.

4.   Write an essay that gives examples of people whose heroic struggles with illnesses demand courage to get through every day.

America's Gambling Craze

James Popkin
with Katia Hetter

Gambling used to be classified as a vice, something to be warned against and eliminated. In recent years, however, many institutions in our society have welcomed the revenues that gambling can produce. The issue of gambling evokes strong feelings pro and con, as people argue the benefits and drawbacks of gambling in our society. In the following essay, we are given many different facts and statistics about gambling. This information educates us about a topic that remains controversial today.

1   No one howled in protest last month when H&R Block set up makeshift tax-preparation offices in four Nevada casinos and offered gamblers same-day "refund-anticipation loans." And few people cared recently when a Florida inventor won a U.S. patent that could someday enable television audiences to legally bet on game shows, football games, and even beauty pageants from their homes.

2   What's the deal? Not that long ago, Americans held gambling in nearly the same esteem as heroin dealing and applauded when ax-wielding police paid a visit to the corner dice room. But moral outrage has become as outmoded as a penny slot machine. In 1955, for example, baseball commissioner Ford Frick considered wagering so corrupt he prohibited major leaguers from overnighting in Las Vegas. Last year, by contrast, Americans for the first time made more trips to casinos than they did to Major League ballparks—some 92 million trips, according to one study.

3   It took six decades for gambling to become America's Pastime, from the legalization of Nevada casinos in 1931 to April Fool's Day 1991, when Davenport, Iowa, launched the Diamond Lady, the nation's first legal riverboat casino. The gradual creation of 37 state lotteries broke down the public's mistrust, conveying a clear message that the government sanctioned° gambling; indeed, is even coming to depend on it as a tax-revenue source. Corporate ownership of casinos helped in its own way, too, replacing shady operators with trusted brand names like Hilton and MGM. Casinos now operate or are authorized in 23 states, and 95 percent of all Americans are expected to live within a three- or four-hour drive of one by the year 2000.

°**sanctioned**
gave approval to

4   Today, the Bible Belt might as well be renamed the Blackjack Belt, with floating and land-based casinos throughout Mississippi and Louisiana and plans for more in Florida, Texas, Alabama and Arkansas. Meanwhile, the Midwest is overrun with slot hogs, none of the porcine variety.° Iowa, Illinois, Indiana and Missouri allow riverboat gambling, and a 50,000-square-foot land-based casino is scheduled to open in mid-May just outside Detroit, in Windsor, Ontario. Low-stakes casinos attract visitors to old mining towns in Colorado and South Dakota, and Indian tribes operate 225 casinos and high-stakes bingo halls nation-wide. Add church bingo, card rooms, sports wagering, dog and horse racing, and jai alai° to the mix and it becomes clear why Americans legally wagered $330 billion in 1992—a 1,800 percent increase over 1976.

°**slot hogs, none of the porcine variety**
slot machines (that greedily consume money), not actual pigs

°**jai alai**
a fast game similar to handball, played on a walled court

5   Like the first bars that opened after Prohibition,° modern gambling halls are enormously successful. "It will be impossible not to make a lot of money," one executive in New Orleans bragged before his casino had even opened. "It's like spitting and missing the floor." Such boasts—and the real possibility that the boom will create 500,000 jobs nationwide this decade—have not been lost on federal, state, and local lawmakers. In the first six weeks of this year alone they introduced more than 200 bills regarding gambling.

°**Prohibition**
the period from 1920 to 1930 in the United States, when all alcoholic beverages were forbidden

6   But casinos and lotteries may not guarantee the jackpots many politicians expect. When urban-planning professor Robert Goodman reviewed the economic-impact studies that 14 government agencies relied upon before deciding to embrace casino gambling, he found that most were written with a pro-industry spin and only four were balanced and factored in° gambling's hidden costs. Goodman's two-year study, due out next week, concludes that newly opened casinos "suck money out of the local economy," away from existing movie theaters, car dealerships, clothing shops and sports arenas. In Atlantic City, for example, about 100 of 250 local restaurants have closed since the casinos debuted in 1978, says Goodman, who teaches at the University of Massachusetts at Amherst.

°factored in
considered as elements

7   States that get hooked on gambling revenues soon suffer withdrawal symptoms when local competition kicks in. Although pioneering casinos and lotteries typically are profitable, gambling grosses decline when lotteries or casinos open in neighboring states. In Biloxi, Mississippi, for example, slot revenues at first topped about $207 per machine per day. A year later when competitors moved in, however, the daily win-per-machine figure dipped to $109.

8   States frequently overestimate the financial impact of gambling revenues, too. "Legalized gambling is never large enough to solve any social problems," says gambling-law professor and paid industry consultant I. Nelson Rose. In New Jersey, for example, horse racing alone accounted for about 10 percent of state revenue in the 1950s. Today, despite the addition of a lottery and 12 casinos, the state earns only 6 percent of its revenue through gambling. "Atlantic City used to be a slum by the sea," says Rose. "Now it's a slum by the sea with casinos."

9   America's love affair with dice and cards has always been a fickle romance, and some academics predict a breakup soon. Legalized gambling in America has been running on a 70-year boom-and-bust cycle since the colonists started the first lotteries. "We're now riding the third wave of legal gambling" that began with the Depression, says Rose, who has written extensively on the subject and teaches at Whittier Law School in Los Angeles. The trend self-destructs after a few decades, when the public simply gets fed up and embraces more conservative values. Rose believes a cheating or corruption scandal will trigger the next crash in about 35 years, an idea that most casino officials think is ludicrous.

10   The sky is not falling yet. Apart from a handful of academics and the odd politician, few Americans are seriously questioning the morality of an industry that is expected to help gamblers lose a record $35 billion in 1995 alone. Religious leaders have been oddly silent, perhaps because so many churches and synagogues rely on bingo revenues. "The biggest things we have to help people are churches and temples and the government," says Arnie Wexler, executive director of the Council on Compulsive Gambling of New Jersey. "And now they're all in the gambling business."

11   The consequences can be damaging. Wexler says he got a phone call late last week from a man in his 70s who ran up $150,000 in debt just by buying lottery tickets. Although most gambling experts believe that only 1 percent to 3 percent of Americans have a serious gambling problem at any given time, a July 1993 Gallup Poll funded by Wexler's group suggests that the figure may be closer to 5 percent. Regardless, now that casinos are no longer located just in Atlantic City and Nevada it's reasonable to assume that the total number of problem gamblers will soar. "If you put a guy who wouldn't cheat on his wife in a room with a gorgeous nude woman, some guys would fall by the wayside," Wexler says. "When you make gambling legal and socially acceptable, people will try it and some of them will get hooked."

12   But try telling that to a gambler happily feeding a slot machine and waiting for a multimillion-dollar payoff. Fifty-one percent of American adults now find casino gambling "acceptable for anyone," and 35 percent describe it as "acceptable for others but not for me," according to a recent Yankelovich Inc. survey paid for by Harrah's Casinos. The attraction is simple. "The action for them is the thrill of what's going to happen in the next pull of that slot-machine handle," explains Harrah's president, Phil Satre.

Questions for Critical Thinking

1. The purpose for an essay may be to entertain, to inform, or to persuade. Which of these do you believe is the authors' purpose?

2. The first paragraph does not present the thesis. Instead, it gives us two examples of how American attitudes about gambling have changed. After reading the essay, write what you believe is the authors' thesis.

3. Read paragraph 4. Write a topic sentence that expresses the main idea of this paragraph.

4. Most good writing includes illustrations of some kind to support the points being made. This essay is composed of one example after another. Go through the essay and find the four times the authors indicate an example by using the expression "for example."

5. Starting in paragraph 6, the authors use quotations from experts to support their points. Each person's qualification or position is carefully indicated within the text. Fill out the following chart to summarize these examples.

Name of expert	Title/position	Idea presented in the quotation
1.		
2.		
3.		
4.		

6. What are the major points the authors make about gambling? Be careful not to confuse main ideas with detailed examples.

Writing in Response

1. Write an essay in which you present your personal position on gambling. Do you recognize different levels of gambling, or do all forms of gambling

seem the same to you? For example, is buying a lottery ticket the same as gambling in a casino?

2. Gambling revenues are widely advertised as helping communities pay for education and other needed social improvements. In many cases, this has not happened. Write an essay about a situation, an organization, or an activity that is supposed to offer a solution to a social problem but actually creates other, possibly more serious problems.

3. In paragraph 2, the authors explain how in the past gambling was seen as a vice. People felt a "moral outrage" when they encountered any kind of gambling. What situation, practice, or failure in our society causes a feeling of "moral outrage" in you? Write an essay in which you argue your position on this topic.

4. Over the years, people's attitudes toward certain social issues have changed. Gambling is just one example of such an issue. Identify one of the changes that you have observed in our society. Present an argument that this change has been for the good or the bad.

On Writing

Stephen King

Stephen King was born in Portland, Maine, in 1947. He tells us that wrote his earliest piece when he was only seven years old; by the time he was twelve, he was submitting his stories to magazines. It was not until he was eighteen, however, that he placed his first short story. King worked as a janitor, as a laborer in an industrial laundry, and as a worker in a New England knitting mill while he practiced his writing. His initial attempt at a full-length novel made him so discouraged he threw the manuscript into the garbage. His wife rescued it, however, and suggested that he expand his story. The result was *Carrie,* a novel that achieved wide success and later was made into a popular movie. Stephen King has published many short stories, novels, and screenplays. The following essay is taken from his book *On Writing: A Memoir of the Craft* published in 2000.

1   If you want to be a writer, you must do two things above all others: read a lot and write a lot. There's no way around these two things that I'm aware of, no shortcut.

2   I'm a slow reader, but I usually get through seventy or eighty books a year, mostly fiction. I don't read in order to study the craft; I read because I like to read. It's what I do at night, kicked back in my blue chair. Similarly, I don't read fiction to study the art of fiction, but simply because I like stories. Yet there is a learning process going on. Every book you pick up has its own lesson or lessons, and quite often the bad books have more to teach than the good ones.

3   When I was in the eighth grade, I happened upon a paperback novel by Murray Leinster, a science fiction pulp writer who did most of his work during the forties and fifties, when magazines like *Amazing Stories* paid a penny a word. I had read other books by Mr. Leinster, enough to know that the quality of his writing was uneven. This particular tale, which was about mining in the asteroid belt,° was one of his less successful efforts. Only that's too kind. It was terrible, actually, a story populated by paper-thin characters and driven by outlandish° plot developments. Worst of all (or so it seemed to me at the time), Leinster had fallen in love with the word *zestful.*

4   Characters watched the approach of ore-bearing asteroids with *zestful smiles.* Characters sat down to supper aboard their mining ship with *zestful anticipation.* Near the end of the book, the hero swept the large-breasted blonde heroine into a *zestful embrace.* For me, it was the literary equivalent of a smallpox vaccination: I have never, so far as I know, used the word *zestful* in a novel or a story. God willing, I never will.

5   *Asteroid Miners* (which wasn't the title, but that's close enough) was an important book in my life as a reader. Almost everyone can remember losing his or her virginity, and most writers can remember the first book he/she put down thinking: *I can do better than this. Hell, I* am *doing better than this!* What could be more encouraging to the struggling writer than to realize his/her work is unquestionably better than that of someone who actually got paid for his/her stuff?

6   One learns most clearly what not to do by reading bad prose—one novel like *Asteroid Miners* (or *Valley of the Dolls, Flowers in the Attic,* and *The Bridges of Madison County,* to name just a few) is worth a semester at a good writing school, even with the superstar guest lecturers thrown in.

7   Good writing, on the other hand, teaches the learning writer about style, graceful narration, plot development, the creation of believable characters, and

°**asteroid belt**
a ring of minor planets revolving around the sun, located mainly between Mars and Jupiter

°**outlandish**
bizarre or strange

°*The Grapes of Wrath*
novel by John Steinbeck

°**spur**
an incentive or stimulus

°**goading**
urging or stimulating

°**nostalgia**
a longing for the past

°**Byzantine**
very complicated or involved

°**aerobic**
physically fit

°**aspiring**
working toward

truth-telling. A novel like *The Grapes of Wrath*° may fill a new writer with feelings of despair and good old-fashioned jealousy—"I'll never be able to write anything that good, not if I live to be a thousand"—but such feelings can also serve as a spur,° goading° the writer to work harder and aim higher. Being swept away by a combination of great story and great writing—of being flattened, in fact—is part of every writer's necessary formation. You cannot hope to sweep someone else away by the force of your writing until it has been done to you.

8   So we read to experience the mediocre and the outright rotten; such experience helps us to recognize those things when they begin to creep into our own work, and to steer clear of them. We also read in order to measure ourselves against the good and the great, to get a sense of all that can be done. And we read in order to experience different styles.

9   You may find yourself adopting a style you find particularly exciting, and there's nothing wrong with that. When I read Ray Bradbury as a kid, I wrote like Ray Bradbury—everything seemed green and wondrous and seen through a lens smeared with the grease of nostalgia.° When I read James M. Cain, everything I wrote came out clipped and stripped and hard-boiled. When I read Lovecraft, my prose became luxurious and Byzantine.° I wrote stories in my teenage years where all these styles merged, creating a kind of hilarious stew. This sort of stylistic blending is a necessary part of developing one's own style, but it doesn't occur in a vacuum. You have to read widely, constantly refining (and redefining) your own work as you do so. It's hard for me to believe that people who read very little (or not at all in some cases) should presume to write and expect people to like what they have written, but I know it's true. If I had a nickel for every person who ever told me he/she wanted to become a writer but "didn't have time to read," I could buy myself a pretty good steak dinner. Can I be blunt on this subject? If you don't have time to read, you don't have the time (or the tools) to write. Simple as that.

10   Reading is the creative center of a writer's life. I take a book with me everywhere I go, and find there are all sorts of opportunities to dip in. The trick is to teach yourself to read in small sips as well as in long swallows. Waiting rooms were made for books—of course! But so are theater lobbies before the show, long and boring checkout lines, and everyone's favorite, the john. You can even read while you're driving, thanks to the audiobook revolution. Of the books I read each year, anywhere from six to a dozen are on tape. As for all the wonderful radio you will be missing, come on—how many times can you listen to Deep Purple sing "Highway Star"?

11   Reading at meals is considered rude in polite society, but if you expect to succeed as a writer, rudeness should be the second-to-least of your concerns. The least of all should be polite society and what it expects. If you intend to write as truthfully as you can, your days as a member of polite society are numbered, anyway.

12   Where else can you read? There's always the treadmill, or whatever you use down at the local health club to get aerobic.° I try to spend an hour doing that every day, and I think I'd go mad without a good novel to keep me company. Most exercise facilities (at home as well as outside it) are now equipped with TVs, but TV—while working out or anywhere else—really is about the last thing an aspiring° writer needs. If you feel you must have the news analyst blowhards on CNN while you exercise, or the stock market blowhards on MSNBC, or the sports blowhards on ESPN, it's time for you to question how serious you really are about becoming a writer. You must be prepared to do some serious turning inward toward the life of imagination, and that means, I'm afraid, that Geraldo, Keith Olbermann, and Jay Leno must go. Reading takes time, and the glass teat° takes too much of it.

°**teat**
a nipple

13   Once weaned from the ephemeral° craving for TV, most people will find they enjoy the time they spend reading. I'd like to suggest that turning off that endlessly quacking box is apt to improve the quality of your life as well as the quality of your writing. And how much of a sacrifice are we talking here? How many *Frasier* and *ER* reruns does it take to make one American life complete? How many Richard Simmons infomercials? How many whiteboy/fatboy Beltway insiders on CNN? Oh man, don't get me started. Jerry-Springer-Dr.-Dre-Judge-Judy-Jerry-Falwell-Donny-and-Marie, I rest my case.

°**ephemeral**
lasting a short time; brief

14   When my son Owen was seven or so, he fell in love with Bruce Springsteen's E Street Band, particularly with Clarence Clemons, the band's burly sax player. Owen decided he wanted to learn to play like Clarence. My wife and I were amused and delighted by this ambition. We were also hopeful, as any parent would be, that our kid would turn out to be talented, perhaps even some sort of prodigy.° We got Owen a tenor saxophone for Christmas and lessons with Gordon Bowie, one of the local music men. Then we crossed our fingers and hoped for the best.

°**prodigy**
a young person with exceptional talent

15   Seven months later I suggested to my wife that it was time to discontinue the sax lessons, if Owen concurred.° Owen did, and with palpable° relief—he hadn't wanted to say it himself, especially not after asking for the sax in the first place, but seven months had been long enough for him to realize that, while he might love Clarence Clemon's big sound, the saxophone was simply not for him—God had not given him that particular talent.

°**concurred**
agreed

°**palpable**
obvious

16   I knew, not because Owen stopped practicing, but because he was practicing only during the periods Mr. Bowie had set for him: half an hour after school four days a week, plus an hour on the weekends. Owen mastered the scales and the notes—nothing wrong with his memory, his lungs, or even his eye-hand coordination—but we never heard him taking off, surprising himself with something new, blissing himself out. And as soon as his practice time was over, it was back into the case with the horn, and there it stayed until the next lesson or practice-time. What this suggested to me was that when it came to the sax and my son, there was never going to be any real play-time; it was all going to be rehearsal. That's no good. If there's no joy in it, it's just no good. It's best to go on to some other area, where the deposits of talent may be richer and the fun quotient° higher.

°**fun quotient**
amount or degree of fun

°**renders**
makes

17   Talent renders° the whole idea of rehearsal meaningless; when you find something at which you are talented, you do it (whatever *it* is) until your fingers bleed or your eyes are ready to fall out of your head. Even when no one is listening (or reading, or watching), every outing is a bravura° performance, because you as the creator are happy. Perhaps even ecstatic.° That goes for reading and writing as well as for playing a musical instrument, hitting a baseball, or running the four-forty. The sort of strenuous° reading and writing program I advocate°—four to six hours a day, every day—will not seem strenuous if you really enjoy doing these things and have an aptitude° for them; in fact, you may be following such a program already. If you feel you need permission to do all the reading and writing your little heart desires, however, consider it hereby granted by yours truly.°

°**bravura**
with brilliant style

°**ecstatic**
extremely happy

°**strenuous**
requiring great effort

°**advocate**
argue in favor of

°**aptitude**
an inborn talent

18   The real importance of reading is that it creates an ease and intimacy with the process of writing; one comes to the country of the writer with one's pa-

°**yours truly**
Stephen King himself

°**trite**
something once forceful
but now stale

°**less apt**
less likely

pers and identification pretty much in order. Constant reading will pull you into a place (a mind-set, if you like the phrase) where you can write eagerly and without self-consciousness. It also offers you a constantly growing knowledge of what has been done and what hasn't, what is trite° and what is fresh, what works and what just lies there dying (or dead) on the page. The more you read, the less apt° you are to make a fool of yourself with your pen or word processor.

Questions **for Critical Thinking**

1. In this essay, Stephen King analyzes how a person becomes a writer. Review paragraph 1 of the essay. What is the writer's thesis?

2. Stephen King tells us he reads a great deal. Is his primary purpose as a reader to learn to write better?

3. What are the lessons Stephen King learned from reading "bad" writing?

4. A transitional expression in paragraph 7 tells us that the writer is changing his topic, from what you can learn by studying bad writing to what you can learn when you read good writing. What is that transitional expression?

5. Explain how all of paragraph 8 works as a transitional paragraph.

6. Which paragraphs in the essay focus on the importance of talent when it comes to making a writer? Mark that place in the essay where the writer gives a personal anecdote to illustrate his point.

7. What process of learning does the saxophone teacher recommend?

8. Writers often use their own creative expressions to better express their feelings or opinions about a particular term. The word *television* is a neutral term. In paragraph 13, what expression does Stephen King use when he writes about television? How does that expression reveal his attitude toward that medium? In other words, what is the connotation of his new term?

9. Review paragraph 11. If you are going to work hard to become the best you can be at some particular skill, do you believe, as Stephen King does, that a person has to be willing to "step on people's toes"?

Writing **in Response**

1. Write an essay in which you discuss how a person can develop a specific talent. (You might choose to write about musical talent, athletic talent, artistic talent, or mathematical talent.)

2. In paragraph 12, Stephen King tells us that a writer who spends significant time watching television is doing something that works against the discipline of writing. Write an essay using process analysis. Suggest very specifically just how people could accomplish more if they did not watch so much television. How would your own life be different if you did not watch any television at all?

3. Teachers and parents often urge young people not to waste their time. Write an essay demonstrating a process that, at first glance, seemed to be a waste of time but later turned out to be something very positive and beneficial. Or write an essay explaining a process that everyone claims is so important but that you have found to be a waste of your time.

How to Mark a Book

Mortimer Adler

Mortimer Adler (1902–2001) dropped out of his New York City high school when he was fifteen, but later attended Columbia University. He failed to obtain his degree there, however, because he did not take the swimming test required for graduation. Despite this, he was given a teaching post at Columbia as an instructor in psychology, and in a few years he wrote a doctoral dissertation—the only student in the country to earn a PhD without the benefit of even a high school diploma. In 1983, Columbia finally excused Adler from the swimming requirement and gave him his BA—sixty years after he should have graduated.

Adler firmly believed that everyone can find a good education by studying areas of knowledge that help people think clearly and exercise their free will, and throughout his life, Adler worked toward proving his theory. In 1946, while he was at the University of Chicago, Adler was instrumental in starting the Great Books Program, which brought adults together regularly to discuss classic works of literature and philosophy. To support this program, *Encyclopaedia Britannica* printed a set of fifty-four books. The idea behind the Great Books Program spread throughout the country, influencing the lives of many people for years.

1   You know you have to read "between the lines" to get the most out of anything. I want to persuade you to do something equally important in the course of your reading. I want to persuade you to "write between the lines." Unless you do, you are not likely to do the most efficient kind of reading.

°**contend**
assert

2   I contend,° quite bluntly,° that marking up a book is not an act of mutilation° but of love.

°**bluntly**
frankly

3   You shouldn't mark up a book which isn't yours. Librarians (or your friends) who lend you books expect you to keep them clean, and you should. If you decide that I am right about the usefulness of marking books, you will have to buy them. Most of the world's great books are available today, in reprint editions, at less than a dollar.

°**mutilation**
damage beyond repair

4   There are two ways in which you can own a book. The first is the property right you establish by paying for it, just as you pay for clothes or furniture. But this act of purchase is only the prelude° to possession. Full ownership comes only when you have made it a part of yourself, and the best way to make yourself a part of it is by writing in it. An illustration may make the point clear. You buy a beefsteak and transfer it from the butcher's icebox to your own. But you do not own the beefsteak in the most important sense until you consume it and get it into your bloodstream. I am arguing that books, too, must be absorbed in your bloodstream to do you any good.

°**prelude**
an introductory action

5   Confusion about what it means to *own* a book leads people to a false reverence° for paper, binding, and type—a respect for the physical thing—the craft of the printer rather than the genius of the author. They forget that it is possible for a man to acquire the idea, to possess the beauty, which a great book contains, without staking his claim by pasting his bookplate inside the cover. Having a fine library doesn't prove that its owner has a mind enriched by books; it proves nothing more than that he, his father, or his wife, was rich enough to buy them.

°**reverence**
deep respect

6   There are three kinds of book owners. The first has all the standard sets and best-sellers—unread, untouched. (This deluded° individual owns woodpulp and ink, not books.) The second has a great many books—a few of them read through, most of them dipped into, but all of them as clean and shiny as the day they were bought. (This person would probably like to make books his own, but

°**deluded**
self-deceived

is restrained by a false respect for their physical appearance.) The third has a few books or many—everyone of them dog-eared and dilapidated,° shaken and loosened by continual use, marked and scribbled in from front to back. (This man owns books.)

°dilapidated
shabby

7 Is it false respect, you may ask, to preserve intact and unblemished° a beautifully printed book, an elegantly bound edition? Of course not. I'd no more scribble all over a first edition of *Paradise Lost*° than I'd give my baby a set of crayons and an original Rembrandt!° I wouldn't mark up a painting or a statue. Its soul, so to speak, is inseparable from its body. And the beauty of a rare edition or of a richly manufactured volume is like that of a painting or a statue.

°unblemished
without a flaw

°Paradise Lost
epic poem by John Milton
(1608–1674)

8 But the soul of a book *can* be separated from its body. A book is more like the score of a piece of music than it is like a painting. No great musician confuses a symphony with the printed sheets of music. Arturo Toscanini° reveres Brahms,° but Toscanini's score of the C-minor Symphony is so thoroughly marked up that no one but the maestro° himself can read it. The reason why a great conductor makes notations on his musical scores—marks them up again and again each time he returns to study them—is the reason why you should mark your books. If your respect for magnificent binding or typography gets in the way, buy yourself a cheap edition and pay your respects to the author.

°Rembrandt
Dutch painter (1606–1669)

°Toscanini
Italian conductor (1867–1957)

°Brahms
German composer (1833–1897)

°maestro
master musician

9 Why is marking up a book indispensable° to reading? First, it keeps you awake. (And I don't mean merely conscious; I mean wide awake.) In the second place, reading, if it is active, is thinking, and thinking tends to express itself in words, spoken or written. The marked book is usually the thought-through book. Finally, writing helps you remember the thoughts you had, or the thoughts the author expressed. Let me develop these three points.

°indispensable
essential

10 If reading is to accomplish anything more than passing time, it must be active. You can't let your eyes glide across the lines of a book and come up with an understanding of what you have read. Now an ordinary piece of light fiction, like say, *Gone With the Wind,*° doesn't require the most active kind of reading. The books you read for pleasure can be read in a state of relaxation, and nothing is lost. But a great book, rich in ideas and beauty, a book that raises and tries to answer great fundamental questions, demands the most active reading of which you are capable. You don't absorb the ideas of John Dewey° the way you absorb the crooning of Mr. Vallee.° You have to reach for them. That you cannot do while you're asleep.

°Gone with the Wind
novel of the American Civil War

°John Dewey
American educator (1859–1952)

11 If, when you've finished reading a book, the pages are filled with your notes, you know that you read actively. The most famous active reader of great books I know is President Hutchins, of the University of Chicago. He also has the hardest schedule of business activities of any man I know. He invariably° reads with a pencil, and sometimes, when he picks up a book and a pencil in the evening, he finds himself, instead of making intelligent notes, drawing what he calls "caviar factories" on the margins. When that happens, he puts the book down. He knows he's too tired to read, and he's just wasting time.

°Mr. Vallee
Rudy Vallee, popular singer
(1901–1986)

°invariably
always

12 But, you may ask, why is writing necessary? Well, the physical act of writing, with your own hand, brings words and sentences more sharply before your mind and preserves them better in your memory. To set down your reaction to important words and sentences you have read, and the questions they have raised in your mind, is to preserve those reactions and sharpen those questions.

13 Even if you wrote on a scratch pad, and threw the paper away when you had finished writing, your grasp of the book would be surer. But you don't have to throw the paper away. The margins (top and bottom, as well as side), the end-papers, the very space between the lines, are all available. They aren't sacred. And, best of all, your marks and notes become an integral° part of the book and stay there forever. You can pick up the book the following week or year, and there are all your points of agreement, disagreement, doubt, and inquiry. It's like re-suming an interrupted conversation with the advantage of being able to pick up where you left off.

°**integral**
essential

14   And that is exactly what reading a book should be: a conversation between you and the author. Presumably he knows more about the subject than you do; naturally, you'll have the proper humility as you approach him. But don't let any-body tell you that a reader is supposed to be solely on the receiving end. Under-standing is a two-way operation; learning doesn't consist in being an empty receptacle.° The learner has to question himself and question the teacher. He even has to argue with the teacher, once he understands what the teacher is say-ing. And marking a book is literally° an expression of your differences, or agree-ments of opinion, with the author.

°**receptacle**
a container

°**literally**
really, exactly

15   There are all kinds of devices° for marking a book intelligently and fruit-fully.° Here's the way I do it:

°**devices**
techniques

°**fruitfully**
producing results

1. *Underlining:* of major points, of important or forceful statements.
2. *Vertical° lines at the margin:* to emphasize a statement already underlined.
3. *Star, asterisk, or other doo-dad at the margin:* to be used sparingly, to emphasize the ten or twenty most important statements in the book. (You may want to fold the bottom corner of each page on which you use such marks. It won't hurt the sturdy paper on which most modern books are printed, and you will be able to take the book off the shelf at any time and, by opening it at the folded-corner page, refresh your recollection of the book.)
4. *Numbers in the margin:* to indicate the sequence of points the author makes in developing a single argument.
5. *Numbers of other pages in the margin:* to indicate where else in the book the author made points relevant to the point marked; to tie up the ideas in a book, which, though they may be separated by many pages, belong together.
6. *Circling of key words or phrases.*
7. *Writing in the margin, or at the top or bottom of the page, for the sake of:* recording questions (and perhaps answers) which a passage raised in your mind; reducing a complicated discussion to a simple state-ment; recording the sequence of major points right through the books. I use the end-papers at the back of the book to make a personal index of the author's points in the order of their appearance.

°**vertical**
up and down lines

16   The front end-papers are, to me, the most important. Some people reserve them for a fancy bookplate.° I reserve them for fancy thinking. After I have fin-ished reading the book and making my personal index on the back end-papers, I turn to the front and try to outline the book, not page by page, or point by point (I've already done that at the back), but as an integrated structure, with a basic unity and an order of parts. This outline is, to me, the measure of my under-standing of the work.

°**bookplate**
a label placed in a book, with the owner's name

17   If you're a die-hard anti-book-marker, you may object that the margins, the space between the lines, and the end-papers don't give you room enough. All

right. How about using a scratch pad slightly smaller than the page-size of the book—so that the edges of the sheets won't protrude? Make your index, outlines, and even your notes on the pad, and then insert these sheets permanently inside the front and back covers of the book.

18 Or, you may say that this business of marking books is going to slow up your reading. It probably will. That's one of the reasons for doing it. Most of us have been taken in by the notion that the speed of reading is a measure of our intelligence. There is no such things as the right speed for intelligent reading. Some things should be read quickly and effortlessly, and some should be read slowly and even laboriously. The sign of intelligence in reading is in the ability to read different things differently according to their worth. In the case of good books, the point is not to see how many of them you can get through, but rather how many can get through you—how many you can make your own. A few friends are better than a thousand acquaintances. If this be your aim, as it should be, you will not be impatient if it takes more time and effort to read a great book than it does a newspaper.

19 You may have one final objection to marking books. You can't lend them to your friends because nobody else can read them without being distracted by your notes. Furthermore, you won't want to lend them because a marked copy is a kind of intellectual diary, and lending it is almost like giving your mind away.

20 If your friend wishes to read your *Plutarch's Lives,*° *Shakespeare,* or *The Federalist Papers,*° tell him gently but firmly to buy a copy. You will lend him your car or your coat—but your books are as much a part of you as your head or your heart.

°*Plutarch's Lives*
famous biography of people from
the ancient world

°*The Federalist Papers*
a series of articles published in
1787 urging the ratification of the
U.S. Constitution

Questions for Critical Thinking

1. Mortimer Adler begins his essay by quite clearly saying he will try to persuade us that we should mark our books when we read. This, of course, means he is writing an argument. Yet the title is the typical title of a process analysis essay. Scan the essay to find where he gets to the process part of the essay. What paragraphs tell us how to mark a book?
2. Where in the essay does Mortimer Adler use classification?
3. Mortimer Adler uses a simile to make clear what he thinks a book is like. What is the simile? Explain the simile in your own words.
4. How would you define "active reading" using Mortimer Adler's viewpoint?
5. Mortimer Adler begins by making some disclaimer about marking up books. What are the cases in which a book should not be marked?
6. In paragraph 9, what are the three transitional words?
7. According to paragraph 12, what is the relationship between writing and memory?
8. In paragraph 14, Mortimer Adler claims that the reader or learner is not an "empty receptacle." Explain what he means by this.

Writing in Response

1. Our culture places a great deal of emphasis on owning things: fancy cars, beautiful jewelry, name-brand clothes. Mortimer Adler has a very different attitude about who owns a book. Explore his idea and expand it to look at other things. Who owns a college degree? Who owns a piece of property?

2. Reread this essay. Using Mortimer Adler's advice, mark his essay.

3. Using Mortimer Adler's ideas, write a guide for college students giving them advice on how to read a chapter in a textbook that they will be tested on.

4. Write an essay about your own reading habits or study habits. What is the process you follow when you do homework or study for an exam?

5. How important is it to have books in your home? Write an essay in which you give advice to someone how to begin collecting books for a home library.

Neat People vs. Sloppy People

Suzanne Britt

Sometimes we learn the most about ourselves when our shortcomings are pointed out in a humorous way. The author of the following essay does just this, as she divides the human population into two basic groups. Suzanne Britt teaches English literature and writing at Meredith College in Raleigh, North Carolina. Her writing has been widely published: her essay and articles have appeared in such periodicals as *Newsweek* and the *New York Times,* and her books have been well received by readers of popular fiction and by students working in college writing classrooms. As you read the following essay, decide which of the two groups described by the author is the better one for you—or which group is the one you would like to join.

1   I've finally figured out the difference between neat people and sloppy people. The distinction is, as always, moral. Neat people are lazier and meaner than sloppy people.

2   Sloppy people, you see, are not really sloppy. Their sloppiness is merely the unfortunate consequence of their extreme moral rectitude.° Sloppy people carry in their mind's eye a heavenly vision, a precise plan, that is so stupendous, so perfect, it can't be achieved in this world or the next.

°**rectitude**
correctness

3   Sloppy people live in Never-Never Land. Someday is their *métier*.° Someday they are planning to alphabetize all their books and set up home catalogues. Someday they will go through their wardrobes and mark certain items for tentative mending and certain items for passing on to relatives of similar shape and size. Someday sloppy people will make family scrapbooks into which they will put newspaper clippings, postcards, locks of hair, and the dried corsage from their senior prom. Someday they will file everything on the surface of their desks, including the cash receipts from coffee purchases at the snack shop. Someday they will sit down and read all the back issues of *The New Yorker.*

°**métier**
French for "a person's specialty"

4   For all these noble reasons and more, sloppy people never get neat. They aim too high and wide. They save everything, planning someday to file, order, and straighten out the world. But while these ambitious plans take clearer and clearer shape in their heads, the books spill from the shelves onto the floor, the clothes pile up in the hamper and closet, the family mementos accumulate in every drawer, the surface of the desk is buried under mounds of paper and the unread magazines threaten to reach the ceiling.

5   Sloppy people can't bear to part with anything. They give loving attention to every detail. When sloppy people say they're going to tackle the surface of the desk, they really mean it. Not a paper will go unturned; not a rubber band will go unboxed. Four hours or two weeks into the excavation, the desk looks exactly the same, primarily because the sloppy person is meticulously creating new piles of papers with new headings and scrupulously stopping to read all the old book catalogs before he throws them away. A neat person would just bulldoze the desk.

6   Neat people are bums and clods at heart. They have cavalier° attitudes toward possessions, including family heirlooms. Everything is just another dustcatcher to them. If anything collects dust, it's got to go and that's that. Neat people will toy with the idea of throwing the children out of the house just to cut down on the clutter.

°**cavalier**
very informal and offhand

7   Neat people don't care about process. They like results. What they want to do is get the whole thing over with so they can sit down and watch the rasslin' on

TV. Neat people operate on two unvarying principles: Never handle any item twice, and throw everything away.

8   The only thing messy in a neat person's house is the trash can. The minute something comes to a neat person's hand, he will look at it, try to decide if it has immediate use and, finding none, throw it in the trash.

9   Neat people are especially vicious with mail. They never go through their mail unless they are standing directly over a trash can. If the trash can is beside the mailbox, even better. All ads, catalogs, pleas for charitable contributions, church bulletins and money-saving coupons go straight into the trash can without being opened. All letters from home, postcards from Europe, bills and paychecks are opened, immediately responded to, then dropped in the trash can. Neat people keep their receipts only for tax purposes. That's it. No sentimental salvaging of birthday cards or the last letter a dying relative ever wrote. Into the trash it goes.

10   Neat people place neatness above everything, even economics. They are incredibly wasteful. Neat people throw away several toys every time they walk through the den. I knew a neat person once who threw away a perfectly good dish drainer because it had mold on it. The drainer was too much trouble to wash. And neat people sell their furniture when they move. They will sell a La-Z-Boy recliner while you are reclining in it.

11   Neat people are no good to borrow from. Neat people buy everything in expensive little single portions. They get their flour and sugar in two-pound bags. They wouldn't consider clipping a coupon, saving a leftover, reusing plastic non-dairy whipped cream containers or rinsing off tin foil and draping it over the unmoldy dish drainer. You can never borrow a neat person's newspaper to see what's playing at the movies. Neat people have the paper all wadded up and in the trash by 7:05 A.M.

12   Neat people cut a clean swath through the organic as well as the inorganic world. People, animals, and things are all one to them. They are so insensitive. After they've finished with the pantry, the medicine cabinet, and the attic, they will throw out the red geranium (too many leaves), sell the dog (too many fleas), and send the children off to boarding school (too many scuffmarks on the hardwood floors).

Questions for Critical Thinking

1.   At what point in your reading of the essay did you become aware that this was a humorous piece of writing?

2.   What explanation does Suzanne Britt give for a sloppy person's behavior? Do you agree with her?

3.   In paragraph 3, what are the examples the writer lists when she presents the projects a sloppy person plans to do? Do these plans seem admirable to you?

4.   Does the author use the block method or the point-by-point method to contrast sloppy people with neat people?

5.   One of the reasons Suzanne Britt's writing is so appreciated is that readers recognize themselves in her essays. In paragraph 11, the author tells us that "neat people are no good to borrow from." What makes her supporting statements for this comment humorous?

6. Review the concluding paragraph of the essay. Do you know anyone who acts in the ways listed in that paragraph? By the time you have finished the essay, have you come to your own conclusion as to which category the writer herself belongs to?

Writing **in Response**

1. Write an essay that takes the opposite viewpoint from the one given by Suzanne Britt. Defend the neat person and criticize the sloppy person.

2. Describe two people you know who have very different approaches to being neat and organized. Explain what it is like to be with each of them.

3. How would you describe the household in which you grew up? In what ways were your parents very organized? In what areas were they disorganized? What are the problems of growing up in a household that is extreme in one way or another?

4. Write an essay in which you give advice to a young couple setting up a household. How would you advise them on being neat and organized?

5. Suzanne Britt claims that sloppy people cannot part with anything. Write an essay in which you analyze your own attitude about possessions. What are the things you have a hard time parting with? What things do you especially like to collect and save?

Dream Houses

Tenaya Darlington

When the author's parents move into a new house, she is confronted with the fact that although it is her parents' "dream house," it does not feel at all like home.

1   The house I grew up in had one bathroom, a tub in it. No shower. The rooms were small, more like clubhouses than rooms, and the basement, which was divided into my father's music room on one side and our playroom on the other, had been decorated by the previous owners who were local football fans. Hence the red and yellow shag.° It was a make-do house. A small ranch-style with a high-sloping driveway on a corner lot. Every year there was talk of putting in a shower, taking down the foil wallpaper over the stove, getting rid of that awful paneling downstairs, and fixing the part of the ceiling that buckled. But every year, the same reply from my parents: *we're waiting for our dream house, we'll probably move next year.*

°**shag**
a rug with long fibers

2   Three years ago, my parents finally moved. After twenty, yes, twenty temporary years, the perfect house in the woods came onto the market: a modern-looking flat-roof with wood siding stained a cool gray. Inside, the back wall is all glass and there are skylights. A huge stone fireplace pipes warmth into the heating ducts to warm the whole house. When my brother and I visit during the holidays we sleep in large rooms that overlook a wooded ravine, snow falling against timber, and somewhere in the distance, a barred owl croons for a matching call. It's the sort of house people smoke pipes in and writers write in. The low-slung pine beams on the upper floor make it feel less like a house real people live in and more like a ski lodge, a retreat for dreamers. And so we watch our parents float in front of the window, my mother in her wool clogs, my father in his moccasins, hands wrapped around chunky mugs of coffee. It feels like a commercial. When my brother and I swap hellos going in and out of the bathroom (with its massager shower and all-white matchingness), I can't help but think of Best Western.

3   In the afternoons at the dream house, we do dream things: walk down the ravine to where there is a river with a small island, find a swatch of fox fur on the path, climb a fallen tree that looks like a reclining woman (two big branches like her legs, two big knots like her breasts). My brother is in college now and I am several years out, yet we act like kids in those woods, running through the trees, skipping rocks, delighting in a nest or a set of deer prints, and dragging home a huge sheet of bark to plant in front of the house like a flag. We live on hot chocolate and hard cookies sent to us by an aunt in Switzerland, and in the evening, at my mother's insistence, we roast hot dogs and marshmallows in front of the fire and eat lying down.

4   My mother gets a little teary during these visits. *It's a shame,* she'll say, shaking her head, *that we didn't live here when you were children. Think how differently you'd look back on your childhood.* What she doesn't know is this: sometimes at night, my brother and I will go for a drive. We'll drive across town, sleet pressing itself against the windshield and the radio tuned to some eighties station, and we'll park in front of our old house. It's in a neighborhood of other small houses like it where, at one time, we knew all the families. Mrs. Berry in the pale blue house who used to give us divinity;° the Clarks in the white colonial with the playhouse and fish pond; the Phillips in the vanilla two-story who threw birthday parties for their bulldogs; the Zimmermans across from them who took us

°**divinity**
a soft, white candy usually containing nuts

arrowhead-hunting on rainy Saturdays; Mr. Cook, diagonally, who helped my father on the car and had a cat lovingly named "Cat."

5   Our old house looks at us like a dejected pet in a pound. It knows we are sitting outside in the car, sharing a bag of Raisinets from the glove compartment. Lights are on in two windows, like eyes—figures passing in the hallway like our own shadows still lingering, still fighting over who gets to take the first bath. Our breath freezes like blank captions in a cartoon of ourselves, and I think of the one bathroom with the ledge where I used to sit and paint my toes. My mother would be taking a bubble bath, my father reading *Stereo Review* on his throne, my brother brushing his teeth and making faces at himself in the mirror while the dog slept on a pile of towels. The whole family crowded in one bathroom, its door never closed. It was the center of everything, the stage with the tubside seating where we watched my mother cut her hair, my father trim his beard. Aside from going to the mall two blocks east, it was the social hub. I can't imagine us like that now, hanging out, sharing gossip in one of the dream bathrooms with its three-way mirrors, fader switches, and cold floors.

6   My brother and I drive back across town, a trail of tire tracks in the snow connecting the old house with the new. *Remember the dent in the door from your moon boot? Remember the mark on the ceiling above the oven that we always thought was a trap door? Remember the space under the stairs where we hoarded Flintstones vitamins and ate them like candy?* When we return, the house is dark, our parents asleep at their end of the house. We pat the walls, hunting for a light switch.

7   The truth about dream houses, especially dream houses out in the woods that are purchased late in life, is that they are like empty beehives, grandiose° combs° with elaborate compartments but without the dreams to fill them. When I go home to visit, I enjoy the beautiful view, the way the seasons pervade° the living room—the changing leaves like changing wallpaper—and I love that raccoons come to the window in the den at night and look in, but they are no substitute for having neighbors. And when my brother and I leave after the holidays are over, I envision my parents rattling around in a house as empty as it is beautiful. I see them spread out in distant corners, my father downstairs in his office, my mother upstairs at her desk, both of them looking out through binoculars at a pheasant or a grouse and seeing only snowflakes magnified many times to look like moths. And beyond that: nothing, and more nothing, and beyond that, perhaps a dream, or the footprints of a dream leading to another house.

°**grandiose**
great in scope or intent

°**combs (honeycombs)**
waxy structures composed of walled cells or rooms made by honeybees for storing honey and larvae

°**pervade**
to completely fill

Questions **for Critical Thinking**

1.   In her essay, the author compares the bathrooms of the two houses (paragraphs 1 and 5) to discuss some larger truths about her family. Why does she focus on that room to illustrate her points?

2.   In paragraph 2, we discover clues as to the author's attitude toward her parents' new house. Review the paragraph and underline those words and phrases that reveal the author's attitudes.

3.   A place some people might consider a perfect home may be less than satisfactory to other people. Compare those aspects of a house that matter to the parents in this essay with those aspects that matter to the children.

4. The writer pays a good deal of attention to childhood memories and how we look back on our experiences during those years. Think back to your own childhood. What are some of the strongest memories you have from childhood?

Writing in Response

1. What room was "the center of everything" in the home where you grew up? Write an essay in which you describe this memorable room and what took place there during your childhood years.

2. Recall a home you lived in as a child or one you visited often, and compare it with the home you live in now.

3. What is your own dream house like? Where is it located? How is it furnished? With whom would you share it?

4. At the conclusion of her essay, the writer emphasizes that, no matter how perfect a place might be to live, there is "no substitute for having neighbors." To what extent do neighbors make up an important part of the quality of life where you live? To what extent do you depend on your neighbors?

5. When people dream of material possessions—anything from a pair of sneakers to a car or a house—they often give these items an emotional significance. Write about a possession that holds emotional significance for you. Or describe a process you went through in attaining something you had wanted for a long time. Was it all you had hoped for?

Why Marriages Fail

Anne Roiphe

Anne Roiphe is noted for her exploration of women's search for personal identity. Themes running through her fiction and nonfiction include feminism, marriage, family, and cultural identity. One commentator has referred to her writing as a "thoughtful and often provocative" analysis of history and of the forces that shape modern culture and society. Anne Roiphe's best-known novel is *Up the Sandbox!* She has also contributed to such magazines as *Redbook* and *Family Circle.* In the following essay, the writer examines one of the striking facts of our modern society, that is, the large number of marriages ending in divorce. As she explores this topic, we notice two impressive aspects of her writing: an analysis that is always clear and convincing, and a voice that is reasonable and calm.

1   These days so many marriages end in divorce that our most sacred vows no longer ring with truth. "Happily ever after" and "Till death do us part" are expressions that seem on the way to becoming obsolete.° Why has it become so hard for couples to stay together? What goes wrong? What has happened to us that close to one-half of all marriages are destined for the divorce courts? How could we have created a society in which 42 percent of our children will grow up in single-parent homes? If statistics could only measure loneliness, regret, pain, loss of self-confidence and fear of the future, the numbers would be beyond quantifying.°

2   Even though each broken marriage is unique, we can still find the common perils, the common causes for marital despair. Each marriage has crisis points and each marriage tests endurance, the capacity for both intimacy and change. Outside pressures such as job loss, illness, infertility,° trouble with a child, care of aging parents and all the other plagues of life hit marriage the way hurricanes blast our shores. Some marriages survive these storms and others don't. Marriages fail, however, not simply because of the outside weather but because the inner climate becomes too hot or too cold, too turbulent or too stupefying.°

3   When we look at how we choose our partners and what expectations exist at the tender beginnings of romance, some of the reasons for disaster become quite clear. We all select with unconscious accuracy a mate who will recreate with us the emotional patterns of our first homes. Dr. Carl A. Whitaker, a marital therapist and emeritus° professor of psychiatry at the University of Wisconsin, explains, "From early childhood on, each of us carried models for marriage, femininity, masculinity, motherhood, fatherhood and all the other family roles." Each of us falls in love with a mate who has qualities of our parents, who will help us discover both the psychological happiness and miseries of our past lives. We may think we have found a man unlike Dad, but then he turns to drink or drugs, or loses his job over and over again or sits silently in front of the T.V. just the way Dad did. A man may choose a woman who doesn't like kids just like his mother or who gambles away the family life savings just like his mother. Or he may choose a slender wife who seems unlike his obese mother but then turns out to have other addictions that destroy mutual happiness.

4   A man and a woman bring to their marriage bed a blended concoction of conscious and unconscious memories of their parents' lives together. The human way is to compulsively° repeat and recreate the patterns of the past. Sigmund Freud so well described the unhappy design that many of us get trapped in: the unmet needs of childhood, the angry feelings left over from frustrations long ago, the limits of trust and the recurrence of old fears. Once an individual senses this

---

°**obsolete**
no longer used

°**quantifying**
expressing an exact amount

°**infertility**
inability to conceive a child

°**stupefying**
amazing; astonishing

°**emeritus**
retired keeping an honorary title

°**compulsively**
unable to resist acting

°**yearning**
a deep desire

entrapment, there may follow a yearning° to escape, and the result could be a broken, splintered marriage.

5   Of course people can overcome the habits and attitudes that developed in childhood. We all have hidden strengths and amazing capacities for growth and creative change. Change, however, requires work—observing your part in a rotten pattern, bringing difficulties out into the open—and work runs counter to the basic myth of marriage: "When I wed this person all my problems will be over. I will have achieved success and I will become the center of life for this other person and this person will be my center, and we will mean everything to each other forever." This myth, which every marriage relies on, is soon exposed. The coming of children, the pulls and tugs of their demands on affection and time, place considerable strain on that basic myth of meaning everything to each other, of merging together and solving all of life's problems.

6   Concern and tension about money take each partner away from the other. Obligations to demanding parents or still-depended-upon parents create further strain. Couples today must also deal with all the cultural changes brought on in recent years by the women's movement and the sexual revolution. The altering of roles and the shifting of responsibilities have been extremely trying for many marriages.

°**erode**
to diminish; to make disappear

°**euphoric**
extremely happy

7   These and other realities of life erode° the visions of marital bliss the way sandstorms eat at rock and the ocean nibbles away at the dunes. Those euphoric,° grand feelings that accompany romantic love are really self-delusions, self-hypnotic dreams that enable us to forge a relationship. Real life, failure at work, disappointments, exhaustion, bad smells, bad colds and hard times all puncture the dream and leave us stranded with our mate, with our childhood patterns pushing us this way and that, with our unfulfilled expectations.

8   The struggle to survive in marriage requires adaptability, flexibility, genuine love and kindness and an imagination strong enough to feel what the other is feeling. Many marriages fall apart because either partner cannot imagine what the other wants or cannot communicate what he or she needs or feels. Anger builds until it erupts into a volcanic burst that buries the marriage in ash.

9   It is not hard to see, therefore, how essential communication is for a good marriage. A man and a woman must be able to tell each other how they feel and why they feel the way they do; otherwise they will impose on each other roles and actions that lead to further unhappiness. In some cases, the communication patterns of childhood—of not talking, of talking too much, of not listening, of distrust and anger, of withdrawal—spill into the marriage and prevent a healthy exchange of thoughts and feelings. The answer is to set up new patterns of communication and intimacy.

10   At the same time, however, we must see each other as individuals. "To achieve a balance between separateness and closeness is one of the major psychological tasks of all human beings at every stage of life," says Dr. Stuart Bartle, a psychiatrist at the New York University Medical Center.

11   If we sense from our mate a need for too much intimacy, we tend to push him or her away, fearing that we may lose our identities in the merging of marriage. One partner may suffocate the other partner in a childlike dependency.

12   A good marriage means growing as a couple but also growing as individuals. This isn't easy. Richard gives up his interest in carpentry because his wife, Helen, is jealous of the time he spends away from her. Karen quits her choir group because her husband dislikes the friends she makes there. Each pair clings° to each other and are angry with each other as life closes in on them. This kind of marital balance is easily thrown as one or the other pulls away and divorce follows.

°**clings**
holds on tightly

13   Sometimes people pretend that a new partner will solve the old problems. Most often extramarital sex destroys a marriage because it allows an artificial split between the good and the bad—the good is projected on the new partner and the bad is dumped on the head of the old. Dishonesty, hiding and cheating create walls between men and women. Infidelity is just a symptom of trouble. It is a symbolic complaint, a weapon of revenge, as well as an unraveler of closeness. Infidelity is often that proverbial° last straw that sinks the camel to the ground.

°**proverbial**
a saying that expresses
a basic truth

14   All right—marriage has always been difficult. Why then are we seeing so many divorces at this time? Yes, our modern social fabric is thin, and yes the permissiveness of society has created unrealistic expectations and thrown the family into chaos. But divorce is so common because people today are unwilling to exercise the self-discipline that marriage requires. They expect easy joy, like the entertainment on TV, the thrill of a good party.

15   Marriage takes some kind of sacrifice, not dreadful self-sacrifice of the soul, but some level of compromise. Some of one's fantasies, some of one's legitimate desires have to be given up for the value of the marriage itself. "While all marital partners feel shackled at times, it is they who really choose to make the marital ties into confining chains or supporting bonds," says Dr. Whitaker. Marriage requires sexual, financial and emotional discipline. A man and a woman cannot follow every impulse, cannot allow themselves to stop growing or changing.

16   Divorce is not an evil act. Sometimes it provides salvation for people who have grown helplessly apart or were frozen in patterns of pain or mutual unhappiness. Divorce can be, despite its initial devastation,° like the first cut of the surgeon's knife, a step toward new health and a good life. On the other hand, if the partners can stay past the breaking up of the romantic myths into the development of real love and intimacy, they have achieved a work as amazing as the greatest cathedrals of the world. Marriages that do not fail but improve, that persist despite imperfections, are not only rare these days but offer a wondrous shelter in which the face of our mutual humanity can safely show itself.

°**devastation**
shock; destruction

Questions for Critical Thinking

1.   When an essay is concerned with answering the question why, we know the method of development is cause and effect. There are many ways to write an introductory paragraph; describe how Anne Roiphe chose to introduce her topic.

2.   Certain transitional words in a piece of writing are used to help the reader understand how one idea connects to another. In paragraph 2, find two words that signal contrast, two words that signal cause, and one expression that signals to us that examples will follow.

3.   Find at least two examples of the author's use of simile or metaphor.

4.   Mark any place in the essay where the author uses an authority to support a point.

5. In paragraph 3, Anne Roiphe claims that "Each of us falls in love with a mate who has the qualities of our parents." Do you agree or disagree with this claim? Do you have any counterevidence?

6. Summarize this essay by making a list of reasons why marriages fail, according to Anne Roiphe.

Writing in Response

1. Anne Roiphe provides a list of major problems that often occur in a person's life: loss of a job, serious illness, infertility, trouble with a child, or caring for an aging parent. Write an essay discussing how the occurrence of even one of these events can effect many of the relationships in a person's life.

2. Many couples go to therapists hoping to work out their problems. Write an essay in which you discuss the benefits of having a third person listen to a couple explaining their problems.

3. In your view, does going through hard times help or hurt a person's ability to sustain relationships? Write an essay answering this question by using your own experience and observations.

4. Many people believe that if they make a change (such as getting married, having a child, moving to another place) they will fix something that is broken in their lives. Write an essay in which you discuss the extent to which a major change can be a benefit for a person, and to what extent making a change will not really solve any of that person's problems.

5. The old expression "Money comes between friends" can also be applied to family relationships. Write an essay in which you discuss how issues of money can have negative effects on people's relationships. How can money issues create several kinds of problems in people's lives?

°**requiem**
a composition (musical or literary) for the dead

June Jordan

Requiem° for the Champ

Many sports figures become heroes, but when one of these heroes falls from grace, a feeling of disillusionment inevitably follows. In the following essay, the late African American poet, essayist, and professor June Jordan reflects on the life and career of one of these heroes, the boxer Mike Tyson. In the process of examining the tragedy of this fighter, who suffered his greatest defeat outside the ring, the writer makes some harsh observations, and even harsher judgments, on American society.

1 Mike Tyson comes from Brooklyn. And so do I. Where he grew up was about a twenty-minute bus ride from my house. I always thought his neighborhood looked like a war zone. It reminded me of Berlin—immediately after World War II. I had never seen Berlin except for black-and-white photos in *Life* magazine, but that was bad enough: Rubble. Barren. Blasted. Everywhere you turned your eyes recoiled from the jagged edges of an office building or a cathedral, shattered, or the tops of apartment houses torn off, and nothing alive even intimated, anywhere. I used to think, "This is what it means to fight and really win or really lose. War means you hurt somebody, or something, until there's nothing soft or sensible left."

2 For sure I never had a boyfriend who came out of Mike Tyson's territory. Yes, I enjoyed my share of tough guys and/or gang members who walked and talked and fought and loved in quintessential° Brooklyn ways: cool, tough, and deadly serious. But there was a code as rigid and as romantic as anything that ever made the pages of traditional English literature. A guy would beat up another guy or, if appropriate, he'd kill him. But a guy talked different to a girl. A guy made other guys clean up their language around "his girl." A guy brought ribbons and candies and earrings and tulips to a girl. He took care of her. He walked her home. And if he got serious about that girl, and even if she was only twelve years old, then she became his "lady." And woe betide any other guy stupid enough to disrespect that particular young Black female.

°**quintessential**
the most typical

3 But none of the boys—none of the young men—none of the young Black male inhabitants of my universe and my heart ever came from Mike Tyson's streets or avenues. We didn't live someplace fancy or middle-class, but at least there were ten-cent gardens, front and back, and coin Laundromats, and grocery stores, and soda parlors, and barber shops, and Holy Roller churchfronts, and chicken shacks, and dry cleaners, and bars-and-grills, and a takeout Chinese restaurant, and all of that usable detail that does not survive a war. That kind of seasonal green turf and daily-life supporting pattern of establishments to meet your needs did not exist inside the gelid° urban cemetery where Mike Tyson learned what he thought he needed to know.

°**gelid**
very cold or icy

4 I remember when the City of New York decided to construct a senior housing project there, in the childhood world of former heavyweight boxing champion Mike Tyson. I remember wondering, "Where in the hell will those old people have to go in order to find food? And how will they get there?"

5 I'm talking godforsaken. And much of living in Brooklyn was like that. But then it might rain or it might snow and, for example, I could look at the rain forcing forsythia into bloom or watch how snowflakes can tease bare tree limbs into temporary blossoms of snow dissolving into diadems° of sunlight. And what did

°**diadems**
crowns

Mike Tyson ever see besides brick walls and garbage in the gutter and disinte-grating concrete steps and boarded-up windows and broken car parts blocking the sidewalk and men, bitter, with their hands in their pockets, and women, bit-ter, with their heads down and their eyes almost closed?

6   In his neighborhood, where could you buy ribbons for a girl, or tulips?

7   Mike Tyson comes from Brooklyn. And so do I. In the big picture of Amer-ica, I never had much going for me. And he had less. I only learned, last year, that I can stop whatever violence starts with me. I only learned, last year, that love is infinitely more interesting, and more exciting, and more powerful, than really winning or really losing a fight. I only learned, last year, that all war leads to death and that all love leads you away from death. I am more than twice Mike Tyson's age. And I'm not stupid. Or slow. But I'm Black. And I come from Brooklyn. And I grew up fighting. And I grew up and I got out of Brooklyn because I got pretty good at fighting. And winning. Or else, intimidating my would-be adversaries with my fists, my feet, and my mouth. And I never wanted to fight. I never wanted anybody to hit me. And I never wanted to hit anybody. But the bell would ring at the end of another dumb day in school and I'd head out with dread and a nervous sweat because I knew some jackass more or less my age and more or less my height would be waiting for me because she or he had nothing better to do than to wait for me and hope to kick my butt or tear up my books or break my pencils or pull hair out of my head.

8   This is the meaning of poverty: when you have nothing better to do than to hate somebody who, just exactly like yourself, has nothing better to do than to pick on you instead of trying to figure out how come there's nothing better to do. How come there's no gym/no swimming pool/no dirt track/no soccer field/no ice-skating rink/no bike/no bike path/no tennis courts/no language arts workshop/no computer science center/no band practice/no choir rehearsal/no music lessons/no basketball or baseball team? How come neither one of you has his or her own room in a house where you can hang out and dance and make out or get on the telephone or eat and drink up everything in the kitchen that can move? How come nobody on your block and nobody in your class has any of these things?

9   I'm Black. Mike Tyson is Black. And neither one of us was ever supposed to win anything more than a fight between the two of us. And if you check out the mass-media material on "us," and if you check out the emergency-room reports on "us," you might well believe we're losing the fight to be more than our enemies have decreed. Our enemies would deprive us of everything except each other: hungry and furious and drug-addicted and rejected and ever convinced we can never be beautiful or right or true or different from the beggarly monsters our en-emies envision and insist upon, and how should we then stand, Black man and Black woman, face to face?

10   Way back when I was born, Richard Wright had just published *Native Son* and, thereby, introduced white America to the monstrous product of its racist hatred.

11   Poverty does not beautify. Poverty does not teach generosity or allow for sucker attributes of tenderness and restraint. In white America, hatred of Black-folks has imposed horrible poverty upon us.

12   And so, back in the thirties, Richard Wright's Native Son, Bigger Thomas, did what he thought he had to do: he hideously murdered a white woman and he viciously murdered his Black girlfriend in what he conceived as self-defense. He did not perceive any options to these psychopathic, horrifying deeds. I do not believe he, Bigger Thomas, had any other choices open to him. Not to him, he who was meant to die like the rat he, Bigger Thomas, cornered and smashed to death in his mother's beggarly clean space.

13   I never thought Bigger Thomas was okay. I never thought he should skate back into my, or anyone's community. But I did and I do think he is my brother. The choices available to us dehumanize. And any single one of us, Black in this white country, we may be defeated, we may become dehumanized, by the monstrous hatred arrayed against us and our needy dreams.

14   And so I write this requiem for Mike Tyson: international celebrity, millionaire, former heavyweight boxing champion of the world, a big-time winner, a big-time loser, an African-American male in his twenties, and, now, a convicted rapist.

15   Do I believe he is guilty of rape?

16   Yes I do.

17   And what would I propose as appropriate punishment?

18   Whatever will force him to fear the justice of exact retribution, and whatever will force him, for the rest of his damned life, to regret and to detest the fact that he defiled, he subjugated, and he wounded somebody helpless to his power.

19   And do I therefore rejoice in the jury's finding?

20   I do not.

21   Well, would I like to see Mike Tyson a free man again?

22   He was never free!

°**condone**
to forgive or overlook

23   And I do not excuse or condone° or forget or minimize or forgive the crime of his violation of the young Black woman he raped!

24   But did anybody ever tell Mike Tyson that you talk different to a girl? Where would he learn that? Would he learn that from U.S. Senator Ted Kennedy? Or from hotshot/scot-free movie director Roman Polanski? Or from rap recording star Ice Cube? Or from Ronald Reagan and the Grenada escapade? Or from George Bush in Panama? Or from George Bush and Colin Powell in the Persian Gulf? Or from the military hero flyboys who returned from bombing the shit out of civilian cities in Iraq and then said, laughing and proud, on international TV: "All I need, now, is a woman"? Or from the hundreds of thousands of American football fans? Or from the millions of Americans who would, if they could, pay

°**surrealistic**
fantastic; unreal; dreamlike

surrealistic° amounts of money just to witness, up close, somebody like Mike Tyson beat the brains out of somebody?

°**citadel**
a fortress or other
place of control

25   And what could which university teach Mike Tyson about the difference between violence and love? Is there any citadel° of higher education in the country that does not pay its football coach at least three times as much as the chancellor and six times as much as its professors and ten times as much as its social and psychological counselors?

°**a priori**
existing from the start
and based on belief, not fact

26   In this America where Mike Tyson and I live together and bitterly, bitterly, apart, I say he became what he felt. He felt the stigma of a priori° hatred and intentional poverty. He was given the choice of violence or violence: the violence of defeat or the violence of victory. Who would pay him to rehabilitate inner-city housing or to refurbish a bridge? Who would pay him what to study the facts of our collective history? Who would pay him what to plant and nurture the trees of a forest? And who will write and who will play the songs that tell a guy like Mike Tyson how to talk to a girl?

27   What was America willing to love about Mike Tyson? Or any Black man? Or any man's man?

28   Tyson's neighborhood and my own have become the same no-win battle-ground. And he has fallen there. And I do not rejoice. I do not.

Questions for Critical Thinking

1. In paragraph 1, June Jordan compares the neighborhood of Mike Tyson's childhood with that of Berlin after World War II. What three words does she use that she wants us to remember? How does she make these three words stand out?

2. In paragraph 2, the author contrasts her own neighborhood in Brooklyn with Tyson's neighborhood. What are the differences?

3. What is June Jordan's definition of poverty? Do you believe her definition is correct?

4. In paragraph 8, June Jordan refers to people who occupy their time by fighting with each other, "instead of trying to figure out how come there's nothing better to do." What are the results when people struggle against each other instead of struggling against their negative circumstances?

5. In paragraph 22, the writer states that Mike Tyson was never free. What does she mean?

6. In paragraph 7, what does June Jordan tell us she has learned during the past year?

7. What should be the social responsibility of a government toward its citizens who are struggling with poverty and lack of opportunity? What mistakes were made by government agencies in the past and continue to be made even now?

Writing in Response

1. Compare and contrast two neighborhoods with which you are familiar. How are they alike? How are they different? How do the physical and social environments of these places play a role in how the people behave?

2. June Jordan points out the historical forces that have conspired against her people. What are these forces? Discuss these forces and the extent to which they continue to influence the direction of our society.

3. Write an essay in which you discuss the social conditions that lead women to be victimized by men.

4. Write an essay in which you propose how children could be better protected from destructive or threatening forces in our society today.

5. How can two people from similar backgrounds turn out so differently?

I'm a Banana and Proud of It

Wayson Choy

Wayson Choy was born in Vancouver, Canada, in 1939, of Chinese ancestry. He studied creative writing at the University of British Columbia before moving to Toronto, where he taught from 1967 to 2004. He has published two novels, *The Jade Peony* (1995) and *All That Matters* (2004), in addition to a book of memoirs, *Paper Shadows: A Chinatown Childhood* (1999). The following autobiographical essay first appeared in a Canadian newspaper, *The Globe and Mail*, in 1997.

1   Because both my parents came from China, I took Chinese. But I cannot read or write Chinese and I can barely speak it. I love my North American citizenship. I don't mind being called a "banana," yellow on the outside and white inside. I'm proud I'm a banana. After all, in Canada and the United States, native Indians are "apples" (red outside, white inside); blacks are "Oreo cookies" (black and white); and Chinese are "bananas." These metaphors° assume, both rightly and wrongly, that the culture here has been primarily anglo-white. Cultural history made me a banana.

°**metaphors**
figures of speech that compare two dissimilar things

2   History: My father and mother arrived separately to the British Columbia coast in the early part of the century. They came as unwanted "aliens."° Better to be an alien here than to be dead of starvation in China. But after the Chinese Exclusion laws were passed in North America (late 1800s, early 1900s), no Chinese immigrants were granted citizenship in either Canada or the United States.

°**aliens**
foreigners; outsiders

3   Like those Old China village men from *Toi San* who, in the 1850s, laid down cliff-edge train tracks through the Rockies and Sierras, or like those first women who came as mail-order wives or concubines° and who as bond-slaves were turned into cheaper laborers or even prostitutes—like many of those men and women, my father and mother survived ugly, unjust times. In 1918, two hours after he got off the boat from Hong Kong, my father was called "chink" and told to go back to China. "Chink" is a hateful racist term, stereotyping the shape of Asian eyes: "a chink in the armor," an undesirable slit. For the elders, the past was humiliating. Eventually, the Second World War changed the hostile° attitudes toward the Chinese.

°**concubine**
in imperial China, a woman contracted to a man

°**hostile**
showing ill will

4   During the war, Chinese men volunteered and lost their lives as members of the American and Canadian military. When hostilities ended, many more were proudly in uniform waiting to go overseas. Record Chinatown dollars were raised to buy War Bonds. After 1945, challenged by such money and ultimate sacrifices, the Exclusion laws in both Canada and the United States were revoked. Chinatown residents claimed their citizenship and sent for their families. By 1949, after the Communists took over China, those of us who arrived here as young children, or were born here, stayed. No longer "aliens," we became legal citizens of North America. Many of us also became "bananas."

5   Historically, "banana" is not a racist term. Although it clumsily stereotypes many of the children and grandchildren of the Old Chinatowns, the term actually follows the old Chinese tendency to assign endearing nicknames to replace formal names, semicomic° names to keep one humble. Thus, "banana" describes the generations who assimilated° so well into North American life. In fact, our families encouraged members of my generation in the 1950s and sixties to "get ahead," to get an English education, to get a job with good pay and prestige. "Don't work like me," Chinatown parents said. "Work in an office!" The *lao wahkiu* (Chinese old-timers) also warned, "Never forget—you still be Chinese!"

°**semicomic**
partly humorous

°**assimilated**
absorbed into the larger culture

6   None of us ever forgot. The mirror never lied.

7   Many Chinatown teenagers felt we didn't quite belong in any one world. We looked Chinese, but thought and behaved North American. Impatient Chinatown parents wanted the best of both worlds for us, but even they bluntly° labeled their children and grandchildren "*juk-sing*" or even "*mo no.*" Not that we were totally "shallow bamboo butt-ends" or entirely "no brain," but we had less understanding of Old China traditions, and less and less interest in their village histories. Father used to say we lacked Taoist ritual, Taoist° manners. We were, he said, "*mo li.*"

°**bluntly**
frankly

°**Taoist**
descriptive of an ancient Chinese philosophy and religion

8   This was true. Chinatown's younger brains, like everyone else's of whatever race, were being colonized by "white bread" U.S. family television programs. We began to feel Chinese home life was inferior. We co-operated with English-language magazines that showed us how to act and what to buy. Seductive° Hollywood movies made some us secretly weep that we did not have movie-star faces. American music made Chinese music sound like noise. By the 1970s and eighties, many of us had consciously or unconsciously distanced ourselves from our Chinatown histories. We became bananas.

°**seductive**
attractively enticing

9   Finally, for me, in my 40s or 50s, with the death first of my mother, then my father, I realized I did not belong anywhere unless I could understand the past. I needed to find the foundation of my Chinese-ness. I needed roots.

10   I spent my college holidays researching the past. I read Chinatown oral histories, located documents, searched out early articles. Those early citizens came back to life for me. Their long toil° and blood sacrifices, the proud record of their patient, legal challenges, gave us all our present rights as citizens. Canadian and American Chinatowns set aside their family tongue differences and encouraged each other to fight injustice. There were no borders. "After all," they affirmed,° "*Daaih ga tohng yahn. . . . We are all Chinese!*"

°**toil**
exhausting labor

°**affirmed**
declared positively

11   In my book, *The Jade Peony,* I tried to recreate this past, to explore the Beginnings of the conflicts trapped within myself, the struggle between being Chinese and being North American. I discovered the truth: These "between world" struggles are universal. In every human being, there is "the Other"—something that makes each of us feel how different we are from everyone else, even family members. Yet, ironically,° we are all the same, wanting the same security and happiness. I know this now.

°**ironically**
contrary to what was intended or expected

12   I think the early Chinese pioneers actually started "going bananas" from the moment they first settled upon the West Coast. They had no choice. They adapted. They initiated° assimilation. If they had not, they and their family would have starved to death. I might even suggest that all surviving Chinatown citizens eventually became bananas. Only some, of course, were more ripe than others.

°**initiated**
took the first step toward

13   That's why I'm proud to be a banana: I accept the paradox° of being both Chinese and not Chinese. Now at last, whenever I look in the mirror or hear ghost voices shouting, "You still Chinese!", I smile. I know another truth: In immigrant North America, we are all Chinese.

°**paradox**
a seeming contradiction that proves to be true

Questions for Critical Thinking

1. In paragraph 1, Wayson Choy states his thesis, "Cultural history made me a banana." How would you define cultural history?

2. When we define a word we put it into a *class* and then give that word *identifying* characteristics. Into what class would you put the word "banana," as it is used by Wayson Choy in his essay? What are the identifying characteristics of a "banana"? Review the essay and find other examples of such terms that the author includes in the essay.

3. We can also define a term by telling what it is *not*. Where in the essay does the writer say what "banana" is not? What is the significance of this point?

4. An *extended definition* provides an analysis of the idea or term, thereby giving us a more in-depth understanding. One method of creating an extended definition is to provide an historical context. Review the essay and mark any paragraphs where the author gives us an historical analysis.

5. In paragraph 7, the writer reports that members of his generation had "less and less understanding of Old China traditions." Is it inevitable that the children and grandchildren of immigrants have less and less of a feeling for the original culture? What is gained? What is lost?

6. Wayson Choy's essay expresses a very optimistic view of assimilating into a new culture. How can an immigrant people have the best of both worlds?

7. What is "the other truth" that Wayson Choy speaks about in the last paragraph? Mark the place in the essay where he describes this "other truth."

Writing in Response

1. How would you define *American culture*? What are the greatest strengths of the American culture, and what are some of its weaknesses?

2. What is "the American Dream"? Write an essay of definition and analysis to explain your understanding of this well-known phrase.

3. Write an essay in which you classify the different types of immigrants in the United States today. How do they differ from the immigrants of one hundred years ago?

4. In some cultures, a person's social class is defined at birth. Write an essay defining the idea of *class* in a particular culture with which you are familiar.

5. In paragraph 11, Wayson Choy tells us that every person is unique, having individual characteristics that make the person different even from other members of his or her own family. Write an essay in which you define yourself by analyzing how you differ from your family, your friends and neighbors, or your own culture.

6. In paragraph 12, the author tells us that the early Chinese immigrants actively began the process of becoming assimilated into American life. Define the term "assimilation" by referring to the many ways people can adapt to the larger culture. You might use food, rituals, religious beliefs, and language to organize the different parts of your essay.

The Ways of Meeting Oppression

Martin Luther King Jr.

Martin Luther King Jr. (1929–1968) earned his BA degree from Morehouse College in Atlanta, Georgia, and finished his graduate studies in theology in Boston, in 1953. It was also in Boston that he met and married Coretta Scott.

The following year, the young minister accepted a position in a church in Montgomery, Alabama. It was in Montgomery, in 1955, that the Reverend King headed the famous boycott that lasted for more than a year in that city. The boycott had been sparked by the refusal of Rosa Parks to give up her seat on one of the Montgomery buses. When at last the Supreme Court declared segregation laws unconstitutional, Martin Luther King instantly became a national figure in the struggle for civil rights.

Throughout the ten-year period that began in 1957, Martin Luther King traveled six million miles and spoke more than twenty-five hundred times, all in the fight to end injustice and inequality. His most famous public moment came in 1963, when he directed a peaceful march on Washington, D.C., and where he delivered his memorable I Have a Dream speech. Five years later, he was assassinated.

In the following essay, the civil rights activist looks at the situation of oppressed people everywhere, from the ancient world to modern American society, and gives us his insights into the different ways subjugated people deal with the unjust situations in which they find themselves.

1   Oppressed people deal with their oppression in three characteristic ways. One way is acquiescence: the oppressed resign themselves to their doom. They tacitly° adjust themselves to oppression, and thereby become conditioned to it. In every movement toward freedom some of the oppressed prefer to remain oppressed. Almost 2800 years ago Moses set out to lead the children of Israel from the slavery of Egypt to the freedom of the promised land. He soon discovered that slaves do not always welcome their deliverers. They become accustomed to being slaves. They would rather bear those ills they have, as Shakespeare pointed out, than flee to others that they know not of.° They prefer the "fleshpots of Egypt" to the ordeals of emancipation.°

°**tacitly**
with silent acceptance

°*see Hamlet, act 3, scene 1*

°**emancipation**
freedom from bondage

2   There is such a thing as the freedom of exhaustion. Some people are so worn down by the yoke° of oppression that they give up. A few years ago in the slum areas of Atlanta, a Negro guitarist used to sing almost daily: "Been down so long that down don't bother me." This is the type of negative freedom and resignation that often engulfs° the life of the oppressed.

°**yoke**
instrument of bondage

°**engulfs**
overwhelms

3   But this is not the way out. To accept passively an unjust system is to cooperate with that system; thereby the oppressed become as evil as the oppressor. Noncooperation with evil is as much a moral obligation as is cooperation with good. The oppressed must never allow the conscience of the oppressor to slumber. Religion reminds every man that he is his brother's keeper. To accept injustice or segregation passively is to say to the oppressor that his actions are morally right. It is a way of allowing his conscience to fall asleep. At this moment the oppressed fails to be his brother's keeper. So acquiescence—while often the easier way—is not the moral way. It is the way of the coward. The Negro cannot win the respect of his oppressor by acquiescing; he merely increases the oppressor's arrogance and contempt. Acquiescence is interpreted as proof of the Negro's inferiority. The Negro cannot win the respect of the white people of the South or the peoples of the world if he is willing to sell the future of his children for his personal and immediate comfort and safety.

°corroding
gradually destructive

4   A second way that oppressed people sometimes deal with oppression is to resort to physical violence and corroding° hatred. Violence often brings about momentary results. Nations have frequently won their independence in battle. But in spite of temporary victories, violence never brings permanent peace. It solves no social problem; it merely creates new and more complicated ones.

5   Violence as a way of achieving racial justice is both impractical and immoral. It is impractical because it is a descending spiral ending in destruction for all. The old law of an eye for an eye leaves everybody blind. It is immoral because it seeks to humiliate the opponent rather than win his understanding; it seeks to annihilate° rather than to convert. Violence is immoral because it thrives on hatred rather than love. It destroys community and makes brotherhood impossible. It leaves society in monologue° rather than dialogue. Violence ends by defeating itself. It creates bitterness in the survivors and brutality in the destroyers. A voice echoes through time saying to every potential Peter, "Put up your sword."° History is cluttered with the wreckage of nations that failed to follow this command.

°annihilate
destroy completely

°monologue
a speech by one person

°see Christ's words to Peter in John 18:11 of the Christian Bible

6   If the American Negro and other victims of oppression succumb° to the temptation of using violence in the struggle for freedom, future generations will be the recipients of a desolate° night of bitterness, and our chief legacy to them will be an endless reign of meaningless chaos.° Violence is not the way.

°succumb
give in to

°desolate
dreary; dismal

7   The third way open to oppressed people in their quest for freedom is the way of nonviolent resistance. Like the synthesis° in Hegelian philosophy,° the principle of nonviolent resistance seeks to reconcile the truths of two opposites—the acquiescence and violence—while avoiding the extremes and immoralities of both. The nonviolent resister agrees with the person who acquiesces that one should not be physically aggressive toward his opponent; but he balances the equation by agreeing with the person of violence that evil must be resisted. He avoids the nonresistance of the former and the violent resistance of the latter. With nonviolent resistance, no individual or group need to submit to any wrong.

°chaos
total confusion

°synthesis
combination of elements

°Hegelian philosophy
Hegel's belief that we arrive at truth by combining theories

8   It seems to me that this is the method that must guide the actions of the Negro in the present crisis in race relations. Through nonviolent resistance the Negro will be able to rise to the noble height of opposing the unjust system while loving the perpetrators° of the system. The Negro must work passionately and unrelentingly° for full stature° as a citizen, but he must not use inferior methods to gain it. He must never come to terms with falsehood, malice, hate, or destruction.

°perpetrators
those responsible for an act

°unrelentingly
without lessening in force

9   Nonviolent resistance makes it possible for the Negro to remain in the South and struggle for his rights. The Negro's problem will not be solved by running away. He cannot listen to the glib° suggestion of those who would urge him to migrate en masse° to other sections of the country. By grasping his great opportunity in the South he can make a lasting contribution to the moral strength of the nation and set a sublime° example of courage for generations yet unborn.

°stature
status

°glib
superficial

10   By nonviolent resistance, the Negro can also enlist all men of good will in his struggle for equality. The problem is not a purely racial one, with Negroes set against whites. In the end, it is not a struggle between people at all, but a tension between justice and injustice. Nonviolent resistance is not aimed against oppressors but oppression. Under its banner° consciences, not racial groups, are enlisted.

°en masse
French for "all together"

°sublime
noble; majestic

°banner
a flag

Questions for Critical Thinking

1. Martin Luther King begins his essay with an extended reference to the situation Moses and the Israelites faced in Egypt nearly three thousand years ago. Why does the author begin his essay with this reminder of the ancient world?

2. How many ways does Martin Luther King give for meeting oppression? Mark each place in the essay where a category or "way" is first presented.

3. To what extent do you agree with Martin Luther King's statement in paragraph 2 that some people "are so worn down by the yoke of oppression that they give up"?

4. When, in paragraph 3, Martin Luther King states, "Nations have frequently won their independence in battle," he adds, almost immediately, that "violence never brings permanent peace." Can you give an example of this seeming paradox?

5. In paragraph 9, Martin Luther King notes that the problem of injustice faced by the African American "will not be solved by running away." What examples do you have, from your own observations of others and from your awareness of history, of people who ran away from their problems? In each case, what were the consequences?

6. In paragraph 10, Martin Luther King stresses that the struggle for equality is not a struggle between people but rather "between justice and injustice." Do you agree with him? Is it not true that the problems people face are created by other people and not by some abstract concept?

Writing in Response

1. Write an essay of persuasion that seeks to convince your classmates that they should participate in a current social issue.

2. Write an essay in which you classify people into types according to how they react to situations that call for a response.

3. Different situations call for different responses. Write an essay in which you suggest which kinds of situations would belong in each of the following categories: (1) those situations where a person should do nothing, (2) those situations where a person should act in a limited or guarded way, (3) those situations where a person has an ethical or legal duty to act, and (4) those extreme cases (if there are any) where a person should act even if it means disobeying a law.

The Changing American Family

Alvin and Heidi Toffler

No one denies that the American family has changed and will continue to evolve. The research and writing team of Alvin and Heidi Toffler have concluded that not all of these changes are necessarily negative. As they share the results of their research, the Tofflers not only provide a broad historical review of some of the most striking changes the family has undergone but also classify families according to different types.

1   The American family is not dying. It is diversifying. This is the "secret" to understanding what is happening to ourselves, our children, and our society. Millions of people today are frightened about the future of the family. Dire° predictions pour from the pulpit, the press, even from the White House. Emotional oratory about the need to "restore" the family is echoing through the nation.

°dire
desperate; urgent;
warning of disaster

2   Unfortunately, our attempts to strengthen family life are doomed unless we first understand what is happening. And all the evidence suggests we don't.

3   Despite misconceptions, the American family system is not falling apart because of immoral television programs or permissive child-rearing or because of some sinister conspiracy. If that were the problem, the solutions would be simpler.

4   To begin with, it is worth noticing that whatever is happening to family life is *not* just happening in the United States. Many of today's trends in divorce, remarriage, new family styles, and attitudes toward children are present in Britain, France, Sweden, Germany, Canada, even in the Soviet Union and Eastern Europe. Something is happening to families in all these countries at once.

°fracturing
breaking up

5   What is happening is that the existing family system is fracturing°—and taking on a new, more diversified form—because of powerful pressures arising from revolutionary changes in energy, technology, work, economics, and communications. If permissiveness and immorality play a role, they are far less important than these other, larger pressures.

6   The whole world is changing rapidly, and it seems reasonable that you cannot have a revolution in all these fields without expecting a revolution in family life as well.

7   Human history has gone through successive phases—each characterized by a certain kind of family. In greatly simplified terms we can sketch these:

8   The First Wave family: Ten thousand years ago, the invention of agriculture launched the First Wave of change in history. As people shifted from hunting, fishing, and foraging, the typical peasant-style family spread: a large household, with grandparents and children, uncles and aunts and sometimes nonblood relatives, as well as neighbors, boarders or others, all living together and—most important—working together as a production team in the fields.

9   This kind of "extended" family was found all over the world, from Japan to Eastern Europe to France to the American colonies. It is still the dominant type of family in the nonindustrial, agricultural countries today.

10   The Second Wave family: Three hundred years ago, the Industrial Revolution exploded in England and triggered the Second Wave of change.

11   The old style family which worked so well as a production team in the fields did not fit well in the new evolving world of factories and offices. The elderly couldn't keep up with the clattering machines. Children were too undisciplined to be really efficient factory hands. And the industrial economy needed workers who could move from city to city as jobs opened up or closed. That was hard to do with a big family.

12 Gradually, under these pressures, families became smaller, more stream-lined, with the husband going out to work in a factory or office, the wife staying home, and the kids marching off to school. Old folks were farmed out to their own apartments or nursing homes. Young people moved into their own apartments as soon as they could afford it. The family adapted to the new conditions and the so-called "nuclear" family became the most popular model.

13 This is the type of family that most of today's evangelists, politicians, and others have in mind when they say we must "protect" the family or "restore" it. They act as though the nuclear family were the only acceptable form of family life.

14 Yet today, as society is struck by a new shock-wave of technological, economic, ecological, and energy changes, the family system is adapting once more, just as it did three hundred years ago.

15 Because the economic and other conditions that made the nuclear family popular are changing, the nuclear family itself is less and less popular. America is no longer a nation of poorly educated blue-collar workers. Most of us work in service occupations or spend our time processing information. And today only some 7 percent of Americans still live in classical nuclear families. The nuclear family is simply no longer the norm—and it is not likely to become the norm again, no matter how much pulpit-pounding or breast-beating we do about it. In its place, a new family system is emerging.

16 The Third Wave family: This new system is harder to describe because it is not based on a single dominant family form but on a dazzling diversity of household structures.

17 For example, look at what is happening to single life. Between 1970 and 1978 alone, the number of people aged 14 to 34 who live alone nearly tripled in the United States. Today fully one-fifth of all households are live-alones. Some are alone out of necessity, others prefer it. Then there are the child-free couples. As James Ramey of the Center for Policy Research has pointed out, we are seeing a massive shift from "child-centered" to "adult-centered" homes. The number of couples who deliberately decide not to have children—whether for economic, psychological, or ecological reasons—has increased dramatically.

18 Next come the single-parent households. Divorce rates may be leveling out in this country, depending upon how they are measured, but broken nuclear households are so widespread that today as many as one out of seven children are raised by a single parent. In big cities that may run as high as one in four.

19 In many countries at once, the single-parent household is becoming a key family form. Sweden gives one-parent households first crack at nursery and day-care facilities. Germany is building special blocks of apartments for them.

20 Then there is what we have called the "aggregate family." That's where two divorced people—each with kids—marry, and the kids from both sides come to know each other and form a kind of tribe. Often the kids get on better than the parents. It has been estimated that, before long, 25 percent of American kids may be part of such "aggregate families."

21   Trial marriages . . . single-sex households . . . communes . . . all can be found as people struggle to find alternatives to the nuclear model. Some of these will turn out to be workable alternatives; others will fall by the wayside.

22   We can also expect to see an increasing number of "electronic cottage" families—families in which one or both spouses work at home instead of commuting to the job. As the cost of gasoline skyrockets and the cost of computers and communication plummets, companies will increasingly supply their employees with simple work-at-home electronic equipment.

23   In such homes, we may well find husband and wife sharing the same work. Even children and old folks might pitch in, as they once did in the agricultural household. In our day, such "electronic cottage" families are as much an outgrowth of changes in energy, technology, and communications, as the nuclear family was a response to the factory system at the time of the Industrial Revolution.

24   In the new environment, nuclear households will no doubt continue to survive. For many people, they work. But this Second Wave family form will hardly dominate the future, as it did the recent past.

25   What we are seeing today, therefore, is not the death of the family, but the rapid emergence of a Third Wave family system based on many different types of family.

26   This historic shift to new, more varied and flexible family arrangements is rooted in and related to parallel changes now fast developing in other fields. In fact, we find the same push toward diversity at every level.

27   The energy system is diversifying, shifting from a near-total reliance on fossil fuels to new, alternative sources of energy. In the world of work, we see a similar trend: Older Second Wave industries engaged in mass production—turning out millions of identical items. Newer Third Wave industries, based on computers, numerical controls, and robots, custom-tailor their goods and turn them out in small runs. At the consumer level, we see an increasing variety of products.

28   The same shift toward diversity is even stronger in communications where the power of the great mass media is increasingly challenged by new "mini-media"—cable television, satellite-based networks, special-interest magazines. This shift toward diversity amounts to the demassification of the media.

29   In short, the whole structure of society is moving toward increased diversity. It is hardly surprising that the family system is in tune with this shift. The recent startling changes in American family structure are part of this larger move from a mass society to one that offers a far greater variety of life choice.

30   Any attempt to go backward to a simpler system dominated by the nuclear family—or by any one model—will fail, just as our attempts to save the economy by "reindustrializing" have failed. For in both cases we are looking backward rather than forward.

31   To help families adapt to the new Third Wave society, with its diversified energy, production, communications, and politics, we should encourage innovations that permit employees to adjust their work hours to personal needs. We should favor "flex-time," part-time work arrangements, job-sharing. We should eliminate housing tax and credit regulations that discriminate against non-nuclear families. We need more imaginative day-care facilities.

32   An idea put forward by one businesswoman: a bank of word-processors and a nursery located in a suburban shopping center, so that busy housewives or husbands can put in an hour or two of paid work whenever it is convenient for them, and actually have their kids right there with them.

33   In short, anything that makes it easier to combine working and self-help, job-work with housework, easier to enter and leave the labor force, could smooth the transition for millions of people who are now caught, as it were, between the old, Second Wave, family arrangements and the fast-emerging Third Wave family system.

°**wallowing**
surrendering to an emotion

34   Rather than wallowing° in nostalgia and praising the "good old days"—which were never as good as they may seem in retrospect—we ought to be finding ways to make the new system more decent, responsible, morally satisfying, and humane. The first step is an understanding of the Third Wave.

Questions **for Critical Thinking**

1.   The Tofflers argue that people should not be so upset about the changing American family. Find the paragraph where they begin using classification as a method of developing their argument.

2.   Explain each of the three distinct categories, or "waves," described by the authors. Do you agree with this historical classification? Can you think of other ways to classify the family?

3.   In paragraphs 16 through 24, find the nine types of families suggested for the Third Wave. Discuss the conditions of our modern world that make these "new" family groupings possible.

4.   The Tofflers point out that only 7 percent of Americans still live in classic nuclear families. This fact frightens many people, even some who themselves are outside a nuclear family. What are some of the reasons for these fears? Do these reasons make you less optimistic than the Tofflers about the new family structures?

5.   In paragraph 30, the writers point out that any "attempt to go backward to a simpler system dominated by the nuclear family . . . will fail" because that would mean looking backward instead of ahead. Do you agree or disagree, and why?

6.   The Tofflers suggest we need to understand the Third Wave to make the new system "more decent, responsible, morally satisfying and humane." What are some of their suggestions? Do you think American society is moving toward greater understanding of the Third Wave family? Discuss.

Writing **in Response**

1.   An often-repeated saying is "The only thing you can be sure of in life is change." Most people have trouble adapting to change in their lives. Write an essay in which you classify the types of changes that can happen to a person during the course of a lifetime. You may want to include categories such as physical change, economic change, and social change. Be sure to provide good examples within each category.

2. Write an essay in which you classify the different types of relationships you have known. Explain what is unique about each type you select. Devote at least one well-developed paragraph to each category.

3. The Tofflers suggest that employers need to make innovations that will permit workers to adjust working hours to their personal needs. Write an essay in which you classify the kinds of innovations that could be made by employers to make life better for families. What is the likelihood that your suggestions will actually be put into effect? Why or why not?

No Comprendo

Barbara Mujica

The following essay appeared on the op-ed page of the *New York Times*. The author, a professor of Spanish at Georgetown University, uses her professional expertise and her personal experience to take a stand on a controversial issue, one that continues to raise very strong feelings in our society.

1   Last spring, my niece phoned me in tears. She was graduating from high school and had to make a decision. An outstanding soccer player, she was offered athletic scholarships by several colleges. So why was she crying?

2   My niece came to the United States from South America as a child. Although she had received good grades in her schools in Miami, she spoke English with a heavy accent and her comprehension and writing skills were deficient. She was afraid that once she left the Miami environment she would feel uncomfortable and, worse still, have difficulty keeping up with class work.

3   Programs that keep foreign-born children in Spanish-language classrooms for years are only part of the problem. During a visit to my niece's former school, I observed that all business, not just teaching, was conducted in Spanish. In the office, secretaries spoke to the administrators and the children in Spanish. Announcements over the public-address system were made in an English so fractured that it was almost incomprehensible.

4   I asked my niece's mother why, after years in public schools, her daughter had poor English skills. "It's the whole environment," she replied. "All kinds of services are available in Spanish or Spanglish.° Sports and after-school activities are conducted in Spanglish. That's what the kids hear on the radio and in the street."

°**Spanglish**
an informal mixture of Spanish and English used in conversation

5   Until recently, immigrants made learning English a priority. But even when they didn't learn English themselves, their children grew up speaking it. Thousands of first-generation Americans still strive to learn English, but others face reduced educational and career opportunities because they have not mastered this basic skill they need to get ahead.

6   According to the 1990 census, 40 percent of the Hispanics born in the U.S. do not graduate from high school, and the Department of Education says that a lack of proficiency in English is an important factor in the dropout rate.

7   People and agencies that favor providing services only in foreign languages want to help people who do not speak English, but they may be doing them a disservice by condemning them to a linguistic ghetto from which they can not easily escape.

8   And my niece? She turned down all of her scholarship opportunities, deciding instead to attend a small college in Miami, where she will never have to put her English to the test.

Questions **for Critical Thinking**

1. Which role gives Barbara Mujica more authority on the topic of bilingual education: her position as a professor of Spanish or the fact that she has a niece with some unhappy educational experiences?

2. In paragraph 5, the author refers to mastering English as a basic skill needed "to get ahead." In your opinion, how important is it for speakers of other languages to know English when they live in this country? To what extent is it possible to survive and get ahead in the United States without learning English?

3. On the basis of your own experience and what you know from the experiences of others, what factors go into the creation of a successful bilingual program? What are some of the mistakes made when bilingual programs are put into operation?

4. In paragraph 7, the author claims that people who live and work using languages other than English are condemned to "a linguistic ghetto." Do you agree that providing services for people in their native languages keeps them from full participation in this society?

5. To what extent do the arguments for or against bilingual education depend on how old a person is when first placed in a bilingual program?

6. Why is English the most important international language in the world today?

Writing **in Response**

1. Agree or disagree with the following statement: *English should be made the official language of the United States.*

2. Agree or disagree with the following statement: *An immigrant should always learn to function in the dominant language of the new country.*

3. Agree or disagree with the following statement: *Parents of schoolchildren should have the right to make the decision as to whether or not their children are placed in bilingual education.*

Why Don't These Women Just Leave?

Elaine Weiss

One of our society's most serious problems is spousal abuse. Elaine Weiss uses her own painful experience as an abused wife to discuss this problem in a direct and compelling way. Her essay argues against the commonly held belief that the problem could be solved if only the abused partner would simply leave the relationship. The writer does not support her argument with any outside facts or statistics, nor does she quote any experts on the matter. All she does is give us a clear and convincing personal history, one that is impossible to contradict.

1   Last May, Neal and I celebrated our sixteenth wedding anniversary. This is his first marriage; my second. Ours is a fine, strong partnership, filled with shared interests, mutual respect, and ever-deepening intimacy. That's not the point of this story. This story is about my first marriage. But to tell the story of my first marriage is to take a risk—and I feel I have to start by establishing that I am capable of a good marriage.

2   I've spent nineteen years trying to make sense of my first marriage: the one that began in 1967 and ended when I left in 1976. I've spent nineteen years trying to unravel the tightly-woven threads of physical and verbal abuse that made up the fabric° of that marriage. I've spent nineteen years, and I may spend nineteen more. Why bother? Why not just be grateful that I found the strength to leave—that I didn't simply become a statistic in a "Domestic Violence" docudrama? Because, I still have nightmares, sometimes. Because, beautiful though *Carousel*° is, I can't watch Billy Bigelow hit Julie Jordan and watch her forgive him. Because when I see Charles Boyer° methodically driving Ingrid Bergman° slowly mad in *Gaslight*, I cry, and then feel silly for overreacting. And because after O. J. Simpson's arrest, during the brief spasm of media interest in domestic violence, I overheard a woman in the beauty parlor proclaim, "You know, the women who let themselves be abused are just as sick as the men who abuse them. She should have walked out the very first time he raised a hand to her. That's what I would have done."

3   She should have . . . our glib° answer to women who are physically and emotionally abused. These days we're far too sophisticated to directly blame the woman for the man's behavior; we no longer say, "Well, if he beat her up, she must have done something to deserve it." Instead, we say, "She should have been more assertive." "She should have been more accommodating." "She should have left." "She should have gotten therapy." "She should have called the police."

4   So, as if the pain of the abusive relationship weren't enough, we tell women that this pain is their fault. They hear *she should*—never *he should*. They hear, "She should have stood up to him"—which, ideally, she should—but they never hear, "He should have stopped being abusive."

5   I know it's not as simple as that. I've read all the books and articles. I know that men who batter their partners are themselves in pain. I know that their behavior is a desperate attempt to make themselves feel in control. I know that many of them were once victims of abuse. I know they can't just stop—that they need professional help. And I sympathize—just as I sympathize with alcoholics and drug addicts. I'm no longer angry with my former husband (though this took me years to accomplish). But I am angry—hotly, fiercely angry—when I hear "Why don't these women just leave?"

°**fabric**
the underlying structure

°***Carousel***
a 1945 Broadway musical composed by Richard Rodgers

°**Charles Boyer** and **Ingrid Bergman**
screen actors who appeared together in the 1944 film drama *Gaslight*

°**glib**
offhand; slick

6   To me, this question is as meaningless as asking the victim of a train wreck "Why didn't you just drive to work that morning?" Nevertheless, I'm going to tell you why I didn't leave; or, rather, why it took me eight years, seven months, and twenty-one days to leave. This is what I wish I had said to the woman in the beauty parlor.

7   I didn't leave . . . because abuse wasn't supposed to happen to people like me. I was only nineteen when I married, halfway through college, with little experience of the world. This was 1967; the term "spouse abuse" didn't exist: No one thought to join those two words, since no one accepted that it happened. Or, if it did, it happened only to impoverished, uneducated women married to men with names like Billy Bob, who turned into mean drunks on Saturday nights. It certainly didn't happen to nice Jewish girls from upper-middle-class families; they went to college, married nice boys, taught school for a while, and then started a family. This is what my friends and I were raised to believe, and this is how I thought the world worked. So when the abuse started, within a week of the wedding, I had no way to frame° what was happening.

8   I didn't leave . . . because I thought it was my fault. My only experience of marriage was the seventeen years I had spent in my parents' home, and there I saw warmth, kindness, and love. If my marriage looked nothing like theirs, I assumed that I must be doing something wrong. My husband would become angry and throw me against a wall—then berate° me for "egging him on." Lying in bed that night, I would replay the scene, trying to pinpoint the exact moment where I had gone wrong. I always found it, too: "I should have laughed it off when he told me the dinner was disgusting." "I should have ignored it when he called me a 'fat dummy, too useless to live.'" "I shouldn't have cried when he announced that he wanted to have affairs with other women—and that if I didn't like it, I was being too possessive."

9   I didn't leave . . . because I believed I could fix it. During our courtship, he was tender and affectionate. He told me I was the most wonderful girl in the world (in 1967 we were all "girls"—as were our mothers and grandmothers). So I held on to the image of the man who was once my loving boyfriend, and was now my menacing husband. He told me I had changed—that I was no longer the cute, bright girl he had married—and I imagined he must be right. Since rational people don't suddenly turn violent without provocation,° I must be provoking him. I thought that if I could just get it right, he would be nice to me again.

10   I didn't leave . . . because I told myself that I was overreacting. Yes, he would occasionally punch me in the stomach or choke me—but at least he never gave me a black eye or a broken arm. Yes, he would delight in pointing out an obese woman on the street and saying "Your ass is even bigger than hers"—but perhaps I did need to lose weight (I was then, as I am now, a size six). Yes, he would indicate another woman, tall, blond, buxom and leggy, and scold "Why can't you look like that?"—but this was the 1960s, when the Beach Boys wished we all could be California Girls, and maybe a petite brunette couldn't hope to be seen as attractive. Yes, he would occasionally put a pillow over my face while I slept, then watch with detached interest as I woke up half-smothered—but I had to be imagining that, didn't I?

11   I didn't leave . . . because there was no support for women like me. There was no place I could tell my story and be told "It's not you—it's him. There's no way you can 'get it right,' because he desperately needs you to get it wrong." I convinced my husband to enter couple therapy, and tried to find the words to pin

°**frame**
to put into words

°**berate**
to scold angrily

°**provocation**
something that causes
a person to become angry

down my husband's actions. "If he goes through a door ahead of me, he gives it an extra push to let it swing back and hit me." "He tells me I'm so ugly that his new nickname for me is 'uggles'." "I feel like I'm constantly walking on egg-shells." The therapist's response was to insist that I had an obligation to stay in the marriage because my husband couldn't function without me. He also insisted that if I stopped being my father's Little Girl and became my husband's Adult Wife, my problems would be solved. Since this advice came from a professional, I assumed it had to be correct. We spent two years in weekly visits to this man, after which I was discharged with the admonition° to put my energy into supporting my husband.

°**admonition**
piece of cautionary advice

12   I didn't leave . . . because I grew accustomed to living a lie. He treated me well in public. To our friends, we were the perfect couple. Maintaining our outward loving appearance became an unspoken conspiracy between us. He called it "not airing our dirty linen in public," and I agreed. Of course I agreed. I was to blame for his behavior, and I couldn't manage to figure out how to be the sort of wife he cherished.° Which, he assured me, he surely would—if I could just learn how to make him happy. A wife who can't make her husband happy—why would I want that to become public knowledge? I agreed to the charade,° and I played my part well. Which probably explains why, when I finally left, he got to keep the friends; no one could see why I'd want to escape such a wonderful marriage.

°**cherished**
held dear

°**charade**
a pretense in which people act out parts

13   I didn't leave . . . and then one day I left. Why? It sounds so trivial in retrospect,° but it was triggered by an encounter with an unknown woman in New York City. This was in 1974, shortly after my husband and I moved to Manhattan. He had taken a job with a prestigious° corporate law firm and, after five years as a schoolteacher, I was beginning graduate school at Columbia University. One afternoon, as we stood on a street corner at a downtown crosswalk, I looked up to see a particularly lovely old building with a magnificent garden on its terraced roof. I pointed and said, "Isn't that building beautiful?" "Which one," sneered my husband, "you mean the one up there that looks exactly like every other building on the street?" A woman standing beside us turned abruptly. "She's right, you know. The building is beautiful—and you are a horse's ass." As the light changed and she stalked off, something shifted inside me. I finally realized that this man was never going to change, and that I deserved better. Within a year I announced that I was leaving.

°**in retrospect**
in looking back

°**prestigious**
having a high standing or reputation

14   Yes, of course it took more than this one encounter. My professors at Columbia told me I was a talented instructional designer, and encouraged me to enter the doctoral program. Fellow students became close friends. Many of them had never met my husband—I was more than half a couple. With professional and personal successes, I stopped caring about, hardly noticed, my husband's abuse. Ironically, the more I ignored him, the nicer he acted. The day I told him the marriage was over (my twenty-eighth birthday), he cried and begged me to stay. He told me how much he needed me. He said he couldn't imagine life without me. He swore he would change. He painted an idyllic° picture of the new life we would build. I barely heard him.

°**idyllic**
simple and carefree

15   And so I left. I am one of the lucky ones. He didn't threaten me. He didn't physically try to stop me. He didn't stalk me. He didn't murder me. Some men do. I am one of the lucky ones. The impact on the rest of my life has been minimal. I didn't become homeless. I didn't turn to drugs or alcohol. I didn't enter into a series of abusive relationships. I didn't commit suicide. Some women do.

16   Instead, I went on to earn a doctorate, develop a successful consulting practice, and build a strong marriage. Life is good. But I still have nightmares, sometimes. I still walk out of movies that show acts of violence against women. And I still, and probably always will, feel anguish° when I hear someone ask "Why don't these women just leave?"

°**anguish**
agonizing mental pain

Questions for Critical Thinking

1.   The author presents the opposing point of view to her own argument when she reports a conversation she once overheard in a beauty salon. Find the quote, underline it, and label it "opposing viewpoint" in the margin of the essay.

2.   An author's thesis is usually found in the opening paragraph of a piece of writing, but that is not the case in this essay. Nevertheless, the writer's thesis is still very clear. We come to realize what that thesis is from the essay's contents, beginning with the title. Using your own words, write a sentence that will provide the thesis of this essay.

3.   Why does the author begin her essay with a picture of her present marriage? What effect does this positive opening have on us as we read the rest of the essay?

4.   In the first six paragraphs, the author presents the traditional thinking about women who find themselves in abusive relationships. What are some of those traditional ideas?

5.   The heart of a persuasive essay is the evidence an author uses to support the essay's thesis. In this selection, which paragraphs present the evidence for the author's thesis? Find these paragraphs and underline the six reasons the writer gives for having stayed in her abusive relationship.

6.   What are the words the author repeats as she introduces each new reason? What is the writer's reason for this repetition?

7.   Paragraphs 11, 13, and 14 point out the roles that other people played in the author's struggle to understand her marriage. Explain the role of each of these persons and the degree of influence each one had on the author's thinking.

8.   What are all the elements that make this essay a convincing argument? Can you find any weak points in the writer's approach? Refer to the guidelines for writing a persuasive essay given in Chapter 31.

Writing in Response

1.   Recall a relationship you remember well. Why did that relationship succeed or fail? Using the Weiss essay as your model, tell the story of that relationship. As you tell that story, make an argument to convince your reader as to why that relationship did or did not work.

2.   Write an essay in which you classify marriages according to their degree of success. Give each of your categories a heading. For instance, one category could be called "marriages doomed to failure."

3.   In this essay, we learn that the image a family member presents in public may be very different from the reality the rest of the family experiences at

home. Write an essay that describes someone you have observed whose actions at home are very different from that person's public image.

4. In paragraph 13 of the essay, Elaine Weiss presents a seemingly unimportant event that turns out to be an epiphany (an incident that is suddenly and profoundly revealing). Write your recollection of an experience you had or a moment in your own life that was an epiphany for you. Explain the effects of this moment of revelation on your life.

5. Many people seek the advice of counselors, therapists, and other experts to help them with their problems. In paragraph 10 of the essay, Elaine Weiss tells us that she received some unfortunate advice from a therapist, advice she assumed had to be correct because it came from a professional. Use your personal experience or experiences of others you know to make an argument for seeking help from experts. How can a person judge the advice of a professional?

6. Write a helpful letter to a friend who has been suffering in an abusive relationship. Advise that person what to do and give the person a step-by-step plan to follow. (Use process as the letter's method of development.)

7. In paragraph 14, the author discusses the people who supported her during a difficult period in her life. Write an essay in which you discuss how the support of other people can be important when an individual is in distress. Your essay could be a *narration* of your personal experience, it could include *classification* of the types of individuals who can be helpful to people in need, or it could present an *argument* that many people need much more support than they are presently getting.

Should Women Go into Combat?

Catherine L. Aspy

Traditionally, military organizations have been male-only organizations, based strictly on authority and excluding any group not thought to be supportive of the world of the military. Until recently, women were among those unwelcome groups, and the issue of women going into combat continues to be a subject of much discussion. In the following essay, Catherine L. Aspy joins this debate. As a person who has served in the Army, Ms. Aspy speaks from first-hand experience. In addition, she has gathered convincing evidence for her position by conducting several interviews with other military personnel.

1 Inside my boots my feet had turned to hamburger. My uniform, even my belt, was soaking with sweat, and my back and shoulders were numb from the 40 pounds of gear in my rucksack. The climax of Army basic training at Fort Jackson, South Carolina, a 12-mile march, was almost over.

2 Determined to keep up, I forced my exhausted muscles to move. But few of the other women in the company remained with me near the front. Many were straggling and some rode the truck that followed to retrieve discarded rucksacks. The men, meanwhile, were swinging along, calling cadence.° They seemed to relish the whole thing.

°**calling cadence**
keeping the beat for marching

3 That march confirmed something which had struck me often during the previous eight weeks: with rare exceptions, the women in my unit could not physically compete with the men. Many were unable to lift heavy weights, scale° barriers or pull themselves along a rope suspended above a safety net. Mixed running groups had inevitably sorted themselves out by sex; in final tests on two-mile runs, the average woman took 18 minutes, the average man about 14. It was apparent that too many of the men weren't challenged enough by the training regimen.°

°**scale**
to climb up or over

°**regimen**
a systematic procedure

4 There were certainly good soldiers among the women in my company; later on, during regular duty at a military-intelligence installation, I saw women of all the service branches perform as well as or better than men in a variety of capacities. Nevertheless, the huge physical performance gap, so obvious in basic training, forced me to consider the implications of placing women in ground combat units.

5 Today the nearly 200,000 women in the nation's armed forces (14 percent of all active-duty personnel) serve as everything from Air Force fighter pilots to military police officers to captains of Navy ships. But the direct combat arms of the Army and Marines—including infantry armor and field artillery—are closed to them.

6 Should women be allowed into these units as well? Many believe they should. After all, we Americans resent being barred from anything; it's part of our instinct for freedom. Former Rep. Patricia Schroeder (D., Colo.) declared, "Combat-exclusion laws have outlived their usefulness and are now nothing more than institutionalized discrimination."

7 It's not an issue I thought about much when I enlisted. I'm sure if I had been asked at the time whether women should be allowed in combat, I would have at least said, "maybe."

8 Now I say, "no." Everything I observed during my hitch in the Army, and later, as I studied the issue and talked to others inside and outside the military, has convinced me this would be a mistake.

9   Combat is not primarily about brains, or patriotism, or dedication to duty. There is no question women soldiers have those in abundance. Combat is about war-fighting capacity and the morale of the unit. Here physical strength can be a life-and-death issue. And that is why the physical disparities between men and women cannot be ignored.

10   For years, Sergeant Kelly Logan* believed that women should be allowed into combat units, that "it didn't matter if you were a man or a woman—there is one standard, we all meet it, bond, and drive on with the mission." Then came her 1997 tour of duty with peacekeeping forces in Bosnia. "I had a complete change in attitude," she says. "When we had to do things like digging and reinforcing bunkers, the guys ended up doing most of the physical work. The women tended to move themselves to the sidelines." Logan watched resentment build until it undermined the unit's morale.

11   She also observed that many women were "so unprepared for heavy-duty soldiering that they would have endangered the unit in a crisis." Patrolling in Bosnia required soldiers to remain on high alert and in full battle gear, including flak° vests and ammo. Says Logan: "The equipment prevented many of the women from moving as quickly as men, let alone being combat effective."

°**flak**
bulletproof

12   While some women may be up to the rigors of combat, she says, "they are the rare exception. And for some individuals, it was only a matter of time before the platonic° bonds progressed to sex, and then all kinds of disruptions ensued."

°**platonic**
reflecting a spiritual as opposed to a physical relationship

13   Logan has reluctantly concluded that "women cannot bond with men in a unit the same way men do." But she cannot say so openly, and insisted that her real name not be used. "It can definitely hurt your career to speak your mind publicly about these things."

14   The expectation in military units has always been that you pull your own load. But an apache helicopter pilot told me that his female crew chief simply refused to carry her tools, which weighed 60–80 pounds.

15   "The Army is supposed to be about not showing favoritism," says Desert Storm veteran Sam Ryskind, who was a mechanic in the famed 82nd Airborne Division. "But the females I trained with were de facto° exempted from any heavy-lifting jobs."

°**de facto**
in reality or fact; actually

16   Whether it was changing truck tires, loading cargo, or even moving heavy cooking pots into position on the chow line, Ryskind says men "always pulled the hard work. Pretty soon this made it an us-and-them situation."

17   While these experiences do not reflect actual combat conditions, they point to the kinds of intractable° problems that would arise if women were in combat units.

°**intractable**
stubborn; difficult to remedy

18   In 1994 an Army rule barring women from hundreds of "combat support" positions was eliminated. Meanwhile the Army tried to institute tests to match a soldier's physical strength to a specific "military occupational specialty," or MOS. Then it was discovered that the tests would have disqualified most Army women from 65 percent of the more than 200 MOSs. The tests were scrapped.

19   To deal with the male-female performance gap, the Army has increased emphasis on "teamwork." No one is against teamwork—that's the essence of the military. But in some cases it has become a euphemism° for defining down° mil-

°**euphemism**
a vague, mild term substituted for a harsh, blunt term

°**defining down**
lowering the standard for

*Not her real name.

itary tasks, as when three or four soldiers are needed to carry an injured comrade instead of two.

°**ludicrous**
laughably absurd

20   "From a combat standpoint this is just ludicrous,°" notes William Gregor, a veteran of combat in Vietnam who is now associate professor of social sciences at the Army's School of Advance Military Studies in Fort Leavenworth, Kansas. "You may not have extra people around. And battle wears you down. A unit where one person can't pull his or her weight becomes a weaker unit."

21   I'm five feet, six inches tall, and I arrived at basic training weighing 135 pounds. I was taller than many women in my unit. But the average female soldier is 4.7 inches shorter and 33.9 pounds lighter than her male counterpart. She has 37.8 pounds less lean body mass. This is critical because greater lean body mass is closely related to physical strength.

°**torso**
the trunk of the body

22   A U.S. Navy study of dynamic upper torso°s strength in 38 men and women found that the women possessed about half the lifting power of the men. In another Navy study, the top 7 percent of 239 women scored in the same range as the *bottom* 7 percent of men in upper-body strength.

23   Even though I had been athletic in high school and had been toughened by two months' training, that final 12-mile march was a killer. One reason: cardio-respiratory capacity—the rate at which the heart, lungs and blood vessels deliver oxygen to working muscles. Trainers know that this capacity is key to sustained physical performance. And numerous studies have revealed differences by sex. "In general," summarized the 1992 Presidential Commission on the Assignment of Women in the Armed Forces, "women have a smaller heart mass, heart volume and cardiac output than men."

24   Some who want women in combat units acknowledge these differences, but claim they're based on stereotyping and can be minimized by extra training. It isn't that simple.

25   In a 1997 Army study, for example, 46 women were given a specially designed 24-week physical-training program to see if they could improve their ability to do "very heavy" lifting. During the training, the number of women who qualified for these jobs increased from 24 percent to 78 percent. Still, on average they were unable to match the lifting performance of men who did not undergo the program.

26   But what about those few women who might qualify for combat units? Gregor, who has done extensive research on male-female physical performance, questions how realistic it is to train 100 women for combat on the chance of finding a handful who will meet—or in exceptional cases exceed—the minimum requirements.

27   The interchangeability of every soldier in a combat emergency is an enduring principle of an army's effectiveness as a fighting force. It assumes that each has received the same training and can perform to the same basic standard. That's still true for men who sign up to go directly into the Army's combat arms. They train "the old way," in a harsh, demanding environment.

28   It's no longer true elsewhere. Under mixed-gender basic training instituted in 1994, men and women are held to different standards. The regimen became less challenging to hide the difference in physical performance between men and women (although the Army denies this).

29   Eventually, the softness of basic training became an object of such widespread public ridicule that "tougher" rules were drawn up. Even with these new standards, scheduled to take effect this month, women can score as well as men who are being tested against a tougher standard. In the 17-to-21 age group, for example, to get a minimum score of 50 points, a male recruit must do 35 push-ups, a female, 13. If women were allowed into combat units and these double standards were made universal, the result would be to put physically weaker forces into the field.

°level the playing field
to give everyone a fair
or equal opportunity

30   An Army publicity release defended these "tougher" standards on the ground that they "promote gender equity" and "level the playing field."°

31   I don't know about the "playing" field. But somehow I think the field of actual combat will not be very level.

Questions **for Critical Thinking**

1.   What is the writer's thesis?
2.   According to the author, what is combat all about (paragraph 9)?
3.   Summarize the three first-hand accounts that give evidence for the thesis:
     - The problem encountered by the author on a 12-mile march during basic training in the Army (paragraphs 1 and 2)
     - The problem encountered by Kelly Logan in Bosnia (paragraphs 10–13)
     - The problem encountered by Sam Ryskind in Desert Storm (paragraphs 15 and 16)
4.   What is the opposing point of view to the author's position, as presented by Representative Pat Schroeder (who never served in the military)?
5.   What is the problem with the opposing argument that states that teamwork will make up for any one individual's weak points (paragraphs 19 and 20)?
6.   Why doesn't offering women extra training solve the problem (paragraphs 25 and 26)?
7.   In addition to first-hand or anecdotal accounts, two studies cited by the author support her thesis. What were the results of these two studies (paragraphs 22 and 23)?

Writing **in Response**

1.   Write a summary of the points the author uses to support her thesis.
2.   Write a persuasive essay of your own in which you begin, as Catherine Aspy did, by giving a first-hand account of an experience that led you to take a position on some controversial subject.
3.   Write a persuasive essay in which you argue for or against the military draft.
4.   Americans take pride in their freedoms, but what kinds of limits should be placed on the rights of individuals? Specifically, what should these limits be and why?
5.   Write an essay in which you classify jobs that at one time were considered to be for men and those that were considered to be for women. To what extent have people's ideas changed?
6.   Write an essay in which you present the positive and negative aspects of a career in the military.
7.   Write a narrative essay in which you tell the story of a person whose job has traditionally been closed to that person's particular group. What have been some of the difficulties that person has experienced?

Where Have All the Fathers Gone?

Chicago Tribune

The following essay appeared as an editorial in the *Chicago Tribune* on Father's Day, June 18, 1995. Instead of the expected tribute to fathers, this editorial is highly critical of a growing number of men who have not faced up to their obligations to support their children. Since that time, the situation has only grown worse.

1   Today is Father's Day, so let's talk about dads. Not the ones who cheer their sons and daughters at baseball and soccer games or the ones who fix dinner for the family every night or the ones who come home dead tired after a day at the Merc° or McDonald's but still have time for a little family conversation.

°**Merc**
Chicago
Mercantile Exchange

2   No, let's talk about the invisible dads, the ones who don't marry mom, don't support their kids and don't hang around for hugs, kisses and helping with homework. There are millions of them in the United States, and their numbers are growing.

3   In 1950, 14 of every 1,000 unmarried women had babies. By 1992, 45 of every 1,000 did. In fact, almost one-third of the children born in the United States in 1992 were born to unwed parents, a 54 percent increase over 1980, according to figures released this month by the National Center for Health Statistics.

°**compiled**
put together or organized

4   And though the figures generally are compiled° in terms of unmarried women and the resulting handwringing is done in the name of unwed mothers, the facts of life are that for every one of those unmarried mothers there is an unmarried father.

5   The moms are a lot more visible though, because in the overwhelming number of cases, they are the ones raising the kids. So who's the real problem here? And why should we care?

6   We *must* care because the social and financial cost of children growing up in households without fathers is immense. Many of the country's most troublesome social problems—poverty, poor performance in schools, gang activity, juvenile crime, mounting welfare costs—have their roots in families where a father has abdicated° responsibility for his children.

°**abdicated**
given up

7   Women who do not marry before having their first child are three times more likely to wind up on welfare for 10 years or more than those who do marry. And census figures indicate that an intact mother-father household has a far better chance for financial security than a single-parent family.

8   Moreover, children who have little or no contact with their fathers are robbed of a crucial role model for fashioning their own lives.

9   What's to be done? For starters, parents, grandparents, churches and schools must hammer home the lesson that a man who conceives a child without marrying and being prepared to support the child for 18 years unfairly burdens his family and his community. He must understand that his action will be met by community disapprobation,° not the respect and awe of his peers.

°**disapprobation**
moral disapproval

10   And while government can't legislate morality, it can encourage responsibility. Legislators should make that a priority by providing tax incentives for couples to marry and by requiring every woman to name her child's father on the birth certificate. Law enforcement officers can (and are beginning to) go after the fathers for child support.

°**squandered**
wasted

11   Fatherhood, like motherhood, is its own reward—as most dads have found. Sadly, for the others, the invisible ones, it is a gift foolishly squandered.°

Questions for Critical Thinking

1.   What is the thesis of the editorial?

2.   What supporting evidence for the thesis is given in the editorial?

3.   Were any outside sources used to support the thesis? If so, mark these in the text.

4.   Does the author say what will happen if nothing is done about the problem?

5.   In paragraph 9, the writer states that if a man fathers a child and does not support that child, he should not look for the respect of those around him but risk disapproval. Is this true? In our society, is a man in this situation vulnerable to this kind of criticism?

6.   Do you agree with the editorial? If not, can you explain your reasons for holding a different point of view?

7.   What is meant by the author's statement in the concluding paragraph, "Fatherhood . . . is its own reward."?

Writing in Response

1.   Write a letter to a "vanished" father. Use your letter as a way to persuade him to become involved in the lives of his children.

2.   Imagine that several of these "vanished" fathers are gathered in one room, and a speaker is trying to convince them to participate in the raising of their children. What do you believe would be some of these fathers' reasons for not participating in the lives of their offspring?

3.   Increasingly, nontraditional individuals and couples are offering to provide a family unit for needy children. What do you believe should be the criteria for adopting a child in this country?

4.   Society is now using the technology of computers to locate deadbeat dads, forcing them to pay child support by garnisheeing their wages. Is this approach to the problem of deadbeat dads better than sermonizing? Is there a single solution to the problem or is the answer a combination of approaches? Write an essay in which you propose a solution to this major social problem.

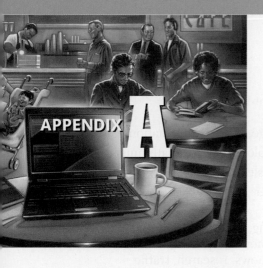

Reference Guide for the ESOL Student

Many students in the United States today have a first language that is not English. These students share similar problems with spoken and written English. The following appendix reviews some of the more common difficulties faced by these students.

Using the Articles *a, an,* and *the*

HOW DO YOU KNOW WHEN TO USE THE ARTICLE *A* OR *AN* BEFORE A NOUN?

Most English nouns are **count nouns;** that is, they can be counted:

one town   two towns
one orange   two oranges

Use *a* or *an* with single count nouns when the noun has not been specifically identified. (Perhaps the noun is being introduced for the first time to the reader.)

A town in Georgia was struck by a tornado.
An orange contains vitamin C.

Noncount nouns cannot be counted easily:

courage   homework   sugar

Do *not* use *a* or *an* with noncount nouns.

We admire people with *courage.*
Do you have *homework* tonight?
I like *sugar* in my coffee.

NOTE: Never add *s* to make a noncount noun plural. Noncount nouns have no plural form.

Learn to recognize common noncount nouns:

Abstract nouns:	beauty, courage, health, information, knowledge
Areas of study:	astronomy, biology, history, math, music
Diseases:	diabetes, measles
Games:	football, soccer
Nouns that indicate a mass of something:	advice, clothing, entertainment, equipment, furniture, homework, jewelry, luggage, machinery, mail, money, news, research, traffic
Food and drink:	flour, sugar, rice, salt, water, coffee, tea, milk, butter, oil
Natural substances:	air, blood, cotton, silk, coal, gasoline, ice, snow

Some nouns can be countable or uncountable, depending on the context:

Count noun:	There is *a time* for work and *a time* for play.
Noncount noun:	*Time* is passing.
Count noun:	He found *a hair* on the lens of the camera.
Noncount noun:	She cuts *hair* for a living.

HOW DO YOU KNOW WHEN TO USE THE ARTICLE *THE* BEFORE A NOUN?

Use *the* with both count and noncount nouns when the noun is specifically identified by its context. Do *not* use *the* if the noun has not been clearly identified or if the meaning carries the idea of *all* or *in general*.

Examples of nouns that are identified		**Examples of nouns that are not identified or whose meaning carries the idea of *all* or *in general***
The city of Macon was struck by a tornado.	but	*A city in Georgia* was struck by a tornado.
The cities of Macon and Savannah were struck by tornadoes.		*Cities in Georgia* were struck by tornadoes.
The jacket with the hood is mine.	but	I would like *a jacket with a hood*.
The jackets with the hoods are new.		*Jackets with hoods* are popular.
The soldier spoke of *the courage that his platoon displayed* in the battle.	but	The soldier spoke of *courage*.

Most singular proper nouns do not take the article *the.*

I live on Walnut Street in Buffalo, New York.

The following categories of proper nouns do *not* take the article *the:*

Countries of one word:	Canada, Mexico
Continents:	Asia, Africa
States:	New Jersey, Arizona
Cities:	Miami, Detroit
Streets:	Elm Street, Rodeo Drive
Parks:	Central Park
Lakes:	Lake Michigan
Persons:	Mayor Fernandez, Captain Cook
Days of the week:	Monday, Tuesday
Months of the year:	January, February

There are many exceptions to this rule, so it is important to learn the following list of categories of nouns that *do* require the article *the.*

The following categories of proper nouns take the article *the:*

Most bodies of water, including oceans, seas, canals, gulfs, and rivers:
the Indian Ocean, the Panama Canal, the Ohio River   but   Lake Louise

Deserts and mountain ranges:
the Sonoma Desert, the Rocky Mountains   but   Mount Everest

Countries whose names suggest plural units:
the United States, the United Arab Emirates,
the Virgin Islands   but   Puerto Rico

Geographical regions and areas:
the Ukraine, the Mississippi Delta, the Northwest Territory

Historical periods and events:
the Depression, the French Revolution, the Civil War

Buildings, bridges, hotels, and highways:
the Sears Tower, the Delaware Memorial Bridge, the Marriott Hotel,
the Dixie Highway

Groups:
the Rotary, the Shriners, the Red Cross

WHAT ARE THE OTHER DETERMINERS BESIDES *A, AN,* AND *THE*?

Determiners are those adjectives that identify and quantify nouns. In a series of adjectives before a noun, these determiners always come first.

For count nouns, you can choose from the following determiners:

Singular: a, one, each, every, this, that

Plural: the, these, those, few, a few, many, more, most, some, several, any, two, three, and so on.

Thus,

I have *one book* to read.

I have *many books* to read.

For noncount nouns, you can choose from somewhat different determiners:

the, this, that, some, little, a little, much, more, any

Thus,

I have *much homework* to do.

Notice you cannot use specific numbers.

Incorrect: I have *five homeworks* to do.

Correct: I have *some homework* to do.

or

Correct: I have *five assignments* to do.

(Changing to the count noun *assignment* allows you to use the number *five.*)

English Word Order

WORD ORDER FOR ADJECTIVES

When more than one adjective is used to modify a noun, use the conventional order:

Determiner: a, each, the, this (see list above)

Judgment: friendly, stunning

Size: tiny, petite

Shape: round, slender

Age: young, elderly

Color: yellow, green

Nationality: Korean, Nigerian

Material: wax, wood

Thus,

I found a beautiful, antique, silver bracelet.

She purchased two large, oval, linen tablecloths.

WORD ORDER FOR ADVERBS

Adverbs showing frequency (*always, often, usually, sometimes, never*) come after forms of the verb *be*, but before other verbs.

My aunt *is usually* on time.

My aunt *usually brings* us candy.

WORD ORDER FOR NEGATION

Not is placed after the first helping verb. When there is no helping verb, insert a form of the verb *do* before *not*.

Statement:	The patient *has been taking* the medicine.
Negation:	The patient *has not been taking* the medicine.
Statement:	The patient *takes* the medicine every day.
Negation:	The patient *does not take* the medicine every day.

The Idiomatic Use of Prepositions

Learning to choose the correct preposition comes mostly from reading and listening to the idiomatic use of prepositions. Some expressions should be carefully studied. Learn these idiomatic uses of prepositions for expressing time.

Use *on* for a specific day or date	Use *in* for a period of time	Use *at* for a specific time
on Thursday	in the morning	at 12 noon
on Friday afternoon	in the afternoon	at 3 a.m.
on August 25, 2003	in the evening (but *at* night)	at dawn
	in 2003	at dusk
	in the summer	at night
	in August	
	in six hours	

Special Problems with English Verbs

THE FIVE FORMS OF ENGLISH VERBS

Most English verbs have five forms. One exception is the verb *be*, which has eight forms.

	Regular	Irregular	Verb *be*
Base form (used for first person, second person, and third-person plural)	walk	go	be (am, are)
-s form (present third-person singular)	walks	goes	is
-ing form (present participle)	walking	going	being
Past tense form	walked	went	was, were
Past participle form	walked	gone	been

THE MEANINGS OF ENGLISH HELPING VERBS

Of the twenty-three helping verbs (including forms of *do, have,* and *be*), ni[ ] called **modals.** These modals function only as helping verbs. They do n[ ] the five forms of the main verbs. They are used to form tenses and to ad[ ] of meaning to the main verb. Be sure you know these meanings. Not[ ] some cases a modal may have an alternate expression that has the same meaning. (See *can*, *must*, and *should* in the following chart.)

	Verb	Meaning	Example
1.	can is able to (another option for *can*)	ability	I *can* paint this room. I *am able to* paint this room.
2.	could (after a past tense)	ability	He said I *could* paint this room.
3.	will	intention	I *will* paint this room.
4.	shall	usually used for questions	*Shall* I paint this room?
5.	would	intention (after a past tense)	I promised him that I *would* paint this room.
6.	may	permission	*May* I paint this room?
7.	might	possibility	I *might* paint this room if you buy the paint.
8.	must have to (another option for *must*)	necessity	I *must* paint this room before we move in. I *have to* paint this room before we move in.
	must	probability	He *must* be ill; he didn't show up for work.
9.	should ought to (another option for *should*)	advisability	The room is shabby; I *should* paint it. The room is shabby; I *ought to* paint it.
	should ought to	expectation	He *should* arrive soon. He *ought to* arrive soon.

VERBS THAT DO NOT OCCUR IN THE CONTINUOUS FORM

The continuous form indicates an ongoing activity:

Continuous form: The chef *is learning* to make pastry.

Some English verbs cannot occur in the continuous form, even though they indicate an ongoing activity. These verbs are called **stative verbs.**

Incorrect: The chef is understanding today's demonstration.

Correct: The chef *understands* today's demonstration.

Incorrect: He is knowing how to make pie crust.

Correct: He *knows* how to make pie crust.

Do not use the continuous form with stative verbs.

Verbs with Stative Meanings

State of being	Mental activity	Sensory perception	Measurement	Relationship
be	believe	appear	cost	belong
	doubt	feel	equal	contain
Emotion	know	hear	measure	entail
desire	remember	see	weigh	have
dislike	think	seem		own
hate	understand	smell		
like		taste		
love				
want				

Note that in some cases a verb may have both a stative meaning and an active meaning.

Stative verb: The child *weighs* sixty pounds.

but

Active verb: The grocer *is weighing* the fruit.

THE VERB FORMS *BEEN* AND *BEING*

Although *been* and *being* may sound similar in speech, in writing there is an important difference. Use *been* when a past participle is needed. *Been* will follow *has, have,* or *had.*

Active voice: The actress *has been studying* her part.

Passive voice: The part *has been studied* by the actress.

Use *being* when a present participle is needed. *Being* will follow some form of the helping verb *be* (*am, is, are, was, were*).

Active voice: The scientists *are being* observant.

Passive voice: The experiment *is being observed* by the scientist.

IDIOMATIC EXPRESSIONS USING *DO* OR *MAKE*

Following are some of the many idiomatic expressions using *do* or *make.*

do the wash	*make* the bed
do the dishes	*make* a pie, cake, meal
do your homework	*make* a decision
do a job	*make* a mistake
do the shopping	*make* a deal
do the laundry	*make* progress
do someone a favor	*make* a speech
do your hair	*make* a living

VERB-PREPOSITION COMBINATIONS

The uses and meanings of prepositions in the English language are very difficult to master. When they are part of two-word and three-word combinations with verbs, the prepositions are called **particles,** and the combinations are called **phrasal verbs.** Some of these particles may be separated from the verb, and others may not be separated. Since there is no clear rule, each one must be learned the same way you would learn a new vocabulary word. Below are a few common verb-preposition combinations.

Separable phrasal verbs

ask out (invite on a date)	He *asked out* the older girl. He *asked* the older girl *out*.
call off (cancel)	Let's *call off* the party. Let's *call* the party *off*.
call up (telephone)	The officer *called up* the applicant. The officer *called* the applicant *up*.
clear up (solve)	Can you *clear up* this problem? Can you *clear* this problem *up*?
fill out (complete)	Please *fill out* these forms. Please *fill* these forms *out*.
get back (recover)	The student *got back* the test results. The student *got* the test results *back*.
leave out (omit)	Don't *leave out* any answers. Don't *leave* any answers *out*.
look over (review)	*Look over* this paper for any errors. *Look* this paper *over* for any errors.
look up (research, check)	*Look up* the number in the telephone book. *Look* the number *up* in the telephone book.
make up (create, invent, lie)	Do you think he *made up* the story? Do you think he *made* the story *up*?
turn down (refuse)	She *turned down* our generous offer. She *turned* our generous offer *down*.
turn off (switch off)	*Turn off* the light. *Turn* the light *off*.

Nonseparable phrasal verbs

call on (visit; choose)	Doctors used to *call on* patients in their homes. The teacher *called on* me for the answer.
get away with (escape the consequences of)	Our dog always tries to *get away with* something when we are out.

get along with (be on good terms with)	The new employee *gets along with* all her coworkers.
get over (recover from)	We took a long time to *get over* the loss of our pet.
get at (hint, suggest)	What do you think the editorial was *getting at?*
get after (scold)	The mother will *get after* the child for being disobedient.
go over (review)	Please *go over* the chapter before taking the test.
let up (diminish in force)	The storm will soon *let up.*
look in on (visit)	Joshua *looks in on* his elderly mother at least twice a week.
look into (investigate)	The federal agents will *look into* the case.
run into (meet)	I always *run into* someone I know at the supermarket.
run out of (become used up)	The printer will soon *run out of* paper.
speak up (talk in a louder voice)	Please *speak up* so that I can hear you.
turn up (appear)	Has the lost child *turned up* yet?
wear out (become unusable through long use)	He *wore out* five pairs of jeans this season.

VERBS FOLLOWED BY GERUNDS OR INFINITIVES

Some verbs may be followed by gerunds (-*ing* form of the verb). Others are followed by infinitives (*to* plus the base form of the verb). Still others may be followed by either a gerund or an infinitive. Because this is a challenging aspect of becoming fluent in English, begin by learning the most commonly used expressions. Then gradually increase your correct usage of these many expressions. Look for them as you read and try to incorporate them into your speaking and writing.

Verbs followed by gerunds

admit	deny	imagine	practice
appreciate	discuss	keep	quit
avoid	enjoy	miss	risk
consider	finish	postpone	suggest

I *imagined going* on a cruise.

I *quit eating* junk food.

Verbs followed by infinitives

agree to	decide to	mean to	promise to
ask to	expect to	need to	refuse to
beg to	have to	offer to	want to
choose to	hope to	plan to	
claim to	manage to	pretend to	

I *expect to visit* you by the end of the summer.

Verbs followed by either gerunds or infinitives

begin	hate	remember	try
continue	like	start	
forget	love	stop	

Stuart *began reading* at age four.

or

Stuart *began to read* at age four.

ESOL Word Confusions

WHEN DO YOU USE *NO* AND WHEN DO YOU USE *NOT?*

Use *no* before a noun. *No* is an adjective.

I have *no food* in the house.

Use *not* before a verb, adverb, or adjective. *Not* is an adverb.

I am *not going.*

They were *not very* satisfied.

We are *not unhappy.*

WHAT IS THE DIFFERENCE BETWEEN *A FEW* AND *FEW* AND BETWEEN *A LITTLE* AND *LITTLE?*

Use *a few* and *a little* to mean *some:*

With count nouns:	We have *a few cans* on the shelf, maybe five or six.
With noncount nouns:	We have *a little money* in the bank.

Use *few* and *little* to mean *not many* or *not much:*

With count nouns:	We have *few cans* left, two or three at most.
With noncount nouns:	We have *little money* in the bank.

Other ESOL Concerns Addressed in *The Writer's Workplace*

Parts of Speech

Words can be divided into categories called **parts of speech.** Understanding these categories will help you work with language more easily, especially when it comes to revising your own writing.

Nouns

> A **noun** is a word that names a person, place, or thing.

Common nouns	Proper nouns
officer	Michael Johnson
station	Grand Central Station
magazine	*Newsweek*

Nouns are said to be **concrete** if they name things you can see or touch.

window   paper   river

Nouns are said to be **abstract** if they name things you cannot see or touch. These words may express concepts, ideas, or qualities.

marriage   democracy   honesty

To find out whether a word is a noun, it may help to ask one or more of these questions:

- Can I make the word plural? (Most nouns have a plural form.)
- Can I put the article *the* in front of the word?
- Is the word used as the subject or object of the sentence?

Pronouns

> A **pronoun** is a word that takes the place of a noun. Like a noun, it can be used as the subject or object of a sentence.

Pronouns can be divided into several classes. Some of them are given in the following chart.

Classes of Pronouns

PERSONAL PRONOUNS

	Subjective		Objective		Possessive	
	Singular	**Plural**	**Singular**	**Plural**	**Singular**	**Plural**
1st person	I	we	me	us	my (mine)	our (ours)
2nd person	you	you	you	you	your (yours)	your (yours)
3rd person	he she it	they	him her it	them	his (his) her (hers) its (its)	their (theirs)

RELATIVE PRONOUNS
(CAN INTRODUCE NOUN CLAUSES AND ADJECTIVE CLAUSES)

who   whom   whose   which   that   what   whoever   whomever   whichever   whatever

DEMONSTRATIVE PRONOUNS
(CAN POINT OUT THE ANTECEDENT)

this   that   these   those

INDEFINITE PRONOUNS
Singular

another	someone	everyone	no one	each	much
anyone	somebody	everybody	nobody	either	one
anybody	something	everything	nothing	neither	such
anything					

Plural

both   few   many   several

Singular or Plural
(depending on meaning)

all   any   more   most   none   some

Adjectives

An **adjective** is a word that modifies, describes, or limits a noun or a pronoun. Adjectives usually come directly before the nouns they modify, but they can also appear later in the sentence.

Here the adjective comes directly in front of the noun it modifies:

The *unusual* package was placed on my desk.

Here the adjective occurs later but refers back to the noun it modifies:

The package felt *cold*.

Verbs

A **verb** is a word that shows action or expresses being. It can change form to show the time (past, present, or future) of that action or being.

Verbs can be divided into three classes: action verbs, linking verbs, and helping verbs.

ACTION VERBS

An **action verb** tells us what the subject is doing and when the action occurs.

In this sentence, the action takes place in the present:

The athlete *runs* five miles every morning.

In this sentence, the action takes place in the past:

The crowd *cheered* for the oldest runner.

LINKING VERBS

A **linking verb** joins the subject of a sentence to one or more words that describe or identify the subject.

Here the linking verb *was* identifies *he* with the noun *dancer:*

He *was* a dancer in his twenties.

Here the linking verb *seemed* describes *she* as *disappointed:*

She *seemed* disappointed with her job.

Common Linking Verbs

act	become	look	sound
appear	feel	remain	taste
be (am, is, are, was, were,	get	seem	turn
has been, have been, had been)	grow	smell	

HELPING VERBS (ALSO CALLED AUXILIARIES)

> A **helping verb** combines with the main verb to form a verb phrase. It always comes before the main verb.

The helping verb could show the *tense* of the verb:

It *will* rain tomorrow.

The helping verb could show the *passive voice:*

The new civic center *has been* finished.

The helping verb could give a *special meaning* to the verb:

Ricky Martin *may be* singing here tonight.

Common Helping Verbs

		Forms of *be*		Forms of *have*	Forms of *do*
can	shall	being	are	has	does
could	should	been	was	have	do
may	will	am	were	had	did
might	would	is			
must					

Adverbs

> An **adverb** is a word that modifies a verb, an adjective, or another adverb. It often ends in *-ly*, but a better test is to ask yourself if the word answers one of the questions *how, when,* or *where.*

The adverb could modify a *verb:*

The student walked *happily* into the classroom.

The adverb could modify an *adjective:*

It will be *very* cold tomorrow.

The adverb could modify another *adverb:*

Winter has come *too* early.

Learn to recognize the common adverbs in the following list.

Common Adverbs

Adverbs of frequency		Adverbs of degree	
always	often	even	only
ever	seldom	extremely	quite
never	sometimes	just	surely
		more	too
		much	very

Prepositions

A **preposition** is a word that may be used to relate a noun or pronoun to some other word in the sentence. The preposition with its noun or pronoun and any modifiers is called a **prepositional phrase.**

The letter is *from* my father.

The envelope is addressed *to* my sister.

Read through the following list of prepositions several times so that you will be able to recognize them. Your instructor may ask you to memorize them.

Common Prepositions

about	behind	except	onto	toward
above	below	for	out	under
across	beneath	from	outside	underneath
after	beside	in	over	unlike
against	between	inside	past	until
along	beyond	into	regarding	up
among	by	like	since	upon
around	concerning	near	through	with
as	despite	of	throughout	within
at	down	off	till	without
before	during	on	to	

Conjunctions

> A **conjunction** is a word that joins or connects words, phrases, or clauses.

A conjunction may connect *two words:*

> Sooner *or* later, you will have to pay.

A conjunction may connect *two phrases:*

> The story was on the radio *and* in the newspaper.

A conjunction may connect *two clauses:*

> Dinner was late *because* I had to work overtime.

Conjunctions

Coordinating conjunctions		Subordinating conjunctions		Correlative conjunctions
and	yet	after	if, even if	though	either . . . or
but	so	although	in order that	unless	neither . . . nor
or		as, as if, as though	provided that	until	both . . . and
nor		as long as	rather than	when, whenever	not only . . . but also
for (meaning		because	since	where, wherever	
because)		before	so that	whether	
		even though	that	while	
		how			

Adverbial conjunctions
(also known as conjunctive adverbs)

To add an idea:	furthermore	*To show an alternative:*	otherwise
	moreover		instead
	likewise		on the other hand
	in addition	*To show likeness:*	likewise
	also		similarly
	besides	*To show emphasis:*	indeed
To contrast:	however		in fact
	nevertheless	*To show time:*	meanwhile
	nonetheless		
	consequently		
To show results:	therefore		
	accordingly		
	hence		
	thus		

Interjections

An **interjection** is a word that expresses a strong feeling and is not connected grammatically to any other part of the sentence.

Oh, I forgot my keys.

Well, that means I'll have to sit here all day.

Studying the Context

Because one word may function differently or have different forms or meanings in different sentences, you must often study the context in which the word is found to be sure of its part of speech. In the following sentence, *for* functions as a preposition:

The parent makes sacrifices *for* the good of the children.

In this next sentence, *for* functions as a conjunction, meaning *because:*

The parent worked two jobs, *for* her child needed a good education.

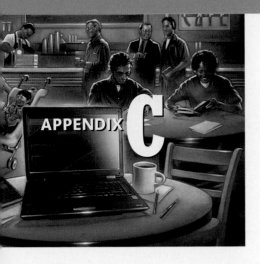

Irregular Verbs

Following is an alphabetical listing of the principal parts of common irregular verbs.

Base form	Past tense	Past participle
arise	arose	arisen
bear	bore	borne
beat	beat	beat or beaten
become	became	become
begin	began	begun
bend	bent	bent
bet	bet	bet
bind	bound	bound
bite	bit	bitten, bit
bleed	bled	bled
blow	blew	blown
break	broke	broken
breed	bred	bred
bring	brought	brought
build	built	built
burst	burst	burst
buy	bought	bought
cast	cast	cast
catch	caught	caught
choose	chose	chosen
cling	clung	clung
come	came	come
cost	cost	cost
creep	crept	crept
cut	cut	cut
deal	dealt	dealt
dig	dug	dug
dive	dived, dove	dived
do	did	done
draw	drew	drawn
drink	drank	drunk
drive	drove	driven
eat	ate	eaten
fall	fell	fallen
feed	fed	fed
feel	felt	felt
fight	fought	fought

Base form	Past tense	Past participle
find	found	found
fit	fit	fit
flee	fled	fled
fling	flung	flung
fly	flew	flown
forbid	forbade, forbad	forbidden
forget	forgot	forgotten
forgive	forgave	forgiven
freeze	froze	frozen
get	got	gotten
give	gave	given
go	went	gone
grind	ground	ground
grow	grew	grown
hang	hung, hanged*	hung, hanged
have	had	had
hear	heard	heard
hide	hid	hidden
hit	hit	hit
hold	held	held
hurt	hurt	hurt
keep	kept	kept
kneel	knelt	knelt
know	knew	known
lay (to put)	laid	laid
lead	led	led
leave	left	left
lend	lent	lent
let	let	let
lie (to recline)	lay	lain
lose	lost	lost
make	made	made
mean	meant	meant
meet	met	met
mistake	mistook	mistaken
pay	paid	paid
plead	pleaded, pled	pleaded, pled
prove	proved	proved, proven
put	put	put
quit	quit	quit
read	read†	read†
ride	rode	ridden
ring	rang	rung
rise	rose	risen
run	ran	run
say	said	said
see	saw	seen
seek	sought	sought
sell	sold	sold
send	sent	sent
set	set	set

* See the dictionary to clarify usage.
† Pronunciation changes in past and past participle forms.

Base form	Past tense	Past participle
sew	sewed	sewn, sewed
shake	shook	shaken
shave	shaved	shaved, shaven
shed	shed	shed
shine	shone	shone
shoot	shot	shot
show	showed	shown, showed
shrink	shrank, shrunk	shrunk, shrunken
shut	shut	shut
sing	sang	sung
sink	sank	sunk
sit	sat	sat
slay	slew	slain
sleep	slept	slept
slide	slid	slid
sling	slung	slung
slink	slunk	slunk
slit	slit	slit
sow	sowed	sown, sowed
speak	spoke	spoken
speed	sped, speeded	sped, speeded
spend	spent	spent
spin	spun	spun
spit	spat	spat
split	split	split
spread	spread	spread
spring	sprang	sprung
stand	stood	stood
steal	stole	stolen
stick	stuck	stuck
sting	stung	stung
stink	stank, stunk	stunk
stride	strode	stridden
strike	struck	struck
string	strung	strung
swear	swore	sworn
sweep	swept	swept
swim	swam	swum
swing	swung	swung
take	took	taken
teach	taught	taught
tear	tore	torn
tell	told	told
think	thought	thought
throw	threw	thrown
wake	woke, waked	woken, waked
wear	wore	worn
weave	wove	woven
weep	wept	wept
wet	wet	wet
win	won	won
wind	wound	wound
wring	wrung	wrung
write	wrote	written

APPENDIX **D**

Spelling

Forming the Plurals of Nouns

Almost all nouns can be made plural by simply adding *s* to the singular form:

girl   girls
dinner dinners

However, each of the following groups of words has its own special rules for forming the plural.

1. **Words ending in -y.** For words ending in -*y* preceded by a *consonant*, change the *y* to *i* and add *es*.

    la*dy*   lad*ies*
    ceremo*ny*   ceremon*ies*

    Words ending in -*y* preceded by a *vowel* form their plurals in the regular way, by just adding *s*.

    d*ay*   d*ays*
    monk*ey*   monk*eys*
    vall*ey*   vall*eys*

2. **Words ending in -o.** Most words ending in -*o* preceded by a *consonant* add *es* to form the plural.

    her*o*   her*oes*
    pota*to*   potat*oes*
    ec*ho*   ech*oes*

    However, musical terms or names of musical instruments add only *s*.

    pian*o*   pian*os*
    sol*o*   sol*os*
    sopran*o*   sopran*os*

    Words ending in -*o* preceded by a *vowel* add *s*.

    pat*io*   pat*ios*
    rad*io*   rad*ios*
    rod*eo*   rod*eos*

    Some words ending in -*o* may form their plural with *s* or *es*.

    memen*to*   mement*os*   or   mement*oes*
    pin*to*   pint*os*   or   pint*oes*
    zer*o*   zer*os*   or   zer*oes*

If you are uncertain about the plural ending of a word ending in *-o*, it is best to consult a dictionary. The dictionary gives all the endings of irregular plurals. If no plural form is given, you know the word forms its plural in the regular way, by adding only *s*.

3. **Words ending in *-ch, -sh, -s, -x,* and *-z*.** For words ending in *-ch, -sh, -s, -x,* and *-z,* add *es*.

   witch*es*   dress*es*   buzz*es*
   dish*es*   tax*es*

4. **Words ending in *-fe* or *-f*.** For some words ending in *-fe* or *-f*, change the *f* to *v* and add *es*. You can hear the change from the *f* sound to the *v* sound in the plural.

   wi*fe*   wi*ves*
   leaf   lea*ves*

   For other words ending in *-fe* or *-f*, keep the *f* and just add *s*.

   sheriff   sheriff*s*
   belie*f*   belief*s*

   Again, you can hear that the *f* sound is kept in the plural. Some words can form their plural either way. If so, the dictionary will give the preferred way first.

5. **Foreign words.** Some words borrowed from other languages use the plurals from those other languages.

   crisi*s*   cris*es*
   phenomen*on*   phenomen*a*
   alumn*us* (masc.)   alumn*i*
   alumn*a* (fem.)   alumn*ae*
   alg*a*   alg*ae*

6. **Compound nouns.** Plurals of compound nouns are formed by putting *s* on the end of the main word.

   brother-in-law   brothers-in-law
   passer-by   passers-by

7. **Irregular plurals.** Some nouns in English have irregular plurals.

   child   children
   deer   deer
   foot   feet
   goose   geese
   man, woman   men, women
   moose   moose
   mouse   mice
   ox   oxen
   sheep   sheep
   tooth   teeth

Adding Endings to Words Ending in *-y*

1. When a *y* at the end of a word is preceded by a consonant, change *y* to *i* and add the ending. (After you have studied the examples, write the other words on the blanks.)

Word		Ending		New word
carry	+	er	=	carr*ier*
merry	+	ment	=	merr*iment*
funny	+	er	=	_____
busy	+	ness	=	_____
vary	+	es	=	_____

Exceptions: Do not change the *y* to *i* if the ending starts with *i*. In English, we seldom have two *i*'s together.

stu*dy*	+	ing	=	stud*ying* (not studiing)
rea*dy*	+	ing	=	_____

Some long words drop the *y* when the ending is added. You can hear that the *y* syllable is missing when you pronounce the word correctly.

milita*ry*	+	ism	=	militar*ism*
accomp*any*	+	ist	=	_____

2. When a *y* at the end of a word is preceded by a vowel, do *not* change the *y* when adding the ending. Simply add the ending.

surv*ey*	+	s	=	surv*eys*
enj*oy*	+	ment	=	_____

Learning to Spell *ie* or *ei* Words

Use this rhyme to help you remember how to spell most *ie* and *ei* words:

i before *e*

except after *c*

or when sounded like *ā*

as in *neighbor* or *weigh*.

i before *e* (*ie* is much more common than *ei*):

believe	friend	yield
chief	shriek	

except after *c:*

ceiling	conceive	receive
conceit	receipt	

or when sounded like *ā* as in *neighbor* or *weigh:*

beige	reins	vein
eight	sleigh	

Once you have learned the rhyme, concentrate on learning the following groups of words, which are exceptions to the rhyme.

Exceptions to the *ie/ei* rule

caffeine	leisure	ancient	either	counterfeit
codeine	seize	conscience	neither	Fahrenheit
protein	seizure	efficient	sheik	foreign
		sufficient	stein	height
			their	
			weird	

When Should the Final Consonant of a Word Be Doubled?

When you add an ending that begins with a vowel (*-ed, -er, -est, -ing*) to a word, how do you know whether you should double the final consonant of that word? The answer to this question involves a complicated spelling rule. However, the rule is well worth learning because once you know it, you will suddenly be able to spell scores of words correctly.

In the examples below, can you explain why the word *trap* doubles its *p* but the word *turn* does not double its *n*?

The final *p* doubles:	trap + ing = tra**pp**ing
The final *n* does not double:	turn + ing = tur**n**ing

Because the last three letters (*rap*) in the word *trap* are a consonant-vowel-consonant combination, you double the final consonant in this one-syllable word (when adding an ending beginning with a vowel). Since the last three letters (*urn*) in the word *turn* are a vowel-consonant-consonant combination, you do not double the final consonant in this one-syllable word (when adding an ending beginning with a vowel).

Double the final consonant of a one-syllable word when adding an ending that begins with a vowel only if the last three letters of the word end with a consonant-vowel-consonant combination.

PRACTICE

Study the list of words that follows. For each of these one-syllable words, decide whether to double the final consonant when adding an ending beginning with a vowel.

One-syllable word	Consonant-vowel-consonant combination?	Double?	Word with -ing ending
1. drag	_____	_____	_____
2. drain	_____	_____	_____
3. slip	_____	_____	_____
4. crack	_____	_____	_____
5. broil	_____	_____	_____
6. win	_____	_____	_____

NOTE: In words with *qu*, like *quit* or *quiz*, think of the *qu* as a consonant: *quit* + ing = qui**tt**ing. The *u* does have a consonant *w* sound.

> **For words of more than one syllable, the rule has one more condition: If the first syllable in the newly formed word is accented, do not double the final consonant.**

Thus,

pre fer´ + ed = pre ferred´

(The new word *preferred* maintains the accent on the second syllable, so the final *r* is doubled.) However,

pre fer´ + ence = pref´ er ence

(In the new word *preference*, the accent is on the first syllable, so the final consonant *r* is not doubled.)

Is It One Word or Two?

Deciding whether certain words should be joined to form compound words is difficult. To avoid confusion, study the following three groups of words.

These words are always written as one word:

another	good-bye,	playroom
bathroom	or good-by	roommate
bedroom	grandmother	schoolteacher
bookkeeper	nearby	southeast, northwest, and so on
cannot	nevertheless	yourself
downstairs	newspaper	

These words are always written as two words:

a lot	dining room	high school	no one
all right	good night	living room	

The following words may be written as one or two words depending on their use. After you have studied the spellings and definitions, write the proper words on the blanks in the sample sentences.

all ready (pron, adj): completely prepared
already (adv): previously; before

He was ——————— there by the time I arrived.

I have ——————— read that book.

We were ——————— for the New Year's Eve party.

all together (pron, adj): in a group
altogether (adv): completely

Our family was ——————— at Thanksgiving.

I am ——————— too upset to concentrate.

Have you gathered your papers ———————?

all ways (adj, noun):   every road or path
always (adv):   on every occasion

> Be sure to check ———————— before you cross that intersection.
>
> ———————— look both ways before you cross that intersection.
>
> She ———————— figures out the homework.

any one (adj, pron):   one person or thing in a specific group
anyone (indefinite pron):   any person at all

> Did ———————— ever find my gloves?
>
> She will talk to ———————— who will listen to her.
>
> I would choose ———————— of those sweaters if I had the money.

every one (adj, pron):   every person or thing in a specific group
everyone (indefinite pron):   all of the people

> ———————— of the books we wanted was out of stock.
>
> ———————— was so disappointed.
>
> ———————— of the workers disapproved of the new rules.

may be (verb):   might be
maybe (adv):   perhaps

> The news broadcast said that there ———————— a storm tomorrow.
>
> If it's bad, ———————— I won't go to work.
>
> ———————— my car won't start.

Spelling Commonly Mispronounced Words

Several common English words are often mispronounced or pronounced in such a way that the result is incorrect spelling. Below are sixty common words that are often misspelled. As you study them, be careful to spell each of the underlined syllables correctly.

1. Remember the *a* in each underlined syllable:

accidentally	literature
basically	miniature
boundary	separate
extraordinary	temperament
incidentally	temperature

2. Remember the *e* in each underlined syllable:

considerable	mathematics
difference	numerous
funeral	scenery
interesting	

Notice, however, that the words below in column 1, which end in *-er,* drop the *e* when they change to the new form in column 2.

disas<u>ter</u>	disas<u>tr</u>ous
en<u>ter</u>	ent<u>r</u>ance
hin<u>der</u>	hind<u>r</u>ance
hun<u>ger</u>	hun<u>gr</u>y
laun<u>der</u>	laun<u>dr</u>y
mons<u>ter</u>	mons<u>tr</u>ous
remem<u>ber</u>	remem<u>br</u>ance

3. Remember the *i* in each underlined syllable:

     asp<u>i</u>rin   fam<u>i</u>ly   simil<u>a</u>r

4. Remember the *o* in each underlined syllable:

choc<u>o</u>late	hum<u>o</u>rous
envir<u>o</u>nment	lab<u>o</u>ratory
fav<u>o</u>rite	soph<u>o</u>more

5. Remember the *u* in each underlined syllable:

     lux<u>u</u>ry   acc<u>u</u>racy

6. Remember the *y* in each underlined syllable:

     stud<u>y</u>ing   carr<u>y</u>ing

7. Remember the underlined consonant in each of the following words:

b	**n**
proba<u>b</u>ly	gover<u>n</u>ment

c	**r**
arc<u>t</u>ic	Feb<u>r</u>uary
	lib<u>r</u>ary
d	su<u>r</u>prise
candi<u>d</u>ate	
han<u>d</u>kerchief	**t**
suppose<u>d</u> to	authen<u>t</u>ic
use<u>d</u> to	iden<u>t</u>ical
	par<u>t</u>ner
g	promp<u>t</u>ly
reco<u>g</u>nize	quan<u>t</u>ity

8. Do not add an extra *e* after the *th:*

     athlete   athletic

9. Do not transpose the underlined letters:

trage<u>dy</u>	
pe<u>r</u>suade	p<u>r</u>efer
pe<u>r</u>form	p<u>r</u>escription

Spelling Two Hundred Tough Words

Word List 1: Silent Letters

b

climb
crumb
debt
doubt

c

indict

d

knowledge
Wednesday

h

exhibit
rhetoric
rhythm
schedule

l

colonel

n

autumn
column
condemn

p

pneumonia
psychology

s

aisle
debris
island

t

depot
listen
mortgage

w

answer

Word List 2: Double Letters

accidentally	committee	possession	suggest
accommodate	exaggerate	preferred	summarize
across	finally	questionnaire	tomorrow
annual	guarantee	recommend	written (but writing)
apparently	necessary	succeed	
arrangement	occasionally	success	

Word List 3: -able or -ible

-able. Usually, when you begin with a complete word, the ending is -able.

acceptable   agreeable

These words keep the e when the ending is added:

knowledgeable   noticeable
manageable   peaceable

These words drop the e when the ending is added:

conceivable   imaginable
desirable   indispensable

-ible. Usually, if you start with a root that is not a word, the ending is -ible.

audible	illegible	possible
compatible	incredible	susceptible
eligible	permissible	tangible
feasible	plausible	

Word List 4: *de-* or *di-*

de-		di-	
decide	despise	dilemma	dispense
decision	despite	dilute	dispute
delinquent	despondent	discipline	dissent
descend	destructive	discuss	divide
describe	develop	disease	divine
despair	device	disguise	division
despicable			

Word List 5: The *-er* Sound

Most words ending with the *-er* sound are spelled with *-er*, like the words *prisoner*, *customer*, and *hunger*. Words that are exceptions to this should be learned carefully.

-ar	-or	-ur
beggar	actor	murmur
burglar	author	
calendar	bachelor	**-yr**
cellar	doctor	martyr
dollar	emperor	
grammar	governor	
pillar	humor	
polar	labor	
similar	motor	
vulgar	neighbor	
	professor	
	sailor	
	scissors	

Word List 6: *-ance* or *-ence*

Most words with the *-ence* sound at the end are spelled *-ence*. Here are a few examples:

audience	intelligence
correspondence	presence
excellence	reference
existence	

Learn these exceptions:

-ance		-ense	-eance
allowance	guidance	license	vengeance
ambulance	ignorance		
appearance	nuisance		
assistance	observance		
attendance	resistance		
balance	significance		
dominance	tolerance		

Word List 7: Problems with *s*, *c*, *z*, *x*, and *k*

absence	criticize	medicine
alcohol	ecstasy	muscle
analyze	emphasize	prejudice
auxiliary	especially	recede
awkward	exceed	sincerely
biscuit	exercise	supersede
complexion	fascinate	vacillate
concede	magazine	vicious
consensus		

Word List 8: Twenty-five Demons

acquire	extremely	occurred
argument	frightening	occurrence
benefit	grateful	privilege
cafeteria	inoculate	ridiculous
category	judgment	secretary
cemetery	lightning	truly
conquer	ninety	until
corroborate	ninth	village
courageous		

Transitions

Transitions are words or phrases that take the reader from one idea to another. Here are some of the most commonly used transitional expressions. They are especially useful when you want to make the connections between ideas clear to your readers.

Transitions for description—to show place

above, on top of	to the left, to the right
beneath, under	beside, near, close by, at hand, next to
ahead, in front of, in the distance	across from, nearby, in the neighborhood
behind, in back of	between, in the middle, in the center
toward, away from	

Transitions for narration—to show a shift in time

recently	suddenly	then
previously	immediately	next, the next day
earlier	meanwhile	several weeks later
in the past	at the same time	the following month
a few days ago	within a few minutes	finally
a hundred years ago	soon, soon afterward	eventually
now, by now	later, later on	in the end
at once	after a little while	

Transitions to show examples

for example	a case in point is . . .	specifically
another example is . . .	one such case	for instance
to illustrate	a typical case	such as
an illustration of this is . . .	consider the case of . . .	

Transitions for process

the first step	while you are . . .	the last step
in the beginning	as you are . . .	the final step
to start with	next	finally
to begin with	then	at last
first of all	the second step	eventually
	after you have . . .	

Transitions for comparison

again	like
also	likewise
as well as	moreover
both	the same
equally	similar to
furthermore	similarly
just as	so
just like	too

Transitions for contrast

although	instead
and yet	nevertheless
but	on the contrary
despite	on the other hand
different from	otherwise
even though	still
except for	though
however	unlike
in contrast with	whereas

Transitions for cause

because
caused by
results from
the reason is that
since

Transitions for effect

accordingly
as a result, resulted in
consequently
for this reason
so, so that
then, therefore, thus

Transitions for classification

divisions, divided into
categories, categorized by
types, kinds
groups, groupings, grouped into
areas, fields

Transitions for definition

is defined as
is understood to be
means that
is sometimes thought to be
signifies

Transitions for persuasion

To signal the thesis:
I agree (disagree)
I (do not) support
I am (not) in favor of
. . . should (not) be changed
. . . should (not) be adopted
I propose

To signal a reason:
a convincing piece of evidence
an additional reason
because
in view of this fact

To admit an opponent's viewpoint:
while it is true
although there are those who . . .
the opposition would have you believe . . .
of course,
some may claim
we have been told that . . .
popular thought is that . . .
most people assume that . . .

To signal a conclusion:
therefore
consequently
as a result

Answer Key to Practices and Selected Exercises

CHAPTER 1: GATHERING IDEAS FOR WRITING

Activity 5: Preparing Questions for an Interview (page 15)

1. What is a typical day at work like?
2. What is the range of salaries that a person could expect to earn as a lawyer?
3. What are the different areas of law practice, and how did you choose which one you wanted to pursue?
4. What is the most interesting case you have ever had?
5. What are some of your greatest challenges, and how do you handle them?

CHAPTER 2: RECOGNIZING THE ELEMENTS OF GOOD WRITING

Activity 1: Choosing an Aspect of a Subject (page 22, sample answers)

1. *A personal story:* the story of my unusual part-time job
2. *How to do something:* how to succeed in school while holding a job.
3. *Persuasion:* three good reasons why you shouldn't work while you're in school
4. *Effects:* the hidden costs of having a job while going to school
5. *Comparison/contrast:* a comparison of two groups of students: those who must work and those who can devote all time to studies

Activity 3: Identifying an Audience and a Purpose (page 23, sample answers)

1. *Audience:* first-aid class; *purpose:* information
2. *Audience:* town council; *purpose:* information and persuasion
3. *Audience:* owners; *purpose:* manual of information

4. *Audience:* community; *purpose:* persuasion
5. *Audience:* classmates; *purpose:* entertainment

CHAPTER 3: FINDING SUBJECTS AND VERBS IN SIMPLE SENTENCES

Practice (page 35)

1. gym   2. coach   3. He   4. cheerleaders
5. People

Practice (page 36)

1. morning, June   2. flowers, grass
3. people, village, square   4. lottery, Mr. Sommers
5. man, time, energy, activities

Practice (page 36)

1. They   2. It   3. They   4. He   5. We
6. Nobody or No one

Practice (page 37)

1. The, confident
2. Her, long, strenuous (*her* is a possessive pronoun used as an adjective)
3. Several, the, finish
4. a, terrible, one
5. A, disappointing, the
Note: *A, an,* and *the* are usually called *articles* or *noun determiners.*

Practice (page 38)

1. Exercise, diet   2. Mothers, fathers
3. factors, factors

Practice (page 38)

1. child: concrete common noun
2. Helen Keller: concrete proper noun
3. She: personal pronoun

4. park: concrete common noun
5. leaves: concrete common noun
6. thought: abstract common noun
7. parents, teacher: compound subject; concrete common nouns

Exercise 1: Finding the Subject of a Sentence (page 38)

1. train   2. Steven Laye   3. He
4. Everything   5. man   6. tunnel
7. Buses, cars   8. People   9. noise
10. Loneliness

Exercise 5: Recognizing Prepositions (page 41)

1. During   2. for   3. by   4. from   5. of
6. within   7. to   8. in   9. at   10. on

Exercise 7: Finding Subjects in Sentences with Prepositional Phrases (page 42)

1. On Friday, January 27, 2006, Western Union sent its last telegram.
2. With the ascendancy of modern technology, the telegram is no longer needed.
3. In 1851 in Rochester, New York, Western Union had its beginings.
4. Messages were transmitted by Morse code over the wires and delivered by couriers.
5. Eventually, telegraph service drove the pony express out of business.
6. Until the emergence of the telegraph, the average delivery time for a message by pony express took ten days.
7. At the height of the telegram business, in 1929, two hundred million telegrams were sent around the world.
8. Now for Wester Union, money transfers, bill payment, and products such as telephone service and Internet access will form the core of their business.
9. In the past, families sent messages of births, deaths, birthdays, and weddings by telegram.
10. In the present era, e-mail and fax messages have taken the place of the telegram.

Practice (page 43)

1. Alex Harkavy, a high school senior, has an auditory-processing disorder.
2. Marcia Rubinstein, an educational consultant, can help him find the right college.

3. For instance, Landmark, a college in Putney, Vermont, specializes in programs for students with learning disabilities.
4. A new federal law, the Americans with Disabilities Act, was enacted in 1990.
5. Now many colleges, both public and private ones, offer support for learning-disabled students.
6. One particular guidebook, *Peterson's Colleges with Programs for Students with Learning Disabilities or Attention Deficit Disorders, ADD,* is especially helpful.

Practice (page 44)

1. Here in America the sale of human organs for transplant is against the law.
2. Unfortunately, there is a disturbing illegal market in the sale of these organs.
3. Where are some people desperately looking for kidneys?
4. Why are so many donors exploited and unprotected?
5. Get invovled.
6. Work toward a solution to this tragic social problem.

Exercise 8: Finding Subjects in Simple Sentences (page 44)

1. child   2. motion   3. mother   4. lights
5. passengers   6. silence   7. people
8. children   9. woman   10. man

Practice (page 46)

1. is   2. has   3. comes

Exercise 11: Finding Action Verbs (page 47)

1. Collectors enjoy   2. people collect

3. collection will give   4. man saved

5. group trades   6. Members gather

7. person keeps   8. Arthur Fiedler hung

9. Tom Bloom finds   10. Collections will entertain

Exercise 13: Finding Linking Verbs (page 48)

1. My dream last night was wonderful.

2. I had been transformed.

3. I looked young again.

4. The house was empty and quiet.

5. In a sunlit kitchen with a book in hand, I appeared relaxed and happy.

6. In the morning light, the kitchen felt cozy.

7. It seemed safe.

8. The brewing coffee smelled delicious.

9. The bacon, my usual Sunday morning treat, never tasted better.

10. In this dreamworld, life felt satisfying.

Exercise 15: Finding Helping Verbs (page 51)

1. We have been driving in a snowstorm for several hours.

2. On Friday, we will have traveled two thousand miles.

3. The travel agent should have warned us about the trip.

4. I had always expected mild weather.

5. We cannot possibly arrive by dark.

6. According to my phone conversation with the hotel, they will hold our reservations.

7. During our stay, we could try the restaurant across the street from the hotel.

8. Shall we swim in the pool?

9. I might not have brought enough money.

10. I am making no promises about the rest of our trip.

Exercise 17: Identifying Parts of Speech (page 52)

1. a   2. c   3. f   4. f   5. b   6. a   7. e
8. d   9. d   10. a

CHAPTER 4: MAKING SUBJECTS AND VERBS AGREE

Practice (page 58)

1. barks   2. wakes   3. become   4. deserve
5. throw

Practice (page 59)

1. doesn't   2. were   3. doesn't   4. Were
5. doesn't

Exercise 1: Making the Subject and Verb Agree (page 59)

1. writers present   2. They nominate
3. writer lives   4. He doesn't   5. we see
6. He wears   7. books center   8. book is
9. He was   10. We don't

Exercise 4: Agreement with Hidden Subjects (page 61)

1. plan is   2. busywork prevents   3. period is

4. People do   5. breaks are   6. clutter causes

7. perfectionists do   8. habit is

9. activities are   10. Children need

Exercise 6: Agreement with Collective Nouns (page 63)

1. crew is   2. union accuses   3. group files

4. team are   5. public voice   6. crowd grows

7. audience interrupt   8. jury hears

9. group have   10. crowd sit

Exercise 8: Agreement with Indefinite Pronouns (page 65)

1. Nobody knows   2. Some argue

3. Most remain   4. All is (and) proves

5. Everybody agrees   6. One is   7. One is

8. Each has been   9. some recommend

10. both are

Exercise 10: Subject-Verb Agreement with Compound Subjects (page 66)

1. Macaroni and cheese is

2. meal (and) others have

3. mother (and) father enjoy

4. habits (or) routine needs

5. salad (or) vegetable is

6. Adults (and) children do

7. pizzas (and) sodas are

8. lack (or) eating causes

9. chips (nor) popcorn is

10. apple (or) grapes make

CHAPTER 5: UNDERSTANDING FRAGMENTS AND PHRASES

Exercise 2: Understanding Fragments (page 77)

1. a   2. b   3. c   4. b   5. b   6. a
7. b   8. a   9. d   10. c

Exercise 4: Finding Fragments That Belong to Other Sentences (page 79)

1. Fishing is one of the oldest sports in the world **and can be one of the most relaxing.** A person with a simple wooden pole and line can have as much fun as a sportsman **with expensive equipment. For busy executives, overworked teachers, and even presidents of nations,** fishing can be a good way to escape from the stress of demanding jobs.
2. The first electric car was built in 1887. It was sold commercially **six years later.** At the turn of the century, people had great faith in new technology. In fact, three hundred electric taxicabs were operating in New York City by 1900. However, electric cars soon lost their popularity. The new gasoline engine became more widely used. **With our concern over pollution,** perhaps electric cars will become desirable once again.
3. Tiger Woods is famous for his success as a championship golfer. He is also known for his work with children. In Anaheim, California, Tiger has recently opened a learning center **for fourth to twelfth graders.** Children can apply for a wide range of classes **including robotics, creative writing, forensics, and photography.** Eventually, the center will serve five thousand children. Tiger is planning the construction of other centers around the country **at a cost of five million dollars apiece.** He is grateful for his loving and supportive family **and wants to help less-fortunate children.**

Practice (page 81)

1. INF   2. PP   3. INF   4. INF   5. PP

Practice (page 82)

1. P   2. G   3. G   4. P   5. P

Exercise 5: Identifying Phrases (page 82)

1. gerund phrase   2. infinitive phrase
3. prepositional phrase   4. participial phrase
5. noun phrase   6. participial phrase
7. verb phrase   8. prepositional phrase
9. verb phrase   10. prepositional phrase

Exercise 12: Correcting the Fragment That Contains a Participle (page 88, sample answers)

Walking through the deserted apartment building, I poked around in piles of junk. The brick walls were crumbling. Two children were playing in the dismal hallways. We are waiting for someone to restore the house to its former glory.

Exercise 14: Correcting Fragments (page 89, sample answers)

1. Early morning is a time of peace in my neighborhood.
2. The gray mist covers up all but the faint outlines of nearby houses.
3. I can barely make out the shapes of cars in the streets and driveways.
4. Often if I have the time, I sit and look out the window.
5. Holding a steaming cup of coffee, I slowly wake up.
6. The only sound to be heard is the rumbling of a truck.
7. It is passing by on the highway a quarter mile away.
8. Children are all tucked in their beds.
9. No barking dogs can be heard.
10. I love to sit by the window in this soft, silent dreamworld.

CHAPTER 6: COMBINING SENTENCES USING THREE OPTIONS FOR COORDINATION

Practice (page 98)

1. The audience was packed, for this was a man with an international reputation.
2. He could have told about all his successes, but instead he spoke about his disappointments.
3. His words were electric, so the crowd was attentive.
4. I should have brought a tape recorder, or at least I should have taken notes.

Exercise 1: Combining Sentences Using Coordinating Conjunctions (page 98)

1. contrast: but
2. reason: for

3. result: so
4. adds an idea when both clauses are in the negative: nor
5. reason: for
6. contrast: but
7. reason: for
8. contrast: but; to emphasize the contrast: yet
9. result: so
10. adds an idea: and

Practice (page 102)

1. The restaurant is always too crowded on Saturdays; nevertheless, it serves the best food in town.

2. The land was not for sale; however, the house could be rented.

3. The lawsuit cost the company several million dollars; consequently, the company went out of business a short time later.

4. The doctor told him to lose weight; furthermore, she instructed him to stop smoking.

Exercise 4: Combining Sentences Using Adverbial Conjunctions (page 102)

1. ; however,   2. ; also,   3. ; however,
4. ; in fact,   5. ; furthermore,   6. ; therefore,
7. ; indeed,   8. ; nevertheless,
9. ; consequently,   10. ; nonetheless,

Exercise 7: Combining Sentences Using the Semicolon (page 105)

1. The assistant wrote the speech; the manager delivered it at the national meeting.
2. no semicolon required
3. The apartment was light and airy; the property was neat and clean.
4. Shoppers were pushing grocery carts down the aisles; workers were stocking the shelves.
5. My sister plans to learn three foreign languages; she already knows two.
6. no semicolon required
7. He tried to explain; nobody gave him a chance.
8. no semicolon required
9. Writing in my journal helps me think through problems; I can relive an incident to think about it more clearly.
10. no semicolon required

CHAPTER 7: COMBINING SENTENCES USING SUBORDINATION

Exercise 1: Identifying Dependent and Independent Clauses (page 114)

1. DC   2. DC   3. IC   4. IC   5. IC
6. DC   7. IC   8. IC   9. DC   10. DC

Practice (page 116)

1. DC   2. PP   3. PP   4. DC   5. PP
6. DC

Practice (page 118)

1. a. Calvin went out to celebrate after he won the wrestling match.
   b. After he won the wrestling match, Calvin went out to celebrate.
2. a. The family was excited when Carla returned from Venezuela this spring.
   b. When Carla returned from Venezuela this spring, the family was excited.

Exercise 5: Combining Sentences Using Subordination (page 119, sample answers)

1. While he was eating breakfast, the results of the election came over the radio.
2. The town council voted against the plan because they believed the project was too expensive.
3. I will see Maya Angelou tonight because she is speaking at the university.
4. The worker hoped for a promotion even though not one person in the department had received a promotion last year.
5. Because the worker hoped for a promotion, he did all his work accurately and on time.

Practice (page 121)

1. The chemistry lab that I attend is two hours long.
2. The student assistant who is standing by the door is very knowledgeable.
3. The equipment that was purchased last year will make possible some important new research.

Practice (page 123)

1. no commas   2. no commas
3. Her biology course, which met four times a week for two hours each session, was extremely demanding.   4. no commas
5. My own poetry, which has improved over the semester, has brought me much satisfaction.

Exercise 8: Combining Sentences Using Relative Pronouns (page 124)

1. Stress, which we experience every day, can do a great deal of harm.
2. People whose jobs are demanding often use food to help them cope. (no commas)
3. The practice of eating to cope with stress, which usually goes back to childhood, is often automatic.
4. Some foods that people turn to in times of stress can actually increase tension. (no commas)
5. Sweet foods, which are popular with people who need a lift, are actually not energy boosters.
6. Another substance that people use to get an energy boost is caffeine. (no commas)
7. One of the biggest mistakes people make is to use alcohol, which is really a depressant, as an aid to achieving calm.
8. People who want to feel a sense of calm should eat three light meals a day and two small snacks. (no commas)
9. Getting enough protein is also important in keeping an adequate energy level which will get you through the day. (no commas)
10. A person should eat regularly to avoid binges, which put on pounds and drain one's energy.

CHAPTER 8: CORRECTING FRAGMENTS AND RUN-ONS

Exercise 1: Recognizing Fragments (page 135)

1. b   2. c   3. a   4. c   5. d   6. c
7. a   8. d   9. b   10. d

Practice (page 138, sample answers)

1. In recent years, several celebrities, including Michael J. Fox, Lance Armstrong, and Melissa Etheridge, have shared their health situations with the public. **T**his has had a beneficial effect.
2. In 1995, Christopher Reeve became a quadriplegic after a horse riding accident. **H**e and his wife worked tirelessly until their untimely deaths to draw attention to the need for better treatments and cures for spinal cord injuries.
3. Katie Couric, the American media personality, lost her husband to colon cancer in 1998. **A**fter his death, Katie became a spokeswoman for colon cancer awareness.
4. In fact, Katie had a colonoscopy on the air in March of 2000, **and** she inspired many to follow her example.

5. Katie Couric's efforts have become known as the "Couric effect;" we now know a celebrity can draw significant attention and support to worthwhile causes.

Exercise 4: Recognizing and Correcting Run-Ons (page 139, sample answers)

I was driving along on Route 80 when my daughter asked my wife to change the radio station. My wife told my daughter to do it herself, so my daughter unhooked her seatbelt and reached over from the back seat to change the station. However, just then her brother tickled her, and she lost her balance and fell on the gear shift. The gear shift was pushed into neutral, causing the car to lose power instantly. That's when we were hit by the van behind us.

CHAPTER 9: CHOOSING CORRECT PRONOUNS

Practice (page 150)

1. I   2. me   3. me

Practice (page 151)

1. he   2. me

Practice (page 153)

1. whom   2. who   3. whoever   4. who
5. who

Exercise 3: Choosing the Correct Pronoun Using *Who/Whom* (page 153)

1. Whom   2. Whoever   3. whom   4. Who
5. whoever   6. whoever   7. Whose
8. Whom   9. Whose   10. Whom

Exercise 5: Choosing Correct Pronoun Forms (page 154)

1. she   2. me   3. whoever   4. she
5. Whoever   6. Who   7. they   8. ours
9. him   10. I

Practice (page 157, sample answers)

1. Everyone should bring suggestions to the meeting.
2. These sorts of clothes are popular now.
3. The students didn't know what they were doing.
4. If the bird watchers hope to see anything, they must get up early.
5. This type of book appeals to me.

Practice (page 157, sample answers)

1. I enjoy math exams because I can show what I know.
2. When I took geometry, I discovered that frequent review of past assignments helped make the course seem easy.
3. People always need to practice their skills to not forget them.
4. Math games can be fun for a student if he or she has a spirit of curiosity.
5. When studying math, you must remember that you have to "use it or lose it."

Practice (page 158, sample answers)

1. The biologist asked the director to bring back the biologist's microscope.
2. The report says that the number of science and engineering students seeking doctoral degrees has fallen 50 percent since the mid-1960s.
3. At the laboratory, the scientists said the research had run into serious difficulties.
4. The testing equipment, which was accidentally dropped onto the aquarium, was badly damaged.
5. I don't watch the ten o'clock news anymore because the programs have become too slick.

Exercise 7: Making Pronouns and Antecedents Agree (page 159)

1. The father mailed his son the son's high school yearbook.
2. No one wants his or her income reduced.
3. When a company fails to update its equipment, it often pays a price in the long run.
4. Women today have many more options open to them than ever before.
5. Everybody knows his or her own strengths best.
6. All of the workers anticipate their summer vacations.
7. If the campers want to eat quickly, they should help themselves.
8. This sort of bathing suit looks ridiculous on me.
9. The application says you must pay a registration fee of thirty-five dollars.
10. The doctor said that those types of diseases are rare here.

CHAPTER 10: WORKING WITH ADJECTIVES, ADVERBS, AND PARALLEL STRUCTURE

Exercise 1: Adjectives and Adverbs Used in Comparisons (page 170)

1. easier   2. tallest   3. more easily   4. better
5. most famous   6. most helpful   7. more slowly
8. worst   9. worse   10. most delicious

Practice (page 173)

1. awfully   2. bad   3. well   4. quickly
5. really

Exercise 3: Revising Misplaced Modifiers (page 175)

1. I gave the puppy with the white paws to my sister.
2. I am looking for the missing keys to the filing cabinets.
3. We decided to buy better sleeping bags before the camping trip.
4. The pilot always put passenger safety first.
5. They need to go directly home immediately after the party.
6. Watching the faces of the judges, the dance contestants waited eagerly.
7. The jeweler wanted to design a special charm bracelet for his new customer.
8. I took my daughter, who loved a day off from school, to my office.
9. The accountant almost forgot to tell his client about the change in the law.
10. There are exactly five tablets in this medicine bottle.

Exercise 4: Revising Dangling Modifiers (page 176)

1. Wearing his tuxedo, Victor fed the dog.
2. While we were visiting Yellowstone National Park, Old Faithful entertained us by performing on schedule.
3. Hoping to see the news, I turned on the television set by seven o'clock.
4. Although I ran up the stairs, the train had already left for Philadelphia.
5. After running over the hill, I could see the farm in the valley below.
6. I thought my son, dressed in a Dracula costume, looked perfect for Halloween.
7. She saw three spiders hanging from the ceiling in her bedroom.

8. After I wiped my glasses, the redbird flew away.
9. We listened to the neighbor's dog howling all evening without a stop.
10. After I had painted in my room all afternoon, my cat demanded her dinner.

Practice (page 179, sample answers)

1. A person should never (or shouldn't ever) go out with something cooking on the stove.
2. You have neither a bike nor a car (or You haven't either a bike or a car).
3. I don't want anything (or I want nothing).
4. I will never (won't ever) break my promise.
5. I can't (or can hardly) wait until summer.

Practice (page 180)

1. dirty   2. sewing her own clothes
3. willingly explain the lesson more than once

Exercise 6: Revising Sentences for Parallel Structure (page 180)

1. bitterly cold   2. fixing an old car
3. a dedicated father   4. dark   5. graceful
6. sunny   7. to work out at the gym
8. work on my term paper for political science
9. imagination   10. head for the homestretch

CHAPTER 11: PRACTICING IRREGULAR VERBS

Practice (page 191)

1. cost   2. quit   3. spread   4. hit
5. become

Practice (page 191)

1. bought   2. spent   3. bled   4. kept
5. thought   6. sought   7. fought   8. taught
9. led   10. sent

Practice (page 192)

1. known   2. began   3. sang   4. grew
5. drove   6. rose   7. rode   8. flown
9. sprung   10. written

Exercise 1: Practicing Irregular Verb Forms (page 193)

1. began   2. written   3. knew   4. bet
5. hit   6. threw   7. kept   8. come
9. shrunk   10. hidden

Exercise 4: Practicing More Irregular Verb Forms (page 194)

1. shot   2. built   3. fled   4. burst
5. mistook   6. slid   7. dealt   8. drawn
9. frozen   10. wrung

CHAPTER 12: MASTERING VERB TENSES

Practice (page 202)

1. went   2. have gone   3. has studied
4. took   5. has been

Practice (page 203)

1. has fascinated   2. has become, have watched
3. have replaced, had existed   4. had lived
5. has built

Exercise 1: Practicing with Sequence of Tenses (page 204)

1. have stopped   2. would have   3. will buy
4. had never been   5. liked   6. will soon be
7. is   8. knew   9. would go   10. had gone

Exercise 3: Correcting Unnecessary Shifts in Verb Tense (page 206)

1. completed   2. was   3. doesn't   4. came
5. didn't   6. told   7. has   8. came
9. prefers   10. arrived

Exercise 6: Forming Active Voice and Passive Voice (page 209)

1. *Active voice:* The child dialed the wrong number.
2. *Active voice:* My grandmother very carefully crocheted the sweater.
3. *Passive voice:* Cherry Creek was struck by a tornado last spring.
4. *Passive voice:* The leaves were blown across the yard (by the wind).
5. *Active voice:* In the seventies, many fashionable young men and women wore platform shoes.

Practice (page 210)

1. When President Roosevelt died in 1945, the law required that Vice President Truman take over immediately.
2. It was essential that President Truman act quickly and decisively.

3. Truman must have wished that he were able to avoid using the atomic bomb to bring an end to World War II.
4. He felt it was necessary that the United States help Europe recover from the destruction of World War II.
5. President Truman always insisted that other countries be economically strong.

CHAPTER 13: USING CORRECT CAPITALIZATION AND PUNCTUATION

Exercise 1: Capitalization (page 218)

1. Italian   2. Canadian Rockies   3. Torah
4. University of Delaware   5. Halloween
6. American Telephone and Telegraph Company, Friday, Portland, Oregon
7. President, Emancipation Proclamation
8. Why   9. United Auto Workers
10. East, *A Prairie Home Companion*

Practice (page 221)

1. On November 14, 1977, officials discovered a major body of polluted water in Oswego, New York.
2. Problems with the water supply of the United States, Europe, Canada, and other parts of the world are growing.
3. Water is colorless, tasteless, odorless, and free of calories.
4. You will use on an average day twenty-four gallons of water for flushing, thirty-two gallons for bathing and washing clothes, and twenty-five gallons for other uses.
5. It took 120 gallons of water to create the eggs you ate for breakfast, 3,500 gallons for the steak you might eat for dinner, and over 60,000 gallons to produce the steel used to make your car.

Practice (page 221)

1. The most overused bodies of water are our rivers, but they continue to serve us daily.
2. American cities often developed next to rivers, and industries followed soon after in the same locations.
3. The people of the Industrial Age can try to clean the water they have used, or they can watch pollution take over.

4. The Great Lakes are showing signs of renewal, yet the struggle against pollution there must continue.
5. Many people have not yet been educated about the dangers to our water supply, nor are all our legislators fully aware of the problem.

Practice (page 222)

1. To many people from the East, the plans to supply more water to the western states seem unnecessary.
2. However, people in the West know that they have no future without a good water supply.
3. When they entered Salt Lake Valley in 1847, the Mormons found dry soil that needed water before crops could be grown.
4. Confidently, the new settlers dug ditches that brought the needed water.
5. Learning from the past, modern farmers are trying to cooperate with nature.

Practice (page 223)

1. Some parts of our country, I believe, do not have ample supplies of water.
2. The rocky soil of Virginia, for example, cannot absorb much rainwater.
3. Johnstown, Pennsylvania, an industrial city of 48,000, is situated in one of the most flood-prone valleys of America.
4. It is not, therefore, a very safe place to live.
5. The Colorado, which is one of our longest rivers, gives up most of its water to farmers and cities before it can reach the sea.

Practice (page 223)

1. Dear, your tea is ready now.
2. I wonder, Jason, if the game has been canceled.
3. Dad, could I borrow five dollars?
4. I insist, sir, on speaking with the manager.
5. Kim, is that you?

Practice (page 224)

1. 4,876,454   2. 87,602   3. 156,439,600
4. 187,000   5. 10,000,000,000,000,000

Practice (page 224)

1. "I won't," he insisted, "be a part of your scheme."
2. He mumbled, "I plead the Fifth Amendment."
3. "I was told," the defendant explained, "to answer every question."

4. "The court case," the judge announced, "will be televised."
5. "The jury," said Al Tarvin of the press, "was handpicked."

Practice (page 224)

1. Kicking, the child was carried off to bed.
2. To John, Russell Baker is the best columnist.
3. When you can, come and visit us.
4. We surveyed the students in the class; out of the twenty, seven were married.
5. Some types of skin cancers can kill, doctors say.

Exercise 4: Using the Comma Correctly (page 224)

1. In Weaverville, California, the local high school administrators made an interesting discovery.
2. At a cost of four hundred dollars a year per student, a private company was offering college-level advanced placement courses on the web.
3. Because some students need these courses to get into more competitive colleges, everyone thought this would be a perfect way to take advantage of the new technology.
4. The problems, however, soon became apparent when two students signed up for a government course.
5. Brian Jones, a senior who wants to be a record producer, and Jeremy Forbes, a classmate who dreams of being a cartoonist, found these problems very frustrating.
6. Their worst problems were long delays getting online, many technical glitches, and the absence of a teacher to encourage persistence.
7. Out of six hundred students who enrolled in one of the company's online courses last year, two-thirds did not complete enough course work to take the final exam.
8. Government officials have praised the use of this electronic support for schools, but others say online courses are a poor replacement for the 180,000 new teachers the country really needs.
9. Still others worry that too many cyberspace offerings provide only supplemental services such as SAT training, college counseling, and virtual field trips.
10. Francisco J. Hernandez, an educator at the University of California at Santa Cruz, says, "Our intent is not to be an alternative to a high-quality teacher and classroom but to be an alternative to nothing because that's what students are getting right now."

Exercise 7: Using the Apostrophe (page 228)

1. sun's   2. press's   3. room's
4. Anthony and Maria's   5. nobody's   6. his
7. Queen Elizabeth's reign   8. That's
9. boys'   10. book's

Practice (page 230)

1. "The Gift of the Magi" is one of the short stories in O. Henry's book *The Four Million*.
2. Franklin Delano Roosevelt said, "We have nothing to fear but fear itself."
3. no quotation marks with indirect speech
4. The term "punk" refers to a particular form of rock music.
5. She read the article "Trouble in Silicon Valley" in a recent issue of *Newsweek*.

Practice (page 230)

1. One of the best ways to remember a vacation is to take numerous photos; one of the best ways to recall the contents of a book is to take notes.
2. The problem of street crime must be solved; otherwise, the number of vigilantes will increase.
3. The committee was made up of Kevin Corey, a writer; Anita Poindexter, a professor; and Jorge Rodriguez, a politician.
4. The bank president was very cordial; however, he would not approve the loan.
5. The retailer wants higher profits; the customer wants lower cost.

Practice (page 231)

1. Three pianists played in New York on the same weekend: André Watts, Claudio Arrau, and Jorge Bolet.
2. The official has one major flaw in his personality: greed.
3. no colon
4. The college offers four courses in English literature: Romantic Poetry, Shakespeare's Plays, The British Short Story, and The Modern Novel.
5. Arriving at 6:15 in the morning, Marlene brought me a sausage and cheese pizza, soda, and a gallon of ice cream.

Practice (page 232)

1. Herbert Simon is—and I don't think this is an exaggeration—a genius.

2. George Eliot (her real name was Mary Ann Evans) wrote *Silas Marner*.
3. You should—in fact, I insist—see a doctor.
4. Unemployment brings with it a number of other problems (see the study by Brody, 1982).
5. Mass media (television, radio, movies, magazines, and newspapers) are able to transmit information over a wide range and to a large number of people.

Exercise 10: Other Marks of Punctuation (page 232)

1. To measure crime, sociologists have used three different techniques: official statistics, victimization surveys, and self-report studies.
2. "The Bells" is one of the best-loved poems of Edgar Allan Poe.
3. The lake this summer has one major disadvantage for swimmers: weeds.
4. E. B. White wrote numerous essays for adults; however, he also wrote some very popular books for children.
5. Tuberculosis (also known as consumption) has once again become a serious health issue.
6. The Victorian Period (1837–1901) saw a rapid expansion of industry.
7. He promised me—I know he promised—that he would come to my graduation.
8. Do you know what the French expression "déjà vu" means?
9. She wanted to go to the movies; he wanted to stay home and watch a movie on the DVD player.
10. She has the qualifications needed for the job: a teaching degree, a pleasant personality, two years' experience, and a love of children.

CHAPTER 14: CHOOSING WORDS THAT WORK

Exercise 1: Using Words Rich in Meaning (page 243)

Thin: 1. c   2. e   3. d   4. a   5. b
Eat: 1. d   2. f   3. a   4. e   5. b   6. c

Exercise 3: Denotation/Connotation (page 245, sample answers)

1. farmhouse   2. trudge   3. lady
4. packages   5. in her eighties   6. wrinkles
7. converse   8. vacant   9. mumbling
10. relaxing

Exercise 6: Revising Wordy Sentences (page 248, sample answers)

1. The deadline for your project is May 18.
2. The thought of the exam is stressful for her.
3. The best place to study is our library.
4. Some people believe that astrology is a science.
5. We all need better organizational skills.
6. Mike is very handy mechanically.
7. She is cooking dinner.
8. The game will be canceled because of the rain.
9. The reasons for unemployment are complex.
10. The box was oblong.

Exercise 8: Recognizing Language Inappropriate for Formal Writing (page 251)

1. stop beating around the bush: get to the point
2. chill out: calm down; relax
3. a bummer: a disappointment; unpleasant
4. businessmen: businesspeople
5. level with: speak honestly with
6. a downer: a disappointment
7. guts: courage; determination
8. a dump: a mess
9. guys: men
10. crash: rest; go to bed

CHAPTER 15: PAYING ATTENTION TO LOOK-ALIKES AND SOUND-ALIKES

Group I (page 260)

oral, aural; By, buy, by; capital, capitol; clothes, close; course, coarse; complement, compliment; forward, foreword; past, passed, past; plain, plane; presence, presents

Exercise 1: Group I Words (page 263)

1. aural, oral   2. By, buy   3. capital, capital
4. cloth, clothes, close   5. course, coarse
6. complement, compliment
7. forward, foreword   8. past, passed
9. plain, plane   10. presents, presents

Group II (page 264)

principal, principal, principle; reign, rain; site, sight, cited; stationary, stationery; two, to, too; vain, vein; waist, waste; whether, weather; hole, whole; write, right, rite

Exercise 3: Group II Words (page 267)

1. principal, principle   2. rein, reign
3. cite, sight   4. stationery, stationary
5. to, to, too   6. vain, vein   7. waste, waist
8. weather, whether   9. whole, hole
10. right, rite

Group III (page 268)

It's, its; They're, there, their; where, Were, we're;
Whose, who's; your, you're

Exercise 5: Group III Words (page 269)

1. It's, its   2. its, it's   3. they're, their, there
4. they're, their, there   5. We're, were, where
6. Where, we're   7. Whose, who's
8. Who's, whose   9. you're, your
10. your, you're

Group IV (page 270)

accept, except; advise, advice; affect, effect; breath,
breathe; choose, chose; conscience, conscious,
conscientious; custom, costume; council, counsel,
consul; desert, dessert; diner, dinner, diners

Exercise 7: Group IV Words (page 272)

1. accept, except   2. advice, advise
3. affect, effect   4. breathe, breath
5. choose, chose   6. conscious, conscience
7. customs, costumes   8. council, counsel
9. dessert, desert   10. dinner, diner

Group V (page 273)

emigrate, immigrate, emigrants, immigrants; further,
farther; loose, lose; personal, personnel; quite, quiet,
quit; receipt, recipe; special, especially; than, then;
thought, thorough, though, threw, through; used to,
used, use

Exercise 9: Group V Words (page 275)

1. emigrated   2. farther   3. loose
4. personnel   5. quiet   6. receipt
7. special   8. than   9. through, though
10. used

Practice Group VI (page 277)

1. rising   2. lie   3. sitting   4. lay
5. rose   6. lying   7. sat   8. risen
9. lain   10. sat

Practice Group VI
(page 278, sample answers)

1. laid the package
2. raised his son
3. set the groceries
4. laying down the new floor
5. lay out my clothes
6. raises many questions
7. set the timer
8. laid the ground rules
9. setting the table
10. raised a substantial amount of money

Exercise 11: Group VI Words (page 279)

1. laid   2. sitting   3. sit   4. raised
5. rose   6. rose   7. raised   8. lie
9. lying   10. laid

CHAPTER 16: WORKING WITH PARAGRAPHS: TOPIC SENTENCES AND CONTROLLING IDEAS

Exercise 2: Finding the Topic Sentence of a Paragraph (page 290)

1. We are the great "Let's junk it" society!
2. Today, the hospital nurse has one of the hardest jobs of all.
3. Anything can happen at a county agricultural fair.
4. This was one of the worst situations I had ever been in.
5. During those summer days, the sunporch was the center of our lives.

Exercise 5: Distinguishing a Topic Sentence from a Title (page 293)

1. T   2. T   3. TS   4. T   5. TS   6. T
7. T   8. TS   9. T   10. TS

Exercise 8: Finding the Topic in a Topic Sentence (page 294)

1. Remodeling an old house
2. two-part topic: College work and high school work
3. A well-made suit
4. Growing up near a museum
5. My favorite room in the house
6. A student who goes to school full time and also works part time
7. One of the disadvantages of skiing
8. Spanking

9. An attractive wardrobe
10. first year

Exercise 11: Finding the Controlling Idea (page 296)

1. *Topic:* vigorous exercise; *controlling idea:* a good way to reduce the effects of stress on the body
2. *Two-part topic:* Buffalo and Toronto; *controlling idea:* differ
3. *Topic:* television violence; *controlling idea:* causes aggressive behavior
4. *Topic:* athletic scholarships available to women; *controlling idea:* increasing
5. *Topic:* caffeine; *controlling idea:* several adverse effects on the body
6. *Topic:* Serena Williams and her sister Venus; *controlling idea:* have dominated the world of women's tennis
7. *Topic:* training a parakeet to talk; *controlling idea:* takes great patience
8. *Topic:* babysitting for a family with four pre-school children; *controlling idea:* difficult
9. *Topic:* the hours between five and seven in the morning; *controlling idea:* productive
10. *Topic:* the foggy night; *controlling idea:* spooky

CHAPTER 17: WORKING WITH PARAGRAPHS: SUPPORTING DETAILS

Practice (page 307)

Topic sentence: Everyone has heard of surefire formulas to prevent getting a cold.
Examples of home remedies: a cold shower, exercise, hot rum toddy, cod-liver oil, tea with honey, citrus fruit juices, keeping one's feet dry
Examples of over-the-counter remedies: vitamins, alkalizers, lemon drinks, antihistamines, decongestants, time-release capsules, antibiotics, antiseptic gargles, bioflavonoids, nose drops and sprays
Fact: Americans average two or three colds a year, each lasting about a week.
Expert and statistic: U.S. Public Health Service; 50 percent of the population experiences a common cold during winter and 20 percent has a cold during the summer.

Exercise 1: Finding the Topic Sentence and Supporting Details (page 308)

1. *Topic sentence:* Saturday afternoon was a blessed time on the farm.
   First reason: no mail—no distressing business letters

Second reason: Everyone looked forward to Sunday, when they would rest or play and the Squatters could work their own land.
Third reason: The oxen would graze all day on Sunday.
2. *Topic sentence:* The popularity of sports is enormous.
   First statistical fact: Fifteen percent of all television programs produced are sports programs.
   Second statistical fact: Professional football games have a yearly attendance of more than ten million spectators, and both baseball leagues together draw more than three million spectators every year.
   Examples of recognizable sports stars: Muhammad Ali, Pelé

Exercise 4: Distinguishing a Supporting Detail from a Restatement of the Main Idea (page 311)

1. a. SD   b. R   c. SD   d. SD
2. a. SD   b. SD   c. R   d. SD
3. a. R   b. SD   c. SD   d. SD
4. a. SD   b. SD   c. R   d. SD
5. a. SD   b. SD   c. SD   d. R

CHAPTER 18: DEVELOPING PARAGRAPHS: ILLUSTRATION

Exercise 1: The Sources for Illustrations (page 322)

1. information from a survey
2. hypothetical example
3. example from personal experience

Exercise 4: Analyzing Paragraphs Using Examples (page 324)

1. *Example of the main idea in one's own words:* As a lover of junk, I have a happily messed-up life.
2. 17
4. yes
5. Like the junk itself, the examples have no obvious order.

CHAPTER 19: DEVELOPING PARAGRAPHS: NARRATION

Exercise 4: Placing Details in Order of Time Sequence (page 341)

1. 3, 1, 4, 2, 5

Exercise 7: Working with Transitions (page 343, sample answers)

The author's choice of transitions:
1. A few months ago   2. Then
3. A few weeks later   4. Twenty-four hours later
5. the next three months   6. Today
7. from time to time

CHAPTER 20: DEVELOPING PARAGRAPHS: DESCRIPTION

Exercise 1: Selecting the Dominant Impression (page 358, sample answers)

1. transformed   2. well lit   3. cluttered
4. well-stocked   5. dusty   6. busy
7. overcrowded   8. raucous   9. welcoming
10. bright

Exercise 3: Revising Vague Dominant Impressions (page 360, sample answers)

1. a brilliant blue   2. cool   3. energizing
4. destructive   5. filled with pickup trucks
6. bustling   7. creamy   8. his happy self again
9. comfortable   10. satisfying for now

Practice (page 361)

1. *Hearing:* loud humming; *touch:* cool; *sight:* large refrigerator case, milk, cream, soda, beer
2. *Smell:* onion, caraway seed, pumpernickel
3. *Sight, smell, and taste:* cheese, smoked meat

Exercise 6: Recognizing Sensory Images (page 362)

Sight: room: wide, dirty, disheveled; ancient typewriters; copyeditors at coffee-stained desks; crumpled paper on floor; green, grimy walls
Sound: clatter from old typewriters; voice of the boss, L. L. Engelking
Smell: smoke from cigarettes and cigars

Exercise 12: Using Spatial Order (page 367)

1. 3, 1, 5, 4, 2   2. 4, 5, 2, 1, 3   3. 2, 3, 1, 4

CHAPTER 21: DEVELOPING PARAGRAPHS: PROCESS ANALYSIS

Exercise 1: Is the Process Complete? (page 382)

Missing steps in the recipe for the Swedish spice cake: a list of ingredients, directions to separate the eggs yolks from the egg whites (saving the egg whites until later), temperature of the oven, how long to bake the cake

Exercise 4: Ordering in Logical Sequence (page 384)

4, 8, 7, 10, 1, 3, 6, 9, 5, 2

CHAPTER 22: DEVELOPING PARAGRAPHS: COMPARISON/CONTRAST

Exercise 1: Evaluating the Two-Part Topic (page 400)

1. too broad   2. suitable   3. suitable
4. suitable   5. too broad   6. suitable
7. too broad   8. suitable   9. too broad
10. too broad

Exercise 4: Recognizing the Two Approaches to Ordering Material (page 403)

1. Block, differences
2. Point-by-point, similarities
3. Block, differences
4. Point-by-point, similarities
5. Point-by-point, similarities

Exercise 7: Using Transitions in Comparisons and Contrasts (page 406, sample answers)

1. Dr. Rappole has a reputation for having an excellent bedside manner, but Dr. Connolly is very withdrawn and speaks so softly we can hardly understand him.
2. In the United States, interest in soccer has become apparent only in recent years; however, in Brazil, soccer has always been immensely popular.
3. Unlike the French Revolution, which was directed by the common people, the Russian Revolution was directed by an elite group of thinkers.
4. Whereas Amy is carefree and fun loving, with little interest in school, Noreen, Amy's sister, is so

studious and hardworking that she is always on the honor role.

5. The first apartment had almost no furniture, was badly in need of painting, and felt chilly even though I was wearing a coat; on the other hand, the second apartment was attractively furnished, had been freshly painted, and was so warm that I had to take off my coat.

CHAPTER 23: DEVELOPING PARAGRAPHS: CAUSE AND EFFECT

Exercise 1: Finding Causes and Effects in Paragraphs (page 426)

Causes of headaches: 1. nervous tension
2. dietary factors   a. dependency on caffeine
b. allergy to salt   c. low blood sugar
3. environmental factors—chemicals
a. polishes   b. waxes   c. bug killers
d. paint
Effects of headaches: 1. nausea
2. interrupted sleep, which can worsen the physical and emotional state
3. reliance on drugs with negative side effects
4. reduced productivity on the job, even absences
5. interruption of family life

Exercise 3: Looking for the Causal Relationship (page 428)

1. U   2. C   3. U   4. C   5. C   6. U
7. C   8. U   9. C   10. U

CHAPTER 25: MOVING FROM THE PARAGRAPH TO THE ESSAY

Practice (page 457)

1. F   2. TH   3. TH   4. T   5. F

Exercise 1: Recognizing a Thesis Statement (page 457)

1. TH   2. T   3. F   4. TH   5. T   6. F
7. F   8. T   9. F   10. TH

Exercise 7: Finding Transitional Expressions (page 468)

Transitional expressions: In the past, Sometimes, many times, For one thing, For another, For example, Naturally, Then, after a short while, Of course, Finally
Pronouns: They, they, it, it, we, all this, we, we, no one, they both, we, itself, ourselves
Repeated terms: appear/disappear/reappear, reasons, geopolitical/geopolitically, supported, ally, bases, ties, moved into, both sides

CHAPTER 32: OTHER COLLEGE WRITING: THE RESEARCH PAPER AND THE ESSAY EXAM

Exercise 2: Methods of Development (page 559)

1. summary   2. comparison/contrast
3. definition   4. classification
5. cause and effect

Credits

PHOTOS

READINGS

Index